P9-CAE-607

PROSE MODELS

PROSE MODELS

ELEVENTH EDITION

GERALD LEVIN
Professor Emeritus, University of Akron

THOMSON
™
WADSWORTH

Australia Canada Mexico Singapore Spain United Kingdom United States

Prose Models
Eleventh Edition
Gerald Levin

Publisher: *Earl McPeek*
Acquisitions Editor: *Julie McBurney*
Marketing Strategist: *John Meyers*
Project Manager: *Barrett Lackey*

Cover design: *Candice M. Carta*

Copyright © 2001, 1996, 1993, 1990, 1987, 1984, 1981, 1978, 1975, 1970, 1964 by Wadsworth, a part of the Thomson Corporation. Wadsworth, Thomson, and the Thomson logo are trademarks used herein under license.
Copyright renewed 1992 by Gerald Levin.

Printed in Canada
8 9 10   06

For more information contact Wadsworth, 25 Thomson Place, Boston, MA 02210 USA, or you can visit our Internet site at http://www.Wadsworth.com

All rights reserved. No part of this work covered by the copyright hereon may be reproduced or used in any form or by any means—graphic, electronic, or mechanical, including photocopying, recording, taping, Web distribution or information storage and retrieval systems—without the written permission of the publisher.

For permission to use material from this text, submit a request online at http://www.thomsonrights.com.
Any additional questions about permissions can be submitted by email to thomsonrights @ thomson.com

ISBN: 0-1550-6404-5

Library of Congress Catalog Card Number: 2001088521

PREFACE

This eleventh edition of *Prose Models* offers more than 110 models for composition from both contemporary and classic writers. The book contains numerous and varied examples of the rhetorical modes of writing as well as detailed discussions of the paragraph, the sentence, and diction. A major part is devoted to argument and persuasion, with particular attention to inductive and deductive reasoning.

To quote James Sledd, "Nobody ever learned to write without reading." In his essay on composition, Mark Twain refers to the "model-chamber" or store of effective sentences gathered by the writer from many kinds of reading. These statements express the philosophy of this book. Student writers need to understand the methods of prose composition and to observe these in practice. The writing process and exercises in invention enhance writing skills, but analysis and discussion of a wide selection of readings are just as essential.

ABOUT THE SELECTIONS

The readings in *Prose Models* will elicit active classroom discussion and thoughtful student writing. They range in topic and are strong rhetorical models. Thirty-two new selections have been added to the more than 70 readings that have proved effective in the classroom. Writers new to *Prose Models* include Irving Lewis Allen, William J. Bennett, Carol Bly, William Buckley, Jr., Stephen L. Carter, I. Bernard Cohen, Michael Dorris, Gretel Ehrlich, Sydney J. Harris, Mark Johnson, George Lakoff, Richard Lanham, John McPhee, Patrick D. Maines, Joshua Micah Marshall, Richard Moran, George Plimpton, Mary Helen Ponce, Robert Sullivan, C. DeLores Tucker, Calvin Trillin, and Gary Wills.

The readings connect in theme in various ways. For example, John Holt, Kenneth B. Clark, John Henry Newman, and William Zinsser discuss the purpose of education. The section on Internet filtering includes sections from the landmark 1996 Supreme Court case and a range of essays discussing censorship and various issues related to it. The thematic table of contents and *Instructor's Manual* suggest other connections.

ORGANIZATION

Part 1 of the book deals with matters of organization in the paragraph and the essay. Part 2 illustrates essay and paragraph development—description, narration, and methods of exposition including example, classification and division, definition, comparison and contrast, analogy, and process and causal analysis. Part 3 addresses with usage, tone, imagery, and other matters of diction; Part 4, with sentence style. Part 5, using on argument and persuasion, includes contrasting essays on Internet filtering and the legalization of drugs. Part 6 concludes with essays on writing by John Ciardi, Walker Gibson, Mark Twain, and William Zinsser.

Each of the readings is introduced by a headnote containing brief information about the author and the reading. Questions and suggestions for writing follow the selections except for The Gettysburg Address and the supplementary essays on writing. Vocabulary studies following most of the readings invite the student to look up unfamiliar words and find the exact meaning of familiar ones.

INSTRUCTOR'S MANUAL

The *Instructor's Manual* that accompanies *Prose Models* Eleventh Edition suggests way to teach the selections and provides answers to the questions. To show how this reader can be combined with a handbook, a one-semester model syllabus links the sections of *Prose Models* with the corresponding sections of the *Harbrace College Handbook*.

ACKNOWLEDGMENTS

I wish to thank the following teachers of writing who made suggestions for the Eleventh Edition: Carl Thum, Dartmouth College: Peggy Richards, The University of Akron; and Susan Tilka, Southwest Texas State University. I owe a continuing debt to William Francis, Alan Hart, Bruce Holland, Robert Holland, Alice MacDonald, Sally K. Slocum, and Linda Weiner, former colleagues at the University of Akron, for advice and support over many years.

I thank my acquisitions editor at Harcourt College Publishers, Julie McBurney, and my developmental editor, Jessie Swigger, for their encouragement and suggestions. I thank also Harcourt Project Manager Barrett Lackey and Manufacturing Manager Elaine Curda; and York Production Services and Production Editor Steve Holtzapple and Cover and Text Designer Candice Carta.

I owe a considerable debt to my wife, Lillian Levin, for her support and help over many editions. Christopher, Daniel, and Sarah Rubin, and Matthew, Meredith, and Katie Ziegler were always in mind. So too Sylvia and David Rubin, Elizabeth and Bill Ziegler.

In memory Gerald Scherba, beloved teacher and dear friend.

Gerald Levin

PREFACE TO THE STUDENT: HOW TO USE THIS BOOK

Part One of *Prose Models* discusses matters essential to various kinds of writing you will be doing in college and later. These include stating your central idea or thesis clearly and highlighting it, organizing your ideas and supporting details effectively, showing how they connect. Part Two addresses ways to develop ideas in expository essays that explain ideas and processes—these first two parts showing how to organize and develop paragraphs, the basic units of the essay. Parts Three and Four discuss effective diction and sentence building. Part Five presents various kinds of arguments and their use in persuasive writing—illustrated in a major court opinion and in series of essays on Internet filtering. Part Six concludes the book with a series of essays on the art of composition.

Spoken and Written English. In your reading, you may have noticed how a particular writer favors similar kinds of sentences and ways of phrasing ideas, even ways of building paragraphs and essays. The word *style* describes these recurrent patterns. Though still connected for many people with what is "correct" or proper in writing (style for the eighteenth-century writer Jonathan Swift was "proper words in proper places"), the word today refers commonly to choices in diction and sentence construction as well as to organization. It is in this sense that people refer to a "Hemingway style" in fiction.

However, much of what we describe as style in speaking and writing is probably not a matter of choice at all. One writer may favor long, heavily coordinated sentences, as in the speech of a nonstop talker. Another person, used to speaking in clipped sentences, may write in very short sentences or very short paragraphs. Hemingway, in fact, used both to great effect in his stories and novels. Style was a conscious choice in these instances. Yet much of the writing you do is governed strongly by habits that develop without your awareness. Habits of speech strongly influence how you write, though written communication requires more attention to such matters as sentence structure, punctuation, and the organization of the whole essay, particularly in the final editing.

Though you will continue to speak and write in ways natural to you, you can make your writing more expressive and effective. The more writing you do, the more aware you will become of your own habitual choices. As your awareness increases, you will have the opportunity to experiment with new ways of expressing your ideas—as college gives you the opportunity to think about new ideas in new ways. The discovery and enhancement of your own style of writing and thinking are important purposes of this book.

Use of Prose Models.   The readings in this book show how various American and British writers develop their ideas and and impressions in effective ways. The readings do not represent every kind of effective writing, nor are they "models" in the sense of representing the best and only way to compose an effective sentence, paragraph, or essay. Rather, they illustrate choices possible in writing—effective solutions to problems writers have faced and you will face in your own writing. The readings have have another purpose—to help you draw on your own experiences and observations. You will discover that many of the readings connect in theme and point of view, offering an opportunity for you to work out your own ideas and to bring your experience to bear on the topic under discussion. Essays that interest or move you can serve as resources that you may return to for inspiration and guidance.

The readings constitute in this way a repertory of choices stored in the "model-chamber" Mark Twain refers to—a repertory that we draw on in various ways. The study and discussion of paragraphs and essays are not the only parts of the process of writing, but are indispensable. For you learn to write as you learn to speak—by reading and listening to the words of others. In planning, drafting, and revising, you will have numerous opportunities to return to your reading and perhaps discover new ways to build and develop your ideas.

In these readings, you will have an opportunity to consider matters of organization and development in both the smaller and larger units of the essay. You will discover that principles of organization and development in paragraphs and sentences occur in the whole essay—the topic sentence of the paragraph bearing a close relationship to the main clause that organizes a sentence, the thesis that organizes the essay. Though each reading illustrates a particular method of organizing and developing ideas, each also employs other methods discussed in the book. The questions frequently call attention to these, and your instructor may use a reading to discuss another topic.

Journals and Other Writing Aids. Here are a few ways you can gain even more from the readings. Glance at the questions that follow before reading a selection. Keep a notebook at hand and, as you read, jot down answers. A few words will usually suffice; you don't want to lose the continuity of the reading or your train of thought. You may want to pause at a break in a longer essay and expand a note or two, writing in complete sentences. Now is the opportunity to review your answers, returning to the selection in doing so. Ideas for an essay may come to mind—perhaps an experience of your own similar to one in the essay, perhaps a response to a statement of the writer. Keep a record of these for later use. Reading notes of this sort are much like those you take in class; the difference is that listening to a lecture or to the give-and-take of classroom discussion, you have fewer opportunities to pause and take stock.

We suggested jotting down a few words or phrases as you read. These are often difficult to recall ten minutes or an hour or day later. The same is true of class notes, as you probably have discovered in reviewing them for a quiz or exam. The solution is to turn these into complete sentences as soon as possible, adding cross-references to the classroom text that clarifies an idea or gives supporting facts. Careful notetaking is indispensable in a chemistry or other science lab: an experiment is worthless unless you make an accurate record as you proceed from stage to stage. The same care in reading a selection or taking notes for a course paper will not be time wasted. You may find the process time-consuming at first. The process will become easier as your note-taking increases. The rewards will be immense.

You may already have discovered the value of keeping a journal—a record of daily experiences, impressions, ideas, and reflections soon lost if not written down. A journal can be an additional resource in searching for a topic or recalling details and experience that support an idea. A well-kept journal will continue to be a resource throughout your college years and beyond.

Preparing To Write. There will be occasions, as in essay exams, when you will need to write impromptu, without advance preparation in style and organization. You may have the opportunity to practice this kind of writing in your composition course. Assigned papers will provide an opportunity to prepare one or more drafts, revising both organization and content. The number of drafts will vary, and you may find at some point that your first or second thoughts were the best—returning to them at a late stage of revision.

In a first or second draft, you may want to get your thoughts down quickly, without full attention to grammar or punctuation until your final version. At times, you will find it best to write slowly, crafting sentences that express your ideas exactly. In the act of writing, you will discover you have clarified your idea, given it shape, brought personal experiences and observations to bear. There is no one best way to proceed. You may already have discovered what best suits your way of thinking and writing.

At times you may find it difficult to get started, even after an initial outline or listing of your thoughts and the details you want to include. Freewriting—putting down ideas and details as quickly as you can—may be the solution. Here, first thoughts may not be the best. The danger is a superficiality of thought and imprecision if freewriting is carried into a first or second draft without thought and careful revision. Each idea, each sentence, needs to be tested and recast until you are satisfied that the latest draft is exactly what you want to say. On matters of revision, William Zinsser and Walker Gibson give valuable advice in Part 6 of this book.

Building Vocabulary. A final word on the vocabulary lists following many of the readings. These lists contain unfamiliar words as well as many you use every day. These are singled out because the author of the reading uses them in a special or unusual way. Often you will recognize the general meaning of a word, but you will need your dictionary to discover the subtle meaning that the author has in mind. In preparing these essays for class discussion, you will gain the most if you keep a dictionary at hand and check the words listed as well as any doubtful ones. A log of unfamiliar words and their definitions can be of immense help in all of your courses.

CONTENTS

---

*Complete section, chapter, or essay.

Contents By Theme

People and Places

Childhood and Adolescence

EDUCATION

URBAN AND RURAL LIFE

DIFFERENT CULTURES, DIFFERENT VALUES

LIFE IN AMERICA

NATIVE AMERICANS, AFRO-AMERICANS, LATINOS

NATURE

MEDIA

The eleventh edition of this respected rhetorical reader provides instructors and students with over 110 models for composition by contemporary and classic authors. *Prose Models,* 11e, contains numerous and varied examples of the rhetorical modes of writing as well as detailed discussions of the paragraph, sentence, and diction.

New to this Edition

- Thirty new selections have been added to the more than 70 established and classroom-tested readings. New authors include Irving Lewis Allen, Gretel Ehrlich, Carol Bly, William Buckley, Jr., Stephen L. Carter, Michael Dorris, Richard Lanham, and George Plimpton.
- A new Section containing contrasting essays on Internet filtering exposes students to contemporary uses of argument and persuasion techniques.

In this Edition

- Each reading is introduced by a headnote containing information about the author and his or her work.
- Questions and suggestions for writing follow each reading and encourage students to think critically and write about their own ideas and experiences.
- Vocabulary studies invite students to look up unfamiliar words and find the exact meaning of familiar ones.
- Part 6 is composed of essays on writing by such highly respected authors as John Ciardi, Mark Twain, and William Zinsser.

I

ORGANIZING THE ESSAY

INTRODUCTION: THE ESSAY AND THE PARAGRAPH

The Nature of the Essay. If asked what an essay is, many would say that it is a piece of writing that states one or more ideas or impressions, develops these fully, and has a clearly marked beginning, middle, and end. The essay may be addressed to a single reader—perhaps in the form of a letter—or to a general audience, the readers of a newspaper or magazine, or a special audience, the readers of a technical journal. Many essays today—those written by newspaper and magazine columnists, television commentators, scholars, students—meet this definition.

But many essays in newspapers, magazines, and journals do not work out ideas completely; the essayist may do no more than explore an idea or an impression of a person or place briefly. The etymology of the word indeed suggests that an essay was for many writers of the past a trying-out or weighing of an idea, a first attempt at expression that might be followed by a second or third attempt. It is sometimes that today. The essayist might put words on paper and not revise them; or might rephrase ideas, introduce new ideas and details, or recast the whole essay or parts of it.

One of the creators of the modern essay; the sixteenth-century French writer Michel de Montaigne, states that some of his late essays added to "other parts of my portrait." "I add, but I do not correct," he writes in the third book of his essays, though he did make corrections later. It would be better to restate ideas in new essays. Montaigne adds that he fears to lose by the change; my understanding does not always advance, it also goes backwards. I do not distrust my thoughts less because they are the second or third, than because they are the first, or my present less than my past thoughts. Besides, we often correct ourselves as foolishly as we correct others. ("Of Vanity," *Essays*)

For Montaigne and for the British essayist and novelist Virginia Woolf, the essay is first of all an expression of personal ideas:

> A very wide definition obviously must be that which will include all the varieties of thought which are suitably enshrined in essays. . . . Almost all essays begin with a capital I—"I think," "I feel"—and when you have said that, it is clear that you are not writing history or philosophy or biography or anything but an essay, which may be brilliant or profound, which may deal with the immortality of the soul, or the rheumatism in your left shoulder, but is primarily an expression of personal opinion. ("The Decay of Essay-Writing")

Since Montaigne's day, the essay has broadened to include "all the varieties of thought," as Woolf states. The contemporary essay sometimes expresses personal opinion and feelings and as such sometimes seems extemporaneous and unfinished. But it also may be entirely objective in tone and approach to the subject, omitting personal opinions and feelings. It may narrate experiences, describe persons and places, explain an idea or a process, give the history of an event, or argue a point and seek to persuade us to accept it.

Organizing and Developing the Essay. Essays indeed have been traditionally classified as narrative, descriptive, expository, and argumentative, depending on the chief method used to organize and develop them. We commonly refer to novels as narratives, word pictures as descriptions, sets of directions as expositions, and defenses of opinion as arguments. This traditional classification does not, however, tell us why the essayist chooses to narrate or describe, explain or argue. We need to know the writer's purpose in doing so.

Thus an autobiographical essay or memoir like Sally Carrighar's recollection of her father (p. 39) may use narrative and description to express the writer's sense of the past or help us to understand it. Narratives in the form of short stories and novels may entertain us, or, like John Steinbeck's *The Grapes of Wrath,* seek to move us or persuade us to take action. An explanatory essay helps us to understand a process or, as in Jearl Walker's essay on how to cook outdoors (p. 200), teaches us to perform it. Usually argument is used as a means of persuasion. Though essays may depend on a single method of development, most depend upon more than one. Description usually gives support to narrative. And exposition often aids in expressing feelings and attitudes, and often joins with argument, as in an advertisement that explains how a product works and gives us reasons to buy it.

The Nature of the Paragraph. In this section and those following in Parts 1 and 2, we will see how individual paragraphs and complete essays illustrate a principle of organization and development of ideas. In looking at paragraphs, we need to remember that they form complete essays and do not stand alone, except where the essay consists of a single paragraph, as in E. B. White's "In an Elevator" (p. 48).

Some paragraphs develop a single impression or idea; some develop related impressions or ideas. The paragraphs that follow in this and later sections are of this type. Other paragraphs, it should be noted, are transitional, marking a turn to a new idea, and some are summary paragraphs—stating or reiterating the central idea or thesis, without developing it:

> [*Transitional*]: But mass transportation needn't necessarily wait for breakthroughs in energy technology. In fact, in the nineteenth century, cities developed their first systems based on the use of one of mankind's oldest suppliers of energy: the horse.

> [*Summary*]: The organization of mass transportation systems was an important step forward in urban social organization, but it hardly marked a major breakthrough in technology. Horses, after all, had been used to pull wagons from time immemorial. Aside from the rather mundane development that saw rails put in city streets, there was very little to distinguish the early-nineteenth-century transportation engineer from his Roman (or even Sumerian) counterpart. (James C. Trefil, *The Growth of Cities*).

The essays and paragraphs that follow by no means show all possible ways of organizing and developing ideas. But the methods illustrated are common ones that all writers draw upon.

I

TOPIC SENTENCE, THESIS, AND UNITY

TOPIC SENTENCE AND UNITY IN THE PARAGRAPH

In reading an essay, we depend on the opening sentence of each paragraph to direct us from one idea to the next. As in the following paragraph from Eric Sevareid's essay describing his hometown in North Dakota (p. 28), the opening sentence sometimes directs us through a topic sentence or statement of the central idea:

> *Sights have changed:* there is a new precision about street and home, a clearing away of chicken yards, cow barns, pigeon-crested cupolas, weed lots and coulees, the dim and secret adult-free rendezvous of boys. An intricate metal "jungle gym" is a common backyard sight, the sack swing uncommon. . . . ("Velva, North Dakota" [italics added])

Not all opening sentences state the central idea fully. Some state just the subject or topic of the paragraph—occasionally through a single word, as in another paragraph of Sevareid's:

> *Consolidation.* The nearby hamlets of Sawyer and Logan and Voltaire had their own separate banks and papers and schools in my days of dusty buggies and Model Ts marooned in the snowdrifts. Now these hamlets are dying. . . . [italics added]

The subject or topic may also be introduced through a question that Sevareid answers in the remainder of the paragraph:

> *But now I must ask myself: Are they nearer to one another?* And the answer is no; yet I am certain that this is good. The shrinking of time and distance has made contrast and relief available to their daily lives.

> They do not know one another quite so well because they are not so much obliged to. . . . [italics added]

In paragraphs that open with a statement of the subject or topic, the central or topic idea may follow immediately, as in the paragraph just cited. Or details and explanatory statements may build from an introductory comment to the central idea or a reflective comment, coming at the end:

> I have read that in the unlikely event that you are caught in a stare-down with a grizzly bear, the best thing to do is talk to him softly and pleasantly. Your voice is supposed to have a soothing effect. I have not yet had occasion to test this out on grizzly bears, but I can attest that it does not work on muskrats. It scares them witless. I have tried time and again. Once I watched a muskrat feeding on a bank ten feet away from me; after I had looked my fill I had nothing to lose, so I offered a convivial greeting. Boom. The terrified muskrat flipped a hundred and eighty degrees in the air, nose-dived into the grass at his feet, and disappeared. The earth swallowed him; his tail shot straight up in the air and then vanished into the ground without a sound. Muskrats make several emergency escape holes along a bank for just this very purpose, and they don't like to feed too far away from them. The entire event was most impressive, and illustrates the relative power in nature of the word and the sneak. (Annie Dillard, *Pilgrim at Tinker's Creek*)

Paragraphs that build in this way may generate a sense of climax, the full impact occurring when we have all the facts.

Paragraphs do not occur in isolation, unless an essay consists of a single one, as in E. B. White's "On the Elevator" (p. 48). Paragraphs link, the topic sentence of one appearing at the end of the one before or the beginning of the next. When the details alone make the point, the paragraph is said to have an *implied* topic sentence—the central idea or the dominant impression remaining unstated, as in the following description of the Kalahari Desert in Southwest Africa:

> That evening we camped beside an omaramba where the air was warm and pale, lit by the three-quarter moon; the wind made the dry leaves of a mangetti tree over our heads tap together and before we went to sleep we heard a leopard coughing far away, then growling nearer, a rattle, a rumble of a growl. In the morning we got up long before dawn because of a veld fire that someone had seen coming toward us; it made a huge red light in the black sky, like the open doors of an inferno, but as the dawn winds lifted it blew back on itself and went out. The sky slowly got gray, then pale rose, and then, hundreds of miles away, the

great sun lifted from the veld's horizon and with the light we found the leopard's footprints which he had left as he had walked around us, in two great circles, as though he had cast a spell. (Elizabeth Marshall Thomas, *The Harmless People*)

The topic sentence, stated or implied, helps in unifying the paragraph. A unified paragraph not only develops one idea at a time but also makes each idea and detail relevant to the topic idea. The reader sees the relation of ideas and details. A disunified paragraph, by contrast, seems disconnected, its ideas and details introduced without transition or apparent reason.

GRETEL EHRLICH

GRETEL EHRLICH traveled to Wyoming to make a documentary for the Public Broadcasting Company, later returning to work on a ranch. She has written about her experiences in two collections of essays—*The Solace of Open Spaces* (1985) and *Islands, the Universe, Home* (1991). Other writings include *Heart Mountain* (1988) a novel about Japanese Americans in Wyoming in World War Two, *Arctic Heart* (1992), a collection of poems, and *A Match to the Heart* (1994), a memoir about a near-death experience.

OBITUARY

A big ranch is a miniature society. Its demise has the impact of a bankruptcy in a small town: another hundred people out of work and a big chunk of the town's business is suddenly gone. A ranch offers more than jobs; whole families are taken in, their needs attended to: housing, food, schools, even a graveyard plot for those who died on the job or liked the place so much they wanted to be buried there. Itinerant cowboys and sheepherders are given tools of their trade—a horse, a working dog, a saddle, rifle, binoculars—if they arrived empty-handed, and the farm hands are provided with air-conditioned tractors. Altogether, this extended ranch family includes not just cowboys and sheepherders but irrigators, mechanics, camp tenders, foremen, and cooks. A loyal veteran of the outfit would always be assured of a place to live out his days. When he became too old or infirm to work, he might live in the ranch yard and feed the dogs or clear the kosha grass from the pens in the spring. In exchange he could eat in the cookhouse or batch it with a year's supply of elk meat or mutton.

VOCABULARY

demise, itinerant

QUESTIONS

1. The opening sentence states the central idea of the paragraph. In how many ways is a big ranch a miniature society?

2. What kind of society does Ehrlich have in mind?

3. What features does she begin and end with? What does she gain in organizing the paragraph as she does?

SUGGESTIONS FOR WRITING

1. In an opening paragraph of your own, discuss the ways your high school formed a miniature society, or how your college or university does.

2. In additional paragraphs, discuss some of the features mentioned in your opening paragraph. Present your central idea early in each paragraph, unless you have reason to present it later.

ABOUT MEN

When I'm in New York but feeling lonely for Wyoming I look for the   1
Marlboro ads in the subway. What I'm aching to see is horseflesh, the glint of a spur, a line of distant mountains, brimming creeks, and a reminder of the ranchers and cowboys I've ridden with for the last eight years. But the men I see in those posters with their stern, humorless looks remind

me of no one I know here. In our hellbent earnestness to romanticize the cowboy we've ironically disesteemed his true character. If he's "strong and silent" it's because there's probably no one to talk to. If he "rides away into the sunset" it's because he's been on horseback since four in the morning moving cattle and he's trying, fifteen hours later, to get home to his family. If he's "a rugged individualist" he's also part of a team: ranch work is teamwork and even the glorified open-range cowboys of the 1880s rode up and down the Chisholm Trail in the company of twenty or thirty other riders. Instead of the macho, trigger-happy man our culture has perversely wanted him to be, the cowboy is more apt to be convivial, quirky, and softhearted. To be "tough" on a ranch has nothing to do with conquests and displays of power. More often than not, circumstances—like the colt he's riding or an unexpected blizzard—are overpowering him. It's not toughness but "toughing it out" that counts. In other words, this macho, cultural artifact the cowboy has become is simply a man who possesses resilience, patience, and an instinct for survival. "Cowboys are just like a pile of rocks—everything happens to them. They get climbed on, kicked, rained and snowed on, scuffed up by wind. Their job is 'just to take it,'" one old-timer told me.

A cowboy is someone who loves his work. Since the hours are long— ten to fifteen hours a day—and the pay is $30 he has to. What's required of him is an odd mixture of physical vigor and maternalism. His part of the beef-raising industry is to birth and nurture calves and take care of their mothers. For the most part his work is done on horseback and in a lifetime he sees and comes to know more animals than people. The iconic myth surrounding him is built on American notions of heroism: the index of a man's value as measured in physical courage. Such ideas have perverted manliness into a self-absorbed race for cheap thrills. In a rancher's world, courage has less to do with facing danger than with acting spontaneously—usually on behalf of an animal or another rider. If a cow is stuck in a boghole he throws a loop around her neck, takes his dally (a half hitch around the saddle horn), and pulls her out with horsepower. If a calf is born sick, he may take her home, warm her in front of the kitchen fire, and massage her legs until dawn. One friend, whose favorite horse was trying to swim a lake with hobbles on, dove under water and cut her legs loose with a knife, then swam her to shore, his arm around her neck lifeguard-style, and saved her from drowning. Because these incidents are usually linked to someone or something outside himself, the westerner's courage is selfless, a form of compassion.

The physical punishment that goes with cowboying is greatly un- 3
derplayed. Once fear is dispensed with, the threshold of pain rises to meet
the demands of the job. When Jane Fonda asked Robert Redford (in the
film *Electric Horseman*) if he was sick as he struggled to his feet one
morning, he replied, "No, just bent." For once the movies had it right.
The cowboys I was sitting with laughed in agreement. Cowboys are
rarely complainers; they show their stoicism by laughing at themselves.

VOCABULARY

paragraph 1: ironically, disesteemed, perversely, convivial, macho, resilience
paragraph 2: iconic, myth, hobble, compassion
paragraph 3: dispensed with, stoicism

QUESTIONS

1. The opening sentences of paragraph 1 introduce the subject or topic
of the essay—the Marlboro man. Which sentence states the idea developed in the paragraph? How does Ehrlich develop it?

2. How does Ehrlich illustrate "the odd mixture of physical vigor and
maternalism" in the cowboy?

3. What is the central or topic idea of paragraph 3, where is it stated,
and how does Ehrlich develop it?

SUGGESTIONS FOR WRITING

1. In one or two well-developed paragraphs, describe the skills needed
in a particular job. Be as specific in your details as you can.

2. Discuss the extent to which a particular advertisement accurately depicts an age group or profession you are familiar with. Open your paragraphs with topic sentences that state the subject or an idea illustrated
by the details that follow.

M A R K   T W A I N

Growing up in Hannibal, Missouri, on the Mississippi River, SAMUEL CLEMENS had one ambition in life—to become a steamboatman. "Boy after boy managed to get on the river," Twain tells us in *Life on the Mississippi* (1883). "The minister's son became an engineer. The doctor's and the postmaster's sons became 'mud clerks'. . . ." Twain left Hannibal in 1853 and worked as a printer in St. Louis and other cities. In 1857 he became a cub pilot on a Mississippi steamboat, secured his license two years later, and worked as a pilot until 1861. Later, working as a newspaper reporter, he adopted the pen name "Mark Twain," after the term leadsmen used on river boats for "two fathoms deep." In the excerpt reprinted below, Twain describes the trials of learning the shape of the Mississippi under a senior pilot, Horace Bixby. Bixby says "I'll learn a man," Twain says in a note, because "'teach' is not in the river vocabulary." In the excerpt in Part 4 of this book (pp. 296), Twain describes his early ambition.

THE SHAPE OF THE RIVER

I went to work now to learn the shape of the river: and of all the eluding and ungraspable objects that ever I tried to get mind or hands on, that was the chief. I would fasten my eyes upon a sharp, wooden point that projected far into the river some miles ahead of me, and go to laboriously photographing its shape upon my brain; and just as I was beginning to succeed to my satisfaction, we would draw up toward it and the exasperating thing would begin to melt away and fold back into the bank! If there had been a conspicuous dead tree standing upon the very point of the cape, I would find that tree inconspicuously merged into the general forest, and occupying the middle of a straight shore, when I got abreast of it! No prominent hill would stick to its shape long enough for me to make up my mind what its form really was, but it was as dissolving and changeful as if it had been a mountain of butter in the hottest corner of the tropics. Nothing ever had the same shape when I was coming down-stream that it had borne when I went up. I mentioned these little difficulties to Mr. Bixby. He said, "That's the main virtue of the thing. If the shapes didn't change every three seconds they wouldn't be of any use. Take this place where we are now, for instance. As long as that hill over yonder is only one hill, I can boom right along the way I'm going; but the moment it splits at the top and forms a V, I know I've got to scratch to starboard in a hurry, or I'll bang this boat's brains out against a rock; and then the moment one of the prongs of the V swings behind the other, I've got to waltz to larboard again, or I'll have a misunderstanding with a snag that would snatch the keelson out of this steamboat as neatly as if it were a sliver in your hand. If that hill didn't change its shape on bad nights there would be an awful steamboat graveyard around here inside of a year."

It was plain that I had got to learn the shape of the river in all the different ways that could be thought of—upside down, wrong end first, inside out, fore-and-aft, and "thort-ships"—and then know what to do on gray nights when it hadn't any shape at all. So I set about it. In the course of time I began to get the best of this knotty lesson, and my self-complacency moved to the front once more. Mr. Bixby was all fixed, and ready to start it to the rear again. He opened on me after this fashion:

"How much water did we have in the middle crossing at Hole-in-the-Wall, trip before last?"

I considered this an outrage. I said:

"Every trip, down and up, the leadsmen are singing through that tangled place for three quarters of an hour on a stretch. How do you reckon I can remember such a mess as that."

"My boy, you've got to remember it. You've got to remember the exact spot and the exact marks the boat lay in when we had the shoalest water, in every one of the five hundred shoal places between St. Louis and New Orleans; and you mustn't get the shoal soundings and marks of one trip mixed up with the shoal soundings and marks of another, either, for they're not often twice alike. You must keep them separate."

When I came to myself again, I said,

"When I get so that I can do that, I'll be able to raise the dead, and then I won't have to pilot a steamboat to make a living. I want to retire from this business. I want a slush-bucket and a brush; I'm only fit for a roustabout. I haven't got brains enough to be a pilot; and if I had I wouldn't have strength enough to carry them around, unless I went on crutches."

"Now drop that! When I say I'll learn a man the river, I mean it. And you can depend on it, I'll learn him or kill him."

VOCABULARY

paragraph 1: starboard, larboard, keelson
paragraph 4: leadsmen

QUESTIONS

1. Twain states the topic idea of paragraph 1 in his opening sentence. How does he illustrate this idea, and in what order does he present his examples?

2. What point is Bixby making in paragraph 2, and where does he state it? How does he develop it?

3. What is Twain showing about himself as a student and about Bixby as a teacher?

SUGGESTIONS FOR WRITING

1. In one or two well-developed paragraphs, describe your own experience learning a difficult job. Like Twain, explain in detail what you had to learn.

2. Describe a similar episode that shows something about you as a student and something about the teacher. Open your paragraphs with topic sentences that state the subject of the paragraph or an idea illustrated by the details that follow.

THESIS AND UNITY IN THE ESSAY

The thesis of an essay is its central or controlling idea, the proposition or chief argument—the point of the essay. The topic sentence of a paragraph may be either a full or a partial statement of the controlling idea. The thesis is always a full statement of it.

Where the thesis appears depends largely on the audience. If we believe that our readers require no introduction to it (no background or explanation of the issue or important terms) we may state it in the opening paragraph. Many newspaper editorials begin this way—a practice consistent with that of putting the essential information in the opening sentences of a news story. Many essayists, by contrast, prefer to build to a full statement of the thesis—introducing it in the opening paragraphs, perhaps with an explanation of important terms and the issues to be discussed. William Zinsser does this in the opening paragraphs of the essay on writing in Part 6 of this book:

> Clutter is the disease of American writing. We are a society strangling in unnecessary words, circular constructions, pompous frills and meaningless jargon. ("Simplicity")

Zinsser illustrates this opening statement in the succeeding paragraph, then states his thesis in the opening sentence of a paragraph that follows shortly:

> But the secret of good writing is to strip every sentence to its cleanest components.

The remainder of the essay shows how to do so, the conclusion restating the thesis in light of what Zinsser has demonstrated:

> Writing is hard work. A clear sentence is no accident. Very few sentences come out right the first time, or even the third time. . . .

If the thesis needs extensive background and discussion to be understood or perhaps is highly controversial, we may decide to build up to it instead of stating it toward the beginning of the essay. In some essays we may not state the thesis at all, letting the reader draw conclusions from the details or facts provided. In such essays the thesis is said to be *implied*.

GEORGE ORWELL

GEORGE ORWELL (1903–1950) was the pseudonym of the English novelist and essayist Eric Hugh Blair. Orwell was born in India, where his father was a customs official in the British civil government. After attending school in England, Orwell took a job with the Imperial Police in Burma, serving from 1922 to 1927. On leaving the police service, he returned to Europe, where he began his career as journalist and novelist.

The rise of totalitarianism in Europe is the subject of numerous essays and books, particularly in his fable *Animal Farm* (1945) and the novel *Nineteen Eighty-four* (1949). In "Shooting an Elephant," Orwell skillfully combines description of a small Burmese town and British colonial officials with a narrative of what happened to him when summoned to deal with a crazed elephant. In narrating the incident, Orwell is arguing a thesis in a special way—through an episode typical of a situation faced by colonial powers. Orwell also has something important to say about human nature. Although Great Britain no longer governs India or Burma, his ideas remain pertinent to today's political issues.

SHOOTING AN ELEPHANT

In Moulmein, in lower Burma, I was hated by large numbers of people — the only time in my life that I have been important enough for this to happen to me. I was subdivisional police officer of the town, and in an aimless, petty kind of way anti-European feeling was very bitter. No one had the guts to raise a riot, but if a European woman went through the bazaars alone somebody would probably spit betel juice over her dress. As a police officer, I was an obvious target and was baited whenever it seemed safe to do so. When a nimble Burman tripped me up on the football field and the referee (another Burman) looked the other way, the crowd yelled with hideous laughter. This happened more than once. In the end the sneering yellow faces of young men that met me everywhere, the insults hooted after me when I was at a safe distance, got badly on my nerves. The young Buddhist priests were the worst of all. There were several thousands of them in the town and none of them seemed to have anything to do except stand on street corners and jeer at Europeans.

All this was perplexing and upsetting. For at that time I had already made up my mind that imperialism was an evil thing and the sooner I chucked up my job and got out of it the better. Theoretically—and secretly, of course—I was all for the Burmese and all against their oppressors, the British. As for the job I was doing, I hated it more bitterly than I can perhaps make clear. In a job like that you see the dirty work of Empire at close quarters. The wretched prisoners huddling in the stinking cages of the lock-ups, the gray, cowed faces of the long-term convicts, the scarred buttocks of the men who had been flogged with bamboos—all these oppressed me with an intolerable sense of guilt. But I could get nothing into perspective. I was young and ill educated and I had had to think out my problems in the utter silence that is imposed on every Englishman in the East. I did not even know that the British Empire is dying, still less did I know that it is a great deal better than the younger empires that are going to supplant it. All I knew was that I was stuck between my hatred of the empire I served and my rage against the evil-spirited little beasts who tried to make my job impossible. With one part of my mind I thought of the British Raj as an unbreakable tyranny, as something clamped down, in *saecula saeculorum*, upon the will of prostrate peoples; with another part I thought that the greatest joy in the world would be to drive a bayonet into a Buddhist priest's guts. Feelings like these are the normal by-products of imperialism; ask any Anglo-Indian official, if you can catch him off duty.

One day something happened which in a roundabout way was enlightening. It was a tiny incident in itself, but it gave me a better glimpse than I had had before of the real nature of imperialism—the real motives for which despotic governments act. Early one morning the sub-inspector at a police station the other end of the town rang me up on the 'phone and said that an elephant was ravaging the bazaar. Would I please come and do something about it? I did not know what I could do, but I wanted to see what was happening and I got on to a pony and started out. I took my rifle, an old .44 Winchester and much too small to kill an elephant, but I thought the noise might be useful *in terrorem*. Various Burmans stopped me on the way and told me about the elephant's doings. It was not, of course, a wild elephant, but a tame one which had gone "must."* It had been chained up, as tame elephants always are when their attack of "must" is due, but on the previous night it had broken its chain and escaped. Its mahout,† the only person who could manage it when it was in that state, had set out in pursuit, but had taken the wrong direction and was now twelve hours' journey away, and in the morning the elephant had suddenly reappeared in the town. The Burmese population had no weapons and were quite helpless against it. It had already destroyed somebody's bamboo hut, killed a cow and raided some fruit-stalls and devoured the stock; also it had met the municipal

3

---

* *must:* state of sexual heat in male elephant. [All notes are the editor's.]

† *mahout:* the elephant driver and sometimes owner.

rubbish van and, when the driver jumped out and took to his heels, had turned the van over and inflicted violences upon it.

The Burmese sub-inspector and some Indian constables were waiting 4 for me in the quarter where the elephant had been seen. It was a very poor quarter, a labyrinth of squalid bamboo huts, thatched with palm-leaf winding all over a steep hillside. I remember that it was a cloudy, stuffy morning at the beginning of the rains. We began questioning the people as to where the elephant had gone and, as usual, failed to get any definite information. That is invariably the case in the East; a story always sounds clear enough at a distance, but the nearer you get to the scene of events the vaguer it becomes. Some of the people said that the elephant had gone in one direction, some said that he had gone in another, some professed not even to have heard of any elephant. I had almost made up my mind that the whole story was a pack of lies, when we heard yells a little distance away. There was a loud, scandalized cry of "Go away, child! Go away this instant!" and an old woman with a switch in her hand came round the corner of a hut, violently shooing away a crowd of naked children. Some more women followed, clicking their tongues and exclaiming; evidently there was something that the children ought not to have seen. I rounded the hut and saw a man's dead body sprawling in the mud. He was an Indian, a black Dravidian coolie, almost naked, and he could not have been dead many minutes. The people said that the elephant had come suddenly upon him round the corner of the hut, caught him with its trunk, put its foot on his back and ground him into the earth. This was the rainy season and the ground was soft, and his face had scored a trench a foot deep and a couple of yards long. He was lying on his belly with arms crucified and head sharply twisted to one side. His face was coated with mud, the eyes wide open, the teeth bared and grinning with an expression of unendurable agony. (Never tell me, by the way, that the dead look peaceful. Most of the corpses I have seen looked devilish.) The friction of the great beast's foot had stripped the skin from his back as neatly as one skins a rabbit. As soon as I saw the dead man I sent an orderly to a friend's house nearby to borrow an elephant rifle. I had already sent back the pony, not wanting it to go mad with fright and throw me if it smelt the elephant.

The orderly came back in a few minutes with a rifle and five car- 5 tridges, and meanwhile some Burmans had arrived and told us that the elephant was in the paddy fields below, only a few hundred yards away.

As I started forward practically the whole population of the quarter flocked out of the houses and followed me. They had seen the rifle and were all shouting excitedly that I was going to shoot the elephant. They had not shown much interest in the elephant when he was merely ravaging their homes, but it was different now that he was going to be shot. It was a bit of fun to them, as it would be to an English crowd; besides they wanted the meat. It made me vaguely uneasy. I had no intention of shooting the elephant—I had merely sent for the rifle to defend myself if necessary—and it is always unnerving to have a crowd following you. I marched down the hill, looking and feeling a fool, with the rifle over my shoulder and an ever-growing army of people jostling at my heels. At the bottom, when you got away from the huts, there was a metalled road and beyond that a miry waste of paddy fields a thousand yards across, not yet ploughed but soggy from the first rains and dotted with coarse grass. The elephant was standing eight yards from the road, his left side toward us. He took not the slightest notice of the crowd's approach. He was tearing up bunches of grass, beating them against his knees to clean them, and stuffing them into his mouth.

I had halted on the road. As soon as I saw the elephant I knew with perfect certainty that I ought not to shoot him. It is a serious matter to shoot a working elephant—it is comparable to destroying a huge and costly piece of machinery—and obviously one ought not to do it if it can possibly be avoided. And at that distance, peacefully eating, the elephant looked no more dangerous than a cow. I thought then and I think now that his attack of "must" was already passing off; in which case he would merely wander harmlessly about until the mahout came back and caught him. Moreover, I did not in the least want to shoot him. I decided that I would watch him for a little while to make sure that he did not turn savage again, and then go home.

But at that moment I glanced round at the crowd that had followed me. It was an immense crowd, two thousand at the least and growing every minute. It blocked the road for a long distance on either side. I looked at the sea of yellow faces above the garish clothes—faces all happy and excited over this bit of fun, all certain that the elephant was going to be shot. They were watching me as they would watch a conjurer about to perform a trick. They did not like me, but with the magical rifle in my hands I was momentarily worth watching. And suddenly I realized that I should have to shoot the elephant after all. The people expected it of me and I had got to do it; I could feel their two thousand wills pressing me forward, irresistibly. And it was at this moment, as I stood there with the rifle in my hands, that I first grasped the hollowness, the futility of the white man's dominion in the East. Here was I, the white man with his gun, standing in front of the unarmed native crowd—seemingly the leading actor of the piece; but in reality I was only an absurd puppet pushed to and fro by the will of those yellow faces behind. I perceived in this moment that when the white man turns tyrant it is his own freedom that he destroys. He becomes a sort of hollow, posing dummy, the conventionalized figure of a sahib. For it is the condition of his rule that he shall spend his life in trying to impress the "natives," and so in every crisis he has got to do what the "natives" expect of him. He wears a mask, and his face grows to fit it. I had got to shoot the elephant. I had committed myself to doing it when I sent for the rifle. A sahib has got to act like a sahib; he has got to appear resolute, to know his own mind and do definite things. To come all that way, rifle in hand, with two thousand people marching at my heels, and then to trail feebly away, having done nothing—no, that was impossible. The crowd would laugh at me. And my whole life, every white man's life in the East, was one long struggle not to be laughed at.

But I did not want to shoot the elephant. I watched him beating his   8
bunch of grass against his knees with that preoccupied grandmotherly air that elephants have. It seemed to me that it would be murder to shoot him. At that age I was not squeamish about killing animals, but I had never shot an elephant and never wanted to. (Somehow it always seems worse to kill a *large* animal.) Besides, there was the beast's owner to be considered. Alive, the elephant was worth at least a hundred pounds; dead, he would only be worth the value of his tusks, five pounds, possibly. But I had got to act quickly. I turned to some experienced-looking Burmans who had been there when we arrived, and asked them how the elephant had been behaving. They all said the same thing: he took no notice of you if you left him alone, but he might charge if you went too close to him.

It was perfectly clear to me what I ought to do. I ought to walk up   9
to within, say, twenty-five yards of the elephant and test his behavior. If he charged, I could shoot; if he took no notice of me, it would be safe to leave him until the mahout came back. But also I knew I was going to do no such thing. I was a poor shot with a rifle and the ground was soft mud into which one would sink at every step. If the elephant charged and I missed him, I should have about as much chance as a toad under a steam-roller. But even then I was not thinking particularly of my own

skin, only of the watchful yellow faces behind. For at that moment, with the crowd watching me, I was not afraid in the ordinary sense, as I would have been if I had been alone. A white man mustn't be frightened in front of "natives"; and so, in general, he isn't frightened. The sole thought in my mind was that if anything went wrong those two thousand Burmans would see me pursued, caught, trampled on, and reduced to a grinning corpse like that Indian up the hill. And if that happened it was quite probable that some of them would laugh. That would never do. There was only one alternative. I shoved the cartridges into the magazine and lay down on the road to get a better aim.

The crowd grew very still, and a deep, low, happy sigh, as of people who see the theater curtain go up at last, breathed from innumerable throats. They were going to have their bit of fun after all. The rifle was a beautiful German thing with crosshair sights. I did not then know that in shooting an elephant one would shoot to cut an imaginary bar running from ear-hole to ear-hole. I ought, therefore, as the elephant was sideways on, to have aimed straight at his ear-hole; actually I aimed several inches in front of this, thinking the brain would be further forward.

When I pulled the trigger I did not hear the bang or feel the kick— one never does when a shot goes home—but I heard the devilish roar of glee that went up from the crowd. In that instant, in too short a time, one would have thought, even for the bullet to get there, a mysterious, terrible change had come over the elephant. He neither stirred nor fell, but every line of his body had altered. He looked suddenly stricken, shrunken, immensely old, as though the frightful impact of the bullet had paralyzed him without knocking him down. At last, after what seemed a long time—it might have been five seconds, I dare say—he sagged flabbily to his knees. His mouth slobbered. An enormous senility seemed to have settled upon him. One could have imagined him thousands of years old. I fired again into the same spot. At the second shot he did not collapse but climbed with desperate slowness to his feet and stood weakly upright, with legs sagging and head drooping. I fired a third time. That was the shot that did for him. You could see the agony of it jolt his whole body and knock the last remnant of strength from his legs. But in falling he seemed for a moment to rise, for as his hind legs collapsed beneath him he seemed to tower upward like a huge rock toppling, his trunk reaching skyward like a tree. He trumpeted, for the first and only time. And then down he came, his belly toward me, with a crash that seemed to shake the ground even where I lay.

I got up. The Burmans were already racing past me across the mud.   12
It was obvious that the elephant would never rise again, but he was
not dead. He was breathing very rhythmically with long rattling gasps,
his great mound of a side painfully rising and falling. His mouth was
wide open—I could see far down into caverns of pale pink throat. I
waited a long time for him to die, but his breathing did not weaken.
Finally I fired my two remaining shots into the spot where I thought
his heart must be. The thick blood welled out of him like red velvet,
but still he did not die. His body did not even jerk when the shots hit
him, the tortured breathing continued without a pause. He was dying,
very slowly and in great agony, but in some world remote from me
where not even a bullet could damage him further. I felt that I had got
to put an end to that dreadful noise. It seemed dreadful to see the great
beast lying there, powerless to move and yet powerless to die, and not
even to be able to finish him. I sent back for my small rifle and poured
shot after shot into his heart and down his throat. They seemed to
make no impression. The tortured gasps continued as steadily as the
ticking of a clock.

In the end I could not stand it any longer and went away. I heard   13
later that it took him half an hour to die. Burmans were bringing dahs*
and baskets even before I left, and I was told they had stripped his body
almost to the bones by the afternoon.

Afterward, of course, there were endless discussions about the   14
shooting of the elephant. The owner was furious, but he was only an
Indian and could do nothing. Besides, legally I had done the right thing,
for a mad elephant has to be killed, like a mad dog, if its owner fails
to control it. Among the Europeans opinion was divided. The older
men said I was right, the younger men said it was a damn shame to
shoot an elephant for killing a coolie, because an elephant was worth
more than any damn Coringhee coolie. And afterward I was very glad
that the coolie had been killed; it put me legally in the right and it gave
me a sufficient pretext for shooting the elephant. I often wondered
whether any of the others grasped that I had done it solely to avoid
looking a fool.

---

* *dahs:* knives for butchering animals.

VOCABULARY

paragraph 2: imperialism, supplant, prostrate
paragraph 4: Dravidian
paragraph 7: dominion, sahib
paragraph 8: squeamish
paragraph 11: glee, sagged, slobbered, senility
paragraph 14: pretext

QUESTIONS

1. Orwell states in paragraph 3: "One day something happened which in a roundabout way was enlightening. It was a tiny incident in itself, but it gave me a better glimpse than I had had before of the real nature of imperialism—the real motives for which despotic governments act." The incident, in its details, reveals the psychology of the imperialist ruler. What effects do the stuffy, cloudy weather and the behavior of the Burmese and their attitude toward the elephant have on his psychology? Why is the dead coolie described in detail in paragraph 4? Why is the shooting of the elephant described in detail in paragraph 11? In general, how does the incident reveal the motives Orwell mentions?

2. The incident reveals more than just the motives of the imperialist ruler: What does it reveal about mob and crisis psychology and the policeman in the middle?

3. Where in the essay is the thesis stated, and how do you account for its placement? Does Orwell restate it?

4. The exact diction contributes greatly to the development of the thesis, for Orwell does not merely *tell us*, he makes us see. In paragraph 11, for example, he states: ". . . I heard the devilish roar of *glee* that went up from the crowd." He might have chosen *laughter, hilarity,* or *mirth* to describe the behavior of the crowd, but *glee* is the exact word because it connotes something that the other three words do not—malice. And the elephant "*sagged* flabbily to his knees," not *dropped* or *sank,* because *sagged* denotes weight and, in the context of the passage, age. What does Orwell mean in the same paragraph by "His mouth *slobbered*" and "An enormous *senility* seemed to have settled upon him"? In paragraph 2 why "*caverns* of pale pink throat" rather than *depths?* In paragraph 4 why is the corpse *grinning* rather than *smiling?* (Consult the synonym listings in your dictionary, or compare definitions).

SUGGESTIONS FOR WRITING

1. Illustrate the last sentence of the essay from your own experience. Build the essay to the moment when you acted to avoid looking like a fool. Make your reader see and feel what you saw and felt.

2. Orwell states: "And my whole life, every white man's life in the East, was one long struggle not to be laughed at." Drawing on your experience and observation, discuss what you see as the feelings and motives of people charged with enforcing rules of some sort—perhaps hall monitors in high school, or lifeguards at a swimming pool, or supervisors at a playground, or babysitters. Use your discussion to draw a conclusion, as Orwell does.

PEGGY AND PIERRE STREIT

PEGGY AND PIERRE STREIT collaborated on numerous articles on life in the Middle East and Asia. Pierre Streit also produced documentaries for television and business corporations. In India, the thousands of subcastes in the Hindu caste system fall into major divisions or varnas in a descending hierarchy–the learned and warrior castes, followed by the merchant, laboring, servant, and other castes. The lowest of these, the outcastes, untouchable because impure in the eyes of the higher castes, perform the menial jobs (Barbara Crossette, *New York Times Magazine*, May 19, 1991). Today thousands of Indian families perform the same work as Shanti. Through the influence of the great Hindu political leader Mahatma Gandhi, the untouchable caste is now called Harijan—meaning "Child of God." In 1949 the Indian government outlawed discrimination against Harijans, but as the Streits show in their 1959 article, traditional attitudes remain powerful.

A WELL IN INDIA

The hot dry season in India. A corrosive wind drives rivulets of sand   1
across the land; torpid animals stand at the edge of dried-up water holes.
The earth is cracked and in the rivers the sluggish, falling waters have
exposed the sludge of the mud flats. Throughout the land the thoughts
of men turn to water. And in the village of Rampura these thoughts are
focused on the village well.

It is a simple concrete affair, built upon the hard earth worn by the feet   2
of five hundred villagers. It is surmounted by a wooden structure over which
ropes, tied to buckets, are lowered to the black, placid depths twenty feet
below. Fanning out from the well are the huts of the villagers—their walls
white from sun, their thatched roofs thick with dust blown from the fields.

At the edge of the well is a semi-circle of earthen pots and, crouched   3
at some distance behind them, a woman. She is an untouchable—a
sweeper in Indian parlance—a scavenger of the village. She cleans la-
trines, disposes of dead animals and washes drains. She also delivers village babies, for this—like all her work—is considered unclean by most
of village India.

Her work—indeed, her very presence—is considered polluting, and   4
since there is no well for untouchables in Rampura, her water jars must
be filled by upper-caste villagers.

There are dark shadows under her eyes and the flesh has fallen away   5
from her neck, for she, like her fellow outcastes, is at the end of a bitter
struggle. And if, in her narrow world, shackled by tradition and hemmed
in by poverty, she had been unaware of the power of the water of the
well at whose edge she waits—she knows it now.

Shanti, 30 years old, has been deserted by her husband, and supports   6
her three children. Like her ancestors almost as far back as history records,
she has cleaned the refuse from village huts and lanes. Hers is a life of
inherited duties as well as inherited rights. She serves, and her work calls
for payment of one chapatty—a thin wafer of unleavened bread—a day
from each of the thirty families she cares for.

But this is the hiatus between harvests; the oppressive lull before the   7
burst of monsoon rains; the season of flies and dust, heat and disease,
querulous voices and frayed tempers—and the season of want. There
is little food in Rampura for anyone, and though Shanti's chores have
continued as before, she has received only six chapatties a day for her
family—starvation wages.

Ten days ago she revolted. Driven by desperation, she defied an ele-   8
mental law of village India. She refused to make her sweeper's rounds—
refused to do the work tradition and religion had assigned her. Shocked
at her audacity, but united in desperation, the village's six other sweeper
families joined in her protest.

Word of her action spread quickly across the invisible line that sep-   9
arates the untouchables' huts from the rest of the village. As the day wore
on and the men returned from the fields, they gathered at the well—the
heart of the village—and their voices rose, shrill with outrage: a *sweeper*
defying them all! Shanti, a sweeper *and* a woman challenging a system
that had prevailed unquestioned for centuries! Their indignation spilled
over. It was true, perhaps, that the sweepers had not had their due. But
that was no fault of the upper caste. No fault of theirs that sun and earth
and water had failed to produce the food by which they could fulfill their
obligations. So, to bring the insurgents to heel, they employed their ultimate weapon; the earthen water jars of the village untouchables would
remain empty until they returned to work. For the sweepers of Rampura
the well had run dry.

No water; thirst, in the heat, went unslaked. The embers of the hearth   10
were dead, for there was no water for cooking. The crumbling walls of
outcaste huts went untended, for there was no water for repairs. There
was no fuel, for the fires of the village were fed with dung mixed with
water and dried. The dust and the sweat and the filth of their lives congealed on their skins and there it stayed, while life in the rest of the village—within sight of the sweepers—flowed on.

The day began and ended at the well. The men, their dhotis wrapped   11
about their loins, congregated at the water's edge in the hushed post-
dawn, their small brass water jugs in hand, their voices mingling in quiet
conversation as they rinsed their bodies and brushed their teeth. The buffaloes were watered, their soft muzzles lingering in the buckets before
they were driven off to the fields. Then came the women, their brass pots
atop their heads, to begin the ritual of water drawing: the careful lowering of the bucket in the well, lest it come loose from the rope; the grat-
ifying splash as it touched the water; the maneuvering to make it sink;
the squeal of rope against wooden pulley as it ascended. The sun rose
higher. Clothes were beaten clean on the rocks surrounding the well as
the women gossiped. A traveler from a near-by road quenched his thirst
from a villager's urn. Two little boys, hot and bored, dropped pebbles
into the water and waited for their hollow splash, far below.

As the afternoon wore on and the sun turned orange through the dust, the men came back from the fields. They doused the parched, cracked hides of their water buffaloes and murmured contentedly, themselves, as the water coursed over their own shoulders and arms. And finally, as twilight closed in, came the evening procession of women, stately, graceful, their bare feet moving smoothly over the earth, their full skirts swinging about their ankles, the heavy brass pots once again balanced on their heads.

The day was ended and life was as it always was—almost. Only the fetid odor of accumulated refuse and the assertive buzz of flies attested to strife in the village. For, while tradition and religion decreed that sweepers must clean, it also ordained that the socially blessed must not. Refuse lay where it fell and rotted.

The strain of the water boycott was beginning to tell on the untouchables. For days they had held their own. But on the third their thin reserve of flesh had fallen away. Movements were slower; voices softer; minds dull. More and more the desultory conversation turned to the ordinary: the delicious memory of sliding from the back of a wallowing buffalo into a pond; the feel of bare feet in wet mud; the touch of fresh water on parched lips; the anticipation of monsoon rains.

One by one the few tools they owned were sold for food. A week passed, and on the ninth day two sweeper children were down with fever. On the tenth day Shanti crossed the path that separated outcaste from upper caste and walked through familiar, winding alleyways to one of the huts she served.

"Your time is near," she told the young, expectant mother. "Tell your man to leave his sickle home when he goes to the fields. I've had to sell mine." (It is the field sickle that cuts the cord of newborn babies in much of village India.) Shanti, the instigator of the insurrection, had resumed her ancestral duties; the strike was broken. Next morning, as ever, she waited at the well. Silently, the procession of upper-caste women approached. They filled their jars to the brim and without a word they filled hers.

She lifted the urns to her head, steadied them, and started back to her quarters—back to a life ruled by the powers that still rule most of the world: not the power of atoms or electricity, nor the power of alliances or power blocs, but the elemental powers of hunger, of disease, of tradition—and of water.

VOCABULARY

paragraph 1: corrosive, rivulets
paragraph 3: untouchable, parlance
paragraph 4: upper-caste
paragraph 7: hiatus, monsoon
paragraph 9: insurgents
paragraph 10: unslaked, congealed
paragraph 13: fetid

QUESTIONS

1. The Streits build to a statement of their thesis at the end of paragraph 5. Why is it necessary to portray the world of the untouchable before stating the thesis?

2. Where in the essay is the thesis restated? Is the restatement more informative or detailed than the original statement of it?

3. What is the attitude of the authors toward the world they portray and the fate of Shanti? Do they seem to be taking sides?

4. Is it important to the thesis that Shanti is a woman? Are the authors concerned with her as a woman, in addition to their concern for her as an untouchable?

5. Is the concern of the essay equally with the power of water and the power of tradition? Or are these considerations subordinate to the portrayal of the untouchable and the courage shown?

6. Are we given a motive directly for what Shanti does—or is the motive implied?

SUGGESTIONS FOR WRITING

1. Develop an idea relating to the power of tradition and illustrate it from personal experience and observation. Provide enough background so that your reader understands why the tradition is important to the people who observe it.

2. Describe a conflict between you and your parents or school officials or between a person and a group of some sort. Explain how the conflict arose from a basic difference in attitude, ideas, or feelings—a difference that reveals something important about you and the other people involved.

ERIC SEVAREID

Born in Velva, North Dakota, ERIC SEVAREID (1912-92) graduated from the University of Minnesota in 1935 and immediately began his career as a journalist with the *Minneapolis Journal*. In 1939 he began his long association with the Columbia Broadcasting Company as a war correspondent in Europe. From 1964 to 1977 he delivered his commentary on the CBS Evening News. His books include *Small Sounds in the Night* (1956) and an autobiography, *Not So Wild a Dream* (1976). Like Orwell in "Shooting an Elephant," Sevareid builds through a careful presentation of detail to increasingly broad truths about the world of his youth and human nature generally.

VELVA, NORTH DAKOTA

My home town has changed in these thirty years of the American story. It is changing now, will go on changing as America changes. Its biography, I suspect, would read much the same as that of all other home towns. Depression and war and prosperity have all left their marks; modern science, modern tastes, manners, philosophies, fears and ambitions have touched my town as indelibly as they have touched New York or Panama City.

Sights have changed: there is a new precision about street and home, a clearing away of chicken yards, cow barns, pigeon-crested cupolas, weed lots and coulees, the dim and secret adult-free rendezvous of boys. An intricate metal "jungle gym" is a common backyard sight, the sack swing uncommon. There are wide expanses of clear windows designed to let in the parlor light, fewer ornamental windows of colored glass designed to keep it out. Attic and screen porch are slowly vanishing and lovely shades of pastel are painted upon new houses, tints that once would have embarrassed farmer and merchant alike.

Sounds have changed; I heard not once the clopping of a horse's hoofs, nor the mourn of a coyote. I heard instead the shriek of brakes, the heavy throbbing of the once-a-day Braniff airliner into Minot, the shattering sirens born of war, the honk of a diesel locomotive which surely cannot call to faraway places the heart of a wakeful boy like the old steam whistle in the night. You can walk down the streets of my town now and hear from open windows the intimate voices of the Washington commentators in casual converse on the great affairs of state; but you cannot hear on Sunday morning the singing in Norwegian of the Lutheran hymns; the old country seems now part of a world left long behind and the old-country accents grow fainter in the speech of my Velva neighbors.   3

The people have not changed, but the *kinds of* people have changed; there is no longer an official, certified town drunk, no longer a "Crazy John," spitting his worst epithet, "rotten chicken legs," as you hurriedly passed him by. People so sick are now sent to places of proper care. No longer is there an official town joker, like the druggist MacKnight, who would spot a customer in the front of the store, have him called to the phone, then slip to the phone behind the prescription case, and imitate the man's wife to perfection with orders to bring home more bread and sausage and Cream of Wheat. No longer anyone like the early attorney, J. L. Lee, who sent fabulous dispatches to that fabulous tabloid, the *Chicago Blade,* such as his story of the wild man captured on the prairie and chained to the wall in the drugstore basement. (This, surely, was Velva's first notoriety; inquiries came from anthropologists all over the world.)   4

No, the "characters" are vanishing in Velva, just as they are vanishing in our cities, in business, in politics. The "well-rounded, socially integrated" personality that the progressive schoolteachers are so obsessed with is increasing rapidly, and I am not at all sure that this is good. Maybe we need more personalities with knobs and handles and rugged lumps of individuality. They may not make life more smooth; more interesting they surely make it.   5

They eat differently in Velva now; there are frozen fruits and sea food and exotic delicacies we only read about in novels in those meat-and-potato days. They dress differently. The hard white collars of the businessmen are gone with the shiny alpaca coats. There are comfortable tweeds now, and casual blazers with a touch in their colors of California, which seems so close in time and distance.   6

It is distance and time that have changed the most and worked the   7
deepest changes in Velva's life. The telephone, the car, the smooth highway, radio and television are consolidating the entities of our country.
The county seat of Towner now seems no closer than the state capital of
Bismarck; the voices and concerns of Presidents, French premiers and
Moroccan pashas are no farther away than the portable radio on Aunt
Jessey's kitchen table. The national news magazines are stacked each week
in Harold Anderson's drugstore beside the new soda fountain, and the
excellent *Minot Daily News* smells hot from the press each afternoon.

Consolidation. The nearby hamlets of Sawyer and Logan and Voltaire   8
had their own separate banks and papers and schools in my days of dusty
buggies and Model T's marooned in the snowdrifts. Now these hamlets
are dying. A bright yellow bus takes the Voltaire kids to Velva each day
for high school. Velva has grown—from 800 to 1,300—because the miners from the Truax coal mine can commute to their labors each morning
and the nearby farmers can live in town if they choose. Minot has tripled
in size to 30,000. Once the "Magic City" was a distant and splendid
Baghdad, visited on special occasions long prepared for. Now it is a
twenty-five minute commuter's jump away. So P. W. Miller and Jay Louis
Monicken run their businesses in Minot but live on in their old family
homes in Velva. So Ray Michelson's two girls on his farm to the west
drive up each morning to their jobs as maids in Minot homes. Aunt Jessey
said, "Why, Saturday night I counted sixty-five cars just between here
and Sawyer, all going up to the show in Minot."

The hills are prison battlements no longer; the prairies no heart-   9
sinking barrier, but a passageway free as the swelling ocean, inviting you
to sail home and away at your whim and your leisure. (John and Helen
made an easy little jaunt of 700 miles that week-end to see their eldest
daughter in Wyoming.)

Consolidation. Art Kumm's bank serves a big region now; its assets   10
are $2,000,000 to $3,000,000 instead of the $200,000 or $300,000 in
my father's day. Eighteen farms near Velva are under three ownerships
now. They calculate in sections; "acres" is an almost forgotten term. Aunt
Jessey owns a couple of farms, and she knows they are much better run.
"It's no longer all take out and no put in," she said. "Folks strip farm
now; they know all about fertilizers. They care for it and they'll hand on
the land in good shape." The farmers gripe about their cash income, and
not without reason at the moment, but they will admit that life is good
compared with those days of drought and foreclosure, manure banked

against the house for warmth, the hand pump frozen at 30 below and the fitful kerosene lamp on the kitchen table. Electrification has done much of this, eased back-breaking chores that made their wives old as parchment at forty, brought life and music and the sound of human voices into their parlors at night.

And light upon the prairie. "From the hilltop," said Aunt Jessey, "the   11
farms look like stars at night."

Many politicians deplore the passing of the old family-size farm, but   12
I am not so sure. I saw around Velva a release from what was like slavery to the tyrannical soil, release from the ignorance that darkens the soul and from the loneliness that corrodes it. In this generation my Velva friends have rejoined the general American society that their pioneering fathers left behind when they first made the barren trek in the days of the wheat rush. As I sit here in Washington writing this, I can feel their nearness. I never felt it before save in my dreams.

But now I must ask myself: Are they nearer to one another? And the   13
answer is no; yet I am certain that this is good. The shrinking of time and distance has made contrast and relief available to their daily lives. They do not know one another quite so well because they are not so much obliged to. I know that democracy rests upon social discipline, which in turn rests upon personal discipline; passions checked, hard words withheld, civic tasks accepted, work well done, accountings honestly rendered. The old-fashioned small town was this discipline in its starkest, most primitive form; without this discipline the small town would have blown itself apart.

For personal and social neuroses festered under this hard scab of con-   14
formity. There was no place to go, no place to let off steam; few dared to voice unorthodox ideas, read strange books, admire esoteric art or publicly write or speak of their dreams and their soul's longings. The world was not "too much with us," the world was too little with us and we were too much with one another.

The door to the world stands open now, inviting them to leave any-   15
time they wish. It is the simple fact of the open door that makes all the difference; with its opening the stale air rushed out. So, of course, the people themselves do not have to leave, because, as the stale air went out, the fresh air came in.

Human nature is everywhere the same. He who is not forced to help   16
his neighbor for his own existence will not only give him help, but his true good will as well. Minot and its hospital are now close at hand, but

the people of Velva put their purses together, built their own clinic and homes for the two young doctors they persuaded to come and live among them. Velva has no organized charity, but when a farmer falls ill, his neighbors get in his crop; if a townsman has a financial catastrophe his personal friends raise a fund to help him out. When Bill's wife, Ethel, lay dying so long in the Minot hospital and nurses were not available, Helen and others took their turns driving up there just to sit with her so she would know in her gathering dark that friends were at hand.

It is personal freedom that makes us better persons, and they are freer   17 in Velva now. There is no real freedom without privacy, and a resident of my home town can be a private person much more than he could before. People are able to draw at least a little apart from one another. In drawing apart, they gave their best human instincts room for expansion.

VOCABULARY

paragraph 1: indelibly
paragraph 4: certified, epithet, tabloid, notoriety, anthropologists
paragraph 5: progressive
paragraph 6: alpaca, blazers
paragraph 7: pashas
paragraph 8: consolidation, commute
paragraph 9: battlements, whim, jaunt
paragraph 10: foreclosure
paragraph 12: deplore, corrodes, trek
paragraph 13: starkest
paragraph 14: neuroses, scab, unorthodox, esoteric

QUESTIONS

1. Where does Sevareid indicate his attitude toward his hometown? What is his thesis?

2. What details in the whole essay support the dominant impression Sevareid creates of the town in his opening paragraph? Is any of this detail unrelated to this impression?

3. What are the causes of the change in life in Velva? Does Sevareid indicate a main cause?

4. What does Sevareid mean by *discipline* in the statement in paragraph 13, "without this discipline the small town would have blown itself apart"?

5. Sevareid points up a series of paradoxes toward the end. What are these, and what do they contribute to the tone of the conclusion?

SUGGESTIONS FOR WRITING

1. Describe important changes that have occurred in the town or the neighborhood in which you grew up, and discuss the reasons. Use these changes to develop a thesis of your own.

2. Sevareid writes that much was lost; the changes that occurred in farming and the general life of Velva were perhaps for the better. Develop your essay further by explaining why you would—or would not—say the same thing about the changes that occurred in your town or neighborhood.

2

MAIN AND SUBORDINATE IDEAS

THE PARAGRAPH

An author may develop the main or central idea of a paragraph through a series of subordinate ideas. Consider the opening sentences of the following paragraph on country superstitions.

In the folklore of the country, numerous superstitions relate to winter weather. Back-country farmers examine their corn husks—the thicker the husk, the colder the winter. They watch the acorn crop—the more acorns, the more severe the season. They observe where white-faced hornets place their paper nests—the higher they are, the deeper will be the snow. They examine the size and shape and color of the spleens of butchered hogs for clues to the severity of the season. They keep track of the blooming of dogwood in the spring—the more abundant the blooms, the more bitter the cold in January. When chipmunks carry their tails high and squirrels have heavier fur and mice come into country houses early in the fall, the superstitious gird themselves for a long, hard winter. Without any scientific basis, a wider-than-usual black band on a woolly-bear caterpillar is accepted as a sign that winter will arrive early and stay late. Even the way a cat sits beside the stove carries its message to the credulous. According to a belief once widely held in the Ozarks, a cat sitting with its tail to the fire indicates very cold weather is on the way. (Edwin Way Teale, *Wandering Through Winter*)

The first sentence is the main idea; the second sentence, a subordinate idea that develops it through illustration:

In the folklore of the country, numerous superstitions relate to
winter weather.
   Back-country farmers examine their corn husks—
      the thicker the husk, the colder the winter.

We have indented to show the levels of subordination in these sentences.
Notice that the third sentence has the same importance as the second in
developing the main idea:

They watch the acorn crop—
   the more acorns, the more severe the season.

Of course, in writing paragraphs you don't indent in this way to show
the relative importance of your ideas. But you do in writing essays: the
break for a new paragraph—through an indentation—tells the reader
that you are introducing a new or related idea or topic. Within the paragraph you need ways of substituting for the indentations shown above.
One of these ways is the use of parallel phrasing to show that ideas have
the same importance:

They watch the acorn crop . . .
They observe . . .
They examine . . .

   In longer paragraphs, you can distinguish the main idea by repeating or restating it at the end. We will see later in the book that the
beginning and ending are usually the most emphatic parts of sentences
because of their prominence. The same is true of paragraphs and essays.

LYTTON STRACHEY

LYTTON STRACHEY (1890–1932), one of England's great biographers, was
particularly interested in revered figures of the nineteenth century and
earlier English history. Strachey looks at the strengths and failings of
his subjects, joining fact with the imagined creation of their inner life.
We see this method in his portrait of Queen Victoria. Born in 1819,
Victoria became queen in 1837 at the age of eighteen, and in 1840 married a first cousin her own age, the German prince Albert of Saxe-Coburg.
When Albert died of a sudden illness in 1861, at the age of 42, she entered

a long period of private mourning—for the remainder of her life preserving her physical surroundings as they had existed in his lifetime. Strachey shows how little the author needs to say when the right details are chosen and organized carefully.

QUEEN VICTORIA
AT THE END OF HER LIFE

[1]She gave orders that nothing should be thrown away—and nothing was. [2]There, in drawer after drawer, in wardrobe after wardrobe, reposed the dresses of seventy years. [3]But not only the dresses—the furs and the mantles and subsidiary frills and the muffs and the parasols and the bonnets—all were ranged in chronological order, dated and complete. [4]A great cupboard was devoted to the dolls; in the china room at Windsor a special table held the mugs of her childhood, and her children's mugs as well. [5]Mementoes of the past surrounded her in serried accumulations. [6]In every room the tables were powdered thick with the photographs of relatives; their portraits, revealing them at all ages, covered the walls; their figures, in solid marble, rose up from pedestals, or gleamed from brackets in the form of gold and silver statuettes. [7]The dead, in every shape—in miniatures, in porcelain, in enormous life-size oil-paintings— were perpetually about her. [8]John Brown stood upon her writing table in solid gold.* [9]Her favorite horses and dogs, endowed with a new durability, crowded round her footsteps. [10]Sharp, in silver gilt, dominated the dinner table; Boy and Boz lay together among unfading flowers in bronze. [11]And it was not enough that each particle of the past should be given the stability of metal or of marble: the whole collection, in its arrangement, no less than its entity, should be immutably fixed. [12]There might be additions, but there might never be alterations. [13]No chintz might change, no carpet, no curtain, be replaced by another; or, if long use at last made it necessary, the stuffs and the patterns must be so identically reproduced that the keenest eye might not detect the difference. [14]No new picture could be hung upon the walls at Windsor, for those already

---

* John Brown (1826–1883) was the Scottish attendant to Victoria's husband, Prince Albert, and after the death of the Prince in 1861, to the Queen herself.—Ed.

there had been put in their places by Albert, whose decisions were eternal. [15]So, indeed, were Victoria's. [16]To ensure that they should be the aid of the camera was called in. [17]Every single article in the Queen's possession was photographed from several points of view. [18]These photographs were submitted to Her Majesty, and when, after careful inspection, she had approved of them, they were placed in a series of albums, richly bound. [19]Then, opposite each photograph, an entry was made, indicating the number of the article, the number of the room in which it was kept, its exact position in the room and all its principal characteristics. [20]The fate of every object which had undergone this process was henceforth irrevocably sealed. [21]The whole multitude, once and for all, took up its steadfast station. [22]And Victoria, with a gigantic volume or two of the endless catalogue always beside her, to look through, to ponder upon, to expatiate over, could feel, with a double contentment, that the transitoriness of this world had been arrested by the amplitude of her might.

VOCABULARY

sentence 3: subsidiary, frills, parasols
sentence 5: mementoes, serried
sentence 11: immutably
sentence 13: chintz
sentence 20: irrevocably
sentence 22: expatiate, transitoriness, amplitude

QUESTIONS

1. In his portrait of Victoria in her old age, Strachey develops and illustrates several major ideas that build to his central or topic idea. What are these ideas?

2. Strachey states in sentence 2 that Victoria saved the dresses of seventy years; in sentence 3, that she saved her furs and bonnets, as well as other articles of clothing—and arranged and dated them chronologically. How does Strachey show that he is moving from one surprising, even astonishing, fact to an even more surprising one?

3. Compare sentences 11 and 12 with those that follow. How does Strachey indicate that he is building the paragraph to even more surprising details?

4. What contributes to the climactic effect of the final sentence of the paragraph?

5. Has Strachey made Queen Victoria human to you? Or is she merely an eccentric?

SUGGESTIONS FOR WRITING

1. Write a character sketch of an unusual friend or teacher, centering on a dominant trait and presenting related traits as Strachey does. Present these related traits in the order of rising importance—as illustrations of the dominant trait.

2. Rewrite Strachey's paragraph, beginning with his concluding sentence and achieving a sense of climax in your reordering of ideas and details.

THE ESSAY

The thesis is the most important idea in an essay. When an essay builds to its thesis through a series of subordinate ideas and details, we may sense a rising importance of ideas, even perhaps a sense of climax. As in the paragraph, it is important that we sense the relative importance of these ideas and details. An essay in which all seem to have the same importance would be extremely hard to read.

We can sense this relative importance of ideas even in the topic sentences, as in these sentences that open the first four paragraphs of Sevareid's essay on Velva, North Dakota. The different indentations show the relative weight of each idea:

My home town has changed in these thirty years . . . .
Sights have changed . . . .
Sounds have changed . . . .
The people have not changed, but the *kinds of* people have changed.

Sevareid builds to his thesis through a series of increasingly broad generalizations. Here are the opening sentences of the last six paragraphs:

> Many politicians deplore the passing of the old family-size farm, but I am not so sure.
> But now I must ask myself: Are they nearer to one another?
> For personal and social neuroses festered under this hard scab of conformity.
> The door to the world stands open now. . . .
> Human nature is everywhere the same.
> It is personal freedom that makes us better persons, and they are freer in Velva now [*thesis*].

Sevareid's sentences show that we do not always need formal transitions to tell us which ideas are main and which are subordinate. The clear, logical relationship of Sevareid's ideas shows their relative importance. But, as in the paragraph, formal transitions are sometimes needed (*thus, however, therefore, moreover*). Having a sense of the relative importance of our ideas and details is important as we write.

SALLY CARRIGHAR

The writer and naturalist SALLY CARRIGHAR was born in Cleveland, Ohio, the scene of the introduction to her autobiography, *Home to the Wilderness* (1973), reprinted here. After graduation from Wellesley College, Carrighar decided to become a nature writer: "There could be no finer subject than woods and fields, streams, lakes, and mountainsides and the creatures who live in that world. It would be a subject of inexhaustible interest, a supreme joy to be learning to tell it all straight and truthfully." For nine years Carrighar lived in an isolated Alaskan village, studying Eskimo life and the animals of the Arctic region. She has written about this experience and about wildlife generally in *Icebound Summer* (1953), *Wild Voice of the North* (1959), *Wild Heritage* (1965), and other books. In the passage that follows, she describes experiences and people that awakened her imagination and curiosity about life.

THE BLAST FURNACE

We were a father and his first-born, a four-year-old girl, setting out every   1
Sunday afternoon to see the industrial marvels of Cleveland, Ohio. The
young man had grown up in a smaller Canadian town and he was
delighted with Cleveland, which hummed and clanged with the vast new
developments steel had made possible. In temperament he was anything
but an engineer; here however he was excited to feel that he had jumped
into the very heart of the torrent of progress.

Most often we walked on the banks of the Cuyahoga River to see   2
the drawbridge come apart and rise up, like giant black jaws taking a
bite of the sky, so that boats could go through: the long freighters that
brought iron ore from Lake Superior, other large and small freighters,
fishing boats, passenger steamers. My father's eyes never tired of watching them make their smooth way up and down the river. His father, born
in Amsterdam of a seagoing family, had been a skipper on the Great
Lakes. Perhaps my father too should have been a sailor, but he was something nearly as satisfying—he worked for a railroad.

And so we went to the roundhouse where the steam engines stood   3
when they were not pulling trains. They had all entered through the same
door but inside their tracks spread apart, as gracefully as the ribs of a
lady's fan. My father knew a great deal about engines, he knew the names
of some of these and he walked among them with pride.

On our way to the roundhouse we passed through the freight yards   4
where long trains of boxcars lay on their sidings. My father said that the
cars belonged to different railroads and came from various parts of the
country, being coupled together here because all those in one train were
bound for the same destination. This was getting too complicated but there
was nothing complicated about my father's emotion when he said. "Working for a railroad is like living everywhere in the country at once!" A characteristic enchantment came into his eyes and voice, a contagious exhilaration which meant that anything it attached to was good. Living everywhere
was something that even a child could grasp vaguely and pleasantly.

My father and I made other trips and best were the ones to the blast   5
furnaces. He explained how the iron ore from the boats was mixed with
coal and carried in little cars to the top of the chimney above the furnace. It was dumped in, and as it fell down "a special kind of very hot
air" was blown into it. The coal and iron ore caught fire, and below they

fell into great tubs as melting metal, a pinkish gold liquid, incandescent as the sun is when it is starting to set. The man and child were allowed to go rather near the vats, to feel the scorching heat and to drown their gaze in the glowing boil. All the rest of the building was dark; the silhouettes of the men who worked at the vats were black shadows. Wearing long leather aprons, they moved about the vats ladling off the slag. That was very skilled work, my father said; the men had to know just how much of the worthless slag to remove. For years afterwards, when we could no longer spend Sunday afternoons on these expeditions, we used to go out of our house at night to see the pink reflections from the blast furnaces on the clouds over Cleveland. We could remember that we had watched the vatfuls of heavily moving gold, and those events from the past were an unspoken bond between us.

Someone once said, "Your father must have been trying to turn you into a boy. He'd probably wanted his first child to be a son." Perhaps; but it was not strange to him to show a girl the achievements of men. He thought of women as human beings and assumed that they, even one very young, would be interested in anything that was interesting to him. He had absorbed that attitude from the women he'd grown up with, his mother and her four sisters, all of whom led adventurous lives. His favorite Aunt Chris had married a clipper captain and sailed with him all her life. When they retired, having seen the entire world, they chose to settle in Burma. Another aunt married one of the Morgan family, who established the famous breed of Morgan horses, and took up a homestead in Manitoba. Aunt Mary, a physician's wife, went with him out to San Francisco during the Gold Rush and stayed there. The fourth aunt had married the inspector of ships' chronometers at Quebec; and my father's mother, of course, had married her skipper from Holland. In the winter when he was not on his ship he ran a factory for making barrel staves that he had established in western Kentucky—all this and the fathering of five children by the time he was twenty-eight, when he lost his life in a notorious Lake Erie storm. His wife, a musician, brought up her five without complaint, just as her mother, also an early widow, had reared her five gallant girls. With his memories of women like these it was not surprising that my father would wish, even somewhat prematurely, to show his daughter the things that were thrilling to him. I did not comprehend all his family history at four, but I did absorb the impression that girls and women reached out

6

for life eagerly and that it was natural for them to be interested in absolutely everything.

VOCABULARY

paragraph 1: temperament
paragraph 4: contagious, exhilaration
paragraph 5: Incandescent, slag
paragraph 6: chronometer

QUESTIONS

1. In paragraph 1 Carrighar develops her opening sentence—the main idea of the paragraph—with specific detail about her father. What is the main idea of paragraph 2, and how does she use the detail of the paragraph to develop it?

2. Paragraph 4 moves from specific detail to the main idea. What is that idea, and how does the author give it prominence?

3. Which of the subordinate ideas in paragraph 5 are in turn illustrated or developed?

4. Paragraphs 1–5 are subordinate to paragraph 6, which draws a conclusion from the experiences described and develops it through details of a different sort. What is this conclusion, and what new details develop it? How is this conclusion—the main idea of the paragraph—restated later in the paragraph and made prominent?

SUGGESTIONS FOR WRITING

1. Write several paragraphs describing childhood experiences that taught you something about the adult world and about yourself. Begin with these truths, or build the paragraphs up to them, as Carrighar does.

2. Write several paragraphs about information you received or impressions you developed about women in your family. If you wish, contrast these impressions with those you received about boys and men. Use these impressions to develop a thesis.

DAVID HOLAHAN

DAVID HOLAHAN has written for numerous magazines and newspapers throughout the United States. After his graduation from Yale in 1971, he published two Connecticut weekly newspapers until their sale in 1982. Holahan writes about his football experiences at Yale from an unusual point of view. He makes the subject his own through concrete details that give insight into college football and the attitudes and feelings of the players.

WHY DID I EVER PLAY FOOTBALL?

Coach kept running the halfback sweep through the projector, clicking the stop, rewind and forward buttons as he dwelled on each "individual breakdown" by our defense. Princeton had gained twenty yards on the play and our individual mistakes added up to a "total Yale breakdown." Gallagher and I sat with the other sophomores, savoring the embarrassment of the first-stringers.   1

The last individual to break down on the play was the defensive safety who started ahead of me. Yale's sports publicity department was touting him as a "pro prospect," but during the eleventh screening of his mistake, he protested that he was not sure how to defense a sweep. After three years on the varsity, our NFL-bound star didn't know how to play your everyday end run.   2

"The first rule," Gallagher said as loudly as he could, "is don't get hurt." Suppressed laughter spread through the room. Everyone knew "the films don't lie" and that "newspaper clippings don't make tackles"; that "you have to want it," even in the Ivy League.   3

I'm not entirely sure why I played football; it might have been because of those great clichés. I certainly didn't enjoy hitting people the way Gallagher did. He liked to bury his helmet into a quarterback's ribs and drive him into the turf. As he returned to the huddle, there would   4 be a strange expression on his face, somewhere between a grimace and a smile. After a game he would be sore, bruised and bloodied, like the other linemen and linebackers, while I would feel about the same as I did after an uneventful mixer at Vassar.

Defensive safeties are not supposed to make a lot of tackles, especially 5 when the people up front are good, which ours were, and that was just fine with me. Still, some of my most vivid memories are of moments of intense pain. Once in junior year I found myself in a dreaded position: one-on-one with a fullback charging as swiftly as his bulky legs would carry him. He was ten yards away and closing fast. He was also growling. "His S. A. T. scores must be beauts," flashed through my mind and the urge to flee became acute. Thousands of eyes were watching—including Coach's camera. If I blew it I would have to see the replay at least a dozen times.

Suddenly I was moving sideways through the air, pain jolting my body, 6 the fullback forgotten. I hit the ground writhing, clutching my side and pulling my knees up to my chest. There was no air in my lungs. For a moment the world stopped at my skin. I wanted to stay crumpled up on the ground, but one of our linemen pulled me to my feet with one hand and half-carried me to the huddle. It must have been their end who hit me. I had seen him split out wide, then I forgot about him. He weighed over 200 pounds; I went about 160. What was I thinking of, playing football? I didn't hear our captain call the defensive signals, but fear slowly returned as the pain subsided. If that quarterback were smart he would try a pass in my zone. The pass never came. Thank God we were playing Harvard.

Continuing to play football was not a particularly rational thing for 7 me to do. In sixth grade I was as big and strong and fast as anyone our six-man team faced. And jocks were popular then. By college virtually everyone I played against was bigger and stronger, and the consensus on campus in the late 1960s was that we were a bunch of neofascists, at best. So much for "Boola, Boola." And when it wasn't a physically grinding ordeal, practice, too, could be as boring as Archeology 101.

Saturday's approach would turn my insides to mush, but the day I 8 dreaded most was Sunday, film day. "Now I want everyone to watch the tackling technique on this play," Coach would say, "Holahan, I hope you squeeze your dates harder than this." Gallagher laughed the loudest.

Oh, I had my moments, usually when the people up front either 9 played badly or were overmatched. Then I got a workout and there was no place to hide. Against Dartmouth, senior year, I turned positively vicious after watching their halfback gloat over one of our players lying injured on the field. I started burying my helmet into people even if they didn't have the ball. Once I made that halfback groan in pain. I also said some ugly things about his mother. I intercepted two passes. And the next day brought sweet soreness; so that's how Gallagher felt after every game.

There were other players who must have had a tougher time figuring   10
out why they were playing football; high-school hotshots who couldn't crack the second string, but who hung on. Some who didn't play in games, never expected to, maybe never even wanted to, for blocking and tackling are clearly unpleasant experiences. A few were not in the least bit athletic. Who knows, they may have been doing it for their résumés, but I suppose they had their moments too, when things would happen that could never take place in Archaeology 101. For me, Coach's films had something to do with why I continued to play.

Sunday afternoon was both a social and a moral occasion—funny,   11
embarrassing, depressing or happy, depending on how the team had done and how each player had performed. Every fall Sabbath was a new Judgment Day. What was shown on the screen was often harsh, but always just. I could fool professors and pass courses without working very hard, but no one could slip anything past that camera. If I played well Saturday, I knew it; still, the camera confirmed it. There was no place to hide in that room, no big linemen up front to take the heat. Film immortalized shirking efforts.

I have often thought of driving forty minutes to New Haven and digging   12
ging up that old Dartmouth game, going back fourteen years to see a younger, stronger, less cautious me. The temptation seems to grow each year, but I will never do it. It would be cheating the camera to look only at that one film.

VOCABULARY

paragraph 1: savoring, first-stringers
paragraph 2: touting, varsity
paragraph 4: clichés, grimace
paragraph 7: virtually, neofascists
paragraph 10: résumés
paragraph 11: shirking

QUESTIONS

1. Holahan might have opened the essay with the question asked in the title instead of building to it through the details of paragraphs 1–3. What does he gain through this buildup of details?

2. In paragraphs 5–6 Holahan describes an experience as a defensive safety in a college game with Harvard. Why does he present this experience before turning to earlier experiences as a football player?

3. Holahan builds to general conclusions through his experiences with football. How does he show that these conclusions are the main ideas of his essay?

4. What is the answer to the question that he asks in the title of the essay and in paragraph 4, and where does he answer the question? What does he gain in answering the question where he does?

SUGGESTIONS FOR WRITING

1. Illustrate your reasons for playing a sport or a musical instrument or for performing a similar activity. Don't state the reasons directly. Let your reader discover them through the details of your essay.

2. Write an essay on one of the following topics or on one of your own choosing. Give your thesis emphasis by introducing it in a prominent place in the essay—perhaps at the end of the opening paragraph, or in the final paragraph. If you begin the essay with your thesis, you can give it emphasis by repeating or restating it at key points:

    a. the art of keeping friends

    b. on not giving advice

    c. the art of persuading children

    d. on living away from home

    e. on waiting in line

3

ORDER OF IDEAS

THE PARAGRAPH

A unified paragraph develops one idea at a time and makes each idea relevant to the topic idea. You will keep a paragraph unified if, as you write and revise, you consider the order in which you want to present your ideas and details. This order is sometimes determined by the subject of the paragraph and sometimes by the audience you have in mind—and sometimes by both. For example, in describing parallel parking for people learning to drive, you probably would present each step as it occurs. But in describing the same process to driving instructors, you might present these steps in the order of their difficulty, to single out those needing the most practice.

An account of a process, or a narrative, is usually chronological. A description of a scene is generally spatial in organization—the details are presented as the eye sees them. The details or ideas can also be ordered in other ways, for example:

- from the easy to the difficult, as in the paragraph written for driving instructors
- from the less to the more important
- from the less to the more interesting or exciting
- from the general to the specific—for example, from the theory of combustion to the details of the process
- from the specific to the general—for example, from simple effects of gravity, like falling off a bike, to a definition of gravity or comment on these effects.

When ideas move from the less to the more important, the sense of importance is sometimes our own. We need to show this to the reader, perhaps through a simple transition like the words *more importantly*. We can dispense with such transitions when the sense of rising importance is expressed directly, as in the famous statement of Julius Caesar— "I came, I saw, I conquered"—or in the details themselves:

> A furious gale attacks him like a personal enemy, tries to grasp his limbs, fastens upon his mind, seeks to rout his very spirit out of him. (Joseph Conrad, *Typhoon*)

As in this sentence, we can achieve climax by making one idea seem to anticipate another and by giving weight to the final idea (in Conrad's sentence, through the word *very*). The terminal position in a sentence or paragraph is a position of natural emphasis because of its prominence— a fact that we can take advantage of in giving weight to ideas or details.

A paragraph may combine two or more orders of ideas. For instance, a paragraph written for driving instructors may move from the easy to the difficult steps of parallel parking, and at the same time from the less to the more important or even interesting.

E. B. WHITE

E. B. WHITE (1899–1985) was one of America's most distinguished writers—an essayist, a poet, a writer of books for children. His long association with *The New Yorker* magazine began in 1926. The columns that appeared in Harper's magazine under the title "One Man's Meat" were collected in 1942 in a book of the same name. Other essays are found in *The Second Tree from the Corner* (1954), *The Points of My Compass* (1962), and *Essays of E. B. White* (1977). In all of these books there is much about Maine, where White lived for many years. But the city of New York was never far from his thoughts, as you can see in his profile of the city later in this book (p. 123).

IN AN ELEVATOR

In an elevator, ascending with strangers to familiar heights, the breath congeals, the body stiffens, the spirit marks time. These brief vertical journeys that we make in a common lift, from street level to office level, past the missing thirteenth floor—they afford moments of suspended animation, unique and probably beneficial. Passengers in an elevator, whether wedged tight or scattered with room to spare, achieve in their perpendicular passage a trancelike state: each person adhering to the unwritten code, a man descending at five in the afternoon with his nose buried in a strange woman's back hair, reducing his breath to an absolute minimum necessary to sustain life, willing to suffocate rather than allow a suggestion of his physical presence to impinge; a man coming home at one A.M., ascending with only one other occupant of the car, carefully avoiding any slight recognition of joint occupancy. What is there about elevator travel that induces this painstaking catalepsy? A sudden solemnity, perhaps, which seizes people when they feel gravity being tampered with—they hope successfully. Sometimes it seems to us as though everyone in the car were in silent prayer.

VOCABULARY

congeals, animation, perpendicular, adhering, impinge, catalepsy, solemnity

QUESTIONS

1. What kind of tensions build in elevator rides, according to White?

2. How does White suggest this buildup of tension through the details of various rides?

3. Why do you think he concluded his description of elevator rides with a ride at one A.M.?

4. To what idea or reflection does White build the paragraph? Would the paragraph have the same effect if he had begun with this idea?

5. How well does White describe your own feelings riding an elevator?

SUGGESTIONS FOR WRITING

1. White asks the following question:

> What is there about elevator travel that induces this painstaking catalepsy?

Write your own answer to this question or another suggested by an elevator ride you have taken recently.

2. Describe an experience similar to those described by White, and build the details to a climax as he does. Conclude with your own comment or reflection on the experience as White does.

THE ESSAY

The subject of a paragraph often suggests how to organize it, as in the step-by-step, chronological description of a process. So does its audience. If the audience is unfamiliar with the subject, it may be preferable to build from simple to more difficult steps, details, and ideas, instead of presenting these chronologically. The same is true of the essay. In a persuasive essay you might introduce the thesis at the beginning if the audience will understand it without explanation. If the thesis requires explanation or is controversial, you might build to it through explanatory details and ideas. Or you may delay it to the end for maximum impact.

The essay of personal experience usually follows a freer course than a formal essay of ideas, the writer presenting a series of reflections or reminiscences, as in Susan Allen Toth's account of a college experience (p. 62). Here are the opening sentences of the first five paragraphs—the author reminded of her Iowa hometown in describing the western Massachusetts campus:

> At first I was so overwhelmed by the Smith campus itself that I did not much wonder what lay beyond it.
> The town I grew up in was not large.
> In winter and early spring, stubbled fields revealed the contours of the land . . . .
> Even when I couldn't see beyond the first few rows of giant stalks, I knew the field rolled on for miles.
> That unconscious assumption of space was part of what made my confinement in Northampton difficult.
> But I did instinctively know that I longed each year for Mountain Day.

An expository or persuasive essay is less free in its build of ideas. These opening sentences of Margaret Mead and Rhoda Metraux's essay on discipline (p. 128) show the logical relationships of ideas:

In the matter of childhood discipline there is no absolute standard.
The Mundugumor, a New Guinea people, trained their children to be self-reliant.
The Arapesh, another New Guinea people, had a very different view of life and personality.
Even very inconsistent discipline may fit a child to live in an inconsistent world.
There are forms of discipline that may be self-defeating.

The order of ideas may reveal a writer's characteristic way of expressing ideas, perhaps a free exploration of feelings and ideas. Expository and argumentative essays, too, may reveal an organization of ideas favored by a writer—perhaps a characteristic building to the thesis instead of introducing it early in the essay.

LEONARD KRIEGEL

LEONARD KRIEGEL contracted polio at the age of 11. "I spent the next two years of my life in an orthopedic hospital, appropriately called a reconstruction home. By 1946, when I returned to my native Bronx, polio had reconstructed me to the point that I walked very haltingly on steel braces and crutches." Kriegel describes this and later experiences in *Working Through* (1972) and *Falling Into Life* (1991), from which the following essay is taken.

THE PURPOSE OF LIFTING

I began lifting weights in May, 1949, a few weeks before my sixteenth 1
birthday. My closest friend and next-door neighbor, Frankie, had quit school—no one used the phrase "high school dropout" back then—to prepare himself for the Marine Corps. He had already enlisted, and he was bound for boot camp at Parris Island at the end of September. He had five months of life as a civilian in which to get his body into the shape the marines demanded.

Frankie bought a used York barbell set and then constructed a press- 2
ing bench from a slatted wooden cocktail table left unclaimed in the cellar
of the Bronx apartment building in which we both lived. As a cripple, I
was certainly not bound for the marines. But the door to Frankie's apartment was only a few feet from the door to our apartment. Curiously
enough, losing the use of my legs to polio had served only to intensify
the natural physical sense of oneself that preoccupies all adolescent boys.
I might walk into Frankie's apartment on braces and crutches, but in my
mind I saw myself as not only physically "normal" but the quintessence
of health. And like any other male adolescent, I was already a sucker for
anything that promised to test my strength and endurance. And so it was
I found myself in Frankie's brightly lit room, lying on the cocktail table
that had been thrust into service as a pressing bench, my brace-bound
legs carefully straddling the bench, surrounded by steel bars, red-metal
screw collars, and black cast-iron weights. On the light blue wall across
from the converted cocktail table Frankie had taped a crayoned chart so
that we could trace the growth of muscles and mass. The smell of our
sweat mingled with the smells of cooking lasagna and baking apple pies
that came from Frankie's mother's kitchen. An unexpected by-product of
lifting was the sense I quickly had that even muscular power and definition were olfactory.

Assuming the role of mentor—he was, after all, a year older and had 3
already invested himself with the proxy authority of the marine he would
soon become—Frankie stood above me, urging me on, as I pressed one
hundred pounds up and down, up and down. The strength surging
through my shoulders and chest was electric, as much with anticipation
as with performance. Frankie and I would take turns on the pressing
bench, encouraging each other. Then we would sit opposite one another
on two hardwood kitchen chairs, vigorously performing set after set of
bicep curls.

Until Frankie left for the marines, our lives were structured by that 4
bedroom gym. Both of us were conscious of the bodies we were remold-
ing. Where we had once passed the time by speaking of the books we
were reading or the ballplayers we admired or how the girls who filed out
of the subway on the corner of 206th Street looked, we now talked about
the geometry of muscularity, our conversation knowingly sprinkled with
references to "lats" and "pecs" and "trapezius." The world of male adolescents has always been curiously hermetic and insular. Lifting weights
fit it like a tight glove, serving to make it even more secretive.

More than anything else I did then, lifting existed beyond the boundaries established by my confrontation with the polio virus. When I first began lifting in Frankie's apartment, I told myself I was doing it to make walking on crutches easier by strengthening my arms and shoulders. But immediately after that first workout, I knew that lifting had as little to do with my need to build up strength in my arms in order to walk on the crutches as it did with Frankie's forthcoming life in the Marine Corps. The passion for working out, a passion each of us felt immediately, was shared by hundreds of thousands of young men throughout the country who were grunting and sweating as we were. All of us were lifting—no one called it "pumping iron" then—in hopes of molding our bodies into some Platonic vision of the ideal male form. Lifting was simply an act of male vanity. And we did it because we wanted to look good.

Of course, I wouldn't admit that in 1949. And neither would Frankie. I don't think anyone who lifted back in 1949 could admit to so flagrant a male vanity. The aspirations we might confess to were limited to bigger biceps, a firmer chest—and, of course, the admiration of the women we knew and the women we wanted to know.

There were other rationalizations for lifting, and at one time or another I probably used them all. I liked to tell myself, for instance, that my private ceremony endowed the world with order and proportion. As I grew older and began a doctorate in American studies, I would try to get myself to believe that by demanding effort, discipline, and patience of my body I was acting in pragmatic American fashion. I was making myself "better." Like the figure in the Charles Atlas ads in comic books I remembered from my childhood, I was making myself strong enough that no one could kick sand in my face.

As I grew less and less concerned with how I looked, I would find myself trying to break myself of the passion for working out with weights. Lifting, I now insisted in debates with an imaginary self, was narcissistic and self-indulgent. It was childish, an attempt to make the body into something greater than it was. And it lacked dignity. I was no longer an adolescent preening for others. I had become a husband, a father, a teacher. Orwell, Mann, Twain, Faulkner—I couldn't even imagine the writers I discussed with the students I taught sweating and straining beneath a burden so mundane as cast-iron weights. A man should learn to make do with the body he had been given. Or so, at least, I tried to convince myself.

But try as I might, I never fully succeeded in breaking the habit. Months would sometimes pass and I would refrain from lifting. And then a morning would arrive and I would suddenly find myself, like a reformed alcoholic trying to maintain his virtue as he stares at the window of a liquor store, staring at the dumbbells I kept stored beneath the bed. And on a day when the world threatened to overwhelm me, when it was simply too much with me, I would find myself seeking refuge in one or another gym laced with the vapors of sweat and Ben-Gay.

For a while, it was as if lifting alone promised to keep me sane. During the 1970s, I would flee the rhetorical excess that came to characterize the profession of college teaching for the very repetitive motions that I had tried to convince myself were senseless. The prospect of a good workout was sometimes the only thing enabling me to swim through that sea of words about " standards" and "relevance" we academics had unleashed upon ourselves and the nation.   10

It was also in the 1970s that I, along with others who had been weaned on free weights, began to use those high-tech machines with names such as Nautilus and Universal. The lush, carpeted spas of chrome and mirrors were a far cry from Frankie's bedroom with its makeshift pressing bench. But in one crucial respect the machines made the purpose of lifting clearer. In my mid-forties, strapped to the chrome and steel and vinyl of a Nautilus double-chest machine, I finally came to accept the idea that lifting had little to do with any kind of vanity, either that of how I looked or that of how I performed. To strap oneself into these gleaming machines was to affirm the surety of habit, to remove the burden of time. It had nothing to do with the virus that had cut me down and it had nothing to do with an adolescent's hunger for a physical sense of his own body. It had to do, rather, not with what I had lost but with what I had gained—an ease of motion that, having been done, could be done over and over and over again. Repetition, concentration, endurance: It was with these I had to concern myself. And it was these that promised to carry me to the idea of a body stripped of any needs other than its own.   11

I still lift—light weights now. But still lifting. And I no longer need any other kind of justification when I feel the urge to do what I first began doing at the age of sixteen. I am neither looking better nor growing particularly stronger. And I have no burning desire to stay in shape. All I want is to lock myself into the sweetness of motion and repetition. I want to continue, one movement following another. How grateful one can become for doing just that.   12

VOCABULARY

paragraph 2: quintessence, olfactory
paragraph 3: mentor, proxy
paragraph 4: hermetic, insular
paragraph 5: Platonic
paragraph 7: rationalizations, pragmatic
paragraph 8: narcissistic, mundane
paragraph 10: rhetorical

QUESTIONS

1. What is the central topic of the essay, and how does Kriegel introduce it through the details of the opening paragraphs?

2. In what order does he present his experiences with weight lifting?

3. What is the order of ideas in the whole essay?

4. What is Kriegel's chief point or thesis, and where does he state it?

SUGGESTIONS FOR WRITING

1. Kriegel shows how a childhood illness shaped later attitudes and interests. Discuss how an illness or another important experience in childhood shaped your own attitudes and interests. Present these in the order of their importance or seriousness or some other order of ideas and details.

2. Use your own experiences and observations to test Kriegel's statement that "the world of male adolescents has always been curiously hermetic and insular," or use them to make a statement about male or female adolescence and illustrate it. Organize your experiences and observations clearly and consistently.

JOAN DIDION

JOAN DIDION first established her reputation as a columnist and magazine editor, and later as a short-story and screen writer and novelist. Her novels include *Play It As It Lays* (1970), *The Book of Common Prayer* (1977), *Democracy* (1984), and *The Last Thing He Wanted* (1996). *Salvador* (1983) is a report on the Central American country; *Miami* (1988), on the Cuban American community. Her many essays are collected in *Slouching Towards Bethlehem* (1968), *The White Album* (1979), and *After Henry* (1992). In her essays and novels, Didion depicts personal and social values often imperceptible to those who live by them. She explores such values in her essay on the marriage business in Las Vegas.

MARRYING ABSURD

To be married in Las Vegas, Clark County, Nevada, a bride must swear   1
that she is eighteen or has parental permission and a bridegroom that he is twenty-one or has parental permission. Someone must put up five dollars for the license. (On Sundays and holidays, fifteen dollars. The Clark County Courthouse issues marriage licenses at any time of the day or night except between noon and one in the afternoon, between eight and nine in the evening, and between four and five in the morning.) Nothing else is required. The State of Nevada, alone among these United States, demands neither a premarital blood test nor a waiting period before or after the issuance of a marriage license. Driving in across the Mojave from Los Angeles, one sees the signs way out on the desert, looming up from the moonscape of rattlesnakes and mesquite, even before the Las Vegas lights appear like a mirage on the horizon: "GETTING MARRIED? Free License Information First Strip Exit." Perhaps the Las Vegas wedding industry achieved its peak operational efficiency between 9:00 P.M. and midnight of August 26, 1965, an otherwise unremarkable Thursday which happened to be, by Presidential order, the last day on which anyone could improve his draft status merely by getting married. One hundred and seventy-one couples were pronounced man and wife in the name of Clark County and the State of Nevada that night, sixty-seven of them by a single justice of the peace, Mr. James A. Brennan. Mr. Brennan did one wedding at the Dunes and the other sixty-six in his office, and charged each couple eight dollars. One bride lent her veil to six others. "I got it down from five to three minutes," Mr. Brennan said later of his feat. "I could've married them *en masse*, but they're people, not cattle. People expect more when they get married."

What people who get married in Las Vegas actually do expect—what,   2
in the largest sense, their "expectations" are—strikes one as a curious
and self-contradictory business. Las Vegas is the most extreme and allegorical of American settlements, bizarre and beautiful in its venality and
in its devotion to immediate gratification, a place the tone of which is
set by mobsters and call girls and ladies' room attendants with amyl ni-
trite poppers in their uniform pockets. Almost everyone notes that there
is no "time" in Las Vegas, no night and no day and no past and no future (no Las Vegas casino, however, has taken the obliteration of the ordinary time sense quite so far as Harold's Club in Reno, which for a
while issued, at odd intervals in the day and night, mimeographed "bul-
letins" carrying news from the world outside); neither is there any logical sense of where one is. One is standing on a highway in the middle of
a vast hostile desert looking at an eighty-foot sign which blinks "STAR-
DUST" or "CAESAR'S PALACE." Yes, but what does that explain? This geographical implausibility reinforces the sense that what happens there has
no connection with "real" life; Nevada cities like Reno and Carson are
ranch towns, Western towns, places behind which there is some historical
imperative. But Las Vegas seems to exist only in the eye of the beholder.
All of which makes it an extraordinarily stimulating and interesting place,
but an odd one in which to want to wear a candlelight satin Priscilla of
Boston wedding dress with Chantilly lace insets, tapered sleeves and a
detachable modified train.

And yet the Las Vegas wedding business seems to appeal to precisely   3
that impulse. "Sincere and Dignified Since 1954," one wedding chapel
advertises. There are nineteen such wedding chapels in Las Vegas, intensely competitive, each offering better, faster, and, by implication, more
sincere services than the next: Our Photos Best Anywhere, Your Wedding
on A Phonograph Record, Candlelight with Your Ceremony, Honey-
moon Accommodations, Free Transportation from Your Motel to Courthouse to Chapel and Return to Motel, Religious or Civil Ceremonies,
Dressing Rooms, Flowers, Rings, Announcements, Witnesses Available,
and Ample Parking. All of these services, like most others in Las Vegas
(sauna baths, payroll-check cashing, chinchilla coats for sale or rent) are
offered twenty-four hours a day, seven days a week, presumably on the
premise that marriage, like craps, is a game to be played when the table
seems hot.

But what strikes one most about the Strip chapels, with their wish-   4
ing wells and stained-glass paper windows and their artificial bouvardia,

is that so much of their business is by no means a matter of simple convenience, of late-night liaisons between show girls and baby Crosbys. Of course there is some of that. (One night about eleven o'clock in Las Vegas I watched a bride in an orange minidress and masses of flame-colored hair stumble from a Strip chapel on the arm of her bridegroom, who looked the part of the expendable nephew in movies like *Miami Syndicate.* "I gotta get the kids," the bride whimpered. "I gotta pick up the sitter, I gotta get to the midnight show." "What you gotta get," the bridegroom said, opening the door of a Cadillac Coupe de Ville and watching her crumple on the seat, "is sober.") But Las Vegas seems to offer something other than "convenience"; it is merchandising "niceness," the facsimile of proper ritual, to children who do not know how else to find it, how to make the arrangements, how to do it "right." All day and evening long on the Strip, one sees actual wedding parties, waiting under the harsh lights at a crosswalk, standing uneasily in the parking lot of the Frontier while the photographer hired by the Little Church of the West ("Wedding Place of the Stars") certifies the occasion, takes the picture: the bride in a veil and white satin pumps, the bridegroom usually in a white dinner jacket, and even an attendant or two, a sister or a best friend in hot-pink *peau de soie,* a flirtation veil, a carnation nosegay. "When I Fall in Love It Will Be Forever," the organist plays, and then a few bars of Lohengrin. The mother cries; the stepfather, awkward in his role, invites the chapel hostess to join them for a drink at the Sands. The hostess declines with a professional smile; she has already transferred her interest to the group waiting outside. One bride out, another in, and again the sign goes up on the chapel door: "One moment please—Wedding."

I sat next to one such wedding party in a Strip restaurant the last 5 time I was in Las Vegas. The marriage had just taken place; the bride still wore her dress, the mother her corsage. A bored waiter poured out a few swallows of pink champagne ("on the house") for everyone but the bride, who was too young to be served. "You'll need something with more kick than that," the bride's father said with heavy jocularity to his new son-in-law; the ritual jokes about the wedding night had a certain Panglossian character, since the bride was clearly several months pregnant. Another round of pink champagne, this time not on the house, and the bride began to cry. "It was just as nice," she sobbed, "as I hoped and dreamed it would be."

VOCABULARY

paragraph 1: mesquite
paragraph 2: allegorical, bizarre, venality, implausibility
paragraph 4: bouvardia, liaisons, expendable, facsimile, nosegay
paragraph 5: jocularity

QUESTIONS

1. One principle of order in Didion's essay is spatial: we see Las Vegas as a visitor would see it from the highway. From what other viewpoints do we see Las Vegas?

2. Didion presents a series of episodes, culminating in the wedding party of the final paragraph. How does she organize these? What sentences indicate this organization?

3. In Voltaire's satirical novel Candide the philosopher Pangloss explains the evils and imperfections of the world in the statement, "All is for the best in the best of all possible worlds." Does Didion agree? What is her attitude to the world she describes? What is the dominant tone of or attitude expressed by the essay, and how does Didion establish it?

4. Does Didion state a thesis, or is she concerned only with giving a picture of Las Vegas and the people who marry there? Does she imply ideas or attitudes rather than state them?

SUGGESTIONS FOR WRITING

1. Compare Didion's way of revealing her attitude toward Las Vegas with Eric Sevareid's way of revealing his attitude toward Velva, North Dakota (p. 28).

2. Characterize another city through an activity typical of its way of life and values. Let your details reveal this way of life and these values.

4

BEGINNING, MIDDLE, AND END

To make your ideas convincing, you need to capture the attention of your readers and hold it. You will lose their attention if, in beginning the essay, you describe in too much detail how you intend to proceed. Sometimes you need to indicate a point of view and suggest how you will develop the essay. The following is an ineffective way of doing so:

> I am going to describe my home town as I saw it on a recent visit. I will illustrate the changes and discuss their causes.

Compare these sentences with the opening paragraph of Eric Sevareid's essay on Velva, North Dakota. Sevareid states his subject and suggests how he will develop his essay—engaging the reader by appealing to common interests:

> My home town has changed in these thirty years of the American story. It is changing now, will go on changing as America changes. Its biography, I suspect, would read much the same as that of all other home towns. Depression and war and prosperity have all left their marks; modern science, modern tastes, manners, philosophies, fears and ambitions have touched my town as indelibly as they have touched New York or Panama City.

If you do need to state your purpose and outline the discussion to follow, you can do so with a minimum of personal reference and without sounding stuffy. Here is a paragraph that states the purpose and outlines the discussion to follow:

> The aim of this book is to delineate two types of clever schoolboy: the converger and the diverger. The earlier chapters offer a fairly detailed description of the intellectual abilities, attitudes and personalities of a few hundred such boys. In the later chapters, this description is then

used as the basis for a more speculative discussion—of the nature of intelligence and originality and of the ways in which intellectual and personal qualities interact. Although the first half of the book rests heavily on the results of psychological tests, and the last two chapters involve psychoanalytic theory, I have done my best to be intelligible, and, wherever possible, interesting to everyone interested in clever schoolboys: parents, school-teachers, dons, psychologists, administrators, clever schoolboys. (Liam Hudson, *Contrary Imaginations*)

This author directly challenges the interest of his reader. The bonus, this introductory paragraph promises, will be the wit of the author, evident in the humorous announcement of a seemingly dry subject.

By contrast, the author of the following paragraph eases his readers into the subject without an immediate statement of purpose. But he does make an immediate appeal to an important concern of his readers—the problem of how to deal with their own failures and those of friends and family members:

The administration of criminal justice and the extent of individual moral responsibility are among the crucial problems of a civilized society. They are indissolubly linked, and together they involve our deepest emotions. We often find it hard to forgive ourselves for our own moral failures. All of us, at some time or other, have faced the painful dilemma of when to punish and when to forgive those we love—our children, our friends. How much harder it is, then, to deal with the stranger who transgresses. (David L. Bazelon, "The Awesome Decision")

Notice that personal references are not out of place in an opening paragraph—or anywhere else in an essay. The risk of too many such references is that they can divert the reader from the subject of the essay to the author. For this reason they should be kept to a minimum.

The opening paragraphs build the expectations of the reader. The middle paragraphs develop ideas introduced at the beginning, the reader needing preparation for a new turn of thought, as Eric Sevareid does:

The people have not changed, but the *kinds of* people have changed. . . .

They eat differently in Velva now. . . .

An effective ending will not let the discussion drop: the reader should not finish the essay with a sense of loose ends, of lines of thought left uncompleted. In the formal essay, the ending may restate the thesis or perhaps even state it for the first time—if you build to the thesis through explanation and details. One of the most effective conclusions, the reference back to ideas that opened the essay, gives the reader a sense of completion:

> It is personal freedom that makes us better persons, and they are freer in Velva now. There is no real freedom without privacy, and a resident of my home town can be a private person much more than he could before. People are able to draw at least a little apart from one another. In drawing apart, they gave their best human instincts room for expansion. ("Velva, North Dakota")

SUSAN ALLEN TOTH

In *Blooming: A Small-Town Girlhood* (1981), SUSAN ALLEN TOTH describes growing up in Ames, Iowa, and in *Ivy Days: Making My Way Out East* (1984), her experiences at Smith College, in Northampton, Massachusetts. In the following excerpt from *Ivy Days,* she describes these two worlds, then gives an account of a fall event at Smith that she looked forward to each year.

MOUNTAIN DAY

At first I was so overwhelmed by the Smith campus itself that I did not   1
much wonder what lay beyond it. I concentrated on learning the campus pathways, exploring the labyrinth of the library, finding my gym locker and the geology lab. I tried to make myself as much at home as possible. In some ways, I succeeded. But I never fully conquered, or even understood, a kind of constriction, a tightness in my chest, that only eased for a time when I took the train home to Iowa at Christmas. Even then I wasn't sure what the feeling was. For four years, I now believe, I lived with a kind of deep claustrophobia, a sense of being closed in. It was part of the price I paid for going "out East."

The town I grew up in was not large. By the time I was a teenager,   2
I knew almost all its streets and connections, its stores and parks and schools. Bicycling everywhere or cruising in cars with my friends, I had

the security of moving freely in a wholly known world. More important, I knew what lay beyond the town. Iowa's peaceful countryside, open fields, and sweeping skies were part of my unconscious landscape, lying in the back of my mind like a stage setting no one ever changed. Although I never lived in the actual country, it was the context in which Ames existed, the sea in which our small town was an important island. Smaller towns were smaller islands, Des Moines a large one. But the land surrounded them all. Driving Highway 30, straight through Ames, one left the endless fields of corn for perhaps ten minutes of houses, gas stations, and stores, and then plunged into the ocean of corn again.

In winter and early spring, stubbled fields revealed the contours of   3 the land, rippling toward the horizon in broken rhythms of bent brown cornstalks or ridged black furrows. By summer, all one saw was waves of green. The corn stood so tall on either side of the highway that it was as if Moses had struck his staff on the sunbaked ground and the green sea had opened a narrow path.

Even when I couldn't see beyond the first few rows of giant stalks,   4 I knew the fields rolled on for miles. Whatever direction we drove from Ames, we passed through the same landscape, black earth, plowed fields, and large clean skies. The farms themselves were tidy dots of house, barn, and sheds, far enough from the road to seem more like Monopoly buildings than real homes with real people. My Iowa landscape was mostly earth and air, plants and sky. Seven miles to the Nevada liquor store, fifteen miles to the park in Boone, thirty miles to shop in Des Moines, fifty or sixty miles to basketball or football games in Newton, Grinnell, Marshalltown: everywhere my mother drove me I absorbed the same sense of space. Outside the towns was a reassuring repetition of fields and farm, fields and farm.

That unconscious assumption of space was part of what made my   5 confinement in Northampton difficult. I didn't have time, or awareness, to ask myself why I sometimes felt almost smothered in Lawrence House, with its fifty-seven girls; why a walk around the artfully landscaped campus didn't always make me feel better; why I spent so much time lying on my bed looking out my small window at a patch of sky.

But I did instinctively know that I longed each year for Mountain   6 Day. Mountain Day was a special Smith holiday, set aside so that students could admire the New England fall foliage. No one ever knew exactly when Mountain Day would fall, but early one crisp October morning, the loud ringing of the carillon signaled the cancellation of all classes. A few determined students remained on campus to study, some fled on buses to see their boyfriends an hour or two away, but most of us scurried about to find bicycles and food for picnic lunches. Soon a flood of girls streamed on their bicycles down the main street of Northampton, like a fall parade, heading to the highways out of town.

All Mountain Days blend into my first one that fall of my fresh-   7
man year. I was curious about whether I could indeed find a mountain close to this Eastern campus. Another freshman across the hall, Meg, who lived in nearby Greenfield, said sure, we could bike to Mount Tom, easily, it wasn't very far, and so, with our roommates, we started off. I am amazed now that we made it. Flabby, out of condition, but high-spirited, we donned sweatshirts, mounted our secondhand, one-speed bikes, and headed for the mountain. On we bicycled, singing loudly, along the edge of a well-traveled highway, through straggling towns that seemed almost continuous, past occasional tobacco fields and vegetable stands. Ahead and behind us, we could see other lines of Smith girls, sometimes waving to us, passing us, or turning onto the Amherst exit.

The sun was high, warming our backs until we had to take off our   8
sweatshirts and tie them around our waists. I looked at everything as hard as I could, every peeling farmhouse, heap of squash, white board fence, to see if I could discern a pattern. It was nice to see people going about ordinary tasks, shopping, working in gardens, trimming hedges. Closed in since my arrival at Smith, I felt miraculously released. The first few miles I scarcely noticed the heaviness of my bike or the unaccustomed strain on my muscles. Stopping occasionally to rest, we plugged onward, puffing and laughing, until finally in early afternoon we found the turnoff to the Mount Tom Lookout Tower. After we climbed the tower ladder, we sank gratefully onto the plank floor in the hot midday sun and decided to go no farther.

Though I recall few details about the surrounding countryside, I know   9
I gasped at the view. We were high above the ground, looking out on a panorama of hills, with fiery masses of leaves everywhere. The fall colors seemed more profuse and vivid than ours at home, probably because my part of Iowa had few hills to provide this sweep of reds, yellows, and golds. "This is it," I thought to myself with an assurance I hadn't had before. "This is New England, just like the pictures." I had foresightedly brought my Brownie, and I took my own pictures. Turning the pages of my photograph album today, I can see us still, rumpled but happy, with the hills behind us, sweatshirts tied around our waists, Coke bottles on

the plank floor, and victorious grins on our faces. That afternoon, while we picnicked and talked and napped for a while on the rough boards, happiness flooded over me with the warm sunshine.

The distance to Mount Tom had been much farther than we'd imag- 10 ined, or than Meg remembered, and so we didn't dare stay too long. After an hour or so, Meg looked at her watch and warned us we'd have to start back. Pedaling home, we were all tired. We didn't talk much, and we didn't want to sing. My roommate, Alice, who'd been doing ski exercises, tried to start "One Hundred Bottles of Beer on the Wall," but no one joined in. My bottom was blistered, and my muscles ached. I began to think of tomorrow, lessons undone, art slides unstudied.

When we dragged in the front door, it was almost time for dinner. 11 As I hurried upstairs to change into a skirt, I brushed by Lee Anderson, an ambitious, competitive girl who was in my Art History class. "Boy, did you get sunburned," she said, stopping to stare. "We went to Mount Tom," I said proudly. "We bicycled all the way. Where did you go?"

"I decided to stay here," Lee said, with more than a trace of self- 12 satisfaction. "It was just great. There was absolutely no one in the art library, so I had yesterday's slides all to myself. I just got caught up a few minutes ago, and am I relieved. Yesterday's lecture was really important, didn't you think?" I didn't answer, except with a kind of grunt. I hurried past Lee toward my room. At least, I thought to myself, now I have seen New England.

QUESTIONS

1. Toth opens her account of her first Mountain Day at Smith with a comment on the Smith campus, then describes the very different world of Ames, Iowa. How do these comments help to explain why she later looked forward to Mountain Day?

2. Why does she mention in paragraph 6 the various ways Smith students spent the special day?

3. What feelings does she highlight in describing the bike ride to Mount Tom and the time spent at the lookout tower?

4. What does the encounter with the classmate tell us about her feelings at the end of the day?

5. Is Toth making a point or developing a thesis in describing this particular Mountain Day?

SUGGESTIONS FOR WRITING

1. Describe an annual high school event that you especially looked forward to, and at some point in your description explain why you did. Describe your feelings in the course of it, letting your details reveal them.

2. Toth describes the experience of returning to the college town in later years:

> Though sometimes I bicycled to a professor's house or to a nearby city park, I really never saw the working side of Northampton, with its factories, commercial developments, and modest residential areas. If I saw, I didn't notice. For me, the East was typified by Smith. Years later, returning for the first time to the college, I was appalled at my ignorance of the town that enclosed it. I didn't even know what streets to take or how far Northampton extended. It was bigger, and less unusual, than I'd ever realized.

Expand your essay to describe your feelings on returning to the town or neighborhood where you once lived. You may wish to describe features that you noticed for the first time.

CALVIN TRILLIN

CALVIN TRILLIN, has written about his travels for *The New Yorker,* his many articles collected in *U.S. Journal* (1971) and other books. His articles on American eating habits are collected in *American Fried* (1974), subtitled "Adventures of a Happy Eater." His narrative of two highly successful ice cream enterpreneurs is taken from *American Stories* (1991). In this excerpt Trillin tells us how Ben Cohen and Jerry Greenfield began selling ice cream in Burlington, Vermont, in a small galvanized-tin former truck repair shop.

BEN & JERRY'S

When Ben & Jerry's began, in 1978, there was no mistaking it for 1
a knockoff of Häagen-Dazs; it seemed more like a knockoff of Steve's,
a homemade ice cream parlor in Somerville, Massachusetts, on the edge
of Cambridge. In fact, what Ben Cohen and Jerry Greenfield, high school
pals from Long Island, had in mind was to move to a relatively quiet
college town and start some more or less entertaining business of the
sort that had already proved itself in places like Cambridge and Berkeley and Ann Arbor. It didn't have to be ice cream. In fact, it is now an
established part of the Ben & Jerry's startup story—a capitalist folktale
that is rapidly becoming almost as well known as the one about Reuben
Mattus—that Cohen and Greenfield were leaning toward a bagel operation before they discovered how much bagel-baking equipment cost.
They simply figured that having a business together would be an improvement over what they had found themselves doing. Greenfield, who
had not been able to get into medical school, was working as a lab technician in North Carolina. Cohen, whose academic aspirations had not
extended much past the pottery-making and jewelry-making courses, was
teaching pottery-making to emotionally disturbed children near Lake
Champlain. Something like a homemade ice cream store, they thought,
would be a way to have some independence and a way to live in a pleasant college town, and maybe even a way to have some fun. They raised
eight thousand dollars for capital. They bought an old-fashioned rock-
salt ice cream maker. They rented an abandoned gas station in Burlington, half a mile or so from the campus of the University of Vermont,
and began fixing it up themselves. They read several books about homemade ice cream. Then they capped off their preparations by sending
away to Pennsylvania State University for a five-dollar correspondence
course in ice cream making—two-fifty apiece. Like a lot of people who
were in college during the late sixties and early seventies, they had been
educated to think small.

College-town ice cream parlors like Steve's seemed to be founded on 2
the principle that the atmosphere of a retail business—at least a retail business selling homemade ice cream to young people—could be more or less
the atmosphere one might expect to find in an Ugliest Man on Campus
contest. In the original Steve's store—which still exists in roughly its original form, even though the business has changed hands and has been

expanded into a franchise operation—there was an old-fashioned home-made ice cream maker in the window producing the store's entire ice cream supply. Steve's also provided a player piano, elaborate rules posted on the wall concerning which combinations of ice cream and toppings and mix-ins were allowed, a bulletin board for notices of yoga classes and rides to New York, and a trivia contest to pass the time spent standing in what always seemed to be a long line. That's the sort of operation Cohen and Greenfield opened in Burlington. Greenfield made the homemade ice cream, which was popular from the start, and Cohen handled the hot food, which wasn't. On summer evenings, they showed free movies on the wall of a building next door. On cold winter days, they instituted an ice cream cone discount scheme they still call POPCDBZWE, pronounced the way it's spelled, which stands for "Penny Off Per Celsius Degree Below Zero Winter Extravaganza." On just about any day, customers were likely to be entertained by Don Rose on his honky-tonk piano. Rose was a volunteer, and his service to the cause earned him the rare distinction of being named a "Ben & Jerry's lifer": he is entitled to free ice cream for the rest of his life.

Ben & Jerry's drifted into the wholesale ice cream business partly because some local restaurants began to ask about being supplied and partly, Cohen always says, because meeting the salesmen who called on the ice cream parlor persuaded him that traveling around the state selling ice cream might be a pleasanter life than being stuck in front of a stove in a former filling station. Ben & Jerry's started to manufacture ice cream by the pint, with Jerry acting as production manager while Ben lived out his traveling-salesman dreams on the roads of Vermont. Their approach to presenting their wares did not have much in common with what Reuben Mattus had done at Häagen-Dazs. Instead of concocting an ersatz European name, they called their ice cream Ben & Jerry's Homemade—although Cohen likes to say that there was some consideration given to putting an umlaut over the "e" in Ben. The picture on the top of their pint container was not a map of Scandinavia but a photograph of the two of them, looking pretty much like two Vermont hippies. The description of the ingredients on the container was done in the sort of hand printing often used on menus that list a variety of herbal teas. The geographical connection Ben & Jerry's tried to project was not with the capitals of Europe but with rural Vermont. Times had changed. For the generation Ben and Jerry belonged to, the Continent had lost its cachet. Cachet had lost its cachet. Cohen and Greenfield were interested not simply in using natural ingredients but in being natural themselves.

They still speak of what they do as being "in our style." From the start, it was their style to be funky. It was their style to be slightly embarrassed at being in business at all. "We grew up in the sixties, when it wasn't cool to be businessmen," Greenfield once said to a trade magazine reporter while trying to explain why Ben & Jerry's has a policy of turning back part of its profits to the community. "Our whole motivation for doing business was never to get rich." It was their style to assume that part of the reason for going into business was to have fun. Their promotional style can be summed up by the fact that a trip to Florida offered as a prize in the Ben & Jerry's "Lick Winter" promotion included not just airfare and hotels but dinner with Jerry's parents, who are retired down there, and a day at Walt Disney World with Ben's uncle.

The two Vermont hippies set out to produce the sort of high-butterfat, low-air-content ice cream that Reuben Mattus had pioneered. Like Mattus, they used natural flavor, and they used plenty of it. (Jerry says that was because it took a strong dose of flavor to get any response from Ben, the sampler, who "doesn't have a real acute sense of taste.") When it came to marketing, though, Ben & Jerry's had practically nothing in common with Häagen-Dazs and Alpen Zauber and Frusen Gladje. Even the flavors were different. When Reuben Mattus began marketing Häagen-Dazs, he carried only vanilla, chocolate, and coffee; Ben & Jerry's seemed to specialize right away in flavors like Chocolate Heath Bar Crunch and White Russian and Dastardly Mash. (Even now, the two brands have only half a dozen flavor names in common.) When Cohen is asked to compare his ice cream with brands like Häagen-Dazs and Alpen Zauber and Frusen Gladje, he often says that Ben & Jerry's is "the only super-premium ice cream you can pronounce." In their strategy of positioning their ice cream in the market, Cohen and Greenfield had, in their own consciously small way, turned around and marched smartly in the opposite direction.

Their sixties sense of limitations was reflected in their motto, "Vermont's Finest All-Natural Ice Cream"—a motto that is, by the standards of ice cream business superlatives, almost pathologically modest. In the summer of 1981, a year after Ben & Jerry's started producing pints, *Time* ran a widely noticed cover story on the popularity of ice cream, and the writer, John Skow, commented on the inflation of ice cream bragging by routinely referring to just about every brand mentioned as the best ice cream in the world. The irony in the way the phrase was being used became clear before the end of the first paragraph, but in the opening sentence of the story the superlative still carried an impact. That sentence said, "What you must understand at the outset is that Ben & Jerry's, in Burlington, Vt., makes the best ice cream in the world."

VOCABULARY

paragraph 3: ersatz, umlaut, cachet
paragraph 6: superlatives, pathological

QUESTIONS

1. On what aspect of the developing enterprise does Trillin give the most detail?

2. How does he introduce it and keep it before the reader in paragraphs 2–5?

3. How does paragraph 6 bring it to a conclusion?

4. Does Trillin express an attitude toward Ben and Jerry and the enterprise, or is his account neutral in attitude?

SUGGESTIONS FOR WRITING

1. Trillin suggests that ice cream parlors and presumably other enterprises often reflect the community they serve. Discuss how true this is of a shop or store in your town or city.

2. Develop your discussion by comparing the shop or store with a similar one in a different community—perhaps a college town or resort.

3. Explain how details in the essay illustrate the sixties' "sense of limitations," referred to in paragraph 6.

5

TRANSITIONS

Transitional words and phrases help us connect ideas and details in our paragraphs and essays. We especially need them when we change the subject or course of discussion, as in the following sentences by Eric Sevareid:

> Sounds have changed. . . .
>
> The people have not changed, but the *kinds of* people have changed. . . .
>
> No, the "characters" are vanishing in Velva. . . .

These sentences, opening a series of early paragraphs, rely on similar phrasing and transitional words (*but, no*). A question marks the turn to another topic in a later paragraph:

> But now I must ask myself: Are they nearer to one another? And the answer is no. . . .

The following paragraph opens with the transitional *for,* telling us that an explanation follows:

> For personal and social neuroses festered under this hard scab of conformity.

The succeeding paragraph concludes with the following sentence— the transitional *so* and *of course* telling us that Sevareid is drawing a conclusion and qualifying it:

> So, of course, the people themselves do not have to leave, because, as the stale air went out, the fresh air came in.

Words like *after* and *since* express relationships of time; words like *above* and *below,* relationships of space. Here are some important transitions that show the relationship of ideas:

- sequence: *first, second, third*
- qualification: *but, however, nevertheless, nonetheless*
- illustration and explanation: *for example, for instance, so, thus*
- comparison: *similarly, in the same way, by comparison, likewise*
- contrast: *by contrast, on the one hand, on the other hand*
- consequence: *thus, so, as a result, consequently, therefore*
- concession: *but, admittedly, nevertheless, however*
- amplification: *and, moreover, furthermore, also, in addition, indeed*
- summation: *in conclusion, to sum up, all in all, finally*

Punctuation also shows us how ideas are related. A colon tells us that an expansion, explanation, or illustration follows; a semicolon, that the ideas joined are closely related or of the same importance.

LEWIS THOMAS

In the course of his long career in medicine, LEWIS THOMAS (1913–1993) served as dean of the medical schools of Yale and New York University and president of Memorial Sloan-Kettering Cancer Center. His first collection of essays, *The Lives of a Cell*, received the National Book Award in 1974. Later collections on medicine, language, and other topics include *The Medusa and the Snail* (1979), *Late Night Thoughts on Listening to Mahler's Ninth Symphony* (1983), and *Et Cetera, Et Cetera* (1990). Thomas gives an account of his professional life in *The Youngest Science* (1983). The paragraphs reprinted here introduce an essay on human language in *The Fragile Species* (1992). An essay by Lewis Thomas appears on p. 325.

COMMUNICATION

Other creatures, most conspicuously from our point of view the social   1
insects, live together in dense communities in such interdependence that
it is hard to imagine the existence of anything like an individual. They

are arranged in swarms by various genetic manipulations. They emerge in foreordained castles, some serving as soldiers for defending the anthill or beehive; some as workers, bringing in twigs of exactly the right size needed for whatever the stage of construction of the nest; some as the food-gatherers tugging along the dead moth toward the hill; some solely as reproductive units for the replication of the community; even some specialized for ventilating and cleaning the nest and disposing of the dead. Automatons, we call them, tiny genetic machines with no options for behavior, doing precisely what their genes instruct them to do, generation after mindless generation. They communicate with each other by chemical signals, unambiguous molecules left behind on the trail to signify all sorts of news items of interest to insects: the dead moth is on the other side of the hill behind this rock, the intruders are approaching from that direction, the queen is upstairs and asking after you, that sort of news. Bees, the earliest and greatest of all geometricians, dance in darkness to tell where the sun is and where it will be in exactly twenty minutes.

We, of course, are different. We make up our minds about the world   2
as individuals, we look around at the world and plan our next move, we remember what happened last week when we made a mistake and got in trouble, and we keep records for longer memories, even several generations back. Also we possess what we call consciousness, awareness, which most of us regard as a uniquely human gift: we can even think ahead to dying, and we cannot imagine an insect, much less a wolf or a dolphin or even a whale, doing *that*. So we are different. And marvelously higher.

Nonetheless, we are a social species. We gather in communities far   3
denser and more complex than any termite nest or beehive, and we depend much more on each other for individual survival than any troupe of army ants. We are compulsively, biologically, obsessively social. And we are the way we are because of language.

Of all the acts of cooperative behavior to be observed anywhere in   4
nature, I can think of nothing to match, for the free exchange of assets and the achievement of equity and balance in the trade, human language. When we speak to each other, it is not like the social insects laying out chemical trails; it contains the two most characteristic and accommodating of all human traits, ambiguity and amiability. Almost every message in human communication can be taken in two or more ways. There are choices to be made all over the place, in the sending of messages and in their reception. We are, in this respect, unlike the ants and bees. We

are obliged to listen more carefully, to edit whatever we hear, and to recognize uncertainty when we hear it, or read it.

Another difference is that the communication systems of animals   5
much older than our species are fixed in place and unchangeable. Our system, language, is just at its beginning, only a few thousand years old, still experimental and flexible. We can change it whenever we feel like, and have been doing so right along. How many of us can speak Chaucerian English, or Anglo-Saxon, or Indo-European, or Hittite? Or read them?

But it is still a genetically determined gift, no doubt about it. We   6
speak and write and listen because we have genes for language. Without such genes, we might still be the smartest creatures on the block, able to make tools and outthink any other animal in combat, even able to think and plan ahead, but we would not be human.

VOCABULARY

paragraph 1: genetic, manipulations, foreordained, replication
paragraph 4: ambiguity, amiability, edit

QUESTIONS

1. What relationships do *even* and *we call them* express in connecting ideas in sentences 3 and 4 of paragraph 1?

2. What idea does the transitional *of course* express in the opening sentence of paragraph 2? What other transitional words occur in paragraph 2, and what relationships do they establish?

3. What relationships do *nonetheless* and *and* (sentences 1 and 4, paragraph 3), *in this respect* (sentence 5, paragraph 4), and *but* (sentence 1, paragraph 6) express? Could any of these transitions be omitted without loss of coherence or clarity?

4. What other transitional words or phrases might Thomas have substituted for the transitions just cited?

5. If we humans are "compulsively, biologically, obsessively social," how are we different from army ants and other social insects?

SUGGESTIONS FOR WRITING

Write a paragraph illustrating from personal experience one of the following ideas or another related to human communication:

a. "Almost every message in human communication can be taken in two or more ways."

b. "There are choices to be made all over the place, in the sending of messages and in their reception."

Restate the idea in light of your own experience and observation, qualifying or disagreeing with it, if you wish, and giving one or more examples. Use transitional words and phrases where needed to connect your ideas and examples.

M A R Y   E .   M E B A N E

Born in 1993 in Durham, North Carolina, MARY E. MEBANE grew up on a farm—the world she describes in her autobiography, *Mary* (1981), and in *Mary, Wayfarer* (1983). Following her graduation from college in Durham, she taught in public schools and took graduate degrees at the University of North Carolina. Like Sally Carrighar and Eudora Welty, Mebane immerses us in the sights, sounds, and smells of childhood in this portrait of her mother.

MARY

Nonnie led a structured, orderly existence. Before six o'clock in the morning, she was up, starting her day. First she turned on WPTF and listened to the news and the weather and the music. Later, when WDNC in Durham hired Norfleet Whitted, the first black announcer in the area, she listened first to one station, then to the other. Some mornings it would be "They Traced Her Little Footprints in the Snow," and other mornings it would be black gospel-singing and rhythm-and-blues. Then she would make a fire in the wood stove and start her breakfast. She prepared some meat—fried liver pudding or fatback, or a streak-of-fat streak-of-lean—and made a hoecake of bread on top of the stove, which she ate with either Karo syrup or homemade blackberry preserves, occasionally with store-bought strawberry preserves, or sometimes with homemade watermelon-rind preserves that she had canned in the summer. Then she would drink her coffee, call me to get up, and leave the house in her blue uniform, blue apron, and blue cap—it would still be dark when she left on winter mornings—and go to catch her ride to the tobacco factory (with Mr. Ralph Baldwin at first, and then, when he retired, with Mr. James Yergan). When Miss Delilah still lived in Wildwood, before she and Mr. Leroy separated, she would come by and call from the road and the two of them would walk together to the end of the road near the highway and wait for Mr. Ralph there.

My job after she left was to see that the fire didn't go out in the wood stove, to see that the pots sitting on the back didn't burn—for in them was our supper, often pinto beans or black-eyed peas or collard greens or turnip salad. Occasionally there was kale or mustard greens or cressy salad. The other pot would have the meat, which most often was neck bones or pig feet or pig ears, and sometimes spareribs. These would cook until it was time for me to go to school; then I would let the fire die down, only to relight it when I came home to let the pots finish cooking.   2

After Nonnie left, I also had the task of getting Ruf Junior up so that he could get to school on time. This presented no problem to me until Ruf Junior was in high school and started playing basketball. Often he would travel with the team to schools in distant towns, sometimes getting home after midnight, and the next morning he would be tired and sleepy and wouldn't want to get up. I sympathized, but I had my job to do. If I let him oversleep, I knew that Nonnie would fuss when she got home. But on the other hand, no matter how often I called to him, he would murmur sleepily, "All right, all right," then go back to sleep. I solved this problem one bitter-cold winter morning. I jerked all the covers off his bed and ran. I knew that the only place he could get warm again would be in the kitchen. (The only fire was in the wood stove.) The fire was already out, so he'd have to make one. After that, I didn't have such a hard time getting him up.   3

My mother worked as a cutter, clipping the hard ends of each bundle of tobacco before it was shredded to make cigarettes. At noon she ate the lunch she had brought from home in a brown paper bag: a biscuit with meat in it and a sweet potato or a piece of pie or cake. Some   4 of the women ate in the cafeteria, but in her thirty years at the Liggett and Myers factory, she never once did. She always took her lunch. Then she worked on until closing time, caught her ride back to Wildwood, and started on the evening's activities. First she had supper, which I had finished preparing from the morning. After I got older we sometimes had meat other than what had to be prepared in a "pot." It would be my duty to fry chicken or prepare ham bits and gravy.

After supper, she'd read the Durham *Sun* and see to it that we did the chores if we hadn't done them already: slop the hogs, feed the chickens, get in the wood for the next day. Then we were free. She'd get her blue uniform ready for the next day, then listen to the radio. No later than nine o'clock, she would be in bed. In the morning she would get up, turn on the radio, and start frying some fatback. Another day would have started.

Saturdays were work days, too, the time for washing, ironing, going to the garden, preparing Sunday dinner (no one was supposed to work on the Sabbath, so we ran the chicken down in the yard and Nonnie wrung its neck or chopped its head off with the ax). Sometimes we went to town on Saturday but not often, for Nonnie went to town every day. Sometimes, at lunchtime, she'd go down to Belk's, and always on Friday she went to the A&P on Mangum Street and bought her groceries; then she'd stop at the Big Star in Little Five Points if she had heard that there was a particularly good buy on something. So the Saturday-in-town ritual that is so much a part of the lives of most country children was not mine at all. I myself sometimes went to Brookstown several times a week when my father was alive, because that is where he went to get trash, sell vegetables, and visit his relatives.

Sunday afternoons she would go to see her friends or they would come to see her. She would say, "I believe I'll go up to Miss Angeline's a little while." Or it would be Miss Pauline's or Claudia's. And she would stay until about dusk and come home, listen to the radio, then go to bed, ready to start Monday morning again.

In the spring and summer after work, my mother would plant in her garden: tomatoes, string beans, okra, and she'd sow a turnip patch. Then, every day after work, she'd go over to the garden on the hill to see how it was doing. On Saturdays she'd get her buckets if it was time for us to go berrypicking. And on hot summer evenings, if the peaches man had been around, she'd can them after work because they wouldn't keep until Saturday, the day she did most of her canning.

This was her routine—fixed, without change, unvarying. And she ac- 9
cepted it. She more than accepted it, she embraced it; it gave meaning to
her life, it was what she had been put here on this earth to do. It was
not to be questioned.

To Nonnie this life was ideal; she saw nothing wrong with it. And 10
she wondered in baffled rage why her daughter didn't value it but rather
sought something else, some other rhythm, a more meaningful pattern to
human life.

Nonnie Mebane was not political. However, a special awe would 11
come into her voice when she said, "And Lee *surrendered*." She was from
Virginia, and I realize now that she probably would have been imbued
with Virginia history in her eight years of schooling there. I myself never
heard Robert E. Lee's name mentioned in any class at Wildwood School.
But my mother loved to say, "And Lee *surrendered*". She also liked to
say sometimes that the Yankee soldiers rode up and said, "Come on out.
Y'all are free this morning."

The way she said it, I could see the men on horseback—the Yan- 12
kees—coming around to the fields and to the cabins and saying to the
blacks who had been slaves for centuries, "Come on out. Ya'll are free
this morning." That was a magical moment. I used to get cold chills when
she said it, for, I now realize, in her voice I heard the voice of my mother's mother as she told Nonnie and her other children how the Yankees
came early one morning and what they had said. My mother's grandmother had heard them.

Nonnie was a good plain cook, but she couldn't sew very well, 13
couldn't fix hair—her own or her daughter's—and, though dutiful, was
an indifferent housekeeper. She was thrifty and paid all of her bills on
time. Work at the tobacco factory was her life.

QUESTIONS

1. How does the opening sentence—"Nonnie led a structured, orderly
existence"—organize the paragraphs that follow?

2. Many of the transitional words are chronological, showing how the
events of the day were connected in time. What examples of such transitions do you find in paragraphs 1, 4, and 8?

3. What transitional ideas do *often, but,* and *on the other hand* express
in paragraph 3? What about *too* and *so* in paragraph 6, *however* in

paragraph 11, and *for* in paragraph 12? Might Mebane have omitted any of these without loss of coherence—that is, without losing the sense of connection between ideas?

4. Does Mebane imply more about her mother's life than she states? What does she reveal about her own feelings or attitudes?

SUGGESTIONS FOR WRITING

1. Mebane describes the work she performed as a member of the family. Describe jobs that you similarly performed, and use this description to say something about the general attitude in your family toward everyday life or the role of children in the family.

2. Mebane refers in paragraph 10 to "some other rhythm, a more meaningful pattern to human life." She is suggesting here the values that children sometimes discover they possess. Discuss a conflict in values between yourself and another member of your family and the origin of this conflict as you see it.

II

DESCRIPTION, NARRATION, EXPOSITION

INTRODUCTION

In exposition, we explain ideas and processes through example, classification and division, definition, comparison and contrast, analogy, process, and cause and effect—methods of analysis discussed in this part of the book. In explaining how to repair a car engine, for example, we might define key terms, trace the process, make comparisons with other kinds of engine repair, and discuss the causes of engine failure. Description and narration often combine with exposition, as in George Orwell's "Shooting an Elephant" (p. 14). A piece of writing may consist entirely of exposition, as in a set of directions, or entirely of description or narration.

In exposition, the kind and number of examples and other methods you use depends on how much information your readers need. Keep in mind that you know more about the subject than your readers do: you are illustrating and analyzing ideas and process for their benefit. And the more explanation you give, the more attention you need to give to organization and transitions. Your readers should understand at every point what method of analysis you are using and why. How you organize the essay depends also on the readers. Some expository essays, like on the causes of a war, often contain a thesis; others, like an essay on repairing an engine, may not. If the essay does contain a thesis, where you place it may depend on how much information readers need to understand it. We shall see that where you place the thesis in the persuasive essay depends on how disposed readers are to accept it and where it has the most impact—aided by description and narration. But, first, some features of descriptive writing.

6

DESCRIPTION

In describing a person, place, or thing, we create a picture. George Orwell does so in describing a quarter of the Burmese town where as a police officer he had been called to deal with an elephant:

> It was a very poor quarter, a labyrinth of squalid bamboo huts, thatched with palm-leaf winding all over a steep hillside. ("Shooting an Elephant")

How much detail the writer gives depends on the purpose of the description. Orwell might have given more details of the town quarter. But additional details would have diverted us from the purpose of the description—to show that the impoverished life of the townspeople made them want to see the elephant shot.

In a descriptive paragraph or essay, the spatial arrangement of details must be clear, the physical point of view obvious and consistent. The writer must be careful to specify the place from which the observation is made. Orwell is careful to do so in describing the shooting of the elephant, and so is James Stevenson in describing a steep road:

> Partway down the long, very steep slope of Loma Vista Drive, descending through Beverly Hills, with the city of Los Angeles spread out far below the houses of sparkling opulence on either side, there is a sign warning "Use Lowest Gear" and, shortly after that, a sign that says "Runaway Vehicle Escape Lane 600 Feet Ahead." ("Loma Vista Drive")

Something more than the physical point of view is suggested here. We discover a dominant mood or attitude. This psychological point of view may be stated directly or conveyed by the details of the description. Orwell does both in describing the crowd of excited spectators:

But at that moment I glanced round at the crowd that had followed me. It was an immense crowd, two thousand at the least and growing every minute. It blocked the road for a long distance on either side . . . . And suddenly I realized that I should have to shoot the elephant after all. The people expected it of me and I had got to do it; I could feel their two thousand wills pressing me forward, irresistibly. ("Shooting an Elephant")

If the writer fails to clarify the point of view or changes it without preparing the reader, details will seem blurred. Abrupt or unexpected shifts in mood or attitude can also be confusing. Brief transitions that bridge these changes are the remedy.

JOHN MCPHEE

A staff writer for *The New Yorker,* JOHN MCPHEE has written on a wide range of subjects from sports to atomic energy, geology, the American wilderness, and the Alaskan frontier. His books include *The Curve of Binding Energy* (1974), *Coming into the Country* (1977), and *The Control of Nature* (1989). McPhee's concern with environmental issues is evident in the following selection from *Irons in the Fire* (1997).

THE WORLD'S LARGEST PILE OF SCRAP TIRES

The world's largest pile of scrap tires is not visible from Interstate 5, in Stanislaus County, California. But it's close. Below Stockton, in the region of Modesto and Merced, the highway follows the extreme western edge of the flat Great Central Valley, right next to the scarp where the Coast Ranges are territorially expanding as fresh unpopulated hills. The hills conceal the tires from the traffic. If you were to abandon your car three miles from the San Joaquin County line and make your way on foot southwest one mile, you would climb into steeply creased terrain that in winter is jade green and in summer straw brown, and, any time at all, you would come upon a black vista. At rest on sloping ground, the tires are so deep that they form their own topography—their own escarpments, their own overhanging cliffs. Deposited from a ridgeline, they border a valley for nearly half a mile. When you first glimpse them, you are not sure what they are. From the high ground on the opposite side, the individual tires appear to be grains of black sand. They look like little eggstones—oolites—each a bright yolk ringed in black pearl. Close to them, you walk in tire canyons. In some places, they are piled six stories high, compressing themselves, densifying: at the top, tires; at the bottom, pucks. From the highest elevations of this thick and drifted black mantle, you can look east a hundred miles and see snow on the Sierra.

The tires are from all sides of the bays of San Francisco and up and down the Great Central Valley from Bakersfield to Sacramento. Even before the interstate was there, a tire jockey named Ed Filbin began collecting them—charging dealers and gas stations "tipping fees" of so much per passenger tire and so much per truck tire, as tire jockeys everywhere do. This was long before people began to worry, with regard to used tires, about mosquitoes, fires, landfills, and compounding environmental concerns, or to look upon old tires as a minable resource. Filbin's pile just grew, and he made enough money to diversify, becoming, as he is today, the largest sheep rancher in Nevada. Meanwhile, his tire ranch near Modesto continued to broaden and thicken, until no one, including Filbin, knew how many tires were there. Eventually, the state took notice—and county zoning authorities—and Filbin felt harassed. When I called him one day in Nevada, he sketched these people as "dirty rotten bureaucrats" and said. "I told them to go jump in a crick. I had grandfather rights." With those words, he cradled his telephone, refusing to say more.

There have been many estimates of the number of tires in the great California pile, but the figures tend to be high or low in direct proportion to the appraiser's economic interest or environmental bias. The variations can be absurd, missing agreement with one another by factors as high as five. Not long ago, while I was at the University of California, Davis, working on something else, I began to muse about the tire pile and the problem of counting its contents. In the university library I found David Lundquist, the map librarian, and asked for his suggestions. The pile does not appear on the 7.5-minute Solyo Quadrangle of the United States Geological Survey, and I thought he might have a more sophisticated map of equally ample scale. He said he had recent low-altitude aerial photographs made by the federal Agricultural Stabilization and Conservation Service that amounted to an eyeball-to-earth mosaic of the state. The prints were nine by ten and were in several map-cabinet drawers. Comparing map and photograph indexes, he rummaged through stacks of pictures. When No. 507-52 was at last before us, a shape in black Rorschach, sharply defined, stood out like a mountain lake. The terrain was veiny with clear draws and ridgelines, which made relatively simple the task of re-creating the dark shape on a copy of the Solyo topographic map. To help determine the acreage covered, a Davis geologist gave me a piece of graph paper whose squares were so small that four thousand four hundred and twenty-two of them covered one square mile on the map. Having seen the great pile and moved around it close, I could assign it an average thickness. Jack Waggoner, of Sacramento, who has spent his career as a distributor of tire-retreading and tire-shredding equipment, supplied figures for average densities of tires compressed by their own weight. On its side, a tire occupies about four square feet. A calculator blended these facts. While I had read or been given estimates of eight, nine, fifteen, twenty-five, forty-two, and forty-four, the calculator was reporting that in the world's largest known pile there are thirty-four million tires.

You don't have to stare long at that pile before the thought occurs   4
to you that those tires were once driven upon by the Friends of the Earth. They are not just the used tires of bureaucrats, ballplayers, and litter-strewing rock-deafened ninja-teen-aged nyrds. They are everybody's tires. They are Environmental Defense Fund tires, Rainforest Action Network tires, Wilderness Society tires. They are California Natural Resources Federation tires, Save San Francisco Bay Association tires, Citizens for a Better Environment tires. They are Greenpeace tires, Sierra Club tires, Earth Island Institute tires. They are Earth First! tires! No one is innocent of scrapping those tires. They who carry out what they carry in have not carried out those tires. Of the problem the tire pile represents, everybody is the cause, and the problem, like the pile, has been increasing. (The California Integrated Waste Management Board has referred to the state's "growing tire population.") Most landfills across the country are refusing tires now, because most landfills are filling up, and, moreover, tires "float." They won't stay covered up. They work their way to the surface like glacial rocks. Intended by their manufacturers to be reliable and durable, they most emphatically are. Nothing about an automobile is safer than its tires, whose ultimate irony is that when they reach the end

of their intended lives they are all but indestructible. When they are thrown away, they are just as tough as they were when they felt Kick One. On the surface or underground or on the beds of rivers, they don't decay. They are one per cent of all municipal solid waste and symbol of the other ninety-nine. Locked into the chemistry of each passenger tire is more than two and a half gallons of recoverable petroleum. California by itself discards twenty million tires a year. The United States throws away two hundred and fifty million tires a year. Strewn about the country at last count are something like three billion trashed tires. A hundred and seventy-eight million barrels of oil.

VOCABULARY

paragraph 1: escarpment, topography, pucks
paragraph 2: jockey
paragraph 3: mosaic, Rorschach

QUESTIONS

1. From what vistas or vantage points does McPhee show us the pile of tires?

2. What point is he making about the tires, and how do these vistas and the order in which they occur help McPhee make it?

3. Where does he state this point, and why at this place in the essay?

4. What information about the tires does he save for the end? What does he gain in not presenting it at the beginning?

SUGGESTIONS FOR WRITING

1. Describe an unusual object or place from more than one physical vantage point to give the reader a full sense of it. For example, you might describe it from a high building or a bridge, then from a moving vehicle.

2. Expand your description to include a view at one or more times of day or seasons of the year. Use your description to make a point as McPhee does. Make this point in the most advantageous place to your point or thesis.

W. S. MERWIN

W. S. MERWIN has had a varied writing career as poet, essayist, playwright, and translator. His many volumes of poetry include *Collected Poems* (1966), *Selected Poems* (1988), and *Travels: Poems* (1993). In 1971 Merwin received the Pulitzer Prize in Poetry. *The Miner's Pale Children* (1970) and *Regions of Memory* (1987) contain essays and other prose. The following excerpt appears in *Unframed Originals* (1982), a book of personal recollections. Merwin gives a vivid picture of a highly valued family car and the trips taken in it.

THE BUICK

But back at the end of their twenties, in the months when my mother 1
was pregnant with me, the First Presbyterian Church of Union City, New Jersey, extended the call—as it was phrased—to my father, and he was happy to accept. They moved. A new place, within sight of Manhattan. In a new state, where people pronounced their words differently. A new church, a city church, and in comparison with the former ones, a rather large one. A new house, new to them at any rate, considerably bigger than any they had lived in. A child on the way, as part of their new life. The pregnancy dated from the beginning of the year. In keeping with the turn of the moment, The Ford was replaced with a new car, The Buick. It represented distance already traversed. And a boast of arrival.

My father remained proud of The Buick for several years, its make, 2
model, everything about it. It is true that I do not remember ever seeing another one just like it. Neither a sedan nor a coupe; a two-door, with a deep back seat, a large hump of luggage compartment on the

rear, and the spare tire bolted on a rack behind that. The middle section stood up like a deck house or a top hat, and was covered with a textured black patent leather. A broad visor extending from the front of it shaded the windshield. The body of the car, from the windowsills down, was a lustrous blue, a twilit sky color. It looked as though you could see far into it, as into water, and my father, and a series of men from the church ritually, indeed reverently, washed and Simonized it. My father pronounced the word Simonize as though it were a spell. When new license plates arrived he called me into his study for the ceremony of removing them from their waxed paper and holding them up with a little "Hm" of pleasure. The rear plate was fastened behind the spare tire, under a small black oval box from which the glass corneas of three lights protruded, one white, one green, and one amber. Each glass was fluted on the inside, like the reverse of an orange squeezer, so that looking at them one saw what appeared to be the undersides of three flowers with precise narrow petals. Only the white light worked, by the time I was old enough to be interested, but I considered all three of them, and the red tail lights—particularly when seen in the dark, with the smoke of the exhaust swirling past them—to be objects of urgent but inexplicable beauty.

Besides, there were the wooden spoke wheels, the spokes enamelled the same lucent blue as the body, with fine black lines along their centers. And running boards on which I yearned to ride. I was never completely content with the plain, almost flat radiator cap with indentations around it for grasping it, once I had seen caps adorned with thermometers standing in metal rings. It made no difference to me that my father shook his head and pursed his lips at the thermometers, and said they worked only for a short time and then were no use. I was not interested in what they were supposed to do. 3

The Buick's importance extended to its housing. It had to itself the whole ground floor of a real (small) barn that walled off half of the back yard: a two story structure with hay-loft doors upstairs above the main ones. The building must have been the same age as the manse. Both of them harked back to the 1870's or '80's at least, the time of horses and carriages. It was obvious that the barn had had other lives that had been concealed but were there in it still. For a while, I learned—I no longer remember from whom—it had been used as a ware house for hides, which had been hoisted from wagons in bales, by means of the pulley that was still there, up under the peak outside the hayloft doors. For 4

us—for me, and later for my sister—the whole building was absolutely
forbidden ground, and only once did I ever see what was on the upper
floor. My father, one day, in an expansive mood, allowed me in beside
the car, where the walls were hung with rakes and shovels and chains
and there were shelves sagging with paint cans. On the far side a ladder went straight up to a hole in the ceiling. He held me up, with my
head above the level of the upper floor, so that I could peer around in
the cardboard light. There was nothing there but bulges. When he lifted
me down he told me that I must never go up there, for any reason. In
time that upper story was populated with wasps, and with assorted people and creatures of my invention, many of whom did not even suspect each other's existence. When my father was about to take the car
out, the barn was called the garage. he would open its doors, and then
open the gates of the fence along New York Avenue and back the car out
onto the white-pebbled driveway, and whoever was going with him would
get in there.

For those trips "back home"—which was another of my father's   5
ways of referring to the periodic journeys across New Jersey and Pennsylvania to New Kensington, where my grandmother had moved after
he left for college, and where he had never lived—he believed in getting
an early start. By one route the distance, according to the Buick's odometer, was 444 miles. He had made it more than once in a single day,
which he and his listeners considered a wonderful achievement. It allowed
him, at any rate, to declare that he *could* do it in a day, though it meant
leaving early and arriving late at night. Most of the trips on which he
managed to do it were ones that he took by himself; usually, when the
family was along, we broke the journey somewhere on the way. But
whatever the plan, or absence of plan, he—who ordinarily did not like
early rising—wanted to be on the road, if possible, by four o'clock in
the morning. You made your best time, he repeated, during the hours
before daylight. So we got up in the hollow dark, my mother cooperat-
ing with the arrangements, but bustling and clucking her tongue at
the proceedings as she went, because getting up so early violated the
children's sleep. Her pursed lips and her impatience with the last minute packings and closings expressed a deepening reluctance concerning
those trips altogether, but I did not understand that, at the begining. My
father assumed full authority for the expeditions, and ignored, or pre-
tended to ignore, her lack of enthusiasm. "The darkest hour," he would
say to me, eyebrows and finger raised, "is just before the dawn." As we

got ready, and floated out of room after room—bedrooms, bathroom, dining room ("the children have to have their breakfast if they're going to be up that long")—the light in the house looked sallow and unlikely, and the smell of wallpaper followed us and then abruptly was gone, replaced by the startling yet elusive scent of what my mother called the night air, which had its dangers. There were no cars at all, at that hour, and the silent darkness was freighted with that odor speaking of the earth. Our footsteps echoed on the gravel walk. The hinges of the back area-way door squeaked behind us. The street car wires hummed above the avenue. The garage doors grated open. The Buick started up, waking huge echoes, and the tail lights moved toward us with the smoke rising around them. My mother spoke to us, and we answered, in whispers, and we climbed in onto the stiff velvet upholstery with its own dusty night smell. In the light of the street lamp its inky blue looked black.

VOCABULARY

paragraph 2: textured, lustrous, fluted
paragraph 3: lucent
paragraph 4: manse
paragraph 5: pursed, sallow, elusive

QUESTIONS

1. To what features of the Buick does Merwin give most attention in paragraphs 2 and 3? What particular idea or impression do the details develop?

2. What idea or impression do those in paragraph 4 develop? Are the details of the upper floor of the barn inessential?

3. What does the final paragraph tell us about the Buick and the family?

4. How are the five paragraphs organized? What do the concluding sentences contribute?

SUGGESTION FOR WRITING

Describe an object that once had special importance for you and your family—perhaps an automobile or other possession, a house or apartment lived in for a time, a park or building in your town or city. Let the details of your description convey the sense of importance the object had. You may find it helpful to write down everything you remember about it, then decide what details you want to include in your description, and in what order you want to present these. An order related to an idea or dominant impression may occur to you in planning your essay.

MARY HELEN PONCE

MARY HELEN PONCE teaches literature and creative writing at the University of California, Santa Barbara. In her autobiography, *Hoyt Street* (1993), she describes the town northwest of Los Angeles in which she grew up. Her other writings include *Taking Control* (1987), a collection of stories, and novel *The Wedding* (1989). Ponce tells us much about the Chicano world of southern California.

HOYT STREET

The town of Pacoima lay to the northeast of Los Angeles, about three   1
miles south of the city of San Fernando. The blue-grey San Gabriel Mountains rose toward the east; toward the west other small towns dotted the area. Farther west lay the blue Pacific and the rest of the world. The barrio, as I Knew it, extended from San Fernando Road to Glenoaks Boulevard on the east and from Filmore and Pierce streets on the north. We lived in the shadow of Los Angeles, twenty odd miles to the south.

Most of the townspeople were Mexican immigrants, as were my par-   2
ents, who had moved to Pacoima in the 1920s. Across the tracks lived the white folks, many of them Okies. There were few blacks in the area up until the early fifties, when the Joe Louis housing tract near Glenoaks Boulevard allowed black ex-GIs to buy there.

Many men in the barrio worked in agriculture, en el fil, weeding, 3
pruning, or watering various crops. Others worked as troqueros, as did
Rocky, my father's compadre, who each fall drove workers in his truck
to the walnut orchards of Camarillo. Men who owned their own trucks
worked for themselves. They lugged fertilizer from poultry farms to
nearby ranches or trucked produce into Los Angeles. Still others took the
bus to the union hall in San Fernando, where they hired out as "casual
laborers" or found work in the packinghouse in that same town. A neighbor,
el Señor Flores, owned a flower nursery; Don Jesús, a kind, rotund
man, had his own grocery store. For the most part men either hired out
as unskilled laborers or worked for themselves, as did my father, who
sold used wood from our backyard.

Pacoima streets were unpaved, full of holes and rocks. During a rain 4
the rich, brown mud clung to our shoes. Van Nuys Boulevard, the main
street, was paved and lit with lamps that burned till late at night; that
was where most stores and businesses were located. The boulevard cut
through the middle of the barrio, then continued west to Van Nuys, North
Hollywood, and other towns.

San Fernando Road, which ran north and south, was the main artery 5
to Los Angeles; it connected Pacoima with Roscoe (later renamed Sun
Valley), Burbank, and Glendale, then curved west to the Hill Street overpass
that led to downtown Los Angeles, called "Elay" or "Los" by the
locals. To the north this highway went over the mountains to become
Highway 99. It cut through the town of Gorman, a truckers' stop with
a huge restaurant and one motel, and on to the "Grapevine," a long,
lonely section constantly filled with huge trucks. Once past the highest
mountain peak, the road no longer curved but shot into the fertile San
Joaquin Valley in an endless straight line.

The barrio was laid out like a huge square. The streets ran up and 6
down with nary a curve or dead end. Streets that ran north and south
started at Filmore Street and came to a screeching halt en la Pierce, where
the Pacoima airport, known as Whiteman Airport, stood. The airstrip
was more like a weed-infested field with cracked pavement. Small shedlike
buildings stood at one end. At one time this area was an empty space
where students playing hookey from school would hide out. During Easter
vacation and in the summer, kids used the unpaved road along the airport
as a shortcut to the nearby hills that dipped and rolled toward
Hansen Dam. In spring they came alive with scrub bushes and other
plants, none of which grew very tall. From the highest peak you could

see Guardian Angel Church and the Pacoima General Store, the two tallest buildings in town. When later a chain link fence and gates with padlocks went up, hiking to the Pacoima hills became less fun.

Homes in Pacas, as we called Pacoima, were modest, ranging from 7 a one-room shack where people slept in the "front room," to the more elegant homes such as Rocky's, which boasted an ample living room, a bathroom with tile and chrome faucets, and a separate bedroom for each child. On our street, and in the immediate neighborhood, houses were one story high except for that of the Torres family; theirs had upstairs bedrooms with tall windows. In the next block was the quasi-Victorian structure belonging to Doña Mercedes. It sat back from the street, as if ashamed to be seen next to older, shabbier homes.

On Hoyt Street the houses were neither fancy nor ugly, but like the 8 houses of poor folks everywhere. While some were constructed of stucco, the majority were of wood, madera. Wood was plentiful and cheaper than cement, so wood it was. The houses, while not uniform, had some similarities: a window on each side and a door smack in the middle. Others appeared lopsided because of the many additions tacked on as a family grew. Still others were of different types of wood bought for price and not appearance. From afar it was easy to spot the short boards nailed next to the smooth planks of polished wood bought at the lumberyard. People were innovative, too, and sometimes built houses of rock and cement.

On Filmore Street sat two stone houses made of the white and gray 9 rocks that filled the Pacoima Wash, a small stream to the east. The sturdy-looking homes, so unlike any others in the barrio, were fascinating. Unlike Rapunzel's castle, they were not surrounded by trees, nor did they have a large tower. Still they were quaint, like the stone huts in the dark German forests where Hansel and Gretel lived. Along the front were large windows embedded in the round stones, with a wooden door in the middle. One rock house even had a fireplace, an anomaly in our town, where few homes even had a spacious living room.

Not all homes had electricity or indoor plumbing. Many casitas on 10 Hoyt Street still had an outhouse somewhere in the back, hidden behind a nopalera or standing blatantly in the middle of the yard. Once the electrical lines reached Van Nuys Boulevard, and local residents were allowed to connect, my father was among the first to do so. After he wired our house, he did that of Doña Luisa, our adopted grandmother, who lived next door. She, like others in our town, continued to use la lámpara de petroleo, which had a long wick and gave only a faint light. She felt that electricity was terribly expensive, and insisted that every time el foco was turned on, it cost a penny! Each time I yanked the string hanging from the light bulb on the ceiling, Doña Luisa pursed her thin lips and reminded me I was wasting electricity—and pennies. She then lit the kerosene lamp and set it next to the trunk alongside her bed.

Mejicanos in our town took pride in their homes and, when money allowed, repaired a dilapidated roof or painted their casitas a bright color. They took special pride in having a yard full of plants and flowers, and these grew well in the rich California soil. La familia Santos had a pretty front yard with bright red geraniums growing in old cans and fruit trees along the side. Like other women in our street, each morning Mrs. Santos raked the front yard, sprinkled water on it to keep the dust down, then trimmed her geraniums. In the Lopez family's yard was a birdbath made of crude cement, rocks, and pipes. It was pretty and the pride of Mr. Lopez, who had designed and made it himself. People said he was un artista. Each day the birdbath was filled with clean water for the many birds that congregated there. In other gardens, bird cages bought at the five and dime in San Fernando hung from the various trees. Still other casitas sported a porch swing where, on warm summer evenings, adults gossiped or told stories of la llorona to pesky children, the soft Spanish words drifting down Hoyt Street and dissolving into the night. While the homes on our street were different in color, shape, and size, they had one thing in common: each had a junk pile somewhere in the back yard.

El yonque was important for folks who were short on money but full of ingenuity. The junk pile held the necessary parts to wire a car together or replace rusted pipes, and it helped keep folks from spending hard-earned cash at the hardware store in town. The Morenos had not one but several junk piles in their huge yard. On one side la Señora Moreno grew flowers and vegetables. On the other were two piles of junk that included automobile parts: engines, carburetors, dented fenders, old batteries, and flat tires. Except for la familia Soto, whose backyard held only a crude table and benches and a row of apricot trees, the junk pile was an accepted part of a Mexican household.

My father, too, clung to junk, a thing that bothered my mother, who functioned best in a clean and orderly household. The yonque, or clutter as I thought of it, was of value to my father as it was to other pobres. Pipes, rusty tin tubs, old tires, wood, wire, and car radios lay scattered here and there. My father was certain that at some point, good use could be made of the stuff. Neighbors and friends would come by for a piece of pipe, a strip of tar paper, or some two-by-fours, all from the junk pile and all freely given to someone in need.

People in Pacoima, I often thought, needed more space than did those 14 in upwardly mobile San Fernando, where homes had sidewalks and paved streets, but sat close together, as if afraid to breathe too much of their neighbor's air. On Hoyt Street most residents had once lived in Mexican ranchitos and had a greater need for land. In the large double lots, they planted fruit trees, vegetable and flower gardens, and assorted hierbas that also grew in Mexico. The Garcias had a nopalera, a wall of prickly pear cactus in the back that served two purposes: it was a fence that kept out errant dogs and kids, and it also provided food. The succulent cactus, nopalitos, were popular during Lent along with deep-fried camarones, shrimp; the prickly pear fruits, or tunas, fell off when ripe and were quickly gobbled up.

We lived at 13011 Hoyt Street, a block from church and the Pacoima 15 General Store (called la tienda blanca), and two blocks from Pacoima Elementary School. Our house sat in the middle of a double lot. The front door, which was rarely used, faced Hoyt Street. The back gate led to the alley and an open field, el llano, which faced Van Nuys Boulevard. To our right lived Doña Luisa. Next to her, in a house that extended the length of the lot, lived the Morenos. To our left was a roomy yellow house with a big garage, occupied on and off by different families. I remember best the Montalvos, a handsome family with light hair and eyes; their daughter Margarita was close to my age.

Our house was built by my father when he and my mother and their 16 three older children moved from Ventura to the San Fernando Valley, sometime in the 1920s. Originally our house had three rooms: a kitchen and two bedrooms. The large kitchen extended the length of the house. Later, as his family grew, my father added on to the house, with some interesting results—our kitchen had a window that opened into the living room! The kitchen floor was covered with dark green linoleum. On one wall was el trastero, the pantry, where flour, sugar, and beans were stored. On the other wall were two large cabinets in which sat assorted dishes and the blue-willow plates that came in a soap box and were used for company. A double sink faced the west wall, and in one corner was the white gas stove with a big griddle. A large window hung with dotted-swiss curtains trimmed in rickrack faced the driveway and framed a huge eucalyptus tree. In the summer my sisters moved the kitchen table next to the window; from there we looked out at the wild birds in the tree branches. In the summer too, my sisters served our dinner outdoors on the cement patio with the roof of palm fronds that my father had also built.

VOCABULARY

paragraph 9: anomaly
paragraph 14: succulent
paragraph 16: rickrack

QUESTIONS

1. How different would the impression given of Hoyt Street be had Ponce begun with the description of the streets and houses of the barrio, omitting its location and the work of many of the men?

2. What do the details of the barrio in paragraph 6 and those of the streets and neighboring houses in paragraphs 7–12 help show what was special about 13011 Hoyt Street?

3. How different would the impression be had Ponce begun by describing the house and moving to the streets and barrio and the location, finally?

4. What point is she making about the junk piles?

SUGGESTIONS FOR WRITING

1. Describe a building you are familiar with—perhaps your own house, a building on campus or in your town or city—that reflects the values of the people who inhabit or work in them. Describe the building from a specific vantage point, or from several—outside as well as inside. Comment on the building as you describe it or following your description.

2. Describe a social or religious ceremony—perhaps a holiday celebration, wedding, memorial service, or funeral—that you once participated in. Give details of the setting, participations, ceremony itself. Then discuss what it reveals about the participants.

barrio: Latino district of a town or city
en el fil: in a row

troquero: trucker
compadre: friend, comrade
la lámpara de petroleo: oil lamp
el foco: light bulb
casita: small house
la llorona: hired mourner
el yonque: junk pile
pobre: impoverished
tienda: shop

RONALD TAKAKI

RONALD TAKAKI, professor of Ethnic Studies at the University of California, Berkeley, is the grandson of Japanese immigrant plantation workers in Hawaii. Takaki writes about their world in *Pau Hana: Plantation Life and Labor in Hawaii* (1983). His other books include *Iron Cages: Race and Culture in Nineteenth-Century America* (1982), *Strangers from a Different Shore* (1990), *A Different Mirror: A History of Multicultural America* (1993), and *Larger Memory* (1998). A selection from Ernesto Galarza's *Barrio Boy,* referred to in the essay, appears on p. 314.

THE BARRIO:
COMMUNITY IN THE COLONY

For many Mexicans, the border was only an imaginary line—one that   1
could be crossed and recrossed at will. Unlike the migrants from Europe,
Africa, and Asia, they came from a country touching the United States.
Standing on the border, migrants had difficulty knowing where one country
began and the other ended. Mexicans had been in the Southwest long
before the Anglos, and they would continue to emigrate despite repatriation programs. In El Norte, there were jobs and also communities.

Indeed, over the years, Chicanos had been creating a Mexican-   2
American world in the barrios of El Norte. In their communities, they
did not feel like aliens in a foreign land as they did whenever they crossed

the railroad tracks and ventured uptown into the Anglo World. Though their neighborhood was a slum, a concentration of shacks and dilapidated houses, without sidewalks or even paved streets, the barrio was home to its residents. The people were all compatriots. They had come from different places in Mexico and had been here for different lengths of time, but together they formed "the *colonia mexicana*." "We came to know families from Chihuahua, Sonora, Jalisco, and Durango," remembered one of them. "Some had come to the United States even before the revolution, living in Texas before migrating to California. Like ourselves, our Mexican neighbors had come this far moving step by step, working and waiting . . ."[1]

In El Norte, Chicanos were recreating a Mexican community and culture. They celebrated national holidays like the Sixteenth of September, Mexican Independence Day. "We are Mexicans," declared a speaker at one of the celebrations, "almost all of us here . . . by our fathers or ancestors, although we are now under a neighboring nation's flag to which we owe respect. Notwithstanding, this respect does not prevent us from remembering our Mexican anniversary." The celebrations, Ernesto Galarza recalled, "stirred everyone in the *barrio*" and gave them the feeling that they were "still Mexicans." At these festive occasions, there were parades in the plazas attended by city and county officials as well as Mexican consuls. The entire town became a *fandango*. Colorful musicians strolled, and people danced in the streets. Excited crowds shouted, "*Viva Mexico!*" and sang Mexican songs as fireworks exploded and *muchachos* (kids) listened to stories about Mexico told by the *viejitos* (old ones). Bands played the national anthems of both countries. The flags and the colors of the United States and Mexico were displayed together—red, white, and blue as well as red, white, and green.[2]

The religion of the Chicanos was a uniquely Mexican version of Catholicism, a blending of a faith brought from the Old World and beliefs that had been in the New World for thousands of years before Columbus. For the Mexicans, God was deeply personal, caring for each of them

3

4

---

[1] Ernesto Galarza, *Barrio Boy: The Story of a Boy's Acculturation* (Notre Dame, IN, 1971), p. 200.

[2] Albert Camarillo, *Chicanos in a Changing Society: From Mexican Pueblos to American Barrios in Santa Barbara and Southern California, 1848–1930* (Cambridge, MA, 1979), p. 62; Galarza, *Barrio Boy*, p. 206; Arnold De Leon, *The Tejano Community, 1836–1900* (Albuquerque, NM, 1982), pp. 180–181.

through their saints. In their homes, they decorated their altars with *santitos,* images of saints dear to them. They had a special relationship with the Virgen de Guadalupe: according to their account, she had visited a poor Indian and felt a particular concern for the people of Mexico. "I have with me an amulet which my mother gave to me before dying," a Mexican told an interviewer. "This amulet has the Virgin of Guadalupe on it and it is she who always protects me." Their Virgin Mary was Mexican: many paintings and statues represented her as dark in complexion.[3]

What bound the people together was not only ethnicity but also class. "We were all poor," a Mexican said, "we were all in the same situation." The barrio was a "grapevine of job information." A frequently heard word was *trabajo* (work), and "the community was divided in two—the many who were looking for it and the few who had it to offer." Field hands, railroad workers, cannery workers, construction laborers, and maids came back to the barrio after work to tell one another where the jobs were and how much they paid and what the food and living quarters were like.[4]

In the colony, unskilled workers from Mexico were welcomed, for they had come from the homeland. "These Mexicans are hired on this side of the Rio Grande by agents of the larger farms, and are shipped in car load lots, with windows and doors locked, to their destination," a local newspaper reported. "After the cotton season the majority will work their way back to the border and into Mexico." But the barrio offered these migrant workers a place to stay north of the border. "Beds and meals, if the newcomers had no money at all, were provided—in one way or another—on trust, until the new *chicano* found a job." Aid was given freely, for everyone knew what it meant to be in need. "It was not charity or social welfare," Ernesto Galarza explained, "but something my mother called *asistencia,* a helping given and received on trust, to be repaid because those who had given it were themselves in need of what they had given. *Chicanos* who had found work on farms or in railroad camps came back to pay us a few dollars for *asistencia* we had provided weeks or months before."[5]

---

[3] Manuel Gamio, *The Mexican Immigrant: His Life Story* (Chicago, 1931), p. 28; De Leon, *Tejano Community,* p. 160.

[4] Camarillo, *Chicanos in a Changing Society,* p. 169; Galarza, *Barrio Boy,* p. 201.

[5] De Leon, *Tejano Community,* p. 65; Galarza, *Barrio Boy,* p. 201.

In the barrio, people helped each other, for survival depended on 7
solidarity and mutual assistance. For example, Bonifacio Ortega had
dislocated his arm while working in Los Angeles. "I was laid up and had
to be in the hospital about three months," he recalled. "Fortunately my
countrymen helped me a lot, for those who were working got something
together every Saturday and took it to me at the hospital for whatever I
needed. They also visited me and made me presents." Ortega's arm healed,
and he returned to work at a brickyard. "We help one another, we fellow countrymen. We are almost all from the same town or from the
nearby farms. The wife of one of the countrymen died the other day and
we got enough money together to buy a coffin and enough so that he
could go and take the body to Jalisco."[6]

Moreover, the barrio was a place where Mexicans could feel at home 8
in simple, day-to-day ways. Women wearing rebozos, or traditional
shawls, were seen everywhere, just as in Mexico. There were Mexican
plays and *carpas*—acrobats and traveling sideshows. Stands and cafés offered tamales and other favorites such as frijoles, tortillas, *menudo* (tripe
stew), and *dulces* made with *piloncillo* (Mexican sugar). Cantinas and
bars were places to hang out and drink beer. *Mercados* stocked Mexican
foods like *chorizo* (sausage), while *panderias* baked fresh bread. Shopping in the *tiendas* was familiar. "In the secondhand shops, where the
barrio people sold and bought furniture and clothing, there were Mexican clerks who knew the Mexican ways of making a sale."[7]

In the early evenings, as the sun began to set, the people sat outside 9
their homes, as they had on the other side of the border in their Mexican
villages. The air still carried the smells of suppertime—"tortillas baking, beans boiling, chile roasting, coffee steaming, and kerosene stench-
ing." The men "squatted on the ground, hunched against the wall of the
house and smoked. The women and the girls . . . put away the kitchen
things, the *candiles* turned down to save kerosene. They listened to the
tales of the day if the men were in a talking mood. "They spoke in two
languages—"Spanish and with gestures." An old man talked about a time
called "Before the Conquest." The Indian tribes had their "own kings
and emperors," he said. "Then the Spaniards [came], killing the Indians
and running them down with hunting dogs. The conquerors took the

---

[6] Gamio, *Mexican Immigrant*, p. 26.
[7] Galarza, *Barrio Boy*, p. 239.

land along the rivers where there was water and rich soil, flat and easy to farm. On these lands the Spaniards set up their haciendas, where the Indians were forced to labor for nothing or were paid only a few centavos for a hard day's work."[8]

Feeling homesick, the people sometimes took out their cedar boxes to display memorabilia from Mexico—a butterfly serape worn to celebrate the Battle of Puebla, tin pictures of grandparents, and "bits of embroidery and lace" made by aunts still in the homeland. They "took deep breaths of the aroma of *puro cedro,* pure Jalcocotan mixed with camphor." A song in Spanish floated in the air: 10

> *I loved a little country girl*
> *She was so shy*
> *She couldn't even talk to me*
> *I would take her hand*
> *And she would sadly cry*
> *Now go away*
> *My mother will be scolding me.*[9]

As darkness descended, the people complained about how they were not allowed to feel at home north of the border: "They [Anglos] would rant at public meetings and declare that this was an American country and the Mexicans ought to be run out." "You can't forget those things. You try to forget because . . . you should forgive and forget, but there is still a pain in there that another human being could do that to you." Someone argued: "I haven't wanted to, nor do I want to learn English, for I am not thinking of living in this country all my life. I don't even like it here." A voice agreed: "They talk to us about becoming citizens, but if we become citizens we are still Mexicans. They look at our hair, and listen to our speech and call us Mexicans." Rejection in the new country reinforced a return mentality.[10]   11

An old man insisted on keeping his Mexican ties: "I have always had and now have my home in El Paso, but I shall never change my [Mexican]   12

---

[8] Ibid., pp. 12, 19, 23, 42.

[9] Ibid., pp. 237, 49.

[10] David Montejano, *Anglos and Mexicans in the Making of Texas, 1836–1986* (Austin, TX, 1987), p. 31; Gamio, *Mexican Immigrant,* p. 13; Mark Reisler, *By the Sweat of Their Brow: Mexican Immigrant Labor in the United States, 1900–1940* (Westport, CT, 1976), p. 113.

citizenship in spite of the fact that [here] I have greater opportunities and protection." Another admitted ambivalence: "I want to go back to Leon because it is my country and I love Mexico. But I like it better here for one can work more satisfactory. No one interferes with one and one doesn't have to fear that there will be or won't be revolutions."[11]

As the night air became chilly, the barrio people pulled their serapes and rebozos around their shoulders. They talked about this land as "occupied" Mexico and the nearness of the border. After arriving in Nogales, Arizona, a young Mexican boy was happy to be finally in the United States. "Look at the American flag," his mother said. As he watched it flying over a building near them, he noticed a Mexican flag on a staff beyond the depot down the street. "We are in the United States," his mother explained. "Mexico is over there." But no matter where they were in the United States, the border was always close to their hearts. Mexican Americans who were citizens by birth were often reminded that they were still Mexicans. By "nationality" my son is "American," a father explained, but he is "Mexicano" "by blood." A local Mexican newspaper criticized some Mexican Americans for not celebrating the Sixteenth of September: "To those 'Agringados' [Americanized Mexicans] who negate that they are Mexicans because they were born in the United States, we ask: what blood runs through their veins? Do they think they are members of the Anglo-Saxon race who only happen to have dark skins because they were born on the border! What nonsense! (Que barbaridad!)" A song chimed: 13

> . . . he who denies his race
> Is the most miserable creature . . .
> A good Mexican
> Never disowns
> The dear fatherland
> Of his affections.[12]

Soon night fell, and the hunched figures blended into the darkness. But no one was sleepy yet, so the people continued to sit in front of their 14

[11] Gamio, *Mexican Immigrant*, pp. 182, 104.

[12] Galarza, *Barrio Boy*, p. 183; Camarillo, *Chicanos in a Changing Society*, p. 149; Mario T. Garcia, *Desert Immigrants: The Mexicans of El Paso, 1880–1920* (New Haven, CT, 1981), pp. 228–229; Gamio, *Mexican Immigrant*, p. 94.

homes. The stars were brighter above Mexico, someone commented, and there were more of them. Sí, yes, another added, and there were coyotes howling nearby. Much was different in El Norte. But as in their old villages, the streets in the barrio had no lights, and now only their voices could be heard. "When they pulled on their cigarettes, they made ruby dots in the dark, as if they were putting periods in the low-toned conversation. The talk just faded away, the men went indoors, the doors were shut . . . there was nothing on the street but the dark. . . ."[13]

VOCABULARY

paragraph 2: barrio, compatriot
paragraph 3: fandango
paragraph 5: ethnicity
paragraph 8: frijole, tortilla, cantina
paragraph 9: hacienda, centavo
paragraph 10: serape
paragraph 13: rebozo, negate

QUESTIONS

1. How detailed is the description of the celebration of Mexican Independence Day in paragraph 3? Does Takaki describe the beginning of the celebration and its end?

2. By comparison, does the description of the barrio in paragraphs 9–14 begin and end at a certain time? Is the description continuous? To what details of barrio life does Takaki give special emphasis?

3. In the course of the essay, what Chicano attitudes and values does Takaki identify? Which of these does he highlight?

4. What is Takaki's thesis or central idea, and where does he first state it? Where does he restate it?

---

[13] Galarza, *Barrio Boy*, p. 12.

SUGGESTIONS FOR WRITING

1. Takaki states that "what bound the people together was not only ethnicity but also class." Explain what he means and show how he illustrates these bonds.

2. Many first- and second-generation Americans, even third- and fourth-generation ones, retain features of the language and culture of their family's origin. Like the Mexican Americans described by Takaki, many are multilingual or retain many of the names and expressions of a language other than American English. Food, art, music, religious practices may also be multicultural. Describe the multicultural world of your own family or neighborhood or another you have observed. Like Takaki, give a picture of this world, focusing on a particular time and place.

7

NARRATION

Description shows a person, place, or thing at a particular time; the ordering of details is spatial—proceeding from left to right or top to bottom or in some other way. The order of details in narration is temporal. Narration shows change occurring—a series of events, personal experiences, and the like presented chronologically, sometimes supported with descriptive details:

> I marched down the hill, looking and feeling a fool, with the rifle over my shoulder and an ever-growing army of people jostling at my heels. At the bottom, when you got away from the huts, there was a metalled road and beyond that a miry waste of paddy fields a thousand yards across, not yet ploughed but soggy from the first rains and dotted with coarse grass. The elephant was standing eight yards from the road, his left side toward us. He took not the slightest notice of the crowd's approach. He was tearing up bunches of grass, beating them against his knees to clean them, and stuffing them into his mouth. (George Orwell, "Shooting an Elephant")

Narration is often found in exposition. In explaining why the Spanish Armada came to defeat or why England survived heavy bombing at the beginning of World War II, the writer may give an account of a decisive event—the wind that blew the Armada off course, the discovery of radar—and subsequent events. Though narration is usually chronological, the writer may have reason to present events in a different order. Transitions are essential in preparing the reader for this change.

JAMES SALTER

A graduate of West Point, JAMES SALTER served in the Air Force from 1945 to 1957. His novel *The Hunters* (1957) is based on his experiences as a fighter pilot in the Korean War. Other writings include the novels *A Sport and a Pastime* (1967) and *Light Years* (1975), and *Dusk and Other Stories* (1988) and *Burning the Days: Recollections* (1997). The following suspenseful account of an early flying experience is taken from Salter's essay "You Must," published in *Esquire* in 1992.

FLYING

At Stewart Field that final spring, nearly pilots, we had the last segment   1
of training. This was near Newburgh, about forty minutes from West Point. We wore flying suits most of the day and lived in long, open-bay barracks. That photograph of oneself, unfading, that no one ever sees, in my case was taken in the morning by the doorway of what must be the dayroom and I am drinking a Coke from an icy, greenish bottle, a delicious prelude to all the breakfastless mornings of flying that were to come. During all the training there had been few fatalities. We were that good. At least I knew I was.

On a May evening after supper we took off, one by one, on a nav-   2
igation flight. It was still daylight and the planes, as they departed, were thrilling in their solitude. On the maps the course was drawn, miles marked off in ticks of ten. The route lay to the west, over the wedged-up Allegheny ridges to Port Jervis and Scranton, then down to Reading, and the last long leg of the triangle back home. It was all mechanical with one exception: The winds aloft had been incorrectly forecast. Unknown to us, they were from a different direction and stronger. Alone and confident we headed west.

The air at altitude has a different smell, metallic and faintly tinged   3
with gasoline or exhaust. The ground floats by with tidal slowness, roads desolate, the rivers unmoving. It is exactly like the map with certain insignificant differences that one ponders over but leaves unresolved. The sun has turned red and sunk lower. The airspeed reads 160. The fifteen or twenty airplanes, invisible to one another, are in a long, phantom

string. Behind, the sky has become a deeper shade. We were flying not only in the idleness of spring but in a kind of idyll that was the end of the war. The color of the earth was muted and the towns seemed empty shadows. There was no one to see or talk to. The wind, unsuspected, was shifting us slowly, like sand.

Of what was I thinking? The inexactness of navigation, I suppose, New York nights, the lure of the city, various achievements that a year or two before I had only dreamed of. The first dim star appeared and then, somewhat to the left of where it should be, the drab scrawl of Scranton.   4

Flying, like most things of consequence, is method. Though I did not know it then, I was behaving offhandedly. There were light lines between cities in those days, like lights on an unseen highway but much further apart. By reading their flashed codes you could tell where you were, but I was not bothering with that. I turned south toward Reading. The sky was dark now. Far below, the earth was cooling, giving up the heat of the day. A mist had begun to form. In it, the light lines would fade away and also, almost shyly, the towns. I flew on.   5

It is a different world at night. The instruments become harder to read, details disappear from the map. After a while I tuned to the Reading frequency and managed to pick up its signal. I had no radio compass but there was a way of determining, by flying a certain sequence of headings, where you were. If the signal slowly increased in strength you were inbound toward the station. If not and you had to turn up the volume to continue hearing it, you were going away. It was primitive but it worked. When the time came I waited to see if I had passed or was still approaching Reading. The minutes went by. At first I couldn't detect a change but then the signal seemed to grow weaker. I turned north and flew watching the clock. Something was wrong, something serious: The signal didn't change. I was lost, not only literally but in relation to reality. Meanwhile the wind, unseen, fateful, was forcing me further north.   6

Among the stars, one was moving. It was the lights of another plane, perhaps from the squadron. In any case, wherever it was headed there would be a field. I pushed up the throttle. As I drew closer, I began to make out what it was, an airliner, a DC-3. It might be going to St. Louis or Chicago. I had already been flying for what seemed like hours and had begun, weakhearted, a repeated checking of fuel. The gauges were on the floor. I tried not to think of them but they were like a wound; I could not keep myself from glancing down.   7

Slowly the airliner and its lights became more distant. I turned north-   8
east, the general direction of home. I had been scribbling illegibly on the
page of memory which way I had gone and for how long. I now had no
idea where I was. The occasional lights on the ground of unknown towns,
lights blurred and yellowish, meant nothing. Allentown, which should
have been somewhere, never appeared. There was a terrible temptation
to abandon everything, to give up, as with a hopeless puzzle. I had the
greatest difficulty not praying and finally I did, flying in the noisy darkness, desperate for the sight of a city or anything that would give me
my position.

In the map case of the airplane was a booklet, *What to Do If Lost,*   9
and suddenly remembering it, I got it out and with my flashlight began
to read. There was a list of half a dozen steps to take in order. My eye
skidded down it. The first ones I had already tried. Others, like tuning
in any radio range and orienting yourself on it, I had given up on. I managed to get the signal from Stewart Field but didn't take up the prescribed
heading. I could tell from its faintness—it was indistinct in a thicket of
other sounds—that I was far away, and I had lost faith in the procedure.
The final advice seemed more practical. If you think you are to the west
of Stewart, it said, head east until you come to the Hudson River and
then fly north or south, you will eventually come to New York or Albany.

It was past eleven, the sky dense with stars, the earth a void. I had   10
turned east. The dimly lit fuel gauges read twenty-five gallons or so in
each wing. The idea slowly growing, of opening the canopy and struggling into the wind, over the side into blackness, parachuting down, was
not as unthinkable as that of giving the airplane itself up to destruction.
I would be washed out, I knew. The anguish was unbearable. I had been
flying east for ten minutes but it seemed hours. Occasionally I made out
the paltry lights of some small town or group of houses, but otherwise
nothing. The cities had vanished, sunken to darkness. I looked down
again. Twenty gallons.

Suddenly off to the left there was a glimmer that became—I was just   11
able to make it out—a faint string of lights and then slowly, magically,
two parallel lines. It was the bridge at Poughkeepsie! Dazed with relief,
I tried to pick out its dark lines and those of the river, turning to keep
it in sight, going lower and lower. Then in the way that all things certain had changed that night, the bridge changed, too. At about a thousand feet above them, stricken, I saw I was looking at the streetlights of
some town.

The gauges read fifteen gallons. One thing that should never be done—   12
it had been repeated to us often—was to attempt a forced landing at
night. But I had no choice. I began to circle, able in the mist to see clearly
only what was just beneath. The town was at the edge of some hills; I
banked away from them in the blackness. If I went too far from the
brightly lit, abandoned main street, I lost my bearings. Dropping even
lower I saw dark roofs everywhere and amid them, unexpectedly, a blank
area like a lake or small park. I had passed it quickly, turned, and lost
it. Finally, lower still, I saw it again. It was not big but there was nothing else. I ducked my head for a moment to look down—the number beneath each index line was wavering slightly; ten gallons, perhaps twelve.

The rule for any strange field was to first fly across at minimum al-   13
titude to examine the surface. I was not even sure it was a field; it might
be water or a patch of woods. If a park, it might have buildings or fences.
I turned onto a downwind leg or what I judged to be one, then a base
leg, letting down over swiftly enlarging roofs. I had the canopy open to
cut reflection, the ghostly duplication of instruments and warning lights.
I stared ahead through the wind and noise. I was at a hundred feet or
so, flaps down, still descending. In front, coming fast, was my field. On
a panel near my knee were the landing light switches with balled tips to
make them identifiable by feel. I reached for them blindly. The instant
they came on I knew I'd made a mistake. They blazed like searchlights
in the mist; I could see more without them but the ground was twenty
feet beneath me, I was at minimum speed and dared not bend to turn
them off. Something went by on the left. Trees, in the middle of the park.
I had barely missed them. No landing here. A moment later, at the far
end, more trees. They were higher than I was, and without speed to climb
I banked to get through them. I heard foliage slap the wings as just ahead,
shielded, a second rank of trees appeared. There was no time to do anything. Something great struck a wing. It tore away. The plane careened
up. It stood poised for an endless moment, one landing light flooding a
house into which an instant later it crashed.

Nothing has vanished, not even the stunned first seconds of silence,   14
the torn leaves drifting down. Reflexively, as a slain man might bewil-
deredly shut a door, I reached to turn off the ignition. I was badly injured, though in what way I did not know. There was no pain. My legs,
I realized. I tried to move them. Nothing seemed wrong. My front teeth
were loose; I could feel them move as I breathed. In absolute quiet I sat
for a few moments at a loss, then unbuckled the harness and stepped over

the cockpit onto what had been the front porch. The nose of the plane was in the wreckage of a room. The severed wing lay back in the street.

The house, as it turned out, belonged to a family that was welcoming home a son who had been a prisoner of war in Germany. They were having a party and had taken the startling noise of the plane as it passed low over town many times to be some sort of military salute and, though it was nearly midnight, had all gone into the street to have a look. I had come in like a meteorite over their heads. The town was Great Barrington. I had to be shown where it was on a map, in Massachusetts, miles to the north and east. 15

That night I slept in the mayor's house, in a feather bed. I say slept but in fact I hung endlessly in the tilted darkness, the landing light pouring down at the large frame house. The wing came off countless times. I turned over in bed and began again. 16

They came for me the next day in a wrecking truck and I rode back with the remains of the plane. In the barracks, which were empty when I arrived, my bed was littered with messages, all mock congratulations. I found myself, unexpectedly, a popular figure. It was as if I had somehow defied the authorities. On the blackboard in the briefing room was a drawing of a house with the tail of an airplane sticking from the roof and written beneath, GEISLER'S STUDENT. I survived the obligatory check rides and the proceedings of the accident board, which were unexpectedly brief. Gradually transformed into a comedy, the story was told by me many times as I felt, for one shameless instant, it would be that night when the boughs of the first trees hit the wings before I saw the second. There was a bent, enameled Pratt and Whitney emblem from the engine that I kept for a long time until it was lost somewhere, and years later a single unsigned postcard reached me, addressed care of the adjutant general. It was from Great Barrington. "We are still praying for you here," it said. 17

QUESTIONS

1. What details in the opening paragraphs help to explain "the inexactness of navigation" in the late 1940s? Could Salter have avoided the dangers of night flying had he been more alert?

2. What rules of night flying did he attempt to follow, discovering he was lost? Did they fail him in his attempt to land the plane?

3. What were Salter's feelings about the crash afterwards, and how does he let us know? Why did he keep the unsigned postcard from Great Barrington?

4. What point is Salter making? Or is he merely reporting a youthful experience?

SUGGESTIONS FOR WRITING

1. Narrate an early experience with an activity important in your own life—perhaps a sport you've continued to play. Explain how you trained for it, what happened in first performing it, and what you discovered about yourself or about the activity. Like Salter, give details of the setting and equipment.

2. The vantage point is as essential in narrative as in purely descriptive writing. Show how essential it is in Salter's narrative, comparing it briefly with that in W. S. Merwin or Mary Helen Ponce.

EUDORA WELTY

EUDORA WELTY was born and raised in Jackson, Mississippi. Her mother was a West Virginian; her father, an Ohioan and the president of a Jackson insurance company. Welty worked at a number of jobs after college before beginning her career as a photographer and writer. She is the author of numerous short stories, novels, and essays, chiefly about Mississippi life. Her novel *The Optimist's Daughter* won the Pulitzer Prize for Fiction in 1973. Welty describes her Jackson girlhood and early career in *One Writer's Beginnings* (1984), from which this account of a summer trip north is taken.

ONE WRITER'S BEGINNINGS

When we set out in our five-passenger Oakland touring car on our summer trip to Ohio and West Virginia to visit the two families, my mother was the navigator. She sat at the alert all the way at Daddy's side as he   1 drove, correlating the AAA Blue Book and the speedometer, often with the baby on her lap. She'd call out, "All right, Daddy: '86-point-2, crossroads. Jog right, past white church. Gravel ends.'—And there's the church!" she'd say, as though we had scored. Our road always became her adversary. "This doesn't surprise me at all," she'd say as Daddy backed up a mile or so into our own dust on a road that had petered out. "I could've told you a road that looked like that had little intention of going anywhere."

"It was the first one we'd seen all day going in the right direction," he'd say. His sense of direction was unassailable, and every mile of our distance was familiar to my father by rail. But the way we set out to go was popularly known as "through the country." 2

My mother's hat rode in the back with the children, suspended over our heads in a pillowcase. It rose and fell with us when we hit the bumps, thumped our heads and batted our ears in an authoritative manner when sometimes we bounced as high as the ceiling. This was 1917 or 1918; a lady couldn't expect to travel without a hat. 3

Edward and I rode with our legs straight out in front of us over some suitcases. The rest of the suitcases rode just outside the doors, strapped on the running boards. Cars weren't made with trunks. The tools were kept under the back seat and were heard from in syncopation with the bumps; we'd jump out of the car so Daddy could get them out and jack up the car to patch and vulcanize a tire, or haul out the tow rope or the tire chains. If it rained so hard we couldn't see the road in front of us, we waited it out, snapped in behind the rain curtains and playing "Twenty Questions." 4

My mother was not naturally observant, but she could scrutinize; when she gave the surroundings her attention, it was to verify something—the truth or a mistake, hers or another's. My father kept his eyes on the road, with glances toward the horizon and overhead. My brother Edward periodically stood up in the back seat with his eyelids fluttering while he played the harmonica, "Old Macdonald had a farm" and "Abdul the Bulbul Amir," and the baby slept in Mother's lap and only woke up when we crossed some rattling old bridge. "*There's* a river!" he'd crow to us all. "Why, it certainly *is*," my mother would reassure him, patting him back to sleep. I rode as a hypnotic, with my set gaze on the landscape that vibrated past at twenty-five miles an hour. We were all wrapped by the long ride into some cocoon of our own. 5

The journey took about a week each way, and each day had my parents both in its grip. Riding behind my father I could see that the road had him by the shoulders, by the hair under his driving cap. It took my 6 mother to make him stop. I inherited his nervous energy in the way I can't stop writing on a story. It makes me understand how Ohio had him around the heart, as West Virginia had my mother. Writers and travelers are mesmerized alike by knowing of their destinations.

And all the time that we think we're getting there so fast, how slowly   7
we do move. In the days of our first car trip, Mother proudly entered in her log, "Mileage today: 161!" with an exclamation mark.

"A Detroit car passed us yesterday." She always kept those logs, with   8
times, miles, routes of the day's progress, and expenses totaled up.

That kind of travel made you conscious of borders; you rode ready for   9
them. Crossing a river, crossing a country line, crossing a state line—especially crossing the line you couldn't see but knew was there, between the South and the North—you could draw a breath and feel the difference.

The Blue Book warned you of the times for the ferries to run; some-   10
times there were waits of an hour between. With rivers and roads alike winding, you had to cross some rivers three times to be done with them. Lying on the water at the foot of a river bank would be a ferry no bigger than somebody's back porch. When our car had been driven on board —often it was down a roadless bank, through sliding stones and run-away gravel, with Daddy simply aiming at the two-plank gangway— father and older children got out of the car to enjoy the trip. My brother and I got barefooted to stand on wet, sun-warm boards that, weighted with your car, seemed exactly on the level with the water; our feet were the same as in the river. Some of these ferries were operated by a single man pulling hand over hand on a rope bleached and frazzled as if made from cornshucks.

I watched the frayed rope running through his hands. I thought it   11
would break before we could reach the other side.

"No, it's not going to break," said my father. "It's never broken be-   12
fore, has it?" he asked the ferry man.

"No sirree."   13

"You see? If it never broke before, it's not going to break this time."   14

His general belief in life's well-being worked either way. If you had   15
a pain, it was "Have you ever had it before? You have? It's not going to kill you, then. If you've had the same thing before, you'll be all right in the morning."

My mother couldn't have more profoundly disagreed with that.   16

"You're such an optimist dear," she often said with a sigh, as she did   17
now on the ferry.

"You're a good deal of a pessimist, sweetheart." 18
"I certainly *am*." 19
And yet I was well aware as I stood between them with the water 20
running over my toes, he the optimist was the one who was prepared
for the worst, and she the pessimist was the daredevil: he the one who
on our trip carried chains and a coil of rope and an ax all upstairs to
our hotel bedroom every night in case of fire, and she the one—before
I was born—when there *was* a fire, had broken loose from all hands and
run back—on crutches, too—into the burning house to rescue her set of
Dickens which she flung, all twenty-four volumes, from the window before she jumped out after them, all for Daddy to catch.

"I make no secret of my lifelong fear of the water," said my mother, 21
who on ferry boats remained inside the car, clasping the baby to her—
my brother Walter, who was destined to prowl the waters of the Pacific
Ocean in a minesweeper.

As soon as the sun was beginning to go down, we went more slowly. 22
My father would drive sizing up the towns, inspecting the hotel in each,
deciding where we could safely spend the night. Towns little or big had
beginnings and ends, they reached to an edge and stopped, where the
country began again as though they hadn't happened. They were intact
and to themselves. You could see a town lying ahead in its whole, as definitely formed as a plate on a table. And your road entered and ran straight
through the heart of it; you could see it all, laid out for your passage
through. Towns, like people, had clear identities and your imagination
could go out to meet them. You saw houses, yards, fields, and people busy
in them, the people that had a life where they were. You could hear their
bank clocks striking, you could smell their bakeries. You would know
those towns again, recognize the salient detail, seen so close up. Nothing was blurred, and in passing along Main Street, slowed down from
twenty-five to twenty miles an hour, you didn't miss anything on either
side. Going somewhere "through the country" acquainted you with the
whole way there and back.

My mother never fully gave in to her pleasure in our trip—for plea- 23
sure every bit of it was to us all—because she knew we were traveling
with a loaded pistol in the pocket on the door of the car on Daddy's side.
I doubt if my father fired off any kind of gun in his life, but he could
not have carried his family from Jackson, Mississippi to West Virginia
and Ohio through the country, unprotected.

QUESTIONS

1. What do the details of the summer trip tell you about motoring in 1917 or 1918? Does Welty highlight any features of the trip or travel generally?

2. What do these and other details reveal about her mother and father? What characteristics does Welty comment on?

3. Is the purpose of the narrative to give a picture of her mother and father and comment on them, or does Welty have another purpose in writing?

SUGGESTIONS FOR WRITING

1. Discuss what the narrative reveals about Eudora Welty as a person and writer. Explain how the narrative reveals these qualities.

2. Narrate a travel experience in which you made an unexpected discovery about yourself, about a place, or about people you were traveling with. You need not give the full details of the trip to let your reader experience what you did and make a point about it.

ESMERALDA SANTIAGO

ESMERALDA SANTIAGO, the oldest in a family of eleven children, lived most of her childhood in rural Puerto Rico, in "a rectangle of rippled metal sheets on stilts hovering in the middle of a circle of red dirt." When she was thirteen, her mother moved the family to New York City—her father remaining in Puerto Rico. Following high school in Brooklyn, she attended Harvard University and Sarah Lawrence College. Santiago is the author of *America's Dream* (1997) and *When I Was Puerto Rican* (1993), in which she tells what happened when American nutritionists came to instruct the women of her village.

THE AMERICAN INVASION OF MACÚN

Lo que no mata, engorda.

What doesn't kill you, makes you fat.

Pollito, chicken
Gallina, hen
Lápiz, pencil
y Pluma, pen
Ventana, window
Puerta, door
Maestra, teacher
y Piso, floor

Miss Jiménez stood in front of the class as we sang and, with her ruler, 1
pointed at the chicks scratching the dirt outside the classroom, at the hen
leading them, at the pencil on Juanita's desk, at the pen on her own desk,
at the window that looked out into the playground, at the door leading
to the yard, at herself, and at the shiny tile floor. We sang along, pointing as she did with our sharpened pencils, rubber end out.

"*¡Muy bien!*" She pulled down the map rolled into a tube at the front 2
of the room. In English she told us, "Now gwee estody about de Jun-
ited Estates gee-o-graphee."

It was the daily English class. Miss Jiménez, the second- and third- 3
grade teacher, was new to the school in Macún. She looked like a
grown-up doll, with high rounded cheekbones, a freckled *café con leche*
complexion, black lashes, black curly hair pulled into a bun at the nape
of her neck, and the prettiest legs in the whole *barrio.* Doña Ana said
Miss Jiménez had the most beautiful legs she'd ever seen, and the next
day, while Miss Jiménez wrote the multiplication table on the blackboard,
I stared at them.

She wore skirts to just below the knees, but from there down, her 4
legs were shaped like chicken drumsticks, rounded and full at the top,
narrow at the bottom. She had long straight hair on her legs, which everyone said made them even prettier, and small feet encased in plain brown
shoes with a low square heel. That night I wished on a star that someday my scrawny legs would fill out into that lovely shape and that the
hair on them would be as long and straight and black.

Miss Jiménez came to Macún at the same time as the community   5
center. She told us that starting the following week, we were all to go to
the *centro comunal* before school to get breakfast, provided by the Estado Libre Asociado, or Free Associated State, which was the official
name for Puerto Rico in the Estados Unidos, or in English, the Jun-ited
Estates of America. Our parents, Miss Jiménez told us, should come to
a meeting that Saturday, where experts from San Juan and the Jun-ited
Estates would teach our mothers all about proper nutrition and hygiene,
so that we would grow up as tall and strong as Dick, Jane, and Sally, the
Americanitos in our primers.

"And Mami," I said as I sipped my afternoon *café con leche*, "Miss   6
Jiménez said the experts will give us free food and toothbrushes and
things . . . and we can get breakfast every day except Sunday . . ."

"Calm down," she told me. "We'll go, don't worry."   7

On Saturday morning the yard in front of the *centro comunal* filled   8
with parents and their children. You could tell the experts from San Juan
from the ones that came from the Junited Estates because the *Americanos*
wore ties with their white shirts and tugged at their collars and wiped
their foreheads with crumpled handkerchiefs. They hadn't planned for
children, and the men from San Juan convinced a few older girls to watch
the little ones outside so that the meeting could proceed with the least
amount of disruption. Small children refused to leave their mothers'
sides and screeched the minute one of the white-shirted men came near
them. Some women sat on the folding chairs at the rear of the room
nursing, a cloth draped over their baby's face so that the experts would
not be upset at the sight of a bare breast. There were no fathers. Most
of them worked seven days a week, and anyway, children and food were
women's work.

"Negi, take the kids outside and keep them busy until this is over."   9

"But Mami . . ."   10

"Do as I say."   11

She pressed her way to a chair in the middle of the room and sat fac-   12
ing the experts. I hoisted Edna on my shoulder and grabbed Alicia's hand.
Delsa pushed Norma out in front of her. They ran into the yard and
within minutes had blended into a group of children their age. Héctor
found a boy to chase him around a tree, and Alicia crawled to a sand
puddle where she and other toddlers smeared one another with the fine
red dirt. I sat at the door, Edna on my lap, and tried to keep one eye on
my sisters and brother and another on what went on inside.

The experts had colorful charts on portable easels. They introduced 13
each other to the group, thanked the Estado Libre Asociado for the
privilege of being there, and then took turns speaking. The first expert opened a large suitcase. Inside there was a huge set of teeth with
pink gums.

"*Ay Dios Santo, qué cosa tan fea,*" said a woman as she crossed her- 14
self. The mothers laughed and mumbled among themselves that yes, it
was ugly. The expert stretched his lips into a smile and pulled a large
toothbrush from under the table. He used ornate Spanish words that we
assumed were scientific talk for teeth, gums, and tongue. With his giant
brush, he polished each tooth on the model, pointing out the proper path
of the bristles on the teeth.

"If I have to spend that much time on my teeth," a woman whis- 15
pered loud enough for everyone to hear, "I won't get anything done
around the house." The room buzzed with giggles, and the expert again
spread his lips, took a breath, and continued his demonstration.

"At the conclusion of the meeting," he said, "you will each receive 16
a toothbrush and a tube of paste for every member of your family."

"*¿Hasta pa' los mellaos?*" a woman in the back of the room asked, 17
and everyone laughed.

"If they have no teeth, it's too late for them, isn't it," the expert said 18
through his own clenched teeth. The mothers shrieked with laughter, and
the expert sat down so that an *Americano* with red hair and thick glasses
could tell us about food.

He wiped his forehead and upper lip as he pulled up the cloth cov- 19
ering one of the easels to reveal a colorful chart of the major food groups.

"*La buena* nutrition is *muy importante para los niños.*" In heavily 20
accented, hard to understand Castilian Spanish he described the necessity of eating portions of each of the foods on his chart every day. There
were carrots and broccoli, iceberg lettuce, apples, pears, and peaches. The
bread was sliced into a perfect square, unlike the long loaves Papi brought
home from a bakery in San Juan, or the round *pan de manteca* Mami
bought at Vitín's store. There was no rice on the chart, no beans, no
salted codfish. There were big white eggs, not at all like the small round
ones our hens gave us. There was a tall glass of milk, but no coffee. There
were wedges of yellow cheese, but no balls of cheese like the white *queso
del país* wrapped in banana leaves sold in bakeries all over Puerto Rico.
There were bananas but no plantains, potatoes but no *batatas,* cereal
flakes but no oatmeal, bacon but no sausages.

"But, *señor,*" said Doña Lola from the back of the room, "none of   21
the fruits or vegetables on your chart grow in Puerto Rico."

"Then you must substitute our recommendations with your native   22
foods."

"Is an apple the same as a mango?" asked Cirila, whose yard was   23
shaded by mango trees.

"*Sí,*" said the expert, "a mango can be substituted for an apple."   24

"What about breadfruit?"   25

"I'm not sure . . ." The *Americano* looked at an expert from San   26
Juan who stood up, pulled the front of his *guayabera* down over his
ample stomach, and spoke in a voice as deep and resonant as a radio
announcer's.

"Breadfruit," he said, "would be equivalent to potatoes."   27

"Even the ones with seeds?" asked Doña Lola, who roasted them on   28
the coals of her *fogón.*

"Well, I believe so," he said, "but it is best not to make substitutions   29
for the recommended foods. That would throw the whole thing off."

He sat down and stared at the ceiling, his hands crossed under   30
his belly as if he had to hold it up. The mothers asked each other where
they could get carrots and broccoli, iceberg lettuce, apples, peaches,
or pears.

"At the conclusion of the meeting," the *Americano* said, "you will all   31
receive a sack full of groceries with samples from the major food groups."
He flipped the chart closed and moved his chair near the window, amid
the hum of women asking one another what he'd just said.

The next expert uncovered another easel on which there was a pic-   32
ture of a big black bug. A child screamed, and a woman got the hiccups.

"This," the expert said scratching the top of his head, "is the mag-   33
nified image of a head louse."

Following him, another *Americano* who spoke good Spanish dis-   34
cussed intestinal parasites. He told all the mothers to boil their water several times and to wash their hands frequently.

"Children love to put their hands in their mouths," he said, making   35
it sound like fun, "but each time they do, they run the risk of infection."
He flipped the chart to show an enlargement of a dirty hand, the tips of
the fingernails encrusted with dirt.

"Ugh! That's disgusting!" whispered Mami to the woman next to   36
her. I curled my fingers inside my palms.

"When children play outside," the expert continued, "their hands 37
pick up dirt, and with it, hundreds of microscopic parasites that enter
their bodies through their mouths to live and thrive in their intestinal
tract."

He flipped the chart again. A long flat snake curled from the corner 38
at the top of the chart to the opposite corner at the bottom. Mami shiv-
ered and rubbed her arms to keep the goose bumps down.

"This," the *Americano* said, "is a tapeworm, and it is not uncommon 39
in this part of the world."

Mami had joked many times that the reason I was so skinny was 40
that I had a *solitaria*, a tapeworm, in my belly. But I don't think she ever
knew what a tapeworm looked like, nor did I. I imagined something like
the earthworms that crawled out of the ground when it rained, but never
anything so ugly as the snake on the chart, its flat body like a deck of
cards strung together.

"Tapeworms," the expert continued, "can reach lengths of nine feet." 41
I rubbed my belly, trying to imagine how long nine feet was and whether
I had that much room in me. Just thinking about it made my insides
itchy.

When they finished their speeches, the experts had all the mothers 42
line up and come to the side of the room, where each was given samples
according to the number of people in their household. Mami got two
sacks of groceries, so Delsa had to carry Edna all the way home while I
dragged one of the bags full of cans, jars, and bright cartons.

At home Mami gave each of us a toothbrush and told us we were 43
to clean our teeth every morning and every evening. She set a tube of
paste and a cup by the door, next to Papi's shaving things. Then she emp-
tied the bags.

"I don't understand why they didn't just give us a sack of rice and 44
a bag of beans. It would keep this family fed for a month."

She took out a five-pound tin of peanut butter, two boxes of corn- 45
flakes, cans of fruit cocktail, peaches in heavy syrup, beets, and tuna fish,
jars of grape jelly and pickles and put everything on a high shelf.

"We'll save this," she said, "so that we can eat like *Americanos* 46
cuando el hambre apriete." She kept them there for a long time but took
them down one by one so that, as she promised, we ate like Americans
when hunger cramped our bellies.

QUESTIONS

1. How does Santiago characterize the Americans who come to the Puerto Rican village from San Juan? Does she tell us anything about them through how they dress and look?

2. What is the attitude of the Americans toward the Puerto Rican women who attend the Saturday meeting at the community center?

3. How does Santiago characterize the Puerto Rican women? Why do they come to the meeting? What is their attitude toward the Americans and what they see and hear, and how does Santiago reveal it?

4. What is her purpose in narrating the episode?

SUGGESTIONS FOR WRITING

1. Narrate a similar episode in which two groups, different in culture and perhaps language, meet. Let the differences between these groups emerge in the details of their dress and appearance and what they say. Let your attitude and the point of the episode emerge in these details.

2. Cultural differences often lead to misunderstanding between friends. Write an account of a misunderstanding you experienced, giving details of how it came about and ended.

8

EXAMPLE

The word *example* originally referred to a sample or a typical instance. The word still has this meaning, and for many writers it is an outstanding instance—even one essential to the idea under discussion, as in the following explanation of right- and left-handedness in the world:

> The world is full of things whose right-hand version is different from the left-hand version: a right-handed corkscrew as against a left-handed, a right snail as against a left one. Above all, the two hands; they can be mirrored one in the other, but they cannot be turned in such a way that the right hand and the left hand become interchangeable. That was known in Pasteur's time to be true also of some crystals, whose facets are so arranged that there are right-hand versions and left-hand versions. (J. Bronowski, *The Ascent of Man*)

Examples are essential in presenting ideas. Those that seem clear to us may not be clear to our readers. Concrete instances like those Bronowski gives help to make our ideas understood.

E. B. WHITE

In this excerpt from a profile of New York City, first published in *Holiday* Magazine in April, 1949, **E. B. White** writes from the point of view of an inhabitant who knows the city well. White conveys the special excitement of the city through a series of examples. Compare this general characterization of New York with the specific picture of a New York street presented by Jane Jacobs (p. 288).

NEW YORK

It is a miracle that New York works at all. The whole thing is implausible. Every time the residents brush their teeth, millions of gallons of water must be drawn from the Catskills and the hills of Westchester. When a young man in Manhattan writes a letter to his girl in Brooklyn, the love message gets blown to her through a pneumatic tube—*pfft*—just like that. The subterranean system of telephone cables, power lines, steam pipes, gas mains and sewer pipes is reason enough to abandon the island to the gods and the weevils. Every time an incision is made in the pavement, the noisy surgeons expose ganglia that are tangled beyond belief. By rights New York should have destroyed itself long ago, from panic or fire or rioting or failure of some vital supply line in its circulatory system or from some deep labyrinthine short circuit. Long ago the city should have experienced an insoluble traffic snarl at some impossible bottleneck. It should have perished of hunger when food lines failed for a few days. It should have been wiped out by a plague starting in its slums or carried in by ships' rats. It should have been overwhelmed by the sea that licks at it on every side. The workers in its myriad cells should have succumbed to nerves, from the fearful pall of smoke-fog that drifts over every few days from Jersey, blotting out all light at noon and leaving the high offices suspended, men groping and depressed, and the sense of world's end. It should have been touched in the head by the August heat and gone off its rocker.

VOCABULARY

implausible, pneumatic tube, subterranean, incision, ganglia, labyrinthine, myriad

QUESTIONS

1. What examples show that "the whole thing is implausible"?

2. White explicitly compares New York City to a human being. What are the similarities, and how does the comparison help to emphasize the "miracle" he is describing?

3. What is the tone or attitude expressed, and how does White convey it?

SUGGESTIONS FOR WRITING

1. In a well-developed paragraph state an idea about your hometown or city and develop it by a series of short examples. Make your examples vivid and lively.

2. Develop one of the following statements by example:

a. "The insupportable labor of doing nothing." (Sir Richard Steele)

b. "The first blow is half the battle." (Oliver Goldsmith)

c. "Ask yourself whether you are happy, and you cease to be so." (John Stuart Mill)

d. "All the modern inconveniences." (Mark Twain)

e. "He had been kicked in the head by a mule when young and believed everything he read in the Sunday papers." (George Ade)

TOM WOLFE

TOM WOLFE is widely known for *The Right Stuff* (1979), his account of the first astronauts in the American space program, and his novels *The Bonfire of the Vanities* (1987) and *Man in Full* (1998). His essays on American life and the youth culture of the 1960s and 1970s are collected in *The Electric Kool-Aid Acid Test* (1968), *The Pump House Gang* (1968), and *The Kandy-Kolored Tangerine-Flake Streamline Baby* (1965), from which the following excerpt is taken. *Hooking Up* (2000) is a recent collection. Wolfe's view of urban life is nowhere better illustrated than in his portrait of New York City teenagers at a subway at morning rush hour.

Thursday Morning in a New York Subway Station

Love! Attar of libido in the air! It is 8:45 A.M. Thursday morning in the   1
IRT subway station at 50th Street and Broadway and already two kids are hung up in a kind of herringbone weave of arms and legs, which proves, one has to admit, that love is not *confined* to Sunday in New York. Still, the odds! All the faces come popping in clots out of the Seventh Avenue local, past the King Size Ice Cream machine, and the turnstiles start whacking away as if the world were breaking up on the reefs. Four steps past the turnstiles everybody is already backed up haunch to paunch for the climb up the ramp and the stairs to the surface, a great funnel of flesh, wool, felt, leather, rubber and steaming alumicron, with the blood squeezing through everybody's old sclerotic arteries in hopped-up spurts from too much coffee and the effort of surfacing from the subway at the rush hour. Yet there on the landing are a boy and a girl, both about eighteen, in one of those utter, My Sin, backbreaking embraces.

He envelops her not only with his arms but with his chest, which has   2
the American teen-ager concave shape to it. She has her head cocked at a 90-degree angle and they both have their eyes pressed shut for all they are worth and some incredibly feverish action going with each other's mouths. All round them, ten, scores, it seems like hundreds, of faces and bodies are perspiring, trooping and bellying up the stairs with arteriosclerotic grimaces past a showcase full of such novel items as Joy Buzzers, Squirting Nickels, Finger Rats, Scary Tarantulas and spoons with realistic dead flies on them, past Fred's barbershop, which is just off the landing and has glossy photographs of young men with the kind of baroque haircuts one can get in there, and up onto 50th Street into a madhouse of traffic and shops with weird lingerie and gray hair-dyeing displays in the windows, signs for free teacup readings and a pool-playing match between the Playboy Bunnies and Downey's Showgirls, and then everybody pounds on toward the Time-Life Building, the Brill Building or NBC.

The boy and the girl just keep on writhing in their embroilment. Her ³ hand is sliding up the back of his neck, which he turns when her fingers wander into the intricate formal gardens of his Chicago Boxcar hairdo at the base of the skull. The turn causes his face to start to mash in the ciliated hull of her beehive hairdo, and so she rolls her head 180 degrees to the other side, using their mouths for the pivot. But aside from good hair grooming, they are oblivious to everything but each other. Everybody gives them a once-over. Disgusting! Amusing! How touching! A few kids pass by and say things like "Swing it, baby." But the great majority in that heaving funnel up the stairs seem to be as much astounded as anything else. The vision of love at rush hour cannot strike anyone exactly as romance. It is a feat, like a fat man crossing the English Channel in a barrel. It is an earnest accomplishment against the tide. It is a piece of slightly gross heroics, after the manner of those knobby, varicose old men who come out from some place in baggy shorts every year and run through the streets of Boston in the Marathon race. And somehow that is the gaffe against love all week long in New York, for everybody, not just two kids writhing under their coiffures in the 50th Street subway station; too hurried, too crowded, too hard, and no time for dalliance.

QUESTIONS

1. Wolfe illustrates "the gaffe against love all week long in New York." What precisely is the "gaffe"? What do the details suggest about the Thursday morning mood of New Yorkers?

2. What does the description of the showcase and of 50th Street imply about the world of the lovers? Would they stand out in any setting? Does Wolfe find the lovers comical, or is he sympathetic and admiring?

3. How similar is Wolfe's view of New York to White's, in the quality of life or its pace?

SUGGESTIONS FOR WRITING

1. Every piece of writing suggests something about the personality, interests, and ideas of the author, even when he or she speaks to us through a narrator. Discuss the impression you receive of the author of this selection.

2. Describe one or two people in a situation made comical by the setting. Allow your reader to visualize the setting as well as the situation through your choice of examples.

M A R G A R E T   M E A D   A N D
R H O D A   M E T R A U X

MARGARET MEAD (1901–1978) was for more than 40 years an ethnologist at the Museum of Natural History in New York City. She taught at numerous universities, mostly at Columbia, and wrote some of the most influential books in the field of social anthropology — including *Coming of Age in Samoa* (1928), *Growing Up in New Guinea* (1930), and *Male and Female* (1949). RHODA METRAUX, an anthropologist also associated with the Museum of Natural History, collaborated with Mead on the writing of several books and a series of magazine essays, later collected in *A Way of Seeing* (1970) and *Aspects of the Present* (1980). Mead and Metraux look at parents and children from the point of view of the anthropologist. Their ideas on how children can be encouraged to develop an independent judgment might be compared with those of John Holt (p. 134).

DISCIPLINE—TO WHAT END?

In the matter of childhood discipline there is no absolute standard. The question is one of appropriateness to a style of living. What is the intended outcome? Are the methods of discipline effective in preparing the child to live in the adult world into which he is growing? The means of discipline that are very effective in rearing children to become headhunters and cannibals would be most ineffective in preparing them to become peaceful shepherds.

The Mundugumor, a New Guinea people, trained their children to be tough and self-reliant. Among these headhunters, when one village was preparing to attack another and wanted to guard itself against attack by a third village, the first village sent its children to the third to be held as hostages. The children knew that they faced death if their own people broke this temporary truce. Mundugumor methods of child-rearing were harsh but efficient. An infant sleeping in a basket hung on the wall was not taken out and held when it wakened and cried. Instead, someone scratched on the outside of the basket, making a screeching sound like the squeak of chalk on a blackboard. And a child that cried with fright was not given the mother's breast. It was simply lifted and held off the ground. Mundugumor children learned to live in a tough world, unfearful of hostility. When they lived among strangers as hostages, they watched and listened, gathering the information they would need someday for a successful raid on this village.

The Arapesh, another New Guinea people, had a very different view 3 of life and human personality. They expected their children to grow up in a fairly peaceful world, and their methods of caring for children reflected their belief that both men and women were gentle and nurturing in their intimate personal relations. Parents responded to an infant's least cry, held him and comforted him. And far from using punishment as a discipline, adults sometimes stood helplessly by while a child pitched precious firewood over a cliff.

Even very inconsistent discipline may fit a child to live in an incon- 4 sistent world. A Balinese mother would play on her child's fright by shouting warnings against nonexistent dangers: "Look out! Fire! . . . Snake! . . . Tiger!" The Balinese system required people to avoid strange places without inquiring why. And the Balinese child learned simply to be afraid of strangeness. He never learned that there are no bears under the stairs, as American children do. We want our children to test reality. We teach our children to believe in Santa Claus and later, without bitter disappointment, to give up that belief. We want them to be open to change, and as they grow older, to put childhood fears and rewards aside and be ready for new kinds of reality.

There are also forms of discipline that may be self-defeating. Training 5 for bravery, for example, may be so rigorous that some children give up in despair. Some Plains Indians put boys through such severe and frightening experiences in preparing them for their young manhood as warriors that some boys gave up entirely and dressed instead as women.

In a society in which many people are socially mobile and may live 6 as adults in a social or cultural environment very different from the one in which they grew up, old forms of discipline may be wholly unsuited to new situations. A father whose family lived according to a rigid, severe set of standards, and who was beaten in his boyhood for lying or stealing, may still think of beatings as an appropriate method of disciplining his son. Though he now lives as a middle-class professional man in a suburb, he may punish his son roughly for not doing well in school. It is not the harshness as such that then may discourage the boy even more, but his bewilderment. Living in a milieu in which parents and teachers reward children by praise and presents for doing well in school—a milieu in which beating is not connected with competence in schoolwork—the boy may not be able to make much sense of the treatment he receives.

There is still another consideration in this question about discipline. 7 Through studies of children as they grow up in different cultures we are coming to understand more about the supportive and the maiming effects of various forms of discipline. Extreme harshness or insensitivity to the child may prepare him to survive in a harsh environment. But it also may cripple the child's ability to meet changing situations. And today we cannot know the kind of world the children we are rearing will live in as adults. For us, therefore, the most important question to ask about any method of discipline is: How will it affect the child's capacity to face change? Will it give the child the kind of strength necessary to live under new and unpredictable conditions?

An unyielding conscience may be a good guide to successful living in 8 a narrow and predictable environment. But it may become a heavy burden and a cruel scourge in a world in which strength depends on flexibility. Similarly, the kind of discipline that makes a child tractable, easy to bring up and easy to teach in a highly structured milieu, may fail to give the child the independence, courage and curiosity he will need to meet the challenges in a continually changing situation. At the same time, the absence of forms of discipline that give a child a sense of living in an ordered world in which it is rewarding to learn the rules, whatever they may be, also may be maiming. A belief in one's own accuracy and a dependable sense of how to find the patterning in one's environment are necessary parts of mature adaptation to new styles of living.

There is, in fact, no single answer to the problem of childhood dis- 9 cipline. But there is always the central question: For what future?

VOCABULARY

paragraph 1: appropriateness
paragraph 3: nurturing
paragraph 6: mobile, environment, milieu
paragraph 8: scourge, maiming

QUESTIONS

1. Do Mead and Metraux give examples of all kinds of childhood discipline, or just of kinds that work well?

2. What thesis do their examples support, and where do Mead and Metraux first state it? Where do they restate it?

3. How do the examples in paragraph 6 help us to understand the kind of society that is "socially mobile"?

4. Would the exposition be as clear if Mead and Metraux had discussed the Arapesh of New Guinea before discussing the Mundugumor? Or does the order of discussion not matter?

5. How do the opening sentences of the nine paragraphs state the relationship of ideas in the whole essay?

SUGGESTION FOR WRITING

State why you agree or disagree with one of the following statements, supporting your ideas with examples from your own experience and observation:

a. "Even very inconsistent discipline may fit a child to live in an inconsistent world."

b. "There are also forms of discipline that may be self-defeating."

c. "In a society in which many people are socially mobile and may live as adults in a social or cultural environment very different from the one in which they grew up, old forms of discipline may be wholly unsuited to new situations."

d. "Extreme harshness or insensitivity to the child may prepare him to survive in a harsh environment. But it also may cripple the child's ability to meet changing situations."

e. "At the same time, the absence of forms of discipline that give a child a sense of living in an ordered world in which it is rewarding to learn the rules, whatever they may be, also may be maiming."

9

CLASSIFICATION AND DIVISION

There are times when you want to show what various objects have in common. To do so, you engage in the process of classification—grouping objects, persons, or ideas that share significant qualities. To show the range of cars manufactured in the United States, you might classify Chevrolets, Dodges, and Fords with other American cars. To illustrate the importance of General Motors in the manufacture of cars, you can classify Chevrolets with Buicks, Oldsmobiles, and other GM cars. The number of classes to which an object can be fitted is obviously wide. Chevrolets might be classified with cars of similar size by other manufacturers.

The process of division begins with a class and shows its subclassifications or divisions. The class may be a broad one, as in the following division of American cars according to manufacturer:

By manufacturer: GM cars, Chrysler cars, Ford cars, etc.

The same class of American cars may be divided in another way:

By transmission: cars with manual transmission, cars with automatic transmission

Any one of the subclasses or divisions may be divided by the same or by another principle—GM cars may be subdivided according to size, engine, color, or place of manufacture, to cite only a few ways:

By size: small, compact, medium, large GM cars

By engine: (GM cars with) four-cylinder, six-cylinder, eight-cylinder engines

Again the basis or principle of division you choose depends on the purpose of the analysis. Here is an example of division in a scientific discussion of meteorites:

purpose of analysis

class: *meteorites*

division or subclassification according to constituent material

first type: *stony*

second type: *iron*

third type: *stony-iron*

subdivision of stony meteorites according to presence or absence of chondrules

further subdivisions

For the investigator of meteorites, the basic challenge is deducing the history of the *meteorites* from a bewildering abundance of evidence. The richness of the problem is indicated by the sheer variety of types of meteorite. The two main classes are the *stony meteorites* and the *iron meteorites*. The stony meteorites consist mainly of silicates, with an admixture of nickel and iron. The iron meteorites consist mainly of nickel and iron in various proportions. A smaller class is the *stony-iron meteorites*, which are intermediate in composition between the other two. Stony meteorites are in turn divided into two groups: the chondrules and the achondrites, according to whether or not they contain chondrules, spherical aggregates of magnesium silicate. With each group there are further subdivisions based on mineralogical and chemical composition. (I. R. Cameron, "Meteorites and Cosmic Radiation" [italics added])

JOHN HOLT

JOHN HOLT (1923–1985) widely influenced ideas on the teaching of children in the 1960s and 1970s—through such books as *How Children Fail* (1964), *How Children Learn* (1967), *Escape from Childhood* (1974), and

Freedom from Beyond (1972), based on his experience as a high school teacher in Colorado and Massachusetts. Holt believed that teachers do their job best when they help students teach themselves. His discussion of the various disciplines that guide our learning reveals other assumptions and beliefs.

KINDS OF DISCIPLINE

A child, in growing up, may meet and learn from three different kinds 1 of disciplines. The first and most important is what we might call the Discipline of Nature or of Reality. When he is trying to do something real, if he does the wrong thing or doesn't do the right one, he doesn't get the result he wants. If he doesn't pile one block right on top of another, or tries to build on a slanting surface, his tower falls down. If he hits the wrong key, he hears the wrong note. If he doesn't hit the nail squarely on the head, it bends, and he has to pull it out and start with another. If he doesn't measure properly what he is trying to build, it won't open, close, fit, stand up, fly, float, whistle, or do whatever he wants it to do. If he closes his eyes when he swings, he doesn't hit the ball. A child meets this kind of discipline every time he tries to *do* something, which is why it is so important in school to give children more chances to do things, instead of just reading or listening to someone talk (or pretending to). This discipline is a great teacher. The learner never has to wait long for his answer; it usually comes quickly, often instantly. Also it is clear, and very often points toward the needed correction; from what happened he can not only see that what he did was wrong, but also why, and what he needs to do instead. Finally, and most important, the giver of the answer, call it Nature, is impersonal, impartial, and indifferent. She does not give opinions, or make judgments; she cannot be wheedled, bullied, or fooled; she does not get angry or disappointed; she does not praise or blame; she does not remember past failures or hold grudges; with her one always gets a fresh start, this time is the one that counts.

The next discipline we might call the Discipline of Culture, of Society, 2 of What People Really Do. Man is a social, a cultural animal. Children sense around them this culture, this network of agreements, customs, habits, and rules binding the adults together. They want to understand it and be a part of it. They watch very carefully what people around them are doing and want to do the same. They want to do right, unless they become convinced they can't do right. Thus children rarely misbehave seriously in church, but sit as quietly as they can. The example of all those grownups is contagious. Some mysterious ritual is going on, and children, who like rituals, want to be part of it. In the same way, the little children that I see at concerts or operas, though they may fidget a little, or perhaps take a nap now and then, rarely make any disturbance. With all those grownups sitting there, neither moving nor talking, it is the most natural thing in the world to imitate them. Children who live among adults who are habitually courteous to each other, and to them, will soon learn to be courteous. Children who live surrounded by people who speak a certain way will speak that way, however much we may try to tell them that speaking that way is bad or wrong.

The third discipline is the one most people mean when they speak of discipline—the Discipline of Superior Force, of sergeant to private, of "you do what I tell you or I'll make you wish you had." There is bound to be some of this in a child's life. Living as we do surrounded by things that can hurt children, or that children can hurt, we cannot avoid it. We can't afford to let a small child find out from experience the danger of playing in a busy street, or of fooling with the pots on the top of a stove, or of eating up the pills in the medicine cabinet. So, along with other precautions, we say to him, "Don't play in the street, or touch things on the stove, or go into the medicine cabinet, or I'll punish you." Between him and the danger too great for him to imagine we put a lesser danger, but one he can imagine and maybe therefore want to avoid. He can have no idea of what it would be like to be hit by a car, but he can imagine being shouted at, or spanked, or sent to his room. He avoids these substitutes for the greater danger until he can understand it and avoid it for its own sake. But we ought to use this discipline only when it is necessary to protect the life, health, safety, or well-being of people or other living creatures, or to prevent destruction of things that people care about. We ought not to assume too long, as we usually do, that a child cannot understand the real nature of the danger from which we want to protect him. The sooner he avoids the danger, not to escape our punishment, but as a matter of good sense, the better. He can learn that faster than we think. In Mexico, for example, where people drive their cars with a good deal of spirit, I saw many children no older than five or four walking unattended on the streets. They understood about cars, they knew what to do. A child whose life is full of the threat and fear of punishment is

3

locked into babyhood. There is no way for him to grow up, to learn to take responsibility for his life and acts. Most important of all, we should not assume that having to yield to the threat of our superior force is good for the child's character. It is never good for *anyone's* character. To bow to superior force makes us feel impotent and cowardly for not having had the strength or courage to resist. Worse, it makes us resentful and vengeful. We can hardly wait to make someone pay for our humiliation, yield to us as we were once made to yield. No, if we cannot always avoid using the Discipline of Superior Force, we should at least use it as seldom as we can.

There are places where all three disciplines overlap. Any very demanding human activity combines in it the disciplines of Superior Force, of Culture, and of Nature. The novice will be told, "Do it this way, never mind asking why, just do it that way, that is the way we always do it." But it probably *is* just the way they always do it, and usually for the very good reason that it is a way that has been found to work. Think, for example, of ballet training. The student in a class is told to do this exercise, or that; to stand so; to do this or that with his head, arms, shoulders, abdomen, hips, legs, feet. He is constantly corrected. There is no argument. But behind these seemingly autocratic demands by the teacher lie many decades of custom and tradition, and behind that, the necessities of dancing itself. You cannot make the moves of classical ballet unless over many years you have acquired, and renewed every day, the needed strength and suppleness in scores of muscles and joints. Nor can you do the difficult motions, making them look easy, unless you have learned hundreds of easier ones first. Dance teachers may not always agree on all the details of teaching these strengths and skills. But no novice could learn them all by himself. You could not go for a night or two to watch the ballet and then, without any other knowledge at all, teach yourself how to do it. In the same way, you would be unlikely to learn any complicated and difficult human activity without drawing heavily on the experience of those who know it better. But the point is that the authority of these experts or teachers stems from, grows out of their greater competence and experience, the fact that what they do *works*, not the fact that they happen to be the teacher and as such have the power to kick a student out of the class. And the further point is that children are always and everywhere attracted to that competence, and ready and eager to submit themselves to a discipline that grows out of it. We hear constantly that children will never do anything unless compelled to by

4

bribes or threats. But in their private lives, or in extracurricular activities in school, in sports, music, drama, art, running a newspaper, and so on, they often submit themselves willingly and wholeheartedly to very intense disciplines, simply because they want to learn to do a given thing well. Our Little-Napoleon football coaches, of whom we have too many and hear far too much, blind us to the fact that millions of children work hard every year getting better at sports and games without coaches barking and yelling at them.

QUESTIONS

1. Does Holt divide discipline according to source or to the uses of discipline in education—or according to some other principle? Is Holt's division exhaustive?

2. Holt states in paragraph 4 that the kinds of discipline distinguished overlap. How do they?

3. Holt's principle of division might have been the effects of discipline on the personality of the young person. Is Holt concerned with effects in the course of his discussion?

4. How else might discipline be analyzed in a discussion of it, and to what purpose?

SUGGESTIONS FOR WRITING

1. Write an essay on jobs or hobbies, developing the topic by division. If you divide by more than one principle, keep each breakdown and discussion separate and consistent.

2. Discuss why you think Holt would agree or disagree with Margaret Mead and Rhoda Metraux on effective and ineffective kinds of discipline (p. 128). Analyze key statements in the two essays to support your answer.

3. Discuss your agreement or disagreement with Holt that people learn best when they are not coerced. Refer to your own experience, perhaps with teachers and sports coaches in high school or college.

A L L A N   N E V I N S

One of America's most important historians, ALLAN NEVINS (1890–1971) wrote important biographies of many famous Americans, including John D. Rockefeller and Henry Ford, and won Pulitzer Prizes in 1933 and 1937 for his lives of Grover Cleveland and Hamilton Fish. His discussion of newspapers shows one important use of division in exposition and also tells us something important about the interpretation of evidence—a subject we will consider later in this book.

THE NEWSPAPER

Obviously, it is futile to talk of accuracy or inaccuracy, authority or lack of authority, with reference to the newspaper as a whole. The newspaper cannot be dismissed with either a blanket endorsement or a blanket condemnation. It cannot be used as if all its parts had equal value or authenticity. The first duty of the historical student of the newspaper is to discriminate. He must weigh every separate department, every article, every writer, for what the department or article or writer seems to be worth. Clearly, a great part of what is printed in every newspaper is from official sources, and hence may be relied upon to be perfectly accurate. The weather report is accurate; so are court notices, election notices, building permits, lists of marriage licenses, bankruptcy lists. Though unofficial, other classes of news are almost totally free from error. The most complete precautions are taken to keep the stock market quotations minutely accurate, both by stock exchange authorities and by the newspaper staffs. An error in stock quotations may have the most disastrous consequences, and mistakes are hence excluded by every means within human power. So with shipping news, news of deaths, and a considerable body of similar matter—sports records, registers of Congressional or legislative votes, and so on. 1

    Thus one great division of material in newspapers can be treated as completely authentic. There is another large division which may in general be treated as trustworthy and authoritative. This is the news which is prepared by experts under conditions exempt from hurry and favorable to the gathering of all the significant facts. The weekly review of a real estate expert is a case in point. The sporting news of the best 2 newspapers, prepared by experts under conditions which make for accuracy, is singularly uniform, and this uniformity is the best evidence that it is truthful and well proportioned. Society news, industrial news, and similar intelligence, especially when it appears in the form of weekly surveys written by known specialists, is worthy of the utmost reliance.

But in dealing with news which contains a large subjective element, and which is prepared under conditions of hurry and strain, the critical faculty must be kept constantly alert. Every conscientious correspondent at an inauguration, or a battle, or a political rally, or in an interview, tries to report the facts. But not one of them can help reporting, in addition to the facts, the impression that he has personally received of them. The most honest and careful observer ordinarily sees a little of what he wishes to see. It is through failure to make critical allowance for this fact that the historical student of newspapers is most likely to be led astray. Beveridge in his life of Lincoln remarks upon the striking difference between the Democratic reports and the Republican reports of the Lincoln–Douglas debates. At Ottawa, Illinois, for example, these two great leaders held their first joint debate on August 21, 1858. Lincoln came on a special train of fourteen cars crowded with shouting Republicans. It arrived at Ottawa at noon and, according to the Republican papers, when Lincoln alighted a shout went up from a dense and enthusiastic crowd which made the bluffs of the Illinois River and the woods along it ring and ring again. Lincoln entered a carriage; according to the *Chicago Tribune* men with evergreens, mottoes, fair young ladies, bands of music, military companies, and a dense mass of cheering humanity followed him through the streets in a scene of tumultuous excitement. But according to the *Philadelphia Press* and other Douglas papers, Lincoln had only a chilly and lackadaisical reception. "As his procession passed," stated the *Philadelphia Press*, "scarcely a cheer went up. They marched along silently and sorrowfully, as if it were a funeral cortege following him to the grave." On the other hand, the Democratic papers declared that the reception of Douglas was perfectly tremendous; the cheers were so thundering, said the *Philadelphia Press*, that they seemed to rend the very air. But the *Chicago Tribune* said that Douglas had no reception of consequence; that the only cheers he got came from the Irish Catholics. Yet both reporters were probably fairly honest. They saw what they wished to see.

VOCABULARY

paragraph 1: endorsement, discriminate
paragraph 2: authentic, authoritative, exempt
paragraph 3: conscientious, tumultuous, lackadaisical, cortege

QUESTIONS

1. On what basis does Nevins divide his paragraphs on material in newspapers? What are the three divisions he distinguishes?

2. What point is he making through these divisions?

3. In referring to the "large subjective element" of certain newspaper accounts, is Nevins referring to bias or prejudice in the reporters? What does his example of the Lincoln–Douglas debates show?

4. What is the order of ideas in the three paragraphs? Why does Nevins save "news which contains a large subjective element" for last?

5. Newspapers might be classified generally with sources of information, as in "Newspapers are one of the many sources of information on how government works. . . ." How many other classes can you think of? What purposes might these classifications serve?

SUGGESTIONS FOR WRITING

1. In one or two paragraphs of your own, divide materials in newspapers by another principle of division and use your division to make a point, as Nevins does.

2. Analyze the front page stories of an issue of a newspaper according to the degree of their reliability. Discuss the "subjective element" of one of the stories, as Nevins discusses the account of the Lincoln–Douglas debates.

GARRISON KEILLOR

Humorist and essayist GARRISON KEILLOR began his radio program *A Prairie Home Companion* in 1974, and he made famous a fictional midwestern town he called Lake Wobegon. Keillor received the George Foster Peabody Broadcasting Award in 1980, and in 1985 the Edward R. Murrow Award of the Corporation for Public Broadcasting for service to public radio. His novels and story collections include *The Book of Guys* (1993), *WLT: A Radio Romance* (1991), and *We Are Still Married* (1989), in which his essay "Hoppers" appears. Keillor uses both classification and division in describing people on a New York City street.

HOPPERS

A hydrant was open on Seventh Avenue above 23rd Street last Friday morning, and I stopped on my way east and watched people hop over the water. It was a brilliant spring day. The water was a nice clear creek about three feet wide and ran along the gutter around the northwest corner of the intersection. A gaggle of pedestrians crossing 23rd went *hop hop hop hop hop* over the creek as a few soloists jaywalking Seventh performed at right angles to them, and I got engrossed in the dance. Three feet isn't a long leap for most people, and the ease of it permits a wide range of expression. Some hoppers went a good deal higher than necessary.

Long, lanky men don't hop, as a rule. The ones I saw hardly paused at the water's edge, just lengthened one stride and trucked on across—a rather flatfooted approach that showed no recognition of the space or occasion. Tall men typically suffer from an excess of cool, but I kept hoping for one of them to get off the ground. Most of the tall men wore topcoats and carried briefcases, so perhaps their balance was thrown off. One tall man in a brown coat didn't notice the water and stepped off the curb into the fast-flowing Hydrant Creek and made a painful hop, like a wounded heron: a brown heron with a limp wing attached to a briefcase bulging full of dead fish. He crossed 23rd looking as though his day had been pretty much shot to pieces.

Short, fat men were superb: I could have watched them all morning. A typical fat man crossing the street would quicken his step when he saw the creek and, on his approach, do a little shuffle, arms out to the sides, and suddenly and with great concentration *spring*—a nimble step all the more graceful for the springer's bulk. Three fairly fat men jiggled and shambled across 23rd together, and then one poked another and they saw the water. They stepped forward, studying the angle, and just before the point man jumped for the curb his pals said something, undoubtedly discouraging, and he threw back his head and laughed over his shoulder and threw himself lightly, boyishly, across the water, followed—*boing boing*—by the others.

The women who hopped the water tended to stop and study the creek 4 and find its narrows and measure the distance and then lurch across. They seemed dismayed that the creek was there at all, and one, in a beige suit, put her hands on her hips and glared upstream, as if to say, "Whose water *is* this? This is utterly unacceptable. I am *not* about to jump over this." But then she made a good jump after all. She put her left toe on the edge of the curb, leaned forward with right arm outstretched—for a second, she looked as if she might take off and zoom up toward the Flatiron Building—and pushed off, landing easily on her right toe, her right arm raised. The longest leap was made by a young woman in a blue raincoat carrying a plastic Macy's bag and crossing west on Seventh. She gathered herself up in three long, accelerating strides and sailed, her coat billowing out behind her, over the water and five feet beyond, almost creaming a guy coming out of Radio Shack. He shrank back as she loped past, her long black hair and snow-white hands and face right *there*, then gone, vanished in the crowd.

And then it was my turn. I waited for the green light, crossed 23rd, 5 stopped by the creek flowing around the bend of curb and heard faint voices of old schoolmates ahead in the woods, and jumped heavily across and marched after them.

VOCABULARY

paragraph 1: gaggle
paragraph 3: jiggle, shamble
paragraph 4: lurch, billowing, creaming, lope

QUESTIONS

1. By what principle does Keillor divide the class *male hoppers?* How do the characteristics shared by "long, lanky men" influence the way they cross the water? How do the characteristics of "short, fat men" influence the way they do?

2. How do most of the women differ from men in how they cross the water?

3. In what class does Keillor put himself in paragraph 5? How does this class differ from the other classes described?

4. Is Keillor making a point or developing a thesis in the essay? Or is his essay descriptive only?

SUGGESTIONS FOR WRITING

1. Like Keillor, identify a group of people on the basis of how they act on the street or at home—for example, how they cross a busy intersection, get up in the morning, or prepare for bed.

2. Like Keillor, who divides the men hopping the stream, divide the class according to a single principle. If you wish, use your classification and division to make a point, perhaps an observation about human nature or differences in age groups or genders.

10

DEFINITION

There are many ways of defining something, and the way we choose depends on our purpose and audience. If we are in a store that advertises "Hero Sandwiches" and a visitor asks what these are, we can point to one on the counter. But pointing may not be enough: we may have to "denote" what a hero sandwich is—that is, distinguish the "hero" from other things like it. In a denotative definition we can start with a classification of things like food and single the hero out from all other kinds. But since the visitor knows a hero is something to eat, we can narrow our class to sandwiches.

A dictionary definition usually gives us a denotative definition of this sort—identifying first the class or genus of objects to which the word belongs and then distinguishing the word by its specific difference. As we noted, the class or genus may be broad (*food*) or it may be narrow (*sandwich*). The following dictionary definition of *hero* chooses a narrow genus:

> **hero** U.S. A sandwich [*genus*] made with a loaf of bread cut lengthwise [*specific difference*]. (*Standard College Dictionary*)

Sometimes we want to do more than merely name or identify an object: we want to present ideas and impressions, the emotional aura we associate with it. The word *rose* has a precise denotation—a particular flower with describable properties. It also has a range of connotations or associations. Thus roses are often associated with success or happiness, and we recognize this association in the popular expression "a rosy future." Connotations may be positive in their implication, or negative. Though the words *inexpensive* and *cheap* both mean low price, *cheap* for many people carries the connotation of poor quality or of something contemptible. *Inexpensive* is an emotionally neutral word; *cheap* is sometimes not.

Denotative and connotative definitions tell us how words are used currently. Sometimes we find it helpful to give the original meaning, or etymology, to clarify the current meaning—for example, to explain that the word *gravity* comes from the Latin *gravitas* meaning weight or heaviness, or the word *placebo* from the Latin *placēre,* meaning to please:

> A placebo in the classical sense . . . is an imitation medicine—generally an innocuous milk-sugar tablet dressed up like an authentic pill—given more for the purpose of placating the patient than for meeting a clearly diagnosed organic need. (Norman Cousins, *Anatomy of an Illness*)

But we must be careful not to assume that a current word possesses, or should be limited to, its original meaning. We would certainly be misunderstood if we used *sinister,* a word of Latin derivation originally meaning left and left-handed, to refer to a left-handed person.

We can also use definitions to fix words that have become indefinite or confused in popular usage. We sometimes call this kind of definition *precising.* Judicial decisions are often of this kind, as in decisions that define obscenity in books and films. Another use of definition is to stipulate or propose a name or term for a newly discovered phenomenon so that we can refer to it. An example is the term *quasar,* proposed in the 1960s for newly discovered "quasi-stellar" sources of light in the sky that seem not to be stars. *Stipulative* definitions are proposed with the understanding that the term may change later as more is discovered. By contrast, *theoretical* definitions propose an explanation or theory of the phenomenon: they do not merely propose a term for discussion and further research. Most textbook definitions of democracy and similar ideas are theoretical. In giving definitions, we should be clear about the use we are making of them. It will matter to the reader whether we are trying to make a commonly used word more exact in its usage or proposing a definition without claiming to know the whole truth about it.

CAROL BLY

CAROL BLY writes about rural Minnesota life in her essays and short stories, collected in *Letters from the Country* (1981), *Backbone* (1985), *The*

Tomcat's Wife and Other Stories (1991), and *My Lord Bag of Rice: New and Collected Stories* (2000). The following is taken from her account of experiences as a farm worker during corn harvest.

MONKEYING

The men have left a gigantic 6600 combine a few yards from our grove, at the edge of the stubble. For days it was working around the farm; we heard it on the east, later on the west, and finally we could see it grinding back and forth over the windrows on the south. But now it has been simply squatting at the field's edge, huge, tremendously still, very professional, slightly dangerous. 1

We all have the correct feelings about this new combine: this isn't the good old farming where man and soil are dusted together all day; this isn't farming a poor man can afford, either, and therefore it further threatens his hold on the American "family farm" operation. We have been sneering at this machine for days, as its transistor radio, amplified well over the engine roar, has been grinding up our silence, spreading a kind of shrill ghetto evening all over the farm. 2

But now it is parked, and after a while I walk over to it and climb up its neat little John-Deere-green ladder on the left. Entering the big cab up there is like coming up into a large ship's bridge on visitors' day—heady stuff to see the inside workings of a huge operation like the Queen Elizabeth II. On the other hand I feel left out, being only a dumbfounded passenger. The combine cab has huge windows flaring wider at the top; they lean forward over the ground, and the driver sits so high behind the glass in its rubber moldings it is like a movie-set spaceship. He has obviously come to dominate the field, whether he farms it or not. 3

The value of the 66 is that it can do anything, and to change it from a combine into a cornpicker takes one man about half an hour, whereas most machine conversions on farms take several men a half day. It frees its owner from a lot of monkeying. 4

Monkeying, in city life, is what little boys do to clocks so they never run again. In farming it has two quite different meanings. The first is small side projects. You monkey with poultry, unless you're a major egg handler. Or you monkey with ducks or geese. If you have a very small milk herd, and finally decide that prices plus state regulations don't make 5 your few Holsteins worthwhile, you "quit monkeying with them." There is a hidden dignity in this word: it precludes mention of money. It lets the wife of a very marginal farmer have a conversation with a woman who may be helping her husband run fifteen hundred acres. "How you coming with those geese?" "Oh, we've been real disgusted. We're thinking of quitting monkeying with them." It saves her having to say, "We lost our shirts on those darn geese."

The other meaning of monkeying is wrestling with and maintaining machinery, such as changing heads from combining to cornpicking. Farmers who cornpick the old way, in which the corn isn't shelled automatically during picking in the field but must be elevated to the top of a pile by belt and then shelled, put up with some monkeying. 6

QUESTIONS

1. How does the description of the combine prepare us for the definition of *monkeying* in paragraphs 4–6?

2. Why does Bly give us the meaning of the word in city life as well as in the side projects of farming? Are these definitions connotative in part or in whole?

3. What kind of definition does Bly give us in paragraph 6, and how does she illustrate it?

4. Invading the quiet farm world, the transistor radio of the combine spreads the piercing noise of a crowded city neighborhood. In what other ways does the combine unsettle the farm workers?

SUGGESTIONS FOR WRITING

1. In acquiring particular skills, you begin to use terms and expressions peculiar to the job or activity. Discuss one such term or expression, defining it and illustrating its uses, including what it expresses toward the activity itself.

2. Use the *Oxford English Dictionary* and other historical and special dictionaries to discover the etymology and distinguishing properties of one of the following words. In other reference books and special studies find information on its history and effects. Use your findings in an informative essay directed to readers unfamiliar with the term:

a. DDT
b. insulin
c. nitroglycerin

d. radar
e. stereo
f. digital recording

g. laser printing
h. computer
   networking

LAWRENCE M. FRIEDMAN

Lawrence M. Friedman, Professor of Law at Stanford University, is the author of *A History of American Law* (1986), *The Republic of Choice* (1990), *Horizontal Society* (1999), and other books. In *Crime and Punishment in American History* (1993), Friedman discusses the social response to crime from colonial times to the present. The definition of crime reprinted here appears in the introduction.

CRIME

There is no real answer to the question, What is crime? There are popular ideas about crime: crime is bad behavior, antisocial behavior, blameworthy acts, and the like. But in a very basic sense, crime is a *legal* concept: what makes some conduct criminal, and other conduct not, is the fact that some, but not others, are "against the law."*

Crimes, then, are forbidden acts. But they are forbidden in a special way. We are not supposed to break contracts, drive carelessly, slander people, or infringe copyrights; but these are not (usually) criminal acts. The distinction between a *civil* and a *criminal* case is fundamental in our

---

* Most criminologists, but not all, would agree with this general formulation; for an exception see Michael R. Gottfredson and Travis Hirschi, *A General Theory of Crime* (1990). [Friedman's note]

legal system. A civil case has a life cycle entirely different from that of a criminal case. If I slander somebody, I might be dragged into court, and I might have to open my checkbook and pay damages; but I cannot be put in prison or executed, and if I lose the case, I do not get a criminal "record." Also, in a slander case (or a negligence case, or a copyright-infringement case), the injured party pays for, runs, and manages the case herself. He or she makes the decisions and hires the lawyers. The case is entirely voluntary. Nobody forces anybody to sue. I can have a good claim, a valid claim, and simply forget it, if I want.

In a criminal case, in theory at least, society is the victim, along 3 with the "real" victim—the person robbed or assaulted or cheated. The crime may be punished without the victim's approval (though, practically speaking, the complaining witness often has a crucial role to play). In "victimless crimes" (gambling, drug dealing, certain sex offenses), there is nobody to complain; both parties are equally guilty (or innocent). Here the machine most definitely has a mind of its own. In criminal cases, moreover, the state pays the bills. It should be pointed out, however, that the further back in history one goes, the more this pat distinction between "civil" and "criminal" tends to blur. In some older cultures, the line between private vengeance and public prosecution was indistinct or completely absent. Even in our own history, we shall see some evidence that the cleavage between "public" and "private" enforcement was not always deep and pervasive.

All sorts of nasty acts and evil deeds are not against the law, and 4 thus not crimes. These include most of the daily events that anger or irritate us, even those we might consider totally outrageous. Ordinary lying is not a crime; cheating on a wife or husband is not a crime in most states (at one time it was, almost everywhere); charging a huge markup at a restaurant or store is not, in general, a crime; psychological abuse is (mostly) not a crime.

Before some act can be isolated and labeled as a crime, there must 5 be a special, solemn, social and *political* decision. In our society, Congress, a state legislature, or a city government has to pass a law or enact an ordinance adding the behavior to the list of crimes. Then this behavior, like a bottle of poison, carries the proper label and can be turned over to the heavy artillery of law for possible enforcement.

We repeat: crime is a *legal* concept. This point, however, can lead to 6 a misunderstanding. The law, in a sense, "creates" the crimes it punishes; but what creates criminal law? Behind the law, and above it, enveloping

it, is society; before the law made the crime a crime, some aspect of social reality transformed the behavior, culturally speaking, into a crime;
and it is the social context that gives the act, and the legal responses,
their real meaning. Justice is supposed to be blind, which is to say impartial. This may or may not be so, but justice is blind in one fundamental sense: justice is an abstraction. It cannot see or act on its own. It
cannot generate its own norms, principles, and rules. Everything depends
on society. Behind every *legal* judgment of criminality is a more powerful, more basic *social* judgment; a judgment that this behavior, whatever
it is, deserves to be outlawed and punished.

VOCABULARY

paragraph 2: infringe, civil, slander, negligence case, valid
paragraph 6: concept, context

QUESTIONS

1. What distinguishes a criminal case from a civil case?

2. Why is Friedman's definition of crime theoretical, as he implies in
paragraph 3, and not denotative or stipulative?

3. What misunderstanding may arise in stating that crime is a "legal concept"? How does Friedman clarify this idea?

4. Friedman states that careless driving and copyright infringement are
not usually defined as crimes. Under what circumstances might they
be?

SUGGESTION FOR WRITING

Examine the definition of the following terms in your collegiate dictionary to determine whether it is denotative, connotative, stipulative, or
theoretical. You may find that the dictionary lists more than one kind;

for example, it may list connotations of the word, in addition to its denotation. Write a brief paragraph on each word, discussing your findings:

a. comedy   d. filibuster   g. unicorn
b. democracy   e. liberal   h. witty
c. fascism   f. neutron star

PHILIP HAMBURGER

A native of Wheeling, West Virginia, PHILIP HAMBURGER became a member of the staff of *The New Yorker* magazine in 1939. During World War II he served in the office of Facts and Figures (later the Office of War Information). On his return to the magazine in 1943, he served as a war correspondent in Europe. Hamburger has written for most of the sections of *The New Yorker*. His many contributions include pieces in "Talk of the Town" and "Notes and Comments," "Reporter at Large" articles, film and music criticism, and columns on television. His "Notes for a Gazetteer," a series of profiles of American cities, were collected in *An American Notebook* (1965). His other books include *Curious World: A New Yorker at Large* (1987) and *Friends Talking in the Night: Sixty Years of Writing for* The New Yorker (1999). In *An American Notebook* Hamburger portrays a particular city through the eyes of its inhabitants, as in his profile of Oklahoma City, from which the following excerpt is taken.

THE SOONERS

No higher compliment can be paid to an Oklahoma City man these days than to call him a Sooner. Call an Oklahoma City man a Sooner, and his chest puffs out and his eyes light up. It means that you appreciate the chap—his vigor, his vitality, his civic pride, his alliance with the tall white buildings that, first glimpsed from miles away and across long stretches of land, appear to be a mirage but turn out, upon a closer approach, to be Oklahoma City. Call a man a Sooner, and you identify him with, among other things, the University of Oklahoma football team—the Sooners—and what man could ask for more? Oklahoma City's most fashionable hotel, the Skirvin (Perle Mesta owns part of the Skirvin; her daddy was a Skirvin), has a Sooner Room, which constitutes semiofficial recognition that the word "Sooner" has reached an impeccable social plateau. The use of "Sooner" as an accolade represents a mellowing process. Up to seventy years ago, to call a man a Sooner was to risk being hit over the head with the spare wheel of a covered wagon, kicked in the stomach, or worse. It all goes back to April 22, 1889, the day of The Run, when the Oklahoma Territory (then called the Indian Territory) was opened to settlers, and when the settlers, poised and in natural Technicolor, awaited the sound of the gun that would permit them to race pell-mell for new land and new homes. There is many a man in Oklahoma City today who remembers The Run, and millions of moviegoers feel that they, too, made The Run, as a result of the numerous cinema epics that have glorified it. When dawn broke on that April 22nd, what was to become Oklahoma City was a sleepy little railroad stop sitting out on the lonely grass. Nothing much to be said about it, really—a few wooden houses, a water tower, some railroad tracks, the usual complement of early-rising roosters, perhaps a barefoot boy with a can of worms, and the West stretching as far as the eye could see. There were also on hand some people called Sooners. These were people who had shown up too soon—who weren't taking any chances on losing out in the race for land, and who had crossed the line before the starting gun. To the thousands of law-abiding citizens who waited patiently behind the line, the Sooners were beneath contempt. "They were chisellers, that's what they were," an old-time Oklahoma City resident said not long ago. He was in the Sooner Room at the time, sipping a brandy. "The organized Sooners, who were sooner than the Sooners, were known as Boomers, and it is hard to say which were worse. They were all mean, dirty, low-life chisellers." By nightfall, after the gun had gone off and The Run had been accomplished, Oklahoma City was a city of ten thousand souls, many of them out looking for the Sooners and the Boomers. Time heals many wounds.

VOCABULARY

mirage, impeccable, social plateau, pell-mell, complement

QUESTIONS

1. What is the denotative definition of *Sooner,* and where in the paragraph does Hamburger present it?

2. What positive and negative connotations does the word *Sooner* have? Why does Hamburger give us information about the Boomers?

3. What do these connotations tell you about Oklahomans and changes in Oklahoma life since 1889?

4. What is the tone of the paragraph—the voice of the writer that you hear in reading it? Specifically, is the tone admiring or sarcastic or amused? Or does Hamburger express no attitude toward the people and the world he describes?

SUGGESTIONS FOR WRITING

1. First give the denotative meaning of a name like the one Hamburger describes—perhaps the name associated with your city or town or with your high school and its teams. Then give its connotations and, if you can, explain their origin. Use your definition to make a point.

2. Advertisers depend on connotative meanings to sell their products. Discuss differences in the connotations of similar products—for example, automobiles with names like "Cougar" and "Charger." Use your discussion to make a point.

CASEY MILLER AND KATE SWIFT

CASEY MILLER worked in publishing and as a freelance writer and editor. KATE SWIFT is a freelance writer and editor and has been a science writer for the American Museum of Natural History and a news director for the Yale School of Medicine. The discussion reprinted here is taken from *Words and Women* (1976)—a book concerned with the influence of language on the lives of women.

"MANLY" AND "WOMANLY"

Webster's Third New International Dictionary (1966) defines *manly* as "having qualities appropriate to a man: not effeminate or timorous; bold, resolute, open in conduct or bearing." The definition goes on to include "belonging or appropriate in character to a man" (illustrated by "manly sports" and "beer is a manly drink"), "of undaunted courage: gallant, brave." The same dictionary's definition of *womanly* is less specific, relying heavily on phrases like "marked by qualities characteristic of a woman"; "possessed of the character or behavior befitting a grown woman"; "characteristic of, belonging to, or suitable to a woman's nature and attitudes rather than to a man's." Two of the examples provided are more informative: "convinced that drawing was a waste of time, if not downright womanly . . ." and "her usual womanly volubility." 1

In its definition of *manly* the *Random House Dictionary of the English Language* (1967) supplies the words "strong, brave, honorable, resolute, virile" as "qualities usually considered desirable in a man" and cites "feminine; weak, cowardly," as antonyms. Its definitions of *womanly* are "like or befitting a woman; feminine; not masculine or girlish" and "in the manner of, or befitting, a woman." The same dictionary's synonym essays for these words are worth quoting in full because of the contrasts they provide: 2

MANLY, MANFUL, MANNISH mean possessing the qualities of a man. MANLY implies possession of the most valuable or desirable qualities a man can have, as dignity, honesty, directness, etc., in opposition to servility, insincerity, underhandedness, etc.: *A manly foe is better than a weak friend.* It also connotes courage, strength, and fortitude: *manly determination to face what comes.* MANFUL stresses the reference to courage, strength, and industry: *manful resistance.* MANNISH applies to that which resembles man: *a boy with a mannish voice.* Applied to a woman, the term is derogatory, suggesting the aberrant possession of masculine characteristics: *a mannish girl; a mannish stride.*

WOMANLY, WOMANLIKE, WOMANISH, mean resembling a woman. WOM-
ANLY implies resemblance in appropriate, fitting ways: *womanly deco-*
rum, modesty. WOMANLIKE, a neutral synonym, may suggest mild dis-
approval or, more rarely, disgust: *Womanlike, she (he) burst into tears.*
WOMANISH usually implies an inappropriate resemblance and suggests
weakness or effeminacy; *womanish petulance.*

What are these parallel essays saying? That we perceive males in   3
terms of human qualities, females in terms of qualities—often negative—
assigned to them as females. The qualities males possess may be good or
bad, but those that come to mind when we consider what makes "a man"
are positive. Women are defined circularly, through characteristics seen
to be appropriate or inappropriate to women—not to human beings. In
fact, when women exhibit positive attributes considered typical of men—
dignity, honesty, courage, strength, or fortitude—they are thought of as
aberrant. A person who is "womanlike" may (although the term is said
to be "neutral") prompt a feeling of disgust.

The broad range of positive characteristics used to define males could   4
be used to define females too, of course, but they are not. The characteristics of women—weakness is among the most frequently cited—are
something apart. At its entry for *women Webster's Third* provides this
list of "qualities considered distinctive of womanhood": "Gentleness, affection, and domesticity or on the other hand fickleness, superficiality,
and folly." Among the "qualities considered distinctive of manhood"
listed in the entry for *man,* no negative attributes detract from the
"courage, strength, and vigor" the definers associate with males. According to this dictionary, *womanish* means "unsuitable to a man or to
a strong character of either sex."

Lexicographers do not make up definitions out of thin air. Their task   5
is to record how words are used, it is not to say how they should be
used. The examples they choose to illustrate meanings can therefore be
especially revealing of cultural expectations. The *American Heritage Dic-*
tionary (1969), which provides "manly courage" and "masculine charm,"
also gives us "Woman is fickle," "brought out the woman in him," "womanly virtue," "feminine allure," "feminine wiles," and "womanish tears."
The same dictionary defines *effeminate,* which comes from the Latin *ef-*
feminare, meaning "to make a woman out of," as "having the qualities
associated with women; not characteristic of a man; unmanly" and "characterized by softness, weakness, or lack of force; not dynamic or vigor-
ous." For synonyms one is referred to *feminine.*

   Brother and *sister* and their derivatives have acquired similar features.   6
A columnist who wrote that "the political operatives known as 'Kennedy
men' and 'Nixon men' have been sisters under their skins" could not possibly have called those adversaries "brothers," with all the mutual respect
and loyalty that word implies. As the writer explained, "Like the colonel's
lady and Judy O'Grady, their styles were different but their unwavering
determination to win was strikingly similar." Other kinds of sisters for
whom no comparable male siblings exist include the sob sister, the weak
sister, and the plain ordinary sissy, whose counterpart in the brotherhood
is the buddy, a real pal. Like *effeminate,* these female-related words and
phrases are applied to males when a cutting insult is intended.

   Masculine, manly, manlike, and other male-associated words used to   7
compliment men are frequently also considered complimentary when applied to women: thus a woman may be said to have manly determination, to have a masculine mind, to take adversity like a man, or to struggle manfully against overwhelming odds. The one male-associated word
sometimes used to insult her is mannish, which may suggest she is too
strong or aggressive to be a true woman, or that she is homosexually oriented, in which case mannish can become a code word.

   Female-associated words, on the other hand, must be hedged, as in   8
"He has almost feminine intuition," if they are used to describe a man
without insulting him. He may be praised for admirable qualities defined
as peculiar to women, but he cannot be said to have womanly compassion
or womanlike tenderness. In exceptions to this rule—for example, when
a medic on the battlefield or a sports figure in some postgame situation
of unusual drama is said to be "as gentle as a woman"—the life-and-
death quality of the circumstances makes its own ironic and terrible commentary on the standards of "masculinity" ordinarily expected of men.

   The role expectations compressed into our male-positive-important   9
and female-negative-trivial words are extremely damaging, as we are beginning to find out. The female stereotypes they convey are obvious, but
the harm doesn't stop there. The inflexible demands made on males,
which allow neither for variation nor for human frailty, are dehumanizing. They put a premium on a kind of perfection that can be achieved
only through strength, courage, industry, and fortitude. These are admirable qualities, but if they are associated only with males, and their
opposites are associated only with females, they become sex-related demands that few individuals can fulfill.

Vocabulary

paragraph 1: effeminate, timorous, undaunted, volubility
paragraph 2: virile, antonym, servility, derogatory, aberrant, decorum, synonym, petulance
paragraph 4: fickleness, superficiality
paragraph 5: lexicographer, wiles
paragraph 6: sibling
paragraph 8: intuition
paragraph 9: stereotype, dehumanizing, fortitude

Questions

1. Miller and Swift state that "Women are defined circularly, through characteristics seen to be appropriate or inappropriate to women—not to human beings." How is the definition of women circular?

2. What attitudes toward men and women underlie the dictionary definition—and current uses—of *manly* and *womanly?* What change in attitude toward men and women do Miller and Swift favor? Do they say what change they favor, or do you infer their beliefs from their analysis?

3. To what extent do Miller and Swift describe your own use of *manly* and *womanly* and your conceptions of manhood and womanhood?

Suggestions for Writing

1. Analyze your own conception of manliness and womanliness, comparing your use of *manly* and *womanly* with those discussed by Miller and Swift.

2. Miller and Swift suggest that the words we commonly use create "role expectations"—attitudes and behavior society looks for in men and women. Discuss "role expectations" promoted in advertisements for a particular product, such as sports equipment.

HERBERT J. GANS

HERBERT J. GANS is Robert S. Lynd Professor of Sociology at Columbia University in New York City. In his article on the word "underclass" published in *The Washington Post* September 10, 1990, Gans shows how a widely accepted word can create an unfair stereotype and influence thinking on issues of welfare and poverty. In exploring the connotations of the term, Gans is also considering the implications of what is for journalists and sociologists a theoretical definition.

THE UNDERCLASS

Sticks and stones may break my bones, but names can never hurt me goes the old proverb. But like many old proverbs, this one is patent nonsense, as anyone knows who has ever been hurt by ethnic, racist or sexist insults and stereotypes. 1

The most frequent victims of insults and stereotypes have been the poor, especially those thought to be undeserving of help because someone decided—justifiably or not—that they had not acted properly. America has a long history of insults for the "undeserving" poor. In the past they were bums, hoboes, vagrants and paupers; more recently they have been culturally deprived and the hard-core poor. Now they are "the underclass." 2

Underclass was originally a 19th-century Swedish term for the poor. In the early 1960s, the Swedish economist Gunnar Myrdal revived it to describe the unemployed and unemployables being created by the modern economy, people who, he predicted, would soon be driven out of that economy unless it was reformed. Twenty years later, in Ronald Reagan's America, the word sprang to life again, this time not only to describe but also to condemn. Those normally consigned to the underclass include: women who start their families before marriage and before the end of adolescence, youngsters who fail to finish high school or find work, and welfare "dependents"—whether or not the behavior of any of these people is their own fault. The term is also applied to low-income delinquents and criminals—but not to affluent ones. 3

"Underclass" has become popular because it seems to grab people's attention. What grabs is the image of a growing horde of beggars, muggers, 4 robbers and lazy people who do not carry their part of the economic load, all of them threatening nonpoor Americans and the stability of American society. The image may be inaccurate, but then insults and pejoratives don't have to be accurate. Moreover, underclass sounds technical, academic, and not overtly pejorative, so it can be used without anyone's biases showing. Since it is now increasingly applied to blacks and Hispanics, it is also a respectable substitute word with which to condemn them.

There are other things wrong with the word underclass. For one, it   5
lumps together in a single term very diverse poor people with diverse problems. Imagine all children's illnesses being described with the same word, and the difficulties doctors would have in curing them.

For example, a welfare recipient often requires little more than a de-   6
cent paying job—and a male breadwinner who also has such a job—to make a normal go of it, while a high school dropout usually needs both a better-equipped school, better teachers and fellow students—and a rationale for going to school when he or she has no assurance that a decent job will follow upon graduation. Neither the welfare recipient nor the high school dropout deserves to be grouped with, or described by, the same word as muggers or drug dealers.

Labeling poor people as underclass is to blame them for their poverty,   7
which enables the blamers to blow off the steam of self-righteousness. That steam does not, however, reduce their poverty. Unfortunately, underclass, like other buzzwords for calling the poor undeserving, is being used to avoid starting up needed antipoverty programs and other economic reforms.

Still, the greatest danger of all lies not in the label itself but in the   8
possibility that the underclass is a symptom of a possible, and dark, American future: that we are moving toward a "post-post-industrial" economy in which there may not be enough decent jobs for all. Either too many more jobs will move to Third World countries where wages are far lower or they will be performed by ever more efficient computers and other machines.

If this happens, the underclass label may turn out to be a signal that   9
the American economy, and our language, are preparing to get ready for a future in which some people are going to be more or less permanently jobless—and will be blamed for their joblessness to boot.

Needless to say, an American economy with a permanently jobless   10
population would be socially dangerous, for all of the country's current social problems, from crime and addiction to mental illness would be

sure to increase considerably. America would then also become politically more dangerous, for various kinds of new protests have to be expected, not to mention the rise of quasi-fascist movements. Such movements can already be found in France and other European countries.

Presumably, Americans—the citizenry and elected officials both—will not let any of this happen here and will find new sources of decent jobs, as they have done in past generations, even if today this requires a new kind of New Deal. Perhaps there will be another instance of what always saved America in the past: new sources of economic growth that cannot even be imagined now.   11

The only problem is that in the past, America ruled the world economically, and now it does not—and it shows in our lack of economic growth. Consequently, the term underclass could become a permanent entry in the dictionary of American pejoratives.   12

Vocabulary

paragraph 1: stereotype
paragraph 2: hoboes, vagrants, paupers
paragraph 4: pejoratives
paragraph 6: rationale
paragraph 8: symptom
paragraph 10: quasi-fascist

Questions

1. Gans shows that the economist Gunnar Myrdal introduced a precising definition for the nineteenth-century Swedish word *underclass* (see p. 146). What was the original meaning of the word, and how did Myrdal make the meaning precise?

2. To what extent has Myrdal's meaning been adopted by Americans, according to Gans? What additional meanings has the word acquired since the early 1960s?

3. Why does Gans consider *underclass* an inaccurate term or label for the poor? What additional danger does he see in the widespread acceptance of the term?

4. Does Gans believe that poverty is irremediable? Or does he believe that remedies exist in America today?

Suggestions for Writing

1. Define one of the following words or another word descriptive of an attitude or behavior by stating what it is and what it is not. Comment on the significance of its etymology.

a. gluttony   **c.** intolerance   **e.** stinginess

b. greed   **d.** laziness

2. Discuss the various meanings of a descriptive term like *cool* or *tacky,* illustrating these meanings by your use of them.

IRVING LEWIS ALLEN

Irving Lewis Allen, Professor of Sociology at the University of Connecticut, writes about ethnic labeling and slurs in *Unkind Words* (1990), and New York City culture and popular speech in *The City in Slang* (1993), from which the following section is taken. Allen writes: "Popular and lexical culture responded effusively to the innovations in mass communication most closely associated with the classic cycle of the metropolitan center—the modern newspaper, the telephone, and the movies. . . . The instruments of communication—newsprint, telephone sets, and motion picture theaters—became objects of folklore and humor and stories about their early days set their popular names into the context of their origin."

Newspapers

Alexis de Tocqueville in *Democracy in America,* written about his nine-month visit to America in 1831–32, noted the intrinsic and pervasive role of the press in our politics and community life. Compared to France, he thought that American newspapers were incredible in number; every city and town seemed to have one. Unlike the press in Europe, the American papers were also given to muckraking, which in the big cities after 1850 was to become a national sport. A century later sociologist Robert E. Park emphasized the importance of the newspaper in metropolitan life.[1] Many studies stemming from Park's influence have shown the role of newspapers in urban social, political, and economic integration and how the papers made the workings of the huge, diverse city imaginable to the masses of people. Newspapers were the first true mass medium and their content interacted inextricably with popular speech. At one time in the second half of the nineteenth century, New York had fourteen dailies, more or less, nearly as many semi-weeklies, and several score of weeklies, many serving immigrant communities in their own languages.

The act of newspaper reading in public places, selling papers in the streets, and even the physical presence of newsprint itself have been close to the consciousness of everyday city life and have influenced popular speech. Discarded newspapers, blowing whole in the streets or left behind in subways, are an abiding part of the disordered urban scene. Many modern artists have used newsprint, or pieces of it, in collages to say things about modern life. The papers "are themselves the city's detritus because yesterday's newspaper is a synonym for waste and the city's amnesia," wrote Peter Conrad in his analysis of New York art and literature.[2] The indifferent city custom of commuters leaving their papers behind on seats or on the floor of els and subways was probably formed in the early days of mass transit. In "The Tunnel," wrote Hart Crane, "Newspapers wing, revolve and wing" in a barreling subway car.[3]

Not surprisingly, people gave slangy names to the ubiquitous product of newsprint itself, which was so visible at newsstands, hawked continuously by newsboys, or held in the hands of straphangers, some of it ending in sidewalk refuse bins, or carelessly discarded, when not put to a number of practical uses. Because newspapers were printed on a large sheet, folded in the center, and designed to be spread out, they were in street speech by 1850 called a *spread*. Early in this century newspapers

---

[1] Robert E. Park, Ernest W. Burgess, and Roderick D. McKenzie, *The City* (Chicago: University of Chicago Press, 1925), pp. 80–98.

[2] Peter Conrad, *The Art of the City: Views and Versions of New York* (New York: Oxford University Press, 1984), p. 302.

[3] Hart Crane, *The Complete Poems of Hart Crane*, ed. Waldo Frank (Garden City, N.Y.: Anchor/Doubleday, 1958), p. 57.

were commonly called a *sheet,* as well. A verse of 1908 mentioned the newsboy "Calling the news that will sell the sheet."

The speech of the large German settlements in New York and other cities in the nineteenth century also influenced slang words for newspapers. One of the largest dailies in New York was the *Staats Zeitung.* The German presence probably accounts for the slang *blat* for any newspaper, from German *Blatt,* which means a newspaper as well as a page or "sheet." Writer Damon Runyon used *bladder,* and this form may have had wider currency, too. *Blab sheet* and *daily blab,* silly names for a gossipy newspaper, are from *to blab,* 'to speak,' especially indiscriminately. Such scandal sheets were also called *rags,* or *dirty rags,* if they were bad enough. These names are apparently from the sense of "rag" as something of contemptuously small value and not, as it might seem, from the rag content of the paper, which in the case of newsprint was becoming mostly wood pulp, anyhow.

Tabloid, originally, a trademark of the 1880s for a tablet, or a little pill, was applied, amid law suits, to other concentrated things. *Tabloid* was extended in a slangy way around 1906 to the new newspapers of the half-size format. Pulitzer's New York *World* had introduced the tabloid-size newspaper on January 1, 1901, in response to the fierce circulation battles of the period. A British newspaper, first published in 1902, actually used the word in its title. By the 1920s a tabloid newspaper in New York was called a *tab* for short. Tabloids, true to their name, compressed the news and (with many pictures) made it graphic and easy to swallow.

Because of its small size, the tabloid was popular with straphangers, who managed to read it while holding the folded paper in one hand. Seated passengers could also spread out the little tabloids without intruding on the social space of their fellow riders. Subways readers of the traditional large format of the *New York Times* were self-reliant and learned a folding technique for reducing the paper to smaller than tabloid size and, moreover, allowing them to read continuously by turning and adjusting the fold. The technique, especially when done with one hand while holding onto a strap, rail, or bar, is genuine city culture. The exact technique is illustrated for out-of-towners and learners in a guide to New York.[4]

---

[4] Saul Miller, *New York Street Smarts* (New York: Holt, Rinehart and Winston, 1983), p. 94.

The kind of sensational, gossipy news favored by some of the tabloids   7
was by 1898 dubbed the *yellow press*. Joseph Pulitzer had bought the
New York *World* from Jay Gould in 1883 and set a new course for American journalism with livelier language, political cartoons, and colored
comics. The first comic strip to run successfully in an American paper
was the *Yellow Kid* introduced by Pulitzer's *World* in 1895. "To attract
attention to the feature, yellow ink was used, and the *World*, which was
pretty sensational in those years, became known as the "yellow paper" —
an epithet later extended in the term *yellow journalism* to any sensation-
mongering newspaper," explain the lexicographers William Morris and
Mary Morris.[5]

There is a little more to the story. Richard F. Outcault, the origina-   8
tor of the "Yellow Kid" at the *World*, left and took the strip with him
to Hearst's New York *Journal*. George Luks, later to become known as
one of the Ashcan painters, was hired to continue a nearly identical car-
toon series in the *World*, as if Outcault had never left. The two "Yellow
Kid" comics flourished side by side, despite law suits. "Other papers referred to the *World* and the *Journal* as 'Yellow Kid journals,' and soon
dropped 'kid' from the phrase, so that 'yellow journalism' came into popular parlance, referring to the competitive sensationalism of the press."[6]
The expression was probably influenced even earlier by the traditional
yellow paper covers on cheaply bound, sensational books and pamphlets
that had been published since mid-century.

After being read or "looked at," newspapers were circulated to a va-   9
riety of other uses, such as food wrappers. Harry Golden in *Only in
America* recalled that street vendors in New York once rolled newsprint
into a cone, as is done traditionally for British fish and chips, and
dispensed hot chickpeas.[7] Children on the Lower East Side called these
horn-like cones *toots*. Certain newspapers were disparagingly called *fish
wrappers*, suggesting what they were mainly good for, and there has been
a worse suggestion of a fitting use for yet other papers. New York housewives of two generations ago, as it is told by their children, spread

---

[5] William Morris and Mary Morris, *Morris Dictionary of Word and Phrase Origins* (New
York: Harper and Row, 1977), p. 616.
[6] Stanley L. Cuba, Nina Kasanof, and Judith O'Toole, *George Luks: An American Artist*
(Wilkes-Barre, Penn.: Sordoni Art Gallery, Wilkes College, 1987), p. 95.
[7] Harry Golden, *Only in America* (New York: World, 1958), p. 60.

newspapers on the linoleum of the kitchen floor after mopping to soak up water and prevent tracking.

Bums and other down-and-outs used newspapers to line their 10 clothing against wintry blasts, to line their shoes against holes in the soles, and not infrequently as blankets for sleeping in doorways and on park benches. The practice has been recorded as early as the 1860s when James D. McCabe, Jr. writing of bums sleeping, on park benches, noticed that "most had old newspapers under them."[8] O. Henry in "The Cop and the Anthem" (1906) wrote: "On the previous night three Sabbath newspapers, distributed beneath his coat, about his ankles and over his lap, had failed to repulse the cold as he slept on his bench." Theodore Dreiser in *The Color of A Great City* recalled a scene from about 1910 of an old woman preparing to sleep on a park bench. "And now she is stuffing old newspapers between her dress and her breast to keep warm."[9] In the cheapest flop houses, a place on the floor was first covered with newspapers. Reflecting all these images, newspapers were called *bum fodder, bum wad,* and *bum's comforter. Blanket* was a hoboes' term for an overcoat and so newspapers were also known facetiously as *California* or *Tucson blankets.*

VOCABULARY

paragraph 1: intrinsic, muckraking, inextricable
paragraph 2: collage, detritus, synonym
paragraph 3: ubiquitous
paragraph 7: epithet, lexicographer

QUESTIONS

1. Which of the slang terms for newspapers does Allen trace to foreign words, and which to low opinions about their content?

[8] James D. McCabe, Jr. [under pseudonym: "Edward Winslow Martin"], *The Secrets of the Great City* (Philadelphia: Jones, Brothers, 1868), p. 279

[9] Theodore Dreiser, *The Color of a Great City* (New York: Boni and Liveright, 1923), p. 220.

2. Which of the terms does he trace to their form, and which to various uses in addition to reporting the news?

3. What mistaken beliefs about these terms does he correct? What does their actual origin tell us about the role of newspapers or changing attitudes toward them?

4. How does Allen organize his discussion of these terms and their origin?

SUGGESTIONS FOR WRITING

1. Define one of the following words, or another word descriptive of an attitude or behavior, by stating what it is and what it is not. Cite various situations illustrating how the word is used:

a. envious
b. greedy

c. intolerant
d. open-minded

e. romantic
f. cynical

2. Discuss the various meanings of a slang term like *cool* or *tacky*, illustrating through your use of them.

I I

COMPARISON AND CONTRAST

Comparison shows the similarities between people, things, or ideas; contrast shows the differences. The word *comparison* sometimes refers to both kinds of analysis, as in this block comparison of President Franklin Roosevelt with Great Britain's wartime prime minister, Winston S. Churchill:

> Roosevelt, as a public personality, was a spontaneous optimistic, pleasure-loving ruler who dismayed his assistants by the gay and apparently heedless abandon with which he seemed to delight in pursuing two or more totally incompatible policies, and astonished them even more by the swiftness and ease with which he managed to throw off the cares of office during the darkest and most dangerous moments. Churchill too loves pleasure, and he too lacks neither gaiety nor a capacity for exuberant self-expression, together with the habit of blithely cutting Gordian knots in a manner which often upset his experts; but he is not a frivolous man. His nature possesses a dimension of depth — and a corresponding sense of tragic possibilities — which Roosevelt's light-hearted genius instinctively passed by. (Sir Isaiah Berlin, "Mr. Churchill")

Block comparisons present the details of the first subject as a whole and then the details of the second. But the author may choose to develop the comparison point by point, as in this succeeding paragraph on Roosevelt and Churchill:

> Roosevelt played the game of politics with virtuosity, and both his successes and his failures were carried off in splendid style; his performance seemed to flow with effortless skill. Churchill is acquainted with darkness as well as light. Like all inhabitants and even transient visitors of inner worlds, he gives evidence of seasons of agonized brooding and

slow recovery. Roosevelt might have spoken of sweat and blood, but when Churchill offered his people tears, he spoke a word which might have been uttered by Lincoln or Mazzini or Cromwell, but not Roosevelt, great-hearted, generous and perceptive as he was.

Both paragraphs build from similarities to differences. Were the similarities more important, the author would probably have built up to them instead. Notice also that the purpose of the comparison is to arrive at a relative estimate of the two men as leaders. We discover the qualities of Roosevelt through Churchill, and those of Churchill through Roosevelt.

Relative estimates help in explaining something strange or new, as in the following extended comparison of a concentration camp inmate of Nazi Germany or the Soviet Union with other kinds of prisoners.

> Forced labor as a punishment is limited as to time and intensity. The convict retains his rights over his body; he is not absolutely tortured and he is not absolutely dominated. Banishment banishes only from one part of the world to another part of the world, also inhabited by human beings; it does not exclude from the human world altogether. Throughout history slavery has been an institution within a social order; slaves were not, like concentration-camp inmates, withdrawn from the sight and hence the protection of their fellow-men; as instruments of labor they had a definite price and as property a definite value. The concentration-camp inmate has no price, because he can always be replaced; nobody knows to whom he belongs, because he is never seen. From the point of view of normal society he is absolutely superfluous, although in times of acute labor shortage, as in Russia and in Germany during the war, he is used for work. (Hannah Arendt, *The Origins of Totalitarianism*)

Though the author is concerned with defining the status of the concentration camp inmate, she does so through a relative estimate that illuminates the special situation of each kind of prisoner.

MARIE WINN

MARIE WINN is the author of numerous articles and books on parents and children—including *Children Without Childhood* (1983) and *Unplugging the Plug-In Drug* (1987). Her book on children and television, *The*

Plug-In Drug (1977), is based on interviews with parents and children, social workers, teachers, and child psychologists in Denver and New York City. Winn is concerned about our experience with television and about what happens to children when it takes the place of reading. She believes that "a disposition toward 'openness,' " acquired through years of television viewing "has influenced adversely viewers' ability to concentrate, to read, to write clearly—in short, to demonstrate any of the verbal skills a literate society requires." Her comparison between reading and television viewing tells us why.

TELEVISION AND READING

A comparison between reading and viewing may be made in respect to the pace of each experience, and the relative control a person has over that pace, for the pace may influence the ways one uses the material received in each experience. In addition, the pace of each experience may determine how much it intrudes upon other aspects of one's life.   1

The pace of reading, clearly, depends entirely upon the reader. He may read as slowly or as rapidly as he can or wishes to read. If he does not understand something, he may stop and reread it, or go in search of elucidation before continuing. The reader can accelerate his pace when the material is easy or less than interesting, and slow down when it is difficult or enthralling. If what he reads is moving, he can put down the book for a few moments and cope with his emotions without fear of losing anything.   2

The pace of the television experience cannot be controlled by the viewer; only its beginning and end are within his control as he clicks the knob on and off. He cannot slow down a delightful program or speed up a dreary one. He cannot "turn back" if a word or phrase is not understood. The program moves inexorably forward, and what is lost or misunderstood remains so.   3

Nor can the television viewer readily transform the material he receives into a form that might suit his particular emotional needs, as he invariably does with material he reads. The images move too quickly. He cannot use his own imagination to invest the people and events portrayed on television with the personal meanings that would help him understand and resolve relationships and conflicts in his own life; he is under the   4 power of the imagination of the show's creators. In the television experience the eyes and ears are overwhelmed with the immediacy of sights and sounds. They flash from the television set just fast enough for the eyes and ears to take them in before moving on quickly to the new pictures and sounds . . . so as *not to lose the thread.*

Not to lose the thread . . . it is this need, occasioned by the irreversible direction and relentless velocity of the television experience, that not only limits the workings of the viewer's imagination, but also causes television to intrude into human affairs far more than reading experiences can ever do. If someone enters the room while one is watching television— a friend, a relative, a child, someone, perhaps, one has not seen for some time—one must continue to watch or one will lose the thread. The greetings must wait, for the television program will not. A book, of course, can be set aside, with a pang of regret, perhaps, but with no sense of permanent loss.

VOCABULARY

paragraph 2: elucidation, accelerate, enthralling
paragraph 3: inexorably
paragraph 5: irreversible, velocity

QUESTIONS

1. What is the purpose of the comparison, according to paragraph 1?

2. What are the differences? In what order does Winn present them?

3. Does Winn say that we should give up television, or is she making no recommendation?

4. Is the experience of watching a sports event on television much the same as reading about the event? If not, what are the differences? Do these similarities give support to Winn, or do they provide contrary evidence?

SUGGESTIONS FOR WRITING

1. In a few well developed paragraphs, make a comparison between one of the following pairs. State the purpose of your comparison somewhere in your essay, and draw conclusions as you discuss the similarities or differences.

    a. playing baseball (or another sport) and watching baseball

    b. listening to a particular kind of music and dancing to it

    c. reading a book and seeing the movie made from it

    d. reading a newspaper or newsmagazine and reading a novel or a textbook

2. The following activities require similar skills. First discuss these similarities, and then discuss the different skills also required:

    a. parallel parking and backing into a garage

    b. pruning a hedge and pruning a tree

    c. learning to ride a bike and learning to drive

    d. painting a chair and painting a room

EDWARD HOAGLAND

EDWARD HOAGLAND's numerous essays have appeared in *The New Yorker, The New York Times,* and other periodicals and newspapers. They are collected in *The Courage of Turtles* (1970), *Red Wolves and Black Bears* (1976), *Seven Rivers West* (1986), *Balancing Acts* (1992), *Tigers and Ice* (1999), and other books. Hoagland writes on a wide range of subjects—from circus experiences to animal life, the environment, and changes in the American scene. He draws on his life in New York City and rural Vermont in the following.

CITY PEOPLE AND COUNTRY PEOPLE

A New York City editor has asked me for an article about "the invigorating effects of silence," and yet I sometimes find silence enervating, and play the radio so much I fall asleep with it still playing. These cutover New England woods are bilingual when they do speak, as when one stumbles over an ancient scrap of reddish barbed wire bound around a line of pasture birches now lost in a new wilderness of outlaw growth. The sugaring trails are all but effaced, and isolated, suffering apple trees, bloomless lately, are slowly strangling to death in what was once a farmer's water meadow but has become an alder swamp. Some coyotes and a bounding white wolf-sized wild dog live here in this brief interval between the rival epochs of farming and of summer-home development.

In the silence in the house one hears the drumming-ticking of the stove and an ovenbird's or veery's song. The wind sounds like the brook and the brook like the wind, though from the way the dog tilts his head I can infer the presence of a deer in the clump of poplars below the house. It would be very well, except that the birds give their best voice at dawn and the deer—a barren doe whose fortunes I have followed for years (she is lonely herself)—only comes down off my neighbor's land to mine to feed at 6:00 P.M., which leaves a lot of time to kill, and I'm a city man and life is short to me.

City people try to buy time as a rule, when they can, whereas country people are prepared to kill time, although both try to cherish in their mind's eye the notion of a better life ahead. Country people do not behave as if they think life is short; they live on the principle that it is long, and savor variations of the kind best appreciated if most days are the same. City people crowd life when they have the chance; and it is nonsense to suppose that they have become "less observant," less alert than old-time country people were. Even that pioneer, whose lumpy, sharp-roofed log house I have a photo of, and who listened each morning for the location of his big neighbor, the bear, was not more on his toes than the Los Angeles denizens who, four abreast and tailgating, drive the Santa Monica Freeway at seventy miles an hour. His hearing and eyesight may have been better, but the city dweller, it should be borne in mind, wears out his eyes and ears from encountering so much so fast.

Country people tend to consider that they have a corner on righteousness and to distrust most manifestations of cleverness, while people in the city are leery of righteousness but ascribe to themselves all manner of cleverness. The countryman in the meantime, however—at least in my experience—drops in his tracks from a coronary just as promptly and endures his full share of ulcers and nervous attacks, so that his famous procrastination, which is as characteristic a tendency as his righteousness, does him little concrete good. Whether it's the local lawyer you have business with, or the carpenter, the highway engineer, a nearby farmer with a tractor, the delays almost defy belief. Conventionally, most of us, both in the city and the country, say, "Oh, they enjoy life more upstate, and so naturally they work slower." More often, instead of that, it's the undifferentiated outlook they take toward work. Not that there is some fuzzy idea abroad in the country that every farmer is as good as any other farmer. But a cow is finally just a cow, a chore is after all a chore, there is small possibility of what is called in the city "advancement," and so many hard chores remain to be performed in a long lifetime that, even allowing for the satisfactions of craftsmanship, if you keep putting some of them off, you may get away with having to do fewer of them in the end.

What the countryman does frequently possess is a face more content with middle age; and this is an important phenomenon to try to understand, because one of the central questions—central in the sense that if we could ever answer it we'd know a lot—is why our faces lose so much of the hopefulness apparent in photographs taken around the age of nineteen. On our deathbed, in the last throes of death, a strangely convinced, calm, smiling hopefulness will capture our faces once again, if we are like most people, displacing the anxiety and pain that had been there and astonishing the relatives left behind. But in between, why is it "heartbreaking," as both my wife and mother like to say, to look at somebody's picture from a time when he or she was young instead of middle-aged? It scarcely matters who is pictured; a sorrowful, protective feeling sweeps over us as we look at his face then: "Little did he know."

VOCABULARY

paragraph 1: enervating, bilingual, effaced, epoch
paragraph 2: ovenbird, veery
paragraph 3: savor, denizens
paragraph 4: procrastination

Questions

1. What leads Hoagland to reflect on the difference between city and country people?

2. Is he writing from the viewpoint of the country person or city dweller, or both? How do you know?

3. Is the contrast in paragraph 3 a block one—country people, then city people—or is it point by point? What is Hoagland showing through this relative estimate?

4. Hoagland considers both differences and similarities in paragraph 4. How does he organize the paragraph to make a point?

5. What point is Hoagland making in paragraph 5?

Suggestions for Teaching

1. Compare two other groups of people you are familiar with—for example, 13- and 14-year olds and older adolescents—citing similarities and differences. Use your relative estimate to make a point.

2. Compare and contrast one of the following pairs of activities, or another you are familiar with, to arrive at a relative estimate and make a point:

   a. football and touch football

   b. tennis and badminton

   c. checkers and chess

   d. tap and another kind of dancing

   e. writing with a typewriter and word processor

E D W A R D   T.   H A L L

Edward T. Hall, professor of anthropology at Northwestern University from 1967 to 1977, has studied the cultures of many peoples of the world, especially that of the Pueblo Indians of the Southwest. His books include

The Silent Language (1959) and *Beyond Culture* (1976). In *The Hidden Dimension* (1966) Hall states a major theme of his many writings on culture and the nonverbal forms of language: "Contrary to common belief, the many diverse groups that make up our country have proved to be surprisingly persistent in maintaining their separate identities. Superficially, these groups may all look alike and sound somewhat alike but beneath the surface there lie manifold unstated, unformulated differences in the structuring of time, space, materials, and relationships. It is these very things that, though they give significance to our lives, so often result in the distortion of meaning regardless of good intentions when peoples of different cultures interact." In this section Hall combines contrast with other methods of analysis in discussing how people perceive space in different ways. The word *proxemics* is a term coined by Hall for "the interrelated observations and theories of man's use of space as a specialized elaboration of culture."

THE ENGLISH AND THE AMERICANS

It has been said that the English and the Americans are two great people   1
separated by one language. The differences for which language gets blamed may not be due so much to words as to communications on other levels beginning with English intonation (which sounds affected to many Americans) and continuing to ego-linked ways of handling time, space, and materials. If there ever were two cultures in which differences of the proxemic details are marked it is in the educated (public school) English and the middle-class Americans. One of the basic reasons for this wide disparity is that in the United States we use space as a way of classifying people and activities, whereas in England it is the social system that determines who you are. In the United States, your address is an important cue to status (this applies not only to one's home but to the business address as well). The Joneses from Brooklyn and Miami are not as "in" as the Joneses from Newport and Palm Beach. Greenwich and Cape Cod are worlds apart from Newark and Miami. Businesses located on Madison and Park avenues have more tone than those on Seventh and Eighth avenues. A corner office is more prestigious than one next to the elevator or at the end of a long hall. The Englishman, however, is born and brought up in a social system. He is still Lord— no matter where you find him, even if it is behind the counter in a

fishmonger's stall. In addition to class distinctions, there are differences between the English and ourselves in how space is allotted.

The middle-class American growing up in the United States feels he 2 has a right to have his own room, or at least part of a room. My American subjects, when asked to draw an ideal room or office, invariably drew it for themselves and no one else. When asked to draw their present room or office, they drew only their own part of a shared room and then drew a line down the middle. Both male and female subjects identified the kitchen and the master bedroom as belonging to the mother or the wife, whereas Father's territory was a study or a den, if one was available; otherwise, it was "the shop," "the basement," or sometimes only a workbench or the garage. American women who want to be alone can go to the bedroom and close the door. The closed door is the sign meaning "Do not disturb" or "I'm angry." An American is available if his door is open at home or at his office. He is expected not to shut himself off but to maintain himself in a state of constant readiness to answer the demands of others. Closed doors are for conferences, private conversations, and business, work that requires concentration, study, resting, sleeping, dressing, and sex.

The middle- and upper-class Englishman, on the other hand, is 3 brought up in a nursery shared with brothers and sisters. The oldest occupies a room by himself which he vacates when he leaves for boarding school, possibly even at the age of nine or ten. The difference between a room of one's own and early conditioning to shared space, while seeming inconsequential, has an important effect on the Englishman's attitude toward his own space. He may never have a permanent "room of his own" and seldom expects one or feels he is entitled to one. Even Members of Parliament have no offices and often conduct their business on the terrace overlooking the Thames. As a consequence, the English are puzzled by the American need for a secure place in which to work, an office. Americans working in England may become annoyed if they are not provided with what they consider appropriate enclosed work space. In regard to the need for walls as a screen for the ego, this places the Americans somewhere between the Germans and the English.

The contrasting English and American patterns have some remarkable 4 implications, particularly if we assume that man, like other animals, has a built-in need to shut himself off from others from time to time. An English student in one of my seminars typified what happens when hidden patterns clash. He was quite obviously experiencing strain in his relationships with Americans. Nothing seemed to go right and it was quite clear from his remarks that we did not know how to behave. An analysis of his complaints showed that a major source of irritation was that no American seemed to be able to pick up the subtle clues that there were times when he didn't want his thoughts intruded on. As he stated it, "I'm walking around the apartment and it seems that whenever I want to be alone my roommate starts talking to me. Pretty soon he's asking 'What's the matter?' and wants to know if I'm angry. By then I am angry and say something."

It took some time but finally we were able to identify most of the   5 contrasting features of the American and British problems that were in conflict in this case. When the American wants to be alone he goes into a room and shuts the door—he depends on architectural features for screening. For an American to refuse to talk to someone else present in the same room, to give them the "silent treatment," is the ultimate form of rejection and a sure sign of great displeasure. The English, on the other hand, lacking rooms of their own since childhood, never developed the practice of using space as a refuge from others. They have in effect in-ternalized a set of barriers, which they erect and which others are sup-posed to recognize. Therefore, the more the Englishman shuts himself off when he is with an American the more likely the American is to break in to assure himself that all is well. Tension lasts until the two get to know each other. The important point is that the spatial and architec-tural needs of each are not the same at all.

VOCABULARY

paragraph 1: intonation, ego-linked, fishmonger

QUESTIONS

1. What is Hall's thesis, and where does he first state it? Where does he restate it later in the essay?

2. How does he organize the contrast between the English and the Amer-icans? Does he contrast the English and American patterns point by point or in blocks? Or does he mix these methods of organization?

3. How does he illustrate these patterns? Does he illustrate all of them?

4. Hall traces cause-and-effect relations through contrast of living patterns. What are the chief relations he traces?

5. How do the examples explain the phrase *internalized a set of barriers,* in the concluding paragraph? What does Hall mean by *screening?*

6. What use does he make of classification in the whole essay? On what basis does he divide the English and the Americans?

SUGGESTIONS FOR WRITING

1. Discuss the extent to which your study habits fit the English or the American pattern. Use your analysis to comment on the accuracy of Hall's thesis.

2. Contrast two of your friends or relatives on the basis of their attitudes toward space and architecture or toward privacy. State the similarities before commenting on the differences. Notice that the differences may be slight ones, and even slight differences may be revealing of people.

RICHARD A. LANHAM

For many years the director of writing programs at University of California, Los Angeles, and later president of Rhetorica, Inc., a media production company, RICHARD A. LANHAM has written about composition and communication in *Style: An Anti-Textbook* (1974), *Literacy and the Survival of Humanism* (1983), and *Electronic Word: Democracy, Technology, and the Arts* (1993). In the following essay he discusses a new kind of literacy and its effects today.

DIGITAL LITERACY

The word "literacy," meaning the ability to read and write, has gradually   1
extended its grasp in the digital age until it has come to mean the ability
to understand information, however presented. Increasingly, information
is being offered in a new way: instead of black letters printed on a white

page, the new format blends words with recorded sounds and images into a rich and volatile mixture. The ingredients of this combination, which has come to be called multimedia, are not new, but the recipe is.

New, too, is the mixture's intrinsic volatility. Print captures utterance—the words are frozen on the page. This fixity confers authority and sometimes even timeless immortality. That is why we value it, want to get things down in "black-and-white," write a sonnet, in Horace's words, "more lasting than bronze." The multimedia signal puts utterance back into time: the reader can change it, reformat and rescale it, transform the images, sounds and words. And yet, at the end of these elegant variations, the original can be summoned back with a keystroke.

Print literacy aimed to pin down information; multimedia literacy couples fixity and novelty in a fertile oscillation. Contrary to the proverbial wisdom, in a digital universe you can eat your cake and have it, too: keep your original and digest it on your own terms. And because digital code is replicable without material cost, you can give your cake away as well.

Printed books created the modern idea of "intellectual property" because they were fixed in form and difficult to replicate. One could therefore sell and own them, and the livelihoods of printer and author could be sustained. This copyright structure dissolves when we introduce the changeable multimedia signal. We will have to invent another scaffolding to fit the new literacy. Judging from the early signs, it won't be easy.

There is one other way in which digital flexibility is radical. If we ask, looking through the wide-angle lens of Western cultural history, "What does multimedia literacy do?", a surprisingly focused answer comes back. It recaptures the expressivity of oral cultures, which printed books, and handwritten manuscripts before them, excluded.

In writing this text, for example, I have been trying to create a credible "speaking voice," to convince you that I am a person of sense and restraint. Now imagine that you can "click" on an "author box." I appear as a moving image, walk into the margin and start to speak, commenting on my own argument, elaborating it, underlining it with my voice, gesture and dress—as can happen nowadays in a multimedia text.

What has changed? Many of the clues we use in the oral culture of daily life, the intuitive stylistic judgments that we depend on, have returned. You can see me for yourself. You can hear my voice. You can feed that voice back into the voiceless prose and thus animate it. Yet the writing remains as well. You can see the author with stereoscopic depth, speaking in a space both literate and oral.

Oral cultures and literate cultures go by very different sets of rules. 8
They observe different senses of time, as you will speedily understand if
you listen to one of Fidel Castro's four-hour speeches. Oral cultures pro-
long discourse because, without it, they cease to be; they exist only in
time. But writing compresses time. An author crams years of work into
some 300 pages that the reader may experience in a single day.

Oral and literate cultures create different senses of self and society, 9
too. The private reflective self created by reading differs profoundly from
the unselfconscious social role played by participants in a culture that
knows no writing. Literacy allows us to see human society in formal terms
that are denied to an oral culture that just plays out its drama.

The oral and written ways of being in the world have contended ran- 10
corously throughout Western history, the rancor being driven more often than not by literate prejudice against the oral rules. Now the great
gulf in communication and in cultural organization that was opened up
by unchanging letters on a static surface promises to be healed by a new
kind of literacy, one that orchestrates these differences in a signal at the
same time more energizing and more irenic than the literacy of print.

If we exchange our wide-angle cultural lens for a close-up, we can ob- 11
serve the fundamental difference between the two kinds of literacies. In
the world of print, the idea and its expression are virtually one. The
meaning takes the form of words; words generate the meaning. Digital
literacy works in an inherently different way. The same digital code that
expresses words and numbers can, if the parameters of expression are
adjusted, generate sounds and images. This parametric variation stands
at the center of digital expressivity, a role it could never play in print.

The multiple facets of this digital signal constitute the core difference 12
between the two media, which our efforts in data visualization and sonification have scarcely begun to explore. If we think of the institutional
practices built on the separation of words, images and sounds—such as
separate departments for literature, art and music—we can glimpse the
profound changes that will come when we put them back together.

To be deeply literate in the digital world means being skilled at de- 13
ciphering complex images and sounds as well as the syntactical subtleties
of words. Above all, it means being at home in a shifting mixture of
words, images and sounds. Multimedia literacy makes us all skilled oper-
agoers: it requires that we be very quick on our feet in moving from one
kind of medium to another. We must know what kinds of expression fit

what kinds of knowledge and become skilled at presenting our information in the medium that our audience will find easiest to understand. We all know people who learn well from books and others who learn by hands-on experience; others, as we say in music, "learn by ear." Digital literacy greatly enhances our ability to suit the medium both to the information being offered and to the audience. Looked at one way, this new sensory targeting makes communication more efficient. Looked at another, it simply makes it more fun.

The multimedia mixture of talents was last advanced as an aristocratic ideal by the Renaissance humanists. The courtly lord and lady were equally accomplished in poetry, music and art. The Renaissance ideal now presents itself, broadened in scope and coarsened in fiber perhaps, as the common core of citizenship in an information society.

At its heart, the new digital literacy is thus profoundly democratic. It insists that the rich mixture of perceptive talents once thought to distinguish a ruling aristocracy must now be extended to everyone. It thus embodies fully the inevitable failures, and the extravagant hope, of democracy itself.

VOCABULARY

paragraph 2: intrinsic, volatility
paragraph 3: oscillation, replicable
paragraph 7: animate, stereoscopic
paragraph 10: rancor, irenic
paragraph 11: parameters
paragraph 12: sonification
paragraph 13: syntactical

QUESTIONS

1. How does Lanham define *multimedia* in paragraph 1? How does he further explain and illustrate the term in paragraph 2?

2. What are the characteristics of print literacy? What are its advantages? How is multimedia literacy an advance over it?

3. Is the comparison of oral and literate cultures in paragraphs 8 and 9 block or point by point? What relative estimate does Lanham reach? What point does he make about the two cultures in paragraph 10?

4. How does the comparison of the two in paragraph 11 advance the discussion of digital literacy?

5. What is Lanham's thesis? Where does he introduce and restate it? How does the comparison of oral and literate cultures support the thesis?

SUGGESTIONS FOR WRITING

1. Lanham states that "oral cultures and literate cultures go by very different sets of rules." Illustrate from your own experience—perhaps the oral culture of phone conversations and talk among friends and written communication with absent ones.

2. A new invention or technology like the Internet may change long-established habits—the way we think, communicate, spend our leisure time. Discuss one such invention or technology—perhaps the Internet—that has changed habits of yours. In the course of the discussion, discuss the gain and loss.

12

ANALOGY

Illustrative *analogy* is a special kind of example, a comparison, usually point by point, between two quite different things or activities for the purpose of explanation—a child growing like a tender plant and needing sun, water, and a receptive soil as well as proper care from a skilled gardener. But there are differences also, and if there is danger of the analogy being carried too far (children are not so tender that they need as much protection as plants from the hazards of living), the writer may state these differences to limit the inferences readers may draw. The writer has chosen the analogy for the sake of vivid illustration and nothing more. We will see later that analogy is often used in argument: children *should* be fully protected from various hazards because they are tender plants. The argument will stand or fall depending on how convinced we are of the similarities and of the unimportance of the differences.

Analogy is often used in explanations of scientific ideas. One of the most famous is Fred Hoyle's analogy between the moving apart of the galaxies in the universe and an expanding raisin cake:

> Suppose the cake swells uniformly as it cooks, but the raisins themselves remain of the same size. Let each raisin represent a cluster of galaxies, and imagine yourself inside one of them. As the cake swells, you will observe that all the other raisins move away from you. Moreover, the farther away the raisin, the faster it will seem to move. When the cake has swollen to twice its initial dimensions, the distance between all the raisins will have doubled itself—two raisins that were initially an inch apart will now be two inches apart; two raisins that were a foot apart will have moved two feet apart. Since the entire action takes place within the same time interval, obviously the more distant raisins must move apart faster than those close at hand. So it happens with the clusters of galaxies.

And Hoyle draws a further conclusion from his analogy:

> No matter which raisin you happen to be inside, the others will always move away from you. Hence the fact that we observe all the other galaxies to be moving away from us does not mean that we are situated at the center of the universe. Indeed, it seems certain that the universe has no center. A cake may be said to have a center only because it has a boundary. We must imagine the cake to extend outward without any boundary, an infinite cake, so to speak, which means that however much cake we care to consider there is always more. ("When Time Began")

Hoyle points out the limits of the analogy in these final sentences. One advantage of the raisin analogy is the disparity of size between a raisin and a galaxy—a system of sometimes billions of stars occupying an enormous amount of space. The disparity in size provides a relative estimate of size in the universe.

LOREN EISELEY

LOREN EISELEY (1907–1977) was Benjamin Franklin Professor of Anthropology at the University of Pennsylvania. His many books on human origins and society and other topics include *The Immense Journey* (1957), *The Firmament of Time* (1960), *The Unexpected Universe* (1969), *The Night Country* (1971), and *The Innocent Assassins* (1973). In his autobiography, *All the Strange Hours* (1975), Eiseley describes his Nebraska boyhood and later experiences that shaped him as an anthropologist and writer. In the following excerpt, he uses an extended analogy and a childhood experience to comment on the resources the personal essayist draws upon.

WHAT MAKES A WRITER

In all the questioning about what makes a writer, and especially perhaps   1
the personal essayist, I have seen little reference to this fact; namely, that
the brain has become a kind of unseen artist's loft. There are pictures

that hang askew, pictures with outlines barely chalked in, pictures torn, pictures the artist has striven unsuccessfully to erase, pictures that only emerge and glow in a certain light. They have all been teleported, stolen, as it were, out of time. They represent no longer the sequential flow of ordinary memory. They can be pulled about on easels, examined within the mind itself. The act is not one of total recall like that of the professional mnemonist. Rather it is the use of things extracted from their context in such a way that they have become the unique possession of a single life. The writer sees back to these transports alone, bare, perhaps few in number, but endowed with a symbolic life. He cannot obliterate them. He can only drag them about, magnify or reduce them as his artistic sense dictates, or juxtapose them in order to enhance a pattern. One thing he cannot do. He cannot destroy what will not be destroyed; he cannot determine in advance what will enter his mind.

By way of example, I cannot explain why, out of many forgotten 2 childhood episodes, my mind should retain as bright as yesterday the peculiar actions of a redheaded woodpecker. I must have been about six years old, and in the alley behind our house I had found the bird lying beneath a telephone pole. Looking back, I can only assume that he had received in some manner a stunning but not fatal shock of electricity. Coming upon him, seemingly dead but uninjured, I had carried him back to our porch and stretched him out to admire his color.

In a few moments, much to my surprise, he twitched and jerked 3 upright. Then in a series of quick hops he reached the corner of the house and began to ascend in true woodpecker fashion—a hitch of the grasping feet, the bracing of the tail, and then, wonder of wonders, the knock, knock, knock, of the questing beak against our house. He was taking up life where it had momentarily left him, somewhere on the telephone pole. When he reached the top of the porch he flew away.

So there the picture lies. Even the coarse-grained wood of the porch 4 comes back to me. If anyone were to ask me what else happened in that spring of 1913 I would stare blindly and be unable to answer with surety. But, as I have remarked, somewhere amidst the obscure lumber loft of my head that persistent hammering still recurs. Did it stay because it was my first glimpse of unconsciousness, resurrection, and time lapse presented in bright color? I do not know. I have never chanced to meet another adult who has a childhood woodpecker almost audibly rapping in his skull.

VOCABULARY

paragraph 1: teleported, mnemonist, transports, obliterate, juxtapose, enhance
paragraph 4: obscure, resurrection

QUESTIONS

1. What are the similarities between the brain of the writer and the "artist's unseen loft"?

2. Would the analogy be more or less exact if Eiseley had compared the writer's mind to the basement of the artist's house?

3. To what extent could a diary or journal serve as another analogy for the special qualities Eiseley is illustrating? Are the differences significant enough to weaken the analogy?

4. What idea is Eiseley illustrating in paragraphs 2–4?

SUGGESTION FOR WRITING

Use an analogy to explain the sensation of being alone in a car in heavy traffic or a storm or to explain a similar experience that invites comparison. At some point in your explanation, comment on the differences between the things you are comparing.

LOREN EISELEY

LOREN EISELEY had the gift of explaining highly complex ideas to the general reader. In this section from *The Invisible Pyramid* (1972), he uses brief, revealing analogies to help the reader understand a series of ideas related to space travel.

THE COSMIC PRISON

This, then, is the secret nature of the universe over which the ebullient senator so recklessly proclaimed our absolute mastery. Time in that universe is in excess of ten billion years. It recedes backward into a narrowing funnel where, at some inconceivable point of concentration, the monobloc containing all the matter that composes the galaxies exploded in the one gigantic instant of creation.

Along with that explosion space itself is rushing outward. Stars and the great island galaxies in which they cluster are more numerous than the blades of grass upon a plain. To speak of man as "mastering" such a cosmos is about the equivalent of installing a grasshopper as Secretary General of the United Nations. Worse, in fact, for no matter what system of propulsion man may invent in the future, the galaxies on the outer rim of visibility are fleeing faster than he can approach them. Moreover, the light that he is receiving from them left its source in the early history of the planet earth. There is no possible way of even establishing their present existence. As the British astronomer Sir Bernard Lovell has so appropriately remarked, "At the limit of present-day observations our information is a few billion years out of date."

Light travels at a little over one hundred and eighty-six thousand miles a second, far beyond the conceivable speed of any spaceship devised by man, yet it takes light something like one hundred thousand years just to travel across the star field of our own galaxy, the Milky Way. It has been estimated that to reach the nearest star to our own, four light-years away, would require, at the present speed of our spaceships, a time equivalent to more than the whole of written history, indeed one hundred thousand earthly years would be a closer estimate—a time as long, perhaps, as the whole existence of *Homo sapiens* upon earth. And the return, needless to state, would consume just as long a period.

Even if our present rocket speeds were stepped up by a factor of one hundred, human generations would pass on the voyage. An unmanned probe into the nearer galactic realms would be gone so long that its intended mission, in fact the country which sent it forth, might both have vanished into the mists of history before its messages began to be received. All this, be it noted, does not begin to involve us in those intergalactic distances across which a radio message from a cruising spaceship might take hundreds of years to be received and a wait of other hundreds before a reply would filter back.

We are, in other words, truly in the position of the blood cell exploring our body. We are limited in time, by analogy a miniature replica of the cosmos, since we too individually ascend from a primordial atom, exist, and grow in space, only to fall back in dissolution. We cannot, in terms of the time dimension as we presently know it, either travel or survive the interstellar distances.

Two years ago I chanced to wander with a group of visiting scholars into a small planetarium in a nearby city. In the dark in a remote back seat, I grew tired and fell asleep while a lecture was progressing. My eyes had closed upon a present-day starry night as represented in the northern latitudes. After what seemed in my uneasy slumber the passage of a long period of time, I started awake in the dark, my eyes fixed in amazement upon the star vault overhead. All was quiet in the neighboring high-backed seats. I could see no one. Suddenly I seemed adrift under a vast and unfamiliar sky. Constellations with which I was familiar had shifted, grown minute, or vanished. I rubbed my eyes. This was not the universe in which I had fallen asleep. It seemed more still, more remote, more enormous, and inconceivably more solitary. A queer sense of panic struck me, as though I had been transported out of time.

Only after some attempt to orient myself by a diminishing pole star did the answer come to me by murmurs from without. I was not the last man on the planet, far in the dying future. My companions had arisen and left, while the lecturer had terminated his address by setting the planetarium lights forward to show the conformation of the heavens as they might exist in the remote future of the expanding universe. Distances had lengthened. All was poised, chill, and alone.

I sat for a moment experiencing the sensation all the more intensely because of the slumber which left me feeling as though ages had elapsed. The sky gave little sign of movement. It seemed drifting in a slow indeterminate swirl, as though the forces of expansion were equaled at last by some monstrous tug of gravity at the heart of things. In this remote night sky of the far future I felt myself waiting upon the inevitable, the great drama and surrender of the inward fall, the heart contraction of the cosmos.

I was still sitting when, like the slightest leaf movement on a flooding stream, I saw the first faint galaxy of a billion suns race like a silverfish across the night and vanish. It was enough: the fall was equal to the flash of creation. I had sensed it waiting there under the star vault of the planetarium. Now it was cascading like a torrent through the ages in my head. I had experienced, by chance, the farthest reach of the star prison. I had similarly lived to see the beginning descent into the maelstrom.

VOCABULARY

paragraph 1: ebullient, monobloc
paragraph 4: intergalactic
paragraph 5: primordial, interstellar
paragraph 7: orient
paragraph 9: maelstrom

QUESTIONS

1. In paragraph 2 Eiseley depends on the simple comparison or analogy of blades of grass to suggest how many stars and galaxies exist. What other such analogies does he use in paragraphs 1 and 9 for explanation?

2. What are the points of similarity in the analogy in paragraph 5? Does the difference in size between humankind and the cosmos increase the effectiveness of the analogy or diminish it?

3. What point is Eiseley making through the experience described in paragraphs 6–9? How is the experience analogous to that of the space traveler as well as to the human being on Earth?

4. Eiseley is arguing against the view that humans have attained or will attain "absolute mastery" over the universe. Is he also implying that exploration of far space is a useless enterprise, given the enormous space between stars and galaxies?

SUGGESTION FOR WRITING

Eiseley states in a later section of *The Invisible Pyramid* that "there are other confinements . . . than that imposed by the enormous distances of the cosmos." Our senses, he suggests, confine us through their limitations. Write an essay developing this point through your own experiences. Focus on one or two of the senses.

M I C H I O   K A K U

MICHIO KAKU, Professor of Theoretical Physics at the City College of the City University of New York, has written widely on quantum physics and the theory of higher dimensional space. His other books include *Beyond Einstein* (1987), with Jennifer Trainer, *Visions: How Science Will Revolutionize the 21st Century* (1997), and *Hyperspace* (1994), from which the following section is taken. Kaku uses an illustrative analogy to explain how his interest in the ideas of Albert Einstein led to scientific experiments of his own.

THE EDUCATION OF A PHYSICIST

Two incidents from my childhood greatly enriched my understanding of the world and sent me on a course to become a theoretical physicist.

I remember that my parents would sometimes take me to visit the famous Japanese Tea Garden in San Francisco. One of my happiest childhood memories is of crouching next to the pond, mesmerized by the brilliantly colored carp swimming slowly beneath the water lilies.

In these quiet moments, I felt free to let my imagination wander; I would ask myself silly questions that only a child might ask, such as how the carp in that pond would view the world around them. I thought, What a strange world theirs must be!

Living their entire lives in the shallow pond, the carp would believe that their "universe" consisted of the murky water and the lilies. Spending most of their time foraging on the bottom of the pond, they would be only dimly aware that an alien world could exist above the surface. The nature of my world was beyond their comprehension. I was intrigued that I could sit only a few inches from the carp, yet be separated from them by an immense chasm. The carp and I spent our lives in two distinct universes, never entering each other's world, yet were separated by only the thinnest barrier, the water's surface.

I once imagined that there may be carp "scientists" living among the fish. They would, I thought, scoff at any fish who proposed that a parallel world could exist just above the lilies. To a carp "scientist," the only things that were real were what the fish could see or touch. The pond was everything. An unseen world beyond the pond made no scientific sense.

Once I was caught in a rainstorm. I noticed that the pond's surface was bombarded by thousands of tiny raindrops. The pond's surface became turbulent, and the water lilies were being pushed in all directions by water waves. Taking shelter from the wind and the rain, I wondered how all this appeared to the carp. To them, the water lilies would appear to be moving around by themselves, without anything pushing them. Since the water they lived in would appear invisible, much like the air and space around us, they would be baffled that the water lilies could move around by themselves.

Their "scientists," I imagined, would concoct a clever invention called a "force" in order to hide their ignorance. Unable to comprehend that there could be waves on the unseen surface, they would conclude that lilies could move without being touched because a mysterious invisible entity called a force acted between them. They might give this illusion impressive, lofty names (such as action-at-a-distance, or the ability of the lilies to move without anything touching them).

Once I imagined what would happen if I reached down and lifted one of the carp "scientists" out of the pond. Before I threw him back into the water, he might wiggle furiously as I examined him. I wondered how this would appear to the rest of the carp. To them, it would be a truly unsettling event. They would first notice that one of their "scientists" had disappeared from their universe. Simply vanished, without leaving a trace. Wherever they would look, there would be no evidence of the missing carp in their universe. Then, seconds later, when I threw him back into the pond, the "scientist" would abruptly reappear out of nowhere. To the other carp, it would appear that a miracle had happened.

After collecting his wits, the "scientist" would tell a truly amazing story. "Without warning," he would say, "I was somehow lifted out of the universe (the pond) and hurled into a mysterious nether world, with blinding lights and strangely shaped objects that I had never seen before. The strangest of all was the creature who held me prisoner, who did not resemble a fish in the slightest. I was shocked to see that it had no fins whatsoever, but nevertheless could move without them. It struck me that the familiar laws of nature no longer applied in this nether world. Then, just as suddenly, I found myself thrown back into our universe." (This story, of course, of a journey beyond the universe would be so fantastic that most of the carp would dismiss it as utter poppycock.)

I often think that we are like the carp swimming contentedly in that 10 pond. We live out our lives in our own "pond," confident that our universe consists of only those things we can see or touch. Like the carp, our universe consists of only the familiar and the visible. We smugly refuse to admit that parallel universes or dimensions can exist next to ours, just beyond our grasp. If our scientists invent concepts like forces, it is only because they cannot visualize the invisible vibrations that fill the empty space around us. Some scientists sneer at the mention of higher dimensions because they cannot be conveniently measured in the laboratory.

Ever since that time, I have been fascinated by the possibility of other 11 dimensions. Like most children, I devoured adventure stories in which time travelers entered other dimensions and explored unseen parallel universes, where the unusual laws of physics could be conveniently suspended. I grew up wondering if ships that wandered into the Bermuda Triangle mysteriously vanished into a hole in space; I marveled at Isaac Asimov's Foundation Series, in which the discovery of hyperspace travel led to the rise of a Galactic Empire.

A second incident from my childhood also made a deep, lasting im- 12 pression on me. When I was 8 years old, I heard a story that would stay with me for the rest of my life. I remember my schoolteachers telling the class about a great scientist who had just died. They talked about him with great reverence, calling him one of the greatest scientists in all history. They said that very few people could understand his ideas, but that his discoveries changed the entire world and everything around us. I didn't understand much of what they were trying to tell us, but what most intrigued me about this man was that he died before he could complete his greatest discovery. They said he spent years on this theory, but he died with his unfinished papers still sitting on his desk.

I was fascinated by the story. To a child, this was a great mystery. 13 What was his unfinished work? What was in those papers on his desk? What problem could possibly be so difficult and so important that such a great scientist would dedicate years of his life to its pursuit? Curious, I decided to learn all I could about Albert Einstein and his unfinished theory. I still have warm memories of spending many quiet hours reading every book I could find about this great man and his theories. When I exhausted the books in our local library, I began to scour libraries and bookstores across the city, eagerly searching for more clues. I soon learned that this story was far more exciting than any murder mystery and more important than anything I could ever imagine. I decided that I would try to get to the root of this mystery, even if I had to become a theoretical physicist to do it.

I soon learned that the unfinished papers on Einstein's desk were an attempt to construct what he called the unified field theory, a theory that could explain all the laws of nature, from the tiniest atom to the largest galaxy. However, being a child, I didn't understand that perhaps there was a link between the carp swimming in the Tea Garden and the unfinished papers lying on Einstein's desk. I didn't understand that higher dimensions might be the key to solving the unified field theory.

Later, in high school, I exhausted most of the local libraries and often visited the Stanford University physics library. There, I came across the fact that Einstein's work made possible a new substance called antimatter, which would act like ordinary matter but would annihilate upon contact with matter in a burst of energy. I also read that scientists had built large machines, or "atom smashers," that could produce microscopic quantities of this exotic substance in the laboratory.

One advantage of youth is that it is undaunted by worldly constraints that would ordinarily seem insurmountable to most adults. Not appreciating the obstacles involved, I set out to build my own atom smasher. I studied the scientific literature until I was convinced that I could build what was called a betatron, which could boost electrons to millions of electron volts. (A million electron volts is the energy attained by electrons accelerated by a field of a million volts.)

First, I purchased a small quantity of sodium-22, which is radioactive and naturally emits positrons (the antimatter counterpart of electrons). Then I built what is called a cloud chamber, which makes visible the tracks left by subatomic particles. I was able to take hundreds of beautiful photographs of the tracks left behind by antimatter. Next, I scavenged around large electronic warehouses in the area, assembled the necessary hardware, including hundreds of pounds of scrap transformer steel, and built a 2.3-million-electron-volt betatron in my garage that would be powerful enough to produce a beam of antielectrons. To construct the monstrous magnets necessary for the betatron, I convinced my parents to help me wind 22 miles of copper wire on the high-school football field. We spent Christmas vacation on the 50-yard line, winding and assembling the massive coils that would bend the paths of the high-energy electrons.

When finally constructed, the 300-pound, 6-kilowatt betatron con- 18 sumed every ounce of energy my house produced. When I turned it on, I would usually blow every fuse, and the house would suddenly become dark. With the house plunged periodically into darkness, my mother would often shake her head. (I imagined that she probably wondered why she couldn't have a child who played baseball or basketball, instead of building these huge electrical machines in the garage.) I was gratified that the machine successfully produced a magnetic field 20,000 times more powerful than the earth's magnetic field, which is necessary to accelerate a beam of electrons.

VOCABULARY

paragraph 2: mesmerized
paragraph 9: nether
paragraph 15: antimatter
paragraph 16: electron volt
paragraph 17: cloud chamber

QUESTIONS

1. In the analogy developed in paragraphs 5–10, to whom does Kaku compare the carp in the Tea Garden pond, and to whom does he compare the carp scientists? To what does he compare the rainstorm that disturbs the pond?

2. In stating that the carp scientist disappears from the pond, then suddenly reappears, is Kaku suggesting that something similar can occur in our world? Or is what happens to the scientist merely fanciful?

3. What is the point of the analogy?

4. What is the link between the unfinished papers on Einstein's desk and the carp in the pond?

5. Is Kaku making a general point, explicitly or implicitly, in describing how his interest in physics developed and what experiments he performed while in high school?

SUGGESTIONS FOR WRITING

1. Describe how your interest in a particular science or art developed. Be specific in describing personal experiences.

2. Develop an analogy that you might use to explain to a child why the sun rises and sets, or to explain a similar phenomenon.

13

PROCESS

A process is a series of connected actions or steps, each one developing from the preceding and leading to a product or an effect. A mechanical process is one that we create, like cooking over an outdoor fire or sharpening a knife or changing a flat tire.

Natural processes, like the growth of a plant or the death of a star or the onset and progression of a disease, are not ones that we create, though in some of these we may play a role in initiating the process, as in the planting of a seed. To historians, economists, and political scientists, a process is a traceable series of events they consider repeatable and believe recur—for example, the sequence of events that lead to economic recession. Here there may be disagreement about what is taking place, or even whether such a process—a definable sequence of events—actually exists.

MARK TWAIN

Earlier in this book (p. 11), Mark Twain describes the difficulty of learning the shape of the Mississippi River. One of the hazards of navigation was the river at low stage, at which the steamboat might founder. Twain traces the process of sounding the river to discover its depth. Later in this book (p. 296), Twain tells us why he wanted to become a river pilot.

Sounding

When the river is very low, and one's steamboat is "drawing all the wa-   1
ter" there is in the channel—or a few inches more, as was often the case
in the old times—one must be painfully circumspect in his piloting. We
used to have to "sound" a number of particularly bad places almost every
trip when the river was at a very low stage.

Sounding is done in this way. The boat ties up at the shore, just above   2
the shoal crossing; the pilot not on watch takes his "cub" or steersman
and a picked crew of men (sometimes an officer also), and goes out in
the yawl—provided the boat has not that rare and sumptuous luxury, a
regularly-devised "sounding-boat"—and proceeds to hunt for the best
water, the pilot on duty watching his movements through a spyglass,
meantime, and in some instances assisting by signals of the boat's whistle, signifying "try higher up" or "try lower down;" for the surface of
the water, like an oil-painting, is more expressive and intelligible when
inspected from a little distance than very close at hand. The whistle signals are seldom necessary, however; never, perhaps, except when the wind
confuses the significant ripples upon the water's surface. When the yawl
has reached the shoal place, the speed is slackened, the pilot begins to
sound the depth with a pole ten or twelve feet long, and the steersman
at the tiller obeys the order to "hold her up to starboard;" or "let her
fall off to larboard;"[1] or "steady—steady as you go."

When the measurements indicate that the yawl is approaching the   3
shoalest part of the reef, the command is given to "ease all!" Then the
men stop rowing and the yawl drifts with the current. The next order
is, "Stand by with the buoy!" The moment the shallowest point is
reached, the pilot delivers the order, "Let go the buoy!" and over she
goes. If the pilot is not satisfied, he sounds the place again; if he finds
better water higher up or lower down, he removes the buoy to that place.
Being finally satisfied, he gives the order, and all the men stand their
oars straight up in the air, in line; a blast from the boat's whistle indicates that the signal has been seen; then the men "give way" on their
oars and lay the yawl alongside the buoy; the steamer comes creeping

---

[1] The term "larboard' is never used at sea, now, to signify the left hand; but was always
used on the river in my time.

carefully down, is pointed straight at the buoy, husbands her power for the coming struggle, and presently, at the critical moment, turns on all her steam and goes grinding and wallowing over the buoy and the sand, and gains the deep water beyond. Or maybe she doesn't; maybe she "strikes and swings." Then she has to while away several hours (or days) sparring herself off.

Sometimes a buoy is not laid at all, but the yawl goes ahead, hunt-   4
ing the best water, and the steamer follows along in its wake. Often there is a deal of fun and excitement about sounding, especially if it is a glorious summer day, or a blustering night. But in winter the cold and the peril take most of the fun out of it.

A buoy is nothing but a board four or five feet long, with one end   5
turned up; it is a reversed school-house bench, with one of the supports left and the other removed. It is anchored on the shoalest part of the reef by a rope with a heavy stone made fast to the end of it. But for the resistance of the turned-up end of the reversed bench, the current would pull the buoy under water. At night, a paper lantern with a candle in it is fastened on top of the buoy, and this can be seen a mile or more, a little glimmering spark in the waste of blackness.

Nothing delights a cub so much as an opportunity to go out sound-   6
ing. There is such an air of adventure about it; often there is danger; it is so gaudy and man-of-war-like to sit up in the stern-sheets and steer a swift yawl; there is something fine about the exultant spring of the boat when an experienced old sailor crew throw their souls into the oars; it is lovely to see the white foam stream away from the bows; there is music in the rush of the water; it is deliciously exhilarating, in summer, to go speeding over the breezy expanses of the river when the world of wavelets is dancing in the sun. It is such grandeur, too, to the cub, to get a chance to give an order; for often the pilot will simply say, "Let her go about!" and leave the rest to the cub, who instantly cries, in his sternest tone of command, "Ease starboard! Strong on the larboard! Starboard give way! With a will, men!" The cub enjoys sounding for the further reason that the eyes of the passengers are watching all the yawl's movements with absorbing interest if the time be daylight; and if it be night he knows that those same wondering eyes are fastened upon the yawl's lantern as it glides out into the gloom and dims away in the remote distance.

VOCABULARY

paragraph 1: circumspect
paragraph 2: shoal, yawl, starboard
paragraph 3: husbands, sparring
paragraph 4: wake
paragraph 6: gaudy

QUESTIONS

1. What are the essential steps in sounding the river? Does Twain present these in the order performed?

2. What shows that Twain is describing the process for those who have traveled the river, as well as those who haven't?

3. Had he been writing for a special audience—namely, river pilots in training—what information would he probably have omitted? What additional information would he have provided?

4. What did he gain by describing the pleasure of a cub pilot given command?

SUGGESTIONS FOR WRITING

1. Describe a difficult process you learned to perform, for readers who have no interest in performing it themselves.

2. Rewrite your description for readers who wish to perform it.

JEARL WALKER

JEARL WALKER, Professor of Physics at Cleveland State University, is the author of *The Flying Circus of Physics* (1977) and *Roundabout: The Physics of Rotation in the Everyday World* (1985). In this excerpt from an article on outdoor cooking in the August 1985 issue of *Scientific*

American, Walker explains the physical basis of various mechanical cooking processes. Proceeding step by step, he allows his readers to visualize each of the processes. In the course of his explanation, he describes the necessary implements.

OUTDOOR COOKING

Outdoor cooking can be a pleasant part of camping or a key to survival   1
in an emergency. It can also provide a study in thermal physics: how heat can be transferred from a heat source to food. This month I analyze several ways of cooking food with flames, coals or charcoal briquettes. The techniques require little or no equipment.

A few fundamental concepts of thermal physics underlie all cooking   2
procedures. One concept involves what is meant by heat and temperature. The atoms and molecules of a substance move randomly at any temperature above absolute zero. In a solid the motion consists in rotation and vibration. In a gas or a liquid the phenomenon also includes the random motion of atoms and molecules that are traveling in straight lines, colliding and then again traveling in straight lines.

When a substance is heated, the heat represents the additional en-   3
ergy imparted to the random motion. Temperature is a measure of the amount of energy in the random motion. Thus when the substance is heated, its temperature increases and the substance is said to be hotter. The heat of cooking increases the energy of the random motion of the atoms and molecules in the food, and the food thereupon cooks by undergoing certain chemical and physical changes.

Conduction, convection and radiation are the three primary ways of   4
transferring heat energy. In conduction the heat is conveyed through some intermediate material such as a metal pan or foil by means of atomic collisions. As the outside surface of the metal warms, the energy in the random motion of the atoms there increases. They collide with atoms somewhat deeper in the metal, giving those atoms some of the kinetic energy derived from the heat source. Eventually atoms on the inside surface receive the energy and collide with atoms on the surface of the food, heating the food. Conduction continues for as long as the temperature of the heat source is above the temperature of the food.

Convection involves the ascent of a heated fluid, either air or a liquid.   5
Heat increases the energy in the random motion of the fluid and decreases

the density of the fluid. The surrounding cooler and denser fluid then pushes the heated fluid upward. As the hot fluid passes the food, the atoms and molecules in the fluid collide with those on the surface of the food and transfer energy to them.

Radiation involves the emission and absorption of electromagnetic waves. In cooking the source is light. The surface of a heat source such as burning coal emits light in the infrared and visible parts of the electromagnetic spectrum. Since light has energy, this emission is a radiation of energy. When the light is absorbed by atoms and molecules on the surface of the food, the energy of their random motion increases, as does the temperature of the surface. Heating by radiation therefore requires that the food absorb some of the light (primarily the infrared) emitted by the heat source.

Many campfire-cooking techniques draw on more than one of these primary means of transferring heat. For example, a fire might heat a metal pan by both convection of hot air and radiation of light. As the metal warms, energy is conducted through it to the food. As the surface of the food then heats up, conduction brings the heat into the food.

One of the easiest ways to cook food such as meat is to spear it with a stick or wrap it around the stick and then suspend it over the fire or coals. The food is heated by the convection of rising hot air and by the radiation from the heated surfaces of the wood and from the hot regions in the flame. You can save work by propping the stick over the fire or suspending it across the fire by means of two forked sticks driven into the ground on opposite sides of the campfire.

A large piece of meat suspended over the fire must be turned frequently, because only the side toward the fire gets the effect of the rising hot air and the radiation. The rig known as a dingle fan, probably from the logging-camp shed called a dingle, is helpful in this task. To make the apparatus attach a short chain to the upper end of a stick that is angled upward over the perimeter of the campfire. Suspend the meat from the chain by a string attached to a hook in one end of the meat. Tie a short stick to the string. One end of the stick holds a fan made of wire or branches wrapped in aluminum foil or leaves. To the other end attach a small rock to serve as a counterweight to the fan. Orient the plane of the fan somewhat off the vertical and arrange the entire assembly so that the fan is in the hot air rising from the campfire. The meat is not in that convection current but is exposed to the radiation from the fire.

The rising hot air pushes against the underside of the fan. The force 10
moves the fan to one side, twisting the chain and rotating the meat. Once
the fan is out of the convection current the chain untwists, rotating the
meat in the opposite direction. It overshoots the original position, again
twisting the chain. The cycle continues indefinitely, exposing about half
of the meat to the radiation. After a while invert the roast and hang
it from a hook on the other end to expose the other half of the meat to
the radiation.

To fry food you can make a stove from an empty No. 10 can. Re- 11
move one end plate of the can and cut a flap at the open end. Bend the
flap outward. Push the loose end plate into the can and against the other
end plate. With a can opener (the kind that punches triangular holes) or
a knife, cut flaps in the can in several places near the closed end. Push
the flaps into the can and against the loose end plate to hold it near the
fixed end one. Place the open end of the can over a heat source. The upper end plate serves as a surface on which eggs, bacon and other items
can be fried.

The can functions as a chimney because cool air is sucked in through 12
the open flap at the bottom to replace the hot air rising to the top and
out through the holes there. The strong flow of air through the can fans
the fire and keeps it burning briskly.

You could make the stove without the loose end plate held near the 13
top. That plate, however, helps to produce a nearly uniform temperature
over the entire cooking surface. Without this plate the part of that surface directly above the heat source would be hotter than the rest of the
surface because it receives more radiation from the source. The loose
plate is intended to heat the small layer of air above it, transferring heat
to the cooking surface evenly by the conduction and convection through
the air.

A popular heat source for the stove is a "buddy burner," a small can 14
filled with corrugated cardboard over which hot paraffin has been poured.
When the can is brought out for cooking, the paraffin is solid. A match
melts and vaporizes some of it, and thereafter the vapor burns. The flame
melts more paraffin, which is drawn to the top of the cardboard, where
it vaporizes and burns. The cardboard also burns, but slowly, like the
wick of a candle. A damper can be placed over part of the burner to slow
things down if the stove gets too hot. Make the damper by folding the
lid from the can over a doubled piece of wire.

VOCABULARY

paragraph 3: atoms, molecule
paragraph 4: kinetic energy
paragraph 5: ascent, density
paragraph 6: infrared spectrum, electromagnetic spectrum
paragraph 9: vertical
paragraph 14: paraffin

QUESTIONS

1. What are the differences between conduction, convection, and radiation? How do the three sometimes work together in the process described in paragraph 7?

2. In the process described in paragraphs 8–10, what aspects does Walker describe in most detail? How do his earlier definitions help him in explaining the process?

3. What devices used in the same process does Walker describe? Does he give a full description of each device, or does he describe only those parts needed in cooking?

4. What devices used in frying food does Walker describe in paragraphs 11–14? How detailed is his description of each device?

5. Is Walker writing to readers unfamiliar with laws of physics and cooking techniques? Or does he assume that his readers vary in knowledge and experience?

SUGGESTION FOR WRITING

Describe one of the following processes or another that you have performed often enough to explain thoroughly. Explain your terms and steps of the process in nontechnical language that readers who are unfamiliar with it will understand:

a. seeding and tending a lawn or garden

b. growing tomatoes or another fruit or vegetable

c. cutting down a dead tree

d. carving a turkey

e. mastering a difficult technique in learning to play a musical instrument or to draw or paint

f. repairing a small motor or other equipment

J O H N   R I C H A R D S

Trained as an engineer, the English nature writer JOHN RICHARDS brings a keen eye to his description of the workings of nature—in the excerpt reprinted here from *The Hidden Country* (1973), the intricate natural process of spinning orb-webs. Richards is describing the web-spinning of the Diadem spider, a brown spider with a large white cross on its abdomen. Richards states: "These web-building spiders have eight eyes, yet in spite of this their sight is not good. Unlike the spiders which hunt and catch their prey by watching for them or by chasing, they do not need to see well; what is much more important is their ability to interpret the meaning of the various tensions in the threads of their webs." The drawing Richards refers to has been omitted.

HOW THE SPIDER SPINS ITS WEB

I have shown the garden spider in the center of its web, but you will   1
rarely find one there during the daytime. This would be a dangerous situation for the spider when birds are about, and it would be unlikely to stay there for long. Instead, it spends the day in a lair by the side of the web, coming out to the center only in the evening, and staying there for the night, unless otherwise engaged.

The orb-webs, as they are called, from their circular shape, are mas- 2
terpieces of construction, and yet are relatively short-lived. They are usually built in the late evening, and may in some cases be virtually demolished
and rebuilt each night. The webs vary considerably in size, and the one
which I have drawn, for the sake of convenience, is one of the smallest.

The spider constructs these webs using two different kinds of silk, 3
which it produces from spinnerets at the end of the abdomen. A more
or less horizontal thread is needed as a start for the web, and the spider
produces this in one of several ways, depending on the circumstances.

If the wind direction is right, it may be enough to stand on one point 4
and to put out a long thread into the wind, so that this eventually becomes fouled on a twig or other projection on the far side of the chosen
gap. The spider can walk across this thread, anchor the other end firmly,
and then reinforce the thread with one or more additional strands.

In other cases, as for example when the web is to be made across a win- 5
dow frame, it may be possible for the spider to walk from one point to the
other, trailing a line as it goes, which can subsequently be tightened as necessary. Yet again, it will sometimes drop on a thread to the bottom of the
window, and then walk up to the required spot, taking the thread with it.

Once this starting line is established, the rest of the outer frame of 6
the web is built in much the same way, until the size and basic outline
has been settled. A couple of radii can now be dropped from points along
the top thread, and when these are crossed over, they locate the point
which is to be the center of the web.

The rest of the radii are now laid in, so that when finished they are 7
all at very nearly the same angle to their neighbors. The spider does this
by walking along one thread as it spins the adjacent one, and it appears
to be able to determine the appropriate distance at which to keep it with
considerable accuracy. This is quite surprising, because as the web does
not have a circular outline, the radii cannot be evenly spaced along the
outer threads.

Once the radii are in position, the spider constructs a flat non-sticky 8
platform at the center of the web, and then uses this same kind of silk
to lay down a spiral, starting from the center and working outwards until
it comes to the outer frame.

This thread serves only as a form of scaffolding, to establish finally 9
how the spiral will go, and to secure the radial threads firmly at the correct distances apart, ready for the next stage. In his last step, the sticky
spiral will be placed in position.

Starting at the outer end of the scaffolding spiral, the spider begins   10
to work inwards, spinning a new sticky thread, anchoring this firmly to
the radii, and destroying the temporary thread as it goes. The real purpose of the temporary spiral now becomes apparent. The sticky thread,
when it first comes from the spinnerets, is smooth, and the spider tenses
and relaxes it repeatedly as it is laid down. In doing this, it breaks up the
gummy material on the silk from a continuous film into strings of small
droplets at intervals along the silk thread. Had the spider not first fixed
the radial threads firmly in the required position with the temporary spiral
thread, this stretching and relaxing would pull them badly out of line.

Vocabulary

paragraph 1: lair
paragraph 2: orb-webs
paragraph 3: spinnerets
paragraph 6: radii
paragraph 9: scaffolding

Questions

1. When must the spider take account of the place or setting and the
weather in spinning the web?

2. How does the spider spin a temporary spiral, and what is its purpose?

3. What details does Richards stress to show that the orb-webs are "mas-
terpieces of construction"?

4. At which points in his description does Richards pause to give additional information or comment on the process?

Suggestion for Writing

Make several observations of a natural process similar to the one Richards
describes—for example, a bird building a nest, a grasshopper leaping
through the grass, a dog swimming, or an ant moving a grain of sand.
Then write a description of the process, explaining your terms and the
steps of the process for readers unfamiliar with it.

14

CAUSE AND EFFECT

There is not just one kind of causal analysis. In explaining why you missed a chemistry exam, you may say that you overslept. In explaining an event like a steep decline in stock prices, a market analyst may cite an event occurring immediately before the decline—for example, the announcement of a rise in interest rates. These are the *immediate* (or *proximate*) causes. Asked why you overslept, you trace the prior events that made you so tired; the market analyst traces the events that led to the rise in interest rates. These are the *mediate* (or *remote*) causes. What one points to as the "cause" depends on the purpose of the analysis. In analyzing an event like a decline in the stock market, an explanation that satisfies a person untrained in economics may not satisfy the professional economist.

Objects, too, have more than one cause. One useful and traditional kind of analysis distinguishes four related ones. Consider a dictionary. Its *material cause* is the paper, ink, and other materials used in its manufacture. The *formal cause* is its shape—the alphabetic arrangement of words, and the arrangements of definitions according to a plan. The *efficient cause* is the dictionary writer, and the *final cause,* the use intended for the dictionary. The analysis of a chemical compound is more rigorous, requiring an account of substances that form the compound as well as the process by which the formation occurs. Process analysis is often an essential part of causal analysis because we want to understand both the how and the why of objects and events. Later in this book we will consider another, more technical kind of causal explanation.

JOHN BROOKS

JOHN BROOKS began writing about American business for *The New Yorker* in 1949. His books include *The Go-Go Years* (1973), *The Games Players* (1980), *Showing Off in America* (1981), and *The Takeover Game* (1987). In the following paragraph from *The Telephone* (1976), a history of AT&T, Brooks refers to the idea of Marshall McLuhan that the telephone is a "cool" medium—one requiring full participation because, unlike print, it is empty of content. The user supplies this content, unlike the reader of a book. Brooks says later in his book: "In the uneasy postwar world, people seemed to be coming to associate the telephone with their frustrations, their fears, and their sense of powerlessness against technology."

THE TELEPHONE

What has the telephone done to us, or for us, in the hundred years of its existence? A few effects suggest themselves at once. It has saved lives by getting rapid word of illness, injury, or famine from remote places. By joining with the elevator to make possible the multistory residence or office building, it has made possible—for better or worse—the modern city. By bringing about a quantum leap in the speed and ease with which information moves from place to place, it has greatly accelerated the rate of scientific and technological change and growth in industry. Beyond doubt it has crippled if not killed the ancient art of letter writing. It has made living alone possible for persons with normal social impulses; by so doing, it has played a role in one of the greatest social changes of this century, the breakup of the multigenerational household. It has made the waging of war chillingly more efficient than formerly. Perhaps (though not provably) it has prevented wars that might have arisen out of international misunderstanding caused by written communication. Or perhaps—again not provably—by magnifying and extending irrational personal conflicts based on voice contact, it has caused wars. Certainly it has extended the scope of human conflicts, since it impartially disseminates the useful knowledge of scientists and the babble of bores, the affection of the affectionate and the malice of the malicious.

But the question remains unanswered. The obvious effects just cited   2
seem inadequate, mechanistic; they only scratch the surface. Perhaps the
crucial effects are evanescent and unmeasurable. Use of the telephone involves personal risk because it involves exposure; for some, to be "hung
up on" is among the worst of fears; others dream of a ringing telephone
and wake up with a pounding heart. The telephone's actual ring—more,
perhaps, than any other sound in our daily lives—evokes hope, relief,
fear, anxiety, joy, according to our expectations. The telephone is our
nerve-end to society.

In some ways it is in itself a thing of paradox. In one sense a metaphor   3
for the times it helped create, in another sense the telephone is their polar
opposite. It is small and gentle—relying on low voltages and miniature
parts—in times of hugeness and violence. It is basically simple in times
of complexity. It is so nearly human, recreating voices so faithfully that
friends or lovers need not identify themselves by name even when talking
across oceans, that to ask its effects on human life may seem hardly more
fruitful than to ask the effect of the hand or the foot. The Canadian
philosopher Marshall McLuhan—one of the few who have addressed
themselves to these questions—was perhaps not far from the mark when
he spoke of the telephone as creating "a kind of extra-sensory perception."

QUESTIONS

1. Why does Brooks consider the effects he discusses in paragraph 1 less
significant than those in paragraph 2? What does he mean by the statement, "Perhaps the crucial effects are evanescent and unmeasurable"?

2. In what ways is the telephone a paradox? Does the author show it to
be a paradox in paragraphs 1 and 2?

3. Has Brooks stated all the effects of the telephone, or has he identified
only a few? What central point is he making?

SUGGESTIONS FOR WRITING

1. Develop one of the ideas in the essay from your personal experience.
You might discuss your own positive and negative attitudes toward the

telephone, and the reasons for them, or you might develop the statement, "In some ways it is in itself a thing of paradox."

2. Write an essay describing what it would be like to live without a telephone, or discuss the impact of the telephone on life in your home. Distinguish the various uses and effects of the telephone for various members of your family.

MARVIN HARRIS

MARVIN HARRIS, Graduate Research Professor of Anthropology at the University of Florida, writes about American life from the point of view of the anthropologist in *Cannibals and Kings: The Origins of Culture* (1977), *Culture, People, Nature* (1997), and *Culture in Postmodern Times* (1999). *Good to Eat* (1986) and *The Sacred Cow and the Abominable Pig* (1987) both concern "riddles of food and culture." In the following excerpt from *America Now: The Anthropology of a Changing Culture* (1981) Harris gives an interesting illustration of Murphy's Law. Notice how he combines several types of exposition, including definition, process, and example.

WHY NOTHING WORKS

According to a law attributed to the savant known only as Murphy, "if anything can go wrong, it will." Corollaries to Murphy's Law suggest themselves as clues to the shoddy goods problem: If anything can break down, it will; if anything can fall apart, it will; if anything can stop running, it will. While Murphy's Law can never be wholly defeated, its effects can usually be postponed. Much of human existence consists of efforts aimed at making sure that things don't go wrong, fall apart, break down, or stop running until a decent interval has elapsed after their manufacture. Forestalling Murphy's Law as applied to products demands intelligence, skill, and commitment. If these human inputs are assisted by special quality-control instruments, machines, and scientific sampling procedures, so much the better. But gadgets and sampling alone will never do the trick since these items are also subject to Murphy's Law. Quality-control instruments need maintenance; gauges go out of order; X rays and laser beams need adjustments. No matter how advanced the technology, quality demands intelligent, motivated human thought and action.

Some reflection about the material culture of prehistoric and preindustrial peoples may help to show what I mean. A single visit to a museum which displays artifacts used by simple preindustrial societies is sufficient to dispel the notion that quality is dependent on technology. Artifacts may be of simple, even primitive design, and yet be built to serve their intended purpose in a reliable manner during a lifetime of use. We acknowledge this when we honor the label "handmade" and pay extra for the jewelry, sweaters, and handbags turned out by the dwindling breeds of modern-day craftspeople.   2

What is the source of quality that one finds, let us say, in a Pomo Indian basket so tightly woven that it was used to hold boiling water and never leaked a drop, or in an Eskimo skin boat with its matchless combination of lightness, strength, and seaworthiness? Was it merely the fact that these items were handmade? I don't think so. In unskilled or uncaring hands a handmade basket or boat can fall apart as quickly as baskets or boats made by machines. I rather think that the reason we honor the label "handmade" is because it evokes not a technological relationship between producer and product but a social relationship between producer and consumer. Throughout prehistory it was the fact that producers and consumers were either one and the same individuals or close kin that guaranteed the highest degree of reliability and durability in manufactured items. Men made their own spears, bows and arrows, and projectile points; women wove their own baskets and carrying nets, fashioned their own clothing from animal skins, bark, or fiber. Later, as technology advanced and material culture grew more complex, different members of the band or village adopted craft specialties such as pottery-making, basket-weaving, or canoe-building. Although many items were obtained through barter and trade, the connection between producer and consumer still remained intimate, permanent, and caring.   3

A man is not likely to fashion a spear for himself whose point will fall off in midflight; nor is a woman who weaves her own basket likely to make it out of rotted straw. Similarly, if one is sewing a parka for a husband who is about to go hunting for the family with the temperature at sixty below, all stitches will be perfect. And when the men who make boats are the uncles and fathers of those who sail them, they will be as seaworthy as the state of the art permits.   4

In contrast, it is very hard for people to care about strangers or about   5
products to be used by strangers. In our era of industrial mass production
and mass marketing, quality is a constant problem because the intimate
sentimental and personal bonds which once made us responsible to each
other and to our products have withered away and been replaced by
money relationships. Not only are the producers and consumers strangers
but the women and men involved in various stages of production and
distribution—management, the worker on the factory floor, the office
help, the salespeople—are also strangers to each other. In larger companies there may be hundreds of thousands of people all working on the
same product who can never meet face-to-face or learn one another's
names. The larger the company and the more complex its division of
labor, the greater the sum of uncaring relationships and hence the greater
the effect of Murphy's Law. Growth adds layer on layer of executives,
foremen, engineers, production workers, and sales specialists to the pay-
roll. Since each new employee contributes a diminished share to the over-
all production process, alienation from the company and its product are
likely to increase along with the neglect or even purposeful sabotage of
quality standards.

QUESTIONS

1. What role does Murphy's Law play in Harris's explanation of why
nothing works? Does he say or imply that the law is irreversible and that
things inevitably break down?

2. How does Harris attempt to prove that quality is not dependent on
technology?

3. Does Harris provide the same kind of evidence for his explanation of
the source of quality in the handmade products he discusses in paragraphs 3–5?

4. We can test the evidence Harris presents in paragraph 2 by examining the museum objects discussed. Can you think of a way to test the
explanation in paragraphs 3–5 if the evidence cannot be tested directly?
How convincing do you find his explanation of these paragraphs?

Suggestions for Writing

1. Write your own explanation of why something you own does not work. In the course of your analysis, discuss the extent to which the ideas of Harris offer an explanation.

2. Write an essay on succeeding in a sport or another topic of your choosing, using causal analysis and examples to develop a thesis. The more limited your focus and discussion, the stronger your thesis will be.

J A M E S   T R E F I L

JAMES TREFIL, Professor of Physics at George Mason University, is the author of *Meditations at Sunset* (1986), *Scientist at the Seashore* (1987), *The Dark Side of the Universe* (1988), *Edge of the Unknown* (1996), and other books on science. In *A Scientist in the City* (1994), he discusses "how energy shapes a city," first when people walk or depend on horses and other animals: "Julius Caesar got around in Rome pretty much the same way that the young Queen Victoria got around London. All of these famous figures had only one way to move from one point to another—they had to use muscles, either their own or those of some animal." In the sections reprinted here, Trefil traces technological changes from the age of "muscle power" to the age of petroleum. The "Rule of 45" that restricts the size of cities is that "most people will not travel more than 45 minutes to work or shop."

The Growth of Cities

MASS TRANSPORTATION IN THE AGE OF MUSCLE POWER

Cities grow. This is the clear message of several centuries of experience. So what can be done to deal with the transportation problems that growth brings? One approach, exemplified by the broad boulevards of Paris and modern eight-lane freeways, is to build bigger roads and more bridges. Another approach is to make the movement of traffic more efficient by grouping travelers together in one vehicle. Bus lines, trams, and trains are examples of this approach. Finally, we can finesse the geometrical constraints completely by moving traffic to a plane different from the city surface. Elevated railways (like Chicago's El) lift traffic above the ground; subways move it below. A recent variation on this theme is found in many cities today: keep vehicular traffic on the ground and build a new "surface" of walkways, parks, and buildings above it. Except for mass transportation, all of these methods of dealing with congestion have obvious limits. There is, after all, only so much space in a central city that can be used for freeways and tunnels.

But mass transportation needn't necessarily wait for breakthroughs in energy technology. In fact, in the nineteenth century, cities developed their first systems based on the use of one of mankind's oldest suppliers of energy: the horse.

As far as I can tell, the first public mass transit system in the world was inaugurated by a man named Henri Baudry in Nantes, France, in 1826. A retired army officer who owned a resort outside of town, he thought he could help business by running a short, regularly scheduled stagecoach line from town to his establishment. The stages left from a location in front of a hatmaker named Omnes, so it quickly acquired the name "omnibus."

Baudry noticed that most of his passengers seemed to be getting off before they got to his place. He must have been a good businessman because instead of getting upset and trying to restrict the use of his stage, he realized that this represented an opportunity and began running stages all over town. His fleet of omnibuses was so successful that it was quickly copied in Paris, London, and New York, which by 1853 had over 600 licensed coaches.

But just putting people in horse-drawn wagons didn't improve transportation all that much. For one thing, the roads were full of potholes and puddles, so the rides tended to be on the bumpy side. For another, there was already so much congestion in the streets that travel was slow—in most places, it was quicker to walk than to ride. The combination of uncomfortable ride and slow progress was probably what the *New York Herald* had in mind when it commented in 1864 that "modern martyrdom may be succinctly described as riding in a New York omnibus."

The development of the horsecar in the mid-nineteenth century eased this burden somewhat. Also called the street railway, the horsecar ran on metal wheels over tracks laid in the street—think of it as a horse-drawn trolley. The ride was smoother and the progress a little more rapid than was possible with an omnibus; horsecars typically moved at speeds of 6 to 8 miles per hour, or about as fast as a jogger. They caught on quickly, particularly in American cities, where they provided transportation to what were then outlying suburbs. In New York, for example, lines on Second and Sixth avenues reached to what is now Central Park, and well-to-do people could commute downtown to work in less than 45 minutes. In the words of one Philadelphian in 1859:

> These passenger cars, which are street railroads with horse power, are a great convenience. Though little more than a year old, they have almost displaced the heavy, jolting, slow and uncomfortable omnibus. . . . They are roomy, their motion smooth and easy, they are clean, well cushioned and handsome, low to the ground so that it is convenient to get on and off, and are driven at a rapid pace. They offer great facility for traversing the city, now grown so large that the distances are very considerable from place to place.

Nor were horsecars confined to large cities on the East Coast. I was very surprised to learn from my father-in-law, for example, that the town of Billings, Montana—hardly a major metropolis—had a horsecar line connecting the downtown to the railroad yards. He can remember the tracks still being in the street when he was a boy (although the cars no longer ran at that time). Many scholars credit the horsecar with beginning the explosive dispersion of American cities by making it possible for people to live far from their place of work. 7

The organization of mass transportation systems was an important step forward in urban social organization, but it hardly marked a major breakthrough in technology. Horses, after all, had been used to pull wagons from time immemorial. Aside from the rather mundane development that saw rails put in city streets, there was very little to distinguish the early-nineteenth-century transportation engineer from his Roman (or even Sumerian) counterpart. 8

MASS TRANSPORTATION IN THE AGE OF STEAM

We usually think of the steam engine as the great driver of change in transportation systems. The first steam railroads were built at mineheads in England in the early nineteenth century. (Some of these early freight lines also offered a passenger service—using, oddly enough, horse-drawn cars.) The first railroad line in the United States, the beginning of the 9

Baltimore & Ohio Railroad, opened in Baltimore in 1830. Long before this time, improvements in the steam engine had made it small enough to be portable and powerful enough to run not only railroads but ships as well.

In fact, that quintessentially American phenomenon, the flight to the suburbs, began in 1814, when the first steam ferry started operating between New York (what we would call Manhattan today) and the small farm town of Brooklyn across the East River. By 1860, the population of the town had grown from less than 5000 to 250,000 as people who worked in New York sought quiet, tree-shaded homes for their families. No less a personage than Walt Whitman, writing for the *Brooklyn Eagle*, talked of "Brooklyn the Beautiful," where "men of moderate means may find homes of moderate rent, whereas in New York City there is no median between a palatial mansion and a dilapidated hovel." He also cast a sardonic eye on the behavior of passengers when the ferry docked. His description will seem familiar to anyone who has ever negotiated a subway during rush hour:

> It is highly edifying to see the phrenzy exhibited by certain portions of the younger gentlemen when the bell (signifying the arrival of the ferry) strikes. They rush forward as if for dear life, and woe to the fat woman or unwieldy person of any kind, who stands in their way.

But it was the steam railroad that really shaped American urban areas. Its effect on cities was governed by one simple fact: a steam locomotive takes a mile or more to get up to its running speed. This means that the most efficient way for a railroad-driven transportation system to operate is to have towns strung every few miles along the railroad track. In this kind of situation, people in the "railroad suburbs" walk or ride to the station, then take the train into town. A typical string of such suburbs are towns along the Main Line near Philadelphia.

Not everyone was happy with the growth of suburbs. In 1849, the *New York Tribune* sounded a complaint that can still be heard in American cities today when it said:

> Property is continually tending from our city to escape the oppressiveness of our taxation. . . . While every suburb in New York is rapidly growing, and villages twenty and thirty miles distant are sustained by incomes earned here and expended there, our City has no equivalent rapidity of growth, and unimproved property here is often unsalable at a nominal price.

When the first urban transportation systems were built—London's   13
Underground and New York's Elevated, for example—they used steam
locomotives because there wasn't anything else available. But this form
of steam technology just didn't fit naturally into city life and was quickly
dropped. Some way had to be found to harness the power of steam in a
form where energy was generated in a fixed spot, then sent out to be
used on the streets.

For a brief period in the 1880s and '90s, cable car networks were   14
built in a number of American cities. Today, we associate them with San
Francisco, but Chicago, New York, and Philadelphia all used them at one
time or another. A cable car works like this: A steam engine is used to
turn a large cylinder that, in turn, pulls a long cable through a groove
between tracks in a city street. The operator of the car pulls a lever that
causes a pair of grippers under the car to grab the cable, and the car then
moves along.

In San Francisco, such a system has obvious advantages. You don't   15
have to lift the motor to get the car over a hill. On flat stretches of land
such as are found in most eastern and midwestern cities, however, the
cable system has proved remarkably inefficient. Up to 90 percent of the
energy generated by the steam engine may go to pulling the cable, and
only 10 percent to the cars themselves. Obviously, there has to be a better way to get the job done.

MASS TRANSPORTATION IN THE AGE OF ELECTRICITY

That "better way" was demonstrated by a man named Frank Sprague   16
in 1887. Working in Richmond, Virginia, he built the first electrically
operated street railroad system—the first trolley. In this system, steam
turbines generated electricity at a central location, and the electricity
was run out to the cars through wires above the streets. A flexibly
mounted pole on top of the car maintained contact with these wires and
fed the electricity to the car's motor. (The word "trolley" is a corruption of "troller," the technical word for a little wheel at the end of
the pole.)

Sprague installed some 12 miles of track in the Richmond system,   17
but he never really cleared a profit on it. His demonstration was such a
technical success, however, that cities all over the country began buying

his equipment and taking out licenses on his patents. By 1893, there were no fewer than 250 electric railway companies in the United States; by 1903, there were some 30,000 miles of electrified street railways. Even in our own age of rapid change, when new subdivisions seem to spring up overnight, it's a little hard to envision such a massive revolution in transportation taking place in just 15 years.

The streetcars accelerated the explosion of American cities. "Street- 18
car suburbs" grew up around every major city, connected to the city by steel tracks and overhead wires. There were even interurban trolleys; for example, you could go from New York to Philadelphia on the streetcar. The "interurbans" also ran to small farm towns outside of cities. I can recall my grandfather talking about how he used to ride them out from Chicago to buy farm produce. Many of what are now established city neighborhoods and close suburbs got their start from the streetcars.

Like the steam railroad, streetcars produced a characteristic pattern 19
of city growth. If a typical ride downtown is 20 minutes, then the Rule of 45 tells us that most people will live within a 25-minute walk (a mile or so) of the track. In this situation, growth will be along a series of fingers spreading away from the city center. This pattern will, in fact, be typical of any system that depends on public transportation built around a central city hub.

MASS TRANSPORTATION IN THE AGE OF PETROLEUM

It was the development of the automobile that filled in the spaces between 20
the urban fingers created by trolleys. It is a product of the most recent change of energy source, from coal to petroleum products. The internal combustion engine, which burns gasoline and uses the resulting energy to turn a shaft that runs wheels, is ubiquitous today. It runs cars, trucks, and buses, of course, but we hear its high-pitched drone on summer afternoons when people are cutting their lawns; in the woods, where chain saws cut down trees; and at construction sites, where a variety of machines are used to excavate and shape the land. The first vehicle powered by an internal combustion engine was built in Germany in 1885 by Karl Benz (whose name survives on one of that country's more upscale products). In 1903, Henry Ford formed the company that bears his name and soon began producing the Model T.

The great advantage of the internal combustion engine was its use of energy derived directly from burning fossil fuels. Thus, all the messy apparatus connected with the use of steam could be eliminated. Both the engine and the fuel in the automobile were compact, so that it was economical to build a vehicle that would carry only a few people at a time.

The "automobilization" of America is a story too well known and too well told to be repeated here. Suffice it to say that it didn't take long for Americans to adopt the automobile. Not long after World War II, there was one car per family in this country; and in the 1970s, one car per worker. By 1985, the number of cars in the United States actually exceeded the number of registered drivers, and it now hovers at about 20 percent more than that number. (I didn't believe this figure, but experts I talked to pointed out that many cars are owned by corporations and rental companies, and many families own seldom-used machines like recreational vehicles in addition to their working cars.)

With the growth of car ownership—with almost all individuals now having a vehicle at their disposal—a new pattern of city growth has developed. Cities now grow in rings, with all the land a given distance from the city center being used before land farther out is built up. This is, of course, the familiar pattern of "urban sprawl." As we pointed out earlier, cities took this shape when individuals controlled their own travel by walking. It's not surprising to find it repeated today, when we control our own travel by driving.

At first, this kind of uniform concentric growth produced a metropolitan area that consisted of a central city full of jobs, surrounded by bedroom suburbs full of commuting workers. Books like *The Lonely Crowd* and *The Organization Man* decried the spiritual aridity of the suburbs and helped create a stereotype of the suburbs that persists to this day.

But whether such sociological views are valid or not, from a technological standpoint there is no question that the modern suburb owes its existence and its organization to the internal combustion engine. This engine has one important use, however, that tends to get overlooked in the story of suburban growth: it can drive trucks as well as automobiles. This means that, like automobiles, trucks can "fill in the blanks" between rail lines in the urban growth ring. Consequently, almost as soon as people started migrating to the suburbs, factories and warehouses started migrating with them. From the very beginnings of urban expansion, there were jobs available in the suburbs.

Vocabulary

paragraph 1: finesse, constraints
paragraph 5: succinctly
paragraph 7: dispersion
paragraph 8: mundane, Sumerian
paragraph 10: quintessential, median, dilapidated, hovel, sardonic
paragraph 20: ubiquitous
paragraph 24: aridity

Questions

1. How did horse-drawn vehicles influence the growth of New York City in the nineteenth century?

2. How did the steam railroad and steamboat later influence its growth and that of other cities?

3. Why was the cable car an efficient means of transportation in San Francisco but not in other cities like Chicago?

4. Why was the electrically operated vehicle more efficient than the steam-powered vehicle? Did the electrically operated streetcar influence city growth in the same way as earlier steam-powered vehicles?

5. Why was the internal combustion engine more efficient than steam-powered vehicles? What influence did it have on the growth and life of cities?

6. What is Trefil's thesis, and does he state it explicitly? How do the changes in mass transportation discussed illustrate it?

Suggestions for Writing

1. James Trefil explains how various kinds of transportation have influenced the social life of people in cities—in particular, where they live and work. Describe how the means of transportation that became available to you where you grew up changed your life.

2. The layout and design of city streets influences the driving habits and attitudes of bikers, cyclists, and motorists. Explain how the streets in a particular town or city influence driving habits and attitudes, giving examples from your own experience.

III

MATTERS OF STYLE: DICTION

INTRODUCTION

The word *diction* refers to the choice of words we make in speaking and writing. The choice may be a matter of vocabulary—as in exposition, when we name a specific tool in performing a job, and in descriptive writing, when we choose concrete words or phrases and vivid images and suggestive metaphors to create a mental picture. In persuasive writing, we look for words that are exact but also move the reader to accept an idea or take action. Diction concerns both the use and the misuse of words. In all kinds of writing, we look for words that have appropriate connotations, avoiding words that have misleading ones.

The first two sections of Part III discuss the matter of usage or appropriateness of words and phrases and show how writers control the tone of their essays to express their attitude toward the subject and audience. The sections that follow define and illustrate various kinds of images and common figurative language, such as simile, metaphor, and personification. The concluding section deals with inappropriate or inexpressive uses of words and singles out words that are meaningless and ugly.

Like earlier discussions and readings, those in this part of the book can serve in drafting essays and revising them. Finding the right tone and "level" of usage for an essay is a major concern in starting to write.

15

USAGE

None of us speaks or writes in the same way on all occasions. The differences depend on how formal or informal the occasion is. A letter of application for a job will be more formal than a letter to a friend; a graduation speech will sound different from a locker-room or school hallway conversation.

Each of us has a formal and an informal language—and standards for judging their effectiveness. These standards come from the different groups we belong to—each with its special idioms and vocabulary. To the California surfer, a "barney" is another surfer who "drops in on" a wave, cutting one off; a "goofy-footer" is a surfer who puts the wrong foot forward on the board. And the wave may be a "filthy" one—awesome in height and power. By the time this is published, these slang terms may have given way to others.

Like these surfers, teenagers in different parts of the country or cities or towns may share a special dialect or spoken language. They may also share a special one with family and friends. Even a family may have its own private language—special words and expressions to describe acts and feelings.

Cutting across these differences is a standardized English we hear on television, read in newspapers, speak and write in school—a language sometimes less colorful and personal, but serving as a medium of communication among diverse groups, not only in the United States but in other English-speaking countries. This standard, of long-term growth, changes less than the informal language and slang of particular groups like the California surfers. This standard, represented in the readings in this book, falls between two extremes—one formal and abstract in its content and sentences, the other informal and concrete.

[Formal] It is simple enough to say that since books have classes—fiction, biography, poetry—we should separate them and take from each what it is right that each should give us. Yet few people ask from books what books can give us. Most commonly we come to books with blurred and divided minds, asking of fiction that it shall be true, of poetry that it shall be false, of biography that it shall be flattering, of history that it shall enforce our own prejudices. If we could banish all such preconceptions when we read, that would be an admirable beginning. (Virginia Woolf, "How Should One Read a Book?")

[*Informal*] Bryant's specializes in barbecued spareribs and barbecued beef—the beef sliced from briskets of steer that have been cooked over a hickory fire for thirteen hours. When I'm away from Kansas City and depressed, I try to envision someone walking up to the counterman at Bryant's and ordering a beef sandwich to go—for me. The counterman tosses a couple of pieces of bread onto the counter, grabs a half-pound of beef from the pile next to him, slaps it onto the bread, brushes on some sauce in almost the same motion, and then wraps it all up in two thicknesses of butcher paper in a futile attempt to keep the customer's hand dry as he carries off his prize. (Calvin Trillin, *American Fried*)

The abstract ideas of Woolf could be stated less formally. But usage is a matter of convention and occasion as well as personal choice, and if we would not be surprised to find her ideas stated informally, we probably would be surprised to find barbecue described in formal language.

As a rule, informal writing is closer to the patterns of everyday speech; formal writing seems impersonal if it departs widely from these patterns. Much standard writing today has both formal and informal features: we find colloquialisms (*grabs a half-pound of beef, slaps it onto*) in company with abstract or less familiar words (*envision*). We also find striking balance and antithesis—a feature of formal sentences—in company with looser, more familiar phrasing and expressions:

What I would like to know is: how should I feel about the earth, these days? Where has all the old nature gone? What became of the wild, writhing, unapproachable mass of the life of the world, and what happened to our old, panicky excitement about it? just in fifty years, since I was a small boy in a suburban town, the world has become a structure of steel and plastic, intelligible and diminished. (Lewis Thomas, "A Trip Abroad")

WILLIAM LEAST HEAT-MOON

WILLIAM LEAST HEAT-MOON states that the name "Least Heat-Moon" is Sioux in origin: "My father calls himself Heat-Moon, my elder brother Little Heat-Moon. I, coming last, am therefore Least." In 1978, he packed a 1975 Ford van that he called Ghost Dancing and began a search for his ancestors in rural America. Heat-Moon traveled east from Columbia, Missouri, to the Atlantic and then clockwise around the United States, on backroads marked blue on roadmaps. In *Blue Highways: A Journey into America* (1982), he tells us that he sought places where "change did not mean ruin and where time and men and deeds connected." In *PrairyErth* (1991) and *River-Horse: The Logbook of a Boat across America* (1999), Heat-Moon describes later travels. The restaurant described in the following section from *Blue Highways* tells us much about the people and customs of rural Georgia.

IN THE LAND OF "COKE-COLA"

In the land of "Coke-Cola" it was hot and dry. The artesian water was   1
finished. Along route 72, an hour west of Ninety-Six, I tried not to look for a spring; I knew I wouldn't find one, but I kept looking. The Savannah River, dammed to an unnatural wideness, lay below, wet and cool. I'd come into Georgia. The sun seemed to press on the roadway, and inside the truck, hot light bounced off chrome, flickering like a torch. Then I saw what I was trying not to look for: in a coppice, a long-handled pump.

I stopped and took my bottles to the well. A small sign: WATER UN-   2
SAFE FOR DRINKING. I drooped like warm tallow. What fungicide, herbicide, nematicide, fumigant, or growth regulant—potions that rebuilt Southern agriculture—had seeped into the ground water? In the old movie Westerns there is commonly a scene where a dehydrated man, crossing the barren waste, at last comes to a water hole; he lies flat to drink the tepid stuff. Just as lips touch water, he sees on the other side a steer skull. I drove off thirsty but feeling a part of mythic history.

The thirst subsided when hunger took over. I hadn't eaten since   3
morning. Sunset arrived west of Oglesby, and the air cooled. Then a
roadsign:

SWAMP GUINEA'S FISH LODGE

ALL YOU CAN EAT!

An arrow pointed down a county highway. I would gorge myself. A record
would be set. They'd ask me to leave. An embarrassment to all.

The road through the orange earth of north Georgia passed an old,   4
three-story house with a thin black child hanging out of every window
like an illustration for "The Old Woman Who Lived in a Shoe"; on into
hills and finally to Swamp Guinea's, a conglomerate of plywood and two-
by-fours laid over with the smell of damp pine woods.

Inside, wherever an oddity or natural phenomenon could hang, one   5
hung: stuffed rump of a deer, snowshoe, flintlock, hornet's nest. The
place looked as if a Boy Scout troop had decorated it. Thirty or so
people, black and white, sat around tables almost foundering under
piled platters of food. I took a seat by the reproduction of a seventeenth-century woodcut depicting some Rabelaisian banquet at the
groaning board.

The diners were mostly Oglethorpe County red-dirt farmers. In Geor-   6
gia tones they talked about their husbandry in terms of rain and nitrogen
and hope. An immense woman with a glossy picture of a hooked bass
leaping the front of her shirt said, "I'm gonna be sick from how much
I've ate."

I was watching everyone else and didn't see the waitress standing   7
quietly by. Her voice was deep and soft like water moving in a cavern. I
ordered the $4.50 special. In a few minutes she wheeled up a cart and
began offloading dinner: ham and eggs, fried catfish, fried perch fingerlings, fried shrimp, chunks of barbecued beef, fried chicken, French fries,
hush puppies, a broad bowl of cole slaw, another of lemon, a quart of
ice tea, a quart of ice, and an entire loaf of factory-wrapped white bread.
The table was covered.

"Call me if y'all want any more." She wasn't joking. I quenched the   8
thirst and then—slowly—went to the eating. I had to stand to reach
plates across the table, but I intended to do the supper in. It was all
Southern fried and good, except the Southern-style sweetened ice tea; still
I took care of a quart of it. As I ate, making up for meals lost, the Old-
Woman-in-the-Shoe house flashed before me, lightning in darkness. I had

no moral right to eat so much. But I did. Headline: STOMACH PUMP FAILS TO REVIVE TRAVELER.

The loaf of bread lay unopened when I finally abandoned the meal. 9 At the register, I paid a man who looked as if he'd been chipped out of Georgia chert. The Swamp Guinea. I asked about the name. He spoke of himself in the third person like the Wizard of Oz. "The Swamp Guinea only tells regulars."

"I'd be one, Mr. Guinea, if I didn't live in Missouri." 10

"Y'all from the North? Here, I got somethin' for you." He went to 11 the office and returned with a 45 rpm record. "It's my daughter singin'. A little promotion we did. Take it along." Later, I heard a husky north Georgia voice let go a down-home lyric rendering of Swamp Guinea's menu:

> That's all you can eat
>
> For a dollar fifty,
>
> Hey! The barbecue's nifty!

And so on through the fried chicken and potatoes.

As I left, the Swamp Guinea, a former antique dealer whose name 12 was Rudell Burroughs, said, "The nickname don't mean anything. Just made it up. Tried to figure a good one so we can franchise someday."

The frogs, high and low, shrilled and bellowed from the trees and 13 ponds. It was cool going into Athens, a city suffering from a nasty case of the sprawls. On the University of Georgia campus, I tried to walk down Swamp Guinea's supper. Everywhere couples entwined like moon-flower vines, each waiting for the blossom that opens only once.

VOCABULARY

paragraph 1: artesian water, coppice
paragraph 2: fungicide, herbicide, nematicide, fumigant, tepid, mythic
paragraph 4: conglomerate
paragraph 5: phenomenon, Rabelaisian
paragraph 6: husbandry
paragraph 7: fingerlings
paragraph 9: chert

QUESTIONS

1. What expressions or grammatical characteristics mark the speech of the diner, the waitress, and the restaurant owner as regional or dialectal?

2. To what extent does Least Heat-Moon depend on colloquial or everyday spoken expressions in writing about his experience? Is his sentence construction loose, or is he writing at a general or formal level?

3. Is he merely describing rural Georgia and the fish restaurant, or is he making a judgment about this world and developing a thesis?

4. Why does he conclude with the description of the couples on the Georgia campus?

SUGGESTION FOR WRITING

Describe a restaurant through its appearance, the food it serves, and the speech of its employees and possibly its owner. Let your details express a judgment or make a point about the restaurant. Don't state the judgment or the point explicitly.

NEWSWEEK

In its special fiftieth anniversary issue, NEWSWEEK magazine traced the history of five families in Springfield, Ohio—typical of the life of Americans from 1933 to 1983. The description here is of Dick Hatfield, the "guru of cool" in Springfield in the 1950s. Hatfield illustrates an attitude and style that require concrete detail to be understood.

BEING COOL

The time then ending had been one in which quietude had been elevated 1
to national policy and a certain insouciance called *cool* became a personal style among the trendier young. The guru of cool in Springfield was Dick Hatfield, Catholic Central High class of '53, known as the Imperial

Debubba of the Hort Club in tribute to two of the nonsense words he contributed to the nearly universal vocabulary of the city's cooler youth. Hatfield had been a precocious student, a high-school graduate at 15, which gave him a long run on the street—he hung out with the classes of '53 through '57—and a recognized seniority in the world of cool. When local advertisers dropped his word "hort" into their copy or bought little blocks of space that said DIGGEDY DIGGEDY DA BUSH BUSH, nothing more, it was a homage to Hatfield, his gift of unintelligible gab and his authority as an arbiter of cool taste.

Being cool, Hatfield remembers now, had to do first with how you looked and what you wore. Cool guys did not wear leather jackets or chinos and sweat socks, either. Cool guys wore pleated gray-flannel pants, custom pegged by a needlewoman named Ma Weiner for 75 cents a pair, with a skinny belt buckled on the side and a shirt with the billowing Mr. B collar popularized by the singer Billy Eckstine, who was *very* cool. Cool guys had cool walks, too, working at them till they had just the right hunch to the shoulders, just the right swing to the arms. "Sometimes," Hatfield recalls, "you would just *stand* there and be cool. Some chick would come by and say, 'He's cool,' just by the way you stood."

Cool guys did not sit home watching family sitcoms or the Mouseketeers. When they were home at all, cool guys watched "77 Sunset Strip" mostly for Kookie, the eighth avatar of cool, or Dick Clark's "American Bandstand"; it was the constant intention of Hatfield's crowd to go to Philly, where the Bandstand was produced, and really show them how to dance, but somehow they never saved up enough money. They did their stepping instead at El Som (for sombrero) dances at the Y on football and basketball Friday nights, or later, when they came of drinking age, at upscale clubs like the Melody Showbar—the Four Freshmen played there once—or funkier joints like the Frolics out on Lagonda Avenue. Hatfield, ultracool, preferred the Frolics for its ambience, which included a bouncer with a .357 magnum and featured a rhythm-and-blues band presided over by a large black man named H-Bomb Ferguson. You could do the dirty boogie at the Frolics, "a modified jitterbug," as Hatfield remembered it, "with like more hips," and find out quickly which guys and chicks were truly cool.

Cool guys hung out, at Frisch's Big Boy for the burgers, or under the clock at Woolworth's for the girl-watching, or at East High Billiards for the action; Hatfield was taking tickets there one March day in 1954 when the great Willie Mosconi came in and sank 526 straight balls for a world's

2

3

4

record. But mostly cool guys cruised, customizing their cars and living an automotive life later imitated by art in the film "American Graffiti." Hatfield's wheels supported a mink-white Chevy with scallops in three colors, regatta blue, Bahama blue and Inca gray, and the what-me-worry likeness of Alfred E. Neuman hand-done on the gas cap by a local painter. For a final touch of style, he installed a dummy telephone with a real-sounding Ma Bell ring, activated by a push button under the dashboard. Sometimes he would set it off with his knee at Frisch's just as one of the carhop girls came over to take his order. "Hold on a second, will you, honey," he would say, picking up the receiver. "I got an important call here."

The cruising route favored by the cool guys was downtown when it   5 still *was* downtown, its streets alive with life; Hatfield figured he spent very nearly every evening for four years going around the core block in the heart of the city, so many times he imagined that his tire tracks must have been indelibly imprinted in the left-hand lane. You cruised for a while, checking out the happenings; then you did the joints, O'Brien's Tavern at 9, then the Savoy, and then, at 1 A.M., the Alibi or the Shady Lane Saloon.

But suddenly everything began changing, and the cool life began to   6 chill. Hatfield noticed it around the time he was called up into the Reserves in 1960, at 22. Guys were getting restless, itchy for something new; some were disappearing into the military, some into marriages. The music was changing; five white guys named the Beach Boys were bleaching out Chuck Berry's black sound, and the dirty boogie was washed under by the twist, the pony and the mashed potato. "It was like everybody knew how to do *our* dance," Hatfield recalls. "The dirty boogie was no longer new." Downtown was changing, too, emptying out and beginning to go seedy. The difference struck Hatfield one day in the early '60s when he pulled up at East High Billiards and found a parking space right across the street. There was nobody around; being cool wasn't cool anymore.

Hatfield grew up when he came home from the Reserves; he went   7 back to work with the railroad for a while, then spun records for Station WBLY for a while more and now sells steel for the Benjamin Steel Co. He sold the '53 Chevy with the tricolor scallops before he went away and bought a 1960 Plymouth Valiant when he came back, a car so square that it couldn't be customized. He restocked his record library with Percy Faith and retooled his nights out to consist of taking a nice girl to a nice dinner at the Holiday Inn.

But some of the cool guys of his day could never let go of the rites 8
of coolness. The world had changed under them; Kennedy had died, with
all that diamond-bright promise; new tribes of the young had divided
American politics, morals and popular culture across a void that came
to be known as the generation gap; Chuck Berry's records were golden
oldies, and Kookie was the answer to a trivia tease. Nothing remains now
of the age of cool in Springfield except its last few survivors, baldish men
in their middle and late 40s with two or three divorces behind them, still
driving the old cruising routes as if in familiar motion they could catch
up with the past and recover the last innocent time.

Vocabulary

paragraph 1: quietude, insouciance, guru, arbiter
paragraph 3: magnum
paragraph 4: regatta
paragraph 8: trivia

Questions

1. How do the details help explain what the phrase "being cool" meant
to teenagers in the late 1950s? Does *Newsweek* state the meaning directly?

2. What other slang does *Newsweek* identify? How do you discover the
meaning of these words or expressions?

3. What does the language of these teenagers tell you about their world
and values? Is the *Newsweek* account a sympathetic one? Or is *Newsweek*
merely reporting what happened to teenagers in the 1950s?

4. How different is the voice of *Newsweek* from the voice of Hatfield
and the other teenagers described? What words and sentences tell you
that the voices are different?

5. How different are Hatfield's world and values from your own? What
language expresses the values of teenagers today? What influence does
popular music have on current teenager slang and values?

SUGGESTIONS FOR WRITING

1. Analyze the language of two sports columnists, noting the degree of informality in each and the extent to which each depends on sports jargon. Use your analysis to define the difference in the voice of each writer.

2. Describe a special jargon or slang that you share with friends or your family. Discuss the special meanings of these words and the values they express.

3. Every profession and trade has a special language or jargon that provides a "shorthand" or concise means of communicating. Examine a trade journal or popular magazine directed to a particular audience—*Popular Mechanics, Field and Stream, Stereo Review*—and identify particular words and phrases of this kind. Discuss the special meanings conveyed by several of these words or phrases.

ROBERT SULLIVAN

ROBERT SULLIVAN has written for *The New York Times Magazine, The New Republic, Rolling Stone,* and other periodicals. He is the author of *The Meadowlands* (1998) and *A Whale Hunt* (2000). His "Memo from Dad" appeared in *The New Yorker* on March 25, 1996.

A MEMO FROM DAD

As your father, I am happy to report that our family had a marvellously 1
successful first quarter this year. Earnings are up, costs are down (despite the new fuel pump on the minivan), and, as you all know by now, we've added a new member, Katherine Anne. At nine pounds two ounces, she is, I believe, another example of the kind of quality work that we've come to expect from your mother—the kind that has made us stand out from other families on the block.

And yet I can't help thinking that we've still got a lot of work left 2
to do, which is why I am circulating this memo today. We can't blame

only ourselves; like families everywhere, we are facing hard times, with new technologies, leaner competition, and inflationary orthodontic costs. But when I look around the kitchen table I see inefficiencies and redundancies, out-of-control allowances—I see a family run like a liberal welfare scam. We need to make some tough choices.

Let's begin with Jimmy. I've been reviewing your contribution to the family, and I'm afraid we're going to have to let you go. Your frequent late night weekend outings have become a drain on me personally, and I think even your mother will admit that at seventeen you're not as cute as you used to be. You will all be happy to know that I am currently in negotiations with Frank Lindgren, our next-door neighbor, hoping to arrange a contractual agreement with his son, Frank, Jr. With a part-time son, our food-and-milk overhead will be significantly reduced. Also, I see some potential synergy in the area of garbage take-out. (A brief personal note: Jimmy, I trust that you will let me know if I can be of assistance should you seek relationships with any other families in the neighborhood. I hear the Wenglers are looking for a freelance cousin, and I'd be happy to recommend you.)

In the matter of Jennifer: I am pleased to report that I have finished reviewing the analysis of last month's phone bill as conducted by Cane & Co., an independent consulting firm, and that I will be redesigning your position, as per the report's recommendation. So, while you will still be referred to as "daughter" at family gatherings and in all interfamily communications, your official title will be "communications specialist," effective immediately. Your aggressive use of late-night calling discounts is to be commended, Princess, and you'll be hearing from me soon regarding the acquisition of your new pager.

There are numerous additional positions within our family that might be merged or downsized with an eye to increased returns. I feel we will operate more efficiently, for instance, with an over-all grandparent-and-great-grandparent-surplus reduction—but attrition may help us out in this area. Likewise, Uncles Fred, Derrick, Rodney, and Harry will be removed from all barbecue-invitation lists and phone logs, and I am especially happy to announce that as of midnight tonight we will permanently discontinue the position of mother-in-law. Denise will retain her post as mother while assuming all the responsibilities that, through this refocussing of the skill mix, have not been reassigned. Here I am thinking primarily of walking Iaccoca, our German shepherd, and the Sunday-afternoon washing of the cars, both of which were formerly Jimmy's department.

As for myself, I will be attending a family-management seminar next week in the company of Frank Lindgren and Don Wengler. The program is entitled "Officer, I've Never Seen These Children Before: How to Survive a Hostile Family Takeover with Quick and Drastic Reductions in Labor Costs," and while I'm there I hope to meet with other fathers who are in the midst of downsizing. This year, it's in Palm Springs, which I think will be the perfect place for us fathers to unwind with one-on-one organizational-strategy sessions and a little golf. If anyone's concerned about the cost of the trip, don't worry: I've been reviewing my own performance, and I have decided to give myself a raise.

QUESTIONS

1. What did you expect to find in "a memo from Dad," and what did you find? What kind of memo does it resemble in language and content?

2. What message is Dad sending to members of his family?

3. What impression do you get of Dad? Does he want to convey this impression?

4. What is Sullivan's purpose in writing, and how do you know?

SUGGESTIONS FOR WRITING

1. Analyze a letter to your local newspaper, discussing the impression you get of the writer, given what he says and how he says it.

2. Show how certain words and sentences in one of the following other readings in this book help you discover the purpose of the writer:

    a. Esmeralda Santiago, "The American Invasion of Macun"

    b. E. B. White, "New York"

    c. Tom Wolfe, "Thursday Morning in a New York Subway Station"

    d. Anonymous, "Who Am I?"

    e. Jonathan Swift, "A Modest Proposal"

16

TONE

By the tone of a piece of writing, we mean the reflection of the writer's attitude toward the subject or reader. The possibilities are many: a piece of writing may be sarcastic, bitter, angry, mocking, whimsical, facetious, joyful, admiring—or indifferent. And we can reveal this attitude in numerous ways—most commonly by stating it directly:

> There should be more sympathy for school children. The idea that they are happy is of a piece with the idea that the lobster in the pot is happy. (H. L. Mencken, "Travail")

Or we can express our attitude indirectly—perhaps by exaggerating sometimes to the point of absurdity for a humorous or satirical effect as in this parody of a course description in a college bulletin:

> Rapid Reading—This course will increase reading speed a little each day until the end of the term, by which time the student will be required to read *The Brothers Karamazov* in fifteen minutes. (Woody Allen, "Spring Bulletin")

Or we can write sarcastically intending to ridicule:

> He has occasional flashes of silence, that makes his conversation perfectly delightful. (Sydney Smith, describing a famous nineteenth-century historian)

Sarcasm is a biting or sometimes angry form of irony:

> The law, in its majestic equality, forbids the rich as well as the poor to sleep under bridges, to beg in the streets, to steal bread and to commit other quality-of-life crimes. (Anatole France, *The Red Lily*)

Irony arises from a startling difference between what we expect and what we are shown:

> The fireboat burned and sank.

Or what we expect to hear and what is said:

> A man cannot be too careful in the choice of his enemies. (Oscar Wilde, *The Picture of Dorian Gray*)

Understatement is another form of irony:

> The reports of my death have been grossly exaggerated. (Mark Twain, cable to the Associated Press)

So are paradoxical statements:

> The most intolerable pain is produced by prolonging the keenest pleasure. (George Bernard Shaw, *Man and Superman*)

And humorous statements like the following are ironic:

> It has been known for years that prisons have been accepting a very low-class type of inmate, some without any education, others who are unstable, and some who are just plain antisocial. (Art Buchwald, "Upping Prison Requirements")

An ironic statement at minimum implies that something more is meant than is actually said; at most, that we mean the opposite of what we say.

As these examples suggest, tone is conveyed by the voice we try to express in writing. Voice depends on the rhythms and nuances of speech, carried into the modulations and rhythms of sentences and paragraphs. False starts in writing are often failures to discover the right voice or tone. Too formal a sentence or choice of words may create the impression of distance or unconcern; a highly informal style may suggest lack of seriousness or flippancy. Not surprisingly, we often find as we write that we need to adjust the tone. For an essay need not express a single dominant tone: the expression of our attitude changes as we turn to new ideas and details.

MARK SINGER

MARK SINGER has written a number of talk pieces and profiles for *The New Yorker* magazine. His books include *Funny Money* (1985),

Mr. Personality (1988), and *Citizen K.* (1996). Singer's account of a karate birthday party in a New York City suburb appeared in "The Talk of the Town"—a collection of short commentaries, profiles, and sketches in *The New Yorker*. The observer in the account at no point makes a personal reference or states an opinion about the party. The tone of the essay is therefore crucial in deciding whether the observer expresses an attitude toward the birthday party through what he reports.

Osu!

The karate-birthday-party concept occurred to Howard Frydman because   1
Howard Frydman is an acutely aware person. To begin with, it was obvious to Howard and his partner, Tokey Hill, who run the Karate Center of Champions, a martial-arts academy that sits right next to the Long Island Rail Road station in Douglaston, Queens, that kids love karate. Then the mother of one of the many fine eight-year-old boys in Nassau County remarked to Howard that virtually every variety of kid's-birthday-party idea you could think of had been done to death. That was about three years ago. Since then, Howard and Tokey—Howard was the captain of the American karate team and a silver-medal winner at the 1981 Maccabiah Games, in Israel, and Tokey has won even more medals than Howard, and they both recently joined the Budweiser National Karate Team and appeared on the cover of the première issue of the magazine *American Karate*—have developed and refined the karate-birthday-party concept. By now, they've done hundreds of parties. For the basic fee—a hundred dollars—you get a thirty-minute karate class for the entire party, plus fifteen minutes of professional kicking, punching, blocking, and board-breaking. Maybe, for a little extra money, Howard and Tokey will arrange for a ninja to come out and terrify the guests with one of the magnificient steel-and-chrome ninja swords that you see advertised in all the martial-arts magazines. After the kicking, punching, blocking, and board-breaking (and the ninja appearance, if that's in the package) come the pizza and cake and ice cream and birthday presents. Howard and Tokey will stage a karate birthday party either way—at your home or at the Karate Center of Champions. They'll even do it in a restaurant; Howard has done a couple of karate birthday parties at Benihana. Another time, he went to New Jersey. For a karate

birthday party in Jersey, though, he charges a pretty penny, because of all the travel.

The Karate Center of Champions has about two thousand square feet of classroom space, plywood floors, white walls, some broad mirrors along the walls, and, just inside the front door, a desk, plenty of framed and mounted photographs and martial-arts-magazine covers, and a Karate Master video game. Howard Frydman has dark hair, a trim, muscular build, a thin, bony face, and twenty years of seniority over this particular Saturday's birthday boy—Joshua Feldman, son of Geoff and Jill, of Great Neck. Joshua has the standard dimensions of an eight-year-old, curly blond hair, freckles, and pouchy cheeks. He wears a white karate robe with a blue belt. The blue belt signifies that Joshua knows how to execute fifteen basic karate movements—low block, chest block, head block, knife-hand block, several kicks, and some other stuff. If you are going to execute any of the fifteen basic karate movements, you first have to spit out your bubble gum. Then you line up and do whatever the sensei (that's an honorific term accorded a senior martial-arts instructor; Tokey Hill is out of town, so Howard is the principal sensei today) tells you to do.

Always—*always*—Sensei Frydman starts things off with a formal Oriental bow and the Japanese greeting *"Osu!"*—which sounds more like "Oos!" There are very few gestures in karate that do not seem nicer with a heartfelt *"Osu!"* tacked on at the end.

Sensei Frydman (bowing): *Osu!*

Joshua and Invited Guests (Adam, Jason, Jeremy, Michael, etc., in chorus, bowing): *Osu!*

S.F.: O.K., spread the feet a little bit. Hands on the hips. Left ear to the left shoulder. Now right ear to the right shoulder. And rotate. Rotate. O.K., rotate the entire head. That's it. Roll it around. Anybody tired yet?

I.G.s (faint chorus): No, Sensei.

S.F. (loud enough to intimidate I.G.s): I CAN'T HEAR YOU!

I.G.s (loud enough to compete with passing train): NO, SENSEI!

S.F.: Good. O.K., shake it out. Now, as part of this demonstration, we demand that Josh cut Adam in half with the sword. Are you ready? Hmm. All right, we'll do that later, after we cut the cake. Now I need some hips. Let's loosen it up. Come on, Feldman. All right, everybody sit down. Heels together, head to toes. Loosen up the back, hold your breath. O.K. Legs apart. Nose to the knee. Come on, Blue Belts, lock those knees. Close it up, Silverman. Good. Shake it out. All right, who knows what "karate" means? (Silence.) The word "karate"—nobody knows what it means?

I.G. in back row: "Self-defense"? 11

S.F.: No, that's what karate *is*. What does it mean? 12

I.G. in front row (wearing white robe and blue belt): "Empty hand." 13

S.F.: Empty hand. Right. Now, what is the main purpose of karate? 14

A different Blue Belt: Self-defense. 15

S.F.: Good. So what does that mean? It means that after class there 16
will be no running around punching and kicking each other. When you leave here and go home and are playing with your friends, there will be no punching and kicking. If you want to punch or kick the air, that's fine. But otherwise no punching or kicking. Does everybody understand?

I.G.s: Yes, Sensei. 17

S.F. (painful to eardrums): I CAN'T HEAR YOU! 18

I.G.s (loud enough to compete with passing train plus low-flying air- 19
craft): YES, SENSEI!

S.F.: O.K., another thing. What is it you can't do if you can't stand 20
up? Come on, Blue Belts—Feldman, Teppel, Stock—you know the answer.

A Blue Belt: Fight. 21

S.F.: Right. Because if you're down, your opponent can do this to 22
you. (Demonstrates incapacitating maneuvers that opponent might, if provoked, consider doing.) O.K., stand up. Up! Too slow. Down again. Now up! Stand straight. Stand strong. Silverman, what happened to you? You're like chopped liver today. You—Stop smiling. You don't have any teeth. Your opponent sees that, you're open to attack. Nice suntan, Levy. O.K., punch-and-twist exercise. That's it, full speed, full power. We're all gonna count in Japanese. Count with me.

S.F. and I.G.s count together in Japanese. 23

S.F.: O.K. Anybody tired yet? Hey, Silverman, what you got there? 24
A gun? Give me that gun. Oh, a toy gun. Control yourself, Silverman. Relax.

At the conclusion of one exercise. Sensei Frydman says, "What, no 25
'*Osu*'? Down. Everyone. Ten pushups." Ten pushups ensue. Next, the sensei demonstrates a U-punch and an elbow strike. Then he announces that Joshua Feldman will demonstrate a flying front kick, whereupon he lifts Joshua by the lapels of his white robe and Joshua incapacitates the air with his bare feet.

Any minute now, thumping sounds will come from the stairway that 26
leads to the basement, and then the door will burst open and one of the

other Karate Center of Champions instructors, Sensei David Gonzalez, will appear wearing the sort of black ninja uniform that you see advertised in all the karate magazines: black jacket with hidden pocket, black pants with leg ties, black hood, black hand wraps, the magnificent sword—the works. After Sensei Frydman has vanquished the ninja, he will say, "All right, who wants to see the ninja break a board?" Then Sensei Frydman will hold an inch-thick board at eye level, and Sensei Gonzalez will try to break it with his left foot, using a spinning-jump-hook kick. On the fifth attempt, he will get it right. Everyone—the twenty birthday celebrators, Sensei Frydman, Sensei Gonzalez—will pose for a group picture, and then it will be time to go downstairs for pizza and soft drinks and cake and ice cream. During the pizza course, Joshua Feldman and some of the other Blue Belts will get tomato-sauce stains on their white robes. After the pizza and before the cake and ice cream (there's a drawing of Hulk Hogan on the cake), the invited guests will suffer a collective mental lapse and get up from the table and run around and kick and punch and scream—all in self-defense. There will be a crucial moment during which Joshua Feldman pauses to catch his breath and to contemplate what he might like to do at his ninth-birthday party: "Go bowling. *Osu!*"

QUESTIONS

1. Is the reporter chiefly concerned with Howard Frydman and the idea of the karate birthday party, or with the party itself and Howard's friends? How do you know?

2. What is the attitude of the reporter toward Howard Frydman and the karate party? Is he admiring, or critical, or amused, or is his account wholly neutral and objective?

3. Does the reporter hold the same attitude toward Joshua Feldman and the other eight-year-old boys? How do you know?

4. Does the tone of the report change?

5. Is the reporter making a point or arguing a thesis? Or is the reporter merely describing a birthday party?

SUGGESTIONS FOR WRITING

1. Describe an event like the karate party from two points of view—from that of a neutral observer and from that of an angry or critical or amused one. Make the tone of each description clear and consistent.

2. Analyze a speech in a recent issue of *Vital Speeches* or another periodical to discover the tone of the speaker. Does the speech have a single, dominant tone, or does it change in tone? Explain how you know.

WILLIAM FINNEGAN

WILLIAM FINNEGAN, staff writer for *The New Yorker,* is the author of a number of books about southern Africa: *Crossing the Line: A Year in the Land of Apartheid* (1986), *Dateline Soweto: Travels with Black African Reporters* (1988; updated edition, 1995), and *A Complicated War: The Harrowing of Mozambique* (1992). *Cold New World: Growing Up in a Harder Country* (1998) is a study of American youth today. His description of surfing in northern California is excerpted from his two-part essay, "Surfing," in *The New Yorker* on August 17 and August 24, 1992.

SURFING

The rain puddles are like small powder-blue windows scattered on the muddy farm road as I hurry down to the beach at Four Mile. It's a soft, clear morning, with not a breath of wind, and a north swell looks to have sneaked in overnight. Remarkably, there's no one around. Four Mile is a reef break in a pristine cove between San Francisco and Santa Cruz. The break isn't visible from the highway, but it's a short walk from the road to a vantage point, and the spot is popular with surfers from Santa Cruz. I have caught Four Mile good before, but have never surfed it alone. While I pick my way across a creek behind the beach, I find myself listening anxiously for howls from the hillside behind me—other surfers

1

arriving and seeing the swell. But the only sound is a tractor chugging down long rows of Brussels sprouts that stretch away to the south.

A deep, reliable channel runs out through the middle of the cove at   2 Four Mile; the wave is on the north side. It's a quirky right, with sections that change with the tide or with any shift in the size and direction of the swell. It can get quite big, and very spooky, but the surf this morning looks benign. I paddle out through the channel, hands stinging, and my heart starts to pound when a good-sized wave hits the outside reef, stands up—bottle-green against the pale-blue sky—pitches out, explodes, and begins to wind down the reef in fine, peeling sections. This may be the best wave I've ever seen break at Four Mile. Two more nearly as good follow, and I take deep breaths to try to control a flurry of adrenaline. Carried on the back of a swift seaward current, I reach the lineup with my hair still dry. I move along a line of broad boils, paddling slowly, watching the horizon for a set, looking for a likely takeoff spot near the head of a chunk of reef, checking my position against a cypress tree on the bluff. Still nobody in sight on shore. Just one wave, I find myself praying, just one wave.

A wave comes. It swings silently through the kelp bed, a long, tapering   3 wall, darkening upcoast. I paddle across the grain of the water streaming toward the wave across the reef, angling to meet the hollow of a small peak ghosting across the face. For a moment, in the gully just in front of the wave, my board loses forward momentum as the water rushing off the reef sucks it back up the face. Then the wave lifts me up—I've met the steepest part of the peak, and swerved into its shoreward track— and with two hard strokes I'm aboard. It's a clean takeoff: a sudden sense of height fusing with a deep surge of speed. I hop to my feet and drive to the bottom, drawing out the turn and sensing, more than seeing, what the wave plans to do ahead—the low sun is blinding off the water looking south. Halfway through the first turn, I can feel the wave starting to stand up ahead. I change rails, bank off the lower part of the face, and start driving down the line. The first section flies past, and the wave— it's slightly overhead, and changing angle as it breaks, so that it now blocks out the sun—stands revealed: a long, steep, satiny arc curving all the way to the channel. I work my board from rail to rail for speed, trimming carefully through two more short sections. Gaining confidence that I will in fact make this wave, I start turning harder, slicing higher up the face and, when a last bowl section looms beside the channel, stalling briefly before driving through in a half crouch, my face pressed close to the glassy, rumbling, pea-green wall. The silver edge of the lip's axe flashes harmlessly past on my left. A second later, I'm coasting onto flat water, leaning into a pullout, and mindlessly shouting "My God!"

VOCABULARY

paragraph 1: pristine
paragraph 2: quirky, benign, adrenaline
paragraph 3: kelp

QUESTIONS

1. What are Finnegan's thoughts and feelings as he walks to the beach at Four Mile? What is the tone of paragraph 1?

2. Is there a change in tone from paragraph 1 to paragraph 2?

3. Is there a further change in paragraph 3?

4. How much of the technique employed would Finnegan need to explain if he were instructing the reader how to surf?

SUGGESTIONS FOR WRITING

1. Compare Finnegan's essay with one of the earlier readings in this book, explaining how each author establishes a tone and perhaps changes to another.

2. Narrate an experience in the course of which your feelings changed. Let the details and tone of your narrative reveal your feelings and reflect the changes.

17

IMAGERY

Images convey sensory impressions: impressions of sight, hearing, smell, taste, or touch. The following passage from a story by James Joyce illustrates most of these:

> The cold air stung us and we played till our bodies glowed. Our shouts echoed in the silent street. The career of our play brought us through the dark muddy lanes behind the houses where we ran the gauntlet of the rough tribes from the cottages, to the back doors of the dark dripping gardens where odors arose from the ashpits, to the dark odorous stables where a coachman smoothed and combed the horse or shook music from the buckled harness. ("Araby")

We think in images constantly. Joyce could not have expressed his sense of a particular street on a particular night in abstract language. The more evocative our imagery when the situation calls for vivid impressions, the more directly will our words express experience. A passage will seem overwritten if a vivid representation of experience is not needed; so-called fine writing tries to be too evocative of sense experience. In the passage quoted above, Joyce selects only those details that give the reader an impression of the physical sensations experienced in the darkness. The imagery suggests the vitality of imagination, a theme of the story; Joyce probably could not have conveyed that vitality without it.

RACHEL CARSON

The American naturalist and conservationist **RACHEL CARSON** (1907–1964) worked as a marine biologist and editor for the U.S. Fish and Wildlife

Service. Carson describes the natural life of the Atlantic coast and waters she studied in *Under the Sea-Wind* (1941), *The Edge of the Sea* (1955), and *The Sea Around Us*, which received the National Book Award in 1951. *Silent Spring* (1962), her most influential book, warned of the increasing pollution of the environment by insecticides and various chemicals. In the following passage from *The Edge of the Sea,* Carson uses various kinds of imagery to describe a walk to a rocky shore in northern New England.

THE ROCKY SHORES

When the tide is high on a rocky shore, when its brimming fullness creeps   1
up almost to the bayberry and the junipers where they come down from the land, one might easily suppose that nothing at all lived in or on or under these waters of the sea's edge. For nothing is visible. Nothing except here and there a little group of herring gulls, for at high tide the gulls rest on ledges of rock, dry above the surf and the spray, and they tuck their yellow bills under their feathers and doze away the hours of the rising water. Then all the creatures of the tidal rocks are hidden from view, but the gulls know what is there, and they know that in time the water will fall away again and give them entrance to the strip between the tide lines.

When the tide is rising the shore is a place of unrest, with the surge   2
leaping high over jutting rocks and running in lacy cascades of foam over the landward side of massive boulders. But on the ebb it is more peaceful, for then the waves do not have behind them the push of the inward pressing tides. There is no particular drama about the turn of the tide, but presently a zone of wetness shows on the gray rock slopes, and offshore the incoming swells begin to swirl and break over hidden ledges. Soon the rocks that the high tide had concealed rise into view and glisten with the wetness left on them by the receding water.

Small, dingy snails move about over rocks that are slippery with the   3
growth of infinitesimal green plants; the snails scraping, scraping, scraping to find food before the surf returns.

Like drifts of old snow no longer white, the barnacles come into view;   4
they blanket rocks and old spars wedged into rock crevices, and their sharp cones are sprinkled over empty mussel shells and lobster-pot buoys

and the hard stipes of deep-water seaweeds, all mingled in the flotsam of the tide.

Meadows of brown rockweeds appear on the gently sloping rocks of the shore as the tide imperceptibly ebbs. Smaller patches of green weed, stringy as mermaids' hair, begin to turn white and crinkly where the sun has dried them.

Now the gulls, that lately rested on the higher ledges, pace with grave intentness along the walls of rock, and they probe under the hanging curtains of weed to find crabs and sea urchins.

In the low places little pools and gutters are left where the water trickles and gurgles and cascades in miniature waterfalls, and many of the dark caverns between and under the rocks are floored with still mirrors holding the reflections of delicate creatures that shun the light and avoid the shock of waves—the cream-colored flowers of the small anemones and the pink fingers of soft coral, pendent from the rocky ceiling.

In the calm world of the deeper rock pools, now undisturbed by the tumult of incoming waves, crabs sidle along the walls, their claws busily touching, feeling, exploring for bits of food. The pools are gardens of color composed of the delicate green and ocher-yellow of encrusting sponge, the pale pink of hydroids that stand like clusters of fragile spring flowers, the bronze and electric-blue gleams of the Irish moss, the old-rose beauty of the coralline algae.

And over it all there is the smell of low tide, compounded of the faint, pervasive smell of worms and snails and jellyfish and crabs—the sulphur smell of sponge, the iodine smell of rockweed, and the salt smell of the rime that glitters on the sun-dried rocks.

One of my favorite approaches to a rocky seacoast is by a rough path through an evergreen forest that has its own peculiar enchantment. It is usually an early morning tide that takes me along that forest path, so that the light is still pale and fog drifts in from the sea beyond. It is almost a ghost forest, for among the living spruce and balsam are many dead trees—some still erect, some sagging earthward, some lying on the floor of the forest. All the trees, the living and the dead, are clothed with green and silver crusts of lichens. Tufts of the bearded lichen or old man's beard hang from the branches like bits of sea mist tangled there. Green woodland mosses and a yielding carpet of reindeer moss cover the ground. In the quiet of that place even the voice of the surf is reduced to a whispered echo and the sounds of the forest are but the ghosts of sounds—the faint sighing of evergreen needles in the moving air; the creaks and heavier groans of half-fallen trees resting against their neighbors and rubbing bark against bark; the light rattling fall of a dead branch broken under the feet of a squirrel and sent bouncing and ricocheting earthward.

But finally the path emerges from the dimness of the deeper forest and comes to a place where the sound of surf rises above the forest sounds— the hollow boom of the sea, rhythmic and insistent, striking against the rocks, falling away, rising again.   11

Up and down the coast the line of the forest is drawn sharp and clean on the edge of a seascape of surf and sky and rocks. The softness of sea fog blurs the contours of the rocks; gray water and gray mists merge offshore in a dim and vaporous world that might be a world of creation, stirring with new life.   12

VOCABULARY

paragraph 2: ebb
paragraph 3: infinitesimal
paragraph 4: barnacles, buoys, flotsam
paragraph 6: sea urchins
paragraph 7: anemones, pendent
paragraph 8: hydroids, coralline, algae
paragraph 9: rime
paragraph 10: lichen, ricocheting

QUESTIONS

1. How does Carson establish a place of observation or physical point of view in paragraphs 1–9? Does the place of observation change in the course of these paragraphs?

2. What changes from high tide to low does Carson focus on? What images of sight highlight these changes?

3. To what extent does she also depend on images of sound and smell? Do you also find images of touch?

4. How does Carson establish a physical point of view in paragraphs 10–12? Does this point of view change in the course of these paragraphs?

5. What kinds of imagery do you find in these paragraphs? Does one or more kind of imagery dominate the description?

6. What feelings does Carson experience in observing the seacoast and walking toward it? Does she name these feelings, or express them through images?

7. Does she make a point or develop a thesis in paragraphs 1–9? Does she in paragraphs 10–12? Or is her purpose in writing descriptive and expressive?

SUGGESTIONS FOR WRITING

1. Show how one of the earlier writers in this books—for example, George Orwell in "Shooting an Elephant" (p. 14) or Joan Didion in "Marrying Absurd" (p. 55)—uses images to convey an idea or express an attitude.

2. Describe an experience that gave you an unexpected picture of the world and revealed a truth about it. Let your details convey the discovery and truth. Don't state these directly.

18

FIGURATIVE LANGUAGE

A simile is an explicit comparison (using *like* or *as*) that usually develops or implies one or more simple points of resemblance:

> His face was as blank as a pan of uncooked dough. (William Faulkner, *The Hamlet*)

> Will Brangwen ducked his head and looked at his uncle with swift, mistrustful eyes, like a caged hawk. (D. H. Lawrence, *The Rainbow*)

A metaphor is an implicit comparison in which an object is presented as if it were something else.

> Constant use had not worn ragged the fabric of their friendship. (Dorothy Parker, *The Standard of Living*)

> He had the gaunt and haunted athletic look of those who stare daily down the bony gullet of the great god Aerobics. (Tom Wolfe, *The Bonfire of the Vanities*)

Personification is the attribution of human qualities to abstract ideas or objects. Simile, metaphor, and personification unite in the following passage:

> Then Sunday light raced over the farm as fast as the chickens were flying. Immediately the first straight shaft of heat, solid as a hickory stick, was laid on the ridge. (Eudora Welty, *Losing Battles*)

One purpose of figures of speech is to evoke the qualities of experience and give shape or substance to an emotion or awareness that up to the moment of its expression may be indefinite. In exposition a writer will depend on metaphor because of its property of expressing an attitude as well as representing an idea:

> My parents' house had an attic, the darkest and strangest part of the building, reachable only by placing a stepladder beneath the trapdoor and filled with unidentifiable articles too important to be thrown out with the trash but no longer suitable to have at hand. This mysterious space was the memory of the place. After many years all the things deposited in it became, one by one, lost to consciousness. But they were there, we knew, safely and comfortably stored in the tissues of the house. (Lewis Thomas, "The Attic of the Brain")

Figurative writing is particularly important in descriptive writing, as in the following paragraph which conveys an unusual experience and sensation through metaphor and other figures:

> Although I was still miles from the ocean, a heavy sea fog came in to muffle the obscure woods and lie over the land like a sheet of dirty muslin. I saw no cars or people, few lights in the houses. The windshield wipers, brushing at the fog, switched back and forth like cats' tails. I lost myself to the monotonous rhythm and darkness as past and present fused and dim things came and went in a staccato of moments separated by miles of darkness. On the road, where change is continuous and visible, time is not; rather it is something the rider only infers. Time is not the traveler's fourth dimension—change is. (William Least Heat-Moon, *Blue Highways*)

DIANE ACKERMAN

DIANE ACKERMAN, poet and essayist, writes on natural history and ecology in *The Moon by Whale Light* (1991) and *Rarest of the Rare: Vanishing Animals, Vanishing Worlds* (1995). Her poems are collected in *Lady Faustus* (1983) and *Reverse Thunder* (1988); *On Extended Wings* (1985) is a memoir. Other books include *A Natural History of Love* (1994), a companion to *A Natural History of the Senses* (1990), in which her essay on a night launching of the space shuttle appears. Ackerman writes: "We live on the leash of our senses. Although they enlarge us, they also limit and restrain us, but how beautifully." Figurative language is one means by which Ackerman helps the reader experience the sensations of the launch.

WATCHING A NIGHT LAUNCH
OF THE SPACE SHUTTLE

A huge glittering tower sparkles across the Florida marshlands. Floodlights reach into the heavens all around it, rolling out carpets of light. Helicopters and jets blink around the launch pad like insects drawn to flame. Oz never filled the sky with such diamond-studded improbability. Inside the cascading lights, a giant trellis holds a slender rocket to its heart, on each side a tall thermos bottle filled with solid fuel the color and feel of a hard eraser, and on its back a sharp-nosed space shuttle, clinging like the young of some exotic mammal. A full moon bulges low in the sky, its face turned toward the launch pad, its mouth open.

On the sober consoles of launch control, numbers count backward toward zero. When numbers vanish, and reverse time ends, something will disappear. Not the shuttle—that will stay with us through eyesight and radar, and be on the minds of dozens of tracking dishes worldwide, rolling their heads as if to relieve the anguish. For hours we have been standing on these Floridian bogs, longing for the blazing rapture of the moment ahead, longing to be jettisoned free from routine, and lifted, like the obelisk we launch, that much nearer the infinite. On the fog-wreathed banks of the Banana River, and by the roadside lookouts, we are waiting: 55,000 people are expected at the Space Center alone.

When floodlights die on the launch pad, camera shutters and mental shutters all open in the same instant. The air feels loose and damp. A hundred thousand eyes rush to one spot, where a glint below the booster rocket flares into a pinwheel of fire, a sparkler held by hand on the Fourth of July. White clouds shoot out in all directions, in a dust storm of flame, a gritty, swirling Sahara, burning from gray-white to an incandescent platinum so raw it makes your eyes squint, to a radiant gold so narcotic you forget how to blink. The air is full of bee stings, prickly and electric. Your pores start to itch. Hair stands up stiff on the back of your neck. It used to be that the launch pad would melt at lift-off, but now 300,000 gallons of water crash from aloft, burst from below. Steam clouds scent the air with a mineral ash. Crazed by reflection, the waterways turn the color of pounded brass. Thick cumulus clouds shimmy and build at ground level, where you don't expect to see thunderheads.

Seconds into the launch, an apricot *whoosh* pours out in spasms, like the rippling quarters of a palomino, and now outbleaches the sun, as clouds rise and pile like a Creation scene. Birds leap into the air along with moths and dragonflies and gnats and other winged creatures, all driven to panic by the clamor: booming, crackling, howling downwind. What is flight, that it can take place in the fragile wings of a moth, whose power station is a heart small as a computer chip? What is flight, that it can groan upward through 4.5 million pounds of dead weight on a colossal gantry? Close your eyes, and you hear the deafening *rat-a-tat-tat* of firecrackers, feel them arcing against your chest. Open your eyes, and you see a huge steel muscle dripping fire, as seven million pounds of thrust pauses a moment on a silver haunch, and then the bedlam clouds let rip. Iron struts blow over the launch pad like newspapers, and shock waves roll out, pounding their giant fists, pounding the marshes where birds shriek and fly, pounding against your chest, where a heart already rapid begins running clean away from you. The air feels tight as a drum, the molecules bouncing. Suddenly the space shuttle leaps high over the marshlands, away from the now frantic laughter of the loons, away from the reedy delirium of the insects and the open-mouthed awe of the spectators, many of whom are crying, as it rises on a waterfall of flame 700 feet long, shooting colossal sparks as it climbs in a golden halo that burns deep into memory.

Only ten minutes from lift-off, it will leave the security blanket of our atmosphere, and enter an orbit 184 miles up. This is not miraculous. After all, we humans began in an early tantrum of the universe, when our chemical makeup first took form. We evolved through accidents, happenstance, near misses, and good luck. We developed language, forged cities, mustered nations. Now we change the course of rivers and move mountains; we hold back trillions of tons of water with cement dams. We break into human chests and heads; operate on beating hearts and thinking brains. What is defying gravity compared to that? In orbit, there will be no night and day, no up and down. No one will have their "feet on the ground." No joke will be "earthy." No point will be "timely." No thrill will be "out of this world." In orbit, the sun will rise every hour and a half, and there will be 112 days to each week. But then time has always been one of our boldest and most ingenious inventions, and, when you think about it, one of the least plausible of our fictions.

Lunging to the east out over the water, the shuttle rolls slowly onto   6
its back, climbing at three g's, an upshooting torch, twisting an umbilical of white cloud beneath it. When the two solid rockets fall free, they
hover to one side like bright red quotation marks, beginning an
utterance it will take four days to finish. For over six minutes of seismic wonder it is still visible, this star we hurl up at the star-studded
sky. What is a neighborhood? One wonders. Is it the clump of wild
daisies beside the Banana River, in which moths hover and dive without the aid of rockets? For large minds, the Earth is a small place. Not
small enough to exhaust in one lifetime, but a compact home, cozy,
buoyant, a place to cherish, the spectral center of our life. But how
could we stay at home forever?

VOCABULARY

paragraph 1: Oz, trellis
paragraph 2: console, obelisk
paragraph 3: incandescent
paragraph 4: palomino, gantry, arcing, haunch, bedlam, reedy
paragraph 5: tantrum, happenstance, plausible
paragraph 6: umbilical, seismic

QUESTIONS

1. What similes and metaphors help to describe the launch pad in paragraph 1? What use does Ackerman make of personification?

2. What similes, metaphors, and personifications help her describe the
launch in paragraphs 3 and 4?

3. How do these and other figures help Ackerman express her feelings
about the launch?

4. What central idea or thesis does she develop? Where does she first
state it? What images and figures help her to express it?

SUGGESTIONS FOR WRITING

1. Write several paragraphs describing an exciting event you once witnessed. Rewrite your description, heightening it through similes, metaphors, and other figures. Keep your audience in mind as you write.

2. Analyze the use Rachel Carson makes of figurative language in one or two paragraphs of her description of the Maine coast (p. 000).

3. Analyze the figurative language in a series of automobile or cosmetic ads, or those for another product. Comment on the effectiveness of the language.

GEORGE LAKOFF AND
MARK JOHNSON

GEORGE LAKOFF, Professor of Linguistics at the University of California, Berkeley, is a major figure in generative semantics, cognitive linguistics, and the neural theory of language. His writings in other fields include *Women, Fire, and Dangerous Things* (1987) and, with Mark Turner, *More Than Cool Reason: A Field Guide to Poetic Metaphor* (1989). MARK JOHNSON, Professor of Philosophy at the University of Oregon, is coauthor of *Metaphors We Live By* (1980) and *Philosophy in the Flesh* (1999). His other writings include *Body in the Mind* (1987) and *Moral Imagination* (1993). Lakoff and Johnson argue that the ideas and concepts, basic to how we think about the world and about ourselves, originate in experience of the body. Metaphor carries our bodily experience into thought.

TIME IS MONEY

To get an idea of how metaphorical expressions in everyday language can give us insight into the metaphorical nature of the concepts that structure our everyday activities, let us consider the metaphorical concept TIME IS MONEY as it is reflected in contemporary English.

TIME IS MONEY

> You're *wasting* my time.
> This gadget will *save* you hours.
> I don't *have* the time to *give* you.
> How do you *spend* your time these days?
> That flat tire *cost* me an hour.
> I've *invested* a lot of time in her.
> I don't *have enough* time to *spare* for that.
> You're *running out* of time.
> You need to *budget* your time.
> *Put aside* some time for ping pong.
> Is that *worth your while?*
> Do you *have* much time *left?*
> He's living on *borrowed* time.
> You don't *use* your time *profitably.*
> I *lost* a lot of time when I got sick.
> *Thank you for* your time.

Time in our culture is a valuable commodity. It is a limited resource   2
that we use to accomplish our goals. Because of the way that the concept of work has developed in modern Western culture, where work is
typically associated with the time it takes and time is precisely quantified, it has become customary to pay people by the hour, week, or
year. In our culture TIME IS MONEY in many ways: telephone message
units, hourly wages, hotel room rates, yearly budgets, interest on loans,
and paying your debt to society by "serving time." These practices are
relatively new in the history of the human race, and by no means do
they exist in all cultures. They have arisen in modern industrialized
societies and structure our basic everyday activities in a very profound
way. Corresponding to the fact that we *act* as if time is a valuable
commodity—a limited resource, even money—we *conceive of* time that
way. Thus we understand and experience time as the kind of thing that
can be spent, wasted, budgeted, invested wisely or poorly, saved,
or squandered.

TIME IS MONEY, TIME IS A LIMITED RESOURCE, and TIME IS A VALUABLE   3
COMMODITY are all metaphorical concepts. They are metaphorical since
we are using our everyday experiences with money, limited resources, and
valuable commodities to conceptualize time. This isn't a necessary way
for human beings to conceptualize time; it is tied to our culture. There
are cultures where time is none of these things.

The metaphorical concepts TIME IS MONEY, TIME IS A RESOURCE, and   4
TIME IS A VALUABLE COMMODITY form a single system based on subcategorization, since in our society money is a limited resource and limited
resources are valuable commodities. These subcategorization relationships characterize entailment relationships between the metaphors. TIME
IS MONEY entails that TIME IS A LIMITED RESOURCE, which entails that
TIME IS A VALUABLE COMMODITY.

We are adopting the practice of using the most specific metaphor-   5
ical concept, in this case TIME IS MONEY, to characterize the entire
system. Of the expressions listed under the TIME IS MONEY metaphor,
some refer specifically to money (*spend, invest, budget, profitably,
cost*), others to limited resources (*use, use up, have enough of, run
out of*), and still others to valuable commodities (*have, give, lose, thank
you for*). This is an example of the way in which metaphorical
entailments can characterize a coherent system of metaphorical concepts and a corresponding coherent system of metaphorical expressions
for those concepts.

VOCABULARY

paragraph 2: quantified, profound
paragraph 7: coherent

QUESTIONS

1. How do the examples in paragraph 3 help to explain what a metaphorical concept is?

2. What is the chief category of which the concepts named in paragraph 4
are subordinate, that is, subcategories? How did Lakoff and Johnson decide which of the concepts was chief?

3. How do the concepts discussed in paragraph 6 form a single system?

SUGGESTION FOR WRITING

Identify the metaphors in the following passages. Then comment on how they help to guide our thinking about the issue.

These are the times that try men's souls: The summer soldier and the sunshine patriot will in this crisis, shrink from the service of his country; but he that stands it Now, deserves the love and thanks of man and woman. Tyranny, like hell, is not easily conquered; yet we have this consolation with us, that the harder the conflict, the more glorious the triumph. What we obtain too cheap, we esteem too lightly:———' Tis dearness only that gives everything its value. Heaven knows how to put a proper price upon its goods; and it would be strange indeed, if so celestial an article as FREEDOM should not be highly rated. Britain, with an army to enforce her tyranny, has declared that she has a right (not only to) TAX but "to BIND *us in* ALL CASES WHATSOEVER", and if being *bound in that manner,* is not slavery, then is there not such a thing as slavery upon earth. Even the expression is impious for so unlimited a power can belong only to God. (Thomas Paine, *The American Crisis*)

Time is but the stream I go a-fishing in. I drink at it; but while I drink I see the sandy bottom and detect how shallow it is. Its thin current slides away, but eternity remains. I would drink deeper; fish in the sky, whose bottom is pebbly with stars. I cannot count one. I know not the first letter of the alphabet. I have always been regretting that I was not as wise as the day I was born. The intellect is a cleaver; it discerns and rifts its way into the secret of things. I do not wish to be any more busy with my hands than is necessary. My head is hands and feet. I feel all my best faculties concentrated in it. My instinct tells me that my head is an organ for burrowing, as some creatures use their snout and fore-paws, and with it I would mine and burrow my way through these hills. I think that the richest vein is somewhere hereabouts; so by the divining-rod and thin rising vapors I judge; and here I will begin to mine. (Henry David Thoreau, *Walden*)

19

CONCRETENESS

Writing is *concrete* when it makes an observation or impression perceptible to the senses. Eric Sevareid makes concrete the changes that occurred in his hometown in North Dakota:

> Sounds have changed; I heard not once the clopping of a horse's hoof, nor the mourn of a coyote. I heard instead the shriek of brakes, the heavy throbbing of the once-a-day Braniff airliner into Minot, the shattering sirens born of war, the honk of a diesel locomotive which surely cannot call to faraway places the heart of a wakeful boy like the old steam whistle in the night. ("Velva, North Dakota")

Complex ideas can be made concrete with vivid examples; indeed, examples are essential to our understanding:

> I have described the hand when it uses a tool as an instrument of discovery. . . . We see this every time a child learns to couple hand and tool together—to lace its shoes, to thread a needle, to fly a kite or to play a penny whistle. With the practical action there goes another, namely finding pleasure in the action for its own sake—in the skill that one perfects, and perfects by being pleased with it. This at bottom is responsible for every work of art, and science too: our poetic delight in what human beings do because they can do it. (J. Bronowski, *The Ascent of Man*)

Imagery and figurative language can increase the vividness of specific details.

Whatever the purpose of the writer, excessive detail will blur the focus and perhaps make the writing incoherent. Voltaire said, "The secret of being a bore is to tell everything." A boring movie may show everything in what seems like an endless stream of detail; a boring paragraph or essay does the same thing. To develop an idea or impression effectively, we must *select* the detail. Good writing is economical.

BAILEY WHITE

A graduate of Florida State University, BAILEY WHITE teaches first grade in Thomasville, Georgia. Her commentaries on her life in the South are heard periodically on National Public Radio. Her essays are collected in *Mama Makes Up Her Mind and Other Dangers of Southern Living* (1993), in which the following appears.

MORTALITY

It really makes you feel your age when you get a letter from your insurance agent telling you that the car you bought, only slightly used, the year you got out of college, is now an antique. "Beginning with your next payment, your insurance premiums will reflect this change in classification," the letter said.

I went out and looked at the car. I thought back over the years. I could almost hear my uncle's disapproving voice. "You should never buy a used car," he had told me the day I brought it home. Ten years later I drove that used car to his funeral. I drove my sister, Louise, to the hospital in that car to have her first baby, and I drove to Atlanta in that car when the baby graduated from Georgia Tech with a degree in physics.

"When are you going to get a new car?" my friends asked me.

"I don't need a new car," I said. "This car runs fine."

I changed the oil often, and I kept good tires on it. It always got me where I wanted to go. But the stuffing came out of the backseat and the springs poked through, and the dashboard disintegrated. At 300,000 miles the odometer quit turning, but I didn't really care to know how far I had driven.

A hole wore in the floor where my heel rested in front of the accelerator, and the insulation all peeled off the fire wall. "Old piece of junk," my friends whispered. The seat-belt catch wore out, and I tied on a huge bronze hook with a fireman's knot.

Big flashy cars would zoom past me. People would shake their fists   7
out the windows. "Get that clunker off the road!" they would shout.

Then one day on my way to work, the car coughed, sputtered, and   8
stopped. "This is it," I thought, and I gave it a pat. "It's been a good car."

I called the mechanic. "Tow it in," I said. "I'll have to decide what   9
to do." After work I went over there. I was feeling very glum. The mechanic laughed at me. "It's not funny," I said. "I've had that car a long time."

"You know what's wrong with that car?" he said. "That car was out   10
of gas." So I slopped a gallon of gas in the tank and drove ten more years. The gas gauge never worked again after that day, but I got to where I could tell when the gas was low by the smell. I think it was the smell of the bottom of the tank.

There was also a little smell of brake fluid, a little smell of exhaust,   11
a little smell of oil, and after all the years a little smell of me. Car smells. And sounds. The wonderful sound when the engine finally catches on a cold day, and an ominous *tick tick* in July when the radiator is working too hard. The windshield wipers said "Gracie Allen Gracie Allen Gracie Allen." I didn't like a lot of conversation in the car because I had to keep listening for a little skip that meant I needed to jump out and adjust the carburetor.

I kept a screwdriver close to hand—and a pint of brake fluid, and a   12
new roter, just in case. "She's strange," my friends whispered. "And she drives so slow."

I don't know how fast I drove. The speedometer had quit working   13
years ago. But when I would look down through the hole in the floor and see the pavement, a gray blur, whizzing by just inches away from my feet, and feel the tremendous heat of internal combustion pouring back through the fire wall into my lap, and hear each barely contained explosion just as a heart attack victim is able to hear his own heartbeat, it didn't feel like slow to me. A whiff of brake fluid would remind me just what a tiny thing I was relying on to stop myself from hurtling along the surface of the earth at an unnatural speed, and when I finally arrived at my destination, I would slump back, unfasten the seat belt hook with trembling hands, and stagger out. I would gather up my things and give the car a last look. "Thank you, sir," I would say. "We got here one more time."

But after I got that letter, I began thinking about getting a new car.   14
I read the newspaper every night. Finally I found one that sounded good. It
was the same make as my car, but almost new. "Call Steve," the ad said.

I went to see the car. It was parked in Steve's driveway. It was a fash-   15
ionable wheat color. There was carpet on the floor, and the seats were
covered with a soft, velvety-feeling stuff. It smelled like acrylic and vinyl
and Steve. The instrument panel looked like what you would need to run
a jet plane. I turned a knob. Mozart's Concerto for Flute and Harp poured
out of four speakers. "But how can you listen to the engine with music
playing?" I asked Steve.

I turned the key. The car started instantly. No desperate pleadings,   16
no wild hopes, no exquisitely paired maneuvers with the accelerator and
the choke. Just instant ignition. I turned off the radio. I could barely hear
the engine running, a low, steady hum. I fastened my seat belt. Nothing
but a click.

Steve got in the passenger seat, and we went for a test drive. We   17
floated down the road. I couldn't hear a sound, but I decided it must be
time to shift gears. I stomped around on the floor and grabbed Steve's
knee before I remembered it had automatic transmission. "You mean you
just put it in 'Drive' and drive?" I asked.

Steve scrunched himself way over against his door and clamped his   18
knees together. He tested his seat belt. "Have you ever driven a car before?" he asked.

I bought it for two thousand dollars. I rolled all the windows up by   19
mashing a button beside my elbow, set the air-conditioning on "Recirc,"
and listened to Vivaldi all the way home.

So now I have two cars. I call them my new car and my real car.   20
Most of the time I drive my new car. But on some days I go out to the
barn and get in my real car. I shoo the rats out of the backseat and crank
it up. Even without daily practice my hands and feet know just what to
do. My ears perk up, and I sniff the air. I add a little brake fluid, a little water. I sniff again. It'll need gas next week, and an oil change.

I back it out and we roll down the road. People stop and look. They   21
smile. "Neat car!" they say.

When I pull into the parking lot, my friends shake their heads and   22
chuckle. They amble into the building. They're already thinking about their
day's work. But I take one last look at the car and think what an amazing thing it is, internal combustion. And how wonderful to be still alive!

Questions

1. How does Bailey White make the differences between the old car and her new one concrete for the reader? How does she make her driving experiences concrete?

2. Is White making a point directly or indirectly in describing the physical differences and her driving experiences in the two cars?

3. What are the sources of humor in the essay? Is the essay satirical as well as humorous?

Suggestions for Writing

1. Write about your own experiences with an old car, using these experiences to develop an idea. Make the idea concrete through the details you provide of the car and your experiences.

2. Compare the use Bailey White makes of her driving experiences with the use W. S. Merwin makes of his (p. 88) or Eudora Welty makes of hers (p. 112). Discuss differences in tone as well as purpose.

GEORGE PLIMPTON

As principal editor of *Paris Review,* George Plimpton edited the nine volumes of *Writers at Work*—interviews with authors who appeared in that periodical. The most recent are collected in *Beat Writers at Work* (1999) and *Playwrights at Work* (2000). Plimpton is also known for books describing his training and participation with athletes in various sports, including professional baseball, in *Out of My League* (1961); football, in *Paper Lion* (1966); hockey, in *Open Net* (1985); golf and the PGA Tournament, in *The Bogey Man.* Some of his other writings are included in *The Best of Plimpton* (1990). The following excerpt is taken from his history of fireworks.

FIREWORKS

"What are fireworks like?" she had asked.
"They are like the Aurora Borealis," said the King, "only much more natural. I pre-
fer them to stars myself, as you always know when they are going to appear . . ."

OSCAR WILDE
The Remarkable Rocket

The great thing was to do it yourself—just the nudge of a lighted punk   1
to a fuse, a small commitment that seemed such an insignificant act, and
yet the result was so decisive and visible . . . the sudden puff of a colored
ball emerging from the long tube of a Roman candle, the quick rush and
fading hiss of a rocket, the popping busyness of lawn fountains that
smoked and sputtered and sent the family cat scurrying under the upstairs bed. Anyone could do it. Even "the snake in the grass," that curious pellet that elongated and convoluted into a length of gray-black ash,
had its quality of mystery. Whoever lit it suddenly had the extraordinary
alchemist's gift of turning an inert object into something else. And fireworks provided a sort of equalizer, especially for those kids who were
not good at sports, and were taken last on the pickup teams, and knew
they were doomed to spend most of the long summer afternoons in the
far reaches of right field when they were not stepping up to the plate and
striking out. They, too, on the Fourth of July had the capacity to create
something just as satisfactory as a ball caught up against the fence—or
a base hit—and make a big racket about it besides . . . with only the requirement of nerve enough to reach forward with the punk to the brightly
papered device on the lawn and touch it to the fuse to set the thing off.

I always thought it was the best day of the year. It was in the mid-   2
dle of the summer, to begin with, and when you got up in the morning
someone would almost surely say, as they did in those times, that it was
going to be a "true Fourth of July scorcher." School had been out long
enough so that one was conditioned for the great day. One's feet were
already leather-hard, so that striding barefoot across a gravel driveway
could be done without wincing, and yet not so insensitive as to be unable to feel against one's soles the luxurious wet wash of a dew-soaked
lawn in the early morning. Of course, the best thing about the day was
the anticipation of the fireworks—both from the paper bag of one's own
assortment, carefully picked from the catalogs, and then, after a day's

worth of the excitement of setting them off, there was always the tradition of getting in the car with the family and going off to the municipal show, or perhaps a Beach Club's display . . . the barge out in the harbor, a dark hulk as evening fell, and the heart-pounding excitement of seeing the first glow of a flare out there across the water and knowing that the first shell was about to soar up into the sky.

Christmas was all right, but it was over too quickly, and was almost   3
inevitably fraught with dashed hopes. Rather than the Savage .475 Special rifle (complete with barrel scope) that one had specifically asked for, the "big present" turned out (the heart sank as one noticed the conformation of the package under the Christmas tree) to be a dartboard. Grandmother—one had counted on her—inevitably turned up at the house with a Norwegian sweater she had bought "especially" on a cruise that summer through the fjords.

The Fourth of July had none of these disappointments, unless it rained,   4
which I do not ever remember happening until fireworks were banned and when it did not make any difference. The day was always bright.

A big part of it when I was growing up were what rightfully became the   5
bane of the fireworks industry—the cherry bombs and silver salutes. They were the first objects, after a scout knife, matches, and one's first BB gun, that a youngster was truly lectured about—vociferously, the admonishing tone, the dire warnings about what the cherry bomb could do to fingers or eyes. I can remember the helter-skelter flight after nervously lighting my first cherry bomb off a stick of punk, peering around the corner of the tree at the steamlike smoke in the grass, and starting at the violent report.

There were various accessories that could be used with a cherry bomb.   6
I remember an iron device like a football kicking-tee on which one balanced a tennis ball; when the cherry bomb went off underneath, it knocked the ball straight up, far above the elm trees and the rooftops, finally just a speck in the sky; the great thing was to circle under the ball with a baseball glove as it began to rematerialize; there was time enough to construct an entire mental scenario—the last out of the World Series, a "loud" foul as they used to say, and a lot depended on its being caught because the bases were loaded, and there was the business of waving everyone off that responsibility, shouting out to one's five-year-old sister, standing by on the lawn, wide-eyed, with a lollipop in her mouth, "I've got it! I've got it!"

There were other uses for the cherry bomb that I heard about among   7
school chums but never had the nerve to try: with its lacquered and thus waterproof fuse, the cherry bomb was a favorite for lighting and flushing

down a toilet at school to see what would happen; the inevitable was a pipe bursting a floor or two below with devastating effect, particularly if a class happened to be in session. Fortunately, the bulk of those devices were around in midsummer when schools were not in session. It was obviously not an experiment one wanted to try in one's own house.

On the Fourth, there were other, more refined items that also utilized a sharp bang. One of my favorites was the SOS Ship—a squat, cardboard ocean liner, about five inches long, with people painted standing along the rail; belowdecks their faces peered out of round portholes; it was a craft quite suitable for launching in a pond or a swimming pool; it had a single funnel with a fuse sticking out of the top which, when lit, caused (according to the catalog) "A Shrill Siren Whistle Followed by Several Loud Reports Ending in Complete Destruction of Ship." For a young boy there was something agreeably satanic to hold the destiny of these painted people in his hand and to launch them on their last journey—one could see their immobile passive faces staring imperturbably out of the portholes as the liner bobbed out into the pool while above them the ship's funnel began to send out its last despairing shriek. 8

A companion piece was a cardboard fire engine that did more or less the same thing, including an equally cataclysmic finale which was described in the catalog as "A Whistle Followed by a Brilliant Flash of Flame, Ending in Complete Conflagration of Fire Engine." Only in the fertile minds of fireworks designers could the notion exist of a fire engine exploding and burning up! 9

There was a whole series of self-destruct items—a "Gothic Castle," among them, and perhaps the most bizarre—"A Wild Elephant . . . A Ferocious Beast That Belches Fire, Goes Mad and Destroys Itself!" 10

The prices were within a youngster's fiduciary parameters. For example, for five dollars in 1935, from the American Fireworks Distributing Co. in Franklin's Park, a suburb of Chicago, one could order a "Children's Assortment," which included four boxes of sparklers, twelve Python Black Snakes, twelve pounds of various-sized firecrackers, a Catherine wheel, firepots, and Roman candles—a total of fifty-six listed items! 11

What one chose was carefully culled from brightly colored pamphlets printed on cheap straw-colored paper with illustrations that could hold the attention of a boy for the better part of a day. Once again, they were at least as exciting as those that arrived in the weeks before Christmas. The Christmas catalogs were geared for adults and they seemed to emphasize kitchen appliances and chinaware, all at enormous expense, whereas the items in the Fourth of July catalogs were not only mostly 12 within one's own means but they were absolutely consistent and to the point: Everything in there was calculated to terrify mothers.

The catalogs had a hyperbolic style (an "Octopus shell" had twenty-four tentacles) that kept one lingering on a page—the imagination ignited by the bright illustrations and the carny prose. "Tom, Dick, and Harry," the description might read, "a red-hot trio! Tom—a powerful No. 2 Flash Bomb; Dick—a beautiful No. 3 Star Shell; Harry—a big No. 3 whistling aerial bomb. Touch a match to it and away goes Tom with a big noise, sailing high in the air before he bursts with a loud report. Dick follows with a terrific shower of beautiful stars. Then away goes Harry with a screaming whistle before he bursts in the air with a big bang. New. Different. Sensational. Order plenty!"

While the copy was always flamboyant and hypnotizing, perhaps the first suspicions in a youngster's mind that one should not believe everything one read came from these catalogs. Even if "Tom, Dick, and Harry" did everything one hoped of them out there on the lawn, there were other items that did not live up to expectations. "Extra-Large Python Snakes," the description would proclaim. "Just light one of the pellets, and out comes a black *snake,* little by little, until it reaches a length of three to four feet!"

I lit perhaps thirty of them—all when I was about ten years old—perhaps the first firework item to which I was ever allowed to touch a piece of lighted punk; and even though I watched their performance prudently, as usual from behind a tree, I never saw one of the "snakes" produce more than half a foot of length until—in a quite touching final convulsion that looked more like a death than a birth—the thin piping of gray-black ash would shrivel up and collapse upon itself.

So one learned to be careful about catalog copy. The choices were made with great care. A couple of weeks before the Fourth, the fireworks themselves arrived. Parents inevitably took the packages and hid them away somewhere, but usually they could be ferreted out and the devices within lined up to be gloated over.

They were inevitably, in their flamboyant colors, pretty, but there was always that fine fringe of danger one was aware of. Indeed, if one learned to suspect the sales pitch in a fireworks catalog, perhaps the first English sentences that one truly absorbed were those on the items themselves: *Do Not Hold in Hand After Lighting,* or (even more awe-inspiring) *Lay on Ground—Light Fuse—Get Away* . . . these were among the first positive indications to a youngster that the written language was of use in imparting extremely important information.

The Fourth itself always seemed to be the longest day of the year. So   18
much went on: when one's own allotment of daytime fireworks was
done—the cherry bombs, the smoke bombs, the parachute shells, and
so forth—there were friends with theirs to join down the block. Twilight
was awaited eagerly, since the bulk of one's "best" fireworks were for use
in the darkness. The colored stars rose from the lawns up above the trees.

VOCABULARY

paragraph 1: elongated, convoluted, alchemist
paragraph 5: vociferously, helter-skelter
paragraph 8: imperturbably
paragraph 11: fiduciary, parameters
paragraph 13: hyperbolic
paragraph 14: flamboyant

QUESTIONS

1. "The great thing was to do it yourself," Plimpton writes. How does
he make this "great thing" concrete in paragraph 1?

2. How does he make concrete his preference for the Fourth of July?

3. What made the cherry bomb a desirable firework? How does Plimpton
make this attraction concrete?

4. How were the SOS Ship and the cardboard fire engine more refined
than the cherry bomb? How different were the pleasures these provided?

5. How does Plimpton illustrate the "hyperbolic style" of the catalogs?
What point is he making about this style?

SUGGESTIONS FOR WRITING

1. Describe the feelings another holiday still arouses in you, and like
Plimpton make these feelings concrete through the objects you associate
with it and the things you did.

2. Show how Mark Twain made "sounding" the Mississippi, or Eudora
Welty her feelings on the summer trip, concrete for the reader.

20

EUPHEMISM AND JARGON

We hear much today about the abuse of language—particularly about euphemism and equivocation like that cited by George Orwell in his classic essay "Politics and the English Language":

> Defenseless villages are bombarded from the air, the inhabitants driven out into the countryside, the cattle machine-gunned, the huts set on fire with incendiary bullets: this is called *pacification*. Millions of peasants are robbed of their farms and sent trudging along the roads with no more than they can carry: this is called *transfer of population* or *rectification of frontiers*.

Writing in 1946, Orwell bluntly tells his readers that "[i]n our time, political speech and writing are largely the defense of the indefensible," and he adds that this language "has to consist largely of euphemism, question-begging, and sheer cloudy vagueness." We can guess what Orwell would have said about political language in our own time—about such phrases as "credibility gap" and "positive reference input" to describe the reputations of office holders and candidates, and in nonpolitical discourse, "interfaces between student and teacher" to describe conferences. Such vague and pretentious language can be comical, as Russell Baker shows in his retelling of "Little Red Riding Hood" (see p. 278), but as Orwell explains, the abuses of language have consequences: "if thought corrupts language, language can also corrupt thought."

Every profession and trade has a special language—technical words and, as Perri Klass shows, sometimes coded expressions— making communication efficient and precise. "It would be well if *jargon* could be confined to the first sense," H. W. Fowler says in *Modern English Usage,* referring to this professional language. "There is plenty of work for it there alone, so copiously does jargon of this sort breed nowadays, especially in the newer sciences such as psychology and sociology, and so readily does it escape from its proper sphere to produce popularized technicalities—words that cloud the minds alike of those who use them and those who read them."

PERRI KLASS

PERRI KLASS graduated from Harvard Medical School in 1986. She describes her experiences there in *A Not Entirely Benign Procedure* (1987), in which the following essay appears. Klass writes about her experiences as a Boston pediatrician in *Baby Doctor* (1992). She is also the author of *I Am Having an Adventure* (1986), a collection of stories, and a novel *Other Women's Children* (1990).

LEARNING THE LANGUAGE

"Mrs. Tolstoy is your basic LOL in NAD, admitted for a soft rule-out   1
MI," the intern announces. I scribble that on my patient list. In other words, Mrs. Tolstoy is a Little Old Lady in No Apparent Distress who is in the hospital to make sure she hasn't had a heart attack (rule out a Myocardial Infarction). And we think it's unlikely that she has had a heart attack (a *soft* rule-out).

If I learned nothing else during my first three months of working   2
in the hospital as a medical student, I learned endless jargon and abbreviations. I started out in a state of primeval innocence, in which I didn't even know that "s̄ CP, SOB, N/V" meant "without chest pain, shortness of breath, or nausea and vomiting." By the end I took the abbreviations so much for granted that I would complain to my mother the English professor, "And can you believe I had to put down *three* NG tubes last night?"

"You'll have to tell me what an NG tube is if you want me to sym-   3
pathize properly," my mother said. NG, nasogastric—isn't it obvious?

I picked up not only the specific expressions but also the patterns of   4
speech and the grammatical conventions; for example, you never say that

a patient's blood pressure fell or that his cardiac enzymes rose. Instead, the patient is always the subject of the verb: "He dropped his pressure." "He bumped his enzymes." This sort of construction probably reflects the profound irritation of the intern when the nurses come in the middle of the night to say that Mr. Dickinson has disturbingly low blood pressure. "Oh, he's gonna hurt me bad tonight," the intern might say, inevitably angry at Mr. Dickinson for dropping his pressure and creating a problem.

When chemotherapy fails to cure Mrs. Bacon's cancer, what we say 5 is, "Mrs. Bacon failed chemotherapy."

"Well, we've already had one hit today, and we're up next, but at 6 least we've got mostly stable players on our team." This means that our team (group of doctors and medical students) has already gotten one new admission today, and it is our turn again, so we'll get whoever is admitted next in emergency, but at least most of the patients we already have are fairly stable, that is, unlikely to drop their pressures or in any other way get suddenly sicker and hurt us bad. Baseball metaphor is pervasive. A no-hitter is a night without any new admissions. A player is always a patient—a nitrate player is a patient on nitrates, a unit player is a patient in the intensive care unit, and so on, until you reach the terminal player.

It is interesting to consider what it means to be winning, or doing 7 well, in this perennial baseball game. When the intern hangs up the phone and announces, "I got a hit," that is not cause for congratulations. The team is not scoring points; rather, it is getting hit, being bombarded with new patients. The object of the game from the point of view of the doctors, considering the players for whom they are already responsible, is to get as few new hits as possible.

This special language contributes to a sense of closeness and profes- 8 sional spirit among people who are under a great deal of stress. As a medical student, I found it exciting to discover that I'd finally cracked the code, that I could understand what doctors said and wrote, and could use the same formulations myself. Some people seem to become enamored of the jargon for its own sake, perhaps because they are so deeply thrilled with the idea of medicine, with the idea of themselves as doctors.

I knew a medical student who was referred to by the interns on 9 the team as Mr. Eponym because he was so infatuated with eponymous terminology, the more obscure the better. He never said "capillary pulsations" if he could say "Quincke's pulses." He would lovingly tell over the multinamed syndromes—Wolff-Parkinson-White, Lown-Ganong-Levine, Schönlein-Henoch—until the temptation to suggest Schleswig-Holstein or Stevenson-Kefauver or Baskin-Robbins became irresistible to his less reverent colleagues.

And there is the jargon that you don't ever want to hear yourself us-   10
ing. You know that your training is changing you, but there are certain changes you think would be going a little too far.

The resident was describing a man with devastating terminal pan-   11
creatic cancer. "Basically he's CTD," the resident concluded. I reminded myself that I had resolved not to be shy about asking when I didn't understand things. "CTD?" I asked timidly.

The resident smirked at me. "Circling The Drain."   12

The images are vivid and terrible. "What happened to Mrs. Melville?"   13
"Oh, she boxed last night." To box is to die, of course.   14

Then there are the more pompous locutions that can make the be-   15
ginning medical student nervous about the effects of medical training. A friend of mine was told by his resident, "A pregnant woman with sickle-cell represents a failure of genetic counseling."

Mr. Eponym, who tried hard to talk like the doctors, once explained   16
to me, "An infant is basically a brainstem preparation." The term "brainstem preparation," as used in neurological research, refers to an animal whose higher brain functions have been destroyed so that only the most primitive reflexes remain, like the sucking reflex, the startle reflex, and the rooting reflex.

And yet at other times the harshness dissipates into a strangely elu-   17
sive euphemism. "As you know, this is a not entirely benign procedure," some doctor will say, and that will be understood to imply agony, risk of complications, and maybe even a significant mortality rate.

The more extreme forms aside, one most important function of med-   18
ical jargon is to help doctors maintain some distance from their patients. By reformulating a patient's pain and problems into a language that the patient doesn't even speak, I suppose we are in some sense taking those pains and problems under our jurisdiction and also reducing their emotional impact. This linguistic separation between doctors and patients allows conversations to go on at the bedside that are unintelligible to the patient. "Naturally, we're worried about adeno-CA," the intern can say to the medical student, and lung cancer need never be mentioned.

I learned a new language this past summer. At times it thrills me to   19
hear myself using it. It enables me to understand my colleagues, to communicate effectively in the hospital. Yet I am uncomfortably aware that
I will never again notice the peculiarities and even atrocities of medical
language as keenly as I did this summer. There may be specific expressions I manage to avoid, but even as I remark them, promising myself I
will never use them, I find that this language is becoming my professional
speech. It no longer sounds strange in my ears—or coming from my
mouth. And I am afraid that as with any new language, to use it properly
you must absorb not only the vocabulary but also the structure, the logic,
the attitudes. At first you may notice these new and alien assumptions
every time you put together a sentence, but with time and increased
fluency you stop being aware of them at all. And as you lose that awareness, for better or for worse, you move closer and closer to being a doctor
instead of just talking like one.

VOCABULARY

paragraph 1: intern
paragraph 2: primeval
paragraph 4: cardiac enzymes
paragraph 6: nitrates
paragraph 8: enamored
paragraph 9: eponym(ous), capillary, syndrome
paragraph 15: locution, sickle-cell (anemia)
paragraph 16: brainstem
paragraph 17: euphemism, dissipates
paragraph 19: atrocities, assumptions, fluency

QUESTIONS

1. In what ways is the special language or medical jargon Klass describes
useful to doctors and medical students?

2. In what way did the pregnant woman with sickle-cell anemia represent "a failure of genetic counseling" to the resident (paragraph 15)?
What point is Klass making in citing this statement?

3. What uses of medical jargon does Klass criticize? What uses if any does she praise? Is she critical of the doctor who refers to "a not entirely benign procedure" (paragraph 17)? Is she critical of doctors who seek to distance themselves from patients? Is she saying that all doctors do?

4. Is Klass critical of herself in mastering the language and putting it to use?

SUGGESTIONS FOR WRITING

1. Like Klass, you have probably had to learn a special language in beginning a course of study or training for a job. Describe how you learned the language and what uses you made of it. Then discuss gains or losses in having learned it.

2. Analyze the special language or jargon in several paragraphs from a textbook in one of your courses. Discuss what uses this language serves, pointing out any terms for which simpler words can be substituted without loss of meaning.

3. Rewrite a paragraph of a business contract using simpler words and sentences. Then discuss what is gained or lost in clarity and precision in rewriting the paragraph.

4. Analyze a published speech of a major political figure (in *Vital Speeches, The Congressional Record, The New York Times* or another newspaper of record). Comment on the uses of euphemism, political jargon, and other language that you consider unfair or dishonest. Give your reasons, showing how the issue could be discussed in fair, honest language.

SYDNEY J. HARRIS

SYDNEY J. HARRIS, for many years a columnist for *The Chicago Daily News,* wrote about contemporary social and political issues from a perspective unusual in journalism at the time—that of the political philosopher and ethicist. His columns have been collected in a number of books, including *Majority of One* (1957), *Last Things First* (1961), and *On the Contrary* (1964). Harris wrote often about everyday language, as in the following essay on common clichés.

NIPPING CLICHÉS IN THE BUD

I should like to read or hear, just once, about an apology that is not abject, a void that is not aching, a test that is not acid, and a swoop that isn't fell.   1

And, just once, about beauty coming before age, the line of greatest resistance, the worse half, better never than late, colonels of industry, and uncheckered careers.   2

And, just once, about leaps without bounds, all without sundry, bags without baggage, ways without shapes or forms, reducible minimums, and a last that was also least.   3

And, just once, unconsidered opinions, indiscreet silences, unblanketed snow, unnipped buds, unblissful ignorance, undue consideration, and a few ill-chosen words.   4

And, just once, a common without a garden variety, an introduction that is badly needed, a few that aren't also far between, a whole fist of destiny, a sublime that shuns the ridiculous, and someone who is inconspicuous by his absence.   5

And, just once, glee that isn't girlish, generosity that isn't faulty, a hale that isn't hearty, the depth of absurdity, and retreats that aren't ignominious.   6

And, just once, in this day without in this age, an unravishing beauty, underwhelming odds, a square of applause, sadder but not wiser, an unseething mass of humanity, and sleeping the sleep of the unjust.   7

And, just once, a softened criminal, a sum without a substance, a strong and loquacious man, an untelling effect, trials without tribulations, speculation that isn't rife, and a body falling with a healthy thud.   8

And, just once, people from every run of life, small hours that aren't wee, unbated breath, the short and stubby arm of coincidence, the heavy fantastic, bolts from the white or green or yellow, and people who are more sinning than sinned against.   9

And, just once, an unforegone conclusion, clean lucre, a badly number, a pink-eyed monster, the benign reaper, a cool argument, a reparable loss, and a labor of hate.   10

And, just once, an impeachable authority, chaos out of order, other things being entirely unequal, an unpronounced success, the seamless side of life, an indiscriminate few, a subhuman effort, a tale that doesn't hang, time memorial, and alloyed pleasure.   11

And, just once, a view without alarm, a point without pride, a smile   12
without wreathes, an injury without insult, and a good time that was had
only by some.

QUESTIONS

1. How does Harris make us aware through the working of phrases that
these are clichés?

2. What does he gain through the series of abrupt, one-sentence paragraphs, opening with the same words?

3. By what other means might he have made us aware?

SUGGESTIONS FOR WRITING

1. Write a humorous essay composed entirely of clichés. Then rewrite it,
saying the same thing in different words. Add a paragraph describing the
ease or difficulty you experienced in dropping the clichés.

2. James Sledd puts in a good word for clichés in a discussion of English prose style:

> At receptions and dinner parties, where silence is rude and conversation
> is impossible, the lubrication of customary phrases on customary sub-
> jects makes the wheels turn smoothly; and it is not only in the parlor
> and at the table that clichés may come in handy. Political speeches and
> reports on diplomatic conferences would be impossible without them,
> listeners to radio and watchers of TV would be uneasy if the expected
> prefabricated phrases did not emerge, and hurried writers of business
> letters and similar documents in which neither personality nor scientific
> precision is essential would never get through the day's work if they had
> to stop and look for exact and lively words. (*A Short Introduction to
> English Grammar*)

Illustrate one of Sledd's ideas from your own experience.

RUSSELL BAKER

RUSSELL BAKER began his career in journalism as a reporter for the *Baltimore Sun,* and in 1954 began his long association with *The New York Times.* His column for the *Times* began in 1962. Baker is a keen observer of life in America and, as the essay reprinted here shows, a satirist of the pretentious language we often speak and write. His essays are collected in a number of books, including *All Things Considered* (1965), *So This Is Depravity* (1980), and *There's a Country in My Cellar* (1990). Baker has written about his life in *Growing Up* (1983) and *The Good Times* (1989). In 1979 he was awarded the Pulitzer Prize for Journalism.

LITTLE RED RIDING HOOD REVISITED

In an effort to make the classics accessible to contemporary readers, I am translating them into the modern American language. Here is the translation of "Little Red Riding Hood":   1

Once upon a point in time, a small person named Little Red Riding Hood initiated plans for the preparation, delivery and transportation of foodstuffs to her grandmother, a senior citizen residing at a place of residence in a forest of indeterminate dimension.   2

In the process of implementing this program, her incursion into the forest was in mid-transportation process when it attained interface with an alleged perpetrator. This individual, a wolf, made inquiry as to the whereabouts of Little Red Riding Hood's goal as well as inferring that he was desirous of ascertaining the contents of Little Red Riding Hood's foodstuffs basket, and all that.   3

"It would be inappropriate to lie to me," the wolf said, displaying his huge jaw capability. Sensing that he was a mass of repressed hostility intertwined with acute alienation, she indicated.   4

"I see you indicating," the wolf said, "but what I don't see is whatever it is you're indicating at, you dig?"   5

Little Red Riding Hood indicated more fully, making one thing perfectly clear—to wit, that it was to her grandmother's residence and with a consignment of foodstuffs that her mission consisted of taking her to and with.   6

At this point in time the wolf moderated his rhetoric and proceeded to grandmother's residence. The elderly person was then subjected to the   7 disadvantages of total consumption and transferred to residence in the perpetrator's stomach.

"That will raise the old woman's consciousness," the wolf said to 8 himself. He was not a bad wolf, but only a victim of an oppressive society, a society that not only denied wolves' rights, but actually boasted of its capacity for keeping the wolf from the door. An interior malaise made itself manifest inside the wolf.

"Is that the national malaise I sense within my digestive tract?" won- 9 dered the wolf. "Or is it the old person seeking to retaliate for her consumption by telling wolf jokes to my duodenum?" It was time to make a judgment. The time was now, the hour had struck, the body lupine cried out for decision. The wolf was up to the challenge. He took two stomach powders right away and got into bed.

The wolf had adopted the abdominal-distress recovery posture when 10 Little Red Riding Hood achieved his presence.

"Grandmother," she said, "your ocular implements are of an extra- 11 ordinary order of magnitude."

"The purpose of this enlarged viewing capability," said the wolf, "is 12 to enable your image to register a more precise impression upon my sight systems."

"In reference to your ears," said Little Red Riding Hood, "it is 13 noted with the deepest respect that far from being underprivileged, their elongation and enlargement appear to qualify you for unparalleled distinction."

"I hear you loud and clear, kid," said the wolf, "but what about 14 these new choppers?"

"If it is not inappropriate," said Little Red Riding Hood, "it might 15 be observed that with your new miracle masticating products you may even be able to chew taffy again."

This observation was followed by the adoption of an aggressive pos- 16 ture on the part of the wolf and the assertion that it was also possible for him, due to the high efficiency ratio of his jaw, to consume little persons, plus, as he stated, his firm determination to do so at once without delay and with all due process and propriety, notwithstanding the fact that the ingestion of one entire grandmother had already provided twice his daily recommended cholesterol intake.

There ensued flight by Little Red Riding Hood accompanied by pur- 17 suit in respect to the wolf and a subsequent intervention on the part of a third party, heretofore unnoted in the record.

Due to the firmness of the intervention, the wolf's stomach under-   18
went ax-assisted aperture with the result that Red Riding Hood's grandmother was enabled to be removed with only minor discomfort.

The wolf's indigestion was immediately alleviated with such effec-   19
tiveness that he signed a contract with the intervening third party to perform with grandmother in a television commercial demonstrating the
swiftness of this dramatic relief for stomach discontent.

"I'm going to be on television," cried grandmother.   20

And they all joined her happily in crying, "What a phenomena!"   21

VOCABULARY

paragraph 2: initiated, indeterminate, dimension
paragraph 3: implementing, incursion, interface, alleged, perpetrator,
ascertaining
paragraph 4: intertwined, alienation
paragraph 6: consignment
paragraph 7: rhetoric
paragraph 8: interior, malaise, manifest
paragraph 9: lupine
paragraph 11: ocular, implements
paragraph 13: elongation
paragraph 15: masticating
paragraph 16: posture, propriety, ingestion, cholesterol
paragraph 18: aperture
paragraph 19: alleviated
paragraph 21: phenomena

QUESTIONS

1. The faddish language Baker parodies reflects faddish ideas. Here is
one example: "An interior malaise made itself manifest inside the wolf."
What current attitude toward human predators is Baker satirizing? How
does the language help him to satirize the idea?

2. Red Riding Hood prefers the farfetched to the simple, as in the expression "ocular implements." What other examples can you find of euphemism, circumlocution, and other faults of diction (see below)?

3. What examples of repetitious phrasing and sentence padding do you find?

4. What kind of advertising language is Baker satirizing toward the end of his version?

5. What is the difference between the wolf's language and Red Riding Hood's? What does the wolf's language tell you about his personality and view of the world?

6. What other ideas is Baker satirizing in his telling of the story?

SUGGESTION FOR WRITING

Rewrite another fairy tale in the modish language of advertising or other contemporary jargons and styles. Let your choice of jargon and style make a point—or several points—as Baker's telling of "Little Red Riding Hood" does.

MORE ON FAULTY DICTION

The following suggestions refer to some of the faults Russell Baker is satirizing.

1. Using the same word more than once in a sentence can be confusing when the senses are different.

> We were present for the presentation of the award.
>
> *Improved:* We were present for the award.

We need not avoid repeating a word if the sense is the same. In the following sentence, though *individual* is a popular synonym for *person,* it has other meanings, and the substitution may confuse the reader:

> The person at the door wasn't the individual I was expecting.

If the repetition sounds awkward, a pronoun may be the solution:

> The person at the door wasn't (the one, who) I was expecting.

2. Needless repetition can make sentences hard to understand.

> There's a simpler, easier, less complicated way to get the job done.
>
> *Revised:* There's a simpler way to get the job done.

3. Words that overlap in meaning can have the same effect.

> The result of the survey should produce a change in policy.

The words *results* and *produce* refer to the same thing.

> *Revised:* The survey should produce a change in policy.

4. A euphemism is a mild or pleasant substitute for a blunt term. We are familiar with euphemisms like "senior citizens" and "golden agers" to describe older people—less frequently described as "chronologically privileged" to avoid using the word *old*. Euphemism, as in this last example, can be a source of ambiguity and humor. When a report card says "needs improvement," it may be referring to something more than mispelled words. When a note from the principal refers to "immature" behavior, it may be referring to cheating or theft or something just as serious. We know the price of speaking bluntly, but also the price of hiding facts.

5. Circumlocution means taking the long way around—in other words, saying something in inflated language: saying "he has difficulty expressing what he knows to be the truth" when we mean "he lies." Euphemisms often depend on inflation of this kind.

6. Equivocal terms deceive or create ambiguity through their double meanings. The word *exceptional* sometimes describes bright children, sometimes those who have trouble learning. We need to know what children we are talking about.

7. A cliché, as Sydney J. Harris shows (p. 275), is a phrase or saying that has become trite through overuse: "sweet as sugar," "conspicuous by his absence," "outwore his welcome." Clichés can rob prose of conviction and vigor.

8. Mixed metaphors create confusion and can also be funny.

> Blows to one's pride stick in the craw.

9. Technical language, borrowed to described nontechnical things can have the same effect. The words *interface* (to describe the connecting of

two machines) and *software* (to describe accessory equipment) are useful words in computer language. Outside the world of computers, they become jargon, "talk that is considered both ugly-sounding and hard to understand" (H. W. Fowler). A conference is not an "interface"; textbooks are not "software." A prospective employer may not understand you are seeking a higher-paying job if you give "creative income maximization" as your reason for writing.

IV

MATTERS OF STYLE: THE SENTENCE

INTRODUCTION

This part of the book will show you how to make your sentences more effective as you draft and revise your paragraphs and essays. Unity and proper emphasis are as important in sentences as they are in paragraphs. In fact, sentences can be loosely viewed as miniature paragraphs. For example, in the same way that the topic sentence of a paragraph states the core idea that the paragraph develops, the main clause of a simple or complex sentence states the core idea that the rest of the sentence develops through its modifiers:

> I *heard* instead the shriek of brakes, the heavy throbbing of the once-a-day Braniff airliner into Minot, the shattering sirens born of war, the honk of a diesel locomotive *which* surely cannot call to faraway places the heart of a wakeful boy like the old steam whistle in the night. (Eric Sevareid, "Velva, North Dakota" [italics added])

The core subject and verb of this complex sentence (I *heard*) is completed by a series of modified objects—the final object further modified by a lengthy subordinate clause beginning with *which*.

Just as a series of main ideas combine in a single paragraph, so can simple and compound sentences form single sentences:

> You can walk down the streets of my town now and hear from open windows the intimate voices of the Washington commentators in casual converse on the great affairs of state [*simple sentence: main clause with compound predicate*]; but you cannot hear on Sunday morning the singing in Norwegian of the Lutheran hymns [*simple sentence: main clause with simple predicate*]; the old country seems now part of a world left long behind and the old-country accents grow fainter in the speech of my Velva neighbors [*compound sentence: two main clauses with simple predicates*]. (Sevareid)

And so can main and subordinate ideas, expressed in main and subordinate clauses and their modifiers:

> Attic and screen porch are slowly vanishing [*main clause*] and lovely shades of pastel are painted upon new houses [*main clause*], tints that once would have embarrassed farmer and merchant alike [*subordinate clause modifying the appositive "tints"*]. (Sevareid)

Though the parallel between paragraphs and sentences suggested here is not exact (main clauses do not always contain the most important idea of a sentence), it does suggest that, like paragraphs, sentences often build from cores to which subordinate ideas and details relate. And sentences, like paragraphs, also can contain two or more core ideas.

We write as we speak—stressing the core idea of a simple sentence and joining several core ideas into compound ones. We also place modifying words, phrases, and clauses in different positions in writing, as in speech, to gain different kinds of emphasis. In addition, we frequently make special use of the beginning and ending of the simple sentence for emphasis. We can, however, achieve emphasis in other ways. The following sections illustrate these possibilities.

21

ADDITION AND MODIFICATION

As a paragraph usually begins with a topic sentence that states the subject or central idea, so the sentence may begin with a main clause followed by a series of explanatory details, which are explained in turn:

> Even some instructors had trouble doing a falling leaf. The plane had to be brought precisely to its stalling point, then dropped in a series of sickening sideways skids, first to one side, then to the other, like a leaf falling in a breeze, by delicate simultaneous manipulations of stick, rudder, pedals, and throttle. (Russell Baker, *Growing Up*)

Here is a sentence from Jane Jacobs's description of a New York City street:

> *Character dancers come on,*
> *a strange old man* with strings of old shoes over his shoulders,
> *motor-scooter riders* with big beards and girl friends who bounce on the back of the scooters and wear their hair long in front of their face as well as behind,
> *drunks* who follow the advice of the Hat Council and are always turned out in hats,
>> but not hats the Council would approve.

The three additions—*strange old man, motor-scooter riders,* and *drunks*—make the main clause specific: they name the character dancers. Notice that these *appositives* (adjacent words or phrases that explain or identify another word) are considerably longer than the main clause. Notice, too, that the third appositive is itself modified. English sentences can be modified endlessly. They are not, however, because the reader would soon lose sight of the central idea. How long a sentence is often depends on how many ideas and details a reader can grasp.

JANE JACOBS

Jane Jacobs has influenced ideas on city architecture—long criticizing city planning that breaks up close-knit neighborhoods with housing projects and "cultural centers" that disperse people. "These thin dispersions lack any reasonable degree of innate vitality, staying power, or inherent usefulness as settlements," she writes in *The Death and Life of Great American Cities* (1961), from which the following description of Hudson Street in New York City is taken. Her other books include *Cities and the Wealth of Nations* (1984), *Systems of Survival* (1992), and *Economies* (2000). We hear a personal voice in her sentences—Jacobs talking to us informally about the everyday world.

HUDSON STREET

Under the seeming disorder of the old city, wherever the old city is working successfully, is a marvelous order for maintaining the safety of the streets and the freedom of the city. It is a complex order. Its essence is intricacy of sidewalk use, bringing with it a constant succession of eyes. This order is all composed of movement and change, and although it is life, not art, we may fancifully call it the art form of the city and liken it to the dance—not to a simple-minded precision dance with everyone kicking up at the same time, twirling in unison and bowing off en masse, but to an intricate ballet in which the individual dancers and ensembles all have distinctive parts which miraculously reinforce each other and compose an orderly whole. The ballet of the good city sidewalk never repeats itself from place to place, and in any one place is always replete with new improvisations.

The stretch of Hudson Street where I live is each day the scene of an intricate sidewalk ballet. I make my own first entrance into it a little after eight when I put out the garbage can, surely a prosaic occupation, but I enjoy my part, my little clang, as the droves of junior high school students walk by the center of the stage dropping candy wrappers. (How do they eat so much candy so early in the morning?)

While I sweep up the wrappers I watch the other rituals of morning: Mr. Halpert unlocking the laundry's handcart from its mooring to a cellar door, Joe Cornacchia's son-in-law stacking out the empty crates from the delicatessen, the barber bringing out his sidewalk folding chair, Mr. Goldstein arranging the coils of wire which proclaim the hardware store is open, the wife of the tenement's superintendent depositing her chunky three-year-old with a toy mandolin on the stoop, the vantage point from which he is learning the English his mother cannot speak. Now the primary children, heading for St. Luke's, dribble through to the south; the children for St. Veronica's Cross, heading to the west, and the children for P.S. 41, heading toward the east. Two new entrances are being made from the wings: well-dressed and even elegant women and men with briefcases emerge from doorways and side streets. Most of these are heading for the bus and subways, but some hover on the curbs, stopping taxis which have miraculously appeared at the right moment, for the taxis are part of a wider morning ritual: having dropped passengers from midtown in the downtown financial district, they are now bringing down-towners up to midtown. Simultaneously, numbers of women in house-dresses have emerged and as they crisscross with one another they pause for quick conversations that sound with either laughter or joint indigna-tion, never, it seems, anything between. It is time for me to hurry to work too, and I exchange my ritual farewell with Mr. Lofaro, the short, thick-bodied, white-aproned fruit man who stands outside his doorway a little up the street, his arms folded, his feet planted, looking solid as earth itself. We nod; we each glance quickly up and down the street, then look back to each other and smile. We have done this many a morning for more than ten years, and we both know what it means: All is well.

The heart-of-the-day ballet I seldom see, because part of the nature of it is that working people who live there, like me, are mostly gone, filling the roles of strangers on other sidewalks. But from days off, I know enough of it to know that it becomes more and more intricate. Longshoremen who are not working that day gather at the White Horse or the Ideal or the In-ternational for beer and conversation. The executives and business lunch-ers from the industries just to the west throng the Dorgene restaurant and the Lion's Head coffee house; meat-market workers and communications scientists fill the bakery lunchroom. Character dancers come on, a strange old man with strings of old shoes over his shoulders, motor-scooter riders with big beards and girl friends who bounce on the back of the scooters and wear their hair long in front of their faces as well as behind, drunks who follow the advice of the Hat Council and are always turned out in hats, but not hats the Council would approve. Mr. Lacey, the locksmith, shuts up his shop for a while and goes to exchange the time of day with

Mr. Slube at the cigar store. Mr. Koochagian, the tailor, waters the luxuriant jungle of plants in his window, gives them a critical look from the outside, accepts a compliment on them from two passers-by, fingers the leaves on the plane tree in front of our house with a thoughtful gardener's appraisal, and crosses the street for a bite at the Ideal where he can keep an eye on customers and wigwag across the message that he is coming. The baby carriages come out, and clusters of everyone from toddlers with dolls to teenagers with homework gather at the stoops.

When I get home after work, the ballet is reaching its crescendo. This is the time of roller skates and stilts and tricycles, and games in the lee of the stoop with bottletops and plastic cowboys; this is the time of bundles and packages, zigzagging from the drug store to the fruit stand and back over to the butcher's; this is the time when teenagers, all dressed up, are pausing to ask if their slips show or their collars look right; this is the time when beautiful girls get out of MG's; this is the time when the fire engines go through; this is the time when anybody you know around Hudson Street will go by.

As darkness thickens and Mr. Halpert moors the laundry cart to the cellar door again, the ballet goes on under lights, eddying back and forth but intensifying at the bright spotlight pools of Joe's sidewalk pizza dispensary, the bars, the delicatessen, the restaurant and the drug store. The night workers stop now at the delicatessen, to pick up salami and a container of milk. Things have settled down for the evening but the street and its ballet have not come to a stop.

I know the deep night ballet and its season best from waking long after midnight to tend a baby and, sitting in the dark, seeing the shadows and hearing the sounds of the sidewalk. Mostly it is a sound like infinitely pattering snatches of party conversation and, about three in the morning, singing, very good singing. Sometimes there is sharpness and anger or sad, sad weeping, or a flurry of search for a string of beads broken. One night a young man came roaring along, bellowing terrible language at two girls whom he had apparently picked up and who were disappointing him. Doors opened, a wary semicircle formed around him, not too close, until the police came. Out came the heads, too, along Hudson Street, offering opinion, "Drunk . . . Crazy . . . A wild kid from the suburbs." *

---

* He turned out to be a wild kid from the suburbs. Sometimes, on Hudson Street, we are tempted to believe the suburbs must be a difficult place to bring up children.

Deep in the night, I am almost unaware how many people are on the 8
street unless something calls them together, like the bagpipe. Who the
piper was and why he favored our street I have no idea. The bagpipe just
skirled out in the February night, and as if it were a signal the random,
dwindled movements of the sidewalk took on direction. Swiftly, quietly,
almost magically a little crowd was there, a crowd that evolved into a
circle with a Highland fling inside it. The crowd could be seen on the
shadowy sidewalk, the dancers could be seen, but the bagpiper himself
was almost invisible because his bravura was all in his music. He was a
very little man in a plain brown overcoat. When he finished and vanished, the dancers and watchers applauded, and applause came from the
galleries too, half a dozen of the hundred windows on Hudson Street.
Then the windows closed, and the little crowd dissolved into the random
movements of the night street.

The strangers on Hudson Street, the allies whose eyes help us natives 9
keep the peace of the street, are so many that they always seem to be different people from one day to the next. That does not matter. Whether
they are so many always-different people as they seem to be, I do not
know. Likely they are. When Jimmy Rogan fell through a plate-glass window (he was separating some scuffling friends) and almost lost his arm,
a stranger in an old T shirt emerged from the Ideal bar, swiftly applied
an expert tourniquet and, according to the hospital's emergency staff,
saved Jimmy's life. Nobody remembered seeing the man before and no
one has seen him since. The hospital was called in this way: a woman
sitting on the steps next to the accident ran over to the bus stop,
wordlessly snatched a dime from the hand of a stranger who was waiting with his fifteen-cent fare ready, and raced into the Ideal's phone booth.
The stranger raced after her to offer the nickel too. Nobody remembered
seeing him before, and no one has seen him since. When you see the same
stranger three or four times on Hudson Street, you begin to nod. This is
almost getting to be an acquaintance, a public acquaintance, of course.

I have made the daily ballet of Hudson Street sound more frenetic 10
than it is, because writing it telescopes it. In real life, it is not that way.
In real life, to be sure, something is always going on, the ballet is never
at a halt, but the general effect is peaceful and the general tenor even
leisurely. People who know well such animated city streets will know how
it is. I am afraid people who do not will always have it a little wrong in
their heads—like the old prints of rhinoceroses made from travelers'
descriptions of rhinoceroses.

On Hudson Street, the same as in the North End of Boston or in any   11
other animated neighborhoods of great cities, we are not innately more
competent at keeping the sidewalks safe than are the people who try to
live off the hostile truce of Turf in a blind-eyed city. We are the lucky
possessors of a city order that makes it relatively simple to keep the peace
because there are plenty of eyes on the street. But there is nothing simple about that order itself, or the bewildering number of components that
go into it. Most of those components are specialized in one way or another. They unite in their joint effect upon the sidewalk, which is not specialized in the least. That is its strength.

QUESTIONS

1. The main clause in the first sentence of paragraph 3 is followed by a
series of appositives explaining the *rituals of morning*. How many appositives do you find? Which of them is modified?

2. The colon in the following sentence introduces an addition that explains the main clause:

> Two new entrances are being made from the wings: well-dressed and
> even elegant women and men with briefcases emerge from doorways
> and side streets.

Does the colon in the succeeding sentence, in paragraph 3, serve the
same purpose? What about the colon in the concluding sentence of the
paragraph?

3. The second sentence of paragraph 5 might have been divided into
four separate sentences. What does Jacobs gain by joining the main
clauses through semicolons? Are the semicolons in paragraph 3 used in
the same way?

4. Notice that the main clause of the first sentence of paragraph 6 is
modified by the opening subordinate clause and by the phrases that follow, beginning with *eddying*. Try rewriting the sentence, beginning with
eddying. What problems do you face in revising the sentence? Does your
revision improve the sentence?

5. What point is Jacobs making about the "daily ballet" of Hudson Street? How do the various details illustrate her point?

6. Jacobs is defining what makes a New York street a neighborhood. How different is this neighborhood from yours?

SUGGESTIONS FOR WRITING

1. Explain why the specialization in each of the "bewildering number of components" that make up the street is the source of its strength. Show how Jacobs illustrates this strength.

2. Develop the following main clauses through addition of your own details. Use colons and semicolons if you wish:

a. "Deep in the night, I am almost unaware how many people are on the street. . . ."

b. "The crowd could be seen on the shadowy sidewalk. . . ."

c. "People who know well such animated streets will know how it is. . . ."

22

EMPHASIS

The speaker of the following sentence, a witness before a congressional committee, repeats certain phrases and qualifies his ideas in a typical way:

> My experience is that we hold people sometimes in jail, young people in jail, for days at a time with a complete lack of concern of the parents, if they do live in homes where parents live together, a complete lack of concern in many instances on the part of the community or other agencies as to where these young people are or what they are doing.

Sentences as complex and disjointed as this one seems when transcribed are understood easily when spoken. In speaking, we often interrupt the flow of ideas to emphasize a word or phrase or to repeat an idea. Written punctuation sometimes clarifies the points of emphasis, but in a limited way. We cannot depend directly on vocal inflection for clarity and emphasis in writing; we can suggest these inflections by shaping the sentence in accord with ordinary speech patterns. Clearly written sentences stay close to these patterns.

The core of English sentences, we saw, can be expanded, and at length, if each modifier is clearly connected to what precedes it. To achieve special emphasis the writer may vary the sentence even more, perhaps by making special use of the end of the sentence—the position that in English tends to be the most emphatic:

> The cold passed reluctantly from the earth, and the retiring fogs revealed an army stretched out on the hills, *resting*. (Stephen Crane, *The Red Badge of Courage* [italics added])

Or the writer may break up the sentence so that individual ideas and experiences receive separate emphasis:

> The youth stopped. He was transfixed by this terrific medley of all noises. It was as if worlds were being rended. There was the ripping sound of musketry and the breaking crash of the artillery. (Crane)

English word order largely controls how we connect subordinate clauses to other elements in a sentence. The position of subordinate clauses that serve as nouns or adjectives (sometimes called noun clauses and adjective clauses) is rather fixed; the position of subordinate clauses that serve as adverbs (sometimes called adverb clauses) is not. The position of the adverb clause depends on its importance as an idea as well as on its length:

> I majored in zoology *because I like working with animals.*
>
> *Because I like working with animals,* I majored in zoology.

The position of the subordinate clause determines what information is stressed. In the first sentence, the subordinate clause seems to express the more important idea because it follows the main clause. In the second sentence, the main clause receives the emphasis. But the end of the sentence will not take the thrust of meaning if ideas appearing toward the beginning are given special emphasis.

Our informal spoken sentences show the least variation and depend heavily on coordination. The *stringy sentence* in writing—a series of ideas joined loosely with *and* and other conjunctions—is a heavily coordinated sentence without the usual vocal markers. The sentence *fragment*—a detached phrase or clause, or a sentence missing either a subject or a verb—sometimes derives from the clipped sentences and phrases common in speech. Writers use both for special emphasis, as in the following descriptions of a crouching lion and of nineteenth-century London on a wet November day:

> His flanks were wet and hot and flies were on the little openings the solid bullets had made in his tawny hide, and his big yellow eyes, narrowed with hate, looked straight ahead, only blinking when the pain came as he breathed, and his claws dug in the soft baked earth. (Ernest Hemingway, "The Short Happy Life of Francis Macomber")

> Implacable November weather. As much mud in the streets, as if the waters had but newly retired from the face of the earth, and it would not be wonderful to meet a Megalosaurus, forty feet long or so, waddling

like an elephantine lizard up Holborn Hill. Smoke lowering down from chimney-pots, making a soft black drizzle, with flake of soot in it as big as full-grown snowflakes—gone into mourning, one might imagine, for the death of the sun. Dogs, undistinguishable in mire. Horses, scarcely better; splashed to their very blinkers. Foot passengers, jostling one another's umbrellas, in a general infection of ill-temper, and losing their foot-hold at street-corners, where tens of thousands of other foot passengers have been slipping and sliding since the day broke (if this day ever broke), adding new deposits to the crust upon crust of mud, sticking at those points tenaciously to the pavement, and accumulating at compound interest. (Charles Dickens, *Bleak House*)

Such sentences, more common in fiction, are best used sparingly for special effect.

M A R K   T W A I N

MARK TWAIN worked as a river pilot from 1857 to 1861, and wrote about these experiences in *Life on the Mississippi,* published in 1883. Like the boy described in the passage reprinted here, Twain ran away to go on the river, but without immediate success: "Months afterward the hope within me struggled to a reluctant death, and I found myself without an ambition. But I was ashamed to go home." Eventually he did become a cub pilot, as we see on p. 11.

THE STEAMBOATMAN

[1]When I was a boy, there was but one permanent ambition among my comrades in our village on the west bank of the Mississippi River. [2]That was, to be a steamboatman. [3]We had transient ambitions of other sorts, but they were only transient. [4]When a circus came and went, it left us all burning to become clowns; the first negro minstrel show that ever came to our section left us all suffering to try that kind of life; now and then we had a hope that, if we lived and were good, God would permit us to be pirates. [5]These ambitions faded out, each in its turn; but the ambition to be a steamboatman always remained.

[6]Once a day a cheap, gaudy packet arrived upward from St. Louis, and another downward from Keokuk. [7]Before these events, the day was glorious with expectancy; after them, the day was a dead and empty thing. [8]Not only the boys, but the whole village, felt this. [9]After all these years I can picture that old time to myself now, just as it was then: the white town drowsing in the sunshine of a summer's morning; the streets empty, or pretty nearly so; one or two clerks sitting in front of the Water Street stores, with their splint-bottomed chairs tilted back against the walls, chins on breasts, hats slouched over their faces, asleep—with shingle-shavings enough around to show what broke them down; a sow and a litter of pigs loafing along the sidewalk, doing a good business in watermelon rinds and seeds; two or three lonely little freight piles scattered about the "levee"; a pile of "skids" on the slope of the stone-paved wharf, and the fragrant town drunkard asleep in the shadow of them; two or three wood flats at the head of the wharf, but nobody to listen to the peaceful lapping of the wavelets against them; the great Mississippi, the majestic, the magnificent Mississippi, rolling its mile-wide tide along, shining in the sun; the dense forest away on the other side; the "point" above the town, and the "point" below, bounding the river-glimpse and turning it into a sort of sea, and withal a very still and brilliant and lonely one. [10]Presently a film of dark smoke appears above one of those remote "points"; instantly a negro drayman, famous for his quick eye and prodigious voice, lifts up the cry, "S-t-e-a-m-boat a-comin'!" and the scene changes! [11]The town drunkard stirs, the clerks wake up, a furious clatter of drays follows, every house and store pours out a human contribution, and all in a twinkling the dead town is alive and moving. [12]Drays, carts, men, boys, all go hurrying from many quarters to a common center, the wharf. [13]Assembled there, the people fasten their eyes upon the coming boat as upon a wonder they are seeing for the first time. [14]And the boat is rather a handsome sight, too. [15]She is long and sharp and trim and pretty; she has two tall, fancy-topped chimneys, with a gilded device of some kind swung between them; a fanciful pilot-house, all glass and "gingerbread," perched on top of the "texas" deck* behind them; the paddleboxes are gorgeous with a picture or with gilded rays above the boat's name; the boiler-deck, the hurricane-deck, and the texas

---

* *"texas" deck:* The deck above the officers' quarters.

deck are fenced and ornamented with clean white railings; there is a flag gallantly flying from the jack-staff; the furnace doors are open and the fires glaring bravely; the upper decks are black with passengers; the captain stands by the big bell, calm, imposing, the envy of all; great volumes of the blackest smoke are rolling and tumbling out of the chimneys—a husbanded grandeur created with a bit of pitch-pine just before arriving at a town; the crew are grouped on the forecastle; the broad stage is run far out over the port bow, and an envied deck-hand stands picturesquely on the end of it with a coil of rope in his hand; the pent steam is screaming through the gaugecocks; the captain lifts his hand, a bell rings, the wheels stop; then they turn back, churning the water to foam, and the steamer is at rest. [16]Then such a scramble as there is to get aboard, and to get ashore, and to take in freight and to discharge freight, all at one and the same time; and such a yelling and cursing as the mates facilitate it all with! [17]Ten minutes later the steamer is under way again, with no flag on the jack-staff and no black smoke issuing from the chimneys. [18]After ten more minutes the town is dead again, and the town drunkard asleep by the skids once more.

[19]My father was a justice of the peace, and I supposed he possessed the power of life and death over all men, and could hang anybody that offended him. [20]This was distinction enough for me as a general thing; but the desire to be a steamboatman kept intruding, nevertheless. [21]I first wanted to be a cabin-boy, so that I could come out with a white apron on and shake a tablecloth over the side, where all my old comrades could see me; later I thought I would rather be the deck-hand who stood on the end of the stage-plank with the coil of rope in his hand, because he was particularly conspicuous. [22]But these were only daydreams—they were too heavenly to be contemplated as real possibilities. [23]By and by one of our boys went away. [24]He was not heard of for a long time. [25]At last he turned up as apprentice engineer or "striker" on a steamboat. [26]This thing shook the bottom out of all my Sunday-school teachings. [27]That boy had been notoriously worldly, and I just the reverse; yet he was exalted to this eminence, and I left in obscurity and misery. [28]There was nothing generous about this fellow in his greatness. [29]He would always manage to have a rusty bolt to scrub while his boat tarried at our town, and he would sit on the inside guard and scrub it where we all could see him and envy him and loathe him. [30]And whenever his boat was laid up he would come home and swell around the town in his blackest

and greasiest clothes, so that nobody could help remembering that he was a steamboatman; and he used all sorts of steamboat technicalities in his talk, as if he were so used to them that he forgot common people could not understand them. [31] He would speak of the "labboard" side of a horse in an easy, natural way that would make one wish he was dead. [32] And he was always talking about "St. Looy" like an old citizen; he would refer casually to occasions when he was "coming down Fourth Street," or when he was "passing by the Planter's House," or when there was a fire and he took a turn on the brakes of "the old Big Missouri"; and then he would go on and lie about how many towns the size of ours were burned down there that day. [33] Two or three of the boys had long been persons of consideration among us because they had been to St. Louis once and had a vague general knowledge of its wonders, but the day of their glory was over now. [34] They lapsed into a humble silence, and learned to disappear when the ruthless "cub"-engineer approached. [35] This fellow had money, too, and hair-oil. [36] Also an ignorant silver watch and a showy brass watch-chain. [37] He wore a leather belt and used no suspenders. [38] If ever a youth was cordially admired and hated by his comrades, this one was. [39] No girl could withstand his charms. [40] He "cut out" every boy in the village. [41] When his boat blew up at last, it diffused a tranquil contentment among us such as we had not known for months. [42] But when he came home the next week, alive, renowned, and appeared in church all battered up and bandaged, a shining hero, stared at and wondered over by everybody, it seemed to us that the partiality of Providence for an undeserving reptile had reached a point where it was open to criticism.

[43] This creature's career could produce but one result, and it speedily followed. [44] Boy after boy managed to get on the river. [45] The minister's son became an engineer. [46] The doctor's and the postmaster's sons became "mud clerks"*; the wholesale liquor dealer's son became a barkeeper on a boat; four sons of the chief merchant, and two sons of the county judge, became pilots. [47] Pilot was the grandest position of all. [48] The pilot, even in those days of trivial wages, had a princely salary— from a hundred and fifty to two hundred and fifty dollars a month, and

---

* *mud clerk:* The second clerk on river steamers who went ashore to take account of freight.

no board to pay. [49]Two months of his wages would pay a preacher's salary for a year. [50]Now some of us were left disconsolate. [51]We could not get on the river—at least our parents would not let us.

[52]So, by and by, I ran away. [53]I said I would never come home again till I was a pilot and could come in glory. [54]But somehow I could not manage it. [55]I went meekly aboard a few of the boats that lay packed together like sardines at the long St. Louis wharf, and humbly inquired for the pilots, but got only a cold shoulder and short words from mates and clerks. [56]I had to make the best of this sort of treatment for the time being, but I had comforting day-dreams of a future when I should be a great and honored pilot, with plenty of money, and could kill some of these mates and clerks and pay for them.

QUESTIONS

1. How does Twain give equal emphasis to the many sights described in sentence 9? How do sentences 15 and 46 resemble sentence 9 in structure and emphasis?

2. How does sentence 11 build in emphasis? Sentence 16?

3. Rewrite sentence 19, subordinating one of the clauses. How does your revision affect the emphasis of ideas in the original sentence?

4. Combine sentences 35, 36, and 37 into a single sentence. What does your revision gain or lose in emphasis?

5. How does Twain build sentences 41 and 42 to give the end of the sentences the greatest emphasis?

6. Where does Twain mix short and long sentences to emphasize certain perceptions and feelings?

7. What emotions does Twain convey, and what examples can you cite of how sentence construction conveys these emotions and creates a mood?

8. How well does Twain convey the sense of childhood aspiration and frustration?

Suggestions for Writing

1. Rewrite several of Twain's sentences, giving different emphasis to his ideas through a different coordination and subordination of sentence elements.

2. Twain says in his autobiography: "The truth is, a person's memory has no more sense than his conscience and no appreciation whatever of values and proportions." Discuss how his picture of the Missouri town and the coming of the steamboat illustrates this statement. Then develop the same idea from your own personal experience and observation.

23

LOOSE AND PERIODIC SENTENCES

Sentences are sometimes classified as loose or periodic to distinguish two important kinds of emphasis: the use made of the beginning or the end of the sentence. The loose sentence begins with the core idea, explanatory and qualifying phrases and clauses trailing behind:

> It was not a screeching noise, only an intermittent hump-hump as if the bird had to recall his grievance each time before he repeated it. (Flannery O'Connor, *The Violent Bear It Away*)

If the ideas that follow the core are afterthoughts, or inessential details, the sentence will seem "loose"—easy and relaxed in its movement, perhaps even plodding if the content of the sentence permits:

> His eyes glittered like open pits of light as he moved across the sand, dragging his crushed shadow behind him. (Flannery O'Connor)

A subordinate element will not seem unemphatic or plodding, however, if it expresses a strong action or idea and the details cumulate:

> He beat louder and louder, bamming at the same time with his free fist until he felt he was shaking the house. (Flannery O'Connor)

Opening with modifiers or with a series of appositives, the periodic sentence ends with the core:

> Living this way by the creek, where the light appears and vanishes on the water, where muskrats surface and dive, and redwings scatter, I have come to know a special side of nature. (Annie Dillard, *Pilgrim at Tinker Creek*)

The strongly periodic sentence is usually reserved for moderate or unusually strong emphasis:

> Partway down the long, very steep slope of Loma Vista Drive, descending through Beverly Hills, with the city of Los Angeles spread out far below the houses of sparkling opulence on either side, there is a sign warning "Use Lowest Gear" and, shortly after that, a sign that says "Runaway Vehicle Escape Lane 600 Feet Ahead." (James Stevenson, "Loma Vista Drive")

> Watching the animals come and go, and feeling the land swell up to meet them and then feeling it grow still at their departure, I came to think of the migrations as breath, as the land breathing. (Barry Lopez, *Arctic Dreams*)

Most contemporary English sentences fall between the extremely loose and the extremely periodic. Compound sentences seem loose when succeeding clauses serve as afterthoughts or qualifications rather than as ideas equal in importance to the opening idea:

> I was very conscious of the crowds at first, almost despairing to have to perform in front of them, and I never got used to it. (George Plimpton, *Paper Lion*)

Periodic sentences are used sparingly, with emphasis distributed more often throughout the whole sentence, as in Dillard's sentence above. Sometimes two moderately periodic sentences will be coordinated, with a corresponding distribution of emphasis:

> Though reliable narration is by no means the only way of conveying to the audience the facts on which dramatic irony is based, it is a useful way, and in some works, works in which no one but the author can conceivably know what needs to be known, it may be indispensable. (Wayne C. Booth, *The Rhetoric of Fiction*)

JOHN STEINBECK

John Steinbeck (1902–1968) was born in the Salinas Valley of California, the setting of many of his stories and novels. In 1962 he received the Nobel Prize for Literature—a testimony to the great reputation of his fiction throughout the world. His greatest work is undoubtedly *The Grapes of Wrath*—an account of the Joads, a family who, dispossessed of their Oklahoma farm during the Great Depression, make an arduous journey to California. Steinbeck's account of Depression poverty and the exploitation of migrant workers—awarded the Pulitzer Prize in 1939—remains a powerful one. Toward the beginning of the novel, Steinbeck describes a turtle making its own difficult journey—a hint of what is to follow. Steinbeck's sentences are notable for the various ways they convey the movement of the turtle up the embankment.

THE TURTLE

[1]The sun lay on the grass and warmed it, and in the shade under the grass the insects moved, ants and ant lions to set traps for them, grasshoppers to jump into the air and flick their yellow wings for a second, sow bugs like little armadillos, plodding restlessly on many tender feet. [2]And over the grass at the roadside a land turtle crawled, turning aside for nothing, dragging his high-domed shell over the grass. [3]His hard legs and yellow-nailed feet threshed slowly through the grass, not really walking, but boosting and dragging his shell along. [4]The barley beards slid off his shell, and the clover burrs fell on him and rolled to the ground. [5]His horny beak was partly open, and his fierce, humorous eyes, under brows like fingernails, stared straight ahead. [6]He came over the grass leaving a beaten trail behind him, and the hill, which was the highway embankment, reared up ahead of him. [7]For a moment he stopped, his head held high. [8]He blinked and looked up and down. [9]At last he started to climb the embankment. [10]Front clawed feet reached forward but did not touch. [11]The hind feet kicked his shell along, and it scraped on the grass, and on the gravel. [12]As the embankment grew steeper and steeper, the more frantic were the efforts of the land turtle. [13]Pushing hind legs strained and slipped, boosting the shell along, and the horny head protruded as far as the neck could stretch. [14]Little by little the shell slid up the embankment until at last a parapet cut straight across its line of march, the shoulder of the road, a concrete wall four inches high. [15]As though they worked independently the hind legs pushed the shell against the wall. [16]The head upraised and peered over the wall to the broad smooth plain of cement. [17]Now the hands, braced on top of the wall, strained and lifted, and the shell came slowly up and rested its front end on the wall.

¹⁸For a moment the turtle rested. ¹⁹A red ant ran into the shell, into the soft skin inside the shell, and suddenly head and legs snapped in, and the armored tail clamped in sideways. ²⁰The red ant was crushed between body and legs. ²¹And one head of wild oats was clamped into the shell by a front leg. ²²For a long moment the turtle lay still, and then the neck crept out and the old humorous frowning eyes looked about and the legs and tail came out. ²³The back legs went to work, straining like elephant legs, and the shell tipped to an angle so that the front legs could not reach the level cement plain. ²⁴But higher and higher the hind legs boosted it, until at last the center of balance was reached, the front tipped down, the front legs scratched at the pavement, and it was up. ²⁵But the head of wild oats was held by its stem around the front legs.

QUESTIONS

1. The base idea in sentence 2 is *a land turtle crawled*. If this clause were moved to the end of the sentence, what change would occur in focus or meaning?

2. How does the structure of sentence 3 help us visualize the movement of the turtle? Is the sentence loose or periodic?

3. Consider this revision of sentence 7:

   His head held high, he stopped for a moment.

Is the meaning of the original sentence changed?

4. Combine sentences 7, 8, and 9 into one sentence. What change in meaning, focus, or emphasis occurs?

5. Consider this revision of sentence 11:

   The hind feet kicking his shell along, it scraped on the grass and on the gravel.

What is gained or lost in meaning or effect by the revision?

6. Sentences 11 and 12 both describe the action of the turtle—moving on the grass at the edge of the embankment, then moving up the steep

part. What difference do you see in the structure of these sentences? How does each structure convey the action in a different way?

7. How does the coordinate structure of sentence 23 show that the movement of the legs and the tipping of the shell are not happening at the same time? How could Steinbeck change the structure of the sentence to show the two actions occurring at the same time?

8. How does the structure of sentence 24 help us to visualize the action here?

SUGGESTION FOR WRITING

Steinbeck's turtle seems to many readers symbolic of the Joad family in *The Grapes of Wrath,* the novel in which this description of the turtle appears. Discuss the qualities or attitudes that Steinbeck might be symbolizing in the turtle.

ANNIE DILLARD

ANNIE DILLARD writes about her life in the Roanoke Valley of Virginia in *Pilgrim at Tinker Creek* (1974)—awarded the Pulitzer Prize in 1975. Dillard later lived in the Pacific Northwest and wrote about Puget Sound in a collection of essays, *Teaching a Stone to Talk* (1982). In *An American Childhood* (1987) she describes her early life in Pittsburgh. Her novel *The Living* was published in 1992. "It's all a matter of keeping my eyes open," Dillard tells us in *Pilgrim at Tinker Creek,* from which the following section is taken. "Nature is like one of those line drawings of a tree that are puzzles for children. Can you find hidden in the leaves a duck, a house, a boy, a bucket, a zebra, and a boot? Specialists can find the most incredibly well-hidden things."

AT TINKER CREEK

[1]Where Tinker Creek flows under the sycamore log bridge to the tear-shaped island, it is slow and shallow, fringed thinly in cattail marsh. [2]At this spot an astonishing bloom of life supports vast breeding populations

of insects, fish, reptiles, birds, and mammals. [3]On windless summer evenings I stalk along the creek bank or straddle the sycamore log in absolute stillness, watching for muskrats. [4]The night I stayed too late I was hunched on the log staring spellbound at spreading, reflected stains of lilac on the water. [5]A cloud in the sky suddenly lighted as if turned on by a switch; its reflection just as suddenly materialized on the water upstream, flat and floating, so that I couldn't see the creek bottom, or life in the water under the cloud. [6]Downstream, away from the cloud on the water, water turtles smooth as beans were gliding down with the current in a series of easy, weightless push-offs, as men bound on the moon. [7]I didn't know whether to trace the progress of one turtle I was sure of, risking sticking my face in one of the bridge's spider webs made invisible by the gathering dark, or take a chance on seeing the carp, or scan the mudbank in hope of seeing a muskrat, or follow the last of the swallows who caught at my heart and trailed it after them like streamers as they appeared from directly below, under the log, flying upstream with their tails forked, so fast.

[8]But shadows spread, and deepened, and stayed. [9]After thousands of years we're still strangers to darkness, fearful aliens in an enemy camp with our arms crossed over our chests. [10]I stirred. [11]A land turtle on the bank, startled, hissed the air from its lungs and withdrew into its shell. [12]An uneasy pink here, an unfathomable blue there, gave great suggestion of lurking beings. [13]Things were going on. [14]I couldn't see whether that sere rustle I heard was a distant rattlesnake, slit-eyed, or a nearby sparrow kicking in the dry flood debris slung at the foot of a willow. [15]Tremendous action roiled the water everywhere I looked, big action, inexplicable. [16]A tremor welled up beside a gaping muskrat burrow in the bank and I caught my breath, but no muskrat appeared. [17]The ripples continued to fan upstream with a steady, powerful thrust. [18]Night was knitting over my face an eyeless mask, and I still sat transfixed. [19]A distant airplane, a delta wing out of nightmare, made a gliding shadow on the creek's bottom that looked like a stingray cruising upstream. [20]At once a black fin slit the pink cloud on the water, shearing it in two. [21]The two halves merged together and seemed to dissolve before my eyes. [22]Darkness pooled in the cleft of the creek and rose, as water collects in a well. [23]Untamed, dreaming lights flickered over the sky. [24]I saw hints of hulking underwater shadows, two pale splashes out of the water, and round ripples rolling close together from a blackened center.

²⁵At last I stared upstream where only the deepest violet remained of the cloud, a cloud so high its underbelly still glowed feeble color reflected from a hidden sky lighted in turn by a sun halfway to China. ²⁶And out of that violet, a sudden enormous black body arced over the water. ²⁷I saw only a cylindrical sleekness. ²⁸Head and tail, if there was a head and tail, were both submerged in cloud. ²⁹I saw only one ebony fling, a headlong dive to darkness; then the waters closed, and the lights went out.

³⁰I walked home in a shivering daze, up hill and down. ³¹Later I lay open-mouthed in bed, my arms flung wide at my sides to steady the whirling darkness. ³²At this latitude I'm spinning 836 miles an hour round the earth's axis; I often fancy I feel my sweeping fall as a breakneck arc like the dive of dolphins, and the hollow rushing of wind raises hair on my neck and the side of my face. ³³In orbit around the sun I'm moving 64,800 miles an hour. ³⁴The solar system as a whole, like a merry-go-round unhinged, spins, bobs, and blinks at the speed of 43,200 miles an hour along a course set east of Hercules. ³⁵Someone has piped, and we are dancing a tarantella until the sweat pours. ³⁶I open my eyes and I see dark, muscled forms curl out of water, with flapping gills and flattened eyes. ³⁷I close my eyes and I see stars, deep stars giving way to deeper stars, deeper stars bowing to deepest stars at the crown of an infinite cone.

QUESTIONS

1. To make sentences 9 and 20 periodic, open them with the modifying phrases that conclude them. Do these revisions change the meaning of the sentences or merely change the emphasis?

2. Revise sentences 23 and 33 to put the opening modifiers at the end. What is gained or lost in emphasis?

3. Break sentence 7 into its component parts and combine them into shorter sentences. Then discuss the differences in effect or meaning from the original sentence.

4. How do the following revisions of sentence 11 change the emphasis and effect:

> **a.** Startled, a land turtle on the bank hissed the air from its lungs and withdrew into its shell.

> **b.** Hissing the air from its lungs, a startled land turtle on the bank withdrew into its shell.

> **c.** A land turtle, hissing the air from its lungs, withdrew into its shell, startled.

Do the words *startled* and *hissing* refer clearly to the turtle in these revisions?

How does the following revision change the effect of sentence 15?

> Tremendous action—big action, inexplicable—roiled the water everywhere I looked.

5. How does sentence 37 build in emphasis?

6. What in the experience at Tinker Creek prompts the feelings Dillard describes in the final paragraph? What is the relationship between water and sky?

7. What implied thesis or idea is Dillard developing in the four paragraphs? What sentence comes closest to stating a thesis?

SUGGESTION FOR WRITING

Develop an implied thesis of your own through the details of an outdoor experience. You might build your description to the insight that you reached into the world of nature, as Dillard does.

24

CLIMAX

Periodic sentences achieve climax by delaying the main idea or its completion until the end of the sentence. Even in loose or coordinated sentences, modifying or qualifying phrases and clauses following the main idea can be arranged in the order of rising importance—as in *I came, I saw, I conquered.* Here are sentences of Annie Dillard that do the same:

> But shadows spread, and deepened, and stayed.

> I close my eyes and I see stars, deep stars giving way to deeper stars, deeper stars bowing to deepest stars at the crown of an infinite cone. (*Pilgrim at Tinker Creek*)

A sense of anticipation, promoted through the ideas themselves, is necessary to climax. Anticlimax will result if the culminating idea is less significant than what has gone before. The resulting letdown may be deliberately comic:

> If once a man indulges himself in murder, very soon he comes to think little of robbery; and from robbing he next comes to drinking and Sabbath-breaking, and from that to incivility and procrastination. (Thomas De Quincey, *Supplementary Papers*)

JOHN UPDIKE

JOHN UPDIKE began his long association with *The New Yorker* early in his career and has published many of his poems, stories, and essays in that magazine. His collection of stories *The Music School* won the O. Henry

Award in 1966. He received the National Book Award in 1963 for his novel *The Centaur*, the Pulitzer Prize and the American Book Award in 1981 for *Rabbit Is Rich*, and the Pulitzer again for *Rabbit at Rest* in 1991. His recent books include *In the Beauty of the Lilies* (1996) and *Gertrude and Claudius* (2000). The speaker in one of Updike's stories is describing his grandmother as he remembers her from his youth: "At the time I was married, she was in her late seventies, crippled and enfeebled. She had fought a long battle with Parkinson's disease; in my earliest memories of her she is touched with it. Her fingers and back are bent; there is a tremble about her as she moved about through the dark, odd-shaped rooms of our house in the town where I was born." His thoughts turn in this passage to happier days.

MY GRANDMOTHER

[1]When we were all still alive, the five of us in that kerosene-lit house, on Friday and Saturday nights, at an hour when in the spring and summer there was still abundant light in the air, I would set out in my father's car for town, where my friends lived. [2]I had, by moving ten miles away, at last acquired friends: an illustration of that strange law whereby, like Orpheus leading Eurydice, we achieve our desire by turning our back on it. [3]I had even gained a girl, so that the vibrations were as sexual as social that made me jangle with anticipation as I clowned in front of the mirror in our kitchen, shaving from a basin of stove-heated water, combing my hair with a dripping comb, adjusting my reflection in the mirror until I had achieved just that electric angle from which my face seemed beautiful and everlastingly, by the very volumes of air and sky and grass that lay mutely banked about our home, beloved. [4]My grandmother would hover near me, watching fearfully, as she had when I was a child, afraid that I would fall from a tree. [5]Delirious, humming, I would swoop and lift her, lift her like a child, crooking one arm under her knees and cupping the other behind her back. [6]Exultant in my height, my strength, I would lift that frail brittle body weighing perhaps a hundred pounds and twirl with it in my arms while the rest of the family watched with startled smiles of alarm. [7]Had I stumbled, or dropped her, I might have broken her back, but my joy always proved a secure cradle. [8]And whatever irony was in the impulse, whatever implicit contrast between this ancient husk, scarcely female, and the pliant, warm girl I would embrace before

the evening was done, direct delight flooded away: I was carrying her who had carried me, I was giving my past a dance, I had lifted the anxious caretaker of my childhood from the floor, I was bringing her with my boldness to the edge of danger, from which she had always sought to guard me.

QUESTIONS

1. How does Updike construct sentence 3 to take advantage of the strong terminal position? Does the context justify the double emphasis given to *beloved?*

2. Sentence 3 develops through an accumulation of detail. Does the sentence develop a single idea? Could Updike break it up without interrupting the meaning or disturbing the effect?

3. What technique aids in achieving the climax in sentences 5 and 8? Does the same kind of sentence construction achieve it?

SUGGESTIONS FOR WRITING

1. Describe an episode involving a close relative or friend that reveals a special relationship. Let your details reveal the relationship; do not state it directly.

2. Lytton Strachey's account of Queen Victoria's final years (p. 35) builds to a climax. Show how certain sentences in Strachey's paragraph contribute to this effect.

25

PARALLELISM

The italicized words in the following sentence are parallel in structure; that is, they perform the same grammatical function in the sentence and, as infinitives, are the same in form:

> So long as I remain alive and well I shall continue *to feel* strongly about prose style, *to love* the surface of the earth, and *to take* a pleasure in solid objects and scraps of useless information. (George Orwell, *Why I Write* [italics added])

In speaking and writing, we make elements such as these infinitives parallel naturally. No matter how many words separate them, we continue the pattern we start. Indeed, our "sentence sense" tells us when a pattern has been interrupted. We know something is wrong when we read

> I shall continue to feel strongly about prose style, to love the surface of the earth, and taking pleasure in solid objects and scraps of useless information.

Parallelism is an important means to concision and focus in sentences. It also allows us to make additions to the sentence without loss of clarity.

A special use of parallelism is the balancing of similar ideas in a sentence for special emphasis:

> Violence ends by defeating itself. It creates bitterness in the survivors and brutality in the destroyers. (Martin Luther King, Jr., *Nonviolent Resistance*)

Notice that the parallel phrases here are of the same weight and length. Writers can balance clauses and occasionally whole sentences in the same way:

> Every landscape in the world is full of these exact and beautiful adaptations, by which an animal fits into its environment like one cog-wheel into another. The sleeping hedgehog waits for the spring to burst its metabolism into life. The humming-bird beats the air and dips its needle-fine beak into hanging blossoms. Butterflies mimic leaves and even noxious creatures to deceive their predators. The mole plods through the ground as if he had been designed as a mechanical shuttle. (J. Bronowski, *The Ascent of Man*)

The marked rhythm of these sentences creates a highly formal effect by slowing the tempo. Such exact balance interrupts the natural flow of the sentence, giving emphasis to most or all of its parts. For this reason it is exceptional to find sentences as studied and formal as these in modern writing. But we do find a moderate balance used to give a greater emphasis to similar ideas than ordinary parallelism provides.

ERNESTO GALARZA

ERNESTO GALARZA (1905–1984), the American labor leader, teacher, and writer, was born in Jalcocotán, Nayarit, Mexico, and came to the United States when he was six. He went to school in Sacramento, and later studied at Occidental College and at Stanford and Columbia universities, receiving his Ph.D. in history and political science in 1947. Galarza's youthful experience as a farm and cannery worker prepared him for his life's work organizing agricultural workers. He taught at various universities and as Regents Professor at the University of California, San Diego. His books include the autobiography *Barrio Boy* (1971), which describes his childhood in Mexico and California. The Ajax to which Galarza refers was his mother's sewing machine; Coronel was the family rooster in Jalcocotán.

BOYHOOD IN A SACRAMENTO BARRIO

Our family conversations always occurred on our own kitchen porch, away from the gringos. One or the other of the adults would begin: *Se*   1 *han fijado?* Had we noticed—that the Americans do not ask permission to leave the room; that they had no respectful way of addressing an elderly person; that they spit brown over the railing of the porch into the yard; that when they laughed they roared; that they never brought *saludos* to everyone in your family from everyone in their family when they visited; that *General Delibree* was only a clerk; that *zopilotes* were not allowed on the streets to collect garbage; that the policemen did not carry lanterns at night; that Americans didn't keep their feet on the floor when they were sitting; that there was a special automobile for going to jail; that a rancho was not a rancho at all but a very small hacienda; that the saloons served their customers free eggs, pickles, and sandwiches; that instead of bullfighting, the gringos for sport tried to kill each other with gloves?

I did not have nearly the strong feelings on these matters that Doña Henriqueta expressed. I felt a vague admiration for the way Mr. Brien could spit brown. Wayne, my classmate, laughed much better than the Mexicans, because he opened his big mouth wide and brayed like a donkey so he could be heard a block away. But it was the kind of laughter that made my mother tremble, and it was not permitted in our house.

Rules were laid down to keep me, as far as possible, *un muchacho bien educado.* If I had to spit I was to do it privately, or if in public, by the curb, with my head down and my back to people. I was never to wear my cap in the house and I was to take it off even on the porch if ladies or elderly gentlemen were sitting. If I wanted to scratch, under no circumstances was I to do it right then and there, in company, like the Americans, but I was to excuse myself. If Catfish or Russell yelled to me from across the street I was not to shout back. I was never to ask for tips for my errands or other services to the tenants of 418 L, for these were *atenciones* expected of me.

Above all I was never to fail in *respeto* to grownups, no matter who they were. It was an inflexible rule; I addressed myself to *Señor* Big Singh, *Señor* Big Ernie, *Señora* Dodson, *Señor* Cho-ree Lopez.

My standing in the family, but especially with my mother, depended on my keeping these rules. I was not punished for breaking them. She simply reminded me that it gave her acute *vergüenza* to see me act thus, and that I would never grow up to be a correct *jefe de familia* if I did not know how to be a correct boy. I knew what *vergüenza* was from feeling it time and again; and the notion of growing up to keep a tight rein over a family of my own was somehow satisfying.

In our musty apartment in the basement of 418 L, ours remained a   6
Mexican family. I never lost the sense that we were the same, from Jalco
to Sacramento. There was the polished cedar box, taken out now and
then from the closet to display our heirlooms. I had lost the rifle shells
of the revolution, and Tio Tonche, too, was gone. But there was the butterfly sarape, the one I had worn through the Battle of Puebla; a black
lace mantilla Doña Henriqueta modeled for us; bits of embroidery and
lace she had made; the tin pictures of my grandparents; my report card
signed by Señorita Bustamante and Don Salvador; letters from Aunt Es-
ther; and the card with the address of the lady who had kept the Ajax
for us. When our mementos were laid out on the bed I plunged my head
into the empty box and took deep breaths of the aroma of *puro cedro,*
pure Jalcocotán mixed with camphor.

We could have hung on the door of our apartment a sign like those   7
we read in some store windows—*Aquí se habla español.* We not only
spoke Spanish, we read it. From the *Librería Española,* two blocks up
the street, Gustavo and I bought novels for my mother, like *Genoveva
de Brabante,* a paperback with the poems of Amado Nervo and a handbook of the history of Mexico. The novels were never read aloud, the
poems and the handbook were. Nervo was the famous poet from Tepic,
close enough to Jalcocotán to make him our own. And in the history
book I learned to read for myself, after many repetitions by my mother,
about the deeds of the great Mexicans Don Salvador had recited so vividly
to the class in Mazatlán. She refused to decide for me whether Abraham
Lincoln was as great as Benito Juarez, or George Washington braver than
the priest Don Miguel Hidalgo. At school there was no opportunity to
settle these questions because nobody seemed to know about Juarez or
Hidalgo; at least they were never mentioned and there were no pictures
of them on the walls.

The family talk I listened to with the greatest interest was about Jalco.   8
Wherever the conversation began it always turned to the pueblo, our
neighbors, anecdotes that were funny or sad, the folk tales and the witch-
craft, and our kinfolk, who were still there. I usually lay on the floor
those winter evenings, with my feet toward the kerosene heater, watching on the ceiling the flickering patterns of the light filtered through the
scrollwork of the chimney. As I listened once again I chased the *zopilote*
away from Coronel, or watched José take Nerón into the forest in a
sack. Certain things became clear about the *rurales* and why the young
men were taken away to kill Yaqui Indians, and about the Germans, the

Englishmen, the Frenchmen, the Spaniards, and the Americans who owned the haciendas, the railroads, the ships, the big stores, the breweries. They owned Mexico because President Porfirio Díaz had let them steal it, José explained as I listened. Now Don Francisco Madero had been assassinated for trying to get it back. On such threads of family talk I followed my own recollection of the years from Jalco—the attack on Mazatlán, the captain of Acaponeta, the camp at El Nanchi and the arrival at Nogales on the flatcar.

Only when we ventured uptown did we feel like aliens in a foreign   9
land. Within the *barrio* we heard Spanish on the streets and in the alleys. On the railroad tracks, in the canneries, and along the riverfront there were more Mexicans than any other nationality. And except for the foremen, the work talk was in our language. In the secondhand shops, where the *barrio* people sold and bought furniture and clothing, there were Mexican clerks who knew the Mexican ways of making a sale. Families doubled up in decaying houses, cramping themselves so they could rent an extra room to *chicano* boarders, who accented the brown quality of our Mexican *colonia*.

VOCABULARY

barrio: neighborhood
Se han fijado?: Did you notice?
saludos: greetings
zopilotes: vultures, buzzards
un muchacho bien educado: a well-bred boy
atenciones: duties
respeto: respect
vergüenza: shame, embarrassment
jefe de familia: head of the family
puro cedro: pure cedar
Aquí se habla español: Spanish spoken here
Librería Española: Spanish Bookstore
rurales: rural mounted police
chicano: American of Mexican descent
colonia: colony

QUESTIONS

1. How does the author use parallelism in the third sentence of paragraph 1 to give equal emphasis to the various ideas?

2. How is the same use made of parallelism in paragraph 6?

3. Whole sentences can be parallel to one another. How much parallelism of this kind do you find in paragraph 3?

4. In general, how loose or how strict to you find the parallelism of Galarza's sentences? How formal an effect do his sentences create?

5. How do you believe children are best taught to respect people who are different from them culturally? How different from Galarza's was your training in manners?

SUGGESTIONS FOR WRITING

1. Galarza uses his account to say something about Mexican and American folkways and the changes brought about in moving from one world to another. Discuss what Galarza is saying, and comment on his attitude toward the changes he experiences.

2. Discuss the increased importance customs have when you find yourself in a new environment, perhaps in a new school or neighborhood. You might want to discuss changes in speech habits as well as changes in behavior.

26

ANTITHESIS

When contrasting ideas are balanced in sentences and paragraphs, they are said to be in antithesis:

> History proves that dictatorships do not grow out of strong and successful governments, but out of weak and helpless ones. (Franklin D. Roosevelt)

> Shallow understanding from people of good will is more frustrating than absolute misunderstanding from people of ill will. (Martin Luther King, Jr., *Letter from Birmingham Jail*)

> We can no longer afford to take that which was good in the past and simply call it our heritage, to discard the bad and simply think of it as a dead load which by itself time will bury in oblivion. (Hannah Arendt, *The Origins of Totalitarianism*)

This moderate balancing to heighten the contrast of ideas is found often in modern writing, though usually in formal discussions. Like the exact balance of similar ideas, the balancing of antithetical phrases is exceptional today. The following passage is the dramatic conclusion to a long book on the history of Roman society:

> Rome did not invent education, but she developed it on a scale unknown before, gave it state support, and formed the curriculum that persisted till our harassed youth. She did not invent the arch, the vault, or the dome, but she used them with such audacity and magnificence that in some fields her architecture has remained unequaled. (Will Durant, *Caesar and Christ*)

MARTIN   LUTHER   KING,   JR.

Born in 1929, MARTIN LUTHER KING JR., was ordained in 1947 in the Atlanta church where his father was the minister. He graduated from Morehouse College the following year and received his Ph.D. from Boston University in 1953. In 1955 he rose to prominence in America and throughout the world as leader of the Montgomery, Alabama, bus boycott, and he continued as one of the leaders of the Civil Rights Movement until his assassination in Memphis on April 4, 1968. "From my Christian background I gained my ideals, and from Gandhi my technique," King said. It is the technique of passive resistance that he describes here. King's style of writing reflects the cadences of his speeches—influenced strongly by the style of the Old Testament prophetic books, to name just one of many sources.

NONVIOLENT RESISTANCE

Oppressed people deal with their oppression in three characteristic ways. One way is acquiescence: the oppressed resign themselves to their doom. They tacitly adjust themselves to oppression, and thereby become conditioned to it. In every movement toward freedom some of the oppressed prefer to remain oppressed. Almost 2800 years ago Moses set out to lead the children of Israel from the slavery of Egypt to the freedom of the promised land. He soon discovered that slaves do not always welcome their deliverers. They become accustomed to being slaves. They would rather bear those ills they have, as Shakespeare pointed out, than flee to others that they know not of. They prefer the "fleshpots of Egypt" to the ordeals of emancipation.

There is such a thing as the freedom of exhaustion. Some people are so worn down by the yoke of oppression that they give up. A few years ago in the slum areas of Atlanta, a Negro guitarist used to sing almost daily: "Ben down so long that down don't bother me." This is the type of negative freedom and resignation that often engulfs the life of the oppressed.

But this is not the way out. To accept passively an unjust system is to cooperate with that system; thereby the oppressed become as evil as the oppressor. Noncooperation with evil is as much a moral obligation as is cooperation with good. The oppressed must never allow the conscience of the oppressor to slumber. Religion reminds every man that he is his brother's keeper. To accept injustice or segregation passively is to say to the oppressor that his actions are morally right. It is a way of allowing his conscience to fall asleep. At this moment the oppressed fails to be his brother's keeper. So acquiescence—while often the easier way—is not the moral way. It is the way of the coward. The Negro cannot win the respect of his oppressor by acquiescing; he merely increases the oppressor's arrogance and contempt. Acquiescence is interpreted as proof of the Negro's inferiority. The Negro cannot win the respect of the white people of the South or the peoples of the world if he is willing to sell the future of his children for his personal and immediate comfort and safety.

A second way that oppressed people sometimes deal with oppression 4
is to resort to physical violence and corroding hatred. Violence often brings about momentary results. Nations have frequently won their independence in battle. But in spite of temporary victories, violence never brings permanent peace. It solves no social problem; it merely creates new and more complicated ones.

Violence as a way of achieving racial justice is both impractical and 5
immoral. It is impractical because it is a descending spiral ending in destruction for all. The old law of an eye for an eye leaves everybody blind. It is immoral because it seeks to humiliate the opponent rather than win his understanding; it seeks to annihilate rather than to convert. Violence is immoral because it thrives on hatred rather than love. It destroys community and makes brotherhood impossible. It leaves society in monologue rather than dialogue. Violence ends by defeating itself. It creates bitterness in the survivors and brutality in the destroyers. A voice echoes through time saying to every potential Peter, "Put up your sword." History is cluttered with the wreckage of nations that failed to follow this command.

If the American Negro and other victims of oppression succumb to 6
the temptation of using violence in the struggle for freedom, future generations will be the recipients of a desolate night of bitterness, and our chief legacy to them will be an endless reign of meaningless chaos. Violence is not the way.

The third way open to oppressed people in their quest for freedom 7
is the way of nonviolent resistance. Like the synthesis in Hegelian philosophy, the principle of nonviolent resistance seeks to reconcile the truths of two opposites—acquiescence and violence—while avoiding the extremes and immoralities of both. The nonviolent resister agrees with the

person who acquiesces that one should not be physically aggressive toward his opponent; but he balances the equation by agreeing with the person of violence that evil must be resisted. He avoids the nonresistance of the former and the violent resistance of the latter. With nonviolent resistance, no individual or group need submit to any wrong, nor need anyone resort to violence in order to right a wrong.

It seems to me that this is the method that must guide the actions of the Negro in the present crisis in race relations. Through nonviolent resistance the Negro will be able to rise to the noble height of opposing the unjust system while loving the perpetrators of the system. The Negro must work passionately and unrelentingly for full stature as a citizen, but he must not use inferior methods to gain it. He must never come to terms with falsehood, malice, hate, or destruction.   8

Nonviolent resistance makes it possible for the Negro to remain in the South and struggle for his rights. The Negro's problem will not be solved by running away. He cannot listen to the glib suggestions of those who would urge him to migrate en masse to other sections of the country. By grasping his great opportunity in the South he can make a lasting contribution to the moral strength of the nation and set a sublime example of courage for generations yet unborn.   9

By nonviolent resistance, the Negro can also enlist all men of good will in his struggle for equality. The problem is not a purely racial one, with Negroes set against whites. In the end, it is not a struggle between people at all, but a tension between justice and injustice. Nonviolent resistance is not aimed against oppressors but against oppression. Under its banner consciences, not racial groups, are enlisted.   1

If the Negro is to achieve the goal of integration, he must organize himself into a militant and nonviolent mass movement. All three elements are indispensable. The movement for equality and justice can only be a success if it has both a mass and militant character; the barriers to be overcome require both. Nonviolence is an imperative in order to bring about ultimate community.

A mass movement of a militant quality that is not at the same time committed to nonviolence tends to generate conflict, which in turn breeds anarchy. The support of the participants and the sympathy of the uncommitted are both inhibited by the threat that bloodshed will engulf the community. This reaction in turn encourages the opposition to threaten and resort to force. When, however, the mass movement repudiates violence while moving resolutely toward its goal, its opponents are revealed as the instigators and practitioners of violence if it occurs. Then public support is magnetically attracted to the advocates of nonviolence, while those who employ violence are literally disarmed by overwhelming sentiment against their stand.

QUESTIONS

1. Note the sentences that conclude paragraph 1:

> They would rather *bear those ills they have,* as Shakespeare pointed out,
> than *flee to others that they know not of.*

> They prefer *the "fleshpots of Egypt"*
> *to the ordeals of emancipation.*

What sentences in paragraph 5 contain antithetical elements? How exact is the antithesis? How many of these sentences are balanced to emphasize similar ideas?

2. How exact is the antithesis of ideas in paragraphs 8 and 10?

3. One way to moderate the tension of a passage containing considerable balance and antithesis is to vary the length of clauses or sentences. To what extent are the sentences of paragraphs 5, 8, and 10 varied in their length?

4. What do balance and antithesis contribute to the tone of the passage? What kind of voice do you hear?

SUGGESTIONS FOR WRITING

1. Compare King's sentence style with that of another of his writings, for example, "Letter from Birmingham Jail." Discuss how the relative exactness of sentence balance and antithesis is used to moderate or increase the tension of the writing.

2. Compare a passage in the King James Version of the Bible with the rendering of the same passage in the Revised Standard Version. Comment on the differences you notice in the use of balance or antithesis.

27

LENGTH

There is nothing inherently effective or ineffective, superior or inferior about long or short sentences, just as there is nothing inherently effective or ineffective in a single note of the scale. How effective a sentence is depends on what it does in a paragraph or essay. The very short, disconnected sentences in a story by Ernest Hemingway effectively express the boredom a young war veteran feels on his return home, but would probably also create a feeling of monotony in a piece of writing on another subject:

> He did not want any consequences. He did not want any consequences ever again. He wanted to live alone without consequences. Besides he did not really need a girl. The army had taught him that. It was all right to pose as though you had to have a girl. Nearly everybody did that. But it wasn't true. You did not need a girl. That was the funny thing. ("Soldier's Home")

A sentence, as we have seen, often starts with the main idea and then develops it:

> She was a spirited-looking young woman, with dark curly hair cropped and parted on the side, a short oval face with straight eyebrows, and a large curved mouth. (Katherine Anne Porter, "Old Mortality")

How much detail a writer can provide depends on how prominent the main ideas are—whether in a sentence consisting of a single core idea followed by a series of modifiers, as in Porter, or in one consisting of a series of connected core ideas or main clauses, modified as in this sentence:

> Morrall would duck his head in the huddle and if it was feasible he would call a play which took the ball laterally across the field—a pitchout, perhaps, and the play would eat up ground toward the girls, the ball carrier sprinting for the sidelines, with his running guards in front of him, running low, and behind them the linemen coming too, so that twenty-two men were converging on them at a fair clip. (George Plimpton, *Paper Lion*)

LEWIS THOMAS

LEWIS THOMAS (p. 72) begins his essay on "matters of doubt" with a discussion of an important controversy of the 1960s. The English scientist and novelist C. P. Snow argued in *The Two Cultures and the Scientific Revolution* (1961) that scientists possess a culture little understood by "literary intellectuals," who have little knowledge of scientific ideas and are hostile to its achievements. "The scientific edifice of the physical world," Snow claimed, is "in its intellectual depth, complexity and articulation, the most beautiful and wonderful collective work of the mind of man." The English literary critic F. R. Leavis attacked these ideas, arguing that the achievements of modern science are not superior to those of the traditional culture, which created the human world and made science possible. Traditional literary culture, Leavis argued, provides a particular kind of "intelligence, a power—rooted, strong in experience, and supremely human," needed to respond to the rapid advances of science and technology. Thomas summarizes their views and, finding the controversy muddled, asks what the sciences and the humanities have in common and what attitude we should take in trying to understand the world.

ON MATTERS OF DOUBT

The "two-cultures" controversy of several decades back has quieted down some, but it is still with us, still unsettled because of the polarized views set out by C. P. Snow at one polemical extreme and by F. R. Leavis at

1

the other; these remain as the two sides of the argument. At one edge, the humanists are set up as knowing, and wanting to know, very little about science and even less about the human meaning of contemporary science; they are, so it goes, antiscientific in their prejudice. On the other side, the scientists are served up as a bright but illiterate lot, well-read in nothing except science, even, as Leavis said of Snow, incapable of writing good novels. The humanities are presented in the dispute as though made up of imagined unverifiable notions about human behavior, unsubstantiated stories cooked up by poets and novelists, while the sciences deal parsimoniously with lean facts, hard data, incontrovertible theories, truths established beyond doubt, the unambiguous facts of life.

The argument is shot through with bogus assertions and false images, and I have no intention of becoming entrapped in it here, on one side or the other. Instead, I intend to take a stand in the middle of what seems to me a muddle, hoping to confuse the argument by showing that there isn't really any argument in the first place. To do this, I must try to show that there is in fact a solid middle ground to stand on, a shared common earth beneath the feet of all the humanists and all the scientists, a single underlying view of the world that drives all scholars, whatever their discipline—whether history or structuralist criticism or linguistics or quantum chromodynamics or astrophysics or molecular genetics.

There is, I think, such a shared view of the world. It is called *bewilderment*. Everyone knows this, but it is not much talked about; bewilderment is kept hidden in the darkest closets of all our institutions of higher learning, repressed whenever it seems to be emerging into public view, sometimes glimpsed staring from attic windows like a mad cousin of learning. It is the family secret of twentieth-century science, and of twentieth-century arts and letters as well. Human knowledge doesn't stay put. What we have been learning in our time is that we really do not understand this place or how it works, and we comprehend our own selves least of all. And the more we learn, the more we are—or ought to be—dumbfounded.

It is the greatest fun to be bewildered, but only when there lies ahead the sure certainty of having things straightened out, and soon. It is like a marvelous game, provided you have some way of keeping score, and this is what seems to be lacking in our time. It is confusing, and too many of us are choosing not to play, settling back with whatever straws of fixed knowledge we can lay hands on, denying bewilderment, pretending one conviction or another, nodding our heads briskly at whatever we prefer to believe, staying away from the ambiguity of being.

We would be better off if we had never invented the terms "science" and "humanities" and then set them up as if they represented two different kinds of intellectual enterprise. I cannot see why we ever did this, but we did. Now, to make matters worse, we have these two encampments not only at odds but trying to swipe problems from each other. The historians, some of them anyway, want to be known as social scientists and solve the ambiguities of history by installing computers in all their offices; the deconstructionists want to become the ultimate scientists of poetry, looking at every word in a line with essentially the reductionist attitude of particle physicists in the presence of atoms, but still unaware of the uncertainty principle that governs any good poem: not only can the observer change the thing observed, he can even destroy it. The biologists have invaded all aspects of human behavior with equations to explain away altruism and usefulness by totting up the needs of genes; the sociobiologists are becoming humanists manqué, swept off their feet by ants. The physicists, needing new terms for their astonishments, borrow "quarks" from Joyce and label precisely quantitative aspects of matter almost dismissively with poetically allusive words like "strangeness," "color," and "flavor"; soon some parts of the universe will begin to "itch."

We have, to be sure, learned enough to know better than to say some things, about letters and about science, but we are still too reticent about our ignorance. Most things in the world are unsettling and bewildering, and it is mistake to try to explain them away; they are there for marveling at and wondering at, and we should be doing more of this.

I do not mean to suggest that we are surrounded by unknowable things. Indeed, I cannot imagine any sorts of questions to be asked about ourselves or about nature that cannot sooner or later be answered, given enough time. I do admit to worrying, late at night, about that matter of time: obviously we will have to get rid of modern warfare and quickly, or else we will end up, with luck, throwing spears and stones at each other. We could, without luck, run out of time in what is left of this century and then, by mistake, finish the whole game off by upheaving the table, ending life for everything except the bacteria, maybe—with enough radiation, even them. If you are given to fretting about what is going on in the minds of the young people in our schools, or on the streets of Zurich or Paris or Sydney or Tokyo or wherever, give a thought to the idea of impermanence for a whole species—*ours*—and the risk of earthly incandescence; it is a brand-new idea, never before confronted as a reality by any rising generation of human beings.

I have an idea, as an aside. Why not agree with the Russians about just one technological uniformity to be installed, at small cost, in all the missiles, theirs and ours: two small but comfortable chambers added to every vehicle before firing, one for a prominent diplomat selected by the other side, one for a lawyer selected at random? It might be a beginning.

Here's a list of things, taken more or less at random, that we do not understand:

I am entitled to say, if I like, that awareness exists in all the individual creatures on the planet—worms, sea urchins, gnats, whales, subhuman primates, superprimate humans, the lot. I can say this because we do not know what we are talking about; consciousness is so much a total mystery for our own species that we cannot begin to guess about its existence in others. I can say that bird song is the music made by songbirds for their own pleasure, pure fun, also for ours, and it is only a piece of good fortune that the music turns out to be handy for finding mates for breeding or setting territorial markers. I can say, if I like, that social insects behave like the working parts of an immense central nervous system: the termite colony is an enormous brain on millions of legs; the individual termite is a mobile neurone. This would mean that there is such a phenomenon as collective thinking, which goes on whenever sufficient numbers of creatures are sufficiently connected to one another, and it would also mean that we humans could do the same trick if we tried, and perhaps we've already done it, over and over again, in the making of language and the meditative making (for which the old Greek word *poesis* is best) of metaphors. I can even assert out loud that we are, as a species, held together by something like affection (what the physicists might be calling a "weak force") and by something like love (a "strong force"), and nobody can prove that I'm wrong. I can dismiss all the evidence piling up against such an idea, all our destructiveness and cantankerousness, as error, error-proneness, built into our species to allow more flexibility of choice, and nobody can argue me out of this unless I choose to wander off to another point of view.

I am inclined to assert, unconditionally, that there is one central, universal aspect of human behavior, genetically set by our very nature, biologically governed, driving each of us along. Depending on how one looks at it, it can be defined as the urge to be useful. This urge drives society along, sets our behavior as individuals and in groups, invents all our myths, writes our poetry, composes our music.

It is not easy to be a social species and, at the same time, such a juvenile, almost brand-new species, milling around in groups, trying to construct a civilization that will last. Being useful is easy for an ant: you just wait for the right chemical signal, at the right stage of the construction of the hill, and then you go looking for a twig of exactly the right size for that stage and carry it back, up the flank of the hill, and put it in place, and then you go and do that thing again. An ant can dine out on his usefulness, all his life, and never get it wrong. 12

It is a different problem for us, carrying such risks of doing it wrong, getting the wrong twig, losing the hill, not even recognizing, yet, the outline of the hill. We are beset by strings of DNA, immense arrays of genes, instructing each of us to be helpful, impelling us to try our whole lives to be useful, but never telling us how. The instructions are not coded out in anything like an operator's manual; we have to make guesses all the time. The difficulty is increased when groups of us are set to work together; I have seen, and sat on, numberless committees, not one of which intended anything other than great merit, feckless all. Larger collections of us—cities, for instance—hardly ever get anything right. And, of course, there is the modern nation, probably the most stupefying example of biological error since the age of the great reptiles, wrong at every turn, but always felicitating itself loudly on its great value. It is a biological problem, as much so as a coral reef or a rain forest, but such things as happen to human nations could never happen in a school of fish. It is, when you think about it, a humiliation, but then "humble" and "human" are cognate words. We are smarter than the fish, but their instructions come along in their eggs; ours we are obliged to figure out, and we are, in this respect, slow learners. 13

The sciences and the humanities are all of a piece, one and the same kind of work for the human brain, done by launching guesses and finding evidence to back up the guesses. The methods and standards are somewhat different, to be sure. It is easier to prove that something is so in science than it is to make an assertion about Homer or Cézanne or Wallace Stevens and have it stand up to criticism from all sides, harder still to *be* Homer or Cézanne or Stevens, but the game is the same game. The hardest task for the scientists, hardly yet begun, is to find out what their findings may mean, deep inside, and how one piece of solid information, firmly established by experimentation and confirmation, fits with that unlike piece over there. The natural world is all of a piece, we all know 14 this in our bones, but we have a long, long way to go before we will see how the connections are made.

If you are looking about for really profound mysteries, essential aspects of our existence for which neither the sciences nor the humanities can provide any sort of explanation, I suggest starting with music. The professional musicologists, tremendous scholars all, for whom I have the greatest respect, haven't the ghost of an idea about what music is, or why we make it and cannot be human without it, or even—and this is the telling point—how the human mind makes music on its own, before it is written down and played. The biologists are no help here, nor the psychologists, nor the physicists, nor the philosophers, wherever they are these days. Nobody can explain it. It is a mystery, and thank goodness for that. The Brandenburgs and the late quartets are not there to give us assurances that we have arrived; they carry the news that there are deep centers in our minds that we know nothing about except that they are there.

The thing to do, to get us through the short run, the years just ahead, is to celebrate our ignorance. Instead of presenting the body of human knowledge as a mountainous structure of coherent information capable of explaining everything about everything if we could only master all the details, we should be acknowledging that it is, in real life, still a very modest mound of puzzlements that do not fit together at all. As a species, the thing we are biologically good at is learning new things, thanks to our individual large brains and thanks above all to the gift of speech that connects them, one to another. We can take some gratification at having come a certain distance in just the few thousand years of our existence as language users, but it should be a deeper satisfaction, even an exhilaration, to recognize that we have such a distance still to go. Get us through the next few years, I say, just get us safely out of this century and into the next, and then watch what we can do.

VOCABULARY

paragraph 1: polarized, polemical, parsimoniously, incontrovertible
paragraph 2: bogus
paragraph 5: encampments, reductionist, sociobiologists, manqué
paragraph 6: reticent

paragraph 7: incandescence
paragraph 10: mobile, neurone, cantankerousness
paragraph 13: stupefying, felicitating
paragraph 15: musicologists

QUESTIONS

1. In sentences containing semicolons in paragraphs 3, 5, 6, 13, and 15, the two parts of each might stand as separate sentences. What does Thomas gain by joining the two parts in each sentence? Could a colon substitute for the semicolon in each?

2. What purposes does the colon serve in paragraphs 5, 7, 9, 10, and 12?

3. Why does Thomas set off phrases with dashes rather than parentheses in paragraphs 3, 13, and 15, and the fifth sentence of paragraph 7? Could dashes substitute for the parentheses in paragraph 10?

4. What is the function of the single dash in paragraphs 2 and 10, and the fourth sentence of paragraph 7?

5. Combine the following sentences into longer ones. What is gained or lost by your revision?

> There is, I think, such a shared view of the world. It is called *bewilderment*. (paragraph 3)

> It is the family secret of twentieth-century science, and of twentieth-century arts and letters as well. Human science doesn't stay put. (paragraph 3)

> The biologists are no help here, nor the psychologists, nor the physicists, nor the philosophers, wherever they are these days. Nobody can explain it. (paragraph 15)

6. Thomas might have broken the fifth sentence ("This would mean") and the final sentence ("I can dismiss") of paragraph 10 into a series of shorter ones. What does he gain by not doing so?

7. What does Thomas mean by *bewilderment*, and how does he illustrate the idea?

8. What are the *humanities*, and how does Thomas explain the term in the course of the essay?

9. How does Thomas explain the statement that "the natural world is all of a piece"? How does the statement relate to his general thesis? Where does Thomas state it? Does he restate it in the course of the essay?

SUGGESTIONS FOR WRITING

1. Paragraph 4 contains a series of compound and compound-complex sentences (that is, sentences containing all main or independent clauses or a mix of independent and subordinate or dependent clauses). Rewrite the paragraph, breaking it into shorter sentences, or subordinating independent clauses where possible. Then discuss how your revision changes the emphasis and tone of the original paragraph.

2. Provide a list of things you would like to understand most about yourself and the world, and suggest ways a college education may help you to reach an understanding. You may wish to discuss why a college education cannot provide full or partial answers.

3. Thomas states that "human knowledge doesn't stay put." Illustrate this statement from your own experience.

V

ARGUMENT AND PERSUASION

28

INDUCTIVE REASONING

Part V discusses how we argue, or seek to prove our ideas, and how we use argument and other means to make our ideas persuasive. The essays in this and the following section show how we reason from various kinds of evidence. The process by which we generalize from personal experience, observation, and other factual evidence is called *induction*. The process by which we show what truths, beliefs, and long-established generalizations imply or entail is called *deduction*.

We reason inductively every day, for example in drawing the conclusion that a painful, red, and swollen finger is probably infected, or predicting that an unusual number of car accidents will probably follow an ice storm. Inductive reasoning often generalizes or makes predictions about a whole class of people or things by observing some of its members. An example is the generalization that drivers in a particular age group will have a higher than average number of car accidents—based on observation of a number of drivers in the group over a ten-month period, or the accident history of the group statewide or nationwide gathered statistically from police reports and insurance claims. In this kind of reasoning, no prediction can be made about any single member, nor can the prediction about the group as a whole be made with absolute certainty.

The problem in inductive reasoning is to choose particular instances that truly represent the group or class about which we are generalizing or making predictions. But, as in the sample precincts that pollsters use to predict the outcome of elections, it is impossible to guarantee that the limited number of people sampled are actually typical or representative. We also may be unaware of special circumstances that, if known, would weaken the generalization. These are important reasons for not claiming certainty.

A "hasty generalization" is a judgment made on the basis of insufficient evidence or on the basis of special cases. Thus someone might argue that, because a large number of drivers 70 years of age or older had car accidents during a three-month period, all drivers in this age group will have a higher than average number of accidents in the future, and therefore should pay higher insurance premiums. The argument might be worth considering if the behavior of sample drivers and the conditions under which they were driving could be shown to be typical. It might have been the case, however, that most of the drivers in these accidents proved to have impaired vision (by no means a characteristic of older people) or that the accidents occurred during a harsh winter. The generalization in question would then have been based both on special cases and on special circumstances.

Many beliefs arise from hasty generalizations like the one just cited: small towns are safer than large cities; redheaded people have short tempers; New Yorkers are rude. Consider the last of these generalizations: the New Yorkers who prompted the statement may have been observed on a crowded, stalled bus on the hottest day of the year. We will consider some special forms of inductive reasoning in the discussions that follow.

EXPERIENCE AND OBSERVATION

The process of reasoning from experience and observation requires careful qualification and repeated testing. Scientists engage in a continuous process of testing promising explanations or hypotheses derived from previous experiments and observations in the laboratory and in the field. They test anew conclusions that seem well established. New hypotheses arise that also require testing; if confirmed, these may lead to a questioning of earlier conclusions.

Reasoning from everyday experience and observation requires the same care taken in reasoning from scientific evidence. But this process of reasoning is perhaps even more difficult, for many ideas originate in attitudes and prejudices that we adopt unknowingly. The more deep-rooted the idea, the less likely we are to test it by experience. Indeed, we are more likely to look for evidence that confirms it. So the advice to think "objectively" about people and the world is not easily followed. We can, however, learn to treat with caution the ideas that we derive from what we hear and read. In writing about ideas, we do best to pause and ask where an idea came from before committing it to paper.

VICKI HEARNE

An animal trainer for many years, VICKI HEARNE has written about her experiences in *Adam's Task: Calling Animals by Name* (1986), *Bandit: Dossier of a Dangerous Dog* (1991), and *Parts of Light* (1994). In 1992 she received an award from the American Academy and Institute of Arts and Letters for distinguished literary achievement. *Animal Happiness* (1994), she tells us in the introduction to this collection of essays, is an account of "the mysteries of connection between different kinds of mind," animal and human. These kinds are evident in Hearne's description of an unusual seeing-eye dog and the woman he serves.

MAX INTO MAXIMILIAN

Mary Stockstill has long put her trust in the Good Book. The two great Braille volumes beside the chair in which she might be found knitting a multicolored blanket or entertaining her grandchildren are a source of light in her life. There is also her dog Max, in whom she believes, and the typewriter in which she has come to believe, the Braille one I used to ask her questions about Max when I went nosing over to her house. Max, a chocolate Labrador, her eyes and ears.

Not just her eyes. Her eyes and ears. Mary Stockstill is both deaf and blind.

Max is in "limited service." Most of the blind who use dogs can communicate through the harness about what they hear in the way of dangers, especially traffic dangers—a matter of some moment, since a dog who is concentrating on avoiding obstacles, particularly obstacles a dog is not naturally given to worrying about, such as overhanging branches, is distracted from auditory cues. Hence, normally, handler and dog guide each other. Guide dogs are justly famous for their "disobedience"; a good guide dog should refuse to obey a command that will take the handler into danger. Similarly, the blind handler should refuse to follow the dog if he or she hears danger. Since Mary Stockstill can't hear, she and Max cannot negotiate traffic, hence the expression "limited service."

But this is some kind of limited service. I watched Stockstill work Max at night, alone on a residential street. He took her safely down the street—skirting a pile of weeds and branches left carelessly on the sidewalk, which could have meant a nasty fall—and stopped at the curb. He also glanced back nervously at me. Stockstill didn't know why he was hesitating, only that his halt wasn't the usual firm halt that signals the presence of a curb. He continued looking back at me each time she urged him forward.

When we got back to the house and could talk again through her Braille typewriter, she wondered if Max had been distracted by barking dogs—if, that is, he had not worked responsibly while I watched.

I thought he had worked beautifully. There had been something suspicious for him to worry about: me, following the two of them in the dark as I scribbled in my notebook and muttered into my tape recorder. Not many young dogs would have kept their cool with such conflicting messages. How would you feel if the person you were supposed to be guiding and watching out for was being trailed by a dubious-looking stranger talking into a tape recorder? I would want to call my mother, or the cops—or Max.

Instead of calling his mother, Max just kept doing his job, which at that point had entailed keeping Stockstill out of the street, not letting her get lost, and watching me. She, deciding to trust Max, asked him to guide her home, which he did, still keeping a wary eye on me.

So Max thinks for himself, but his human handlers don't always appreciate his wisdom. There was the time, for example, out shopping, when Max decided it was too warm in the store and simply led Stockstill out, without being requested to do so. Her husband, Chuck, panicked, then found them outside the door. He said in the somewhat cross relief one feels under such circumstances, "I wasn't through shopping!"

Mary said, "Well, Max decided you were."

Stockstill became blind in 1939 at the age of ten. Her deafness "bottomed out" in 1959, which was also the year she thought she had to give up on having a dog, because there were no facilities then that trained dogs to deal with people who were both deaf and blind. It was nearly three decades before she got Max—years of I don't know what grief, frustration, and despair that go with being housebound and pretty much cut off. I don't know about all that because Mary Stockstill wouldn't tell me about it. "Just make Max look good."

Well, that isn't hard. He used to be, as Stockstill said, "just a puppy named Max. Now he's Maximilian."

QUESTIONS

1. Under what circumstances is a guide dog in "limited service," and by implication, in full service?

2. How does Hearne illustrate this kind of service in paragraph 4? What explanation does Hearne give for Max's hesitation at the curb? How did she reach an understanding of his behavior?

3. What idea about animal behavior does Max confirm? What further confirmation does Hearne provide? How has she reasoned inductively?

4. Why does she emphasize in the title of the essay and the concluding paragraph that Max is now Maximilian?

SUGGESTIONS FOR WRITING

1. Describe an experience with a particular breed of dog or cat that led you to generalize about the breed. You may wish to discuss other experiences with the breed that confirmed or led you to question your generalization or reject it.

2. We often generalize about people observed in a city or part of the country we have visited. We often hear complaints about Boston or Los Angeles or New York City drivers. Discuss what you would consider a fair generalization about drivers in your own town or city or part of the country. Explain what circumstances would make a generalization unfair.

EDWARD TENNER

EDWARD TENNER attended Princeton University and received his Ph.D. in European history from the University of Chicago. He has been a junior fellow in the Harvard Society of Fellows, has worked in scientific and trade publishing, and has held visiting positions at Princeton and the Institute for Advanced Study. Tenner's description of how mechanical devices take revenge upon the user deserves comparison with Marvin Harris's explanation of "why nothing works" (p. 211).

REVENGE THEORY

Why are the lines at automatic cash dispensers longer in the evening than those at tellers' windows used to be during banking hours? Why do helmets and other protective gear help make football more dangerous than rugby? Why do filter-tip cigarettes usually fail to reduce nicotine intake? Why are today's paperback prices starting to overtake yesterday's clothbound prices? Why has the leisure society gone the way of the leisure suit?

The world we have created seems to be getting even, twisting our cleverness against us. Or we may be the ones who are unconsciously twisting. Either way, wherever we turn we face the ironic unintended consequences of mechanical, chemical, medical, social, and financial ingenuity—revenge effects, they might be called.

Revenge effects don't require space-age technology. As the humorist Will Cuppy observed of the first pyramids, "Imhotep the Wise originated the idea of concealing the royal corpse and his treasure in a monument so conspicuous that it could not possibly be missed by body snatchers and other thieves." At Elizabethan hangings of cutpurses, their surviving colleagues worked the distracted throngs.

Cognizance of revenge effects is much more recent. Craftworkers and farmers before the nineteenth century, as far as I can tell, didn't seem to blame their tools or materials when things went wrong. They recognized providence and luck, and some of them (notably miners) discerned malicious spirits, but not ornery ordinary *things*. For all the prophecy of Mary Shelley and the insight of Henry David Thoreau, the critic Friedrich Theodor Vischer (1807–1887) probably deserves the honor of propelling revenge theory into common speech in a novel, *Auch Einer (Another)*, published in 1867. His eccentric—critics say, autobiographical—hero is convinced that everyday objects, like pencils, pens, inkwells, and cigars, harbor a perverse and demonic spirit. Although not quite in today's literary canon even in his native Germany, Vischer did achieve immortality through the phrase *die Tücke des Objekts*—the malice of things.

In 1878 Thomas Edison, possibly echoing telegraphers' slang, first wrote of a *bug* as a hidden problem to be removed from a design. According to a later article in *The Pall Mall Gazette,* he was implying "that some imaginary insect has secreted itself inside and is causing all the trouble." It appears that by the mid-1930s, "ironing the bugs out" had become American engineering slang.

By the 1940s the complexity of technological systems raised the con-   6
sciousness of troops and civilians alike about how many things could go
wrong. The London *Observer* acknowledged in 1942 that the behavior
of machines "couldn't always be explained by . . . laws of aerodynamics. And so, lacking a Devil, the young fliers . . . invented a whole hierarchy of devils. They called them Gremlins. . . ."

In 1949 revenge theory took a giant step when Col. P. J. Stapp of   7
Edwards Air Force Base referred to (his colleague Captain Ed) Murphy's
Law—that if something can go wrong, it will—in a press conference.
Aeronautical manufacturers soon were exploiting it in their advertising,
and it passed into folklaw, that vast body of free-form theorizing. Only
a year later the British humorist Paul Jennings published, as a parody of
the Paris avant-garde, an essay on "Resistentialism," a movement supposedly sweeping the Left Bank with the watchword, *"Les choses sont
contre nous."* Our growing "illusory domination over Things," the Re-
sistentialists believed, "has been matched . . . by the increasing hostility
(and greater force) of the Things arrayed against [us]."

In 1955 C. Northcote Parkinson (an expatriate historian then as ob-   8
scure as Murphy himself) began an article in *The Economist* with the
"commonplace observation that work expands so as to fill the time available for its completion. Thus, an elderly lady of leisure can spend the entire day in writing and dispatching a postcard to her niece at Bognor
Regis." He pointed out that there were nearly 68 percent fewer ships in
the Royal Navy in 1928 than in 1914, but more than 78 percent more
Admiralty officials.

What all this speculation had in common was a sense that technology and   9
the bureaucracies that sustained it had sometimes amusing and sometimes
troubling sides. There probably is no single way to classify the tendencies
that these and others have seen—whole books of folklaw principles have
been compiled—but at least five are noteworthy. They might be called *repeating, recomplicating, recongesting, regenerating,* and *rearranging*.

Repeating is the most universal. When a chore becomes easier or
faster, people assume they will be able to spend less time on it and more   10
on important matters. Instead, they may have to or want to do it more
often, or to do new things. The historian of technology Ruth Schwartz
Cowan has shown in *More Work for Mother* that while vacuum clean-
ers, washing machines, and other "labor-saving" appliances did gradually improve the working-class standard of living, they saved no time for

middle-class housewives. Women who had sent soiled clothing to a commercial laundry began to do more and more loads of washing. And as laundries and other services went out of business, fewer choices remained.

Much computing is information housekeeping. The billions of dollars of microcomputers installed in the 1980s replaced batch processing and mainframes, just as home appliances had defeated the laundries. If this unprecedented power had performed as advertised, productivity in services should have soared. Instead, it increased only 1.3 percent a year between 1982 and 1986. In 1989–90 it grew by only 0.5 percent. The largely precomputer postwar average growth had been fully 2.3 percent.   11

Experts disagree about the reasons for what *Fortune* called "the puny payoff from office computers," but repeating effects are surely involved. When spreadsheets were laborious, people did them as seldom and as cautiously as possible. Now recalculations can be done much more easily, but at the cost of having to do them much more often, and of learning to use the software. Meanwhile, competitors have their own spreadsheets (and faxes and cellular telephones), so there isn't even a relative advantage. Likewise, the time spent revising a computerized letter or memo may cancel the advantage of not having to retype. And of course mass-produced "personal" letters and memos eat into the time of the recipients.   12

Computers also force repeating, because often at least some essential data aren't on line. Patrons at libraries with electronic catalogues usually have to search the old printed catalogue too, probably increasing total search time. And they may discover that precious data are almost inaccessible in tapes in obsolete formats.   13

Even the body rebels against repeating. According to the U.S. Bureau of Labor Statistics, repetitive motion disorders (including hand injuries related to computer keyboards) accounted for fully 147,000 of 284,000 occupational illnesses in 1989.   14

Recomplicating is another ironic consequence of the simplifying abilities of computers. Wands, bar codes, on-screen displays, have failed to demystify the operations of video cassette recorders. Touch-tone telephones began as a small saving in dialing time for gadget-minded subscribers. By now the time savings of punching rather than dialing has been more than consumed by the elaborate systems built to take advantage of it. When the carrier access code and credit card number are added to the number itself, a single call may require thirty digits. And a voice mail system may then take over, demanding still more digits and waiting.   15

Powerful mainframes have allowed airlines to maximize income with   16
fare structures that are ever more difficult to understand. A single carrier routinely makes tens of thousands of fare changes each day. The Airline Tariff Publishing Company, the industry cooperative, has processed
as many as 600,000 changes in 24 hours. Dozens of fares may apply on
the same route. The system may benefit the airlines or the public, but it
makes it almost impossible for either to understand without tying into
the computer networks that made it possible.

Even safety devices can recomplicate fatally. In *Normal Accidents* the   17
sociologist Charles Perrow mentions, among other merchant marine
perils, "radar-assisted collisions" caused in part by difficulties of plotting
multiple and moving targets. One study even determined that as many
vessels changed course *toward* a radar-detected target as went in the other
direction.

Recomplicating may be political rather than technological or eco-   18
nomic. The 1986 tax code, introduced as fairer and simpler, has relieved
some taxpayers of itemizing, but the cost of preparing a tax return may
now be as much as 2 percent of a small company's revenue. *The Wall
Street Journal* points out that the rules on passive-loss deductions alone
take 196 pages to define *activity*. In 1988 the Business Council on the
Reduction of Paperwork estimated an average time of 18.6 hours to complete Form 1040, as opposed to the 2.6 hours claimed by the Internal
Revenue Service.

In *recongesting*, the system doesn't necessarily become harder to un-   19
derstand. It's just slower and less comfortable. Technological change
opens new frontiers but soon clogs them up again.

The automobile-based suburb once seemed to show that new ma-   20
chines could break the stranglehold of grasping railroads and monop-
olistic center-city landlords. Only decades later did rapid traffic flow turn
out to be a mirage. As Parkinson observed of bureaucrats and budgets,
cars and car trips have multiplied to saturate the roads built for them,
and even the hours of the day. The lunchtime rush hour in the
Washington, D.C., area is now as congested as those in the morning and
evening. Traffic approaching New York City between 4 and 7 A.M. grew
60 percent from 1967 to 1987. Average travel speed in Los Angeles is
projected to slow from 35 miles per hour to under twenty in the next
twenty years. Daniel Patrick Moynihan predicts that at present rates,
Interstate 95 between Fort Lauderdale and Miami will need 44 lanes in
another thirty years.

The historian and critic Ivan Illich estimates that the average American now spends a combined 1,600 hours either driving or earning the money to support automotive costs "to cover a year total of 6,000 miles, four miles per hour. This is just as fast as a pedestrian and slower than a bicycle."

It's no longer unusual to spend more time on transportation to and from airports, waiting and connection times, and flight delays, than on actual time in the air. Congestion continues even within the aircraft cabin, as coach seats have shrunk from the formerly standard 22 inches to nineteen inches, and pitch (front-to-back spacing) from 34 to 31 inches.

Space itself is not immune. Between 30,000 and 70,000 pieces of space debris, each measuring a centimeter or more in diameter and capable of shattering a spacecraft, now clutter the earth's orbit, endangering future missions. Over 6,600 pieces are the size of a softball, or larger. Donald Kessler of the Johnson Space Center in Houston told *The Washington Post* that by 2050, space junk might reach "critical density" and "grind itself to dust," making low earth orbit unusable.

Regenerating, unlike recongesting, usually appears after a problem seems to have been solved. Instead, the solution turns out to have revived or amplified the problem. Some teachers reinforce the traditional European preference for pencils with plain, painted ends, banning built-in rubber tips as encouragements to sloppy work—a revenge hypothesis, of course. Their pupils respond by finding great big erasers that can rub out entire lines with ease.

More seriously, pest control regenerates pests. In the 1950s and 1960s the pesticides heptachlor and later Mirex devastated wildlife and endangered human health when the U.S. Department of Agriculture deployed them over more than 130 million acres of the South. These tragic costs were tradeoffs, not revenge effects. The revenge effect was that the chemicals also killed the natural ant predators of the targets of the spraying, fire ants, which were able to move into their rivals' territory. Likewise in the 1950s, application of DDT wiped out natural wasp predators of Malaysian caterpillars, bringing defoliation until spraying was stopped. And it should hardly be news that anti-rattlesnake drives in the United States are leading to a surge in reported rattlesnake bites—after a period when there were so few that the Red Cross had discontinued snakebite courses.

Bacteria have a hydralike way of multiplying in response to bathing and even surgical scrubbing, possibly because heat and moisture split large colonies into smaller ones. Michael Andrews reports in *The Life That Lives on Man* that "tests on volunteers who have showered and soaped for ten minutes showed a marked increase in the number of bacteria floating in the air on their rafts of shed skin when they were dressing."

Insects and bacteria that resist pesticides and drugs are an even more alarming regenerating effect, the products of nature's own genetic engineering. Excessive use of antibiotics in livestock feed and over-the-counter drugs has made the problem urgent in the Third World, where resistant strains of bacteria causing ear infections, pneumonia, tuberculosis, and gonorrhea are now common. Even in the United States, antimicrobials in animal feed have helped select and promote resistant strains of salmonella. In 1987 the University of Illinois entomologist Robert Metcalf declared that "we may be rushing headlong back into the agricultural and medical dark ages that existed before the discovery of modern insecticides and antibiotics." 27

Finally, *rearranging* is the revenge effect that shifts a problem in time or space. To be a true revenge effect it must, of course, fall on the same population. For example, if air conditioning raises the ambient temperature of city dwellers who lack it, the result may be uncomfortable and possibly unjust, but it is no revenge effect. But air conditioning in subway systems may be a different story. A spokesman for the New York Transit Authority recently acknowledged that air-conditioned subway cars may provide a cooler ride, "but the stations and the tunnels themselves have become a lot hotter. We seem to be averaging about ten degrees warmer than the outside temperature, so on a day when it's 92 outside, it can be over 100 inside the stations." In fact, heat can actually damage the train air-conditioning units themselves. Then the train windows can't be opened, or opened much—a form of compound revenge. 28

As heat is pushed around beneath the cities, disaster is deferred in the countryside and suburbs. The Caltech geologist W. Barclay Kamb, in John McPhee's *The Control of Nature,* describes efforts to channel debris flow from the San Gabriel Mountains with crib structures. "You're not changing the source of the sediment," says Kamb. "Those cribworks are less strong than nature's own constructs. . . . Sooner or later, a flood will wipe out those small dams and scatter the debris. Everything you store might come out in one event." 29

The environmental historian Stephen J. Pyne points out in *Fire in America* that suppressing forest fires may promote long-term accumulation of combustible materials, leading to even larger conflagrations, just 30 as water control projects may make still heavier flooding possible by blocking off a river's normal channels. And of course all forms of disaster control and relief (including deposit insurance) risk increasing the casualties of disaster by encouraging people to move into and remain in risk-prone areas.

Problems are rearranged above the earth as well as in and on it. The 1970 Clean Air Act, by requiring high smokestacks to protect the surroundings of Midwestern coal-burning plants, ensured the windborne transport of sulfur dioxide, spreading acid rain to woodlands and waters hundreds of miles away.

Do revenge effects teach a political and social lesson? Scholars of unintended consequences draw different conclusions. The historian William H. McNeill points out that Chinese engineers managing the Yellow River in 600 B.C. faced the same cycle as the Army Corps of Engineers does today on the lower Mississippi: levees concentrating sediment and raising water levels, requiring higher levees. The prosperity of the industrial West after World War II, he says, has depended in part on its ability to transfer much of the cost of fluctuations in the business cycle to the loosely organized raw materials producers and immigrant workers of less developed countries. He suggests that "every gain in precision in the coordinating of human activity and every heightening of efficiency in production" may be matched by "a new vulnerability to breakdown," and (while rejecting fatalism) wonders whether "the conservation of catastrophe may indeed be a law of nature like the conservation of energy."

The economist Albert O. Hirschman suggests in his new book, *The Rhetoric of Reaction* (Harvard University Press), that right-wing critics of social and economic reforms exaggerate the seriousness of unintended consequences. He labels the argument that change is counterproductive the "perversity thesis," the assertion that it is useless the "futility thesis," and the claim that it endangers already achieved reforms the "jeopardy thesis." And he shows how closely related the neoconservative critique of the welfare state is to the earlier conservative polemics against the French Revolution and, later, against the spread of the right to vote.

While McNeill sees what I call revenge effects as serious consequences probably fated by increasing economic and technological scale, Hirschman regards them as second-order problems magnified by the smug and self-interested. But the fact that all reactionaries invoke unintended consequences doesn't mean that all who take them seriously have been friends of the status quo ante or even the status quo. Consider George Orwell's observation in *The Road to Wigan Pier* (1937): "If the unemployed learned to be better managers they would be visibly better off, and I fancy it would not be long before the dole was docked correspondingly."

Fifty years later, liberals are as likely as conservatives to invoke revenge effects. Some cite them in arguing that new road construction may increase traffic congestion, others in insisting that increasing police and prisons actually promotes criminality, and still others in arguing that advanced medical technology may be unhealthy, that pesticides and fertilizers endanger food production in the long run, and that new weapons systems make nations less secure. As the Right took over technological optimism from the Left in the 1970s and 1980s, liberal social critics (Hirschman does not deny this) countered with perversity and futility theories of their own. It is Ivan Illich who first suggested the tormented mythological figure of Tantalus as a symbol of the frustrations of modern life in his book *Medical Nemesis*. 35

Can there be a strategy against revenge effects? Observers of ironies have been better at posing paradoxes than at resolving them. But that might be because they haven't paid enough attention to how revenge effects have been overcome or at least managed successfully. Think back to the gremlins of World War II aviation. Human ingenuity overcame them. The very jokes about gremlins must have done wonders for morale. And the Axis had gremlins (or Vischerian treacherous objects) of its own. 36

After the war, Murphy's Law entered the dictionary only because Captain Murphy and his technician finally managed to get the strain gauge bridges wired to assure operation of the balky strap transducer that inspired his law in the first place. Despite tragic episodes, both aircraft design and air traffic control show how engineering practice is able to ensure a remarkably high level of safety in apparently fragile and complex systems. Entire textbooks deal with reliability engineering, though Charles Perrow has argued that nuclear weapons and nuclear power have risks that are inherently and unacceptably high. 37

Clarity about our expectations also helps. There's nothing wrong with wanting to use higher productivity to repeat some activities, like washing clothing, instead of having more free time. Nor is it wicked or foolish to print out three or four drafts of a document or to withdraw cash at 38 all hours from bank accounts. The pleasure of a cool ride, especially for longer-distance subway travelers, may more than offset the discomfort of a hotter platform. The point is to understand choices.

Manufacturers and programmers probably should think more about designing products that can be switched easily among different levels of difficulty. There would be nothing wrong with a complex airline fare system if computer interfaces gave travel agents and eventually the public a clearer overview of alternatives. And individuals could learn to avoid revenge effects by developing their abilities to work without technology. People who can do rapid mental and back-of-the-envelope calculations are most likely to catch costly spreadsheet errors. Those who can write fluently with pencil and paper are best able to use the computer's powers of revision. People who can work with constraint are able to get the most out of power.

Revenge theory doesn't oppose change. It just favors preventive pessimism. As the computer pioneer John Presper Eckert wrote: "If you have a radical idea . . . for God's sake don't be a radical in how you carry it out. . . . Become a right-wing conservative in carrying out a left-wing idea."

VOCABULARY

paragraph 4: cognizance, discerned, malicious, perverse
paragraph 6: aerodynamics, hierarchy
paragraph 7: avant-garde
paragraph 8: expatriate
paragraph 11: batch processing, mainframe, unprecedented, productivity
paragraph 12: spreadsheet, fax, cellular phone
paragraph 13: obsolete, format
paragraph 23: immune, debris, critical density
paragraph 26: hydralike
paragraph 27: genetic engineering, resistant
paragraph 28: ambient
paragraph 29: cribwork
paragraph 30: conflagration, casualty
paragraph 32: levee, fluctuations, coordinating

paragraph 33: neoconservative, polemics
paragraph 34: reactionary, status quo, ante
paragraph 35: Tantalus
paragraph 36: paradox
paragraph 39: interface, constraint

QUESTIONS

1. In what order does Tenner present the five "folklaw principles" discussed?

2. What is "repeating," and what kind of evidence does Tenner present for it?

3. How is "recomplicating" different from "recongesting," and what evidence does Tenner present for these?

4. What evidence does Tenner present for "regenerating," and how is this process different from "recongesting"?

5. How is "rearranging" different from the other folklaws, and what evidence does Tenner present for it?

6. What kinds of inductive evidence—personal experience, observation, statistical studies, for example—does Tenner present in support of his thesis?

7. What thesis concerning technological progress does Tenner develop, and where does he first state it? Does he argue that technological progress is a myth? Does he accept the view of the Left or the Right toward technological progress, or does he reject both views?

SUGGESTIONS FOR WRITING

1. Present personal experiences and observations that lead you to agree with Tenner's analysis about one of the five folklaws, or lead you to doubt or qualify his analysis.

2. State your own view of technological progress, and explain why you hold it. In the course of the discussion, explain why your view of technological progress is the same as or different from Tenner's.

RICHARD MORAN

RICHARD MORAN, Professor of Sociology at Mount Holyoke College, has written on criminal law and crime in America in *Knowing Right from Wrong: The Insanity Defense of Daniel McNaughton* (1981) and numerous articles in *Newsweek* and other periodicals. His article on policing and the rate of crime is inductive in drawing inferences from particulars of experiences and statistical evidence. His article appeared in *The New York Times* on February 27, 1995.

MORE POLICE, LESS CRIME, RIGHT? WRONG

In the raucous debate over the Republicans' anti-crime package, which the Senate is to take up next month, the hiring of more police officers has become the major point of contention. The outcome of this battle will no doubt be significant for Congressional politics, but it will do little to reduce crime in America.

As hard as it may be to believe, there is no direct relationship between the number of police officers and the rate of crime in a community.

In 1991, San Diego and Dallas had about the same ratio of police officers to the population, yet twice as many crimes were reported in Dallas. Cleveland and San Diego had comparable crime rates even though Cleveland had twice as many police officers per capita. As of 1992, Washington, D.C. had the highest murder rate—and the most police per square foot—of any city.

Although police departments were established more than 150 years ago, no one has been able to demonstrate convincingly that adding more police officers lowers the crime rates.

Take Kansas City, Missouri. For research purposes, the city's 15 police beats were divided into three comparable groups in the early 1970's. In one, patrols were doubled or tripled. In another, patrols were eliminated entirely, although the police continued to respond to citizens' calls. In the third, no changes were made. After a year, guess what happened? Absolutely nothing. The crime rate remained the same in all three groups.

What about foot patrols? Don't they reduce crime by improving the   6
exchange of information between the public and the police? Apparently
not. The most thorough study ever done, a 1981 analysis of police beats
in Newark, New Jersey, found that foot patrols had virtually no effect
on crime rates. A cop walking the beat did make people feel safer, but,
since such patrols can produce a false sense of security, they may actually be a bad policing strategy.

Obviously this is not to say that we could simply disband the police   7
and crime would not increase. Indeed, during the Boston Police Strike of
1919, crime—especially looting—increased enormously. But adding more
cops will not significantly reduce the crime rate for a simple reason: police
work is essentially reactive. The police are far better at arresting criminals than preventing crimes. Research has shown that the police discover
only about 2.5 percent of all crimes in progress.

Community policing is designed to address this problem. But since   8
the police actually spend less than 20 percent of their time fighting
crime—as against, say, answering nuisance calls, responding to traffic accidents and doing office work—community policing is mostly public relations. Besides, does anyone seriously believe that a cop on patrol can
do anything about the social, political and economic causes of crime?

But wouldn't adding more officers result in more arrests, more   9
people going to jail and thus fewer criminals on the streets? Not really.
With our prisons dreadfully overcrowded, there is no place to lock up
convicted felons. The number of criminals sent to prison does not depend on how many people police arrest but on how much space there
is in prison.

In 1992, the police arrested more than 14 million people, even though   10
local jails and state prisons can hold only 1.2 million. It doesn't make
much sense to arrest more people unless you have a place to put them.
In any event, there isn't a fixed population of crooks out there. Arresting a drug dealer, prostitute or fence merely opens up a new job opportunity for someone else.

Adding more police officers may be a good way for Republicans and   11
Democrats to demonstrate that they are tough on law and order, but it
is not an effective strategy to reduce crime. The awful truth is that there
is no law enforcement solution to the crime problem; it is embedded in
the social and moral fiber of our society. An insufficient police presence
did not cause the problem, and more officers will not solve it.

QUESTIONS

1. What point is Moran making in paragraphs 3–5? What kind of inductive evidence does he present to support it?

2. What kind does he present in paragraphs 6 and 8 to argue that foot patrols and community policing may be poor or ineffective strategies?

3. Does he present a new kind of evidence in paragraphs 9 and 10?

4. Is Moran trying to *prove* that the crime problem is a social and moral one, or does he have another purpose in writing?

SUGGESTIONS FOR WRITING

1. Those writing to newspapers following the report of a particular crime often seek to explain it or suggest a solution. Analyze the reasoning in two or more such letters, distinguishing the kinds of evidence presented and the use made of these. You may find that the evidence is not inductive, consisting instead of assumptions or beliefs about the nature of crime and prevention rather than the kind of inductive evidence Moran presents.

2. Describe how your high school dealt with infractions and misbehavior. Then discuss how effective or ineffective these policies and measures were, explaining why you think so.

WILLIAM ZINSSER

WILLIAM ZINSSER has had wide opportunity to study American culture as a journalist and teacher. His long career includes experience as a film critic, a feature writer for *The New York Herald Tribune,* and a columnist for *Life* magazine and *The New York Times.* He has published several collections of essays on life in America, including *The Lunacy Boom* (1970). Zinsser taught writing at Yale for a number of years and gives valuable advice on the subject in his book *On Writing Well* (Sixth Edition, 1998), a chapter from which appears on p. 577.

THE RIGHT TO FAIL

I like "dropout" as an addition to the American language because it's brief and it's clear. What I don't like is that we use it almost entirely as a dirty word. 1

We only apply it to people under twenty-one. Yet an adult who spends his days and nights watching mindless TV programs is more of a dropout than an eighteen-year-old who quits college, with its frequently mindless courses, to become, say, a VISTA volunteer. For the young, dropping out is often a way of dropping in. 2

To hold this opinion, however, is little short of treason in America. A boy or girl who leaves college is branded a failure—and the right to fail is one of the few freedoms that this country does not grant its citizens. The American dream is a dream of "getting ahead," painted in strokes of gold wherever we look. Our advertisements and TV commercials are a hymn to material success, our magazine articles a toast to people who made it to the top. Smoke the right cigarette or drive the right car—so the ads imply—and girls will be swooning into your deodorized arms and caressing your expensive lapels. Happiness goes to the man who has the sweet smell of achievement. He is our national idol, and everybody else is our national fink. 3

I want to put in a word for the fink, especially the teen-age fink, because if we give him time to get through his finkdom—if we release him from the pressure of attaining certain goals by a certain age—he has a good chance of becoming our national idol, a Jefferson or a Thoreau, a Buckminster Fuller or an Adlai Stevenson, a man with a mind of his own. We need mavericks and dissenters and dreamers far more than we need junior vice-presidents, but we paralyze them by insisting that every step be a step up to the next rung of the ladder. Yet in the fluid years of youth, the only way for boys and girls to find their proper road is often to take a hundred side trips, poking out in different directions, faltering, drawing back, and starting again. 4

"But what if we fail?" they ask, whispering the dreadful word across the Generation Gap to their parents, who are back home at the Establishment, nursing their "middle-class values" and cultivating their "goal-oriented society." The parents whisper back: "Don't!" 5

What they should say is "Don't be afraid to fail!" Failure isn't fatal. Countless people have had a bout with it and come out stronger as a result. Many have even come out famous. History is strewn with eminent 6 dropouts, "loners" who followed their own trail, not worrying about its odd twists and turns because they had faith in their own sense of direction. To read their biographies is always exhilarating, not only because they beat the system, but because their system was better than the one that they beat.

Luckily, such rebels still turn up often enough to prove that individualism, though badly threatened, is not extinct. Much has been written, for instance, about the fitful scholastic career of Thomas P. F. Hoving, New York's former Parks Commissioner and now director of the Metropolitan Museum of Art. Hoving was a dropout's dropout, entering and leaving schools as if they were motels, often at the request of the management. Still, he must have learned something during those unorthodox years, for he dropped in again at the top of his profession.

His case reminds me of another boyhood—that of Holden Caulfield in J. D. Salinger's *The Catcher in the Rye,* the most popular literary hero of the postwar period. There is nothing accidental about the grip that this dropout continues to hold on the affections of an entire American generation. Nobody else, real or invented, has made such an engaging shambles of our "goal-oriented society," so gratified our secret belief that the "phonies" are in power and the good guys up the creek. Whether Holden has also reached the top of his chosen field today is one of those speculations that delight fanciers of good fiction. I speculate that he has. Holden Caulfield, incidentally, is now thirty-six.

I'm not urging everyone to go out and fail just for the sheer therapy of it, or to quit college just to coddle some vague discontent. Obviously it's better to succeed than to flop, and in general a long education is more helpful than a short one. (Thanks to my own education, for example, I can tell George Eliot from T. S. Eliot, I can handle the pluperfect tense in French, and I know that Caesar beat the Helvetii because he had enough frumentum.) I only mean that failure isn't bad in itself, or success automatically good.

Fred Zinnemann, who has directed some of Hollywood's most honored movies, was asked by a reporter, when *A Man for All Seasons* won every prize, about his previous film *Behold a Pale Horse,* which was a box-office disaster. "I don't feel any obligation to be successful," Zinnemann replied. "Success can be dangerous—you feel you know it all. I've learned a great deal from my failures." A similar point was made by Richard Brooks about his ambitious money loser, *Lord Jim.* Recalling the three years of his life that went into it, talking almost with elation about the troubles that befell his unit in Cambodia, Brooks told me that he learned more about his craft from this considerable failure than from his many earlier hits.

It's a point, of course, that applies throughout the arts. Writers, play- 11 wrights, painters, and composers work in the expectation of periodic defeat, but they wouldn't keep going back into the arena if they thought it was the end of the world. It isn't the end of the world. For an artist—and perhaps for anybody—it is the only way to grow.

Today's younger generation seems to know that this is true, seems 12 willing to take the risks in life that artists take in art. "Society," needless to say, still has the upper hand—it sets the goals and condemns as a failure everybody who won't play. But the dropouts and the hippies are not as afraid of failure as their parents and grandparents. This could mean, as their elders might say, that they are just plumb lazy, secure in the comforts of an affluent state. It could also mean, however, that they just don't buy the old standards of success and are rapidly writing new ones.

Recently it was announced, for instance, that more than two hun- 13 dred thousand Americans have inquired about service in VISTA (the domestic Peace Corps) and that, according to a Gallup survey, "more than three million American college students would serve VISTA in some capacity if given the opportunity." This is hardly the road to riches or to an executive suite. Yet I have met many of these young volunteers, and they are not pining for traditional success. On the contrary, they appear more fulfilled than the average vice-president with a swimming pool.

Who is to say, then, if there is any right path to the top, or even to 14 say what the top consists of? Obviously the colleges don't have more than a partial answer—otherwise the young would not be so disaffected with an education that they consider vapid. Obviously business does not have the answer—otherwise the young would not be so scornful of its call to be an organization man.

The fact is, nobody has the answer, and the dawning awareness of 15 this fact seems to me one of the best things happening in America today. Success and failure are again becoming individual visions, as they were when the country was younger, not rigid categories. Maybe we are learning again to cherish this right of every person to succeed on his own terms and to fail as often as necessary along the way.

VOCABULARY

paragraph 3: swooning, fink
paragraph 4: mavericks, dissenters
paragraph 6: exhilarating
paragraph 7: extinct, unorthodox
paragraph 8: shambles, fanciers
paragraph 9: coddle, frumentum
paragraph 12: affluent
paragraph 14: vapid

QUESTIONS

1. What is Zinsser's thesis, and what kinds of evidence support it in paragraphs 1–4?

2. How does he defend his thesis in paragraphs 5–8? Why does he cite the hero of *The Catcher in the Rye?*

3. How do paragraphs 9–12 explain further what Zinsser means by "the right to fail"?

4. How do paragraphs 13–15 provide additional evidence that the maverick has a role to play in American society? How does Zinsser restate his thesis?

SUGGESTIONS FOR WRITING

1. Discuss the extent of your agreement or disagreement with Zinsser on the demands made on teenagers today by parents and others. Don't try to speak for all teenagers. Limit yourself to your own experience and personal goals and that of friends your age.

2. Discuss how your high school courses influenced your choice of a college, a major, and the development of long-term goals.

3. Write an essay on one of the following topics, stating a thesis and defending it with supporting evidence. You may need to qualify it as Zinsser does, explaining what you do not mean and limiting your generalizations. Restate your thesis in concluding the essay:

a. unintended lessons taught in high school classes

b. lessons that can't be taught in school

c. discovering the nature of prejudice

d. rules that work at home or at school

e. rules that don't work

ELLEN GOODMAN

ELLEN GOODMAN worked for *Newsweek* and the *Detroit Free Press* before joining the *Boston Globe* in 1967 as feature writer and columnist. In 1980 she received the Pulitzer Prize for Commentary. Her columns on a wide range of social and political issues appear regularly in the *Globe* and other newspapers in the United States. They are collected in *At Large* (1981), *Keeping in Touch* (1985), *Making Sense* (1989), and *Value Judgments* (1993). The column reprinted here first appeared on June 19, 1990, in *The Washington Post*.

WAIT A MINUTE

The cop and the rap singer went on the air together last Wednesday. It's the American way. One minute you're arresting a guy and the next minute you're in the greenroom with him. One day he's putting cuffs on you, the next day he's your co-guest.

When the lights went on at *Geraldo,* the Florida sheriff, Nick Navarro, and the leader of 2 Live Crew, Luther Campbell, played their parts like polished performers assigned the role of enemies. Navarro portrayed himself as a lawman and Campbell as his obscene lawbreaker. Campbell cast himself as the rap singer and Navarro as his "Communist and racist."

Then the two parted company and Campbell went on to *Donahue* and then to *Live at Five*. Another opening, another show. That's entertainment.

The scene wasn't much more heartening in Congress, where the players are feeling the dramatic heat of flag burning. Those who were for and against a constitutional amendment to ban the desecration of the flag were worrying about the reviews. Some, like Nebraska senator Bob Kerrey, imagined bleakly how they would look: "Bob Kerrey votes for gun control and he won't vote to protect the flag. It's a great thirty-second spot."

These days, it seems every issue becomes instant theater. Every advocate worries about how his act will play. Every conflict becomes a Punch and Judy show. Are you in favor of Robert Mapplethorpe's photographs? Are you against censors?

In public, people swing beliefs at each other like fists. The audience is expected to identify a hero and a villain. Which do you prefer: the First Amendment or pornography, the Bill of Rights or the flag, freedom of speech or obscenity?

What is so appalling about these one-acts is that they lead the audience to assume that every issue must be equally polarized. Like guests on a talk show, we either have to buy *Me So Horny* or ban it. We must favor the flag or the flag burners. We have to choose between license and crackdown. Now.

Indeed, at the ends of the American spectrum there are people who can only scream at each other across a stage. Americans do feel differently about symbols and speech.

Over the years, the passion to crack down on dissent or on speech has come from those who believe there's a natural human drift down to the lowest common denominator of behavior. Unchecked, they say, the human heart of darkness grows.

Those who have defended free speech have put their faith in reason, persuasion, what was once called enlightenment. In the free marketplace of ideas, they wager, the 2 Live Crew will lose and the flag burners will simmer down.

Over the course of American history, the value of free speech has outlasted both its abusers and its attackers. Over time, the Bill of Rights has been shielded from those who want to express their outrage by repressing outrageousness. But I wonder if these days, we have the time.

Out of the limelight, most Americans are not as certain as talk-show guests or as polarized as attack ads. There are First Amendment absolutists who would like to throttle Andrew Dice Clay and be there when Luther Campbell's daughter asks him to explain his work. There are people who neither want a Mapplethorpe on their wall nor want to dine with his censors.

But today public debate has been pared down to its speed-racing   13
form, a sleek and simplistic shape. Even the Senate now pushes for an amendment with the urgency of a television host trying to wrap things up before the political commercial break.

When asked about the flag amendment, Arkansas senator Dale   14
Bumpers said, "I belong to the wait-just-a-minute club." It's a club with a shrinking membership.

I don't think we need to imprison a rap singer to express our ab-   15
horrence of sexual assault songs. Like profanity on *Geraldo*, 2 Live Crew is a bleep in time. Nor do I think we need to singe the Constitution to punish the few who torch a symbol. Flag burning isn't even a fad.

How do you defend a two-hundred-year-old principle in the era of   16
the thirty-second spot? How do you wait-a-minute, and listen-a-while, in the passionate and polarizing ethic of the moment?

The Bill of Rights is on the political entertainment schedule now.   17
And, it appears, the producers are only worried about today's show.

VOCABULARY

paragraph 6: pornography, obscenity
paragraph 12: polarized, absolutists
paragraph 13: simplistic

QUESTIONS

1. How does Goodman support her generalization in paragraph 5: "These days, it seems every issue becomes instant theater"?

2. What is "instant" about this kind of theater?

3. Does Goodman believe that most Americans are at one end or the other of the American political spectrum—the far left or far right?

4. Does she propose a remedy for instant theater and the polarization of public issues? How should the country deal with offensive song lyrics and photographs and with flag burning?

5. How does she connect her discussion of censorship to that of political discourse in America today? Does she give both problems equal attention?

6. What is Goodman's thesis, and where does she state it?

SUGGESTIONS FOR WRITING

1. Discuss your experience in trying to debate a controversial issue with a friend or a member of your family. To what extent does your personal experience confirm the views Goodman presents in her essay?

2. In the course of a classroom debate on a current issue, one of the students engages in name calling, using language and stereotypes offensive to others in the class. Discuss how you would deal with this situation as the instructor. Would you impose limits on the discussion at the beginning of the debate, telling the class what terms, references, and topics are not permissible? Would you encourage the class to impose its own limits, or would you discourage—and refuse to impose—any limits whatever? State your reasons and defend them.

ANALOGY

We discussed earlier the use of analogy, or point-by-point comparison of two things, for the purpose of illustration (p. 184). In reasoning about everyday decisions and choices you often use analogy, as in deciding to buy a book similar in subject and setting to an author's earlier book you enjoyed. Since arguments from analogy make predictions only, the fact that you enjoyed the earlier book does not guarantee you will enjoy the author's new one. But you can increase the probability by noting similarities with other enjoyable books of the same author.

The greater the number of relevant similarities, the stronger the argument. A candidate for governor may argue that she has the same record and personal characteristics as a much admired former governor; her case becomes stronger if she cites several similarities and not just one, and it becomes even stronger if she makes the comparison with several former governors instead of one. Thus she may point out that, like them, she was a mayor of a large city, held office in years of economic hardship, had a successful career as a state legislator, and served for several years in Congress.

Dissimilarities between the candidate and former governors cited must not be significant enough to weaken the argument. Differences in height or in color of hair are obviously insignificant and irrelevant to the conclusion. But the candidate may have to persuade some members of her audience that her being a woman is an insignificant difference, too. She may even use dissimilarities to strengthen her case. If the governors cited have the same record of service as she yet are different in gender, race, or background—some coming from small towns and some from large cities—the probability increases that the similarities cited support her claim to be qualified.

The points of similarity must be relevant to the conclusion: the similarities noted do support the claim of the candidate that she has the experience needed to deal intelligently with unemployment and the state budget deficit. But much more evidence would be needed to show that she is fit to serve as Treasury secretary or in a comparable governmental post. A limited conclusion may be drawn from a limited analogy if the points of similarity are clearly specified or agreed upon, if these points are relevant to the conclusion, and if inferences are drawn from these points only.

BROOKS ATKINSON

BROOKS ATKINSON (1894–1984) was associated throughout his long career as a journalist with *The New York Times* as war correspondent, dramatic critic, and essayist. In 1947 he received the Pulitzer Prize for Foreign Correspondence. His books include *Henry Thoreau: The Cosmic Yankee* (1927), *East of the Hudson* (1931), and *Brief Chronicles* (1966). Atkinson wrote often about environmental issues. The essay reprinted here first appeared in *The New York Times* on November 23, 1968. The essay, one of Atkinson's finest on this subject, is particularly effective in its use of analogy.

THE WARFARE IN THE FOREST
IS NOT WANTON

After thirty-five years the forest in Spruce Notch is tall and sturdy. It began during the Depression when work gangs planted thousands of tiny seedlings in abandoned pastures on Richmond Peak in the northern Catskills. Nothing spectacular has happened there since; the forest has been left undisturbed.

But now we have a large spread of Norway spruces a foot thick at the butt and 40 or 50 feet high. Their crowns look like thousands of dark crosses reaching into the sky.

The forest is a good place in which to prowl in search of wildlife. But also in search of ideas. For the inescapable fact is that the world of civilized America does not have such a clean record. Since the seedlings were planted the nation has fought three catastrophic wars, in one of which the killing of combatants and the innocent continues. During the lifetime of the forest 350,000 Americans have died on foreign battlefields.

Inside America civilized life is no finer. A President, a Senator, a man of God have been assassinated. Citizens are murdered in the streets. Riots, armed assaults, looting, burning, outbursts of hatred have increased to the point where they have become commonplace.

Life in civilized America is out of control. Nothing is out of control in the forest. Everything complies with the instinct for survival—which is the law and order of the woods.

Although the forest looks peaceful it supports incessant warfare, most of which is hidden and silent. For thirty-five years the strong have been subduing the weak. The blueberries that once flourished on the mountain have been destroyed. All the trees are individuals, as all human beings are individuals; and every tree poses a threat to every other tree. The competition is so fierce that you can hardly penetrate some of the thickets where the lower branches of neighboring trees are interlocked in a blind competition for survival.

Nor is the wildlife benign. A red-tailed hawk lived there last summer—slowly circling in the sky and occasionally drawing attention to himself by screaming. He survived on mice, squirrels, chipmunks and small birds. A barred owl lives somewhere in the depth of the woods. He hoots in midmorning as well as at sunrise to register his authority. He also is a killer. Killing is a fundamental part of the process. The nuthatches kill insects in the bark. The woodpeckers dig insects out. The thrushes eat beetles and caterpillars.

But in the forest, killing is not wanton or malicious. It is for survival. Among birds of equal size most of the warfare consists of sham battles in which they go through the motions of warfare until one withdraws. Usually neither bird gets hurt.   8

Nor is the warfare between trees vindictive. Although the spruces predominate they do not practice segregation. On both sides of Lost Lane, which used to be a dirt road, maples, beeches, ashes, aspens and a few red oaks live, and green curtains of wild grapes cover the wild cherry trees. In the depths of the forest there are a few glades where the spruces stand aside and birches stretch and grow. The forest is a web of intangible tensions. But they are never out of control. Although they are wild they are not savage as they are in civilized life.   9

For the tensions are absorbed in the process of growth, and the clusters of large cones on the Norway spruces are certificates to a good future. The forest gives an external impression of discipline and pleasure. Occasionally the pleasure is rapturously stated. Soon after sunrise one morning last summer when the period of bird song was nearly over, a solitary rose-breasted grosbeak sat on the top of a tall spruce and sang with great resonance and beauty. He flew a few rods to another tree and continued singing: then to another tree where he poured out his matin again, and so on for a half hour. There was no practical motive that I was aware of.   10

After thirty-five uneventful years the spruces have created an environment in which a grosbeak is content, and this one said so gloriously. It was a better sound than the explosion of bombs, the scream of the wounded, the crash of broken glass, the crackle of burning buildings, the shriek of the police siren.   11

The forest conducts its affairs with less rancor and malevolence than civilized America.   12

Vocabulary

paragraph 8: wanton, malicious
paragraph 9: segregation, intangible
paragraph 10: discipline, resonance, matin
paragraph 12: rancor, malevolence

QUESTIONS

1. One sometimes hears the argument that violence is natural to human beings, since we are a part of a warring world. How does Atkinson implicitly reject this analogy? More specifically, what are the points of dissimilarity between the world of the forest and the world of humans?

2. How might the world of the forest be used to challenge the argument that competition in the world of humans need destroy some of those competing—as the argument that only the "fit" survive in the world of business implies?

3. How does Atkinson strengthen his argument through the details he marshals in support of it?

SUGGESTION FOR WRITING

Each of the following statements suggests an analogy. Write on one of them, discussing points of similarity and dissimilarity and using this discussion to argue a thesis.

a. The family is a small nation.

b. The nation is a large family.

c. College examinations are sporting events.

d. Choosing a college is like buying a car.

JOHN HENRY NEWMAN

JOHN HENRY NEWMAN (1801–1890), one of the influential English religious leaders of the nineteenth century, entered the Catholic Church in 1845 and two years later was ordained as a priest. In 1879 he was appointed cardinal of the Church. Rector of the Catholic University of Dublin from 1851 to 1858, Newman delivered a series of lectures on university education—published in 1873 as *The Idea of a University*. The chief purpose of a university is to develop the power to think, Newman argues. Though knowledge is a means to "material and moral advancement," it is "an end in itself," and should be valued for its own sake. Newman argues this point by analogy in this section from a discourse late in the book, *Knowledge Viewed in Relation to Professional Skill*.

THE END OF EDUCATION

You will see what I mean by the parallel of bodily health. Health is a good in itself, though nothing came of it, and is especially worth seeking and cherishing; yet, after all, the blessings which attend its presence are so great, while they are so close to it and so redound back upon it and encircle it, that we never think of it except as useful as well as good, and praise and prize it for what it does, as well as for what it is, though at the same time we cannot point out any definite and distinct work or production which it can be said to effect. And so as regards intellectual culture, I am far from denying utility in this large sense as the end of Education, when I lay it down, that the culture of the intellect is a good in itself and its own end; I do not exclude from the idea of intellectual culture what it cannot but be, from the very nature of things; I only deny that we must be able to point out, before we have any right to call it useful, some art, or business, or profession, or trade, or work, as resulting from it, and as its real and complete end. The parallel is exact: As the body may be sacrificed to some manual or other toil, whether moderate or oppressive, so may the intellect be devoted to some specific profession; and I do not call *this* the culture of the intellect. Again, as some member or organ of the body may be inordinately used and developed, so may memory, or imagination, or the reasoning faculty; and *this* again is not intellectual culture. On the other hand, as the body may be tended, cherished, and exercised with a simple view to its general health, so may the intellect also be generally exercised in order to its perfect state; and this is its cultivation.

Again, as health ought to precede labor of the body, and as a man in health can do what an unhealthy man cannot do; and as of his health the properties are strength, energy, agility, graceful carriage and action, manual dexterity, and endurance of fatigue, so in like manner general culture of mind is the best aid to professional and scientific study, and educated men can do what illiterate cannot; and the man who has learned to think and to reason and to compare and to discriminate and to analyze, who has refined his taste, and formed his judgment, and sharpened his mental vision,

will not indeed at once be a lawyer, or a pleader, or an orator, or a states-
man, or a physician, or a good landlord, or a man of business, or a soldier, or an engineer, or a chemist, or a geologist, or an antiquarian, but he
will be placed in that state of intellect in which he can take up any one of
the sciences or callings I have referred to, or any other for which he has a
taste or special talent, with an ease, a grace, a versatility, and a success, to
which another is a stranger. In this sense then, and as yet I have said but
a very few words on a large subject, mental culture is emphatically *useful*.

If then I am arguing, and shall argue, against Professional or Scientific
knowledge as the sufficient end of a University Education, let me not be
supposed, Gentlemen, to be disrespectful towards particular studies, or arts,
or vocations, and those who are engaged in them. In saying that Law or
Medicine is not the end of a University course, I do not mean to imply that
the University does not teach Law or Medicine. What indeed can it teach
at all, if it does not teach something particular? It teaches all knowledge by
teaching all *branches* of knowledge, and in no other way. I do but say that
there will be this distinction as regards a Professor of Law, or of Medicine,
or of Geology, or of Political Economy, in a University and out of it, that
out of a University he is in danger of being absorbed and narrowed by his
pursuit, and of giving Lectures which are the Lectures of nothing more than
a lawyer, physician, geologist, or political economist; whereas in a University he will just know where he and his science stand, he has come to it, as
it were, from a height, he has taken a survey of all knowledge, he is kept
from extravagance by the very rivalry of other studies, he has gained from
them a special illumination and largeness of mind and freedom and self-
possession, and he treats his own in consequence with a philosophy and a
resource, which belongs not to the study itself, but to his liberal education.

This then is how I should solve the fallacy, for so I must call it, by
which Locke and his disciples would frighten us from cultivating the intellect, under the notion that no education is useful which does not teach us
some temporal calling, or some mechanical art, or some physical secret. I
say that a cultivated intellect, because it is a good in itself, brings with it a
power and a grace to every work and occupation which it undertakes, and
enables us to be more useful, and to a greater number. There is a duty we
owe to human society as such, to the state to which we belong, to the sphere
in which we move, to the individuals towards whom we are variously related, and whom we successively encounter in life; and that philosophical
or liberal education, as I have called it, which is the proper function of a
University, if it refuses the foremost place to professional interests, does but

postpone them to the formation of the citizen, and, while it subserves the larger interests of philanthropy, prepares also for the successful prosecution of those merely personal objects, which at first sight it seems to disparage.

VOCABULARY

paragraph 1: utility, inordinately
paragraph 2: dexterity, culture, antiquarian
paragraph 3: extravagance
paragraph 4: grace, philanthropy

QUESTIONS

1. What analogy does Newman employ in paragraphs 1 and 2 to argue his thesis, and how does he develop it?

2. In saying that law, medicine, and other professional studies are not the "sufficient end" of university education, is Newman saying that these studies do not develop the mind? What does he mean by the word *sufficient?*

3. How does the university teach "*all* knowledge by teaching all *branches* of knowledge"? Is Newman saying that students need to study all branches, including law and medicine, to be fully educated?

4. According to the *Oxford English Dictionary,* what is the origin of the word *liberal* with reference to education? What does Newman mean by *liberal education* in the final sentence of paragraph 3?

SUGGESTIONS FOR WRITING

1. Discuss how Newman probably would answer the objection that we value physical exercise and a healthy diet, not as ends in themselves, but as means to keeping alive and working efficiently.

2. Develop your discussion by explaining why you agree or disagree with Newman's analogy.

CAUSE AND EFFECT

Earlier (p. 208) we discussed some ways of analyzing cause and effect in paragraphs and essays. These include tracing an effect to its recent or immediate cause (death because of famine) and to its more distant or remote causes (drought, soil erosion, ignorance, indifference, neglect). We also discussed the "four causes" of an object—the materials of its manufacture (material cause), the shape given it (formal cause), its maker (efficient cause), and use (final cause).

Cause may also be analyzed through the words *necessary* and *sufficient*, as when we say that getting an "A" on the final exam is necessary but not sufficient for an "A" in the course: an "A" on the final would be sufficient only if the exam solely determined the course grade. A necessary condition is one that must be present for something to happen. The condition is sufficient if the event must happen. When scientists say that a necessary condition of getting a cold is exposure to a virus, they mean that a virus of some kind must be present—not that the virus always produces a cold. Other conditions obviously need to be present, but scientists do not now claim to know what all of these are. If all necessary conditions of the cold were known, we would consider their joining sufficient to produce the cold. But one or more conditions may be judged sufficient in absence of full knowledge.

> Working and thinking ecologically, Dubos reformulated the theory of disease causation by implicating the total environment. He showed that a microbe is necessary but not sufficient to cause disease. (Carol L. Moberg and Zanvil A. Cohn, "René Jules Dubos," Scientific American, May 1991)

> Biologists have agreed upon no general definition of life. Our experience of its possible forms is too limited. . . . None the less, while there is a lack of agreement as to what properties are *necessary* for something to be called "living," there is a reasonable consensus about those features which would be *sufficient* for something to be termed "living." (John D. Barrow, *Theories of Everything*)

In reasoning about cause in this way, we implicitly recognize that events, like the reasons for our actions, are complex. Yet this is not what some of our statements show. Statements that generalize about *the* cause of a cold, or some other complex physical or social or political ill, often mistakenly assume that a single cause can be identified. Another hasty generalization arises from the idea that one event must be the cause of another because it precedes it: I caught the cold "because" I was soaked in a rainstorm. Temporal sequence does not necessarily make one event the cause of the next. Clearly we might have caught the cold even if we had not been soaked, and we cannot know whether getting soaked will always give one a cold—even if it has always in the past. This kind of reasoning is given a Latin name—the *post hoc* fallacy, from the expression *post hoc, ergo propter hoc* ("after this, therefore because of this").

N O R M A N   C O U S I N S

NORMAN COUSINS (1915–1990) is inseparably linked with the *Saturday Review,* which he edited from 1940 to 1977. Cousins won numerous awards for his journalism and his work on behalf of world peace, including the Peace Medal of the United Nations in 1971. His columns, collected in a number of books, provide a continuous commentary on postwar America and the world. His essay on Benny Paret raises important questions about boxing and spectator sports generally—and also about the responsibility of the public for the violence encouraged in them. Emile Griffith knocked out Paret in the twelfth round of a world championship welterweight bout at Madison Square Garden on March 25, 1962. Paret died on April 3, still in a coma, at the age of 24. The essay first appeared in *Saturday Review* on May 5, 1962.

WHO KILLED BENNY PARET?

Sometime about 1935 or 1936 I had an interview with Mike Jacobs, the prize-fight promoter. I was a fledgling newspaper reporter at that time; my beat was education, but during the vacation season I found myself on varied assignments, all the way from ship news to sports reporting. In this way I found myself sitting opposite the most powerful figure in the boxing world.

There was nothing spectacular in Mr. Jacobs's manner or appearance; but when he spoke about prize fights, he was no longer a bland little man but a colossus who sounded the way Napoleon must have sounded when he reviewed a battle. You knew you were listening to Number One. His saying something made it true. 2

We discussed what to him was the only important element in successful promoting—how to please the crowd. So far as he was concerned, there was no mystery to it. You put killers in the ring and the people filled your arena. You hire boxing artists—men who are adroit at feinting, parrying, weaving, jabbing, and dancing, but who don't pack dynamite in their fists—and you wind up counting your empty seats. So you searched for the killers and sluggers and maulers—fellows who could hit with the force of a baseball bat. 3

I asked Mr. Jacobs if he was speaking literally when he said people came out to see the killer. 4

"They don't come out to see a tea party," he said evenly. "They come out to see the knockout. They come out to see a man hurt. If they think anything else, they're kidding themselves." 5

Recently a young man by the name of Benny Paret was killed in the ring. The killing was seen by millions; it was on television. In the twelfth round he was hit hard in the head several times, went down, was counted out, and never came out of the coma. 6

The Paret fight produced a flurry of investigations. Governor Rockefeller was shocked by what happened and appointed a committee to assess the responsibility. The New York State Boxing Commission decided to find out what was wrong. The District Attorney's office expressed its concern. One question that was solemnly studied in all three probes concerned the action of the referee. Did he act in time to stop the fight? Another question had to do with the role of the examining doctors who certified the physical fitness of the fighters before the bout. Still another question involved Mr. Paret's manager; did he rush his boy into the fight without adequate time to recuperate from the previous one? 7

In short, the investigators looked into every possible cause except the real one. Benny Paret was killed because the human fist delivers enough impact, when directed against the head, to produce a massive hemorrhage in the brain. The human brain is the most delicate and complex mechanism in all creation. It has a lacework of millions of highly fragile 8 nerve connections. Nature attempts to protect this exquisitely intricate machinery by encasing it in a hard shell. Fortunately, the shell is thick enough to withstand a great deal of pounding. Nature, however, can protect man against everything except man himself. Not every blow to the head will kill a man—but there is always the risk of concussion and damage to the brain. A prize fighter may be able to survive even repeated brain concussions and go on fighting, but the damage to his brain may be permanent.

In any event, it is futile to investigate the referee's role and seek to   9
determine whether he should have intervened to stop the fight earlier. This is not where the primary responsibility lies. The primary responsibility lies with the people who pay to see a man hurt. The referee who stops a fight too soon from the crowd's viewpoint can expect to be booed. The crowd wants the knockout; it wants to see a man stretched out on the canvas. This is the supreme moment in boxing. It is nonsense to talk about prize fighting as a test of boxing skills. No crowd was ever brought to its feet screaming and cheering at the sight of two men beautifully dodging and weaving out of each other's jabs. The time the crowd comes alive is when a man is hit hard over the heart or the head, when his mouthpiece flies out, when blood squirts out of his nose or eyes, when he wobbles under the attack and his pursuer continues to smash at him with poleax impact.

Don't blame it on the referee. Don't even blame it on the fight man-   10
agers. Put the blame where it belongs—on the prevailing mores that regard prize fighting as a perfectly proper enterprise and vehicle of entertainment. No one doubts that many people enjoy prize fighting and will miss it if it should be thrown out. And that is precisely the point.

Vocabulary

paragraph 1: fledgling
paragraph 2: colossus
paragraph 3: adroit, feinting, parrying
paragraph 8: hemorrhage
paragraph 9: poleax

QUESTIONS

1. Cousins distinguishes between the immediate and the remote causes of Paret's death (see p. 208). What does he show to be the immediate cause, and why can this cause be stated with near certainty?

2. Cousins is concerned chiefly with the remote cause of Paret's death. How is this concern basic to his purpose in writing the essay? What are the chief indications of that purpose?

3. How would a different purpose have required Cousins to focus instead on the immediate cause?

4. How does Cousins establish the remote cause? Is his evidence statistical—based on a sample of statements of boxing fans? Is it theoretical—based on a discussion of "human nature"? Is he concerned with the psychology of the crowd or the sociology of boxing? Is his analysis of the event intended to offer a complete explanation?

SUGGESTIONS FOR WRITING

1. Analyze two or more pro football or hockey games to determine the extent of their appeal to violent emotions.

2. Discuss the immediate and remote (or mediate) causes of an important event in your life, for example, your decision to attend a particular college, to enter a particular field, or to play a sport. Highlight the causes you consider the most important, and explain why you do.

STEPHEN L. CARTER

Professor of Law at Yale University, STEPHEN L. CARTER has written widely on religion and moral issues in American life. His books include *Reflections of an Affirmative Action Baby* (1991), *The Culture of Disbelief* (1993), *Integrity* (1996), *Civility* (1998), and *Dissent of the Government* (1998). In the following excerpt from *Civility,* Carter investigates the causes of an unusual kind of modern incivility.

COMPUTER VIRUSES

There is—or recently was—a shameful bit of software floating around the Internet. Known as AOL4FREE, the program evidently helped users to break the law by setting up America OnLine accounts without the inconvenience of paying for them. Then, in the late spring of 1997, the United States Department of Energy distributed an alert about a fake version of AOL4FREE. This fake theft program looked like the real theft program but was actually a deadly computer virus. Any user who tried to run it received a surprise. Rather than establishing an illegal America OnLine account, the program would erase the entire contents of the user's hard drive.

There is a certain existential irony in the image of a federal agency issuing a warning that a program somebody uses because he thinks it is designed to abet fraud may actually be a fraudulent copy of a program designed to abet fraud and may do harm to the would-be defrauder. But I suppose this is less unusual than it seems. After all, government agencies publish studies all the time on the harm that is caused by illegal drugs, in what is presumably an effort at deterrence. And the attorney general of one of our largest states, it is said, once pursued a consumer fraud action against an individual who offered "grass by mail" at low prices—grass that turned out to be the kind mowed from the lawn, not the kind hidden under the mattress. So perhaps the warning was not as bizarre as it first appeared.

Nevertheless, my own initial reaction to the warning was, "Serves them right!" That is, I quickly decided that anybody who would try to steal computer time deserved to lose a hard drive or two. And although I soon recognized that this rather uncivil and certainly un-Christian response was a little bit like saying that people who decline to feed parking meters deserve to have their cars vandalized, a part of me clings to it still. My dislike for theft is, I confess, visceral.

My more sober reaction, the same reaction I have to the problem of computer viruses generally, was, "Why would anybody do such a thing?" Because lots of people undeniably do. From the creation of the first computer virus, apparently in 1983, to the present day, more than seven thousand different types of viruses have been created—recently at the rate of two or three new ones per day.[1] Although some viruses are relatively benign, others can cause losses ranging into the millions of dollars. Viruses are metaphorically violent—a typical name of one of the many virus-making kits easily available on the Internet is Nightmare Joker—and, in what cannot be an accident, many of the most vicious target only the products of Microsoft. (I also find it rather interesting that *every* identified virus writer has turned out to be male.)[2]

Nobody seems to know exactly why people create viruses, although experts talk confidently about pathological levels of loneliness, alienation, rejection, anger, and frustration, all the usual causes of vandalism, as well as, for that matter, suicide. "I don't have any real-life friends," moans one nineteen-year-old virus creator.[3] And, for the student of civility, that is the moral of the story. The virus writer never seeks recognition. Viruses are sent out to attack people the writer does not know. The virus writer who thinks the activity a big joke (as some evidently do) is able to play it with aplomb in part because the victims are strangers.

And here, indeed, is a point on which most students of civility seem to agree. A big part of our incivility crisis stems from the sad fact that we do not know each other or even want to try; and, not knowing each other, we seem to think that how we treat each other does not matter. For the virus writer, whose alienation from others may be extreme, this is particularly true: the same anonymity behind which the virus's creator hides also cloaks the virus's victims. To the virus writer, whether motivated by anger, perverse pleasure, or ideology, the infection of other people's computers is an end in itself. The people who pay the costs may not seem real . . . assuming he thinks of them at all.

The creation of a virus to harm a complete stranger perfectly exemplifies much that is uncivil in our turbulent age. An important part of civility, as we have already seen, is simple good manners as a signal of respect for others and for the community. Another important part, which has lately occasioned a substantial literature, is about reconstruction of our social institutions. But civility is, fundamentally, an ethic for relating

---

[1] Michael Alexander, "Computer Security: How Much Backup Is Needed?" (book excerpt), *Computer Reseller News*, August 19, 1996, p. 164.

[2] See Adrian Mars, "Keys to the Plague," *Guardian Online* (May 1, 1997), URL: http://go2.guardian.co.uk/computing/archive/863011510virus.html.

[3] Quoted in ibid.

to the stranger. Indeed, much of civility is premised on the notion that the concept of stranger actually exists—that everybody will not in fact come to know, still less grow close to, everybody else. Yet we live in a society in which each of us encounters strangers every day, by the dozens, the hundreds, even the thousands. Civility is about how we treat each and every one of them. So civility is not the same as affection, and when we try to treat the two of them as the same, we end up making matters worse.

Vocabulary

paragraph 2: existential, irony
paragraph 3: visceral
paragraph 4: benign, metaphorically
paragraph 5: pathological, aplomb
paragraph 6: alienation, perverse, ideology
paragraph 7: premised

Questions

1. Carter uses computer viruses to illustrate a common feature of life today. What is that feature, and what details of the viruses and their creators does Carter stress?

2. What are some of the causes cited for computer viruses? Does Carter dismiss these?

3. What point is Carter making about civility in paragraph 7? What is its relation to how we rebuild social institutions today?

Suggestions for Writing

1. Explain what Carter means by *incivility,* illustrating from your own experience. Comment on Carter's explanation for incivility in paragraphs 6 and 7.

2. Discuss other kinds of vandalism you have experienced, explaining why you think they occur. Carter states that "the virus writer never seeks recognition." Is that the case in the vandalism you discuss?

●

A L A N   W E R T H E I M E R

ALAN WERTHEIMER, Professor of Political Science at the University of Vermont, writes often on issues of public policy. His essay, reprinted here, first published in the *New York Times* on April 25, 1980, explores the dilemma that he believes underlies much discussion about government spending—the choice between "helping identifiable lives and saving statistical lives." Knowing that a large segment of his audience supports what he refers to as "welfare-state humanitarianism," Wertheimer uses the dilemma to force a recognition that the issue is complex, does not present a simple choice between right and wrong, and demands an examination of basic assumptions.

STATISTICAL LIVES

Suppose the following were true:

At least some money spent on open-heart surgery could be used to prevent heart disease. True, patients in need of such surgery might die, but many more lives would be saved.

Some money spent treating tooth decay among low-income children might be used on fluoridation and dental hygiene. True, some decay would go untreated, but fewer children would ever need such treatment.

We could prohibit ransom payments to kidnappers. True, kidnapped children might die, but by lowering the incentive to kidnap, fewer children would be taken.

We could drastically reduce unemployment compensation. True, the unemployed would suffer, but by converting the money saved to private investment and by lowering the incentive to stay jobless, there would be substantially less unemployment.

These cases exhibit a similar structure. All involve choosing between a policy designed to help specific persons and one that seeks to prevent the need for such help. These choices are especially difficult because we know who needs help. The patient requiring open-heart surgery, the kidnapped child, the unemployed auto worker—they have names and faces; they are "identifiable" lives. On the other hand, we do not know whose lives will be saved or who will benefit from the prevention of heart disease, tooth decay, kidnappings, or creation of new jobs. Some people will, and we may be able to estimate their numbers with precision. These are real lives, but they are only "statistical" lives.

We might say we do not have to choose between helping those in need and preventing future needs. After all, we could do both. But resources are scarce, and even when resources are not at issue (as in the kidnapping case), we often must choose between competing persons or goals. We cannot do everything we might like to the extent we might like. We must often choose between helping identifiable lives and saving statistical lives.

I wish to make three points about these dilemmas. First we do seem to favor the interests of identifiable lives (saving the kidnapped child) and it may not be irrational to do so. Second, we nevertheless do see the need to attend to the interests of statistical lives, even if this injures identifiable lives. Thus it is now common to hear people advocating directing more medical resources to primary prevention of disease and fewer to treatment. Israel's policy of refusing to negotiate with terrorists may risk the lives of some hostages, but we do see the point. Third, welfare-state policies focus on identifiable lives, whereas conservative economists prefer to focus on statistical lives.

Monetary theory and other technical issues aside, the new Adam Smiths tells us that however well-intentioned, welfare-state policies have not (always) worked—on the policies' own terms. Minimum-wage laws, unemployment compensation, consumer protection, occupational safety, Medicaid, Social Security—by interfering with market efficiency, by discouraging individual initiative, by impeding private-capital formation, by incurring large-scale expenditures on governmental bureaucracies—all these policies (and others) have been self-defeating. They argue that liberal economics, filled with concern for the genuine needs of identifiable lives, has swelled the future ranks of statistical lives in need. Welfare-state humanitarianism is shortsighted, they say, and is thus less humanitarian than we may believe.

We need not dwell on the accuracy of this account. Conservative economists may be wrong about the facts. We certainly need not assume that market choices and private-capital formation always serve the interests of all social groups, that regulation always does more harm than good. But suppose conservative economists are (sometimes) right about the facts. Suppose that attempts to serve the needs of identifiable lives do end up harming future statistical lives. Should we turn our back on the needs that we see in order to prevent those that we cannot see? Regrettably, the answer may sometimes be yes.

Vocabulary

paragraph 4: incentive
paragraph 6: statistical
paragraph 8: dilemmas
paragraph 9: impeding, incurring, humanitarianism

Questions

1. Wertheimer's argument is in part inductive in showing that well-established facts and expert testimony make the dilemma real, not fictitious. What are these facts and testimony? What in the wording of paragraphs 9–10 shows that Wertheimer considers this evidence highly probable and not certain?

2. If we choose to save specific persons, what would be the consequences? What would they be if we choose to save "statistical" lives?

3. One way of refuting a dilemma is to "grasp the horns" and show that at least one of the alternatives is false or would not lead to the alleged consequences. Another way is to "go between the horns" and show that a third alternative exists—a policy that would save specific persons and "statistical" lives both. In paragraphs 7–8, how does Wertheimer anticipate refutation of the dilemma and answer it?

4. Do you agree with Wertheimer's response to the dilemma in paragraph 10? On what evidence do you base your agreement or disagreement—facts, expert testimony, or assumptions that you regard as self-evident?

SUGGESTIONS FOR WRITING

1. Present examples of your own of the dilemma Wertheimer presents, and use them to explore their implications for your own beliefs and conclusions.

2. Present a dilemma that you believe should concern Americans today. Introduce facts or expert testimony to show that the dilemma is a real one, anticipate a refutation of your dilemma and answer it, and state your own views on what can or should be done.

ROGER D. STONE

ROGER D. STONE worked for *Time* magazine from 1955 to 1970, serving in the 1960s as bureau chief in San Francisco, Rio de Janeiro, and Paris. He was vice-president of Chase Manhattan Bank until 1975, and in 1976 he joined the World Wildlife Fund—becoming vice-president in 1982. Stone is author of *Dreams of Amazonia* (1985), a history of the Brazilian rain forest. Stone's article on saving the world's forests appeared in *The New York Times* on November 11, 1986.

WHY SAVE TROPICAL FORESTS?

Many Americans feel that saving the world's tropical forests warrants about as much concern as the snail darter. In Europe and the United States, they say, deforestation was the inevitable and desirable consequence of economic progress; why, therefore, should it be any different in the largely underdeveloped nations where the world's tropical forests are to be found?

It *is* different, and our failure to appreciate the difference stems largely from our inability to distinguish between temperate and tropical conditions. The rich soils and relative biological simplicity of the temperate world enhance forest conversion and eventual reforestation. In tropical forest regions, soils tend to be poor. Life supporting nutrients are stored not in soils but in the trees. Remove them and the whole fragile system collapses. History is littered with examples of failed efforts to convert large areas of tropical forest to agriculture, cattle ranching or other "modern" uses.

People and nature both end up losers when the tropical forest is clum- 3
sily invaded. To begin with, such forests supply the world with goods—hardwoods, rubber, fruits and nuts, drugs and medicines and fragrances and spices—that often cannot be successfully raised in any but natural conditions. Harvesting beyond sustainable limits has already brought some of the tropical forests' best hardwoods—Brazilian rosewood for example—close to extinction.

The tropical forest is also a biological warehouse. Estimates of the 4
total number of species on the planet range up to 30 million, of which only 1.6 million have been identified. It is further estimated that tropical forests, while occupying only 7 percent of the earth's surface, may contain as many as half of all the earth's forms of life. This means that only a tiny fraction of all tropical forest species has so far been studied, and despite the drug industry's increasing reliance on computer modeling, genetic engineering and other laboratory devices, concerned biologists regard the heedless squandering of the tropical forests' known and unknown resources as a major tragedy.

Similarly, we depend on a small group of plants—corn, rice, wheat 5
and the like—for a large part of our sustenance. From time to time, plant pathologists have found, the commonly used strains of these plants require genetic fortification from the wild to protect them from blight and disease. Since many such plants originated in tropical areas and only later were cultivated elsewhere, the primeval forests of the tropics represent a vast genetic storehouse of great potential value to everyone.

Left untouched, tropical forests also contribute to the stability of 6
the world's climate. But when the forests are burned, the carbon released plays an important role in the buildup of atmospheric gases producing the "greenhouse effect," which is causing a warming trend on the planet. The consequences of this trend could be profound. America's corn belt could become a subtropical region, while the melting of the polar ice cap could cause sea levels to rise and lead to drastic losses of coastal land.

In view of all these factors, one might ask why the attack against 7
the tropical forest continues so relentlessly. The answer is that even the infertile tropical forest is often capable of providing short-term economic benefits to individuals and corporations. Given the human propensity to

enjoy one last meal if the alternative seems to be no meal at all, the present defoliation will probably continue unless a revolution in public and official attitudes—equivalent to the dramatic change of the 1980's in how smoking is perceived and handled—comes to the rescue at the eleventh hour.

VOCABULARY

paragraph 1: deforestation
paragraph 4: computer modeling, genetic engineering, squandering
paragraph 5: plant pathologists, blight
paragraph 6: "greenhouse effect"
paragraph 7: defoliation

QUESTIONS

1. Why must we distinguish between temperate and tropical conditions in discussing deforestation and its consequences for the planet? What argument in defense of tropical deforestation is Stone refuting in making this distinction?

2. What causes of tropical deforestation does Stone cite? Does he claim to have cited all of them?

3. What would be the short-range effects of tropical deforestation—those that would immediately change our lives? What would be the remote or long-range effects that would change our lives in the future or speed a process now occurring? In what order does Stone present these effects?

4. Is Stone addressing a general audience—some of whom are unfamiliar with the issues and the scientific facts of tropical deforestation? Or is he addressing a special audience—all of whom are familiar with the issues and facts? In addressing a different audience, would he need to argue in a different way?

SUGGESTION FOR WRITING

Analyze the causal arguments for and against a current policy that affects the environment—for example, restricting land development and logging to protect endangered species. In the course of your analysis, discuss how people who are for or against an issue distinguish these effects and use them in making their case.

HERBERT HENDIN

HERBERT HENDIN, is the author of *Black Suicide* (1969), *The Age of Sensation* (1975), and *Wounds of War: The Psychological Aftermath of Combat in Vietnam* (1984), and other psychosocial studies. Hendin states the basic assumptions of his study of drug users in his preface to *The Age of Sensation:* "Social facts are empty numbers unless translated into psychosocial facts that reflect the dynamism of life, the emotion behind the fact, the cause for the statistic. Culture is a two-way street, a flow between individuals and institutions, single minds and collective forces." In this section from the book, Hendin identifies conditions present in the lives of particular users, without trying to suggest that these are necessary—that is, are always present.

STUDENTS AND DRUGS

No more dramatic expression of the dissatisfaction students feel with themselves can be found than students abusing drugs. Students often become drug abusers, that is, heavy and habitual users, in an attempt to alter their emotional lives, to transform themselves into the people they wish they could be, but feel they never could be without drugs. What they crave is to restructure their own emotions, not to be themselves, but to live as some "other." What this "other" is like and how it can be achieved cut to the center of the changing American psyche.

The turmoil over performance, achievement, and success, the increasing terror of becoming "too" involved with anyone; the attempt to find in fragmentation the means of effecting a pervasive change in one's total relation to life—all these are everywhere prevalent on campus. Students abusing drugs are often attempting to cure themselves of the malaise they see everywhere around them and in themselves.

Why do some students take LSD or heroin while others take mari- 3 juana or amphetamines? Why do still others take anything and everything? Students who are intrigued by drugs can learn through trial and error and from other students to find and favor the drugs which most satisfy their particular emotional needs. They rapidly become expert psychopharmacologists, able to locate the specific drug cure for what disturbs them. One student who by seventeen had tried just about everything and had become a daily, intravenous heroin user, had rejected LSD early in his drug career, explaining, "I can't see what anyone gets out of it. It just sort of makes you schizy—quiet one minute and freaked out the next."

Some students were initially drawn to the "cops-and-robbers" qual- 4 ity of drug abuse. While they were clearly out to defy their parents and the whole structure of authority, they were often unaware that their abuse had anything to do with their families, so profoundly had they pushed their rage at them out of their consciousness. Such students were invariably unable to deal with their parents directly and were bound in a need to defy them and a simultaneous need to punish themselves for their rebellion.

Drugs provided these students with both crime and punishment, while 5 removing their defiance out of the direct presence of their parents. One student would "let his mind float away" and concentrate on music he liked whenever his father berated him. Afterward he went out and took whatever drugs he could buy. While he never connected his drug abuse with his anger toward his father, he often dreamed of it as a crime for which he would be punished. He had a dream in which a riot was going on in another part of town while he was shooting heroin. He was afraid that somehow he would be arrested along with the rioters. Drugs were clearly his way of rioting, of diverting the crime of rebellion to the crime of drug abuse and focusing his destructive potential on himself. The expectation this student had that he would be arrested was typical, and revelatory of the appeal of drugs for him. Jail signified to such students a concrete way of locking up their rage. Drugs permitted them to both contain their rage and to express it in a way that gave them a sense of defiance, however self-damaging that defiance may be. Often, students who are most in trouble with the police over drugs are those for whom the need for crime and punishment was more significant than the need for drugs.

For most of the students who abused them, drugs also provided the   6
illusion of pleasurable connection to other people while serving to detach
them from the emotions real involvement would arouse. Drugs were, for
these students, the best available means of social relations. Heroin abusers
found in the junkie underworld a sense of security, belonging, and acceptance derived from the acknowledgement and the shared need for
heroin. LSD abusers felt their most intimate experiences involved trip-
ping with another person. Marijuana abusers felt that drugs "took the
edge off their personality" enough to permit them to be gentle and to
empathize with other people. Amphetamine abusers were pushed into the
social round on amphetamine energy, often being enabled to go through
sexual experience they would otherwise have found unendurable.

For many students drug abuse is the means to a life without drugs.   7
Such students take drugs to support the adaptation they are struggling
to make. Once it is established, they are often able to maintain it without drugs. The period of heavy drug abuse often marks the crisis in their
lives when they are trying to establish a tolerable relation to the world
and themselves. Appealing, tumultuous, sometimes frighteningly empty,
the lives of students who turn to drugs are an intense, dramatic revela-
tion of the way students feel today, what they are forced to grapple with
not only in the culture, but in themselves.

Vocabulary

paragraph 1: psyche
paragraph 2: fragmentation, malaise
paragraph 3: amphetamines, psychopharmacologists, intravenous
paragraph 5: berated, revelatory
paragraph 6: illusion, empathize
paragraph 7: tumultuous

Questions

1. Does Hendin single out a sufficient cause of drug use among students,
or instead identify a number of related (or unrelated) necessary causes?

2. Does he distinguish psychological from social causes, or does he assume these are one and the same?

3. Is Hendin generalizing about all students—even those who do not use drugs—or is he commenting merely on student drug users?

4. How does drug use foster "fragmentation" in the drug user? How can "fragmentation" provide a solution to the problems Hendin identifies in paragraph 2?

5. What does Hendin mean by the statement, "For many students drug abuse is the means to a life without drugs"?

SUGGESTIONS FOR WRITING

1. Describe tensions you have observed in yourself or in fellow students, and discuss the extent to which these tensions resemble those that Hendin identifies. Suggest some of the causes for those you have experienced or observed.

2. Hendin's book appeared in 1975. Investigate recent studies of drug use in a particular class of people—for example, children sixteen and younger—and compare the causes identified by the authors.

29

DEDUCTIVE REASONING

Induction, as we saw, sometimes reasons from particular instances to a general conclusion or truth:

> I studied the equations but didn't do the practice problems, and I failed algebra. I studied French but skipped the language lab and did poorly on the exam. I studied the formulas and performed the experiments carefully and passed Chemistry [*three particular instances*]. Learning seems to depend on practice as well as study [*probable truth*].

Deduction, by contrast, is the process of inference—of reasoning from a general truth to another general truth or a particular instance:

> The act of learning [is an act that] depends on study and practice.
> The mastery of French is an act of learning.
> Therefore, the mastery of French [is an act that] depends on study and practice.

Usually the argument is shortened and worded less formally:

> Learning depends on study and practice, and therefore so does mastery of French.

In shortened arguments such as this, the major premise, or minor premise (as in the example), or conclusion may be implied. A shortened argument is called an *enthymeme*. In ordinary conversation we may say, in different words, "I passed French because I studied and went to the language lab."

Where inductive arguments depend on the weight of factual evidence beyond the premises, deductive arguments depend on the premises alone as evidence for the conclusion. No other evidence is required because the premises are taken to be true—as in the Declaration of Independence:

> We hold these truths to be self-evident: that all men are created equal; that they are endowed by their creator with certain unalienable rights; that among these are life, liberty, and the pursuit of happiness.

> Society is to be improved, not by forcing a program of social reform down its throat, through the schools or otherwise, but by the improvement of the individuals who compose it. As Plato said, "Governments reflect human nature. States are not made out of stone or wood, but out of the characters of their citizens: these turn the scale and draw everything after them." The individual is the heart of society. (Robert Maynard Hutchins, *The Conflict in Education*)

> Any law that uplifts human personality is just. Any law that degrades human personality is unjust. All segregation statutes are unjust because segregation distorts the soul and damages the personality. (Martin Luther King, Jr., *Letter from Birmingham Jail*).

From truths such as these—long-held beliefs, generalizations established by long experience, scientific "laws" confirmed by repeated observation and laboratory experiments—we draw conclusions, make inferences, as in our original example. Thus, if it is true that learning depends on study and practice and true also that mastery of French is an act of learning, it must be true that mastering French depends on study and practice. In a deductive argument, we look to see what other truths such premises imply or entail.

Though no other evidence but the premises *need* be provided, we may decide to illustrate or back up one or both. Most arguments in fact contain illustration and backing of some kind. For a true statement is not always obvious to everyone. In one kind of argument we may cite the experimental data that supports a scientific truth. In another we may cite laws, statutes, precedents, and judicial rulings. How detailed or technical the backing is depends on the audience being addressed. A trial lawyer shares with the judge and other lawyers certain assumptions, standards, and legal knowledge that usually need to be presented to a jury unacquainted with the applicable law.

The deductive argument must satisfy two requirements: the propositions that form the premises must be true, and the process of reasoning must be correct, or to use the technical term, must be *valid*.

Note that "valid" does not mean "true": an argument may be false in its premises, but still be valid if the process of inference from these premises is correct. Here is a valid argument, both of whose premises are false:

All Texans are taxpayers.
All property owners are Texans.
Therefore, all property owners are taxpayers.

We ask of an argument that it be valid in its reasoning and true in its premises. A valid argument whose premises are true is called *sound*. The argument just cited would be sound, if, in fact, all Texans do pay taxes, and all property owners (everywhere) are Texans. The argument is, of course, unsound. Logicians have complex techniques for testing the validity of the many kinds of syllogism; we cannot review them here. But we need to keep in mind a few of the characteristics that invalidate deductive arguments:

Someone says to us: "My neighbors must all be property owners because they all pay taxes." Something strikes us as wrong with the statement, but what is it? We can construct the whole argument as follows:

All property owners are taxpayers.
My neighbors are taxpayers.
Therefore, my neighbors are property owners.

The trouble is with the middle term, *taxpayers*. The major term of a syllogism is the predicate term of its conclusion; the minor term is the subject. The term that appears in the premises but not in the conclusion is called the middle term.

All	A _____ middle	is	B _____ MAJOR
All	C _____ MINOR	is	A _____ middle
All	C _____ MINOR	is	B _____ MAJOR

A valid argument may not have more than these three terms. The middle term must also be "distributed" in at least one of the premises; that is, it must refer to—that is, be distributed among—all members of the class named. In the argument above, the middle term, *taxpayers,* is undistributed in both premises—referring in each to some members of the class taxpayers, but not necessarily to all:

> All property owners are taxpayers.
> My neighbors are taxpayers.

Though all property owners are taxpayers, not all taxpayers may own property. And though all my neighbors are taxpayers, not all taxpayers may be my neighbors. The argument is thus invalid. In a course on logic, you would study other failures of this kind.

Other invalid arguments can be analyzed more easily. The middle term must not be ambiguous, as in the following argument:

> Whoever helps himself is helped by God.
> A thief helps himself.
> Therefore, a thief is helped by God.

And both premises must be affirmative if the conclusion is so: if one of the premises is negative, so must be the conclusion. And, if both premises are negative, no conclusion follows. The following argument is invalid for this reason:

> No dogs are welcome visitors.
> No children are dogs.
> Therefore, children are welcome visitors.

In developing arguments of our own, we need to remember that an argument may seem "logical" because the process of reasoning is correct, and yet be unsound because the premises are questionable or false. In reading arguments, we need to consider both the premises that form it and the way the writer reasons from them.

SYDNEY J. HARRIS

SYDNEY J. HARRIS, whose essay on clichés appears on p. 275, wrote on important issues of the day. How we think about such issues is of concern to Harris. He says the following in a companion essay: "We should be firmly resistant toward ideas we believe to be wrong, but immensely tolerant toward the people who hold such ideas, never for a moment confusing the person with the idea, which is the besetting sin of bigotry in all its manifold forms." ("Opposing Threats to Civilization") His essay on freedom and security is deductive in showing what various assumptions about these entail.

FREEDOM AND SECURITY

One of the main reasons people think so poorly (and therefore draw such mistaken conclusions from their thinking) is that they fail to understand the nature of opposites.

Most of us reason something like this: "wet" and "dry" are opposites. Therefore, the more wet you are, the less dry you are, and vice versa. This is impeccable logic, and is also true.

We then proceed from there to abstract qualities, like freedom and security. In one sense, freedom and security are opposites; and so we reason: the more freedom we have, the less security, and the more security, the less freedom.

But this is utterly false. Freedom and security are polarities along the same axis, and not opposites on the same order as wet and dry. They do not deny or cancel out one another, but sustain each other.

Consider what the idea of freedom is rooted in. It is rooted in choice. If you have no choice, you have no freedom. If you are hungry, you must eat what is available, or you will die. If you are hungry, you must satisfy your appetite before anything else; you have no real freedom to choose other or higher goals when your stomach is empty.

If freedom is rooted in choice, and if the man who has no choice has no freedom, then the larger the number of choices, the larger the amount of freedom.

And what gives us the largest number of choices? The amount of security we enjoy. If many kinds of jobs are available, we have the freedom to choose any; if only one, we must choose that. If we live in a society that will not let us starve, we have more freedom than if we live in a society where we must support certain leaders or parties in order to make sure we get enough food.

In the personal, social and political realms, freedom and security are 8
not opposites like wet and dry, but polarities that work together to sustain the human person at the maximum of his abilities. Without freedom,
security is slavery; without security, freedom is an illusion.

Of course, these two may be combined in different measures, and 9
neither must overwhelm the other—freedom must not degenerate into
anarchy, nor security into servitude. Each society has the task of finding
the just and proper equation for the best operation of its system.

But the point is that freedom and security are not contraries that 10
deny each other; rather they are as essential to each other as the two
blades in a pair of scissors. To fail to understand this is to fail totally in
grasping the true needs of the human animal.

VOCABULARY

paragraph 4: polarities, axis
paragraph 9: anarchy, equation

QUESTIONS

1. Harris states that "freedom and security are not contraries that deny
each other; rather they are as essential to each other as the two blades
in a pair of scissors." In formal logic, it is impossible for contrary statements to both be true—for example, all Americans are taxpayers, no
Americans are. Yet, like these statements, they can both be false. Why
are freedom and security not contraries as Harris defines them?

2. In what sense are they "polarities along the same axis"?

3. How do freedom and security "sustain each other"?

4. What inferences does Harris draw about people and society from
this truth?

SUGGESTIONS FOR WRITING

1. Harris suggests that we sometimes think of freedom and security as opposites—the more we have of one, the less we have of the other. Write about a situation in which you found yourself thinking in this way. Discuss both the situation and its outcome.

2. Harris suggests that "the larger the number of choices, the larger amount of freedom." Write about how true this has been of choices open to you, possibly in your work experiences or education.

H . L . M E N C K E N

HENRY LOUIS MENCKEN (1880–1956) wrote for Baltimore newspapers and other periodicals most of his life and was one of the founders and editors of the *American Mercury* magazine. His satirical essays on American life and politics were collected in six volumes under the title *Prejudices*. His three volumes of autobiography describe his youth in Baltimore and his later career in journalism. Mencken's interests were wide, and he wrote extensively about American democracy and American English, whose characteristics he describes in *The American Language* (Fourth Edition, 1936). His reflections on war were published in *Minority Report* (1956).

REFLECTIONS ON WAR

The thing constantly overlooked by those hopefuls who talk of abolishing war is that it is by no means an evidence of decay but rather a proof of health and vigor. To fight seems to be as natural to man as to eat. Civilization limits and wars upon the impulse but it can never quite eliminate it. Whenever the effort seems to be most successful—that is, whenever man seems to be submitting most willingly to discipline, the spark is nearest to the powder barrel. Here repression achieves its inevitable work. The most warlike people under civilization are precisely those who submit most docilely to the rigid inhibitions of peace.

Once they break through the bounds of their repressed but steadily accumulating pugnacity, their destructiveness runs to great lengths. Throwing off the chains of order, they leap into the air and kick their legs. Of all the nations engaged in the two World Wars the Germans, who were the most rigidly girded by conceptions of renunciation and duty, showed the most gusto for war for its own sake.

The powerful emotional stimulus of war, its evocation of motives and ideals which, whatever their error, are at least more stimulating than those which impel a man to get and keep a safe job—this is too obvious to need laboring. The effect on the individual soldier of its very horror, filling him with a sense of the heroic, increases enormously his self-respect. This increase in self-respect reacts upon the nation, and tends to save it from the deteriorating effects of industrial discipline. In the main, soldiers are men of humble position and talents—laborers, petty mechanics, young fellows without definite occupation. Yet no one can deny that the veteran shows a certain superiority in dignity to the average man of his age and experience. He has played his part in significant events; he has been a citizen in a far more profound sense than any mere workman can ever be. The effects of all this are plainly seen in his bearing and his whole attitude of mind. War may make a fool of man, but it by no means degrades him; on the contrary, it tends to exalt him, and its net effects are much like those of motherhood on women.   2

That war is a natural revolt against the necessary but extremely irksome discipline of civilization is shown by the difficulty with which men on returning from it re-adapt themselves to a round of petty duties and responsibilities. This was notably apparent after the Civil War. It took three or four years for the young men engaged in that conflict to steel themselves to the depressing routine of everyday endeavor. Many of them, in fact, found it quite impossible. They could not go back to shovelling coal or tending a machine without intolerable pain. Such men flocked to the West, where adventure still awaited them and discipline was still slack. In the same way, after the Franco-Prussian War, thousands of young German veterans came to the United States, which seemed to them one vast Wild West. True enough, they soon found that discipline was necessary here as well as at home, but it was a slacker discipline and they themselves exaggerated its slackness in their imagination. At all events, it had the charm of the unaccustomed.   3

We commonly look upon the discipline of war as vastly more rigid than any discipline necessary in time of peace, but this is an error. The   4 strictest military discipline imaginable is still looser than that prevailing in the average assembly-line. The soldier, at worst, is still able to exercise the highest conceivable functions of freedom—that is, he is permitted to steal and to kill. No discipline prevailing in peace gives him anything even remotely resembling this. He is, in war, in the position of a free adult; in peace he is almost always in the position of a child. In war all things are excused by success, even violations of discipline. In peace, speaking generally, success is inconceivable except as a function of discipline.

The hope of abolishing war is largely based upon the fact that men have 5 long since abandoned the appeal to arms in their private disputes and submitted themselves to the jurisdiction of courts. Starting from this fact, it is contended that disputes between nations should be settled in the same manner, and that the adoption of the reform would greatly promote the happiness of the world.

Unluckily, there are three flaws in the argument. The first, which is 6 obvious, lies in the circumstance that a system of legal remedies is of no value if it is not backed by sufficient force to impose its decisions upon even the most powerful litigants—a sheer impossibility in international affairs, for even if one powerful litigant might be coerced, it would be plainly impossible to coerce a combination, and it is precisely a combination of the powerful that is most to be feared. The second lies in the fact that any legal system, to be worthy of credit, must be administered by judges who have no personal interest in the litigation before them— another impossibility, for all the judges in the international court, in the case of disputes between first-class powers, would either be appointees of those powers, or appointees of inferior powers that were under their direct influence, or obliged to consider the effects of their enmity. The third objection lies in the fact, frequently forgotten, that the courts of justice which now exist do not actually dispense justice, but only law, and that this law is frequently in direct conflict, not only with what one litigant honestly believes to be his rights, but also with what he believes to be his honor. Practically every litigation, in truth, ends with either one litigant or the other nursing what appears to him as an outrage upon him. For both litigants to go away satisfied that justice has been done is almost unheard of.

In disputes between man and man this dissatisfaction is not of serious consequence. The aggrieved party has no feasible remedy; if he doesn't like it, he must lump it. In particular, he has no feasible remedy against 7 a judge or a juryman who, in his view, has treated him ill; if he essayed vengeance, the whole strength of the unbiased masses of men would be exerted to destroy him, and that strength is so enormous, compared to his own puny might, that it would swiftly and certainly overwhelm him. But in the case of first-class nations there would be no such overwhelming force in restraint. In a few cases the general opinion of the world might be so largely against them that it would force them to acquiesce in the judgment rendered, but in perhaps a majority of important cases there would be sharply divided sympathies, and it would constantly encourage resistance. Against that resistance there would be nothing save the counter-resistance of the opposition—*i.e.,* the judge against the aggrieved litigant, the twelve jurymen against the aggrieved litigant's friends, with no vast and impersonal force of neutral public opinion behind the former.

VOCABULARY

paragraph 1: repression, docilely, inhibitions, pugnacity, girded, gusto
paragraph 2: stimulus, evocation, impel, deteriorating, profound
paragraph 3: endeavor
paragraph 6: litigants, coerced
paragraph 7: feasible, aggrieved, essayed, puny

QUESTIONS

1. In paragraphs 1–4, Mencken argues that war will not be easily abolished, and he states his major premise explicitly: "To fight seems to be as natural to man as to eat." How do the wording of his statement and the wording of others in these paragraphs show that Mencken regards these premises as certain and decisive evidence for his conclusions? What conclusions does he reach based on these premises?

2. Though he regards his premises as certain, Mencken explains and illustrates them. What examples does he present? Does he discuss one civilization or instead generalize about "warlike people" on the basis of observations made over a period of time?

3. Paragraph 1 of the Mencken essay contains the making of several syllogisms. In the first of these, the major premise may be stated in these words: "The expression of a natural instinct is evidence of health and vigor." What are the minor premise and conclusion?

4. In paragraph 1 Mencken argues that repression of a natural instinct leads to increased destructiveness. What are the minor premise and the conclusion?

5. L. A. White, in *Science of Culture,* argues that the need for military conscription refutes the assumption that people are naturally warlike. Given his assumptions and evidence, how might Mencken answer this objection? What do paragraphs 5–7 suggest?

6. In paragraphs 5–7 Mencken challenges "the hope of abolishing war," a hope based on the assumption that people have long since "submitted themselves to the jurisdiction of courts." What flaws does Mencken find in the argument, and what kind of evidence does he present in refutation? Does he deal with particular instances or instead generalize from observations made over a period of time?

7. Decide whether the following arguments are sound (see p. 388). It may be necessary to reword the premises:

   a. Since all voters are citizens and I am a voter, I am a citizen.

   b. Since all voters are citizens and I am a citizen, I am a voter.

   c. Since the Irish are vegetarians and Bernard Shaw was Irish, Shaw was a vegetarian.

   d. Those who made 93 or better on the exam will receive an A in the course. Seven of us received an A in the course and therefore must have made 93 or better on the exam.

   e. Since beneficent acts are virtuous and losing at poker benefits others, losing at poker is virtuous.

8. An *enthymeme* is a condensed syllogism (see p. 386). In the following enthymemes, reconstruct the original syllogism by supplying the missing premise, and then evaluate the argument. The premises and conclusion may need rewording:

   a. John F. Kennedy was a good president because he supported the space program and other kinds of scientific research.

b. Capital punishment protects society from depraved individuals.

c. I am successful at business because I once had a paper route.

d. I am an independent voter, just as my father and grandfather were.

SUGGESTION FOR WRITING

Write an argument for or against one of the following. In an additional paragraph identify one or more assumptions that underlie your argument, and explain why you hold these assumptions:

a. setting the drinking age at 21

b. a ban on smoking in restaurants

c. mandatory voting in federal and state elections

d. periodic examination of licensed drivers

e. required attendance in college classes

KENNETH B. CLARK

KENNETH B. CLARK, Distinguished Professor of Psychology at City College of New York from 1970 to 1975, began teaching at City College in 1942. His writings have exerted wide influence on social legislation and judicial thinking about civil rights—his research was used in the case against segregated public schools in Brown vs. Board of Education in 1954. His many influential books include *Dark Ghetto* (1965) and *Pathos of Power* (1974), from which this section on "relevance" in education is taken.

THE LIMITS OF RELEVANCE

As one who began himself to use the term "relevant" and to insist on its   1
primacy years ago, I feel an obligation to protest the limits of relevance or to propose a redefinition of it to embrace wider terms.

Definitions of education that depend on immediate relevance ignore 2
a small but critical percentage of human beings, the individuals who for
some perverse reason are in search of an education that is not dominated by
the important, socially and economically required pragmatic needs of a
capitalist or a communist or a socialist society. Such an individual is not
certain what he wants to be; he may not even be sure that he wants to be
successful. He may be burdened with that perverse intelligence that finds
the excitement of life in a continuous involvement with ideas.

For this student, education may be a lonely and tortuous process not 3
definable in terms of the limits of course requirements or of departmental
boundaries, or the four- or six-year span of time required for the bachelor's or graduate degree. This student seems unable to seek or to define or
to discuss relevance in terms of externals. He seems somehow trapped by
the need to seek the dimensions of relevance in relation to an examination and re-examination of his own internal values. He may have no choice
but to assume the burden of seeking to define the relevance of the human
experience as a reflection of the validity of his own existence as a value-
seeking, socially sensitive, and responsive human being. He is required to
deny himself the protective, supporting crutch of accepting and clutching
uncritically the prevailing dogmatisms, slogans, and intellectual fashions.

If such a human being is to survive the inherent and probably in- 4
evitable aloneness of intellectual integrity, he must balance it by the
courage to face and accept the risks of his individuality; by compassion
and empathetic identification with the frailties of his fellow human beings as a reflection of his own; by an intellectual and personal discipline
which prevents him from wallowing in introspective amorphousness and
childlike self-indulgence. And, certainly, he must demonstrate the breadth
of perspective and human sensitivity and depth of affirmation inherent
in the sense of humor which does not laugh at others but laughs with
man and with the God of Paradox who inflicted upon man the perpetual practical joke of the human predicament.

American colleges, with few notable exceptions, provide little room 5
for this type of student, just as American society provides little room for
such citizens. Perhaps it is enough to see that institutions of higher education do not destroy such potential. One could hope wistfully that our
colleges and even our multiuniversities could spare space and facilities to
serve and to protect those students who want to experiment without being required to be practical, pragmatic, or even relevant.

Is it possible within the complexity and cacophony of our dynamic, power-related, and tentatively socially sensitive institutions for some few to have the opportunity to look within, to read, to think critically, to communicate, to make mistakes, to seek validity, and to accept and enjoy this process as valid in itself? Is there still some place where relevance can be defined in terms of the quest—where respect for self and others can be taken for granted as one admits not knowing and is therefore challenged to seek? 6

May one dare to hope for a definition of education which makes it possible for man to accept the totality of his humanity without embarrassment? This would be valuable for its own sake, but it might also paradoxically be the most pragmatic form of education—because it is from these perverse, alone-educated persons that a practical society receives antidotes to a terrifying sense of inner emptiness and despair. They are the font of the continued quest for meaning in the face of the mocking chorus of meaninglessness. They offer the saving reaffirmation of stabilizing values in place of the acceptance of the disintegration inherent in valuelessness. They provide the basis for faith in humanity and life rather than surrender to dehumanization and destruction. From these impracticals come our poets, our artists, our novelists, our satirists, our humorists. They are our models of the positives, the potentials, the awe and wonder of man. They make the life of the thinking human being more endurable and the thought of a future tolerable. 7

Vocabulary

paragraph 2: relevance, pragmatic, perverse
paragraph 3: dimensions, dogmatisms
paragraph 4: empathetic, introspective, amorphousness, paradox
paragraph 5: wistfully
paragraph 6: cacophony, validity
paragraph 7: antidotes, font, reaffirmation, dehumanization, satirists, humorists

QUESTIONS

1. How does Clark explain the meanings of the term *relevant?* Why does he briefly review these meanings?

2. What assumptions does Clark make about the educational needs of people?

3. What conclusions does he derive from his assumptions?

4. Do you agree that American colleges have little room for the kind of student described in paragraph 4? What is your answer to the questions Clark asks in paragraph 6?

5. Does Clark seek to refute those who argue the "pragmatic needs" of education? Or does he present confirming arguments only?

6. To what extent does Clark describe your goals in seeking an education?

SUGGESTION FOR WRITING

Evaluate one of the following statements on the basis of your experience and observation:

a. "American colleges, with few notable exceptions, provide little room for this type of student, just as American society provides little room for such citizens."

b. "[I]t is from these perverse, alone-educated persons that a practical society receives antidotes to a terrifying sense of inner emptiness and despair."

KARL L. SCHILLING AND KAREN MAITLAND SCHILLING

KARL L. SCHILLING wrote the following as director of the American Association for Higher Education's Assessment Program and associate dean of the Western College Program at Miami University, in Oxford, Ohio; KAREN MAITLAND SCHILLING as is university director of liberal education at the same university. Their article appeared in the *Chronicle of Higher Education*, February 2, 1994.

FINAL EXAMS DISCOURAGE
TRUE LEARNING

While we were visiting another campus recently, a faculty member mentioned his bewilderment about what he saw happening to students as they moved from semester to semester. He frequently taught students in the "intro" course in his discipline during the fall semester and later, in the spring semester of the same academic year, taught many of the same students in the second course in his department's introductory sequence. He was dismayed at the blank stares he received in the spring when he'd say: "As you remember from last semester, we discussed. . . ."

Indeed, the ideas he was recalling had played an important role in the final exam that students had taken only three weeks before. Yet many looked at him as though he had started to speak a foreign language. Was he mistaken? Had he covered this material the year before but forgotten to talk about it this year? When he checked his syllabus, his notes, and his final exam, they all confirmed that he had covered the material and that the students had performed very well on the final-exam questions on the topic. What was happening?

Comprehensive final exams are one of the cherished traditions of higher education. Institutions stop teaching and set aside entire weeks for these tests. Some even give students extra days without classes before exam week to prepare. Legends of all-nighters during this period abound. Clearly, many alumni hold fond memories of these academic hell weeks—of having survived and proved themselves. Yet maybe this great tradition is dysfunctional.

Thinking about the underlying symbolic communication in the way we use final exams may provide an answer to our colleague's frustration. "Final" conveys a conclusion, a *terminus*. If we faculty members think of the curriculum that our department offers as an educational program, as opposed to a collection of discrete courses, that exam at the end of a semester is not really a terminus, but a pause to review and reflect before moving onward.

However, students may mistake the pause as the end of their need to know the material that they have just covered. To students, our assessment practices may be unwittingly communicating the idea that they are finished with a particular set of ideas and concepts. They will move on in the next semester to discrete new chunks of material, they believe; recollection or connection seems unnecessary.

Students may not understand that ideas and concepts run through   6
and connect courses, rather than falling neatly under course titles. They
may not realize that the way material is "chunked" into courses is arbi-
trary. They probably haven't guessed that the institution's bureaucratic
need to organize knowledge into billable units structures their courses
more than any compelling educational rationale does. They may not realize, for example, that Freud did not separate his considerations of human psychology into separate topics such as personality development and
abnormal psychology—although students are exposed to his thought in
courses that package these topics into discrete one-week units.

Many of our current testing practices, particularly final exams, en-   7
courage the development of academic bulimia: binge-and-purge learning.
If we were to graph the time that students spend studying, we would find
a disappointingly low level of effort until the week or two before a major exam. (Most research shows that students spend less than an hour a
day on academic work outside of the classroom.) Right before the exam,
the graph would rise steeply, peaking the day before the exam, followed
by a precipitous fall to near zero for the weeks following the exam. If
we measured students' understanding and retention of material, we would
find a similar curve—including the precipitous decline following the
exam. Although objective tests, particularly multiple-choice final exams
that rely heavily on superficial recall, may be the clearest perpetrator of
this approach to learning, all forms of evaluation that communicate that
the exam is a terminal event encourage it.

How might we signal students that education occurs in a continuum?   8
Giving exams to students as they enter courses could serve this purpose,
by providing an assessment of—and emphasis on—students' learning in
previous courses. Indeed, one might imagine an "entrance-exam week"
in which students would show that they had mastered the material necessary to enroll in subsequent courses.

A student would take an entrance exam (or undergo some other form   9
of assessment) that would evaluate whether he or she had the knowledge
and skills needed for the next class. Any student who failed to demonstrate the required competencies could take a short review course based
on the material covered in the previous course. If a student failed the entrance test a second time, but had passed the previous course given as a
prerequisite, he or she should be allowed to repeat the previous course,
for no additional credit and at no financial cost. If a student insisted on
taking the more-advanced course, he or she would be allowed to enroll,

but "against educational advice." Clearly, if numerous students who had passed a course could not pass the entrance exam for the following class, the failure could be seen as that of the instructor or the curriculum.

Entrance exams would allow students who have been out of school for a while or who have transferred from another institution to place themselves more accurately in the curriculum. Indeed, one could imagine that if faculty members became skilled enough at preparing these assessments, a first-year student who was well-prepared might be able to go right into more demanding, upper-level courses. Many institutions already allow students to take tests in certain disciplines, such as foreign languages, for advanced placement; the practice deserves expansion.

Most important, entrance exams would help students see the connections among courses within a major (or between any upper-level course and the prerequisites that it requires). Entrance exams also would signal that an instructor was not going to re-teach material covered in the previous course. Having passed the entrance exam, the students should have the earlier material fresh in mind and be ready to apply it in the new course.

Instructors would have to be clear about their expectations for students entering a particular course. The expectations would need to be communicated to faculty members teaching introductory courses and any other classes listed as prerequisites for upper-level courses. What better index of teaching effectiveness could there be than one tied to students' mastery of material needed in a subsequent course? Similarly, what better corrective measure for grade inflation than having another faculty member assess students' readiness to begin a subsequent course?

Clear course goals would make both students and faculty members more accountable for what goes on in the classroom. They also would provide clear expectations about the level at which students should be performing, which could help meet the concerns of public officials about rampant grade inflation and a lack of high educational standards.

Giving entrance exams would force faculty members to talk with each other about what they do in their classes, what the goals are for their majors, where in the curriculum the goals should be met, and maybe even what their courses have to offer to the liberal education of all students in the institution.

We have championed a "John Wayne" model for faculty members' behavior—a model of rugged individualists who, under a mistaken understanding of academic freedom, believe that what they do in their classrooms should not necessarily be subject to what happens in any other classroom. In doing so, we have conveyed the notion to students that they are performing for individual professors rather than developing themselves as learners.

Currently, students receive little encouragement to view their edu- 16 cation as a continuous process, even if they are "traditional" students who graduate in four years and are not among those whose education is spread over 10 years or more. But the vision of a continuum of education is crucial if faculty members are to break the current cycle of having to repeat much of the same introductory material in course after course. We must signal students that they need to carry material forward, that we cannot continue to re-teach ideas as we do now. In short, we can change our educational system to promote a healthier way of thinking about learning.

Vocabulary

paragraph 3: dysfunctional
paragraph 4: discrete
paragraph 7: bulimia, precipitous, perpetrator
paragraph 8: continuum

Questions

1. What is the specific problem that the authors wish to solve? How do they show in paragraphs 1–5 that the problem exists?

2. What do they assume is the purpose of education? Do they state this assumption directly and defend it, or do they instead imply it in discussing examination systems?

3. The authors state that education is a continuum, not independent "chunks of material" (paragraph 8). Do they offer proof for this assumption, or present it as a given truth?

4. How does the assumption that education is a continuum guide their reasoning on what should be done to solve the problem discussed in paragraphs 1–5?

5. What are the advantages of the solution they propose? What difficulties do they foresee in reforming the examination system? Do they suggest ways to overcome these difficulties?

6. Are the authors addressing their proposal to teachers, administrators, or students, or to some or all of these? How do you know? Do they take account of objections that might be made be each of these groups?

7. The authors organize their discussion in a persuasive way. To what extent does it contain the elements of the persuasive essay described on p. 513?

SUGGESTIONS FOR WRITING

1. Describe your own study habits, including the amount of time you spend out of class on each subject. Comment on how adequate these habits and the time spent are.

2. State your own ideas on what education should be, and use these to judge how well these courses prepared you for college work. Explain how you came to hold these ideas.

3. Argue for or against entrance exams for prerequisites, based on your own ideas about education and your own educational experience.

WILLIAM RASPBERRY

WILLIAM RASPBERRY has written for the *Washington Post* since 1962, first as a reporter and editor, then as a columnist, commenting on urban and national affairs. Raspberry wrote the following article shortly before the November 3, 1992, referendum on capital punishment in Washington, D.C. In his article he asks his readers to consider how they think about criminal justice.

WHO DESERVES THE DEATH PENALTY?

Capital punishment, which will be on the Nov. 3 ballot here, defies reasonable argument. Produce statistics "proving" that the prospect of capital punishment does not deter the crimes that frighten us most, and proponents change their tack. Maybe it doesn't, they say, but certain kinds of behavior *earn* the death penalty; it's a matter of just desserts. But are all offenders who commit the same offense under the same circumstances deserving of the same punishment?

I put the question to a judicial conference a few years ago. Most people, I said, no matter their views on standardized testing, recognize that identical scores may not be equal. Take the prep-school grandson of a physicist, whose parents are a diplomat and a research scientist, who scores 1300 on the SAT. Now take a youngster who is not sure what sort of work his grandfather did and whose family income, for most of his life, has consisted of his mother's AFDC check. He is a senior at the drug-ridden and academically dreadful public school. And his combined SAT score is 1300.

Not one of the judges would, given the disparity of opportunity afforded the two applicants, rate their identical scores equal, I told them. Well, I reminded them, they *are* admissions officers: not to Penn State but to the state pen. Should they take account of the fact that the defendants before them for sentencing, however comparable their offenses, had unequal chances to avoid criminal involvement?

Should they deal with two "applicants" for a prison cell—both 24-year-olds convicted of selling cocaine—when one is a graduate student at Georgetown and the other a jobless dropout from the ghetto? Are their identical offenses equal? Or should they deny "admission" to the young man whose lack of economic and social advantages makes it a snap for him to pass the prison entrance test—and give admissions preference to the Georgetown student who had to overcome a background of social advantage to qualify?

But if it's common sense to acknowledge that identical crimes may not be equal, doesn't it follow that ostensibly identical punishments may also be unequal? Can a judge properly consider the fact that a youngster from the projects would be less likely to be destroyed by a stint in prison, while the kid from Georgetown might not survive the experience?

Is it unreasonable, for example, for a judge to look at one offender and conclude that, given his unhealthy background, the odds are overwhelming that he will commit new offenses unless he is properly punished? Or to look at the second and guess that the shock of being arrested (and putting at risk his career and social standing) has straightened him out?

Obviously judges cannot postpone the punishment of criminals until society learns what to do about the underclass. But just as obviously, they cannot ignore the social circumstances that predispose some young men to lawlessness. It's one thing to punish people for what they do; quite another to add to that punishment because they've got nothing to lose.

QUESTIONS

1. Raspberry believes that the judges he spoke to at a judicial conference would not have rated two applicants for college equal on the basis of identical scores on the SAT. Why not?

2. If the judges agree that they would not do so, what view must they then take of comparable crimes in sentencing two young men convicted of selling cocaine?

3. What then does Raspberry demonstrate in paragraphs 5 and 6 from what he has shown about identical crimes?

4. What general conclusion does he draw about punishment in paragraph 7? What is his thesis, and where does he first state it? Where does he restate it?

5. What part of Raspberry's argument is deductive, and what in the wording shows that it is?

SUGGESTIONS FOR WRITING

1. State whether you would rate two applicants for college equal on the basis alone of identical scores on the SAT. Explain why, identifying the assumptions that guide your reasoning.

2. Explain why judges should or should not take the background and the chances of surviving prison into account in determining a sentence. Identify the assumptions that guide your reasoning, and explain why you hold them.

30

CONTROVERSY

Inductive and deductive reasoning often work together, depending on the particular argument and the point at issue. Proponents of nuclear power plants may, for example, insist that the issue in making the decision to build a plant in a particular region is economic—the increasing power needs of industry. Opponents may argue that the issue is the danger of an accident or the difficulty of disposing of nuclear waste. The argument in such a debate probably will be inductive: statistical information on productivity and nuclear fuel, eyewitness accounts of nuclear plant operations, scientific reports on waste disposal, and the like. The argument will also be deductive in the inferences drawn from certain assumptions: that a high standard of living is a desirable goal in the community; that risk must be taken into account in making a decision about nuclear power; that high productivity depends on a dependable source of electrical power.

Sometimes both assumptions and conclusions are debated; sometimes the assumptions are accepted as "givens" and not debated. In all debate, fairness and sound argument ideally should prevail. It hardly needs to be said that they often do not. Here are a few important "logical fallacies" that a good argument avoids:

> *Arguing in a circle* is closely related to begging the question, where we assume as true what we are trying to prove. "No person who cares about jobs would oppose the bill because it is one that those who care about jobs in Ohio can support." The speaker has not given a reason to support the bill, but has merely restated the opening assertion, arguing in a circle.

Non sequitur ("it does not follow"): The assertion, "I oppose nuclear power because my father does," contains a hidden premise or assumption—that father knows best. Since this assumption is hidden, the second part of the statement does not follow from the first part clearly. An assumption of this sort may be hidden because, once stated, it shows the statement to be questionable or absurd.

Irrelevant conclusion: If the point at issue is whether nuclear plants present a risk, the argument that they are needed is an irrelevant argument. It may, of course, be relevant later in the debate.

Ad hominem argument ("to the person"): I may attack my opponents rather than the issue—for example, by arguing that proponents of nuclear power are selfish and greedy. Even if they were people of bad character, their proposals must be judged on their merits. In other circumstances, such as an election campaign, the character of a person may be the issue.

Ad populum argument ("to the people"): I may also appeal to popular feeling or prejudice to gain support—suggesting that some highly revered and usually long-dead person would have favored (or opposed) nuclear power. Appeals to authority may also depend on fear. An appeal to authority is legitimate when the person cited is a recognized expert and has stated an opinion on the subject.

Either-or hypothesis: I may set up two alternatives—nuclear power or economic depression—without allowing for other solutions.

Complex question asks two questions in the guise of asking one. "Are you in favor of closing nuclear plants to remove an uncontrollable source of radiation?" The person answering no is forced to admit that nuclear power is in fact uncontrollable—a question that deserves to be debated separately.

Hasty generalization draws on a conclusion from an insufficient number of facts, sometimes even from a single fact (see p. 336). Even if one or more nuclear power plants have operated without an accident, we cannot draw the conclusion that all nuclear power plants are necessarily safe. Conversely, a large number of accidents, even a major one like that at Three Mile Island and at Chernobyl in the 1980s, does not prove conclusively that nuclear power plants cannot be operated safely. Numerous facts and possibilities including human and mechanical error need to be considered. Usually the greater number of relevant instances cited, the more probable the generalization. But the probability may be qualified by unstated or unknown facts—for example, the risk presented by aging equipment. And, as in the example of Three Mile Island and Chernobyl, a single serious instance or fact may have great force in argument.

Argument from ignorance: We cannot draw the conclusion that something *must* exist because no evidence has been found to prove it does not. Nor can we assert that nuclear power is not a threat to the environment or is not the cause of increasing cancer on the ground that no evidence exists to prove it is. Judgment on such questions must remain open in light of possible new evidence. However, we can make qualified judgments and recommendations on the basis of available scientific evidence.

INTERNET FILTERING

Title V of the Telecommunications Act of 1996—referred to as the Communications Decency Act, or CDA—contains two provisions governing access of minors to the Internet. The first of these penalizes the communication of anything "obscene" or "indecent" to anyone under eighteen; the second, the sending or depiction of "sexual or excretory activities or organs" in ways offensive to prevailing standards. The American Civil Liberties Union and other plaintiffs—among them library and publishing, newspaper, and Internet-related associations—challenged these articles as unconstitutional in the U.S. District Court for the Eastern Division of Pennsylvania. The court agreed they were unconstitutional, ruling that CDA, in the words of one of the three judges, "sweeps more broadly than necessary and thereby chills the expression of adults"—a violation of the First Amendment guarantee of free speech—and that CDA, in its vagueness, further violates the Fifth Amendment.

The Justice Department appealed the ruling to the U.S. Supreme Court. On June 26, 1997, Justice John Paul Stevens, joined by six of the nine justices, affirmed the District Court ruling—Justice Sandra Day O'Connor joined by Chief Justice William Rehnquist, dissenting in part. The majority opinion, rejecting the Justice Department's arguments, held that, among other defects, CDA gives parents no role in their children's access and fails to give a clear definition of "indecent" and "obscene" and is overbroad in its prohibitions. Nor does it stipulate that "patently offensive material" may have socially redeeming value under the First Amendment. CDA fails in seeking to govern a medium fully protected as a form of speech or expression. Justice O'Connor agreed with the majority that CDA violates the free speech rights of adults, but in her view "does not burden a substantial amount of minors' constitutionally protected speech." The court did not rule on the Fifth Amendment issue.

Reprinted below are sections 1, 7–9, and 11 of Justice Stevens's majority opinion, and the opening and the second half of Justice O'Connor's partial dissent. Omitted are footnotes and some of the citations in the text to federal law, the District Court and earlier Supreme Court rulings, and testimony of a government witness. Following these excerpts are a series of responses concerned with Internet filtering, access, and censorship. Included are two essays not directly related to the ruling—a commentary on the decision of Wal-Mart not to stock compact discs considered offensive, and a defense of censorship written several years before CDA. The full court opinion is available on the Internet at various sites.

JANET RENO, ATTORNEY GENERAL OF THE UNITED STATES, ET AL., APPELLANTS V. AMERICAN CIVIL LIBERTIES UNION ET AL.

ON APPEAL FROM THE UNITED STATES DISTRICT COURT
FOR THE EASTERN DISTRICT OF PENNSYLVANIA

[June 26, 1997]

JUSTICE STEVENS delivered the opinion of the Court.

At issue is the constitutionality of two statutory provisions enacted   1
to protect minors from "indecent" and "patently offensive" communications on the Internet. Notwithstanding the legitimacy and importance of the congressional goal of protecting children from harmful materials, we agree with the three-judge District Court that the statute abridges "the freedom of speech" protected by the First Amendment.

I

The District Court made extensive findings of fact, most of which were based on a detailed stipulation prepared by the parties. The findings describe the character and the dimensions of the Internet, the availability of sexually explicit material in that medium, and the problems confronting age verification for recipients of Internet communications. Because those findings provide the underpinnings for the legal issues, we begin with a summary of the undisputed facts.

The Internet

The Internet is an international network of interconnected computers. It is the outgrowth of what began in 1969 as a military program called "ARPANET," which was designed to enable computers operated by the military, defense contractors, and universities conducting defense-related research to communicate with one another by redundant channels even if some portions of the network were damaged in a war. While the ARPANET no longer exists, it provided an example for the development of a number of civilian networks that, eventually linking with each other, now enable tens of millions of people to communicate with one another and to access vast amounts of information from around the world. The Internet is "a unique and wholly new medium of worldwide human communication."

The Internet has experienced "extraordinary growth." The number of "host" computers—those that store information and relay communications—increased from about 300 in 1981 to approximately 9,400,000 by the time of the trial in 1996. Roughly 60% of these hosts are located in the United States. About 40 million people used the Internet at the time of trial, a number that is expected to mushroom to 200 million by 1999.

Individuals can obtain access to the Internet from many different sources, generally hosts themselves or entities with a host affiliation. Most colleges and universities provide access for their students and faculty; many corporations provide their employees with access through an office network; many communities and local libraries provide free access; and an increasing number of storefront "computer coffee shops" provide access for a small hourly fee. Several major national "online services" such as America Online, CompuServe, the Microsoft Network, and Prodigy offer access to their own extensive proprietary networks as well as a link to the much larger resources of the Internet. These commercial online services had almost 12 million individual subscribers at the time of trial.

Anyone with access to the Internet may take advantage of a wide va-   6
riety of communication and information retrieval methods. These methods are constantly evolving and difficult to categorize precisely. But, as
presently constituted, those most relevant to this case are electronic mail
("e-mail"), automatic mailing list services ("mail exploders," sometimes
referred to as "listservs"), "newsgroups," "chat rooms," and the "World
Wide Web." All of these methods can be used to transmit text; most can
transmit sound, pictures, and moving video images. Taken together, these
tools constitute a unique medium—known to its users as "cyberspace"—
located in no particular geographical location but available to anyone,
anywhere in the world, with access to the Internet.

E-mail enables an individual to send an electronic message—gener-   7
ally akin to a note or letter—to another individual or to a group of ad-
dressees. The message is generally stored electronically, sometimes waiting
for the recipient to check her "mailbox" and sometimes making its receipt known through some type of prompt. A mail exploder is a sort of
e-mail group. Subscribers can send messages to a common e-mail address,
which then forwards the message to the group's other subscribers. Newsgroups also serve groups of regular participants, but these postings may
be read by others as well. There are thousands of such groups, each serving to foster an exchange of information or opinion on a particular topic
running the gamut from, say, the music of Wagner to Balkan politics to
AIDS prevention to the Chicago Bulls. About 100,000 new messages are
posted every day. In most newsgroups, postings are automatically purged
at regular intervals. In addition to posting a message that can be read
later, two or more individuals wishing to communicate more immediately
can enter a chat room to engage in real-time dialogue—in other words,
by typing messages to one another that appear almost immediately on
the others' computer screens. The District Court found that at any given
time "tens of thousands of users are engaging in conversations on a huge
range of subjects." It is "no exaggeration to conclude that the content
on the Internet is as diverse as human thought."

The best known category of communication over the Internet is   8
the World Wide Web, which allows users to search for and retrieve
information stored in remote computers, as well as, in some cases, to
communicate back to designated sites. In concrete terms, the Web consists
of a vast number of documents stored in different computers all over the
world. Some of these documents are simply files containing information.
However, more elaborate documents, commonly known as Web "pages,"
are also prevalent. Each has its own address—"rather like a telephone

number." Web pages frequently contain information and sometimes allow the viewer to communicate with the page's (or "site's") author. They generally also contain "links" to other documents created by that site's author or to other (generally) related sites. Typically, the links are either blue or underlined text—sometimes images.

Navigating the Web is relatively straightforward. A user may either type the address of a known page or enter one or more keywords into a commercial "search engine" in an effort to locate sites on a subject of interest. A particular Web page may contain the information sought by the "surfer," or, through its links, it may be an avenue to other documents located anywhere on the Internet. Users generally explore a given Web page, or move to another, by clicking a computer "mouse" on one of the page's icons or links. Access to most Web pages is freely available, but some allow access only to those who have purchased the right from a commercial provider. The Web is thus comparable, from the readers' viewpoint, to both a vast library including millions of readily available and indexed publications and a sprawling mall offering goods and services.

From the publishers' point of view, it constitutes a vast platform from which to address and hear from a world-wide audience of millions of readers, viewers, researchers, and buyers. Any person or organization with a computer connected to the Internet can "publish" information. Publishers include government agencies, educational institutions, commercial entities, advocacy groups, and individuals. Publishers may either make their material available to the entire pool of Internet users, or confine access to a selected group, such as those willing to pay for the privilege. "No single organization controls any membership in the Web, nor is there any centralized point from which individual Web sites or services can be blocked from the Web."

Sexually Explicit Material

Sexually explicit material on the Internet includes text, pictures, and chat and "extends from the modestly titillating to the hardest-core." These files are created, named, and posted in the same manner as material that is not sexually explicit, and may be accessed either deliberately or unintentionally during the course of an imprecise search. "Once a provider posts its content on the Internet, it cannot prevent that content from entering any community." Thus, for example, "when the UCR/California Museum of Photography posts to its Web site nudes by Edward Weston and Robert Mapplethorpe to announce that its new exhibit will travel to Baltimore and New York City, those images are available not only in Los Angeles, Baltimore, and New York City, but also in Cincinnati, Mobile, or Beijing—wherever Internet users live. Similarly, the safer sex instructions that Critical Path posts to its Web site, written in street language so that the teenage receiver can understand them, are available not just in Philadelphia, but also in Provo and Prague."

Some of the communications over the Internet that originate in foreign countries are also sexually explicit.

Though such material is widely available, users seldom encounter   12
such content accidentally. "A document's title or a description of the document will usually appear before the document itself . . . and in many cases the user will receive detailed information about a site's content before he or she need take the step to access the document. Almost all sexually explicit images are preceded by warnings as to the content." For that reason, the "odds are slim" that a user would enter a sexually explicit site by accident. Unlike communications received by radio or television, "the receipt of information on the Internet requires a series of affirmative steps more deliberate and directed than merely turning a dial. A child requires some sophistication and some ability to read to retrieve material and thereby to use the Internet unattended."

Systems have been developed to help parents control the material   13
that may be available on a home computer with Internet access. A system may either limit a computer's access to an approved list of sources that have been identified as containing no adult material, it may block designated inappropriate sites, or it may attempt to block messages containing identifiable objectionable features. "Although parental control software currently can screen for certain suggestive words or for known sexually explicit sites, it cannot now screen for sexually explicit images." Nevertheless, the evidence indicates that "a reasonably effective method by which parents can prevent their children from accessing sexually explicit and other material which parents may believe is inappropriate for their children will soon be available."

Age Verification

The problem of age verification differs for different uses of the Internet.   14
The District Court categorically determined that there "is no effective

way to determine the identity or the age of a user who is accessing material through e-mail, mail exploders, newsgroups or chat rooms." The Government offered no evidence that there was a reliable way to screen recipients and participants in such fora for age. Moreover, even if it were technologically feasible to block minors' access to newsgroups and chat rooms containing discussions of art, politics or other subjects that potentially elicit "indecent" or "patently offensive" contributions, it would not be possible to block their access to that material and "still allow them access to the remaining content, even if the overwhelming majority of that content was not indecent."

Technology exists by which an operator of a Web site may condition access on the verification of requested information such as a credit card number or an adult password. Credit card verification is only feasible, however, either in connection with a commercial transaction in which the card is used, or by payment to a verification agency. Using credit card possession as a surrogate for proof of age would impose costs on non-commercial Web sites that would require many of them to shut down. For that reason, at the time of the trial, credit card verification was "effectively unavailable to a substantial number of Internet content providers." Moreover, the imposition of such a requirement "would completely bar adults who do not have a credit card and lack the resources to obtain one from accessing any blocked material."

Commercial pornographic sites that charge their users for access have assigned them passwords as a method of age verification. The record does not contain any evidence concerning the reliability of these technologies. Even if passwords are effective for commercial purveyors of indecent material, the District Court found that an adult password requirement would impose significant burdens on noncommercial sites, both because they would discourage users from accessing their sites and because the cost of creating and maintaining such screening systems would be "beyond their reach."

In sum, the District Court found:

> "Even if credit card verification or adult password verification were implemented, the Government presented no testimony as to how such systems could ensure that the user of the password or credit card is in fact over 18. The burdens imposed by credit card verification and adult password verification systems make them effectively unavailable to a substantial number of Internet content providers."

VII

We are persuaded that the CDA lacks the precision that the First Amend-   21
ment requires when a statute regulates the content of speech. In order to
deny minors access to potentially harmful speech, the CDA effectively sup-
presses a large amount of speech that adults have a constitutional right
to receive and to address to one another. That burden on adult speech is
unacceptable if less restrictive alternatives would be at least as effective
in achieving the legitimate purpose that the statute was enacted to serve.

In evaluating the free speech rights of adults, we have made it per-   22
fectly clear that "[s]exual expression which is indecent but not obscene
is protected by the First Amendment." *Sable,* 492 U.S., at 126.* See also
Carey v. *Population Services Int'l,* 431 U.S. 678, 701 (1977) ("[W]here
obscenity is not involved, we have consistently held that the fact that protected speech may be offensive to some does not justify its suppression").
Indeed, *Pacifica* itself admonished that "the fact that society may find
speech offensive is not a sufficient reason for suppressing it."

It is true that we have repeatedly recognized the governmental in-   23
terest in protecting children from harmful materials. See *Ginsberg,* 390
U.S., at 639; *Pacifica,* 438 U.S., at 749. But that interest does not justify
an unnecessarily broad suppression of speech addressed to adults. As we
have explained, the Government may not "reduc[e] the adult population . . . to . . . only what is fit for children." *Denver,* 518 U.S., at ___
(slip op., at 29) (internal quotation marks omitted) (quoting *Sable,* 492
U.S., at 128). "[R]egardless of the strength of the government's interest"
in protecting children, "[t]he level of discourse reaching a mailbox simply
cannot be limited to that which would be suitable for a sandbox." *Bolger*
v. *Youngs Drug Products Corp.,* 463 U.S. 60, 74–75 (1983).

The District Court was correct to conclude that the CDA effectively   24
resembles the ban on "dial-a-porn" invalidated in *Sable.* 929 F. Supp., at
854. In *Sable,* 492 U.S., at 129, this Court rejected the argument that we
should defer to the congressional judgment that nothing less than a total

---

* The citations in this and the following paragraph are to the following Supreme Court
rulings: *Sable Communications of Cal., Inc. versus FCC* (1989), *Ginsberg versus New York*
(1968), *FCC versus Pacifica Foundation* (1978), and *Denver Area Ed. Telecommunications
Consortium, Inc. versus FCC* (1996). [Ed.]

ban would be effective in preventing enterprising youngsters from gaining access to indecent communications. *Sable* thus made clear that the mere fact that a statutory regulation of speech was enacted for the important purpose of protecting children from exposure to sexually explicit material does not foreclose inquiry into its validity. As we pointed out last Term, that inquiry embodies an "over-arching commitment" to make sure that Congress has designed its statute to accomplish its purpose "without imposing an unnecessarily great restriction on speech." *Denver,* 518 U.S., at ___ (slip op., at 11).

In arguing that the CDA does not so diminish adult communication, the Government relies on the incorrect factual premise that prohibiting a transmission whenever it is known that one of its recipients is a minor would not interfere with adult-to-adult communication. The findings of the District Court make clear that this premise is untenable. Given the size of the potential audience for most messages, in the absence of a viable age verification process, the sender must be charged with knowing that one or more minors will likely view it. Knowledge that, for instance, one or more members of a 100-person chat group will be minor—and therefore that it would be a crime to send the group an indecent message—would surely burden communication among adults.

The District Court found that at the time of trial existing technology did not include any effective method for a sender to prevent minors from obtaining access to its communications on the Internet without also denying access to adults. The Court found no effective way to determine the age of a user who is accessing material through e-mail, mail exploders, newsgroups, or chat rooms. As a practical matter, the Court also found that it would be prohibitively expensive for noncommercial—as well as some commercial—speakers who have Web sites to verify that their users are adults. These limitations must inevitably curtail a significant amount of adult communication on the Internet. By contrast, the District Court found that "[d]espite its limitations, currently available *user-based* software suggests that a reasonably effective method by which *parents* can prevent their children from accessing sexually explicit and other material which *parents* may believe is inappropriate for their children will soon be widely available." (emphases added).

The breadth of the CDA's coverage is wholly unprecedented. Unlike the regulations upheld in *Ginsberg* and *Pacifica,* the scope of the CDA is not limited to commercial speech or commercial entities. Its open-ended prohibitions embrace all nonprofit entities and individuals posting

indecent messages or displaying them on their own computers in the presence of minors. The general, undefined terms "indecent" and "patently
offensive" cover large amounts of nonpornographic material with serious educational or other value. Moreover, the "community standards"
criterion as applied to the Internet means that any communication available to a nation-wide audience will be judged by the standards of the
community most likely to be offended by the message. The regulated subject matter includes any of the seven "dirty words" used in the Pacifica
monologue, the use of which the Government's expert acknowledged
could constitute a felony. It may also extend to discussions about prison
rape or safe sexual practices, artistic images that include nude subjects,
and arguably the card catalogue of the Carnegie Library.

For the purposes of our decision, we need neither accept nor reject the   28
Government's submission that the First Amendment does not forbid a blanket prohibition on all "indecent" and "patently offensive" messages communicated to a 17-year old—no matter how much value the message may
contain and regardless of parental approval. It is at least clear that the
strength of the Government's interest in protecting minors is not equally
strong throughout the coverage of this broad statute. Under the CDA, a
parent allowing her 17-year-old to use the family computer to obtain information on the Internet that she, in her parental judgment, deems appropriate could face a lengthy prison term. Similarly, a parent who sent
his 17-year-old college freshman information on birth control via e-mail
could be incarcerated even though neither he, his child, nor anyone in
their home community, found the material "indecent" or "patently offensive," if the college town's community thought otherwise.

The breadth of this content-based restriction of speech imposes an   29
especially heavy burden on the Government to explain why a less restrictive provision would not be as effective as the CDA. It has not done
so. The arguments in this Court have referred to possible alternatives
such as requiring that indecent material be "tagged" in a way that facil-
itates parental control of material coming into their homes, making exceptions for messages with artistic or educational value, providing some
tolerance for parental choice, and regulating some portions of the Internet—such as commercial web sites—differently than others, such as chat
rooms. Particularly in the light of the absence of any detailed findings by
the Congress, or even hearings addressing the special problems of the
CDA, we are persuaded that the CDA is not narrowly tailored if that requirement has any meaning at all.

VIII

In an attempt to curtail the CDA's facial overbreadth, the Government advances three additional arguments for sustaining the Act's affirmative prohibitions: (1) that the CDA is constitutional because it leaves open ample "alternative channels" of communication; (2) that the plain meaning of the Act's "knowledge" and "specific person" requirement significantly restricts its permissible applications; and (3) that the Act's prohibitions are "almost always" limited to material lacking redeeming social value.

The Government first contends that, even though the CDA effectively censors discourse on many of the Internet's modalities—such as chat groups, newsgroups, and mail exploders—it is nonetheless constitutional because it provides a "reasonable opportunity" for speakers to engage in the restricted speech on the World Wide Web. Brief for Appellants 39. This argument is unpersuasive because the CDA regulates speech on the basis of its content. A "time, place, and manner" analysis is therefore inapplicable. See *Consolidated Edison Co. of N. Y. v. Public Serv. Comm'n of N. Y.*, 447 U.S. 530, 536 (1980). It is thus immaterial whether such speech would be feasible on the Web (which, as the Government's own expert acknowledged, would cost up to $10,000 if the speaker's interests were not accommodated by an existing Web site, not including costs for database management and age verification). The Government's position is equivalent to arguing that a statute could ban leaflets on certain subjects as long as individuals are free to publish books. In invalidating a number of laws that banned leafletting on the streets *regardless of* their content—we explained that "one is not to have the exercise of his liberty of expression in appropriate places abridged on the plea that it may be exercised in some other place." *Schneider v. State (Town of Irvington)*, 308 U.S. 147, 163 (1939).

The Government also asserts that the "knowledge" requirement of both §223(a) and (d), especially when coupled with the "specific child" element found in §223(d), saves the CDA from overbreadth. Because both sections prohibit the dissemination of indecent messages only to persons known to be under 18, the Government argues, it does not require transmitters to "refrain from communicating indecent material to adults; they need only refrain from disseminating such materials to persons they know to be under 18." Brief for Appellants 24.

This argument ignores the fact that most Internet fora—including chat rooms, newsgroups, mail exploders, and the Web—are open to all comers. The Government's assertion that the knowledge requirement somehow protects the communications of adults is therefore untenable. Even the strongest reading of the "specific person" requirement of §223(d) cannot save the statute. It would confer broad powers of censorship, in the form of a "heckler's veto," upon any opponent of indecent speech who might simply log on and inform the would-be discoursers that his 17-year-old child—a "specific person . . . under 18 years of age," 47 U.S.C.A. §223(d)(1)(A) (Supp. 1997)—would be present.

Finally, we find no textual support for the Government's submission that material having scientific, educational, or other redeeming social value will necessarily fall outside the CDA's "patently offensive" and "indecent" prohibitions.

IX

The Government's three remaining arguments focus on the defenses provided in §223(e)(5). First, relying on the "good faith, reasonable, effective, and appropriate actions" provision, the Government suggests that "tagging" provides a defense that saves the constitutionality of the Act. The suggestion assumes that transmitters may encode their indecent communications in a way that would indicate their contents, thus permitting recipients to block their reception with appropriate software. It is the requirement that the good faith action must be "effective" that makes this defense illusory. The Government recognizes that its proposed screening software does not currently exist. Even if it did, there is no way to know whether a potential recipent will actually block the encoded material. Without the impossible knowledge that every guardian in America is screening for the "tag," the transmitter could not reasonably rely on its action to be "effective."

For its second and third arguments concerning defenses—which we can consider together—the Government relies on the latter half of §223(e)(5), which applies when the transmitter has restricted access by requiring use of a verified credit card or adult identification. Such verification is not only technologically available but actually is used by commercial providers of sexually explicit material. These providers, therefore, would be protected by the defense. Under the findings of the District Court, however, it is not economically feasible for most noncommercial speakers to employ such verification. Accordingly, this defense would not significantly narrow the statute's burden on noncommercial speech. Even

33

34

35

with respect to the commercial pornographers that would be protected by the defense, the Government failed to adduce any evidence that these verification techniques actually preclude minors from posing as adults. Given that the risk of criminal sanctions "hovers over each content provider, like the proverbial sword of Damocles," the District Court correctly refused to rely on unproven future technology to save the statute. The Government thus failed to prove that the proffered defense would significantly reduce the heavy burden on adult speech produced by the prohibition on offensive displays.

We agree with the District Court's conclusion that the CDA places an unacceptably heavy burden on protected speech, and that the defenses do not constitute the sort of "narrow tailoring" that will save an otherwise patently invalid unconstitutional provision. In *Sable*, 492 U.S., at 127, we remarked that the speech restriction at issue there amounted to "'burn[ing] the house to roast the pig.'" The CDA, casting a far darker shadow over free speech, threatens to torch a large segment of the Internet community.

XI

In this Court, though not in the District Court, the Government asserts that—in addition to its interest in protecting children—its "[e]qually significant" interest in fostering the growth of the Internet provides an independent basis for upholding the constitutionality of the CDA. Brief for Appellants 19. The Government apparently assumes that the unregulated availability of "indecent" and "patently offensive" material on the Internet is driving countless citizens away from the medium because of the risk of exposing themselves or their children to harmful material.

We find this argument singularly unpersuasive. The dramatic expansion of this new marketplace of ideas contradicts the factual basis of this contention. The record demonstrates that the growth of the Internet has been and continues to be phenomenal. As a matter of constitutional tradition, in the absence of evidence to the contrary, we presume that governmental regulation of the content of speech is more likely to interfere with the free exchange of ideas than to encourage it. The interest in encouraging freedom of expression in a democratic society outweighs any theoretical but unproven benefit of censorship.

For the foregoing reasons, the judgment of the district court is affirmed.

It is so ordered.

JUSTICE O'CONNOR, with whom THE CHIEF JUSTICE joins, concurring   40
in the judgment in part and dissenting in part.

I write separately to explain why I view the Communications De-   41
cency Act of 1996 (CDA) as little more than an attempt by Congress to
create "adult zones" on the Internet. Our precedent indicates that the
creation of such zones can be constitutionally sound. Despite the soundness of its purpose, however, portions of the CDA are unconstitutional
because they stray from the blueprint our prior cases have developed for
constructing a "zoning law" that passes constitutional muster.

Appellees bring a facial challenge to three provisions of the CDA. The   42
first, which the Court describes as the "indecency transmission" provision,
makes it a crime to knowingly transmit an obscene or indecent message or
image to a person the sender knows is under 18 years old. What the Court
classifies as a single "'patently offensive display'" provision, is in reality two
separate provisions. The first of these makes it a crime to knowingly send
a patently offensive message or image to a specific person under the age of
18 ("specific person" provision). The second criminalizes the display of
patently offensive messages or images "in a[ny] manner available" to minors ("display" provision). None of these provisions purports to keep indecent (or patently offensive) material away from adults, who have a First
Amendment right to obtain this speech. *Sable Communications of Cal., Inc.
v. FCC*, 492 U.S. 115, 126 (1989) ("Sexual expression which is indecent
but not obscene is protected by the First Amendment"). Thus, the undeni-
able purpose of the CDA is to segregate indecent material on the Internet
into certain areas that minors cannot access. (CDA imposes "access restrictions . . . to protect minors from exposure to indecent material").

The creation of "adult zones" is by no means a novel concept.   43
States have long denied minors access to certain establishments frequented by adults. States have also denied minors access to speech
deemed to be "harmful to minors." The Court has previously sustained such
zoning laws, but only if they respect the First Amendment rights of adults
and minors. That is to say, a zoning law is valid if (i) it does not unduly
restrict adult access to the material; and (ii) minors have no First Amendment right to read or view the banned material. As applied to the Internet
as it exists in 1997, the "display" provision and some applications of the
"indecency transmission" and "specific person" provisions fail to adhere
to the first of these limiting principles by restricting adults' access to protected materials in certain circumstances. Unlike the Court, however,
I would invalidate the provisions only in those circumstances.

II

Whether the CDA substantially interferes with the First Amendment   4.
rights of minors, and thereby runs afoul of the second characteristic of
valid zoning laws, presents a closer question. In *Ginsberg*, the New York
law we sustained prohibited the sale to minors of magazines that were
"harmful to minors." Under that law, a magazine was "harmful to minors" only if it was obscene as to minors. Noting that obscene speech is
not protected by the First Amendment, *Roth* v. *United States*, 354 U.S.
476, 485 (1957), and that New York was constitutionally free to adjust
the definition of obscenity for minors, the Court concluded that the law
did not "invad[e] the area of freedom of expression constitutionally secured to minors." New York therefore did not infringe upon the First
Amendment rights of minors. Cf. *Erznoznik* v. *Jacksonville*, 422 U.S. 205,
213 (1975) (striking down city ordinance that banned nudity that was
not "obscene even as to minors").

The Court neither "accept[s] nor reject[s]" the argument that the   4
CDA is facially overbroad because it substantially interferes with the
First Amendment rights of minors. I would reject it. *Ginsberg* established that minors may constitutionally be denied access to material that
is obscene as to minors. As *Ginsberg* explained, material is obscene as
to minors if it (i) is "patently offensive to prevailing standards in the
adult community as a whole with respect to what is suitable . . . for minors"; (ii) appeals to the prurient interest of minors; and (iii) is "utterly
without redeeming social importance for minors." Because the CDA de-
nies minors the right to obtain material that is "patently offensive"—
even if it has some redeeming value for minors and even if it does not
appeal to their prurient interests—Congress' rejection of the *Ginsberg*
"harmful to minors" standard means that the CDA could ban some
speech that is "indecent" (*i.e.*, "patently offensive") but that is not obscene as to minors.

I do not deny this possibility, but to prevail in a facial challenge,   4
it is not enough for a plaintiff to show "some" overbreadth. Our cases
require a proof of "real" and "substantial" overbreadth, *Broadrick* v.
Oklahoma, 413 U.S. 601, 615 (1973), and appellees have not carried
their burden in this case. In my view, the universe of speech constitutionally protected as to minors but banned by the CDA—*i.e.*, the
universe of material that is "patently offensive," but which nonetheless has some redeeming value for minors or does not appeal to their

prurient interest—is a very small one. Appellees cite no examples of speech falling within this universe and do not attempt to explain why that universe is substantial "in relation to the statute's plainly legitimate sweep." *Ibid.* That the CDA might deny minors the right to obtain material that has some "value," is largely beside the point. While discussions about prison rape or nude art, may have some redeeming education value for *adults,* they do not necessarily have any such value for *minors,* and under *Ginsberg,* minors only have a First Amendment right to obtain patently offensive material that has "redeeming social importance *for minors*" (emphasis added). There is also no evidence in the record to support the contention that "many [e]-mail transmissions from an adult to a minor are conversations between family members," and no support for the legal proposition that such speech is absolutely immune from regulation. Accordingly, in my view, the CDA does not burden a substantial amount of minors' constitutionally protected speech.

Thus, the constitutionality of the CDA as a zoning law hinges on the extent to which it substantially interferes with the First Amendment rights of adults. Because the rights of adults are infringed only by the "display" provision and by the "indecency transmission" and "specific person" provisions as applied to communications involving more than one adult, I would invalidate the CDA only to that extent. Insofar as the "indecency transmission" and "specific person" provisions prohibit the use of indecent speech in communications between an adult and one or more minors, however, they can and should be sustained. The Court reaches a contrary conclusion, and from that holding I respectfully dissent.   46

Vocabulary

paragraph 3: redundant
paragraph 5: proprietary
paragraph 7: purged
paragraph 12: sophistication
paragraph 25: untenable
paragraph 28: incarcerated

Questions

1. What special problems of age verification does the Internet present? How dependable is existing technology in verifying age?

2. Justice Stevens argues that "CDA lacks the precision that the First Amendment requires" (paragraph 21). How is it imprecise, what are the consequences?

3. What features of the Internet, discussed in paragraphs 3–10, does Justice Stevens stress? How is the medium different from radio and television—media that, like the Internet, minors can access? What role do these features play in the argument that CDA imposes unlawful restrictions on adults (paragraphs 24-29)?

4. How does he rebut the government's argument in paragraph 30 that CDA offers "alternative channels" of communication?

5. How does he rebut the remaining arguments cited in paragraph 30?

6. Justice O'Connor rejects the argument that CDA is overbroad in interfering with "the First Amendment rights of minors" (paragraph 44). How limited are those rights, and why is the interference not substantial enough to invalidate the provision?

7. What would she invalidate specifically in CDA?

Suggestions for Writing

1. Analyze the evidence presented in support of the majority opinion, or one of the dissents, in one of the following Supreme Court rulings:

a. *Butler* v. *Michigan* (1957)

b. *Roth* v. *United States* (1957)

c. *Ginsberg* v. *New York* (1968)

d. *Miller* v. *California* (1973)

e. *FCC* v. *Pacifica Foundation* (1978)

f. *Renton* v. *Playtime Theatres, Inc.* (1986)

2. Discuss the bearing of the opinion on one or more issues raised in *Reno* v. *ACLU.*

WILLIAM F. BUCKLEY, JR.

The founder, long-time editor, and columnist of *National Review*, WILLIAM F. BUCKLEY, JR. is known as the host of *Firing Line* on the Public Broadcasting System. His writings on social and political issues include *God and Man at Yale* (1951), *Right Reason* (1985), and *Gratitude: What We Owe to Our Country* (1990). In the following column from the August 11, 1997, issue of *National Review,* Buckley discusses the recent Supreme Court decision on the constitutionality of the 1996 Communications Decency Act.

INTERNET: THE LOST FIGHT

The Supreme Court decision on the Internet and pornography is analytically infuriating. Justice John Paul Stevens used as the principal argument for the majority opinion invalidating the congressional act the assertion that the Internet is going to do more good than harm. He went so far in this line of argument as to say that such harm as it does is unmeasured and perhaps impalpable—the old argument: Who ever got hurt by pornography? But to argue that more good than harm can come from the Internet is on the order of saying that more good than harm can come from drugs and therefore commerce in prussic acid should not be forbidden.

My own judgment of the Internet is that it is the most exciting technological research and information tool of the century, but this has nothing at all to do with the challenge of ensuring that only adults would have access to its darker corners. If Mr. Justice Stevens had said simply that there probably isn't any way to keep porn off teenage screens, he'd have been persuasive—letting the case rest on that utilitarian point. We know it wasn't possible to keep liquor outside national boundaries, and every day we learn what are the sacrifices necessary to make it hard for subintelligent people to buy marijuana—moderately resourceful people have no problem.

But of course the Court had to accost the legal question, Was the Communications Decency Act constitutional? Ever since its passage in early 1996 it was expected that the Act would be shot down quickly by the courts, as indeed it was, first by the D.C. Court of Appeals, now by the Supreme Court. But the question is left open: Is this a matter of defective constitutional architecture, or do we have a circle-squaring problem? Is it simply impossible? "I don't think some members of Congress have ever read the Constitution," said Rep. Anna Eshoo of California. Her insight is interesting. But it invites the comment that if the Founding Fathers had lived in an age of Internet, they might have reworded the First Amendment.

The utilitarian argument is the one to take on, and it isn't easy. There are devices for the Internet similar to those being attempted to bar porn from television screens. One system would block twenty thousand websites, another would authorize only three thousand, and both would require weekly adjustments to compensate for the ingenuity of young porn-seekers. "Right now," comments Mariam Bell, the vice president of Enough Is Enough, an anti-pornography group, "it's like a defective condom." One might add as relevant here that any 13-year-old can go to any magazine stand or bookstore and pull up anything (I am assuming) that the Internet can give him. The public has the satisfaction of vague laws that classify movies and push television pornography up from kiddie-time to 8 P.M., mildly inconveniencing 10-year-olds. But the local VHS store makes available stuff that would have soothed the Marquis de Sade. The public will to protest the crowning of King Porn ended when the Supreme Court's decision to okay *Deep Throat* went substantially unprotested.

David Kalish of the Associated Press suggests the frustration of parents who have experienced the technical problem of diverting unwanted material. "Type in the word 'toy' on the popular AltaVista site-search engine and the second choice that blinks up isn't GI Joe or Barbie. It's the Nice N Naughty Adult Toy Store, hawking the Felicia Fantasy Doll, the Testicular Stimulator, and the Precision Power Pump."

Sex is a powerful stimulant to the curiosity and to the masturbatory human inclination. The *Washington Post*'s Rajiv Chandrasekaran and Elizabeth Corcoran write nicely on the evolution of the Internet. The fable of the sorcerer's apprentice comes to mind. But here Justice Stevens correctly remarks, however irrelevantly, that more good is going to come from the Internet than non-good. If the printing press hadn't evolved, *Mein Kampf* would have had to be hand-copied, but so too Shakespeare. The Post's story notes, "When Defense Department researchers wired together a set of university computers 31 years ago, creating a communications network that became today's global Internet, the goal was not to make something that could deliver photos from a service called . . ."—but I'll put it in Pig Latin: to discourage the kids—Iancabay's Mutsay Hacksay.

Parents who care will of course encourage and patronize the block- 7 ing devices. But in the back of their minds they will know that this fight, on this front, is lost.

QUESTIONS

1. To what statements of Justice Stevens is Buckley referring in paragraph 1? What is his objection to the argument Stevens is making?

2. What difficulties is Buckley referring to in citing the failure of Prohibition and current efforts to deny access to marijuana?

3. What is the "utilitarian point" that might better have made been? Why is the utilitarian argument difficult to answer?

4. Why might the Founding Fathers have reworded the First Amendment, given the Internet?

5. Does Buckley believe the fight to regulate the Internet is entirely lost?

SUGGESTIONS FOR WRITING

1. The movie rating system is another kind of blocking, designed in part to deny access of children and teenagers to certain kinds of movies. Describe how the system works, then comment on its effectiveness, drawing on your experience with it and observations.

2. Continue your essay, discussing whether the system goes too far or not far enough or perhaps ought to be abolished. In the course of your discussion, introduce objections that might be made to your judgments, and answer these.

GEORGE F. WILL

GEORGE F. WILL served as Washington editor of *National Review* from 1972 to 1976, and began his political column in *Newsweek* in 1975. His columns also appear in the *Washington Post* and other newspapers. In 1977 he received the Pulitzer Prize for distinguished commentary. The following essay dealing with CDA appeared in *Newsweek* on July 7, 1997.

SEX, FAT AND RESPONSIBILITY

Today's subject is sex in cyberspace, but first let's talk about fat. The two subjects have something in common, as public policy pertains to them.

Obesity is one of America's largest and worsening public health problems. A third of all adults and one quarter of all children are obese, in that they are at least 20 percent heavier than they should be. The toll obesity takes in preventable illnesses and premature deaths (300,000 a year, principally due to heart disease, stroke and cancer) is not far behind that taken by tobacco.

But political and other leaders are as reticent about obesity as they are clamorous against tobacco. Michael Fumento, whose book on the subject, "The Fat of the Land," is coming in September, says one salient difference is that obesity cannot be blamed on corporations and their advertising. If obesity is not a badge of victimhood, we lack a public vocabulary for talking about it.

Fumento, a medical journalist associated with the American Enterprise Institute, argues that the ascription of obesity to genetic predisposition is usually almost entirely mistaken. Obesity is largely the responsibility of individuals' choices concerning diet and exercise. Americans are becoming fatter because they are becoming more slothful and self-indulgent. And those attributes are no longer stigmatized and ridiculed as gauche, as smoking is. We have become less judgemental, Fumento says. Kinder and gentler, perhaps. Fatter, certainly. In any case, obesity is a voluntary problem. There is no solution other than a revival of personal responsibility.

Which brings us to sex in cyberspace, and the immunity from government regulation that it enjoys now that the Supreme Court has laid down the law about the law Congress passed last year.

When television came along, a wit said that it enabled you to view in your living room people you would not invite into your living room. Now anyone with access to the Internet is able to see things that no sensible person wants to see and every responsible adult wants children not to see. So last year Congress passed the Communications Decency Act to protect children. The district court that heard the challenge to the CDA said: "It is no exaggeration to conclude that the Internet has achieved, and continues to achieve, the most participatory marketplace of mass speech that this country—and indeed the world—has yet seen."

Last week the Supreme Court rendered its first decision about government regulation of the Internet. In perhaps the most important free speech case in the last quarter of this century, the Court declared the CDA's two principal provisions incompatible with the Constitution's speech protection.

One provision criminalized the use of a telecommunications device, such as a modem, to knowingly transmit indecent communication to an underage recipient. The other criminalized sending or displaying to anyone under age 18 a communication depicting or describing "in terms patently offensive as measured by contemporary community standards, sexual or excretory activities or organs." The Court (Justice Stevens for the Court, joined by everyone but O'Connor and Rehnquist, who concurred in the judgment in part, and dissented in part) ruled that these provisions lack the precision required when regulating the content (as distinct from the "time, place and manner") of speech.

Defenders of the CDA got nowhere trying to argue that regulating the Internet is akin to regulating radio. Radio is characterized by the scarcity of spectrums; the Internet is characterized by expansiveness. On unregulated radio, a child might encounter inappropriate material unexpectedly during a random roam across the dial. But cyberspace is defined by vastness. As Scot Powe of the University of Texas Law School writes, defenders of the CDA are right that "there is vastly more indecency on the Internet than there ever was on radio; but there is vastly more of everything on the Internet." So the real problem the CDA was supposed to deal with was a determined and technologically nimble child actively looking for the wrong stuff and knowing where to look.

And how exactly would censors administer censorship by the CDA's criteria? For example, what—where—is the pertinent "community" when assessing "community standards" in cyberspace? As O'Connor wrote, before the CDA case the Court had considered only "laws that operated in the physical world," a world of "geography and identity." But the electronic world "is no more than the interconnection of electronic pathways." And cyberspace "allows speakers and listeners to mask their identities."

However, cyberspace is malleable in its own peculiar way. It is possible to construct barriers there, making it possible to screen for identity and have arrangements analogous to zoning laws. Someday the same sort of inventive minds who have produced the Internet may produce "filtering" or "gateway" technologies that will enable parents and others to keep children out of adult "zones."

Until market demand for them produces better "blockers" to restrict children's access to the Internet, many parents will opt to keep their households off-line, perhaps comforted by the fact that Thomas Lincoln's log cabin was not wired and his son turned out all right. The government, arguing for the Court to sustain the CDA, said that protecting children was one aim but "equally important" was the aim of fostering growth of the Internet: the CDA would allow parents to be confident that it is safe to have the Internet in their homes. That is, censorship would actually stimulate free speech by encouraging expansion of the Internet marketplace of ideas. The Court swatted aside that argument as "singularly unpersuasive," not least because the growth of the Internet, indecency and all, has been "phenomenal."

For now, the Internet, although an exotic technology, is in one sense mundane. It is a redundant reminder of the law's limits in making life restful. The law can do only so much in removing the burden of living vigilantly and responsibly, for our own sake and our children's. So click off the Internet and go for a brisk walk. You look as though you could use the exercise.

QUESTIONS

1. What point is Will making about obesity in Americans? Why does he introduce the use of tobacco in the course of the discussion?

2. What is his point in connecting sex on the Internet and obesity, and where does he state it?

3. How does his discussion of the majority Supreme Court opinion and Justice O'Connor's partial dissent help to develop this point?

SUGGESTIONS FOR WRITING

1. George Will and William Buckley, Jr. commented on the June 26, 1997 Supreme Court decision shortly after it was delivered. How similar are these comments in opinion and emphasis and in their stated or implied solutions to the problem CDA was intended to remedy?

2. Government intervenes today in the manufacture and use of drugs like cocaine. Argue what in your view justifies this intervention, or what does not. In the course of your discussion, introduce one or more possible objections to your argument, and answer them.

PATRICK D. MAINES

PATRICK D. MAINES is president of the Media Institute, Washington, D.C. His article appeared in *Editor and Publisher,* on September 14, 1996, before the Supreme ruling on the Communications Decency Act. Maines considers Internet filtering within the broader framework of censorship— government censorship in particular—and its consequences.

THE NEW CENSORSHIP

There are some laws and regulations that, taken together, define the "new   1
censorship" that is all the rage these days in Washington, and perhaps in your town, as well.

You have probably heard of some of these issues, like the V-chip, the   2
TV device which its proponents claim will save children from viewing, and hence from committing violent acts.

Or, the Communications Decency Act, whose purpose is to rid the   3
Internet of indecent material that could be accessed by youngsters.

Or, maybe you've been following the fireworks as the Federal Com- 4
munications Commission's chairman attempts to hitch license renewals
to a qualified standard for "educational" children's programming.

There are four characteristics common to all these laws: 5

- They are offered as ways to protect children, who have become
  the new rationale for censorship.
- They will not, and indeed cannot, achieve their own objectives.
- They are backward-looking technologically, and as a matter of
  policy.
- They are almost certainly unconstitutional under the First
  Amendment.

Other than these things, they seem like real good ideas. 6

Take the V-chip, for instance. Here is a device that, if it is to do any- 7
thing at all, must first be activated by the set owner. But how many people will actually do this, when to do so means surrendering their personal taste to that of some anonymous ratings board? Supposedly, the
allure of this device will be especially strong in TV households with children, but one wonders.

In those households where parental concern is high, the risk of vio- 8
lent behavior is relatively low. Moreover, the parents in such households
are probably the kind of people who can distinguish between artistically
warranted and gratuitous depictions of violence—something the V-chip
will not be able to do.

In households where parental concern is low, on the other hand, 9
the risk of violent behavior is relatively high. But precisely because of
their lack of concern, it's hard to believe that large numbers of such
parents are going to attach much importance to the V-chip, even to
activate it.

Beyond the questionable assumptions about the use and effect of it, 1
the V-chip—as now mandated by law—is primitive technologically. Far
better would be a device, which the marketplace alone may well yet provide, that would allow parents to input many, including their own,
program-blocking criteria.

Nobody knows for sure, of course, what the practical impact of the
V-chip will be. But as somebody once said, there is a difference between
a lack of complete knowledge and a complete lack of knowledge.

We don't yet know everything about the V-chip, but we know
enough to predict that it will be used in only a small fraction of all TV

households, and that its impact on crime in society will be so slight as to be unmeasurable.

Almost three years ago, representatives of the broadcasting, cable, production and syndication industries gathered in Los Angeles for a "TV Violence Summit." 13

Prodded by Congress to do something, or else, the networks agreed "voluntarily" to run parental advisories before and during "excessively violent" programming. It was the hope, and the conviction, of those who agreed to run those advisories that this action would head off legislation. 14

I attended that conference, and wrote an op-ed piece that was published on the opening day in the *L.A. Times*. I'd like to quote two sentences of that piece—not to suggest that I'm the smartest kid in the class, but to make an important point: "There is (no) guarantee that critics of TV violence will be content with advisories only. . . . By bowing to congressional pressure, the networks have tacitly admitted that government can, if it so chooses, regulate television content." 15

And the rest, as they say, is history. 16

In the end, the legacy of the V-chip will not be observed in the content of programming, much less in the incidence of violent crime, but in the degree to which government establishes, as a matter of law and policy, its right to coerce speech of its liking. 17

In the meantime, those who have ridiculed the idea of a slippery slope in such matters have been proven right. There is no slippery slope. It's a cliff. 18

Another milestone in the March of the New Censors was passage this year of the so-called Communications Decency Act, or CDA. Like the V-chip, the CDA was designed to protect children—in this case from indecent words and images on the Internet. 19

The whole of the CDA betrays a woeful ignorance of what the Internet is and how it works. Without owners, managers or headquarters, the Internet is now home to perhaps 9.4 million host computers worldwide, not including the millions of personal computers that access the Internet through modems. 20

Much more importantly, compared to traditional media, such as newspapers and broadcasting, the Internet is not a forum for one-way communication, but for two-way communication. And not communication by the few to the many, but by the many to the many. 21

What all this means is that even if the Supreme Court were to uphold the constitutionality of the CDA (and the bet here is that it won't), 22 this law will not and cannot prohibit the display of material deemed "patently offensive" to a person under 18. It can't because the universe of content providers, even within this country, is just too large—while those Internet providers who are citizens of foreign countries are beyond the effective reach of the act. And it won't because adults are simply not going to countenance a legal or regulatory scheme that has the practical effect of reducing most speech to that which is suitable just for children.

The heart of the problem with the Communications Decency Act is that it attempts speaker-based blocking, whereas a better solution—and one that would not traduce the First Amendment—lies in the development and deployment of user-based blocking technology, a fair amount of which is already available.

Like lots of the "new" media before it, the interactive communications industry will probably have to earn its First Amendment stripes the old-fashioned way—by fighting for them.

Children's television is the subject of the other big dust-up initiated by the new censors. Under the zealous leadership of chairman Reed Hundt, the FCC is considering new rules, or "processing guidelines" as the euphemism goes, that would require the airing of a certain minimum number of hours and of a certain type of programming, to satisfy the Children's Television Act of 1990.

This act, which is arguably the most intrusive law in the history of television, has never been challenged in court. In large part this is because the act was written in a manner that allows broadcasters substantial discretion in the way they meet their obligations to the educational and informational needs of children.

Like his predecessors, Hundt would like to see more and better children's programs. Unlike his predecessors, Hundt displays little tolerance for roadblocks, even when those roadblocks spring straight from the Constitution.

These constitutional concerns have split the FCC right down the middle, with two of the commissioners refusing to go along with any scheme that is too inflexible or regulatory in nature.

As with the CDA and the V-chip, the Children's Television Act, even without rigid guidelines, is uninformed technologically in that it imposes obligations and sanctions on that part of the electronic media least able—as a matter of technology and commerce—to deliver the kind of programming at issue.

Contrast, for instance, the single channel and single revenue source of broadcasters with the multiple channels and dual revenue stream of cable and DBS systems, not to mention the interactive media. Which is not to say that they should be the targets of governmental mandates on children's programming.

Rather, that it just seems likely that these other media will, as a matter of course, develop educational children's programming of a sort and number that broadcasters can't match. 31

Indeed, some of the most poignant testimony on this subject at FCC hearings came from several of the most revered of children's TV programmers. Their principal concern was that broadcast TV, as a medium, demands that all programming be first and foremost entertaining, and that therefore the FCC's designs not just on children's programming but "educational" children's programming, might produce—at the point of a regulatory gun—programs that nobody watched. 32

Given the explosive growth of new media and the startling increase in entertainment and information programming, one might wonder why this new censorship has arisen at this precise moment in history. In part, I think it is because of this growth; or more precisely because of the commercial and technological turmoil that surrounds the entertainment and information industries today. This turmoil has left companies, and whole industries, vulnerable not just to the marketplace but to the coercive power of government. 33

Broadcasters, who are the target of the V-chip legislation and the Children's Television Act, are especially vulnerable right now. They are vulnerable because, though much of their programming is still among the best and most popular on TV, they need to transition from an analog to a digital standard—a task that government can make hard or easy. 34

And government overseers—from the White House to the Congress to the FCC—know this and are counting on it as leverage to win broadcast acquiescence in their schemes to advance content controls over violence and indecency. 35

Against this background, both the V-chip and the children's TV controversy look like nothing so much as a vast and continuing governmental shakedown of the broadcast industry. 36

Another reason for the new censorship appears to be a fierce and relatively new competition between Republicans and Democrats over which party is seen to be the most "family friendly." 37

For many years, the Republicans seemed to have this turf, and the censorship component especially, pretty much to themselves. In recent years, however, the Democrats have climbed aboard this politically 38 popular bandwagon, and in the process have become some of the most—if not the most—censorial people in American life.

Whatever the causes of the new censorship, thanks to an independent judiciary and the U.S. Constitution it is likely that there is still going to be time to consider a better way of advancing media excellence and the welfare of our children.

I believe that way lies in the confident embrace of two general policies: deregulation of the media and communications industries; and an absolute prohibition of governmental sway over the content they carry.

For as long as this country has existed, the cure for bad or hurtful speech has been more and better speech. Happily, the very technologies now being deployed promise a kind of abundance and diversity and excellence beyond anything we have known—provided only that we get government out of the way and give these technologies a chance.

QUESTIONS

1. What is "new" about the censorship discussed in paragraphs 1–5?

2. Why does Maines reject the V-chip as a means of protecting children? Is he prepared to accept some or total restriction? What kind of evidence does he present in making this case in paragraphs 6–12?

3. Is he arguing for unrestricted access of children to the Internet and against parental interference?

4. Why does he consider the Communications Decency Act both dangerous and ineffective? And why the Children's Television Act of 1990? Does he favor governmental regulation of any kind?

SUGGESTIONS FOR WRITING

1. These comments were originally part of a longer address to the Television Critics Association. Discuss how Maines builds his argument in light of concerns of television critics and the broadcasting industry, and highlights these concerns as the argument progresses.

2. Newspapers were once the chief source of news for most people. Radio and television brought additional sources, and so now does the Internet. Discuss on which of these media you depend for news of the day, and how effective you find each of them to be.

W I L L I A M   J .   B E N N E T T   A N D
C .   D E L O R E S   T U C K E R

WILLIAM J. BENNETT, Chairman of the National Endowment for the Humanities and Secretary of Education in the 1980s, is a codirector of Empower America and a fellow of the Heritage Foundation. C. DELORES TUCKER is a founding member of the National Women's Caucus and cofounder of the Black Women's Political Caucus, and was chairwoman of the National Political Congress of Black Women at the time their article on Wal-Mart appeared in *The New York Times* on December 9, 1996. In an earlier article Bennett and Tucker appealed to the music industry to end sponsorship of "vulgar and misogynistic lyrics that glorify violence and promote it among children." They add: [W]hile music and art can elevate and inspire, they can also debase and degrade. Not Aristotle but Timothy White of *Billboard* magazine stated that such music leads to 'the death of conscience, corruption of the spirit and ultimately the destruction of the individual and community.' We are not calling for censorship. We are both virtual absolutists on the First Amendment. Our appeal is to a sense of corporate responsibility and simple decency. There are things no one should sell." ("Lyrics from the Gutter," *New York Times,* June 2, 1995)

WAL-MART'S FREE CHOICE

There is news worth celebrating on the popular-culture front. Wal-Mart, the nation's largest retailer, has refused to stock compact disks with lyrics and cover art that it finds objectionable. If the artists and the record companies want Wal-Mart to carry their albums, they can alter the product to eliminate the offensive material. 1

Wal-Mart has a lot of clout—it accounts for 52 million of the 615 million compact disks sold in the United States each year—and it is using 2 that power to help clean up the music industry. For this the chain deserves great praise.

But Wal-Mart's stand has sent many in the artistic community into a tizzy. Some say that Wal-Mart is imposing a new form of censorship. But it is not forcing anyone to remove songs, change lyrics or alter artwork. It is simply saying that there are minimal standards a record company must meet if its compact disks are going to be sold at Wal-Mart.

In short, Wal-Mart is exercising quality control—which it does every day for every product. It is absurd to call this censorship. Such claims are akin to accusing a homeowner of censorship for keeping someone out of his house who intends to step all over the sofa and curse the in-laws. The issue cuts both ways: Gospel singers are not invited to perform at raunchy nightclubs, but the fact that they are not welcome does not mean they are being censored.

Many artists consider any change to their original work an assault on their artistic integrity. But they have a choice: Clean up your lyrics, or your product won't be sold at Wal-Mart. Some artists refuse, but they are the exception. Of course, there are those who have changed their work for financial reasons but who have the chutzpah to whine that "Wal-Mart made us do it!" This is not censorship; this is greed combined with self-righteousness.

Some have charged that Wal-Mart's policy will have a chilling effect on artists' creativity. Nina Crowley, executive director of the Massachusetts Music Industry Coalition, says that some young performers "are wondering if they are going to have to change what they do if they want to make any money." Translation: Wal-Mart is creating market pressure to elevate the quality and standards of what is being sold to children. The response from many of us is: It's about time.

Another argument from the recording companies is that they already met their responsibilities when they agreed (reluctantly) to put "parental advisory" labels on recordings that use profanity or glorify violence. Warning labels are probably better than nothing, but not much better. An analogy: If a toxic-waste dump is polluting the environment, would nearby residents be mollified if the corporate polluters agreed merely to put up a sign saying, "Danger: Toxic Waste"? Of course not.

For years, concerned parents and politicians of both parties have asked the recording industry to stop selling music with lyrics that are so vile that newspapers refuse to print them. We have appealed to simple decency and their sense of corporate responsibility. But for the most part our appeals have fallen on deaf ears. Corporations like BMG, Sony, Time Warner and MCA continue to peddle filth for profit—so we will continue to exercise our First Amendment rights to criticize them for doing so.

The controversy over Wal-Mart is a perfect illustration of the intel-   9
lectual confusion and moral obtuseness of the record companies. They still don't get it.

Questions

1. How do Bennett and Tucker answer the charge that Wal-Mart is engaging in censorship?

2. How do they answer other charges in defending Wal-Mart?

3. What assumptions or beliefs, stated or implied, underlie the argument?

Suggestions for Writing

1. State your own opinion on Wal-Mart's decision not to stock CD's they consider offensive. Explain what assumptions or beliefs govern your opinion, and why you hold them. In the course of your discussion, state what in Bennett and Tucker's defense you agree or disagree with, and why.

2. Discuss how much authority the parents of a sixteen-year-old should exercise in choices of dress or music or even friends. In the course of the discussion, answer possible objections parents or sixteen-year-olds may raise.

JOSHUA MICAH MARSHALL

JOSHUA MICAH MARSHALL, a graduate student in the Department of History at Brown University at the time of writing, examines the implications of the Supreme Court decision in *Reno* vs. *ACLU*. Marshall focuses on a project to filter content as well as products coming into the market in 1997. He turns, then, to "the unfortunate convergence between this growing power of nongovernmental censorship and the declining value of open expression as a positive social idea." The build of argument, beginning with the extended narrative or background of the issue, is a model for discussion of an important contemporary issue. Marshall's essay appeared in the January/February 1998 issue of *The American Prospect*.

WILL FREE SPEECH GET TANGLED IN THE NET?

When the Supreme Court overturned the Communications Decency Act (CDA) last summer, its decision seemed to put to rest much of the controversy over internet free speech. But there are now a host of more limited efforts afoot to prune back the range of internet content and limit access to various kinds of online material. Such technical innovations as "content filtering" and "censor-ware" make it possible for individuals, employers, internet service providers, and others to block out selected portions of the online world. While the CDA's criminal penalties for publishing "indecent" material made an easy mark for free speech advocates, these new forms of control pose more subtle and incremental threats— and should force us to confront whether keeping the government out of the censorship business will be sufficient to assure freedom online.

The new world of online media is inevitably changing the terms of debate about freedom of speech and of the press. Words, ideas, and images are being liberated from their original connection to such physical objects as books, papers, magazines, and photographs, and the costs of copying and transmitting information are dropping sharply. Just what constitutes "publishing," for instance, becomes blurred when books, articles, and even casual notes can be distributed to the entire world, instantaneously and at negligible cost. Must of the difficulty of crafting good public policy for the Internet stems from the fact that the Net removes all the incidental and often overlooked ways in which we have traditionally used physical space to segregate and restrict information. Consider the fact that *Playboy* magazine is behind the counter and not on the magazine rack at the local convenience store, or that certain subterranean activities can only be found in the seedier sections of our central cities. If these tacit ways of organizing information are to be reproduced on the Internet, they must be explicitly reconstituted. But often these barriers can only be rebuilt with meddlesome and obtrusive changes in the way the Web works.

THE PICS IS IN

Much of the debate over how to reconstitute the old barriers and regulate the flow of online information centers on "content filtering" and something called PICS (the Platform for Internet Content Selection). PICS originated in the minds of the men and women who designed the World Wide Web. While Congress was hashing out what would become the Communications Decency Act, a group of internet policy planners began to formulate a system that would allow individual users to decide what could and could not appear on their computer screens. Rather than banning information at the "sending" end, internet users would be able to block offensive material at the "receiving" end. Everybody could then carve out his or her own zone of comfort on the Internet, with just the right mix of Puritanism and prurience. It was an ingenious solution—a kinder, gentler version of the CDA. It would assuage the fears of parents, conciliate free speech advocates, and short-circuit the political argument for a broad regime of internet censorship.

The PICS project was coordinated and directed through the World Wide Web Consortium, an independent body that has taken a leading role in formalizing standards and protocols for the Web, with support from many of the biggest internet industry companies. The designers went to great lengths to make the system unobjectionable to both civil libertarians and those who wanted to limit the circulation of indecent material. In fact, their literature betrays an almost quaint sensitivity to the theory and language of multiculturalism. They designed PICS not as a set of ratings or categories but as a format for devising a variety of different ratings systems, each reflecting different cultural and political perspectives. To understand the distinction, consider the difference between a word processing format like Microsoft Word and the infinite variety of documents that one could author in that format. PICS is not a rating system; it is a format that can be used to create many different rating systems.

PICS envisions at least two basic models in which rating systems might operate. The first—and conceptually more straightforward—is self-rating. Publishers of Web sites rate their own material, alerting viewers to coarse language, nudity, or violence. Publishers would choose whether to rate their sites and, if so, what ratings system to use. PICS would also allow third-party rating. Different organizations or companies could set up "rating bureaus" that would rate sites according to their own political, cultural, or moral standards. Thus the Christian Coalition might set up its own rating bureau, as could the National Organization for Women. Individual users could then decide whether to filter material using the voluntary self-ratings or subscribe to a rating bureau that suited their personal sensibilities.

Given the obvious similarities, many have compared PICS to an internet version of the much-touted V-chip. But the V-chip analogy is only partly correct, and the differences are telling. The weight of the argument for the content filtering approach is that individuals decide what they will and will not see. But PICS-based content filtering is actually much more flexible and scalable than this standard description implies. There are many links in the information food chain separating your personal computer from the source of information. And what you see on the Internet can potentially be filtered at any of those intermediate points. You can block material at your computer, but so can libraries, your employer, your internet service provider, your university, or even—depending on where you live—your nation-state. With the V-chip you control what comes on your television set. But with PICS the choice may not be yours.

There are already a host of new software products on the market that allow this sort of "upstream" content filtering. They are being introduced widely in the workplace and, to a lesser degree, in schools and libraries. This so-called internet access management software makes possible not just filtering and blocking but also detailed monitoring of internet usage. It can monitor what *individual* users view on the Web and how long they view it. It can even compile percentages and ratios of how much viewing is work related, how much is superfluous, and how much is simply inappropriate. These less savory uses of the technology won't necessarily be used. But the opportunities for abuse are obvious and they reach far beyond issues of free speech into elemental questions of personal privacy.

The other problem with PICS is more subtle and insidious. You often do not know just what you are not seeing. Because of a perverse but seemingly inevitable logic, companies that provide content filtering or site blocking services must keep their lists hidden away as trade secrets. The logic is clear enough. The companies expend great resources rating and compiling lists of prohibited sites; to make those lists public would divest them of all their value. But whatever the rationale, this practice leads to numerous tangled situations. Public libraries that have installed site blocking software are in the position of allowing private companies to determine what can and cannot be viewed in the library. Even the librarians don't know what is blocked and what is not.

BECOMING INVISIBLE

The possible integration of search engine technology and PICS-based rating holds out the prospect of a Web where much of the material that would not appear on prime-time television just slips quietly out of view. Even more unsettling, many internet search engine companies—with a good deal of prodding from the White House—have announced plans to begin refusing to list sites that will not, or cannot, rate themselves. Again, the implications are far-reaching. With the increasing size and scope of material on the Web, most people use search engines as their gateway to finding information online. Not being listed is akin to having the phone company tell you that you are welcome to have as many phone numbers as you like but no listings in the phone book. This is one of the ways in which "voluntary" self-rating can quickly become a good deal less than voluntary. There are also bills pending before Congress that would either mandate self-rating or threaten sanctions for "mis-rating" internet content. This is the sort of creeping, indirect censorship that makes PICS so troubling.

9

One of the compensations of real-world censorship is that school boards and city councils actually have to ban unpopular books and look like fools doing it. The crudeness and heavy-handedness of the state's power to censor is always one of the civil libertarians' greatest advantages in battles over the banning and burning of books. But content filtering makes censorship quiet, unobtrusive, and thus all the more difficult to detect or counter. It is difficult to quantify just what is different about the new information technology. But the essence of it is an increasing ability to regulate the channels over which we communicate with one another and find out new information.

10

To all these criticisms the creators of PICS say simply that they and their technology are neutral. But this sort of "Hey, I just make the guns" attitude is hardly sufficient. To their credit, they also point to the more

11

positive uses of content filtering. And here they have a point. In its current form the Internet is a tangled jumble of the useful, the useless, and the moronic. PICS could help users cut through the clutter. Topic searches could become more efficient. In one oft-cited example, content filtering could allow internet searches for information about a particular medical condition that would produce only material from accredited medical organizations. Of course, the question then becomes, who accredits? There are standards of authority and discrimination we will gladly accept about information for treating breast cancer that we would never accept if the topic is, say, art or political speech. And in any case none of these potentially positive uses negate, or really even speak to, the reality of possible abuses.

THE APPEAL OF CENSORSHIP

This new debate over content filtering has sliced apart the once potent coalition of interests that banded together to defeat the Communications Decency Act. One of the striking features of the anti-CDA fight was how it lined up technologists, civil libertarians, and major corporations on the same side. What became clear in the aftermath, however, was that companies like Microsoft, Netscape, and IBM were not so much interested in free speech, as such, as they were in preventing government regulation—two very distinct concepts that we now tend too often to conflate.

In fact, the seamless and adaptable censoring that makes civil libertarians shudder is precisely what makes it so attractive to business. Businesses do not want to refight culture wars in every locale where they want to expand internet commerce. If parents from the Bible Belt are afraid that their children will find gay rights literature on the Web, they won't let them online to buy Nintendo game cartridges either. The same logic is even more persuasive when commerce crosses international borders. International internet commerce is widely seen as one of the most lucrative prospects for the internet industry, and much of that trade would take place with countries that either do not share American standards of cultural permissiveness or that routinely censor political material. Content filtering will let American companies sell goods to China over the Internet without having to worry that pro-Tibetan independence Web sites will sour the Chinese on the Internet altogether. Content filtering allows us to carve the Internet up into countless gated communities of the mind.

These concerns about "cyber-rights" can seem like overwrought digital chic—an activism for the affluent. And often enough, that is just what they are. But it is important to take a broader view. Today the Internet remains for most a weekend or evening diversion and only relatively few of us use it intensively in the workplace. But the technologies and principles that we formulate now will ripple into a future when the Internet—and its successor technologies—will be more and more tightly stitched into the fabric of everyday communication. In a world of books and print, the "Government shall make no law" formulation may be adequate. But in a world of digitized information, private power to censor may be just as deleterious as public power, and in many respects may be more so. 14

FREE EXPRESSION AT RISK

There is also an unfortunate convergence between this growing power of nongovernmental censorship and the declining value of open expression as a positive social ideal. In a political climate such as ours, which is generally hostile to government power, a subtle and perverse shift can take place in our understanding of the First Amendment and the importance of free speech. We can begin to identify the meaning of free speech simply as a restriction on governmental power and lose any sense that free speech has value on its own merits. One might say that it is the difference between free speech and free expression, the former being narrow and juridical, based largely on restrictions on government action, and the latter being a more positive belief not in the right but in the value of open expression for its own sake. We seem to be moving toward a public philosophy in which we would shudder at the thought of government censoring a particular book or idea but would be more than happy if major publishing companies colluded together to prevent the same book's publication. 15

Our political and cultural landscape is replete with examples. We see it is support for the V-chip, government's strong-arming of TV networks to adopt "voluntary" ratings, and in the increasingly fashionable tendency for political figures to shame entertainment companies into censoring themselves. The sort of public shaming of which Bill Bennett has made a career has a very good name in our society, and too few speak up against it. The move to rate television programming may well be benign or, at worst, innocuous in itself. But it points to a broader trend for government to privatize or outsource its powers of censorship. This sort 16 of industry self-regulation is said to be voluntary. But more and more often it is "voluntary" in the sense that Senator John McCain must have had in mind when he threatened to have the Federal Communications Commission consider revoking the broadcasting licenses of NBC affiliates if the network did not agree to adopt the new "voluntary" TV rating system.

The idea that there will be a great multiplicity of rating systems may also be deceptive. Despite the possibility of an infinite variety of rating systems for a multitude of different cultural perspectives, everything we know about the computer and internet industries tells us that pressures lead not toward multiplicity but toward concentration. Aside from Microsoft's various anticompetitive practices, basic structural forces in the computer and software industries make it likely that we will have one or two dominant operating systems rather than five or six. The Web browser market has followed a similar trend toward consolidation. There would likely be a greater demand for a diversity of options in the market for content filtering and site blocking services. But the larger, overarching economic pressures—and the need to create vast economies of scale—would be simply overwhelming. Effectively rating even a minute portion of the Web would be an immense undertaking. The resources required to rate the Web and constantly update those ratings could be recouped only by signing up legions of subscribers. Far more likely than the "let a hundred flowers bloom" scenario is one in which there would be a few large companies providing content filtering and site blocking services. And these would be exactly the kind of companies that would become the targets of crusading "family values" politicians trying to add new candidates to the list of material to be blocked.

THE FIRST AMENDMENT, UPDATED

The novelty of this new information technology calls on us to think and act anew. We cannot now foresee what changes in technology are coming or what unexpected implications they will have. What is clear, however, is that there is no easy translation of real-world standards of intellectual freedom into the online world. Our current conceptions of First Amendment rights are simply unequal to the task. It is easy enough to say that the First Amendment should apply to cyberspace, but crude applications of our current doctrines to the online world involve us in unexpected and dramatic expansions and contractions of intellectual freedoms and free speech. In the architecture of the new information economy, private power will have a much greater and more nimble ability to regulate and constrict the flow of information than state power will. Taking account of this will mean updating both the jurisprudence and the public philosophy of free speech rights. Much like the law of intellectual property, public policy toward free speech must undertake a basic reconsideration of the values it seeks to protect and the goals it seeks to serve.

Partly this will mean focusing more on the goals of First Amendment 19 freedoms and less on the specific and narrow mechanics of preventing government regulation of speech. It may even mean considering some informational equivalent of antitrust legislation—a body of law that would intervene, not to regulate the content, but to ensure that no private entity or single corporation gained too great a degree of control over the free flow of information. What it certainly does mean is that we must abandon that drift in public policy that allows government to outsource its power to censor under the guise of encouraging industry self-regulation. Government may not be fully able to alter some of the pernicious directions in which information technology is evolving—and it may be good that it cannot. But government can at least avoid policies that reinforce the negative tendencies. "Voluntary" industry self-regulation should really be voluntary and we should inculcate within ourselves—and particularly our policymakers—a critical awareness of the implications of new technologies. Whatever the merits of creating PICS and the infrastructure of content filtering, now that it exists we must be vigilant against potential abuses. We should make critical distinctions between the narrow but legitimate goals of content regulation—like providing mechanisms for parents to exercise control over what their children see—and the illegitimate uses to which these technologies can easily be applied.

There are many ways in which we can subtly adjust the law of in- 20 tellectual property, civil liability, and criminal law to tip the balance between more or less restrictive regimes of free speech, privacy, and individual expression. The federal government might limit the ability to claim intellectual property rights in lists of blocked sites. Such a policy would limit the profitability of commercial ventures that compiled them. We can also limit, as much as possible, internet service providers' liability for what material flows through their hardware. This would remove one of the incentives that they would have for filtering content before it reached the individual user. Yet another tack is to rethink the civil liabilities we impose on employers when rogue employees download obscene or conceivably harassing material on their computer terminals. This, again, would remove at least one of the rationales for pervasive content filtering in the workplace. Sensible public policy can be devised to safeguard the values of an open society in the information age. But too often we are letting technology lead public policy around by the nose.

What we need is a wholesale reevaluation of our collective attitudes   21
toward the meaning and value of free speech and the role it plays in our society. Though we strain mightily to avoid government censorship, there is little public commitment in our society today to a culture of free expression on its own merits. Public calls from Bill Bennett to shame media companies into "doing the right thing" are widely acclaimed. Political leaders too often take a wink-and-a-nod approach when private bodies take on the censoring role that government itself cannot. But the myopic focus on government as the singular or most significant threat to free speech rests on a basic misreading of our history. In America, the really pointed threats to free speech and free expression do not come from government. They never have. They have always come from willful majorities intent on bullying dissenters into silence. The new information technology and content filtering make that even more feasible than it has been in the past. And that is the problem.

VOCABULARY

paragraph 1: incremental
paragraph 3: Puritanism, prurience, assuage
paragraph 4: protocols
paragraph 12: conflate
paragraph 14: chic, affluent, digitized, deleterious
paragraph 15: juridical, colluded
paragraph 18: jurisprudence

QUESTIONS

1. How has online media changed the debate about freedom of speech and the press?

2. How did the World Wide Web Consortium seek to make the system unobjectionable through PICS?

3. How is "PICS-based content filtering" different from the V-chip? What possible abuse does it make possible, in contrast to the V-chip? And what possible governmental abuse does Marshall point to?

4. What possible abuse of PICS-based filtering does Marshall cite in paragraphs 9–14?

5. How do the creators of PICS-based filtering answer this charge? Does Marshall disagree entirely with their goals, given what he says in these paragraphs and later in the essay?

6. What danger does Marshall see in the attraction of content-filtering to business? Does he see the same danger in governmental mandates?

7. What threat do structural forces in the Internet industries cited in paragraph 17 present in addition?

8. What is Marshall's main concern, and where does he state it?

9. What proposals does he recommend to deal with the threats discussed? What limits must be acknowledged in taking action? What role should government and private individuals play in controlling the new technology?

SUGGESTIONS FOR WRITING

1. Discuss whether Marshall is addressing his argument to a general audience—one varying in ideas and attitudes and knowledge of current technology—or a particular audience—one holding the same ideas and much the same knowledge. Explain why you think so, citing evidence from the essay.

2. Explain how Marshall builds his argument, keeping sight of the knowledge and ideas and attitudes of his audience.

STANLEY C. BRUBAKER

In his essay on censorship, STANLEY C. BRUBAKER, Professor of Political Science at Colgate University, distinguishes two schools of thought that shaped American democracy. The "enlightened liberalism" of John Locke,

David Hume, and other seventeenth- and eighteenth-century philosophers believed government should concern itself with the welfare of the body rather than with human perfection. "Toward the soul, the state should be indifferent, or tolerant," Brubaker writes. "The ends or needs of the soul we cannot know with any degree of certainty." Classical republicanism, best represented by the ancient Greek philosophers Plato and Aristotle, believed the opposite—the concern of government is "the elevation, the ennoblement of mankind." In Brubaker's words again, "[T]he community persists and develops for the sake of the good life, that is, for human happiness, not merely the pursuit of happiness. And at the core of happiness is excellence of the soul." A third school of thought today, postmodernism, departs from the liberal and republican tradition in seeking total freedom—the human being defined "not by a soul, but by a 'self.' And the product of this self is not culture, but adversary culture."

Brubaker refers to these contrasting views in the second half of his essay, reprinted here. Though his subject is government funding of the arts, his discussion of censorship is pertinent to the debate on Internet filtering. Late in the essay, he refers to ideas of the influential nineteenth-century English poet and critic, Matthew Arnold. Culture, Arnold wrote, is "the acquainting ourselves with the best that has been known and said in the world, and thus with the history of the human spirit." The perfection that culture aims for is impossible for the individual apart from society. "The individual is required, under pain of being stunted and enfeebled in his own development if he disobeys, to carry others along with him in his march toward perfection. . . ." Brubaker's essay appeared in the Winter 1994 issue of *The Public Interest.*

In Praise of Censorship

The case for moderate censorship and support of the arts builds from the presuppositions of the American constitutional system, which are both liberal and republican, a complex synthesis of the first two schools of thought. No one can question that our constitutional system flows largely from the liberal tradition, and in fact helped shape it. With unprecedented boldness and lucidity, our Declaration of Independence set its action and the birth of the nation on the self-evident truths of natural, unalienable rights. These rights are enshrined in the Constitution's contract clause, the Bill of Rights, and the Fourteenth Amendment. Life, liberty, property, and the pursuit of happiness are essential to our constitutional tradition. Nonetheless, they provide an incomplete account of the vision that informed the Framers and our constitutional tradition, for they fail to explain the appeal of self-government, or republican government. As the Declaration itself makes clear, natural rights may be secured by many forms of government, including kingship, and it was not kingship itself that the document set itself against, but a particular king who had become a tyrant by his denial of rights.

Yet Americans would accept only a republican form of government. "No other form," Madison wrote in *The Federalist*, "would be reconcilable with the genius of the people of America; with the fundamental principles of the revolution; or with that honorable determination which animates every votary of freedom to rest all our political experiments on the capacity of mankind for self-government." Self-government, however, makes a sort of moral claim distinct from natural rights. That the American self is capable and worthy of governing itself is less a fully matured claim of the individual than a standard of public aspiration, less a matter of inherent rights than of honorable determination. Even in its modern guise, the republican ideal thus quietly echoes the classical idea of a human good; it seeks authority not just in the preservation of rights, but in the elevation of man. 2

The case for censorship in a modern republic also echoes that of classical republicanism. Oligarchies and tyrannies can be broadly indifferent toward the character of those they rule. But a republic cannot, for those whom it rules are also the rulers. Each has a stake in the character of his fellow citizens. Since the arts shape our taste and habituate our character, a republic thus cannot be indifferent to them. As Walter Berns asks rhetorically: 3

> Is it politically uninteresting whether men and women derive pleasure from performing their duties as citizens, parents, and spouses or, on the other hand, from watching their laws and customs and institutions ridiculed on the stage? Whether the passions are excited by, and the affections drawn to, what is noble or what is base? Whether the relations between men and women are depicted in terms of an eroticism wholly divorced from love and calculated to destroy the capacity for love and the institutions, such as the family, that depend on love?

That is the import of the republican tradition. But ours is a liberal republic. And the liberal tradition gives us reason to question the competence 4 and authority of government to shape the character of its citizens. Thus, any case for censorship must respect liberalism's arguments for toleration: The higher reaches of human character, or soul, cannot be known with confidence, certainly not enough to justify coercion. Freedom is so central a feature of the human good that the worth of most other goods is destroyed by the act of their coercive imposition. Attempting to impose a rigid notion of the human good is likely to cause civil strife and even warfare. The censorship that our Constitution has traditionally allowed and that I wish to defend mediates the tension between the republican concern for character and the liberal suspicion of that concern. It is a liberal form of censorship. Can this be a middle ground rather than a contradiction?

Let me make a few preliminary points. First, the liberal tradition permits a distinction between coercion and persuasion. Employing coercion for the sake of virtue at its higher reaches is a contradiction in terms, for as the tradition emphasizes, such ends can only be chosen. But persuasion leaves freedom intact, seeking only to inform it.

Second, we can affirm freedom as central to the human good and still recognize its worth as conditional. Or, in other words, we can distinguish liberty from license. We esteem freedom most highly when it is directed toward other aspects of the human good such as truth, fulfillment, or self-government. When it utterly fails to serve such ends, and serves instead only the harm or debasement of man, it ceases to compel our respect. Liberalism issues strong counsels of caution for officials attempting to distinguish liberty from license, noting it is hard at times to tell the difference and that drawing a controversial line can engender strife. But a stern counsel of caution is not an absolute principle. On occasion, the difference between liberty and license is marked, and the failure to mark a clear difference is as likely to breed decay as the attempt to act on a murky line is to breed strife.

Third, if we can distinguish liberty from license, we can distinguish morally and psychologically between preventing vice and compelling virtue. The illogic of the latter does not impugn the former. Our inability to compel a love of beauty should not prevent us from prohibiting the sale of pornography.

TWO KINDS OF CENSORSHIP

In considering censorship as permitted in our liberal republic in light of these points, we should distinguish what, for simplicity, and following the vernacular of contemporary liberalism, I joined together: true censorship, making criminal the publication and distribution of certain materials, and so-called "censorship," restricting the content of what is to be funded. Consider first the case of true censorship. Here, constitutional analysis has long recognized the distinction between liberty and license, vigorously protecting speech when it is plausibly directed toward truth, fulfillment, and self-government, and only weakly protecting it when such speech is disconnected from such ends and directed more closely to harm and debasement. As Justice Murphy observed more than fifty years ago in *Chaplinsky v. New Hampshire*:

> There are certain well-defined and narrowly limited classes of speech, the prevention and punishment of which have never been thought to raise any constitutional problem. These include the lewd and obscene, the profane, the libelous, and the insulting or 'fighting' words. . . . [S]uch utterances are not an essential part of any exposition of ideas, and are of such slight social value as a step to truth that any benefit that may be derived from them is clearly outweighed by the social interest in order and morality.

The law of obscenity is a good example. The Court has consistently ruled that obscenity stands outside of First Amendment protection, and the reason for this is found in the Court's very definition of obscenity. Material is obscene, the Court has held, if taken as a whole and judged by contemporary community standards it appeals to a "prurient interest," is "patently offensive," and fails to make a significant contribution to literature, arts, politics, or science. From the flat perspective of pure liberalism, unleavened by a republican concern with man's soul, this definition appears to contradict itself. It seems to hold that such material must simultaneously turn us on and gross us out. Liberalism's descendant, economic analysis, lacking the ability to distinguish the worth of preferences, would be similarly impatient: does the consumer want this material or not? But this rather contrived mystery vanishes from the more elevated perspective of republican government. Obscenity appeals to what is base in us, a prurient interest. In defining this as a shameful or morbid interest in sex, the Court acknowledges there are pleasures that debase us as individuals and make us unfit for self-government. Obscenity offends, patently, what is high in us. In this the Court affirms there are sensibilities that elevate us as individuals and render us fit for self-government.

The classical republican element in this is apparent. But it is also liberal. In the tension between virtue and liberty, it leans quite substantially in favor of liberty. For one thing, there is no attempt here to coerce virtue, only to curb a bit of vice. For another, the definition recognizes that something may be obscene by the first two elements of the definition (appeal to prurient interest, and patently offensive) and yet make a significant contribution to the arts. If that is the case, it is constitutionally protected.

What about restrictions on funding? In one sense this is an easier question, but it also involves a prior question. What's the constitutional basis for funding at all? The liberal tradition views with suspicion funding for the purpose of recognizing and cultivating man's soul. Further, the constitutional text itself warrants skepticism, for as noted above, its recognition of federal authority to further the "useful" arts indicates some doubt about its authority to promote the "fine" arts. Indeed, for the nation's first century and a half, it was seriously disputed whether the authority of the federal government to spend was limited to the enumerated powers of Article One, Section Eight or whether spending was permitted to advance a broader understanding of the "general welfare." Madison himself took the restricted interpretation, but the expansive understanding has of course prevailed. But if spending has not been confined to the enumerated powers, it has for the most part been limited to goods and services justified (plausibly or not) by economic arguments such as "public goods." To be sure, such arguments were put forward when federal funding of the arts was first considered. But the only plausible argument is that stated by the Eisenhower Commission on National Goals: The federal government should fund the arts, not to employ impoverished artists, or attract industry, or to win the cold war. The federal government should encourage the arts "as an expression of what is noblest in people's lives."

Liberalism remains suspicious of such a goal, but the republican element in our constitutional scheme, if strong enough to curb vice through the law of obscenity, surely is strong enough to encourage virtue through the gentle persuasion of noble example. Yet an element of coercion remains, for it is only through the extraction of tax dollars under threat of force from the citizenry that funding is possible. Thus, now as in Arnold's time, culture must prove itself worthy of public support, by providing a "criticism of life" according to "the laws of poetic truth and poetic beauty." And the standard for such criticism remains "what is noblest in people's lives," that is, the beauty of the perfected soul.

Such a rationale entails content restrictions, either by formal legisla-   13
tion or by the discerning judgment of a strong agency head. Especially
when much of the arts community remains more confident of the mission of adversary culture than culture, this means rejecting much of
what it believes merits public support. Artists have been and would
continue to be unhappy about this. But their claims of unconstitutional-
ity are extraordinarily weak. Government has broad discretion to fund
what it thinks promotes the general welfare without being therefore
obliged to fund what it thinks does not. Assuming that the project in
question falls within First Amendment protection, the artist remains free,
just not subsidized.

THE LIBERAL'S RETORT

The pure natural rights theorist will find these conclusions too lofty, out-   14
stretching the narrow purposes of the state. The classical republican will
find them too mundane. But the most bitter opposition will come from
contemporary liberalism, which consciously or unconsciously aligns itself with postmodernism in the celebration of human autonomy, though
it does so in the apparently modest guise of a right to "equal respect."
According to the legal philosopher Ronald Dworkin, for instance, government must not distribute goods and opportunities nor constrain liberty on the presumption that some ways of life are more worthy than
others. Doing so would violate an individual's right to "moral independence." Thus, while the government should subsidize the arts, its "ruling
star" should be "diversity and innovation," not "(what public officials
take to be) excellence."[1] And certainly, there should be no censorship.
Arguments of the sort I have made above violate the principle of moral
independence, for they depend on the judgement "that the attitudes about
sex displayed or nurtured in pornography are demeaning or bestial or
otherwise unsuitable to human beings of the best sort."[2] That is, they
fail to accord equal respect to the bestial and the best way of life.

Yet one must wonder whether this indiscriminate respect secures the   15
arts as well as contemporary liberalism would wish. If the question is,
what right have you to impose your value judgment on the artist, the
freedom of the artist seems secure. If no standard beyond the human will

---

[1] *A Matter of Principle* (Cambridge, MA: Harvard University Press, 1985), p. 233.
[2] Ibid., p. 354.

can justify censorship, we have no right to impose our value judgments on the artist. This is especially true, it might seem, if we follow postmodernism in thinking it is the artist who creates values for us. But if we shift the burden of proof from the censorious community to the artist, contemporary liberalism leaves the artist's case weak. Without a standard external to the human will, what makes the artist's doing as he likes superior to the community's doing as it likes? Or for that matter, what have we to say to the tyrant who wishes to do as he likes? Indeed, if we follow postmodernism, are not the tyrant and the poet simply different sorts of artists, creators working in different media? Hitler wished to create an authentic German community. Lenin wished to create a new communist man. Here in postmodernism lies the true eclipse of the soul. For by it there is no standard external to the human will; no soul by which to judge the will. The artist or the tyrant wills it, and that is sufficient. As Julius Caesar said, the reason is in the will. Only some wills are more powerful than others.

The human good, or soul, is not the enemy of freedom but the guarantor of its worth. Only if we can place reason above passion in a hierarchy of the human soul can we distinguish an argument from an aphrodisiac; on such a distinction alone can we say that real speech, and art, unlike pornography, should be protected when it offends or even causes some harm. Only if art makes life better by making us better persons can it claim exemption from the marketplace and ask for our tax dollars. And of course this means making some distinctions, that is, imposing restrictions, on the content of the art that we fund.

The soul of American politics is subtle. "[T]here is a degree of depravity in mankind which requires a certain degree of circumspection and distrust," Madison wrote in *The Federalist*. Accordingly, the Constitution was designed with separation of powers, checks and balances, and limited powers. Yet, Madison continued, "so there are other qualities in human nature which justify a certain portion of esteem and confidence. Republican government presupposes the existence of these qualities in a higher degree than any other form." While presupposing virtue, our Constitution grants only limited power for its cultivation. Subtlety should not be mistaken for dispensability, however, for self-government must in a way be soul-government, government by our better selves, if it is to maintain its dignity and authority. A liberal republic cannot avoid engaging in what William Bennett has aptly called the "architecture of the soul."

VOCABULARY

paragraph 1: lucidity
paragraph 2: votary
paragraph 3: oligarchies, eroticism
paragraph 4: coercion, mediates
paragraph 8: vernacular
paragraph 9: prurient, unleavened
paragraph 11: expansive
paragraph 14: mundane
paragraph 16: aphrodisiac

QUESTIONS

1. How does the republican view of character differ from the liberal? What is the role of government, given each of these views?

2. How does the censorship permitted by the Constitution provide a middle ground between these views? How does the law of obscenity currently in force illustrate this middle ground?

3. Why is it possible to distinguish liberty from license, and why is this distinction crucial in defending censorship?

4. Given present law and practice, what should be the policy of government in choosing what arts to fund?

5. How does Brubaker answer those who oppose oversight of any kind on the ground that it violates the "moral independence" of the artist?

6. Brubaker states that "subtlety should not be mistaken for dispensability" in regard to constitutional safeguards. What does he mean?

SUGGESTIONS FOR WRITING

1. Discuss what you think Brubaker's position would be on Internet filtering, given what he says in the essay.

2. Write a report on arguments pro and con in a continuing controversy—for example, government funding of the National Endowment for the Humanities and art exhibitions. You will find various accounts in the editorial and op-ed columns and letters to the editor of *The New York Times* and other newspapers and periodicals. Use this report as background for a statement of your own position on the issue.

LEGALIZING DRUGS

M A R K H . M O O R E

Analogies with past historical events are popular in dealing with current issues. The Munich Pact, signed by Great Britain, Germany, Italy, and France in September of 1938, is commonly cited in discussions on dealing with dictatorial regimes; but, Peter McGrath argues, "It is not at all clear that the 'lessons of Munich' are easily translated to other contexts" (*Newsweek,* October 3, 1988). To cite Munich, McGrath suggests, "is inevitably to suggest that nothing has really changed since the world of the late 1930s, that if it was proper to risk war then, it is proper to do so now." **MARK H. MOORE**, Professor of Criminal Justice at Harvard University's Kennedy School of Government, warns against another popular analogy in discussions of the current drug war. His article appeared in *The New York Times* on October 16, 1989.

ACTUALLY PROHIBITION WAS A SUCCESS

History has valuable lessons to teach policy makers but it reveals its lessons only grudgingly. Close analyses of the facts and their relevance is required lest policy makers fall victim to the persuasive power of false analogies and are misled into imprudent judgments. Just such a danger is posed by those who casually invoke the "lessons of Prohibition" to argue for the legalization of drugs.

What everyone "knows" about Prohibition is that it was a failure. It did not eliminate drinking; it did create a black market. That in turn spawned criminal syndicates and random violence. Corruption and widespread disrespect for law were incubated and, most tellingly, Prohibition was repealed only 14 years after it was enshrined in the Constitution.

The lesson drawn by commentators is that it is fruitless to allow moral- 3
ists to use criminal law to control intoxicating substances. Many now say
it is equally unwise to rely on the law to solve the nation's drug problem.

But the conventional view of Prohibition is not supported by the facts. 4

First, the regime created in 1919 by the 18th Amendment and the 5
Volstead Act, which charged the Treasury Department with enforcement
of the new restrictions, was far from all-embracing. The amendment prohibited the commercial manufacture and distribution of alcoholic bever-
ages; it did not prohibit its use, nor production for one's own consumption. Moreover, the provisions did not take effect until a year after
passage—plenty of time for people to stockpile supplies.

Second, alcohol consumption declined dramatically during Prohibi- 6
tion. Cirrhosis death rates for men were 29.5 per 100,000 in 1911 and
10.7 in 1929. Admissions to state mental hospitals for alcoholic psychosis
declined from 10.1 per 100,000 in 1919 to 4.7 in 1928.

Arrests for public drunkenness and disorderly conduct declined 7
50 percent between 1916 and 1922. For the population as a whole, the
best estimates are that consumption of alcohol declined by 30 percent to
50 percent.

Third, violent crime did not increase dramatically during Prohibition. 8
Homicide rates rose dramatically from 1900 to 1910 but remained
roughly constant during Prohibition's 14 year rule. Organized crime may
have become more visible and lurid during Prohibition, but it existed before and after.

Fourth, following the repeal of Prohibition, alcohol consumption in- 9
creased. Today, alcohol is estimated to be the cause of more than 23,000
motor vehicle deaths and is implicated in more than half of the nation's
20,000 homicides. In contrast, drugs have not yet been persuasively linked
to highway fatalities and are believed to account for 10 percent to 20
percent of homicides.

Prohibition did not end alcohol use. What is remarkable, however, 10
is that a relatively narrow political movement, relying on a relatively weak
set of statutes, succeeded in reducing, by one-third, the consumption of
a drug that had wide historical and popular sanction.

This is not to say that society was wrong to repeal Prohibition. A 11
democratic society may decide that recreational drinking is worth the
price in traffic fatalities and other consequences. But the common claim
that laws backed by morally motivated political movements cannot reduce
drug use is wrong.

Not only are the facts of Prohibition misunderstood, but the lessons are misapplied to the current situation.

The U.S. is in the early to middle stages of a potentially widespread cocaine epidemic. If the line is held now, we can prevent new users and increasing casualties. So this is exactly *not* the time to be considering a liberalization of our laws on cocaine. We need a firm stand by society against cocaine use to extend and reinforce the messages that are being learned through painful personal experience and testimony.

The real lesson of Prohibition is that society can, indeed, make a dent in the consumption of drugs through laws. There is a price to be paid for such restrictions, of course. But for drugs such as heroin and cocaine, which are dangerous but currently largely unpopular, that price is small relative to the benefits.

Vocabulary

paragraph 2: spawned, syndicates, random, incubated
paragraph 3: moralist
paragraph 6: psychosis
paragraph 8: lurid
paragraph 13: epidemic, liberalization

Questions

1. Moore warns against the "persuasive power of false analogies" in discussing legalization of drugs and other issues. What analogy is often cited in favor of legalization of drugs, and why does Moore consider it false?

2. What kind of evidence does Moore present to show that the analogy is false?

3. Does Moore believe that society was right to repeal Prohibition? How do you know?

4. What is the thesis of the essay, and where does Moore state it?

SUGGESTIONS FOR WRITING

1. Explain why, in your view, society was right or wrong to repeal Prohibition, or is right or wrong to prohibit heroin and cocaine.

2. Moore states that, contrary to popular opinion, restrictions, on alcohol and drugs can work, but "there is a price to be paid for such restrictions." Explain what price would be paid for restrictions on the use of alcohol, tobacco, or firearms. Then explain why, in your opinion, the price would or would not be too high for society to pay.

ALAN M. DERSHOWITZ

ALAN M. DERSHOWITZ, Professor of Law at Harvard University, writes about civil liberties and other contemporary issues in *The Best Defense* (1982), *Taking Liberties* (1988) *The Abuse Excuse* (1994), and *Contrary to Popular Opinion* (1992), in which the following proposal to legalize heroin appears. The call for legalization of heroin and other addictive drugs has come from many quarters, as the rate of addiction and drug-related crime has risen in the United States. Opposition to legalization is equally strong, as the statement that follows by Congressman Charles B. Rangel of New York shows.

THE CASE FOR MEDICALIZING HEROIN

When *Time* magazine has a cover story on the legalization of drugs, and when Oprah Winfrey devotes an entire show to that "unthinkable" proposition, you can be sure that this is an issue whose time has come—at least for serious discussion.

But it is difficult to get politicians to *have* a serious discussion about alternatives to our currently bankrupt approach to drug abuse. Even thinking out loud about the possibility of decriminalization is seen as being soft on drugs. And no elected official can afford to be viewed as less than ferocious and uncompromising on this issue.

Any doubts about that truism were surely allayed when Vice President Bush openly broke with his president and most important supporter over whether to try to make a deal with Panamanian strongman Manuel Noriega, whom the United States has charged with drug-trafficking.

I was one of the guests on the recent Oprah Winfrey show that debated drug decriminalization. The rhetoric and emotions ran high, as politicians and audience members competed over who could be tougher in the war against drugs.

"Call out the marines, "bomb the poppy fields," "execute the drug dealers"—these are among the "constructive" suggestions being offered to supplement the administration's simpleminded "just say no" slogan.

Proposals to medicalize, regulate, or in another way decriminalize any currently illegal drug—whether it be marijuana, cocaine, or heroin—were greeted by derision and cries of "surrender." Even politicians who *in private* recognize the virtues of decriminalization must continue to oppose it when the cameras are rolling.

That is why it is so important to outline here the politically unpopular case for an alternative approach.

Ironically, the case is easiest for the hardest drug—heroin. There can be no doubt that heroin is a horrible drug: It is highly addictive and debilitating; taken in high, or unregulated, doses, it can kill; when administered by means of shared needles, it spreads AIDS; because of its high price and addictive quality, it makes acquisitive criminals out of desperate addicts. Few would disagree that if we could rid it from the planet through the passage of a law or the invention of a plant-specific herbicide, we should do so.

But since we can neither eliminate heroin nor the demand for it, there is a powerful case for medicalizing as much of the problem as is feasible. Under this proposal, or one of its many variants, the hard-core addict would receive the option of getting his fix in a medical setting, administered by medical personnel.

The setting could be a mobile hospital van or some other facility close to where the addicts live. A doctor would determine the dosage for each addict—a maintenance dosage designed to prevent withdrawal without risking overdose. And the fix would be injected in the medical facility so the addict could not sell or barter the drug or prescription.

This will by no means solve all the problems associated with heroin addiction, but it would ameliorate some of the most serious ones. The maintained heroin addict will not immediately become a model citizen. But much of the desperation that today accounts for the victimization of innocent home-dwellers, store employees, and pedestrians—primarily in urban centers—would be eliminated, and drug-related crime would be significantly reduced.

Today's addict is simply not deterred by the law. He will get his fix by hook or by crook, or by knife or by gun, regardless of the risk. That is what heroin addiction means. Giving the desperate addict a twenty-four-hour medical alternative will save the lives of countless innocent victims of both crime and AIDS.   12

It will also save the lives of thousands of addicts who now kill themselves in drug shooting galleries by injecting impure street mixtures through AIDS-infected needles.   13

There will, of course, always be a black market for heroin, even if it were medicalized. Not every addict will accept a medically administered injection, and even some of those who do will supplement their maintenance doses with street drugs. But much of the desperate quality of the constant quest for the fix will be reduced for at least some heroin addicts. And this will have a profound impact on both the quantity and violence of inner-city crime.   14

Nor would new addicts be created by this medical approach. Only long-term adult addicts would be eligible for the program. And the expenses would be more than offset by the extraordinary savings to our society in reduced crime.   15

If this program proved successful in the context of heroin addiction, variants could be considered for other illegal drugs such as cocaine and marijuana. There is no assurance that an approach which is successful for one drug will necessarily work for others. Many of the problems are different.   16

We have already decriminalized two of the most dangerous drugs known to humankind—nicotine and alcohol. Decriminalization of these killers, which destroy more lives than all other drugs combined, has not totally eliminated the problems associated with them.   17

But we have come to realize that criminalization of nicotine and alcohol causes even more problems than it solves. The time has come to consider whether that is also true of heroin and perhaps of other drugs as well.   18

QUESTIONS

1. What reasons does Dershowitz give for legalizing heroin? Does he give these reasons equal weight?

2. How does he answer objections to legalization? Does he cite differing attitudes and concerns among those opposed?

3. To what extent does his statement of the case and answer to objections fit the pattern of the persuasive essay described on p. 513?

SUGGESTIONS FOR WRITING

1. Compare the case Dershowitz makes for legalization with that of Louis Nizer in the June 8, 1986, issue of *The New York Times,* or Frederick B. Campbell in the January 23, 1990, issue of the same newspaper, or another writer in a book or periodical. Discuss points on which they agree as well as differences in approach as well as argument: one writer may focus on addiction in children; another on addiction in adults. Comment on similarities and differences in kinds of evidence presented—personal experience, testimony of drug users, analogies, statistical studies, authoritative studies, and the like—as well as in the arguments presented.

2. Discussion of legalization in the United States sometimes centers on drug policies in Holland and other European countries. Report on several studies of drug use and addiction rates in one or more of these countries, commenting on what support these studies provide for or against legalization.

CHARLES B. RANGEL

A graduate of New York University and St. John's College of Law, Congressman CHARLES B. RANGEL has represented the 16th District of New York since 1970. Between 1976 and 1994 he was chairman of the House

Select Committee on Narcotics Abuse and Control. Representing a large metropolitan area, he has long been involved in efforts to curb drug use in city neighborhoods. His article opposing legalization of drugs appeared in *The New York Times* on May 17, 1988.

Legalize Drugs? Not On Your Life

The escalating drug crisis is beginning to take its toll on many Americans. And now growing numbers of well-intentioned officials and other opinion leaders are saying that the best way to fight drugs is to legalize them. But what they're really admitting is that they're willing to abandon a war that we have not even begun to fight.   1

For example, the newly elected and promising Mayor of Baltimore, Kurt Schmoke, at a meeting of the United States Conference of Mayors, called for a full-scale study of the feasibility of legalization. His comments could not have come at a worse time, for we are in the throes of the worst drug epidemic in our history.   2

Here we are talking about legalization, and we have yet to come up with any formal national strategy or any commitment from the Administration on fighting drugs beyond mere words. We have never fought the war on drugs like we have fought other legitimate wars—with all the forces at our command.   3

Just the thought of legalization brings up more problems and concerns than already exist.   4

Advocates of legalization should be reminded, for example, that it's not as simple as opening up a chain of friendly neighborhood pharmacies. Press them about some of the issues and questions surrounding this proposed legalization, and they never seem to have any answers. At least not any logical, well thought out ones.   5

Those who tout legalization remind me of fans sitting in the cheap seats at the ballpark. They may have played the game, and they may think they know all the rules, but from where they're sitting they can't judge the action.   6

Has anybody ever considered which narcotic and psychotropic drugs would be legalized?   7

Would we allow all drugs to become legally sold and used, or would we select the most abused few, such as cocaine, heroin and marijuana?   8

Who would administer the dosages—the state or the individual?

What quantity of drugs would each individual be allowed to get?

What about addicts: Would we not have to give them more in order to satisfy their craving, or would we give them enough to just whet their appetites?

What do we do about those who are experimenting? Do we sell them the drugs, too, and encourage them to pick up the habit?

Furthermore, will the Government establish tax-supported facilities to sell these drugs?

Would we get the supply from the same foreign countries that support our habit now, or would we create our own internal sources and "dope factories," paying people the minimum wage to churn out mounds of cocaine and bales of marijuana?

Would there be an age limit on who can purchase drugs, as exists with alcohol? What would the market price be and who would set it? Would private industry be allowed to have a stake in any of this?

What are we going to do about underage youngsters—the age group hardest hit by the crack crisis? Are we going to give them identification cards? How can we prevent adults from purchasing drugs for them?

How many people are projected to become addicts as a result of the introduction of cheaper, more available drugs sanctioned by government?

Since marijuana remains in a person's system for weeks, what would we do about pilots, railroad engineers, surgeons, police, cross-country truckers and nuclear plant employees who want to use it during off-duty hours? And what would be the effect on the health insurance industry?

Many of the problems associated with drug abuse will not go away just because of legalization. For too long we have ignored the root cause, failing to see the connection between drugs and hopelessness, helplessness and despair.

We often hear that legalization would bring an end to the bloodshed and violence that has often been associated with the illegal narcotics trade. The profit will be taken out of it, so to speak, as will be the urge to commit crime to get money to buy drugs. But what gives anybody the impression that legalization would deter many jobless and economically deprived people from resorting to crime to pay for their habits?

Even in a decriminalized atmosphere, money would still be needed to support habits. Because drugs would be cheaper and more available, people would want more and would commit more crime. Does anybody really think the black market would disappear? There would always be opportunities for those who saw profit in peddling larger quantities, or improved versions, of products that are forbidden or restricted.

Legalization would completely undermine any educational effort we 22 undertake to persuade kids about the harmful effects of drugs. Today's kids have not yet been totally lost to the drug menace, but if we legalize these substances they'll surely get the message that drugs are O.K.

Not only would our young people realize that the threat of jail and 23 punishment no longer exists. They would pick up the far more damaging message that the use of illegal narcotics does not pose a significant enough health threat for the Government to ban its use.

If we really want to do something about drug abuse, let's end this 24 nonsensical talk about legalization right now.

Let's put the pressure on our leaders to first make the drug problem 25 a priority issue on the national agenda, then let's see if we can get a coordinated national battle plan that would include the deployment of military personnel and equipment to wipe out this foreign-based national security threat. Votes by the House and more recently the Senate to involve the armed forces in the war on drugs are steps in the right direction.

Finally, let's take this legalization issue and put it where it belongs— 26 amid idle chit-chat as cocktail glasses knock together at social events.

Questions

1. In what order does Rangel ask questions about legalization of drugs in paragraphs 7–17? Does he proceed from less damaging effects to more damaging ones? Or from lesser costs to greater costs of making drugs available? Or from difficulties in making the system work to moral objections to legalization? Or does he ask questions in another order?

2. Rangel might have stated his objections in declarative sentences, for example, "Nobody has yet considered which narcotic and psychotropic drugs would be legalized." What does he gain by presenting his objections in the form of questions?

3. What shows that Rangel is addressing a general audience—readers of a large metropolitan newspaper—and not a special audience or segment of that readership? Were he addressing a city police force, what objections might he have highlighted? What if he were addressing health care and social workers?

4. Does Rangel assume that the majority of his readers are willing to consider legalization, or instead are opposed, or have not made up their minds? How do you know?

SUGGESTION FOR WRITING

The "war" against drugs, still in progress, is controversial. Some observers consider it a success; others, a failure. Compare two articles that present opposite views on an aspect of the drug war—for example, efforts by the federal government to reduce entry of drugs into the United States, cooperative efforts with foreign countries, penalties for drug possession.

31

INTERPRETATION OF EVIDENCE

In explaining your ideas or beliefs, or in debating an issue, you usually draw on personal experience and observation for illustration and evidence. And sometimes you must turn to other sources of information. Opinions need the support of facts.

In investigating an event, you may find evidence in primary sources—firsthand accounts by participants and observers—and in secondary sources—reports and interpretations by those not present. An eyewitness account is a different kind of evidence from the reconstruction of the event by a historian in later years. Though primary evidence might seem the more reliable, it may be contradictory in itself or be contradicted by other eyewitnesses. At the time of the killing of President John F. Kennedy, eyewitnesses disagreed on what they saw and heard. More than thirty years after the event, researchers continue to disagree on what evidence to consider and how to interpret the evidence they do accept.

Secondary sources are often indispensable in deciding how to use primary sources and in determining their reliability. But establishing the reliability of secondary sources can also be difficult. For evidence seldom speaks for itself, and no presentation can be totally neutral or objective, even when the writer seeks to present the evidence fairly; all interpretations are shaped by personal and cultural attitudes. In judging a secondary source, you need to consider the weight given to various kinds of evidence, and need to be alert to special circumstances or biases that limit the usefulness of the source or make it unreliable. Primary and secondary sources both are necessary in the search for facts, and both must be used with care.

I. BERNARD COHEN

A physicist and science historian, I. BERNARD COHEN is Victor S. Thomas
Professor Emeritus of the History of Science at Harvard University. His
numerous writings include *Revolution in Science* (1985), *The Newtonian
Revolution* (1987), and *Science and the Founding Fathers* (1995). In his
essay on Christopher Columbus, Cohen draws on various kinds of evidence in showing how culture and religion shaped the attitude of Columbus to the first Native Americans encountered in 1492. Later in Part V,
M. Scott Momaday and Michael Dorris discuss the fate of Native Americans in later years. Cohen's essay appeared in the December 1992 issue
of *Scientific American.*

WHAT COLUMBUS "SAW" IN 1492

This year, the 500th anniversary of Christopher Columbus's famous voyage, has been the occasion for much reflection on the true nature of the
admiral's achievement. Many writers have remarked that the "New
World" found by Columbus was actually an old world that had long
been inhabited by a culturally diverse, native civilization. It was also an
old world in a less obvious sense: Columbus's perceptions of the lands
he discovered were profoundly influenced by his intellectual and cultural preconceptions. In that way, his reactions were like those of any
person confronting the unfamiliar, whether an explorer seeking new
realms of the earth or a scientist trying to fathom the mysteries of nature. Ideas derived from the Bible, from the reports of previous adven-
turers, from mapmakers and from general lore all worked their way into
Columbus's "discoveries."

Much of the extant information about Columbus's thoughts regarding the New World is contained in two documents, a diary and a
letter. Unlike most mariners of the time, Columbus kept a regular day-
to-day record of his 1492 voyage; he may in fact have been the first sea-
farer to keep such a log. On his return to Spain, Columbus presented
the log to his patroness, Queen Isabella, who had a copy of it made for
Columbus and retained the original for herself. Although both versions
have disappeared, Bartolomé de las Casas, a historian and missionary

known as the Apostle of the Indies, made his own version of Columbus's text (part transcription, part summary), copies of which still survive. Las Casas, who was the first priest to be ordained in the New World, devoted his later life to the cause of Native Americans and preached against their enslavement.

Early in 1493, shortly after his return to Spain, Columbus wrote a   3
lengthy letter, a popular and summary version of his log. This letter was addressed to Luis de Santángel, who had helped Columbus solicit funds for his voyage, and to several others. The letter was widely read and was printed a number of times. It became the primary source of information about the first discoveries made by Columbus.

Modern readers of the two documents may be surprised by Columbus's   4
general lack of interest in details concerning the lands he had visited and by the scant attention he paid to the animals and plants there. His descriptions of locations are so laconic that additional research is often required to determine exactly where Columbus was at the time of writing. For instance, on October 12, 1492, after a 36-day journey from the Canary Islands, Columbus landed on an island he called Guanahaní (now known as San Salvador), one of the Bahama Islands. His main description is remarkably brief: "This island is very large and very flat and with many green trees and much water and a very large lake in the middle, without any mountain; and everything [so] green that it is a pleasure to look at it."

When Columbus did pay attention to details of geography, he gen-   5
erally noted only the outstanding features of the land. He also indulged in the kind of exaggeration that is the accompaniment of wonder. He wrote that Guanahaní has "a port large enough for as many ships as there are in Christendom," an overstatement comparable to Marco Polo's estimate that the shipping on the Yangtze River exceeded that on all the European waterways put together.

Columbus's observations were colored by his search for useful goods   6
to bring back to King Ferdinand and Queen Isabella, who had financed his trip. His reports therefore include mentions of gold, silver, pearls and gems. But Columbus did not recognize the greater significance of the islands he had discovered. He was seeking the kingdom of the Great Khan, the islands of Japan and the riches of India. What he found was not what he wanted to discover, so the details of the land were, in that

sense, irrelevant. In contrast, he had come across a strange new people who were not Europeans or Africans, yet neither were they Asians. The Native Americans attracted Columbus's attention all the more so because their natural beauty contradicted the possibility that he had reached a forbidden part of the earth inhabited by monsters. For these reasons, Columbus recorded in vivid detail the appearance of the natives he encountered without evincing too much concern for the land they inhabited.

Columbus's earlier reading reinforced his belief that his ocean voyage had brought him most of the way to the Far East. He made extensive marginal notes in his copy of *Imago Mundi* of Pierre d'Ailly, a 15th-century geographer. In chapter 11, Columbus writes (partly quoting and partly paraphrasing the text): "The limit of the habitable earth toward the east and the limit of the habitable earth toward the west are quite close, and in between is a small sea." This passage encouraged Columbus in his plan to sail westward from Europe to China or to the region of India.

A disregard for geographic details was common among other explorers of Columbus's time. Amerigo Vespucci, for instance, wrote exquisitely detailed accounts of the natives of South America but gave only cursory information about the land itself. Not until well into the 16th century, when the Americas came to be recognized as previously unknown continents, did explorers begin to pay full attention to the flora and fauna of the New World.

In marked contrast to his lack of concern regarding the natural aspects of the islands he visited, Columbus showed acute interest in his encounters with the people who came to be mistakenly known as Indians. As Leonardo Olschki, the Italian historian of science, observed, Columbus was "meticulous and exhaustive" in reporting the appearance of the natives, their customs and peculiarities, "even depicting their life and habits with a keen and expressive realism."

Columbus's perceptions of the Native Americans were guided by the tales of his seafaring predecessors, by Judeo-Christian mythology and by his own expectations. The books that survive from the library of Columbus include annotated copies of works by Pliny, Aeneas Sylvius (Pope Pius II), Pierre d'Ailly and Marco Polo. Polo repeatedly told of strange sights in strange lands. Nevertheless, readers of his *Milione* cannot help but be struck by his constant comparison of what he witnessed on his travels with similar beings or objects at home. He thus sought to render the unfamiliar acceptable to the mind by relating bizarre features and exotic experiences to the ordinary life of the writer and the prospective readers. Columbus behaved in much the same way.

Based on his intellectual and cultural background, Columbus might have anticipated meeting five distinct kinds of people in the course of his 1492 journey. First, if he had indeed reached the Far East, as he expected and desired, the natives would have had to be Asians. The first natives he met, the Tainu on San Salvador, were obviously not the highly civilized denizens of India, China or Japan. Columbus tried to console himself by searching for hints that he might have reached islands off the coast of Asia. 11

Second, the natives whom Columbus encountered might have been men and women of some other familiar type (Europeans, perhaps, or Africans), in which case he would have reached not the Indies but some unknown pocket of the world. Columbus's log clearly dispels such a thought. Equally unpleasant was the third, opposite possibility that he would confront a previously unrecognized race of men and women—that is, he might have reached some terra incognita. Columbus's unwillingness to admit that potentiality is well documented in his log. 12

A fourth prospect was that the newly discovered peoples would be inhabitants of an earthly paradise. One of the most enduring images associated with the Bible is the Garden of Eden, where a human couple, sublime in their nakedness, inhabited an idyllic wilderness. Columbus may well have been thinking of that image when he commented repeatedly on the surprising nakedness of the native people he confronted. Subsequent writers went much further in drawing parallels between Eden and the New World. 13

The final possibility that Columbus faced was that he might have reached one of the distant, forbidden parts of the world where monsters dwell. Tales of humanoid monsters were a common component of the travel literature and legends with which Columbus was familiar. They became an important part of Columbus's writings as well. 14

The mythical monsters known to Columbus included giants, one-eyed cyclopes and hairy men and women, as well as more exotic creatures. Amazon fighting women cut off the right breast so they could use bows and arrows more efficiently. Anthropophagi devoured human flesh and drank from human skulls. Blemmyae had heads located in their chests. Panotii were endowed with gigantic ears that they used as blankets or as 15 wings for flying. Cynocephali had human bodies but dogs' heads. Sciopods possessed a single leg and a huge foot; they would stretch on their backs and hold the foot above themselves to act as parasols.

Information about those beings appeared in many written accounts and literary works. The alleged correspondence of Alexander the Great, for example, and Pliny the Elder's *Natural History* contain early mentions of humanoid monsters. Marco Polo's *Milione* included descriptions of monstrous races. Anyone who had read about distant places could have expected that such creatures would dwell there. References to monsters were still very much in evidence in 15th-century scholarly books such as d'Ailly's *Imago Mundi* and the *Historia Rerum Ubique Gestarum* of Aeneas Sylvius, both of which were read by Columbus.

Medieval maps gave graphic expression to the ideas concerning the strange beings that appeared in the literature. The earth of the medieval cartographers included terrifying boundaries of haunted seas inhabited by loathsome creatures. The Hereford map of the world, made in the late 13th century, depicted sciopods, blemmyae and other monsters dwelling in far-off lands. Other maps, both earlier and later, offered similar visual representations. Monsters were both a source of fear and of expectations for sailors.

Columbus transcribed and summarized the information about monsters that he found in *Imago Mundi,* indicating the passages that he found most significant. In a postil to chapter 12, Columbus writes that "at these two extremities [toward the north and south] there are savages who eat human flesh; they have vile and horrible faces. The cause is the intemperate climate; because of this they have bad habits and are savage." And in his marginalia to chapter 16, entitled "The Wonders of India," Columbus notes what he might expect to see in that land: pygmies, tall Macrobians, barbarians who kill and eat their elderly relatives, women who give birth only once and produce offspring with white hair that grows dark as they age, as well as the river Ganges, near which d'Ailly locates people who live on the smell of a certain fruit.

When Columbus reached the New World, he inquired again and again about the presence of humanoid monsters. Perhaps his informants did not understand what he was asking, or perhaps they attempted to please him by telling him what he seemingly wanted to hear. Columbus recounts in his letter that he received information about people with tails, people having no hair and women living and fighting on an island devoid of men, for example.

The tales to which Columbus paid attention, and the manner in which he interpreted them, undoubtedly reflected both his expectations and his hopes. The poor communication between Columbus and the Indians (often based on just a few words and on sign language) gave him considerable leeway in imposing his own meanings on the Indians' stories. His wavering attitudes toward those stories expressed both his need to consider seriously the existence of monsters and his desire, for various practical reasons, to deny their existence. [20]

While in Cuba, on November 4, one of the Indians who had been taken on board described a place where "there were one-eyed men, and others, with snouts of dogs, who ate men." Columbus later noted that the captive Indians feared the people living on Bohío (Hispaniola) "who had one eye in their foreheads, and others whom they called cannibals." The word "cannibal" was thus introduced into Western language. Columbus judged his informants were lying; he believed the people whom they dreaded and who had captured some of them "must have been under the rule of the Great Khan." His desire to believe he was near Asia outweighed his inclination to accept the reality of the monsters. In this instance, Columbus manifested a fascinating mix of what he actually heard, what he expected to find, and what he feared to encounter. [21]

In his letter to Santángel, Columbus felt compelled to discuss the reports of monsters, if only to dismiss them as mere rumor. "In these islands I have so far found no human monstrosities, as many expected, but on the contrary the whole population is very well-formed," he wrote. He added that "as I have found no monsters, so I have had no report of any, except in an island Quaris, which is inhabited by people who are regarded in all the islands as very fierce and who eat human flesh." To prove to Ferdinand and Isabella, and to the people of Europe in general, that he had not traveled to lands inhabited by monsters, Columbus brought home to Spain some captive Indians who could display their well-formed bodies. [22]

Columbus also specified in his log that some of the inhabitants of the islands he visited were quite submissive. I cannot help but take note of this aspect of Columbus's character. Of course he lived in an age when there was as yet no general belief in human freedom and dignity. But Columbus did more than acquiesce in the standards of his age; his first thought on encountering a group of simple people was of enslaving them. Columbus referred again to the docility of the Tainu. "They bear no arms, and are all unprotected," he recorded for the information of the king and [23] queen, and are "so very cowardly that a thousand could not face three [armed Spaniards]." He concluded that "they are fit to be ordered about and made to work, to sow and do aught else that may be needed."

Such sentiments distressed Las Casas, who later wrote that "the natural, simple and kind gentleness and humble condition of the Indians, and want of protection, gave the Spaniards the insolence to hold them of little account, and to impose on them the hardest tasks they could, and to become glutted with oppression and destruction . . . the Admiral enlarged himself in speech more than he should, and what he here conceived and set forth from his lips was the beginning of the ill usage he afterwards inflicted upon them." Clearly, the ability to lead a successful expedition does not necessarily imply nobility of character. Or, as Sigmund Freud commented of Columbus, "great discoverers are not necessarily great men."

Most of the time, however, Columbus's observations of the natives were connected to his effort to understand what part of the world he had reached. He described in detail the physical characteristics of the local inhabitants in order to prove that they were not deformed and that they differed in appearance from the known European or African peoples. After his first meeting with the natives at Guanahaní, on October 12, Columbus again wrote that they "are very well-formed, with handsome bodies and very fine faces." He noted that their "hair is not kinky but straight, and coarse like horsehair." They "wear their hair short over their eyebrows, but they have a long hank in the back that they never cut."

Columbus remarked that all the people of Guanahaní were "tall people and their legs, with no exceptions, are quite straight"; none was seen to have a paunch. Their eyes, he found, "are large and very pretty." He did judge, however, that "their appearance is marred somewhat by very broad heads and foreheads, more so than I have ever seen in any other race." He later learned that this feature of their appearance came from the pressure of a board on the forehead of infants. Columbus also recorded that some of the natives had painted their faces, others their whole bodies.

During the same leg of his journey, Columbus observed that the natives' "skin is the color of Canary Islanders or of sunburned peasants, not at all black." This last attribute, like many of the others he had entered in his log, struck him as important in establishing that the island on which he had landed was not a part of Africa. He then added, "Nor should anything else be expected since this island is on an east-west line with the island of Hierro [Ferro] in the Canaries," a reference to Aristotle's theory that all forms of life at the same latitude should be identical.

Some days later, when Columbus arrived in Cuba, he observed that 28 "the people are meek and shy" and "go naked like the others"; he found them to be "without weapons and without government." He may well have been making an implicit comparison to the Garden of Eden. Just before his departure from Cuba, on November 6, Columbus made a final entry about the natives. "These people are free from evil and war," he wrote, adding that they are "not as dark as the people of the Canaries." Some observations were discreetly omitted from Columbus's log. Samuel Eliot Morison, one of the foremost biographers of Columbus, pointed out that Columbus refrained from mentioning "any sporting between the seamen and the Indian girls," whose habits were "completely promiscuous," no doubt because "his Journal was intended for the eyes of a modest Queen."

Despite Columbus's numerous statements in his log and letter about 29 the true nature of the natives he encountered, other writers continued to endow the New World with the kind of monsters that for centuries people had come to regard as inhabiting such remote lands. In 1493 Giuliano Dati made a verse adaptation of Columbus's letter, a very popular work that rapidly went through four editions. Dati then wrote two poems that may be considered sequels, the second of which described monsters supposedly found in the East Indies. The second book even presented woodcuts depicting eight of the humanoid creatures.

The force of popular tradition also is seen in a famous map of the Amer- 30 icas made in 1513 by Piri Re'îs, a Turkish cartographer who wrote about the discoveries of Columbus. The map delineated the east coast of South America with an impressive degree of accuracy. On the land, the map portrays various real creatures such as parrots and monkeys. But he also included a unicorn, a dog-headed man and even a version of a man with a head beneath his shoulders.

Other explorers continued to entertain serious thoughts that monsters 31 might reside in the New World. In 1518 Diego Velásquez de Cuéllar, the governor of Cuba, specifically told Hernán Cortés to watch for people with gigantic ears and dogs' faces. In 1522 Cortés sent back to King Charles V huge fossil bones supposed to have come from the skeletons of giants. The Amazon River was given its name by Francisco de Orellana, who believed it flowed through a region of warrior women lacking breasts and therefore resembling those described by ancient chroniclers. I suspect he mistook male Indian warriors wearing elaborate headdresses for women and therefore for Amazons.

Although Columbus did not find monsters, he did bring back news of living beings even more unexpected: the "Indians," who were unlike any known human race in their appearance and customs. The reaction of European society illustrates the human tendency to search for familiar elements in unfamiliar information; in the words of physicist J. Robert Oppenheimer, "We cannot, coming into something new, deal with it except on the basis of the familiar and the old-fashioned."

The Bible offered one source of inspiration for understanding the Native Americans. Letter-writers of the time commenting on Columbus's expedition frequently cited the nakedness of the Indians, sometimes adding details about the use of a leaf or a swath of cloth to hide the genitals. Morison remarked that the "one touch of nature that made all newsmongers kin was the naked natives, especially the women who wore nothing but a leaf." He observed that the "points in Columbus's discovery that chiefly interested people were the new things that recalled something very old, like Adam and Eve in the Garden of Eden." Morison noted that "the lack of religion among the natives, their timid and generous nature, and ignorance of lethal weapons" were characteristics that, "combined with their prelapsarian innocence, suggested to anyone with a classical education that the Golden Age still existed in far-off corners of the globe." He thus stated explicitly a theme implicit in Columbus's log.

Columbus's insistence that the people of the New World were perfectly formed, beautiful human beings had an interesting by-product. Artistic representations of Native Americans made by the next generation of explorers highlighted that perfection of form, transforming it into a positive statement rather than a mere denial. A result is that 16th- and 17th-century artists depicted Native Americans as if each one were a Greek athlete posing for the sculptor Phidias. In this sense, the earthly paradise had indeed been found.

The nature of kinship between Europeans—that is, Spaniards—and the people of the New World became a central issue in the debate over how to introduce the Native Americans to Christianity. In 1550 Las Casas argued that the Indians were fellow humans and that they should accordingly be treated with tolerance and kindness, leading up to their peaceful conversion to Christianity. Juan Ginés de Sepúlveda, canon of Salamanca and royal historian of Spain, responded that even if those creatures were "more men than beasts"—of which he was by no means certain—they were without question of an inferior sort. Their natural condition was servitude toward their Spanish conquerors, and their conversion should be effected by force, he believed.

The superior virtue of the Spaniards made them fit to rule over the Indians, Sepúlveda continued, just as was the case for the Greeks ruling over the barbarians. He characterized the Indians as showing "every kind of intemperance and wicked lust," including cannibalism. Among the Spanish virtues were "prudence, talent, magnanimity, temperance, humanity and religion"—qualities that seem rather ironic, especially given the history of the treatment of the Native Americans by the Spanish conquistadors. 36

Attitudes toward the culture of the Indians also varied considerably. The 16th-century Spanish explorers José de Acosta and Gonzalo Fernández de Oviedo y Valdés attempted to record, in a relatively sympathetic manner, the beliefs, practices and social organization of the Native Americans. At the same time, Bishop Diego de Landa of Mexico considered some of the habits and customs of the Mayans so savage and repulsive that he systematically destroyed documents recording their civilization. 37

These divergent interpretations of the people of the New World should come as no surprise. A succession of philosophers of science—most recently Thomas S. Kuhn—have convincingly demonstrated that even the ostensibly objective facts of science are to a large degree laden with theory. The history of science shows that the force of theory in interpreting experiments and observations is much like the power of preconception so abundantly evident in Columbus's accounts of the natives of the New World and in those produced by his contemporaries. 38

Columbus hoped to discover the realm of the Great Khan, and to his death he fervently believed he had done so. He knew that he might encounter monsters and heard stories that exactly fitted his concerns. Even as he began to learn something about the beliefs and customs of the Native Americans, Columbus imposed his expectations and pragmatic goals on his perceptions of them. In a real sense, the root of his achievement may have resided in the way he combined his fears and his beliefs so that, both in spite of and because of them, he not only committed grave errors but also achieved marvelous discoveries. 39

VOCABULARY

paragraph 4: laconic
paragraph 7: paraphrasing
paragraph 8: cursory, flora, fauna
paragraph 11: denizens
paragraph 12: terra incognita
paragraph 13: idyllic
paragraph 14: humanoid
paragraph 15: cyclopes, anthropophagi
paragraph 17: cartographers
paragraph 25: hank
paragraph 33: prelapsarian
paragraph 36: conquistadors
paragraph 38: ostensibly
paragraph 39: pragmatic

QUESTIONS

1. Cohen tells us that Columbus "manifested a fascinating mix of what he actually heard, what he expected to find, and what he feared to encounter" (paragraph 21). How do the various writings cited illustrate this mix?

2. How did the Bible further guide Columbus's observations?

3. How do maps of the time reveal the force of popular tradition?

4. What point is Cohen making about scientific investigation and the claim of objectivity, and how do the observations Columbus made illustrate it?

SUGGESTIONS FOR WRITING

1. Cohen concludes that "in a real sense, the root of his achievement may have resided in the way he combined his fears and his beliefs so that, both in spite of and because of them, he not only committed grave errors but also achieved marvelous discoveries." Explain how the writings support this statement.

2. Explain how a preconception you once held about a class of people—perhaps those of another country or region of your own—influenced your first contact and beginning relationship, and how your conception changed if it did.

DEBORAH TANNEN

DEBORAH TANNEN, Professor of Linguistics at Georgetown University, discusses the "talking voices" of men and women in *That's Not What I Mean* (1986), *Talking 9 to 5* (1994), and *You Just Don't Understand* (1990), from which the following excerpt is taken. Tannen shows how different conversational styles create misunderstanding and conflict. She concludes her discussion of these "asymmetries" as follows:

> We look to our closest relationships as a source of confirmation and reassurance. When those closest to us respond to events differently than we do, when they seem to see the same scene as part of a different play, when they say things that we could not imagine saying in the same circumstances, the ground on which we stand seems to tremble and our footing is suddenly unsure. Being able to understand why this happens—*why* and *how* our partners and friends, though like us in many ways, are *not* us, and different in other ways—is a crucial step toward feeling that our feet are planted on firm ground.

ASYMMETRIES

Talking about troubles is just one of many conversational tasks that women and men view differently, and that consequently cause trouble in talk between them. Another is asking for information. And this difference too is traceable to the asymmetries of status and connection.

A man and a woman were standing beside the information booth at the Washington Folk Life Festival, a sprawling complex of booths and displays, "You ask," the man was saying to the woman. "I don't ask."

Sitting in the front seat of the car beside Harold, Sybil is fuming. They have been driving around for half an hour looking for a street he is sure is close by. Sybil is angry not because Harold does not know the way, but because he insists on trying to find it himself rather than stopping and asking someone. Her anger stems from viewing his behavior through the lens of her own: If she were driving, she would have asked directions as soon as she realized she didn't know which way to go, and they'd now be comfortably ensconced in their friends' living room instead of driving in circles, as the hour gets later and later. Since asking directions does not make Sybil uncomfortable, refusing to ask makes no sense to her. But in Harold's world, driving around until he finds his way is the reasonable thing to do, since asking for help makes him uncomfortable. He's avoiding that discomfort and trying to maintain his sense of himself as a self-sufficient person.

Why do many men resist asking for directions and other kinds of information? And, it is just as reasonable to ask, why is it that many women don't? By the paradox of independence and intimacy, there are two simultaneous and different metamessages implied in asking for and giving information. Many men tend to focus on one, many women on the other.

When you offer information, the information itself is the message. But the fact that you have the information, and the person you are speaking to doesn't, also sends a metamessage of superiority. If relations are inherently hierarchical, then the one who has more information is framed as higher up on the ladder, by virtue of being more knowledgeable and competent. From this perspective, finding one's own way is an essential part of the independence that men perceive to be a prerequisite for self-respect. If self-respect is bought at the cost of a few extra minutes of travel time, it is well worth the price.

Because they are implicit, metamessages are hard to talk about. When Sybil begs to know why Harold won't just ask someone for directions, he answers in terms of the message, the information: He says there's no point in asking, because anyone he asks may not know and may give him wrong directions. This is theoretically reasonable. There are many countries, such as, for example, Mexico, where it is standard procedure for people to make up directions rather than refuse to give requested information. But this explanation frustrates Sybil, because it doesn't make sense to her. Although she realizes that someone might give faulty directions, she believes this is relatively unlikely, and surely it cannot happen every time. Even if it did happen, they would be in no worse shape than they are in now anyway.

Part of the reason for their different approaches is that Sybil be-   7
lieves that a person who doesn't know the answer will say so, because
it is easy to say, "I don't know." But Harold believes that saying "I
don't know" is humiliating, so people might well take a wild guess.
Because of their different assumptions, and the invisibility of framing,
Harold and Sybil can never get to the bottom of this difference; they
can only get more frustrated with each other. Keeping talk on the
message level is common, because it is the level we are most clearly
aware of. But it is unlikely to resolve confusion since our true motiva-
tions lie elsewhere.

To the extent that giving information, directions, or help is of use to   8
another, it reinforces bonds between people. But to the extent that it is
asymmetrical, it creates hierarchy: Insofar as giving information frames
one as the expert, superior in knowledge, and the other as uninformed,
inferior in knowledge, it is a move in the negotiation of status.

It is easy to see that there are many situations where those who give   9
information are higher in status. For example, parents explain things to
children and answer their questions, just as teachers give information to
students. An awareness of this dynamic underlies one requirement for
proper behavior at Japanese dinner entertainment, according to anthropologist Harumi Befu. In order to help the highest-status member of the
party to dominate the conversation, others at the dinner are expected to
ask him questions that they know he can answer with authority.

Because of this potential for asymmetry, some men resist receiving   10
information from others, especially women, and some women are cau-
tions about stating information that they know, especially to men. For
example, a man with whom I discussed these dynamics later told me that
my perspective clarified a comment made by his wife. They had gotten
into their car and were about to go to a destination that she knew well
but he did not know at all. Consciously resisting an impulse to just drive
off and find his own way, he began by asking his wife if she had any
advice about the best way to get there. She told him the way, then added,
"But I don't know. That's how I would go, but there might be a better
way." Her comment was a move to redress the imbalance of power created by her knowing something he didn't know. She was also saving face
in advance, in case he decided not to take her advice. Furthermore, she
was reframing her directions as "just a suggestion" rather than "giving
instructions."

"I'LL FIX IT IF IT KILLS ME"

The asymmetry implied in having and giving information is also found in having and demonstrating the skill to fix things—an orientation that we saw in men's approaches to troubles talk. To further explore the framing involved in fixing things, I will present a small encounter of my own.

Unable to remove the tiny lid that covers the battery compartment for the light meter on my camera, I took the camera to a photography store and asked for help. The camera salesman tried to unscrew the lid, first with a dime and then with a special instrument. When this failed, he declared the lid hopelessly stuck. He explained the reason (it was screwed in with the threads out of alignment) and then explained in detail how I could take pictures without a light meter by matching the light conditions to shutter settings in accordance with the chart included in rolls of film. Even though I knew there wasn't a chance in the world I would adopt his system, I listened politely, feigning interest, and assiduously wrote down his examples, based on an ASA of 100, since he got confused trying to give examples based on an ASA of 64. He further explained that this method was actually superior to using a light meter. In this way, he minimized the significance of not being able to help by freeing the battery lid; he framed himself as possessing useful knowledge and having solved my problem even though he couldn't fix my camera. This man wanted to help me—which I sincerely appreciated—but he also wanted to demonstrate that he had the information and skill required to help, even though he didn't.

There is a kind of social contract operating here. Many women not only feel comfortable seeking help, but feel honor-bound to seek it, accept it, and display gratitude in exchange. For their part, many men feel honor-bound to fulfill the request for help whether or not it is convenient for them to do so. A man told me about a time when a neighbor asked him if he could fix her car, which was intermittently stalling out. He spent more time than he could spare looking at her car, and concluded that he did not have the equipment needed to do the repair. He felt bad about not having succeeded in solving her problem. As if sensing this, she told him the next day, and the next, that her car was much better now, even though he knew he had done nothing to improve its performance. There is a balance between seeking help and showing appreciation. Women and men seem equally bound by the requirements of this arrangement: She was bound to show appreciation even though he hadn't helped, and he was bound to invest time and effort that he really couldn't spare, in trying to help.

Another example of the social contract of asking for help and show- ing appreciation occurred on a street corner in New York City. A woman emerged from the subway at Twenty-third Street and Park Avenue South, and was temporarily confused about which direction to walk in to reach Madison Avenue. She knew that Madison was west of Park, so with a little effort she could have figured out which way to go. But without planning or thinking, she asked the first person to appear before her. He replied that Madison did not come down that far south. Now, she knew this to be false. Furthermore, by this time she had oriented herself. But instead of saying, "Yes, it does," or "Never mind, I don't need your help," she found a way to play out the scene as one in which he helped her. She asked, "Which way is west?" and, on being told, replied, "Thank you. I'll just walk west." 14

From the point of view of getting directions, this encounter was ab- surd from start to finish. The woman didn't really need help, and the man wasn't in a position to give it. But getting directions really wasn't the main point. She had used the commonplace ritual of asking direc- tions of a stranger not only—and not mostly—to find her way on emerg- ing from the subway, but to reinforce her connection to the mass of peo- ple in the big city by making fleeting contact with one of them. Asking for help was simply an automatic way for her to do this. 15

"I'LL HELP YOU IF IT KILLS YOU"

Martha bought a computer and needed to learn to use it. After studying the manual and making some progress, she still had many questions, so she went to the store where she had bought it and asked for help. The man assigned to help her made her feel like the stupidest person in the world. He used technical language in explaining things, and each time she had to ask what a word meant she felt more incompetent, an im- pression reinforced by the tone of voice he used in his answer, a tone that sent the metamessage "This is obvious; everyone knows this." He ex- plained things so quickly, she couldn't possibly remember them. When she went home, she discovered she couldn't recall what he had demon- strated, even in cases where she had followed his explanation at the time. 16

Still confused, and dreading the interaction, Martha returned to the store a week later, determined to stay until she got the information she needed. But this time a woman was assigned to help her. And the experi- ence of getting help was utterly transformed. The woman avoided using 17 technical terms for the most part, and if she did use one, she asked whether Martha knew what it meant and explained simply and clearly if she didn't. When the woman answered questions, her tone never implied that everyone should know this. And when showing how to do something, she had Martha do it, rather than demonstrating while Martha watched. The different style of this "teacher" made Martha feel like a different "student": a competent rather than stupid one, not humiliated by her ignorance.

Surely not all men give information in a way that confuses and humiliates their students. There are many gifted teachers who also happen to be men. And not all women give information in a way that makes it easy for students to understand. But many women report experiences similar to Martha's, especially in dealing with computers, automobiles, and other mechanical equipment; they claim that they feel more comfortable having women explain things to them. The different meanings that giving help entails may explain why. If women are focusing on connections, they will be motivated to minimize the difference in expertise and to be as comprehensible as possible. Since their goal is to maintain the appearance of similarity and equal status, sharing knowledge helps even the score. Their tone of voice sends metamessages of support rather than disdain, although "support" itself can be experienced as condescension.

If a man focuses on the negotiation of status and feels someone must have the upper hand, he may feel more comfortable when he has it. His attunement to the fact that having more information, knowledge, or skill puts him in a one-up position comes through in his way of talking. And if sometimes men seem intentionally to explain in a way that makes what they are explaining difficult to understand, it may be because their pleasant feeling of knowing more is reinforced when the student *does not* understand. The comfortable margin of superiority diminishes with every bit of knowledge the student gains. Or it may simply be that they are more concerned with displaying their superior knowledge and skill than with making sure that the knowledge is shared.

A colleague familiar with my ideas remarked that he'd seen evidence of this difference at an academic conference. A woman delivering a paper kept stopping and asking the audience, "Are you with me so far?" My colleague surmised that her main concern seemed to be that the audience understand what she was saying. When he gave his paper, his main concern was that he not be put down by members of the audience—and as far as he could tell, a similar preoccupation was motivating the other men presenting papers as well. From this point of view, if covering one's tracks to avoid attack entails obscuring one's point, it is a price worth paying.

This is not to say that women have no desire to feel knowledgeable 21
or powerful. Indeed, the act of asking others whether they are able to
follow your argument can be seen to frame you as superior. But it seems
that having information, expertise, or skill at manipulating objects is not
the primary measure of power for most women. Rather, they feel their
power enhanced if they can be of help. Even more, if they are focusing
on connection rather than independence and self-reliance, they feel
stronger when the community is strong.

"TRUST ME"

A woman told me that she was incredulous when her husband dredged 22
up an offense from years before. She had been unable to get their VCR
to record movies aired on HBO. Her husband had looked at the VCR
and declared it incapable of performing this function. Rather than accepting his judgment, she asked their neighbor, Harry, to take a look at
it, since he had once fixed her VCR in the past. Harry's conclusion was
the same as that of her husband, who was, however, incensed that his
wife had not trusted his expertise. When he brought it up years later, the
wife exclaimed in disbelief, "You still remember that? Harry is dead!"
The incident, though insignificant to the wife, cut to the core of the husband's self-respect, because it called into question his knowledge and skill
at managing the mechanical world.

Trust in a man's skill is also at issue between Felicia and Stan, another 23
couple. Stan is angered when Felicia gasps in fear while he is driving.
"I've never had an accident!" he protests. "Why can't you trust my driving?" Felicia cannot get him to see her point of view—that she does not
distrust *his* driving in particular but is frightened of driving in general.
Most of all, she cannot understand why the small matter of involuntar-
ily sucking in her breath should spark such a strong reaction.

"BE NICE"

Having expertise and skill can reinforce both women's and men's sense 24
of themselves. But the stance of expert is more fundamental to our notion
of masculinity than to our concept of femininity. Women, according to
convention, are more inclined to be givers of praise than givers of information. That women are expected to praise is reflected in a poster that
was displayed in every United States post office branch inviting customers
to send criticism, suggestions, questions, and compliments. Three of these

four linguistic acts were represented by sketches of men; only compliments were represented by a sketch of a woman with a big smile on her face, a gesture of approval on her fingers, and a halo around her head. The halo is especially interesting. It shows that the act of complimenting frames the speaker as "nice."

Giving praise, like giving information, is also inherently asymmetrical. It too frames the speaker as one-up, in a position to judge someone else's performance. Women can also be framed as one-up by their classic helping activities as mothers, social workers, nurses, counselors, and psychologists. But in many of these roles—especially mothers and nurses—they may also be seen as doing others' bidding.

Overlapping Motivations

When acting as helpers, women and men typically perform different kinds of tasks. But even the same task can be approached with eyes on different goals, and this difference is likely to result in misjudgments of others' intentions. The end of my camera story underlines this. At a family gathering, I brought the camera to my brother-in-law, who has a reputation in the family for mechanical ability. He took it to his workshop and returned an hour and a half later, having fixed it. Delighted and grateful, I commented to his daughter, "I knew he would enjoy the challenge." "Especially," she pointed out, "when it involves helping someone." I felt then that I had mistaken his displayed concern with the mechanics of the recalcitrant battery cover as reflecting his ultimate concern. But fixing the camera was a way of showing concern for me, of helping me with his effort. If women directly offer help, my brother-in-law was indirectly offering help, through the mediation of my camera.

A colleague who heard my analysis of this experience thought I had missed an aspect of my broken-camera episode. He pointed out that many men get a sense of pleasure from fixing things because it reinforces their feeling of being in control, self-sufficient, and able to dominate the world of objects. (This is the essence of Evelyn Fox Keller's thesis that the conception of science as dominating and controlling nature is essentially masculine in spirit.) He told me of an incident in which a toy plastic merry-go-round, ordered for his little boy, arrived in pieces, having come apart during shipping. His wife gave the toy to her uncle, renowned in the family as a fixer and helper. Her uncle worked for several hours and repaired the toy—even though it was probably not worth more than a few dollars. The uncle brought this up again the next time he saw them, and said he would have stayed up all night rather than admit he couldn't put it together. My colleague was convinced that the motivation to gain dominion over the plastic object had been stronger than the motivation to help his sister and nephew, though both had been present.

Furthermore, this man pointed out that he, and many other men, take special pleasure in showing their strength over the world of objects for the benefit of attractive women, because the thanks and admiration they receive is an added source of pleasure and satisfaction. His interpretation of my revised analysis was that my niece and I, both women, would be inclined to see the helping aspect of an act as the "real" or main motive, whereas he still was inclined to see the pleasure of demonstrating skill, succeeding where the camera expert had failed, and whacking the recalcitrant battery lid into line as the main ones.   28

The element of negotiating status that characterizes many men's desire to show they are knowledgeable and skillful does not negate the connection implied in helping. These elements coexist and feed each other. But women's and men's tendencies to place different relative weights on status versus connection result in asymmetrical roles. Attuned to the metamessage of connection, many women are comfortable both receiving help and giving it, though surely there are many women who are comfortable only in the role of giver of help and support. Many men, sensitive to the dynamic of status, the need to help women, and the need to be self-reliant, are comfortable in the role of giving information and help but not in receiving it.   29

QUESTIONS

1. How do the details of paragraph 3 and the discussion of "metamessages" in paragraph 5 explain the meaning of the term? What metamessages are Harold and Sybil delivering in the incident described?

2. Why are metamessages always implicit? Why is talk on the "message level" common in marriages?

3. How do the examples given show how "asymmetry" creates "hierarchy"? What do these words mean?

4. What different kind of asymmetry Tannen experiences in the photography shop illustrate? What is the "social contract" referred to in paragraph 13, and why are men and women both bound to it?

5. How does Tannen further illustrate the same kind of asymmetry in paragraphs 14–21 and paragraphs 22 and 23?

6. What new asymmetry does she illustrate in paragraphs 24 and 25? What added one in paragraph 26? How do these paragraphs reinforce the point about asymmetry and "hierarchy" in paragraph 8?

7. What kinds of evidence does Tannen use to support her ideas? What additional kinds might further support them?

SUGGESTIONS FOR WRITING

1. Discuss how your own experience and observations support one of Tannen's ideas, or perhaps qualify or contradict it. Be as specific in your details as Tannen is.

2. Social contracts also exist between women and between men, as well as in families. Discuss one or more existing in your own relations with friends or with a brother or sister.

LEANNE G. RIVLIN

LEANNE G. RIVLIN is Professor of Environmental Psychology at the Graduate School and University Center, City University of New York. She (with M. Wolfe) is the author of *Institutional Settings in Children's Lives* (1985). Her essay on homelessness was adapted from an invited address to the Society for the Psychological Study of Social Issues, presented at the American Psychological Association meeting in August, 1985. In discussing the causes of homelessness in the early 1980s, Rivlin draws on her own research and that of other social psychologists. Her conclusions have bearing on homelessness in the new century.

A NEW LOOK AT THE HOMELESS

The problem of homelessness has escalated into a critical contemporary social issue. Repeatedly, we hear the phrase, "not since the Great Depression of the 30s" have we faced such numbers of people without stable shelter, yet the efforts to deal with this tidal wave of miseries have been limited, at best.

In the last few years it has been difficult, if not impossible, to open the daily newspaper and fail to find at least one article on the homeless. Although attention to the problem declines in mild weather, it does not disappear. Accounts of suffering and deaths, reports of insufficient and brutal shelters, and deaths on the streets are commonplace. The problem is especially grave for homeless families who are housed in sleazy hotels in the Times Square area of New York City, where streets that are crowded with tourists, pimps, prostitutes, and drug pushers are the children's playgrounds.

Other homeless persons have been observed in public transportation stations such as Grand Central Terminal and the Port Authority Bus Terminal in New York. These are the homeless who find temporary havens in public places subject to the changing policies of the public officials who administer these sites and the private individuals who manage them. Open spaces such as parks, plazas, and the entrances of public buildings uncover other homeless persons who find a temporary perch in mild weather as these locations become public hotels for the needy.

By now most of us have had some contact with the homeless, especially but not exclusively in cities. Even if we have not seen or recognized homeless persons, we are familiar with accounts of the problem. However, many may not be aware of the extensiveness of homelessness and the numbers of persons involved.

INCIDENCES OF HOMELESSNESS

Accurate statistics on homelessness are impossible to obtain since the very nature of being homeless makes people difficult to count, unless they come into contact with an official agency. According to the U.S. Department of Housing and Urban Development (1984), in the winter of 1983–1984, there were between 250,000 and 350,000 homeless per night. These statistics have been criticized as inaccurate by many, among them the research team of the Community Service Society of New York, a group that has done some landmark work on the homeless. They prefer to use an estimate of the *total numbers* of people homeless over the course of a year (Hopper and Hamburg, 1984), which might extend well beyond two million. They also raise the question of the definition of a homeless person, offering Caro's view—a person "without an address which assures them of at least the following 30 days of sleeping quarters which meet minimal health and safety standards" (Caro, 1981). While governmental guidelines are more restrictive, they are based largely on emergency needs, although a month of assured residence does not constitute the security of a home. Since many of the homeless persons today are children, especially minority children, this criterion becomes even more questionable.

Homelessness exists in many different forms and degrees based on the time period involved, the alternative shelter available, and the nature of the person's social contacts. The stereotypic "Bowery bum" is a *chronic, marginal* kind associated with alcoholism and drug abuse, with life on the street most of the day, and with just enough money for a "flop-house" bed. These people may have consistent social contacts and many have a social network or support system of persons like themselves. In some cases they form small communities of persons with similar life styles.

Another kind is *periodic* homelessness—persons who leave home when pressures become intense, leading them to the shelter or the streets, but the home is still available when the tensions subside. A form of periodic homelessness occurs when migrant workers must move with or without their families to the seasonal work that is the source of their livelihoods. This homelessness is time-limited and fairly predictable, with alternative shelter provided, however inadequate it may be. Still, it does involve periodic uprooting and temporary loss of home-based social and emotional needs.

Temporary homelessness is more time-limited than the other forms and is usually a response to a crisis that arises—a fire, hospitalization, a move from one community to another. The assumption here is that the ability to create a home has not been threatened and that once the person leaves the hospital, returns to the damaged home, or reaches a new one the home-building will continue. Their roots are damaged but not destroyed.

The most catastrophic form of homelessness may be the *total* form involving the sudden and complete loss of home and roots through natural, economic, industrial, or interpersonal disasters. Beds may be provided in city shelters, gymnasiums, or church basements, but there is no home left and the physical and psychological process of home-building must begin anew. Although the prospects for the future will differ across individuals and families, the trauma of the total devastation of social and physical supports seriously threatens the recuperative powers of the people involved. It is this group that we see increasing in catastrophically huge numbers.

SOURCES OF HOMELESSNESS

There are many assumptions as to why people are homeless, which in-   10
fluence the ways they are perceived and dealt with, ultimately shaping the policies of various levels of governmental agencies. This raises the question of how much we really know about why people are homeless.

Most people move over the course of a lifetime, sometimes volun-   11
tarily, sometimes forced by circumstances over which they have little power. In fact, statistics indicate that one in five persons in the United States moves each year. But as Peter Rossi (1980) has described it, once the realization that one must move occurs, it is followed by a search for a new home, the assessment of an alternative or alternatives, and the selection of the place. Rossi has examined what he calls an "accounting scheme" that leads to the moving process. Although the scheme acknowledges that some families have very limited opportunities—in some cases a single alternative—the homeless have less than that one choice. Given the present housing market, all but the affluent have had their options seriously reduced, although usually not totally removed.

Studies such as those of the Community Service Society of New York   12
have laid to rest many unwarranted myths about the homeless (Baxter and Hopper, 1981). One such myth is that people are homeless by choice, that they prefer a nomadic existence. Thus, the term "urban nomad" that often is applied to them. This is a dangerous view, one that can give us license *not* to address the problems that lead to homelessness and fail to search out the root causes and take appropriate measures. Very few people choose to be homeless. Most are forced into this existence by poverty, the elimination of services, fires that demolish homes, and evictions that have resulted from the difficult economic circumstances in which people are finding themselves today.

Another myth relates to family responsibility: all homeless persons   13
have relatives who should take care of them. This view shifts the burden

away from agencies and ordinary citizens, denying the needs that exist, and failing to recognize the devastation and pain that separate homeless persons from their families and friends, if, indeed, they exist.

Who are the homeless? In truth, many different kinds of persons are affected: single men and women and poor elderly who have lost their marginal housing, ex-offenders, single-parent households, runaway youths, "throwaway" youths (abandoned by their families or victims of family abuse), young people who have moved out of foster care, women escaping from domestic violence, undocumented and legal immigrants, Native Americans leaving the reservation after federal cutbacks and un-employment, alcoholics and drug abusers, ex-psychiatric patients, and the so-called "new poor," who are victims of unemployment and changes in the job market (Hopper and Hamburg, 1984). Minorities are among the most affected groups (Mercado-Llorens and West, 1985), and there is persistent evidence that the homeless are getting younger and younger (Hopper and Hamburg, 1984; Salerno, Hopper and Baxter, 1984; U.S. Department of Housing and Urban Development, 1984).

Deinstitutionalization has been accused of being the major contrib-utor to the ranks of the homeless. In fact, many assume that *most* of the homeless are formerly hospitalized mental patients since they often are quite conspicuous. But this is another myth. Again, statistics are inade-quate, but it is now estimated that the deinstitutionalized make up 20 to 30 percent of the total numbers of homeless. There is no question that emptying hospitals and failing to provide adequate back-up services led many ex-patients to the streets. Lacking the necessary skills for daily life after years of institutionalization, unable to maintain their fragile hold on housing and nourishment, many end up homeless. These victims of years of deprivation are likely to suffer in a situation where housing is costly and difficult to locate and maintain.

However, the major victims of homelessness are not ex-patients but children, who are forced to live with their families under the most desperate conditions—in overcrowded shelters or welfare hotels. In some parts of the country families searching for employment have been living in their automobiles.

On an international scale the problem of homeless children is remarkably widespread. Their numbers, estimated at 90 million in 1983, have been increasing—with a 90 percent increase anticipated for Brazil (Jupp, 1985). There are children without their families who roam the streets in many countries, but we hear most about them in South and Central America, Africa, India, Bangladesh, Thailand, and the Philippines.

A widely used typology makes the distinction among "children *on* the street," "children *of* the street," and "abandoned" children (Jupp, 1985). Children on the street, over 60 percent of the total according to Felsman (1981; 1984), are children who work on the streets while still maintaining contacts with their families. Children of the streets (over 30 percent of the group) are those living independently with occasional contacts with families. The final group, perhaps 7 percent of the total, are "throwaway" children, abandoned by their families and lacking stable long-term housing and the security of a home. 18

Basic to most homelessness, in this country and elsewhere, is the critical shortage of low-cost housing created by a combination of factors. One factor is the shrinking housing picture—each year about 2.5 million persons in this country lose the places where they live. Over half-a-million low-rental housing units are burned out, demolished, or upgraded and priced out of the market for low-income people. When this depressing loss of housing is placed against other changes—deindustrialization and loss of unskilled and semiskilled jobs, a rise in the poorly paid service economy, the feminization of poverty and persistent unemployment, reduction of benefits due to tightened eligibility requirements (Hopper and Hamburg, 1984) —a disaster scenario emerges. The single-room occupancy hotels, rooming and boarding houses, and other inexpensive, marginal housing that were used by low-income people in the past have all but disappeared, leaving few alternatives. There is little doubt that housing policies and resulting housing shortages are at the base of much of the homelessness we see. 19

Most homeless persons do try to find places to live—with families, friends, or housing offered by municipal agencies. In most cases these arrangements break down, in time, as families and friends become taxed by the additional burdens, forcing the extra members to leave. But there is no low-cost housing to turn to. Public housing has waiting lists years long. In many cities like New York, the homeless end up in shelters or hotels. Federal funds pay exorbitant monthly rates—generally well over $1,000 and often more than $2,000 for families—for a single substandard hotel room. Those going to municipal shelters find huge dormitories of hundreds of beds, impersonal service, unsanitary conditions, and threats to their person and belongings that may drive them back to the streets and total homelessness. 20

At a recent meeting on homelessness, a mother with two young chil- 21
dren described her shelter experiences—being shifted from one unfamiliar neighborhood to another while city agencies were trying to locate a
replacement for her condemned apartment. She was appalled at the dirt,
the closeness of the shelter beds, the mixture of people who, from her
view, were threats to herself and her children. Coping with her four-year-
old son's toileting needs made an ordinary activity into a major obsta-
cle, since she had been warned against letting him use the men's room
alone and the child was terrified of getting lost. It was a calamity every
time the toilet had to be used.

Other homeless persons are victims of various kinds of disasters that 22
are as painful as fires, loss of income, or gentrification. Tidal waves and
floods in Bangladesh is one such natural catastrophe, leaving thousands
in a state of homelessness. The drought in Africa created another group
of wanderers looking for food with many dying in the process, especially
the children. In some cases the disaster is far from natural: the result
of pollution, contamination, or nuclear accidents. The victims of Three
Mile Island or Buffalo Creek are no less homeless than the tidal wave
or drought survivor. So, too, the refugees of war, the boat people from
Vietnam, the thousands of Central Americans who have fled their homes
as a result of war, poverty, or political conflict are examples of the
homeless. These victims share the fate of the burned-out or evicted families in their search for a haven, although the conditions and the needs
may differ.

Although the homelessness that results from fire, floods, famine, or 2
political conditions that redefine national boundaries or wars that scatter populations can occur almost anywhere, there is evidence that in some
societies the homeless are quickly absorbed, taken in and helped by
friends, neighbors, and family. There are places and times in history where
all participate in the reconstruction of the home. However, if the catastrophe affects a large enough area, rendering all residents victims, few
resources or people may remain to provide help. The so-called "safety
net" of the present Administration in Washington has great gashes that
permit many to drop through.

We might suspect that some people are more vulnerable than oth- 2
ers for various reasons. For some, social or cultural supports may be
strong, providing resources that others lack. Clearly, those with financial
ability can find housing substitutes that are not available to the poor.
Illness can exacerbate the condition of loss of home. Minority status offers

both economic and social disadvantages in finding shelter and starting over. But we really know little about the contribution of people's past to their management of homelessness. Before decisions are made about what to do and where to direct resources, we need to know much more about homelessness.

THE HOMELESS EXISTENCE

Wherever we find the homeless their days are filled with constant battles to find places to rest or sleep, to keep clean, to find food, to be safe, to retain personal belongings, and, for some, to fill up the empty hours that stretch ahead. A woman describes the effort to find places where she can wash her hair. Men in a small voluntary shelter launder their clothing in a tiny washroom, drying garments over radiators. The hunger of the homeless is overwhelming as is their eagerness and gratitude for white bread and peanut butter, for hot coffee and oranges. The children play in huge armories around lines and lines of cots or in the plazas near welfare hotels dominated by drug pushers and alcoholics. This is the "life world" of homeless citizens: 25

> the taken-for-granted pattern and context of everyday life in which people routinely conduct their daily affairs without having to bring each gesture, behavior, and event to conscious attention. (Seamon, 1984, p. 124)

For the homeless person, little can be taken for granted: the lifeworld is threatened at the core. The struggle to satisfy the very basic needs taken for granted by most of us—for food, rest, protection from the elements, and safety—must be constantly and consciously negotiated. Life in the public shelters or welfare hotels can be as precarious and difficult as the streets. In the welfare hotels in New York, a parent must prepare meals on a limited daily food allowance in a room with no refrigerator and a single hotplate, difficult, indeed, when there are a number of persons to feed.   26

The public shelters for single persons and families are enormous barrack-like structures allowing no privacy and few comforts. The meals that are provided may be unfamiliar foods served at odd hours. The number of personal possessions that can be maintained is sorely limited since storage is non-existent and the loss of belongings persistent. These places share many of the qualities of other institutions—impersonality, routine, and lack of privacy and control (Rivlin, Bogert and Cirillo, 1981).   27

The challenges to daily life activities come from many sources—criminals who prey on the homeless, space managers who want them out of places, and others who find it uncomfortable to be around homeless persons. But the resourcefulness of many of the homeless is impressive. Some are able to "pass"—to cloak themselves in sufficiently ordinary ways so as to look like the people they are not. Others are able to find safe places for themselves, where there is warmth and some measure of security against the array of threats to their well-being.

There is also a great deal of supportiveness within homeless groups: the sharing of survival tips, of job possibilities, where to go to keep warm, as well as cigarettes, reading material, food, and clothing. It would be well to identify these strengths and build on them in the process of dealing with homelessness. There is cleverness and street-wisdom in the woman who found a place to shampoo her hair and clean herself or the man in Grand Central Terminal who converted an old wardrobe trunk into a portable earth station, neatly filled with an array of life-sustaining possessions—clothing, cleaning materials, and dishes. These are capable survivors, whose coping strategies and the competence that supports them need to be documented, rather than their weaknesses and needs alone.

ATTITUDES TOWARD THE HOMELESS

Some of the challenges faced by homeless persons come from the attitudes of those around them. Mobile people tend to be mistrusted by governments that want to count, tax, and control those living within their boundaries. Indeed, over the years there have been direct and indirect measures taken to sedentarize nomadic groups, to keep them in defined areas, often in the name of economic development. If governments have been unsympathetic toward mobile persons, there also is a long history of mixed reactions toward all kinds of strangers, especially destitute ones. Homeless strangers have been the object of pity, charity, and hospitality, but they also have been feared, rejected, and abused.

In literature the stranger is often the subject of suspicion, at the very least. The Torah speaks of the "ger" (resident strangers), non-Israelites who were unable to rely on their tribes for protection (Union of American Hebrew Congregations, 1981). The kindness that was extended to these strangers derived from the Biblical injunction "You shall not wrong a stranger or oppress him for you were strangers in the land of Egypt" (Exodus 22,20). These were not homeless persons, in the sense that we have today. Our homeless were made strangers by their loss of permanent shelter and community connections. However, the concept of "resident stranger" is a useful one.

In many ways homeless people have become "resident strangers," people who have lost their roles within society, along with their homes. Evidence for this can be found in the generic term "homeless": an undifferentiated form rather than mothers, children, fathers, sons, and daughters whose misfortunes and society's failures have led them to the streets, the welfare hotels, or the shelters. The label serves to obscure their heterogeneity. By depersonalizing them, the impact of their plight is blunted; we distance them from our own lives and fail to address the serious and complex social problems that have produced them in the numbers we see today. It is critical that the psychological, economic, and political dimensions of homelessness be understood and that the distorted, romantic, and inaccurate images of homeless life be disabused.   32

The current social context becomes apparent when we look *historically* at homelessness and how it defines a relationship between people and environments. There has been a long history of prejudice toward strangers, mobile people, and the poor. The most prevalent homeless persons were paupers, a term that included the indigent, sick or aged, widows and orphans, and also the insane. For example, in colonial times there was concern with the financial consequences of "all adverse conditions, not their idiosyncratic attributes" (Rothman, 1971, p. 5). Although there was some concern for "needy neighbors" there was none for "needy outsiders" (Rothman, 1971). The bases for these attitudes were the religious and social traditions of the colonists that reflected, in part, their English heritage. Almshouses and workhouses for the most "suspect" among the poor, a model adapted from English forms, along with various benevolent societies, became the means of dealing with poverty. The presence of the poor was seen as a way for people "to do good" (Rothman, 1971).   33

Paupers were some of this country's earliest homeless citizens and seen from afar the manner of dealing with them may seem to reflect different policies than we have today. However, there are some uncomfortable similarities in the generalizing, the victimization of children, and the ambivalence reflected in the attitudes of the community.   34

Today, our most powerful images of homelessness come from the media with their emphasis on the most visible homeless—usually the mentally disturbed—and from stereotypes of homeless life—gypsies,   35 hoboes, and bag ladies, people who have been portrayed either as vagabonds with carefree lives or secret millionaires hoarding and hiding their affluence. But the homeless also have been greeted with suspicion and contempt and viewed as non-persons since they defy the largely middle-class moral order of the city, a moral order that frequently views homelessness as vagrancy (Duncan, 1975).

In his study of hoboes the British writer Kenneth Allsop (1967) looked for an explanation of mobility in this country and found considerable ambivalence in our attitudes. "My starting point was not the belief that mobility is unique to America, only that America has a unique kind of mobility." He goes on to a broad, admittedly risky generalization:

> To the European impermanence and change are bad, restlessness reveals the flaw of instability; whereas to an American restlessness is pandemic; entrenchment means fossilization, a poor spirit. (Allsop, 1967, p. 31)

He sees a prizing of "fluidity," mobile executives (as Toffler would later describe them in *Future Shock,* 1970) and millions on the road in automobiles, vans, trailers, and campers, using supermarket plazas, malls, drive-in banks, fast-food and open-air restaurants. Allsop suggests that there is a certain amount of official support for this migratory style especially for unemployed workers.

> Mobility is unarguably an indispensable component in an economy of the American character and in a nation of America's size, and so is justifiably prized and commended. But the idea itself has come to be qualified by a cluster of subordinate clauses. Mobility with money is, of course, laudable and desirable—you are then a tourist or envoy of business. Mobility between firms and cities is proof of a professional man's initiative and ambition. Mobility is also proof of a workless working man's grit, of his determination to hunt down the breach in the wall and find readmission to the commonwealth. Finally, mobility without these objectives or rationalizations—therefore, mobility for its own feckless sake—must be held to be bad, for it is the act of a renegade and puts in jeopardy the American declaration of intent. (Allsop, 1967, p. 436)

Although there is ambivalence about mobility, in fact, we know little about specific attitudes toward homeless persons. It is clear, however, that people are not happy about having shelters in their neighborhoods. Public shelters tend to be concentrated in marginal areas, places where local residents have little political influence or the organization to resist.

A *Newsweek* article on the homeless in Arizona describes one kind   37
of local resistance that seems to be working (Alter, 1984). A "fight back"
campaign mounted by Phoenix community leaders to "wipe out the
'unacceptable behavior' of the area's 1,500 street-people" features an ad
campaign that has an illustration of a man on a bench, sleeping. A red
line is "drawn through it like an international traffic sign." Intended to
discourage "outsiders" and abolish soup kitchens and other homeless
hangouts, the effort to maintain an image of a clean and conventional
community persists even as homelessness increases in the Southwest.

SIGNIFICANCE OF HOMELESSNESS

What does it mean to be homeless? On a practical level it means loss of   38
the right to vote, to receive regular social services, to maintain contacts
through mail and telephone. It includes loss of roles, loss of being a neighbor and having neighbors, of hosting visitors, of being a worker, a
provider of shelter and nurturance. The homeless are perpetual guests
and often unwelcome ones.

Loss of a home must be considered one of life's most profound trau-   39
mas (Dohrenwend and Dohrenwend, 1974; Marris, 1975). Although residential mobility often is a response to stress (Shumaker and Stokols,
1982), it also is a producer of stress even when the decision to relocate
is a voluntary one and a sign of upward mobility (Rossi, 1980). The slum
clearance projects of the 50s and 60s have left us with vivid descriptions
of "grieving for a lost home" (Fried, 1963), after the destruction of a
neighborhood for urban renewal.

A home may be viewed as a slum by city officials and urban plan-   40
ners, but it is a place rich with social connections, familiar people, and
deep personal meanings. When the uprooted residents of the West End
of Boston were interviewed, the sadness that they felt for the loss of their
old homes, and neighborhood was of major proportions. In fact, half of
the 566 men and women studied described severe depression or other
disturbances ("It was like a piece being taken from me." "Something of
me went with the West End").

This pattern also has been documented by Michael Young and   41
Peter Willmott for the relocation of families from the East End of
London (1957; 1966), by Marris for Lagos, Nigeria (Marris, 1961;
1975), and Kai Erikson (1976) for the Buffalo Creek Dam disaster. In
some cases grief can result from local changes that render a home

geography unfamiliar. Nora Rubinstein's (1983) study of the Pine Barrens of New Jersey, a semi-rural area near Atlantic City, identified people deeply troubled by changes happening around them. A number of residents could make enormous profits from the sale of their homes and property, but for many the transformation of the area is a painful reminder of a lost past and, most of all, their own limited power to control their immediate environment. Although the grief over the loss of a home and neighborhood, or profound changes to it, may subside over time and be replaced by attachment to the new setting (Willmott, 1963), it is useful to ask why the deep emotion over places exists and how it develops.

We are accustomed to discussions of attachment to people—parents, families, friends—or even attachment to pets. In fact, the developmental literature from infancy through the later years defines growth largely in terms of social experiences. We are less likely to find the context, or setting, of this growth the subject of serious concern, although this is changing (Rivlin and Wolfe, 1985). The recognition that settings and objects within them are components of growth and development, in interactive participation with social experiences, provides a good deal of the answer of why people grieve for lost places and why homelessness is so profoundly painful. As we explore the meaning of home to people, we are learning about the attachments to place and the significance of change and loss (Marris, 1975). 42

We are beginning to appreciate the contribution of environmental experiences to a person's identity (Proshansky, Fabian and Kaminoff, 1983), the power of enduring memories of home, and their effects on both the course of development and on the ability to make a home (see, for example, Cooper Marcus, 1978a; b; Hester, 1978; Horwitz and Klein, 1978; Horwitz and Tognoli, 1982; Rowles, 1978; 1980; 1981). The restorative qualities of a home as "a place to rest, whose familiarity and security permit the person to recuperate for future ventures away from home" (Seamon, 1984, p. 758) are being recognized. These are affective ties to place that the geographer Yi-Fu Tuan has described as *topophilia*, "love of place" (Tuan, 1974), giving people a sense of roots and a feeling of security (Tuan, 1980). 43

It is essential to question the impact of a homeless experience for anyone, but especially for children. Robert Coles (1970) has provided some powerful descriptions of periodic homelessness in the lives of migrant farm workers' children. Whether by accident, poverty, or corruption, 44 large numbers of urban children today lack permanent homes, live in temporary shelters and hotel rooms, in neighborhoods ill-equipped to support healthy childhood activities. Their education often is interrupted until emergency arrangements can be set up. In New York City, school buses now circulate among the welfare hotels and shelters, transporting children to schools. But it took a long time to set this system in place, and few children receive continuous schooling.

There is recent evidence that homelessness has serious consequences 45 for children. Some preliminary data from a study conducted by Dr. Ellen Bassuk, of Harvard University Medical School, found that 78 children (from 51 families) living in shelters had signs of anxiety, severe depression, and serious developmental lags (Bassuk, 1985). Some of the symptoms were severe enough to be considered a state of "acute psychiatric crisis." Emotional difficulties were only part of the problems—there were physical and learning disabilities, as well.

Attachments to place are strongest when large portions of a person's 46 life are laid down in an area (Rivlin, 1982). This occurs when a person resides in an area over an extended time and when a person uses the area for purposes central to life—working, shopping, raising children, playing, socializing, and attending religious services. The greater the *number* of domains of life that take place in an area and the more concentrated these domains are within an area, "the deeper the roots are likely to be in the place" (Rivlin, 1982, p. 89). Although it might be argued that the quality of life today does not encourage the development of roots, that people move widely over their geographies with few deep connections to place, the impact of each setting and the enduring memories of home that parallel these experiences must be acknowledged. Home as an ideal image or a real place acts to anchor, shelter, and personally define an individual to herself or himself.

Rootedness and place attachment do not depend on the quality of a 47 place, its amenities, its services, or the housing stock. Rootedness can occur in places defined as slums, as well as in modest and affluent areas. Although victims of urban homelessness are likely to come from poorer areas, their roots and attachments are as strong and their losses no less painful than victims of floods and fires. The young, disabled, and elderly are particularly vulnerable. For them uprooting means loss of familiar objects, possessions, people, and places and the need to adjust to a series of alternatives under difficult conditions over which they have little or no control.

CONCLUSION

Homelessness takes many forms, in terms of chronic, temporary, peri-   48
odic, and total types. They involve people who may be victims of poverty,
many of them ill, or old, or very young, some alcoholic or with severe
psychological problems. These are people caught in a reality in which
programs developed to enable them to survive intact in their homes have
been systematically dismantled by the current Administration, widening
the possibility of who can become homeless. Homelessness itself creates
a plethora of problems and personal risks, not the least of which is a
severe threat to the person's identity and sense of self.

We can do something about this epidemic in personal, political, and   49
professional ways and we must do it soon, before the homeless become
resigned to their state and other people become desensitized to the problems. We can identify the ecology of homelessness, how it happens, the
series of stages that exist in the progress to the streets, in order to catch
the problem before it escalates. We also need to know what happens to
these people over time and determine how many are able to escape from
the shelters, hotels, and streets and re-establish themselves. We can help
to define the varied needs of the different types of homeless persons—
for housing, food, jobs, vocational training. We can recognize their
capabilities and provide resources for self-help efforts wherever possible.
We need to document coping strategies and competence, not just pathology. Most critically, we must recognize the most threatened among the
group—the children.

We must work with communities to have them accept shelters and   50
other housing for the homeless, politic for affordable housing, and edu-
cate the public about the enormity of the problem. We have had emergency measures for dealing with acute homeless situations for some time.
The Red Cross and Salvation Army have long histories of stepping in and
offering assistance to victims of floods, fires, and the like. But there is a
totally different condition today: an enormous pool of homeless persons
largely created by contemporary social policies. We require new policies
to deal with these numbers.

Temporary shelters are a small move toward resolving the problem   5
of homeless people. But unless people consider other alternatives to
accommodate the homeless within their neighborhoods, we will end up
with enormous shelter-institutions removed from communities and more
and more families in hotels. Action research is needed to work with

communities toward accepting diversity within their boundaries and to work with the homeless to provide housing and services.

In the end the images of homeless individuals, particularly people that we see or read about, provide the strongest motivation to do something. I am reminded of a character in *The Street,* a novel by Israel Rabon, published in 1928 but recently translated from the Yiddish language. It describes the experiences of a veteran of World War I, a man without family who goes to the city of Lodz in Poland when discharged and ends up penniless and on the street. There is a brief passage that is the essence of the homeless experience:

> In the several weeks since I had been hanging around town, I had become acquainted with—and made only too much use of—the places where one could hope to get in out of the rain, or where one might run into somebody one knew. In the waiting rooms of the town's two train stations I was already well known as a bad penny. To the women who kept the buffet counters and to the people at the newspaper kiosks, I was a suspicious character. I did not leave those places because anyone threatened me in any way but because I felt myself overwhelmed by pity—self-pity.
>
> How could a healthy, vigorous person like me be down and out?
>
> In those weeks of knocking about in Lodz, I had grown accustomed to the pathetic silence of my life. I felt my soul being swallowed up in the rhythms of idleness, of futility. There is something about wandering the strange streets of a large industrial city, trying to warm oneself by the light of a chilly sun, turning weaker and weaker with hunger—there is something in all this that separates, alienates one from the entire world.

Our efforts now must be directed toward preventing this alienation, and the bitter loss that goes with it.

REFERENCES

K. Allsop, *Hard Travellin': The Hobo and His History* (New York: The New American Library, 1967).

J. Alter, "Homeless in America," *Newsweek* (Jan. 2, 1984), pp. 20–28.

E. L. Bassuk, *The Feminization of Homelessness: Homeless Families in Boston's Shelters.* Keynote address at the yearly benefit of Shelter, Inc. Cambridge, MA (July 11, 1985).

E. Baxter, and K. Hopper, *Private Lives/Public Spaces* (New York: Community Service Society of New York, 1981).

F. Caro, *Estimating Numbers of Homeless Families* (New York: Community Service Society of New York, 1981).

R. Coles, *Uprooted Children: The Early Life of Migrant Farmworkers* (Pittsburgh: University of Pittsburgh Press, 1970).

C. Cooper Marcus, "Remembrance of Landscapes Past," *Landscape*, Vol. 22, No. 3 (1978), pp. 34–43.

———, "Environmental Autobiography," *Childhood City Newsletter* (Dec. 1978), pp. 3–5.

B. P. Dohrenwend, and B. S. Dohrenwend, *Stressful Life Events: Their Nature and Effects* (New York: John Wiley, 1974).

J. S. Duncan, *Men Without Property: The Tramp's Classification and Uses of Urban Space.* Unpublished manuscript, Syracuse University, Department of Geography (1975).

K. T. Erikson, *Everything in Its Path* (New York: Simon and Schuster, 1976).

J. K. Felsman, "Street Urchins of Colombia," *Natural History* (April 1981).

———, "Abandoned Children: A Reconsideration," *Children Today* (May–June 1984), pp. 13–18.

M. Fried, "Grieving for a Lost Home," in L. J. Duhl (ed.), *The Urban Condition* (New York: Basic Books, 1963).

R. Hester, "Favorite Spaces," *Childhood City Newsletter* (Dec. 1978), pp. 15–17.

K. Hopper, and J. Hamburg, *The Making of America's Homeless: From Skid Row to New Poor* (New York: Community Service Society of New York, 1984).

J. Horwitz, and S. Klein, "An Exercise in the Use of Environmental Autobiography for Programming and Design of a Day Care Center," *Childhood City Newsletter* (Dec. 1984), pp. 18–19.

J. Horwitz, and J. Tognoli, "The Role of Home in Adult Development," *Journal of Family Relations* (July 1982), pp. 134–140.

M. Jupp, "From Needs to Rights: Abandoned/Street Children," *Ideas Forum* (1985).

P. Marris, *Family and Social Change in an African City* (London: Routledge & Kegan Paul, 1961).

———, *Loss and Changes* (Garden City, NY: Anchor Books, 1975).

S. Mercado-Llorens, and S. L. West, "The New Grapes of Wrath: Hispanic Homelessness in the Urban Highland," *U.S. Hispanic Affairs Magazine* (Summer 1985).

H. M. Proshansky, A. K. Fabian, and R. Kaminoff, "Place Identity: Physical World Socialization of the Self," *Journal of Environmental Psychology* (1983), pp. 57–83.

I. Rabon, *The Street* (New York: Schocken, 1985).

L. G. Rivlin, "Group Membership and Place Meanings in an Urban Neighborhood," *Journal of Social Issues*, Vol. 38, No. 3 (1982), pp. 75–93.

L. G. Rivlin, V. Bogert, and R. Cirillo, "Uncoupling Institutional Indicators," in A. E. Osterberg, C. P. Tiernan and R. A. Findlay (eds.), *Design Research*

Interactions: Proceedings of the Twelfth International Conference of the Environmental Design Research Association, Ames, IA (1981).

L. G. Rivlin, and M. Wolfe, *Institutional Settings in Children's Lives* (New York: John Wiley, 1985).

P. H. Rossi, *Why Families Move,* 2nd ed. (Beverly Hills, CA: Sage Publications, 1980).

D. Rothman, *The Discovery of the Asylum: Social Order and Disorder in the New Republic* (Boston: Little, Brown, 1971).

G. D. Rowles, *Prisoners of Space? Exploring the Geographical Experience of Older People* (Boulder, CO: Westview Press, 1978).

————, "Toward a Geography of Growing Old," in A. Buttimer and D. Seamon (eds.), *The Human Experience of Space and Place* (New York: St. Martin's Press, 1980).

————, "Geographical Perspectives on Human Development," *Human Development* (1981), pp. 67–76.

N. Rubinstein, A *Psycho-social Impact Analysis of Environmental Change in New Jersey's Pine Barrens.* Unpublished doctoral dissertation, City University of New York (1983).

D. Salerno, K. Hopper, and E. Baxter, *Hardship in the Heartland: Homelessness in Eight American Cities* (New York: Community Service Society, 1984).

D. Seamon, "Emotional Experience of the Environment," *American Behavioral Scientist,* Vol. 27, No. 6 (1984), pp. 757–770.

S. A. Shumaker, and D. Stokols, "Residential Mobility As a Social Issue and Research Topic," *Journal of Social Issues,* Vol. 38, No. 3 (1982), pp. 1–19.

A. Toffler, *Future Shock* (New York: Random House, 1970).

Y. Tuan, *Topophilia: A Study of Environmental Perceptions, Attitudes and Values* (Englewood Cliffs, NJ: Prentice Hall, 1974).

————, "Rootedness versus Sense of Place," *Landscape,* Vol. 24, No. 1 (1980), pp. 3–8.

Union of American Hebrew Congregations, *The Torah: A Modern Commentary* (1985).

U. S. Department of Housing and Urban Development, *Report to the Secretary on the Homeless and Emergency Shelters* (1984).

P. Willmott, *Evolution of a Community* (London: Routledge & Kegan Paul, 1963).

P. Willmott, and M. Young, *Family and Class in a London Suburb* (London: Routledge & Kegan Paul, 1966).

M. Young, and P. Willmott, *Family and Kinship in East London* (London: Routledge & Kegan Paul, 1957).

VOCABULARY

paragraph 6: chronic
paragraph 9: trauma
paragraph 11: affluent
paragraph 12: nomadic
paragraph 15: deinstitutionalization
paragraph 18: typology
paragraph 19: deindustrialization, feminization
paragraph 22: gentrification
paragraph 24: exacerbate
paragraph 30: sedentarize
paragraph 32: heterogeneity, depersonalizing
paragraph 33: idiosyncratic
paragraph 36: ambivalence, pandemic, entrenchment, fossilization, feckless
paragraph 38: nurturance
paragraph 48: plethora
paragraph 49: ecology, pathology

QUESTIONS

1. By what principle does Rivlin distinguish types of homelessness in paragraphs 6–9? Why does she stress that there are different types?

2. Which type is of most concern to Rivlin? In the remainder of the essay, does she discuss this type only, or does she give attention to other types?

3. Rivlin states that "Homelessness exists in many different forms and degrees based on the time period involved, the alternative shelter available, and the nature of the person's social contacts" (paragraph 6). What kind of evidence does she present to support this statement? To what extent does she depend on the testimony of the homeless? On statistical evidence? On studies by psychiatrists and sociologists?

4. What popular views of homelessness does Rivlin reject? How do these views impede a solution to the problem?

5. Why does Rivlin give particular attention to Kenneth Allsop's view of American life (paragraph 36)? Does she accept or reject his view? Does his view illuminate the causes of homelessness, or present a mistaken analysis, or suggest a solution?

6. Why does Rivlin give attention to "rootedness and place attachment" (paragraph 47)? Does her discussion bear on causes or solutions?

7. To what extent does the solution depend for Rivlin on a change in perception or understanding of the causes, or on sympathy for the homeless? How do you know?

8. Does Rivlin suggest a single social or political remedy—for example, restoration of government programs, increase in state and federal spending on the homeless? Or does she suggest various remedies?

SUGGESTIONS FOR WRITING

1. In seeking to persuade the audience, a writer may appeal to emotion as well as to reason. The character of the writer displayed—in the reasoned judgment and the concern and sympathy shown—also makes an ethical appeal. What evidence do you find of these kinds of appeal in Rivlin's essay?

2. Rivlin discusses the condition of the homeless and causes of homelessness in the 1980s. Discuss an important recent development relating to one of the following topics or a related one. Include discussion of differing attitudes or alternate proposals. Base your discussion on newspapers, magazines, journal articles, and government publications available in your college library.

    a. "throwaway" children on American streets

    b. educating homeless children

    c. housing homeless families

    d. homeless women and their problems

    e. removing homeless people from public places

    f. medical care of the homeless

    g. improving homeless shelters

    h. public attitudes toward the homeless

32

Methods of Persuasion

How you develop an essay depends on your purpose and audience. In describing how to conserve fuel by driving properly, for example, you need to make the process clear; if your purpose is also to persuade drivers to change their driving habits, you need to choose the best means of doing so, given what you know about your audience. If most are hostile or indifferent to the idea of conservation, you might discuss conservation of fuel and make various appeals—for example, to conscience, public spirit, practical concerns—before turning to the matter of driving. If most are friendly to the idea, you probably need only remind them of the importance of conservation.

Persuasive arguments present additional challenges. You must construct a sound argument, arouse the interest of the audience through a legitimate appeal to their emotions, and show that you are well informed on the issue and honest in your presentation and therefore deserve a hearing. Though some writers seek to avoid emotional appeals in the belief the soundness of the argument guarantees its persuasiveness, few arguments are entirely free of emotion or need to be free of it. The problem is not how to rid the argument of emotion but how to balance emotion and reason so that the aroused reader considers the argument fully, gives rational assent to it, and is free to disagree with it in whole or in part.

Persuasive arguments are based on facts that the reader can verify. The facts alone may generate emotion without a direct appeal, as in the following description of homeless people in New York City:

> Many homeless people, unable to get into shelters, or frightened of disease or violence, or intimidated by the regulations, look for refuge in such public places as train stations and church doorways. Scores of people sleep in the active subway tunnels of Manhattan, inches from

six-hundred-volt live rails. Many more sleep on the ramps and the station platforms. Go into the subway station under Herald Square on a December night at twelve o'clock and you will see what scarce accommodations can mean. Emerging from the subway, walk along Thirty-third Street to Eighth Avenue. There you will see another form of scarce accommodations: hot-air grates outside the buildings on Eighth Avenue are highly prized. Homeless people who arrive late often find there is no vacancy, even for a cardboard box over a grate. (Jonathan Kozol, "The Homeless")

The author may build to even more shocking facts—homeless people stabbed and set on fire, or crushed to death as they sleep in trash compactors heated by rotting food. The author knows that some facts challenge belief:

Even phone-booth vacancies are scarce in New York City: as in public housing, people are sometimes obliged to double up. One night, I saw three people—a man, a woman, and a child—jammed into a single booth. All three were asleep.

Kozol does make direct comments on the situation of the homeless, but he usually lets the facts make their own appeal. Anna Quindlen and Hilary de Vries, in the essays on the homeless that follow, express their personal feelings, but ground them in fact and their reliability as witnesses.

ORDER OF IDEAS IN PERSUASIVE ESSAYS

Persuasive essays have a traditional organization, derived from the oratory of the law courts and legislatures of ancient Greece and Rome. We find this organization in many of the expository and argumentative essays we have been considering: the introduction states the purpose and gives pertinent background, the main discussion or central argument, the conclusion that summarizes and may make predictions. The persuasive essay today, like the orations of ancient times, contains these general divisions and, as in Charles B. Rangel's essay on legalizing drugs (p. 466), expands them to meet the needs of the particular argument:

Introduction, or what was called the exordium or exhortation to the audience, appealing to the interest and good will of the audience, and stating the subject of the oration or essay (Rangel: paragraph 1);

narration or background, stating the facts of the case (paragraphs 2–3);

division of proofs, stating the thesis partly or fully, and summarizing the evidence and arguments to be presented (paragraph 4: Rangel's thesis restated in paragraph 19; summary of evidence and proof omitted);

confirmation or proof, arguing the thesis (paragraphs 5–18);

refutation, answering opponents (paragraphs 20–24);

conclusion, reinforcing and summarizing the main argument, and reinforcing the original appeal to the audience (paragraphs 24–26, restating the thesis and calling for study of the issue).

These divisions may be combined or arranged in a different order—the narration or background perhaps combined with the confirming arguments, or the refutation coming before the confirmation. Often the division or outline of the arguments is omitted, and instead of coming early in the argument, the thesis may be delayed until the conclusion for reasons discussed earlier (see p. 14).

ANNA QUINDLEN

In her column "About New York" and the later "Life in the 30's" in *The New York Times,* Anna Quindlen described daily life in New York City. From 1990 to 1994 she wrote an op-ed column for the *Times,* "Public and Private." In 1992 she was awarded the Pulitzer Prize for Commentary. Her novels include *Object Lessons* (1991), *One True Thing* (1994), and *Black and Blue* (1998). Her columns for the *Times* are collected in *Thinking Out Loud* (1993) and *Living Out Loud* (1988), in which the following essay on her encounter with a homeless woman in New York City appears.

HOMELESS

Her name was Ann, and we met in the Port Authority Bus Terminal several Januarys ago. I was doing a story on homeless people. She said I was wasting my time talking to her; she was just passing through, although she'd been passing through for more than two weeks. To prove to me that this was true, she rummaged through a tote bag and a manila envelope and finally unfolded a sheet of typing paper and brought out her photographs.

They were not pictures of family, or friends, or even a dog or cat, its eyes brown-red in the flashbulb's light. They were pictures of a house. It was like a thousand houses in a hundred towns, not suburb, not city, but somewhere in between, with aluminum siding and a chain-link fence, a narrow driveway running up to a one-car garage and a patch of backyard. The house was yellow. I looked on the back for a date or a name, but neither was there. There was no need for discussion. I knew what she was trying to tell me, for it was something I had often felt. She was not adrift, alone, anonymous, although her bags and her raincoat with the grime shadowing its creases had made me believe she was. She had a house, or at least once upon a time had had one. Inside were curtains, a couch, a stove, potholders. You are where you live. She was somebody.

I've never been very good at looking at the big picture, taking the global view, and I've always been a person with an overactive sense of place, the legacy of an Irish grandfather. So it is natural that the thing that seems most wrong with the world to me right now is that there are so many people with no homes. I'm not simply talking about shelter from the elements, or three square meals a day or a mailing address to which the welfare people can send the check—although I know that all these are important for survival. I'm talking about a home, about precisely those kinds of feelings that have wound up in cross-stitch and French knots on samplers over the years.

Home is where the heart is. There's no place like it. I love my home with a ferocity totally out of proportion to its appearance or location. I love dumb things about it: the hot-water heater, the plastic rack you drain dishes in, the roof over my head, which occasionally leaks. And yet it is precisely those dumb things that make it what it is—a place of certainty, stability, predictability, privacy, for me and for my family. It is where I live. What more can you say about a place than that? That is everything.

Yet it is something that we have been edging away from gradually during my lifetime and the lifetimes of my parents and grandparents. There was a time when where you lived often was where you worked and where you grew the food you ate and even where you were buried.

When that era passed, where you lived at least was where your parents had lived and where you would live with your children when you became enfeebled. Then, suddenly, where you lived was where you lived for three years, until you could move on to something else and something else again.

And so we have come to something else again, to children who do   6
not understand what it means to go to their rooms because they have never had a room, to men and women whose fantasy is a wall they can paint a color of their own choosing, to old people reduced to sitting on molded plastic chairs, their skin blue-white in the lights of a bus station, who pull pictures of houses out of their bags. Homes have stopped being homes. Now they are real estate.

People find it curious that those without homes would rather sleep   7
sitting up on benches or huddled in doorways than go to shelters. Certainly some prefer to do so because they are emotionally ill, because they have been locked in before and they are damned if they will be locked in again. Others are afraid of the violence and trouble they may find there. But some seem to want something that is not available in shelters, and they will not compromise, not for a cot, or oatmeal, or a shower with special soap that kills the bugs. "One room," a woman with a baby who was sleeping on her sister's floor, once told me, "painted blue." That was the crux of it; not size or location, but pride of ownership. Painted blue.

This is a difficult problem, and some wise and compassionate peo-   8
ple are working hard at it. But in the main I think we work around it, just as we walk around it when it is lying on the sidewalk or sitting in the bus terminal—the problem, that is. It has been customary to take people's pain and lessen our own participation in it by turning it into an issue, not a collection of human beings. We turn an adjective into a noun: the poor, not poor people; the homeless, not Ann or the man who lives in the box or the woman who sleeps on the subway grate.

Sometimes I think we would be better off if we forgot about the   9
broad strokes and concentrated on the details. Here is a woman without a bureau. There is a man with no mirror, no wall to hang it on. They are not the homeless. They are people who have no homes. No drawer that holds the spoons. No window to look out upon the world. My God. That is everything.

QUESTIONS

1. What appeal is Quindlen making to her readers? Is she asking them to take action to reduce homelessness, or to change their thinking about its causes, or to change their attitude toward the homeless? Or does she have another purpose in writing?

2. How is a "global view" of homelessness different from the view Quindlen takes? How does she justify this view?

3. How is this view of the homeless different from the view Hilary de Vries presents? Is her view a global one?

SUGGESTIONS FOR WRITING

1. Describe an encounter with a stranger that aroused your concern or changed your thinking on a particular issue. Like Quindlen, be specific in your detail, but select it carefully so that each detail is pertinent to your thesis.

2. Quindlen says that home is "something that we have been edging away from gradually during my lifetime and the lifetimes of my parents and grandparents." Explain what she means, then discuss whether or not the statement applies to you and your family. Be specific in your detail without turning your essay into a narrative or story.

HILARY DE VRIES

HILARY DE VRIES graduated from Ohio Wesleyan University in 1976. In 1981 she received an M.A. in creative writing from Boston University. In 1983, she was named Magazine Writer of the Year by the New England Women's Press Association. Her essay describing a visit to a Boston shelter for the homeless was published in *The Christian Science Monitor* on September 17, 1987. Like Anna Quindlen, de Vries gives a face to the homeless and in this way urges the reader to reject a stereotype.

"I THINK I WILL NOT FORGET THIS"

I never learned her name. But she spotted me across the room—the common area of the shelter for the homeless which served as her living room. If I wasn't exactly a guest in her house, then I was just another reporter doing another story on the homeless. She was the one who lived here. She was the one with a story to tell.

I arrived at the shelter in the early evening. Just before supper. Just in time to catch the nightly intake of the hundreds of men and women who, through alcoholism, or mental illness, or just plain hard times, had nowhere to call home but this shelter. It was one of a dozen in dozens of cities, tucked away in a commercial part of town where warehouses and loading docks didn't form neighborhood coalitions against the housing of the homeless.

I was here to put a face on what I thought was an all-too-faceless social problem. I had stepped around my share of breathing bodies lying on the sidewalk in front of department stores. I had argued with myself over whether to feel anger or pity or simply gratitude that it wasn't me lying there gloveless and filthy. Mostly, I wondered how people could live like that.

That's where the woman came in. The woman with neatly filed nails and beautiful skin who didn't wait for me but simply walked across the room and asked me if I was from a newspaper. Her breath smelled faintly of mint and she wore a yellow sweater. I thought at first she was a staff member, and told her I was touring the facility. Come back and talk to me, she said. I'll tell you what it's like to live here.

I was taken first to the men's side of the shelter, to their front door where I watched them being frisked, a man in a black baseball jacket running his hands lightly down their sides as the men stood silently in the first of many lines—a line for admittance, a line for supper, a line for bed. Here, there are only two rules: no guns, no violence. The men had only to get across the threshold to get a bed for the night. If they came late, they joined the 200 others lying on benches or the floor of the day room or the lobby. Every night it was the same. No one was turned away.

One man was lying in the doorway with a pink electric blanket wrapped around him, cradling a boom box. The man next to him was snoring. His coat was greasy with dirt and served as a pillow for both of them. Neither of them noticed me stepping over them, or the officer who stood a few feet away. A policeman was posted here 24 hours. Just in case. Overhead fluorescent lights blazed. They stay on all night, I am told. All night someone will be awake—awake and walking, awake and talking to someone or to themselves. All night the phone will ring.

Upstairs in the painted cement block rooms, I walk by rows of twin   7
beds with rounded edges—nothing sharp here—and plastic-covered mattresses. Three hundred men on secondhand designer sheets and under donated blankets. Each bed is made up for the night. Outside in the hall, someone's heels click by, and the low rumble from the men standing downstairs, crowded and jostling, rises up the stairwell.

It must be easier to be a woman here, I think. It is less crowded for   8
them. They are neater. No torn bread crusts and spilled cups of soup in the corners. No loud bursts of laughter.

When I am taken to their side of the shelter, a woman pushes open   9
the door wearing a rabbit fur coat and suede boots. For a minute I think she works here, until I am told that the donations here are good ones, that the bulging sacks under the stairwell belong to the bag ladies, that the women do not steal from one another, that some of them do arts and crafts here. There are homemade paintings hanging on the wall.

Now, it is dinner time for the women. They sit on benches alongside   10
a wall waiting for an empty chair. It is almost like a restaurant, I think, but not quite. Women from a local church are serving the meal, cafeteria-style. The handwritten menu is posted at the head of the line: three kinds of sandwiches, pea soup, and fruit. At the plastic-covered picnic tables, the women eat neatly. They do not talk, only peel back the wax paper from the sandwiches and take small bites. They do not look at one another or anyone else.

Soon it will be time for bed. Lights here go out at 9 p.m. No excep-   11
tions. The women will go upstairs, stand in line, put their clothes in a bin, put a rubberized band around their wrist. The band has a metal tab with a number on it. It is the number for their bed. In the middle of the night, if someone should call, the woman can be located by number. Next, a woman staff member takes their clothes, hands them a nightgown and a towel. Both are clean and folded. There is some lace on one of the nightgowns. The women's own clothes are put into the "oven," where they bake all night. This is to dry them and to kill lice. Then they take a shower. No exceptions. The women's showers are stalls fitted with curtains, not like the men's, a bare room with a guard posted. "No more

than 5 minutes in the shower," says a sign taped to the wall. It is almost like being back in gym class, I think. But it isn't. It isn't a school. It isn't even a home. And I still wonder how people can live like this.

I make my way down the stairs, under the cold fluorescent lights and with the smell of antiseptic all around me. Now the woman in the yellow sweater finds me again, corners me here in the common room. She doesn't wait for my questions, but starts to tell me that all the women here are unique, that it is not easy or right to categorize them. That is her word, categorize. She tells me that the women are divorced or displaced or just couldn't deal with the life they were dealt. She tells me that it is hard to get stabilized when you do not have a job. She has lived here $3\frac{1}{2}$ weeks; this is her address. She tells me she is going back to school, that she is working on her secretarial skills. She tells me she is from Cleveland, has a job here now but not the $600 a month for an apartment. "You know they give foot soaks here every night," she says. "Some of the women really need them."

Outside it has begun to snow. I would like to go home. Or sit down, just for a minute. But the woman hasn't finished. She hands me a scrap of paper she took from the bulletin board that morning. "This says it for a lot of us," she says, looking right at me. She is not smiling. Someone yells for her to come pick up her things from the floor. I look down at the paper. The handwriting is in faint blue ink: "These times remind me of a situation I never want to realize again."

I look up at the woman. She is not smiling. Remember, she says, everyone here is different, everyone here is an individual. I think I will not forget this, when I am out walking and see a woman pulling bottles from a trash can with dirty, ungloved hands and I start to wonder how can people live like this.

I think I will remember this when I am tired and want to go home or sit down, just for a minute. I will remember the woman with no home, the woman with the neatly filed nails practicing her typing skills. I think I will remember that persistence does not have any particular address or wear any specific outfit; that courage can be found in a gnarled hand gripping the lip of a garbage can.

But mostly I think I will remember that compassion is not limited to those who can write checks or their representative or articles for newspapers, that empathy might be most easily found among those with their heads bowed over bowls of donated soup, and that concern for one's fellow human beings, as in the case of this one woman, does not even have to come with a name.

QUESTIONS

1. de Vries says of the woman who showed her the shelter: "I never learned her name." Why does she stress this fact at the beginning of the essay and return to it at the end?

2. What details does she give us about the woman? What point is she making through these details? Is she arguing a thesis?

3. How does the visit to the shelter change her image of homeless people or of how they live? How does the visit change her attitude and feelings toward them?

4. Is de Vries contrasting the men's shelter with the women's or merely giving us a picture of both? What does she gain by focusing on a single shelter and homeless person?

5. A writer may appeal to our reason, our feelings, and our respect for qualities of the writer's character evident in the essay (ethical appeal). What appeals does de Vries make in her essay? How successful do you find the appeal that de Vries makes to you?

SUGGESTION FOR WRITING

Report an experience that changed your thinking and feelings about a group of people or a current social problem. Build your discussion to a judgment or a comment, as de Vries does in her essay.

GEORGE F. WILL

GEORGE F. WILL's essay on the Supreme Court decision in *Reno* v. *ACLU* appears earlier in this book. His columns on a wide range of political and social issues have been collected in a number of books, including

The Pursuit of Virtue, and Other Tory Notions (1982), *The Morning After* (1986), *Suddenly: The American Idea Abroad and at Home* (1990), *Political Essays* (1990), and *The Woven Figure* (1997). He writes in an earlier essay, "Bearbaiting and Boxing": "From Plato on, political philosophers have taken entertainment seriously, and have believed the law should too. They have because a society is judged by the kind of citizens it produces, and some entertainments are coarsening." Will returns to this idea in the essay reprinted here.

"EXTREME FIGHTING" AND THE MORALS OF THE MARKETPLACE

Here are some sounds of entertainment in a nation entertaining itself into barbarism:

> I was hitting him to the brain stem, which is a killing blow, and when he covered up I'd swing back with upswings to the eye sockets with two knuckles and a thumb. There was no other place on his body you could hurt him.

> There's the toe stomp! . . . There's an open thigh there—he should do some punching. . . . His tooth went flying out of the ring! . . . He's going to snap his arm—he did, too!

Those are words from a participant and some announcers involved in "ultimate fighting" or "extreme fighting," which involves two combatants in an octagonal pen, governed by minimal rules: no biting or eye gouging. There are no rounds, no judges, no weight classifications. (The man pounding the brain stem and eye sockets was fighting a 650-pound wrestler.) The combatants fight until one is unconscious, disabled, or "taps out"—taps the canvas, signaling surrender. The referee's job is to watch for the tapping, occasionally summon a doctor to see if a participant can continue, and exhort the combatants to pour it on.

Six states have permitted such a spectacle. One permissive state is enough to make this a flourishing amusement on pay-per-view television. Three months ago about 300,000 subscribers paid twenty dollars each to see the seventh Ultimate Fighting Championship.

More are coming, but if you can't wait, your neighborhood Blockbuster, which will not rent sexual pornography, probably offers cassettes of some UFC events like the one in which a man's face was pounded to a pulp while he crawled across the canvas, leaving a broad smear of blood. Especially memorable is slow-motion footage from an overhead camera showing a man pounding the face of a pinned opponent. Aficionados savor full-force kicks to faces and elbows smashed into temples.

Participants in these events are frightening, but less so than the pay-   5
ing customers. They include slack-jawed children whose parents must be cretins, and raving adults whose ferocity away from the arena probably does not rise above muttering epithets at meter maids.

Senator John McCain (R., Ariz.), a former naval aviator who was   6
a boxer at Annapolis and spent more than five years being tortured as a prisoner by the North Vietnamese, knows appropriate manliness and is exhorting governors and local officials to ban "extreme fighting" events because they pose "an unacceptable risk to the lives and health of the contestants." To the objection that the contestants are consenting adults, McCain, arguing within the severe limits imposed by our society's respect for choice, contends that the consent may be somehow illusory. He says perhaps a contestant is "driven by profits or the enticements of publicity associated with it and unknowingly is placing his or her life at risk."

To which libertarians respond: If you ban being driven by profits   7
and enticed by publicity, what remains of modern life? Besides, no one has yet been killed in "extreme fighting," which is more than can be said for boxing.

Although in one letter to a governor, McCain says he is "solely" concerned with damage done to combatants, he also worries about the "glorification of cruelty," which raises the problem of virtue: What do we want government to do in the name of that?

The historian Macaulay, disdaining the Puritans, said they banned   8
bearbaiting not because it gave pain to bears but because it gave pleasure to spectators. The Puritans were, of course, tiresome, but were they wrong? Surely there are ignoble, unwholesome pleasures.

Washington manages to make even a concern about virtue seem lu-   9
dicrous, but "extreme fighting" forces a commercial society to decide when the morals of the marketplace are insufficient. Do we really ban cockfighting only because the birds cannot consent? Suppose (one hates to give entertainment entrepreneurs any of the few odious ideas they have not yet had) someone offers a $10 million prize for a Russian

roulette competition—winner take all, necessarily. Imagine the pay-per-view potential.

Would—should—we so respect "consumer sovereignty" that we would allow that? The question is hypothetical, but perhaps not for long. In entertainment, competition does not elevate. Competition for audiences in an increasingly jaded, coarsened, and desensitized society causes competitors to devise ever-more lurid vulgarities to titillate the sated. If you think "extreme fighting" is as extreme as things can get, just wait.

QUESTIONS

1. In Will's judgment, when should government, state or federal, intervene in televised sporting events?

2. On what assumptions about the role of government does he base his argument? Does he argue these assumptions, present them as givens, or merely imply them?

3. Are Will and Senator McCain arguing for a ban on all boxing? If not, why do they single out "ultimate fighting"?

4. Will might have stated the argument for intervention without quoting announcers and one of the participants. What did he gain by doing so?

SUGGESTIONS FOR WRITING

Argue for or against one of the following. State your reasons and, in the course of your argument, answer one or more objections to your position:

a. a ban on blood sports generally

b. a ban on televised blood sports

c. optional use of seatbelts in automobiles

d. periodic driving exams, not less than one every five years

e. school uniforms in public schools

N. SCOTT MOMADAY

Poet, artist, and novelist, N. Scott Momaday is descended from the Kiowa Indians of Oklahoma on his father's side and an Anglo-American pioneer family on his mother's. Momaday describes these contemporary worlds in his novel *House Made of Dawn*—awarded the Pulitzer Prize for Fiction in 1969. *The Walk to Rainy Mountain* (1968) celebrates his Kiowan heritage. "The Morality of Indian Hating," written as a student at Stanford University in the early 1960s. The first part is reprinted here. In the second part, Momaday discusses federal management of Indian affairs. Momaday writes in an afterword:

> My convictions have grown stronger. I believe what most threatens the American Indian is sacrilege, the theft of the sacred. Inexorably the Indian people have been, and are being, deprived of the spiritual nourishment that has sustained them for many thousands of years. This is a subtle holocaust, and it is ongoing. It is imperative that the Indian defines himself, that he finds the strength to do so, that he refuses to let others define him.

THE MORALITY OF INDIAN HATING

In the winter of 1833 the Kiowas were camped on Elm Fork, a branch of the Red River west of the Wichita Mountains. In the preceding summer they had suffered a massacre at the hands of the Osages, and Tai-me, the sacred Sun Dance doll and most powerful medicine of the tribe, had been stolen. At no time in the history of their migration from the north, and in the evolution of their plains culture, had the Kiowas been more vulnerable to despair. The loss of Tai-me was a deep psychological wound. In the early cold of November 13 there occurred over North America an explosion of meteors. The Kiowas were awakened by the sterile light of falling stars, and they ran out into the false day and were terrified.

The year the stars fell is among the earliest entries in the Kiowa calendars, and it is permanent in the Kiowa mind. There was symbolic meaning in that November sky. With the coming of natural dawn there began a new and darker age for the Kiowa people; the last culture to evolve on this continent began to decline. Within four years of the falling stars the

Kiowas signed their first treaty with the government; within twenty, four major epidemics of smallpox and Asiatic cholera destroyed more than half their number; and within scarcely more than a generation their horses were taken from them and the herds of buffalo were slaughtered and left to waste upon the plains.

It is expedient to begin with a particular people and a symbolic event. In a certain sense it is also necessary; one is obliged, by the nature of the subject, to focus upon particulars and their symbols. The unique position of the Indian in this society is anomalously fixed and mutable, here and there, truth and fiction. The Indian has been for a long time generalized in the imagination of the white man. Denied the acknowledgment of individuality and change, he has been made to become in theory what he could not become in fact, a synthesis of himself. This is not semantic trickery. The Navajo, to illustrate, is an American Indian, but "the American Indian" is not conversely a Navajo; he is rather, to the public mind, that lonely specter who stood for two hundred years in the way of civilization, who was removed time and again by force, and who was given in defeat that compensation we call savage nobility, after the example of Rousseau.

The persistent attempt to generalize the Indian has resulted in a delusion and a nomenclature of half truths. The so-called Indian problem is impossible to define. The term is furthermore misleading and dangerous, for it holds up the attractive suggestion that there is *one* problem and, by implication therefore, *one* solution. The suggestion is naive and fallacious, of course; yet it has been the basis of a historical diplomacy. Federal management of Indian affairs has always been expressed in general and uniform policy. Predictably that policy has had but slight and accidental relevance to a random majority of the Indian people and none at all to a struggling, perhaps desperate, minority. Diversity is the principal barrier in the way of cultural assimilation; it will continue to be a barrier for generations to come. There are several hundred societies of Indians. Our reservations now support, with bare adequacy, nearly four hundred thousand inhabitants. And there are more than a hundred living Indian languages.

The history of Indian-white relations conforms to a pattern which has come to be associated with the evolution of the democratic faith: a geographical expansion from east to west and a succession of events which mark the development of American nationalism from the seventeenth century to the twentieth. The outlines of that pattern form the character of my own ideas on the subject of Indian cultural integration, and throughout this essay I shall hold a part of my attention on them for the sake of perspective. There is a meaningful symmetry in the shape of the past. More important than the tangible history of Indian-white relations, however, is the interaction of ideas and attitudes which inform that relationship and transcend it. Those ideas and attitudes are on both sides, matters of morale and morality.

The military campaigns which were waged on the receding frontier   6
of the last century were less consequential by far than was the intrusion of the white man's "civilization" upon the sanctity of the red man's faith. The Indian can recognize and understand malice, and he can bear pain with legendary self-possession. What he can neither recognize nor understand is that particular atmosphere of moral and ideological ambiguity in which the white man prevails, a traditional milieu which is characterized in part by a sense of finality in thought, an immediacy in judgment, and a general preoccupation with efficiency.

Implicit in these characteristics is the inclination to impose the most   7
convenient identities upon friends and acquaintances, strangers and enemies. The Indian has been compelled to make his way under an imposed identity of defeat. He has been made to live for a long time with the conviction—now indivisibly his and the white man's—that the best possessions of his mind and soul are inane. Moralities can be violated and destroyed. Moral degeneration is conceived in guilt and nurtured in prejudice. It is among the most hideous of psychological deformities, and it perpetuates itself in its own infection. The Indian has been afflicted with that for which society prescribes neither prevention nor cure.

In 1705 there appeared an American book entitled *History of the*   8
Present State of Virginia in which the author, Robert Beverly, described the contemporary circumstances of the Virginia Indians in these words:

> They have on several accounts reasons to lament the arrival of the Europeans, by whose means they seem to have have lost their Felicity, as well as their Innocence. The *English* have taken away great part of their Country and consequently made everything less plenty amongst them. They have introduced Drunkenness and Luxury amongst them, which have multiply'd their Wants, and put them upon desiring a thousand things, they never dreamt of before.

The rule of convenience had begun already to enchant the neolithic mind. It is an unbroken spell; in the nearly three centuries since Beverly made his observation, the Indians have regained neither felicity nor innocence, and time has brought them new reasons to lament.

Colonel John Moredock of Illinois, whose story is related indirectly by Melville in *The Confidence Man,* was one who, even in the nineteenth century, had outlived his cause. The Indian hater is no more current than are the atrocities upon which he fed. Yet the particular morality of which Moredock is the spokesman is a cornerstone in the Puritan ethic.

The relationship between the white man and the red was doomed from the outset by a conflict of attitudes and a disposition of intolerance. The initial experience of that relationship was agitated by the cross-purposes of European imperial design. The immediate problems which arose out of colonial establishment are, with reference to the Indian, the common denominators of subsequent history: the question of Indian ownership of land, the development of natural resources, and an uncompromising determination on the part of the white man either to "civilize" the Indian or to eliminate him.

Even so, there was no unanimity in the white man's approach. The Spanish were committed to a system of feudalism; the French were concerned chiefly to exploit the economics of the fur trade; and the English were bound to an agrarian tradition. From the Indian point of view, history has resolved this plurality of interests with a sad significance. It was the English who prevailed in the New World, and it was they whose temperament could concede no usefulness to the Indian. The motives of Spanish and French settlement were sufficiently international in kind to encourage and to realize cooperation. The Indian could be useful to both nations in America; and at the same time, he was well suited to serfdom, and he knew no peer as a hunter. In the New World colonies of France and Spain, therefore, there was no alternative to joint occupation of the land. The Indian was invited to participate in the colonial enterprise, and his participation extended to, and included, intermarriage. But the English could respect the Indian neither as hind nor hunter. Indeed, he was worse than useless; he was an impediment.

The moral aspect of the confrontation between Puritan and Indian is given sharp relief in the context of intercultural relations by the very nature of Calvinism itself and by the sometimes sudden and violent actualities of history. Such an actuality was the so-called Pequod War, of which many have doubtless heard, but of which very few know the causes and effects. It is no wonder. The war is of little historical significance in itself; but, in symbolic terms, it represents a moral precedent upon which a tradition of oppression has been based.

The Pequods were a weak branch of the Algonquin stock which 13 had been severed and driven to the sea by an old warfare with the powerful Iroquois nation. In 1637 the Pequods elected to defend the rich Connecticut Valley against the encroachment of white settlement. Moreover, they threatened to make good their resistance by creating a confederation of local tribes. They were on the point of forming an alliance with the Narragansetts when the recollection of ancient enmities made them pause.

Taking full advantage of the hesitation, the English moved swiftly 14 against the Pequods in a campaign that virtually exterminated the entire tribe. The colonists surprised the Indian stronghold at Fort Mystic in modern-day Connecticut and burned it to the ground. In just more than an hour, some six hundred Indians were shot or burned to death. The English lost two men in the encounter. The grim business of annihilation went on. There began a relentless pursuit of the Pequod survivors. Homeless and grieving, they were easily found and destroyed.

The devastation of the Pequods was a triumph of the Puritan spirit. 15 There was celebration in the New England towns, and the Reverend Cotton Mather called upon his congregation to thank God that "on this day we have sent six hundred heathen souls to hell."

A historian of the Pequod War wrote in 1910: 16

> No comment which analysts of later times might attempt could possibly compass the vindictiveness of the English upon this occasion. The only palliation available to the historian recording these transactions is to imagine himself surrounded with the perils which menaced the meager population of the English at that time . . . If one could imagine himself in a wilderness of woods beset by a pack of hungry wolves he might better appreciate the situation . . . It is barely possible that in the consummation of these killings of the Pequods the intolerancy of the Puritan found a natural vent, and that he carried on this work with a grim satisfaction.

There is a curious and troubled indecision behind these words. The historian is bending under the weight of an old and malignant confusion of attitudes and loyalties. In the same breath he deplores and defends the morality in which his own prejudices have their roots. He is eminently honest, but he cannot be objective. The story he is concerned to tell has become in his own mind the parable of the solitary man and the hungry wolves. His dilemma is one that concerns us all.

A final word on the Pequod War. The Pequods were one of the few peoples who were undiminished by a plague which ravaged the entire coastal plain from Connecticut to Maine in the decade preceding the founding of Plymouth Plantation. It has been estimated that two thirds of all the inhabitants of that region were consumed by pestilence between the years 1613 and 1618. The white men who subsequently touched upon that land were peculiarly alert to the signs of providence. It was their mandate to secure against all impediments the indulgence of an angry and merciless God. They recognized at once their Old Testament foe in the New World wilderness; the Fiend was everywhere present in the painted faces which peered from behind the trees and in the suspicious forms which strode noiselessly over the brittle leaves. The Indian was one whose very existence opposed the will of God; so much was made certain by the fact that God had visited a contagion upon the savage race. He had cleared the way for his faithful and enlightened few through the agency of disease.

That conviction, refined and fortified by such historical phenomena as the Pequod War, made once and for all unacceptable Roger Williams's queer notion of giving value for Indian land, of purchasing that land, as in Europe, however foreign that notion would have been to the inhabitants of the so-called New World. Implicit in that conviction are two assumptions which have acquired the status of truth in this society. One is the assumption, already expressed, that the Indian is an impediment to the progress of civilization; the other is the related assumption that the rights, both natural and legal, which dignify the white man are unavailable to the Indian. The particular morality which can accommodate these ideas is pragmatic and malleable rather than ideal and absolute. It is the morality (to borrow the juxtaposition made famous by Henry Adams) of the dynamo rather than that of the Virgin. It is relevant to the present context that the assumptions here specified suggest a kind of logical syllogism the conclusion of which is a condition of intolerance and aversion. Whatever else he might have been, Colonel Moredock of Illinois was a man who came honestly by his bias.

The Kiowas who watched the strange commotion of the stars on the morning of November 13, 1833, were a people whose way of life was relatively new. It was a good life, for it enabled the Kiowas to possess dignity and well-being. In order to understand what happened to the Kiowas when their way of life was destroyed, it is necessary to raise an

old religion from the dead. There are two legends in the unwritten literature of the Kiowa people which I shall recount. They are brief, and they
will give emphasis to certain points I wish later to make.

The first is the story of the man who found Tai-me: 20

> Long ago there were bad times. The Kiowas were hungry and there was
> no food. There was a man who heard his children cry from hunger, and
> he began to search for food. He walked four days and became very
> weak. On the fourth day he came to a great canyon. Suddenly there was
> thunder and lightning. A Voice spoke to him and said, "Why are you
> following me? What do you want?" The man was afraid. The thing
> standing before him had the feet of a deer, and its body was covered
> with feathers. The man answered that the Kiowas were hungry. "Take
> me with you," the Voice said, "and I will give you whatever you want."
> From that day Tai-me has belonged to the Kiowas.

The second legend is that of two warrior brothers: 21

> On a raid against the Utes, one of two Kiowa brothers was captured.
> The other stole into the Ute camp and tried to set his brother free, but
> he too was captured. The chief of the Utes had respect for the man's
> bravery, and he made a bargain with him. If he could carry his brother
> on his back and walk upon a row of greased buffalo heads without
> falling to the ground, both brothers would be given horses and allowed
> to return in safety to their home. The man bore his brother on his back
> and walked upon the heads of the buffalo and kept his footing. The Ute
> chief was true to his word, and the Kiowa brothers returned to their
> people on horseback.

I relate these stories not only because they are eloquent and venerable but
also because they express the truest response to being that man can make.
That is their essential value. They are the true reflections of that response,
that most moral of human acts. These particular legends grow out of different times and experiences, and they reveal different ways of thinking.

Tai-me came to the Kiowas as they were about to enter upon the   22
southern plains. They had no horses, and they were preoccupied with the
simple problem of survival. Their culture was based upon the principle
of mobility, and they followed the herds of animals which grazed upon
a seemingly boundless expanse of land. They knew no better than to hunt
on foot with crude weapons. When they found rare moments in which
to explain their world to themselves, they did so in terms of suffering
and hope. The Tai-me myth is not an entertainment, nor even the journal

of an old salvation; it is infinitely more. It is an emotional reaction to the elemental experience of being, the affirmation of an eternal reality behind all appearances; it is sacred.

But, in itself, myth is an inadequate expression of the human spirit. Ritual, that ancient effort of man to fashion his very bone and muscle into essential prayer, enabled the Kiowas to have existence in a world that was beyond the capacity of the senses to perceive. With Tai-me came the Sun Dance religion.

When my father was a boy, an old man used to come to the house which my grandfather built near Rainy Mountain Creek. He was a lean old man in braids and was impressive in his age and bearing. His English name was Cheyney. Every morning, my father tells me, Cheyney would paint his wrinkled face, go out, and pray aloud to the rising sun. I like to hear of that old man. I like to watch him make his prayer with the eyes of my mind, though I am nearly ashamed to intrude upon his privacy. Old man Cheyney had come to terms with himself and the world. He did not for a moment doubt the source of his strength, and each morning he returned to it his wonder and his words.

The earth where Cheyney prayed is a deep red, and it bears the innumerable wounds of erosion. It is a huge land—so huge that only sound can possess it; a single tree can dominate the plain, but nothing can fill it. It is the kind of landscape in which a man is seen always against the sky—and a man on the back of a horse is regal. The air is hot and clear and filled with an essence that qualifies all objects in the eye and ear. There, in early summer, I have seen the sun rise out of the ground an immense red-orange disk, scarcely brighter than the moon, beautiful and strange and health-giving. It was old man Cheyney's god.

The Sun Dance was the great medicine dance of the Kiowas. It was held at least once each year at a time and place designated by the Tai-me keeper. All the bands of the tribe coverged upon the Sun Dance place and camped in the presence of the great ancestral medicine. The institution of the Sun Dance was a concerted expression of tribal integrity. As a social event it was a time for the exchange of gossip and wares, an opportunity to show off prize possessions, a festive occasion upon which to take stock of blood resources and prospects.

But the Sun Dance was preeminently an act of faith. It restored power to the people; it invested them with purpose, thus dignity and strength; it enabled them for a moment to partake of divinity, to send their voices— however frail—against the silence at the edge of the world. During the dance Tai-me was exposed to view. It was suspended from a branch of the sacred tree in the Sun Dance lodge. The rest of the time it was—and is now—kept in parfleche which is wrapped in a blanket and bound with strips of ticking. The Sun Dance lasted four days and nights. A buffalo bull was killed, its hide draped on the limbs of the sacred tree and its head impaled at the top. The buffalo was from the beginning the thread of life; it was food and shelter, god and beast. The head of a buffalo bull, uppermost on the Tai-me tree, its dead eyes fixed on the skyline to the east, was the symbol of life itself. And nothing could have been more perfectly symbolic. The Kiowas could have conceived of no greater sacrifice. The principal dancers fasted the four days through and danced to the edge of exhaustion. Paintings of the sun and moon were made on their bodies, and later the flesh was cut away so that the images were permanent. But the dancers were not bled; they were not made to endure torture as were the dancers of certain other tribes on the plains. Far more intimately than we can easily imagine, the Kiowas bound themselves to their religion. Their commitment to faith and morality was total and deliberate. Though the Sun Dance became the supreme religious institution of a young and short-lived culture, it was unspeakably old in itself—as old as the need of man to know his god.

The Sun Dance died away because the white man forbade it and because the white man destroyed the buffalo. The last Kiowa Sun Dance was held in 1887 on a tributary of the Washita river above Rainy Mountain Creek. The buffalo were gone. In order to have their dance, the Kiowas had to buy an animal from the domestic herd which Charles Goodnight preserved in Texas. In 1889 a Sun Dance was planned, but it was found out and prevented by the soldiers at Fort Sill. The Kiowas were going to suspend an old buffalo from the sacred tree. Perhaps the most immoral act ever committed against the land was the senseless killing of the buffalo. 28

The loss of the Sun Dance was the blow that killed the native Kiowa culture. The Kiowas might have endured every privation but that, the desecration of their faith. Without their religion there was nothing to sustain them. Subsequent acceptance of the Ghost Dance, peyote, and Christianity were for the Kiowas pathetic attempts to revive the old deities; they had become a people whose spirit was broken. 29

My grandmother lived in the old house where Cheyney came frequently to visit. It pleased her to dwell on the past, and her memory was keen. On the last day of a visit with her, she told me again of the 30 red horse my grandfather trained to race. I have heard the story many times. The horse belonged to my great aunt, but my grandfather trained it, and it was his to race. When the Sun Dance was gone, the Kiowas came together to race their horses; it was their social time. The red horse was the swiftest runner in the territory. Again and again the Comanches and the Cheyennes and the Pawnees and the Caddoes matched their finest animals against it, but it always won. Half a century or less earlier, the red horse would have been anointed with the medicine of war—it would have been a hunter. When the red horse died, my grandfather placed its bones in a box and kept them in a barn. I can remember seeing them when I was a child. They were stolen some years ago.

It is appropriate to speak of the red horse. It is by no means coinci- 3
dental that it should be in the foreground of my grandmother's memory. Nor is it remarkable that my grandfather should have preserved the bones of a horse—nor, for that matter, that they should have been thought valuable enough to steal. The horse is the factor which accounts for the fundamental difference between the legend of the man who found Tai-me and the tale of the Kiowa brothers. In the earlier setting, before there were horses, the storyteller is sharply aware of his own frailty; he is inhibited by the eternal prospects of pain, hunger, and despair. His mind is compelled to look beyond itself for ease; it recoils from the present world and fastens upon another. All this is turned quite around in the legend of the brothers. In the very motion of that story, there is a satisfaction in the here and now, an enthusiasm for the moment. This is not to imply that the reliance upon myth and religion has become less than integral; it is merely to observe that the storyteller has begun to find his world so various that it can fill and fascinate his whole mind.

About the time of the Pequod War, the Kiowa and the horse came 3
simultaneously upon the southern plains. Then for a hundred years and more the Kiowa and the horse were one. The horse exerted a crucial influence upon virtually every aspect of Kiowa culture. It brought about a revolution.

From the pre-horse culture the Kiowas brought only a nomadism and 3
a mythology; the horse brought a new and material way of life. The Kiowa pulled up the roots which had always held him to the ground. He was given the means to prevail against distance. For the first time he could move beyond the limits of his human strength, of his vision, even of his former dreams. No longer was it necessary to stalk the herds, to construct traps, and to carry the meat of the kill on foot. With the horse

the Kiowa could acquire enough food in one day to last him many months. He could transport his possessions at will and with only a fraction of his former time and effort.

But the greatest change was psychological. Seated behind the with-   34
ers of a horse, elevated to a height from which the far world was made a possession of the eye, sensually conscious of an immense fund of living power under him and nearly part of him, the Kiowa was greater than he was. When a Kiowa died, the throat of his hunting horse was cut over his grave. The horse bred in the Kiowa a certain defiance. It gave him a taste for danger and an inclination to belligerence. A predatory society is said to bear the seeds of its own destruction. Even at the high tide of the horse culture, when they were most warlike and most feared, the Kiowas could not defend all the quarters of their sway. They ranged over hundreds of miles in quest of quarrels and trophies. They resisted to the death every attempt on the part of the white man to take their land, even after all resistance was known to be futile.

When the principle of mobility by which they lived was stifled, when   35
they were driven like cattle into the corrals at Fort Sill and their horses and weapons confiscated, the Kiowas degenerated. When the buffalo were gone and the Sun Dance was prohibited they suffered the loss of their last hope, hope itself. Degeneration is both the cause and effect of despair. The Kiowas had no immunity against the flood of alien forces which fell upon them in defeat. The white man's diseases ravaged them, his conveniences spoiled them, his liquor enslaved and corrupted them. They had returned to the ground actually and symbolically. The centaur was dead.

The sense of defeat is not easily overcome. As do all unrelieved con-   36
ditions of life, it becomes in time personal and definitive—almost welcome, almost comfortable. In one respect the Pequods were spared the ultimate price of resistance, for they were made to surrender their lives only. The moral nature of the force which destroyed the Pequods and beggared the Kiowas had changed but little in two hundred years. Superficially, a witch-burning psychology had given way to an age of philanthropy. Substantially, however, the soldiers who turned from each other at the Wilderness and Gettysburg to oppose their common enemy on the frontier were moved by the same morality which had created violence elsewhere and before.

The morality of intolerance has become in the twentieth century a   37
morality of pity. The American people might well be sensitive on the subject of Indian welfare. The very survival of the Indian race in its homeland

has been an inglorious, not infrequently desperate, journal of abuse and shame. The contact with the white man's civilization—it was all too clear at the turn of the century—had failed entirely to enrich the Indian. To the contrary, that civilization had debased him. Surely the white man was hard put to retain his image of the noble savage. For what he saw in actuality—if he dared to look—was not the creature of his imagination but a poor, syphilitic, lice-infested wastrel whose only weapon against despair was alcohol. The death rate among Indians had begun to exceed the birth rate. The reservations had at last become contagious colonies and concentration camps.

The relaxation of intolerance and the rise of pity are significant footnotes to the evolution of American morality. The Americanist Roy Harvey Pearce has written a unique book on the Indian and the idea of civilization. He observes quite accurately that pity and censure have suffused our understanding of the Indian: "The historical fact is that our civilization in subduing the Indian, killed its own creature, the savage. The living fact is that it has not yet been able entirely to kill the Indian, but having subdued him, no longer needs or cares to."

VOCABULARY

paragraph 3: expedient, synthesis, semantic
paragraph 4: nomenclature, diversity, assimilation
paragraph 5: perspective, symmetry
paragraph 6: ideological, milieu
paragraph 8: neolithic, felicity
paragraph 10: denominator
paragraph 16: palliation
paragraph 27: parfleche

QUESTIONS

1. Why is it necessary to begin with a particular Native American society and a symbolic event? How does Momaday defend this necessity?

2. What still active ideas and attitudes have injured Native Americans more than past military campaigns?

3. How did the religious beliefs of the early colonists shape their attitude toward the Native American?

4. In what way was the symbolic Pequod War a precedent for events that were to follow?

5. How does the statement of the historian quoted in paragraph 16 reveal "a curious and troubled indecision"? How is the statement representative of attitudes Momaday has discussed?

6. Momaday states that the assumptions and conclusion discussed in paragraph 18 "suggest a kind of logical syllogism"? What syllogism does he have in mind?

7. What did the Sun Dance symbolize to the Kiowas? How did its loss help to destroy the Kiowa culture?

8. What role did the horse play in that culture and its destruction?

9. What does the destruction of Kiowan culture add to our understanding of the morality Momaday discusses?

SUGGESTIONS FOR WRITING

1. Momaday says that "the very nature of Calvinism itself" promoted conflict in the colonial period. Investigate the writings of Cotton Mather and other early New England settlers to test this statement.

2. Investigate the ideas and attitudes that promoted the decline of another Native American society—for example, the Sioux of the northern Plains.

MICHAEL DORRIS

MICHAEL DORRIS (1945–1997) was for many years professor of anthropology and chairman of Native American studies at Dartmouth College. His numerous writings include the novels *The Crown of Columbus* (1991), with Louise Erdrich, and *Cloud Chamber* (1997); *Working Men* (1993), a collection of stories; *Paper Trail* (1994), a collection of essays; and *The Broken Cord: A Father's Story* (1989), an account of fetal alcohol syndrome—awarded the National Book Critics Circle Award. Dorris wrote often on issues concerning Native Americans.

FOR INDIANS, NO THANKSGIVING

Maybe those Pilgrims and Wampanoags actually got together for a   1
November picnic, maybe not. It matters only as an ironical footnote.

For the former group, it would have been a celebration of a precar-   2
ious hurdle successfully crossed on the path to the political domination,
first of a continent and eventually of a planet. For the latter, it would
have been, at best, a naive extravaganza—the last meeting as equals with
invaders who, within a few years, would win King Philip's War and dec-
orate the entrances to their towns with rows of stakes, each topped with
an Indian head.

The few aboriginal survivors of the ensuing violence were either sold   3
into Caribbean slavery by their better-armed, erstwhile hosts or ruthlessly
driven from their Cape Cod homes. Despite the symbolic idealism of the
first potluck, New England—from the emerging European point of
view—simply wasn't big enough for two sets of societies.

An enduring benefit of success, when one culture clashes with an-   4
other, is that the victorious group controls the record. It owns not only
the immediate spoils but also the power to edit, embellish, and concoct
the facts of the original encounter for the generations to come. Events,
once past, reside at the small end of the telescope, the vague and hazy
antecedents to accepted reality.

Our collective modern fantasy of Thanksgiving is a case in point. It   5
has evolved into a ritual pageant that almost every one of us, as children,
either acted in or were forced to watch—a seventeenth-century vision
that we can conjure whole in the blink of an eye.

The cast of stock characters is as recognizable as those in any   6
Macy's parade: dour-faced Pilgrim men, right-to-bear-arms muskets at
their sides, sitting around a rude outdoor table while their wives,
dressed in long dresses, aprons, and linen caps, bustle about lifting
the lids off steaming kettles—pater- and materfamilias of New World
hospitality.

They dish out the turkey to a scattering of shirtless Indian invitees.   7
But there is no ambiguity as to who is in charge of the occasion, who
could be asked to leave, whose protocol prevails.

Only "good" Indians are admitted into this tableau, of course, as in   8
those who accept the Manifest Destiny of a European presence and are
prepared to adopt English dining customs and, by inference, English
everything else.

These compliant Hollywood extras are, naturally enough, among the blessings the Pilgrims are thankful for—and why not? Holiday Indians are colorful, bring the food, and vanish after dessert. They are something exotic to write home about, like a visit to Frontierland. In the sound bite of national folklore, they have metamorphosed into totems of America as evocative, and ultimately as vapid, as a flag factory.

And members of this particular make-believe tribe did not all repair to the happy hunting grounds during the first Christmas rush. They lived on, smoking peace pipes and popping up at appropriate crowd-pleasing moments.

They lost mock battles from coast to coast in Wild West shows. In nineteenth-century art, they sat bareback on their horses and stoically watched a lot of sunsets. Entire professional sports teams of them take the home field every Sunday afternoon in Cleveland, Atlanta, or Washington, D.C.

They are the sources of merit badges for Boy Scouts and the emblem of purity for imitation butter. They are, and have been from the beginning, predictable, manageable, domesticated inventions without depth or reality apart from that bestowed by their creators.

These appreciative Indians, as opposed to the pesky flesh and blood native peoples on whom they are loosely modeled, did not question the enforced exchange of their territories for a piece of pie. They did not protest when they died by the millions from European diseases.

They did not resist—except for the "bad" ones, the renegades—when solemn pacts made with them were broken or when their religions and customs were declared illegal. They did not make a fuss in courts in defense of their sovereignty. They never expected all the fixings anyway.

As for Thanksgiving 1988, the descendants of those first party-goers sit at increasingly distant tables, the pretense of equity all but abandoned. Against great odds, Native Americans have maintained political identity, but, in a country so insecure about heterogeneity that it votes its dominant language as "official," this refusal to melt into the pot has been an expensive choice.

A majority of reservation Indians reside in the most impoverished counties in the nation. They constitute the ethnic group at the wrong extreme of every scale: most undernourished, most short-lived, least educated, least healthy. For them, Thanksgiving was perhaps their last square meal.

VOCABULARY

paragraph 2: precarious, naive
paragraph 3: aboriginal, erstwhile, potluck
paragraph 4: antecedents
paragraph 6: pater- and materfamilias
paragraph 7: protocol
paragraph 8: tableau, Manifest Destiny
paragraph 9: metamorphosed, totems, vapid
paragraph 11: stoically
paragraph 14: renegades
paragraph 15: equity, heterogeneity

QUESTIONS

1. Whether or not the colonial gathering actually occurred, Dorris considers it an "ironical footnote" to what followed. Why ironical? And why a "naive extravaganza" to the Wampanoags?

2. What tone of voice do you hear in the opening paragraphs? Is it possibly sad and reflective, or instead mildly or strongly sarcastic, or even stronger than these—angry to the point of outrage? Does the voice you hear change in the course of the essay?

3. What does Dorris assume about the audience he is addressing? Is it indifferent to the treatment of Native Americans, perhaps ignorant of the facts?

4. Tone of voice is an essential consideration in how we choose to persuade the audience addressed. If we wish to conciliate, we speak in one tone; if we wish to shame, we speak in another. What does Dorris wish to do, given the audience he has in mind?

5. What is his purpose in writing about Thanksgiving? What ways does he try to achieve it?

Suggestions for Writing

1. Compare the way Dorris seeks to persuade his audience with the way N. Scott Momaday does in "The Morality of Indian Hating." Comment on the audience each writer has in mind, as well as the various means of persuasion each employs.

2. Write about a minority that you believe has been mistreated, and seek to persuade your readers of this fact. Before writing you will need to decide what audience you wish to reach—what are its knowledge, ideas, and assumptions—and what action if any you wish it to take.

3. Write about a person you know who, in your view, has been misunderstood or judged unfairly and deserves to be honored. Before writing consider what ways to best persuade the audience you have in mind.

A N O N Y M O U S

The anonymous writer of this essay makes a direct appeal to the reader, like Anna Quindlen and Hilary de Vries grounding it in facts. The essay illustrates the traditional ethical appeal of the speech maker—in the words of Edward P. J.Corbett, "the persuasive value of the speaker's or writer's character." "The *whole* discourse," Corbett states, "must maintain the 'image' that the speaker or writer seeks to establish. The ethical appeal, in other words, must be pervasive throughout the discourse." The anonymous writer is highly successful in meeting this test.

Who Am I?

After I tell you who I am you may not know me. You may not recognize me. You may deny that I exist. Who am I? I'm a product of myself. I'm a product of you and of my ancestors.

Now, one half of my ancestors were the Spanish who were Western European, but who were also part African and part Middle Eastern. They came to this country and met with the other side of my family—the

Indians. The Indians also were a great race—people of a great culture. There were many kinds of Indians, as there were many kinds of Spaniards. They mixed, they married, they had children. Their children were called Mestizos, and this is what I am.

We came to California long before the Pilgrims landed at Plymouth Rock. We settled California and all of the southwestern part of the United States, including the states of Arizona, New Mexico, Colorado, and Texas. We built the missions, and we cultivated the ranches. We were at the Alamo in Texas, both inside and outside. You know, we owned California—that is, until gold was found there.

I think it was a mistake to let you into the southwestern states, because eventually you took away our lands. When we fought to retain what was ours, you used the vigilantes to scare us away, to hang us, and to take away our lands. We became your slaves. Now we cook your food, we build your railroads, we harvest your crops, we dig your ditches, we stand in your unemployment lines—and we receive more than 20 percent of your welfare. But we've done some good things, too: We won more Medals of Honor during World War II than any other ethnic group. We've never had a turncoat, even during the Korean War. Yes, we have had outstanding war records. But, you know, we don't complain. By the same token, we don't get much attention, either.

We don't live in your neighborhoods unless we let you call us Spanish, French, or something else, but not what we are. We usually attend our own schools at the elementary or junior high level; and if we get to high school, we may go to school with you. However, even before we finish high school, more than 50 percent of us drop out, and you know we don't go to college. We make up less than 1 percent of the college students, yet we are 12 percent of the total school population. We don't use government agencies because our experiences with them have been rather poor; they haven't been very friendly or helpful. The Immigration Department has never really been our friend. The land offices help to take away our lands—we couldn't exactly call them friendly. The Farm Labor Bureau has never truly served us. The schools haven't really lifted us educationally. The police—well, they haven't been the most cooperative agency in the government either. You accept our Spanish words as long as we don't speak them, because if we do, you say they're "poor" Spanish—not Castilian; so our language can't be very good—it's almost like swearing. We are usually Catholics and sometimes Protestants, but in either case we have our own churches. You say we can leave our *barrios* to live near you—that is, only if we stay in our own place. When we attend your parties to meet your friends, you usually introduce us as being Spanish or something else that we are not. You are ashamed of what we are, and your attitude makes us feel that we, too, should be ashamed of what we are. When we go to school, we don't take part in your school activities; we don't think we're wanted. We seldom participate in sports; we don't run for student offices; we don't go to your school dances; we aren't valedictorians at graduations; we seldom win recognition as students, even in Spanish; we seldom receive scholarships; we are seldom given consideration in school plans; we are seldom given lead parts in school plays. The higher in education we go, the more obvious are the double standards; yet, we haven't given up.

Who are we? Some call us the forgotten people; others call us chili   6
snappers, tacos, spics, mexs, or greasers. Some ignore us and pretend that we don't exist. Some just wish that we would go away. The late U.S. Senator Chavez from New Mexico once said, "At the time of war we are called 'the great patriotic Americans,' and during elections politicians call us 'the great Spanish-speaking community of America.' When we ask for jobs, we are called 'those damn Mexicans.'"

Who am I? I'm a human being. I have the same hopes that you have,   7
the same fears, same drives, same desires, same concerns, and same abilities. I want the same chance that you have to be an individual. Who am I? In reality, I am who you want me to be.

VOCABULARY

paragraph 5: Castilian, barrios, valedictorians

QUESTIONS

1. How does the author create an image of the class of people described? What defining qualities or facts does the author delay in presenting, and why?

2. What is the purpose of the essay, and what audience is the author addressing? Is the author seeking to persuade readers to change their thinking and possibly take action on discrimination or federal policies?

3. How do the persuasive means employed serve this purpose?

4. What does the author gain in persuasiveness by remaining anonymous?

5. How persuasive do you find the essay, and why?

SUGGESTION FOR WRITING

Write your own persuasive essay on who you are. Use the information you give about yourself and your ethnic, racial, religious, professional, or age group to persuade your readers to change their image of the group and possibly take action on a related issue.

JONATHAN SWIFT

JONATHAN SWIFT (1667–1745), the son of English Protestant parents, was born and educated in Ireland. In 1688 he went to England to seek a career in literature. Swift wrote satirical poems, essays, pamphlets, and tracts on the major issues of the day and became involved in many of its political and religious controversies. During his stay, Swift was ordained in the Church of England. In 1713 he became Dean of St. Patrick's Cathedral in Dublin and in the succeeding years wrote widely on various questions bearing on Ireland and England. His most famous satirical work, *Gulliver's Travels,* was published in 1726. Swift was deeply concerned about the sufferings observed in his country from boyhood. Ireland, under the control of the British government, was an impoverished country—restricted in selling its goods, incapable of producing enough food to feed the population. Most of the poor were Catholic, a point Swift emphasizes in his "modest proposal"—written in 1729 to suggest a remedy for the widespread starvation and misery of the country. Swift writes as a disinterested observer, anxious to perform a service to both the English and the Irish with his proposal. The persuasive means that Swift uses deserves the closest study.

A MODEST PROPOSAL

*For Preventing the Children of Poor People in Ireland from Being a Burden
to Their Parents or Country, and for Making Them Beneficial to the Public*

It is a melancholy object to those who walk through this great town, or   1
travel in the country, when they see the streets, the roads, and cabin-
doors crowded with beggars of the female sex, followed by three, four,
or six children, all in rags, and importuning every passenger for an alms.
These mothers, instead of being able to work for their honest livelihood,
are forced to employ all their time in strolling to beg sustenance for their
helpless infants: who, as they grow up, either turn thieves for want of
work, or leave their dear native country to fight for the Pretender in
Spain, or sell themselves to the Barbadoes.

I think it is agreed by all parties, that this prodigious number of chil-   2
dren in the arms, or on the backs, or at the heels of their mothers, and
frequently of their fathers, is in the present deplorable state of the kingdom, a very great additional grievance; and, therefore, whoever could
find out a fair, cheap, and easy method of making these children sound
and useful members of the commonwealth, would deserve so well of the
public, as to have his statue set up for a preserver of the nation.

But my intention is very far from being confined to provide only for   3
the children of professed beggars; it is of a much greater extent, and shall
take in the whole number of infants at a certain age, who are born of
parents in effect as little able to support them as those who demand our
charity in the streets.

As to my own part, having turned my thoughts for many years   4
upon this important subject, and maturely weighed the several schemes
of other projectors, I have always found them grossly mistaken in their
computation. It is true, a child, just dropped from its dam, may be supported by her milk for a solar year with little other nourishment; at most,
not above the value of two shillings, which the mother may certainly get,
or the value in scraps, by her lawful occupation of begging; and it is
exactly at one year old that I propose to provide for them in such a manner, as, instead of being a charge upon their parents or the parish, or
wanting food and raiment for the rest of their lives, they shall, on the
contrary, contribute to the feeding, and partly to the clothing, of many
thousands.

There is likewise another great advantage in my scheme, that it will   5
prevent those voluntary abortions, and that horrid practice of women
murdering their bastard children, alas, too frequent among us, sacrificing
the poor innocent babes, I doubt more to avoid the expense than the
shame, which would move tears and pity in the savage and inhuman breast.

The number of souls in this kingdom being usually reckoned one mil-   6
lion and a half, of these I calculate there may be about two hundred thousand couple whose wives are breeders; from which number I subtract thirty
thousand couple, who are able to maintain their own children (although
I apprehend there cannot be so many, under the present distresses of the
kingdom); but this being granted, there will remain an hundred and seventy thousand breeders. I again subtract fifty thousand for those women
who miscarry, or whose children die by accident or disease within the year.
There only remain a hundred and twenty thousand children of poor parents annually born. The question therefore is how this number shall be
reared and provided for? which, as I have already said, under the present
situation of affairs, is utterly impossible by all methods hitherto proposed.
For we can neither employ them in handicraft or agriculture; we neither
build houses (I mean in the country) nor cultivate land: they can very seldom pick up a livelihood by stealing until they arrive at six years old, except where they are of towardly parts; although I confess they learn the
rudiments much earlier; during which time they can, however, be properly
looked upon only as probationers; as I have been informed by a principal
gentleman in the county of Cavan, who protested to me, that he never
knew above one or two instances under the age of six, even in a part of
the kingdom so renowned for the quickest proficiency in that art.

I am assured by our merchants that a boy or a girl before twelve   7
years old is no salable commodity; and even when they come to this age
they will not yield above three pounds or three pounds and half-a-crown
at most, on the exchange; which cannot turn to account either to the parents or kingdom, the charge of nutriment and rags having been at least
four times that value.

I shall now, therefore, humbly propose my own thoughts, which I   8
hope will not be liable to the least objection.

I have been assured by a very knowing American of my acquaintance   9
in London, that a young healthy child, well nursed, is, at a year old, a
most delicious, nourishing, and wholesome food, whether stewed, roasted,
baked, or boiled; and I make no doubt that it will equally serve in a fricassee or a ragout.

I do therefore humbly offer it to public consideration, that of the   10
hundred and twenty thousand children already computed, twenty thousand may be reserved for breed, whereof only one-fourth part to be
males; which is more than we allow to sheep, black cattle, or swine;
and my reason is, that these children are seldom the fruits of marriage,
a circumstance not much regarded by our savages, therefore one male
will be sufficient to serve four females. That the remaining hundred
thousand may, at a year old, be offered in sale to the persons of quality
and fortune through the kingdom; always advising the mother to
let them suck plentifully in the last month, so as to render them
plump and fat for a good table. A child will make two dishes at an
entertainment for friends; and when the family dines alone, the fore or
hind quarter will make a reasonable dish, and, seasoned with a little
pepper or salt, will be very good boiled on the fourth day, especially
in winter.

I have reckoned, upon a medium, that a child just born will weigh   11
twelve pounds, and in a solar year, if tolerably nursed, increaseth to
twenty-eight pounds.

I grant this food will be somewhat dear, and therefore very proper   12
for landlords, who, as they have already devoured most of the parents,
seem to have the best title to the children.

Infants' flesh will be in season throughout the year, but more   13
plentifully in March, and a little before and after: for we are told by a
grave author, an eminent French physician, that fish being a prolific diet,
there are more children born in Roman Catholic countries about nine
months after Lent than at any other season; therefore, reckoning a year
after Lent, the markets will be more glutted than usual, because the number of popish infants is at least three to one in this kingdom; and therefore,
it will have one other collateral advantage, by lessening the number of
papists among us.

I have already computed the charge of nursing a beggar's child (in   14
which list I reckon all cottagers, labourers, and four-fifths of the farmers)
to be about two shillings per annum, rags included; and I believe no gentleman would repine to give ten shillings for the carcass of a good fat
child, which, as I have said, will make four dishes of excellent nutritive
meat, when he has only some particular friend, or his own family, to dine
with him. Thus, the squire will learn to be a good landlord, and grow
popular among his tenants; the mother will have eight shillings net profit,
and be fit for work till she produces another child.

Those who are more thrifty (as I must confess the times require) may   15
flay the carcass; the skin of which artificially dressed, will make admirable
gloves for ladies, and summer-boots for fine gentlemen.

As to our city of Dublin, shambles[1] may be appointed for this pur-   16
pose in the most convenient parts of it, and butchers we may be assured
will not be wanting; although I rather recommend buying the children
alive, and dressing them hot from the knife, as we do roasting pigs.

A very worthy person, a true lover of this country, and whose virtues   17
I highly esteem, was lately pleased, in discoursing on this matter, to offer a refinement upon my scheme. He said, that many gentlemen of this
kingdom, having of late destroyed their deer, he conceived that the want
of venison might be well supplied by the bodies of young lads and maidens, not exceeding fourteen years of age, nor under twelve; so great a
number of both sexes in every county being now ready to starve for want
of work and service; and these to be disposed of by their parents, if alive,
or otherwise by their nearest relations. But, with due deference to so excellent a friend, and so deserving a patriot, I cannot be altogether in his
sentiments; for as to the males, my American acquaintance assured me
from frequent experience, that their flesh was generally tough and lean,
like that of our schoolboys, by continual exercise, and their taste dis-
agreeable; and to fatten them would not answer the charge. Then as to
the females, it would, I think, with humble submission, be a loss to the
public, because they soon would become breeders themselves: and besides, it is not improbable that some scrupulous people might be apt to
censure such a practice (although indeed very unjustly) as a little bor-
dering upon cruelty; which, I confess hath always been with me the
strongest objection against any project, how well soever intended.

But in order to justify my friend, he confessed that this expedient   18
was put into his head by the famous Psalmanazar,[2] a native of the island
Formosa, who came from thence to London above twenty years ago; and
in conversation told my friend, that in his country, when any young person
happened to be put to death, the executioner sold the carcass to persons
of quality as a prime dainty; and that in his time the body of a plump
girl of fifteen, who was crucified for an attempt to poison the emperor,

---

[1] *Shambles*: butcher shops.

[2] *Psalmanazar*: A French writer, George Psalmanazar, who posed as a native of Formosa
in a fake book he published about that country in 1704, in England.

was sold to his Imperial Majesty's prime minister of state, and other great mandarins of the court, in joints from the gibbet, at four hundred crowns. Neither indeed can I deny, that if the same use were made of several plump young girls in this town, who, without one single groat to their fortunes, cannot stir abroad without a chair, and appear at playhouse and assemblies in foreign fineries which they never will pay for, the kingdom would not be the worse.

Some persons of a desponding spirit are in great concern about that   19 vast number of poor people who are aged, diseased, or maimed; and I have been desired to employ my thoughts what course may be taken to ease the nation of so grievous an encumbrance. But I am not in the least pain upon that matter, because it is very well known, that they are every day dying, and rotting, by cold and famine, and filth and vermin, as fast as can be reasonably expected. And so to the younger labourers, they are now in almost as hopeful a condition: they cannot get work, and consequently pine away for want of nourishment, to a degree, that if at any time they are accidentally hired to common labour, they have not strength to perform it; and thus the country and themselves are happily delivered from the evils to come.

I have too long digressed, and therefore shall return to my subject. I   20 think the advantages by the proposal which I have made are obvious and many, as well as of the highest importance.

For first, as I have already observed, it would greatly lessen the num-   21 ber of papists, with whom we are yearly overrun, being the principal breeders of the nation as well as our most dangerous enemies; and who stay at home on purpose with a design to deliver the kingdom to the Pretender, hoping to take their advantage by the absence of so many good Protestants, who have chosen rather to leave their country than stay at home and pay tithes against their conscience to an idolatrous Episcopal curate.[3]

Secondly, the poorer tenants will have something valuable of their   22 own, which by law may be made liable to distress, and help to pay their landlord's rent; their corn and cattle being already seized, and money a thing unknown.

Thirdly, whereas the maintenance of an hundred thousand children,   23 from two years old and upwards, cannot be computed at less than ten

---

[3] Swift is attacking the prejudice against Irish Catholics in his time, and also the motives of a number of Protestant dissenters from the Church of England.

shillings a piece per annum, the nation's stock will be thereby increased fifty thousand pounds per annum; besides the profit of a new dish introduced to the tables of all gentlemen of fortune in the kingdom who have any refinement in taste. And the money will circulate among ourselves, the goods being entirely of our own growth and manufacture.

Fourthly, the constant breeders, besides the gain of eight shillings sterling per annum by the sale of their children, will be rid of the charge of maintaining them after the first year.

Fifthly, this food would otherwise bring great custom to taverns; where the vintners will certainly be so prudent as to procure the best receipts for dressing it to perfection, and, consequently, have their houses frequented by all the fine gentlemen, who justly value themselves upon their knowledge in good eating: and a skillful cook, who understands how to oblige his guests, will contrive to make it as expensive as they please.

Sixthly, this would be a great inducement to marriage, which all wise nations have either encouraged by rewards, or enforced by laws and penalties. It would increase the care and tenderness of mothers towards their children, when they were sure of a settlement for life to the poor babes, provided in some sort by the public, to their annual profit instead of expense. We should soon see an honest emulation among the married women, which of them could bring the fattest child to the market. Men would become as fond of their wives during the time of their pregnancy, as they are now of their mares in foal, their cows in calf, or sows when they are ready to farrow; nor offer to beat or kick them (as is too frequent a practice) for fear of a miscarriage.

Many other advantages might be enumerated. For instance, the addition of some thousand carcasses in our exportation of barrelled beef; the propagation of swine's flesh, and improvement in the art of making good bacon, so much wanted among us by the great destruction of pigs, too frequent at our tables, which are no way comparable in taste or magnificence to a well-grown, fat yearling child, which, roasted whole, will make a considerable figure at a Lord Mayor's feast, or any other public entertainment. But this, and many others, I omit, being studious of brevity.

Supposing that one thousand families in this city would be constant customers for infants' flesh, besides others who might have it at merry meetings, particularly weddings and christenings, I compute that Dublin would take off annually about twenty thousand carcasses; and the rest of the kingdom (where probably they will be sold somewhat cheaper) the remaining eighty thousand.

I can think of no one objection that will possibly be raised against   29
this proposal, unless it should be urged, that the number of people will
be thereby much lessened in the kingdom. This I freely own, and it was
indeed one principal design in offering it to the world. I desire the reader
will observe that I calculate my remedy for this one individual kingdom
of Ireland, and for no other that ever was, is, or I think ever can be, upon
earth. Therefore let no man talk to me of other expedients: of taxing our
absentees at five shillings a pound: of using neither clothes nor household-
furniture except what is of our own growth and manufacture: of utterly
rejecting the materials and instruments that promote foreign luxury: of
curing the expensiveness of pride, vanity, idleness, and gaming in our
women; of introducing a vein of parsimony, prudence, and temperance:
of learning to love our country, wherein we differ even from Laplanders,
and the inhabitants of Topinamboo:[4] of quitting our animosities and fac-
tions, nor act any longer like the Jews, who were murdering one another
at the very moment their city was taken:[5] of being a little cautious not
to sell our country and consciences for nothing: of teaching landlords to
have at least one degree of mercy towards their tenants: lastly, of putting
a spirit of honesty, industry, and skill into our shopkeepers; who, if a res-
olution could now be taken to buy only our native goods, would immediately unite to cheat and exact upon us in the price, the measure, and
the goodness, nor could ever yet be brought to make one fair proposal
of just dealing, though often and earnestly invited to it.

Therefore I repeat, let no man talk to me of these and the like ex-   30
pedients, till he hath at least some glimpse of hope that there will ever
be some hearty and sincere attempt to put them in practice.

But, as to myself, having been wearied out for many years with of-   31
fering vain, idle, visionary thoughts, and at length utterly despairing of
success, I fortunately fell upon this proposal; which as it is wholly new,
so it hath something solid and real, of no expense and little trouble, full
in our own power, and whereby we can incur no danger in disobliging
England. For this kind of commodity will not bear exportation, the flesh
being of too tender a consistence to admit a long continuance in salt, although perhaps I could name a country which would be glad to eat up
our whole nation without it.

---

[4] *Topinamboo:* A district of Brazil notorious for its barbarism and ignorance.
[5] Swift is referring to the fall of Jerusalem to the Romans in 70 A.D.

After all, I am not so violently bent upon my own opinion as to reject 32
any offer proposed by wise men which shall be found equally innocent,
cheap, easy, and effectual. But before something of that kind shall be
advanced in contradiction to my scheme, and offering a better, I desire
the author, or authors, will be pleased maturely to consider two points.
First, as things now stand, how they will be able to find food and raiment
for a hundred thousand useless mouths and backs? And, secondly, there
being a round million of creatures in human figure throughout this kingdom, whose whole subsistence put into a common stock would leave
them in debt two millions of pounds sterling, adding those who are beggars by profession, to the bulk of farmers, cottagers, and labourers, with
the wives and children who are beggars in effect; I desire those politicians
who dislike my overture, and may perhaps be so bold as to attempt an
answer, that they will first ask the parents of these mortals, whether they
would not at this day think it a great happiness to have been sold for
food at a year old, in the manner I prescribe, and thereby have avoided
such a perpetual scene of misfortunes as they have since gone through,
by the oppression of landlords, the impossibility of paying rent without
money or trade, the want of common sustenance, with neither house nor
clothes to cover them from the inclemencies of weather, and the most
inevitable prospect of entailing the like, or greater miseries, upon their
breed for ever.

I profess, in the sincerity of my heart, that I have not the least per- 33
sonal interest in endeavouring to promote this necessary work, having
no other motive than the public good of my country, by advancing our
trade, providing for infants, relieving the poor, and giving some pleasure
to the rich. I have no children by which I can propose to get a single penny;
the youngest being nine years old, and my wife past child-bearing.

VOCABULARY

paragraph 1: importuning
paragraph 2: prodigious
paragraph 4: schemes, projectors, raiment
paragraph 6: apprehend, rudiments, probationers, renowned

paragraph 9: fricassee, ragout
paragraph 13: prolific, papists
paragraph 14: squire
paragraph 15: flay
paragraph 17: venison
paragraph 18: mandarins, gibbet
paragraph 19: encumbrance
paragraph 20: digressed
paragraph 21: tithes, idolatrous, Episcopal curate
paragraph 25: vintners
paragraph 26: emulation, foal, farrow
paragraph 27: yearling
paragraph 29: expedients, parsimony, animosities
paragraph 31: consistence
paragraph 32: effectual, entailing

QUESTIONS

1. How does Swift establish the basic character and motives of his proposer in the opening paragraphs?

2. How does he reveal his attitude toward the proposer? Is he in accord with his general view of the English and of absentee landlords? Are their motives stated directly or implied?

3. Is the proposer—and perhaps Swift himself—critical of the Irish, or does he exonerate them entirely?

4. Short of adopting the actual "modest proposal," is there another way of remedying the evils exposed in the course of the essay? In other words, does Swift suggest other policies that would reduce poverty and starvation in Ireland?

5. In general, what strategy does Swift employ to deal with English policies and motives and perhaps Irish attitudes too?

6. How persuasive do you find the essay? Is it an essay of historical interest or literary interest only, or does it have something to say to people today?

SUGGESTION FOR WRITING

Write your own "modest proposal" for dealing with a current social or political evil. You may wish to write as yourself or, like Swift, impersonate someone who wishes to make a modest proposal. Maintain a consistent tone throughout your essay, or at least make any shifts in tone consistent with the character of your speaker and his or her motives in writing.

ABRAHAM LINCOLN

The Battle of Gettysburg, fought in southeastern Pennsylvania July 1–3, 1861, left fifty thousand dead from both sides of the conflict. On November 19, 1863, a national cemetery was dedicated on the site. Edward Everett, a former secretary of state and U.S. senator from Massachusetts, delivered a two-hour oration, followed by President Lincoln's brief address. Historian Garry Wills says in *Lincoln at Gettysburg:* "Abraham Lincoln transformed the ugly reality into something rich and strange—and he did it with 272 words. The power of words has rarely been given a more compelling demonstration." His analysis of Lincoln's words follows.

THE GETTYSBURG ADDRESS

Four score and seven years ago our fathers brought forth on this continent, a new nation, conceived in Liberty, and dedicated to the proposition that all men are created equal.

Now we are engaged in a great civil war, testing whether that nation, or any nation so conceived and so dedicated, can long endure. We are met on a great battlefield of that war. We have come to dedicate a portion of that field, as a final resting place for those who here gave their lives that that nation might live. It is altogether fitting and proper that we should do this.

But, in a larger sense, we can not dedicate—we can not consecrate—we can not hallow—this ground. The brave men, living and dead, who struggled here, have consecrated it, far above our poor power to add or detract. The world will little note, nor long remember what we say here, but it can never forget what they did here. It is for us the living, rather, to be dedicated here to the unfinished work which they who fought here have thus far so nobly advanced. It is rather for us to be here dedicated to the great task remaining before us—that from these honored dead we take increased devotion to that cause for which they gave the last full measure of devotion—that we here highly resolve that these dead shall not have died in vain—that this nation, under God, shall have a new birth of freedom—and that government of the people, by the people, for the people, shall not perish from the earth.

GARRY WILLS

GARRY WILLS, former Henry R. Luce Professor of American Culture and Public Policy at Northwestern University, has written on a wide range of social, political, and religious topics. His many books include *Nixon Agonistes* (1970), *Inventing America* (1978), *Reagan's America* (1987), and *Necessary Evil: A History of American Distrust of Government* (1999). Wills says in *Lincoln at Gettysburg* (1992): "Lincoln's speech at Gettysburg worked several revolutions, beginning with one in literary style . . . . Lincoln's remarks anticipated the shift to vernacular rhythms that Mark Twain would complete twenty years later. Hemingway claimed that all modern American novels are the offspring of *Huckleberry Finn*. It is no greater exaggeration to say that all modern political prose descends from the Gettysburg Address." In the following excerpt Wills shows why it did.

THE GETTYSBURG ADDRESS

In his quest to use the right words himself, Lincoln often achieved a clarity that is its own source of aesthetic satisfaction. There is no better description of this effect than Blair's:

> Perspicuity in writing is not to be considered as only a sort of negative virtue, a freedom from defect. It has a higher merit. It is a degree of positive beauty. We are pleased with an author, we consider him as deserving praise, who frees us from all fatigue of searching for his

meaning, who carries us through his subject without any embarrassment or confusion, whose style flows always like a limpid stream where we see to the very bottom.[1]

In a text like Lincoln's famous letter to Horace Greeley, even the sentence structure seems to present its own case. The grammar argues. By ordering a series of simple and disjunctive sentences, Lincoln patiently exhausts all alternatives. Beginning his sentences with repeated "If"s (anaphora), Lincoln rings all changes on the concessive clause (granting irrelevant assertions or assumptions for now) and the hypothetical clause (posing case after case for its own treatment). The analysis of every permutation of the subject seals off misunderstandings as if Lincoln were quietly closing door after door. The points are advanced like a series of theorems in Euclid, as clear, as sequential, as compelling:

> I have just read yours of the 19th instant, addressed to myself through the *New York Tribune*.
>
> If there be in it any statements or assumptions of fact which I may know to be erroneous, I do not now and here controvert them.
>
> If there be in it any inferences which I believe to be falsely drawn, I do not now and here argue against them.
>
> If there be perceptible in it an impatient and dictatorial tone, I waive it, in deference to an old friend whose heart I have always supposed to be right.
>
> As to the policy I "seem to be pursuing," as you say, I have not meant to leave anyone in doubt. I would save the Union. I would save it the shortest way under the Constitution.
>
> The sooner the national authority can be restored, the nearer the Union will be—the Union as it was.
>
> If there be those who would not save the Union unless they could at the same time save slavery, I do not agree with them.
>
> My paramount object in this struggle is to save the Union, and not either to save or destroy slavery.
>
> If I could save the Union without freeing any slave, I would do it; if I could save it by freeing all the slaves, I would do it; and if I could save it by freeing some and leaving others alone, I would also do that.
>
> What I do about slavery and the coloured race, I do because I believe it helps to save the Union; and what I forbear, I forbear because I do not believe it would help to save the Union.

2

---

[1] Hugh Blair, *Lectures on Rhetoric and Belles Lettres* (Edinburgh, 1783), in the facsimile edited by Harold F. Harding (Southern Illinois University Press, 1965), vol. 1, p. 186.

I shall do less whenever I shall believe that what I am doing hurts the cause; and I shall do more whenever I shall believe doing more will help the cause.

I shall try to correct errors where shown to be errors, and I shall adopt new views as fast as they shall appear to be true views.

I have here stated my purpose according to my views of official duty, and I intend no modification of my oft-expressed personal wish that all men everywhere be free.[2]

This is the highest art, which conceals itself. The opening sentences   3
perform the classical role of an exordium, limiting one's task, disarming hostility, finding common ground with one's audience. The traditional *captatio benevolentiae* (claim on good will) could not be better exemplified than in Lincoln's address to his old friend's heart.

While making his own position clear, Lincoln professes a readiness to   4
alter course if he is proved wrong. But he promises to do that only within the framework he has constructed. (He will change *only* if the change saves the Union.) He sounds deferential rather than dogmatic, yet he is in fact precluding all norms but his own. It is the same kind of rhetorical trap he used in his most famous statement of alternative possibilities:

"A House divided against itself cannot stand."

I believe this government cannot endure, permanently half *slave* and half *free*.

I do not expect the Union to be *dissolved*—I do not expect the house to *fall*—but I *do* expect it will cease to be divided.

It will become *all* one thing or *all* the other.

Either the *opponents* of slavery will arrest the further spread of it, and place it where the public mind shall rest in the belief that it is in course of ultimate extinction; or its *advocates* will push it forward, till it shall become alike lawful in *all* the states, *old* as well as *new*—*North* as well as *South*.

Have we no *tendency* to the latter condition?[3]

Lincoln's own underlinings reinforce sentence structure in suggesting that these two and only these two outcomes are possible.

---

[2] Abraham Lincoln, *Speeches and Writings*, edited by Don E. Fehrenbacher (Library of America, 1989), vol. 2, pp. 357–58. I print the text as Charles N. Smiley did in *Classical Journal* 13 (1917), pp. 125–26. Smiley, a classical rhetorician, counted in this letter "six completely balanced sentences, eight cases of anaphora, six instances of similar word endings [homoeoteleuton], six antitheses."

[3] *Speeches and Writings*, vol. 1, p. 426.

The language seems stripped of all figurative elements—though Lincoln has begun with a biblical figure that seems to pre-empt criticism of its premise. Lincoln's logic can be, and has been, challenged; but the ordering of the words *seems* logical, perspicuous. It is also, in its clipped quality, urgent. The rapid deployment of all options seems to press on the reader a need to decide. Lincoln's language is honed to a purpose.

Looking back to the nineteenth century's long speeches and debates, we might deplore the more disjunct "blips" of communication in our time. Television and other modern developments are blamed for a shortening of the modern attention span. But a similar process was at work in Lincoln's time, and he welcomed it. The railroad, the telegraph, the steamship had quickened the pace of events. Thoughts and words took on new and nervous rhythms. Lincoln, who considered language the world's great invention, welcomed a cognate invention, telegraphy. He used the telegraph to keep up with his generals—he even experimented with telegraph wires strung to reconnaissance balloons.[4] As president, Lincoln worked intimately with the developer of telegraphy in America, Joseph Henry, the president of the Smithsonian Institution.[5] He had praised the lightning "harnessed to take his [man's] tidings in a trifle less than no time."[6] Lincoln spent long hours in the telegraph center at the War Department, and was impatient with the fumbling and imprecise language still being used on this instrument, which demands clarity as well as concision.[7] Hay reflects Lincoln's relief when he found an efficient user of modern language in one of his military engineers:

> This is Herman Haupt, the railroad man at Alexandria. He has, as Chase says, a Major General's head on his shoulders. The President is

---

[4] Robert V. Bruce, *Lincoln and the Tools of War* (University of Illinois Press, 1989), pp. 85–88.

[5] Samuel F. B. Morse just developed the code to be used on Henry's transmitter: Robert V. Bruce, *The Launching of Modern American Science, 1846–76* (Alfred A. Knopf, 1987), pp. 141, 150–57, 275–76.

[6] *Speeches and Writings*, vol. 2, p. 3.

[7] See the memoirs of the War Department's telegrapher, David Homer Bates, *Lincoln in the Telegraph Office* (Century Co., 1907). By setting up telegraphic liaison with his generals, through Henry Halleck, Lincoln created what T. Harry Williams has called the first "modern system of command for a modern war," one "superior to anything achieved in Europe until von Moltke forged the Prussian staff machine of 1865 and 1870" (*Lincoln and His Generals* [Vintage, 1952], pp. 302–3).

particularly struck with the business-like character of his dispatch, telling in the fewest words the information most sought for, which contrasted strongly with the weak, whiney, vague, and incorrect dispatches of the whilom General-in-Chief [McClellan].[8]

Lincoln's respect for General Grant came, in part, from the contrast between McClellan's waffling and Grant's firm grasp of the right words to use in explaining or arguing for a military operation. Lincoln sensed what Grant's later publisher, Mark Twain, did, that the West Pointer who once taught mathematics was a master of expository prose. Sitting his horse during a pause in battle, Grant could write model instructions for his subordinates—a skill John Keegan compares to the Duke of Wellington's. Keegan even says: "If there is a single contemporary document which explains 'why the North won the Civil War,' that abiding conundrum of American historical inquiry, it is *The Personal Memoirs of U. S. Grant.*"[9] In an answering hyperbole, James McPherson has claimed that Lincoln won the war by his language.[10] The two half-truths contain at least one whole truth—that well-focused words were the medium through which Grant and Lincoln achieved their amazing degree of mutual sympathy and military accord.[11]

There was no possibility of misunderstanding a dispatch like Lincoln's of August 17, 1864, "Hold on with a bull-dog gripe, and chew & choke, as much as possible"—a message that made Grant burst into laughter and say, "The President has more nerve than any of his advisers."[12] Lincoln's telegraphic eloquence has a monosyllabic and staccato beat:

---

[8] *Lincoln and the Civil War Diaries and Letters of John Hay*, edited by Tyler Bennett (Dodd, Mead, 1939), p. 46. Lincoln used Haupt to circularize scientists for suggestions on war-related research (Robert V. Bruce, *Tools of War*, [University of Illinois Press, 1989], pp. 215–17). Haupt's reciprocal esteem for Lincoln is expressed in the *Reminiscences of General Herman Haupt* (Wright and Joys Co., 1901), pp. 297–301.

[9] John Keegan, *The Mask of Command* (Penguin, 1987), p. 202.

[10] James M. McPherson, "How Lincoln Won the West with Metaphors," in *Abraham Lincoln and the Second American Revolution* (Oxford University Press, 1990), pp. 93–112. Not all the language McPherson adduces is metaphorical, but it is all clear and most of it is brief.

[11] For evidence of that accord, see *The Papers of Ulysses A. Grant*, edited by John Y. Simon (Southern Illinois University Press), vol. 9 (1982), pp. 196–97; vol. 10 (1982), p. 381; vol. 11 (1984), pp. 45, 263, 280, 360, 425, 441; vol. 12 (1984), p. 185.

[12] *Speeches and Writings*, vol. 2, p. 620. Horace Potter, *Campaigning with Grant* (1897, reprinted by Da Capo, 1986), p. 279.

Have none of it. Stand firm.[13]

On that point hold firm, as with a chain of steel.[14]

Watch it every day, and hour, and force it.[15]

Events were moving too fast for the more languid phrases of the past. As a speaker, Lincoln grasped ahead of time Twain's insight of the postwar years: "Few sinners are saved after the first twenty minutes of a sermon."[16] The trick, of course, was not simply to be brief but to say a great deal in the fewest words. Lincoln justly boasted, of his Second Inaugural's six hundred words, "Lots of wisdom in that document, I suspect."[17] The same is even truer of the Gettysburg Address, which uses roughly half that number of words.

The unwillingness to waste words shows up in the Address's telegraphic quality—the omission of most coupling words—that rhetoricians call asyndeton.[18] Triple phrases sound as to a drumbeat, with no "and" or "but" to slow their insistency:

> *we are engaged . . .*
> *We are met . . .*
> *We have come . . .*
>
> *we can not dedicate . . .*
> *we can not consecrate . . .*
> *we can not hallow . . .*
>
> *that from these honored dead . . .*
> *that we here highly resolve . . .*
> *that this nation, under God . . .*
>
> *government of the people,*
> *by the people,*
> *for the people . . .*

---

[13] *Speeches and Writings,* vol. 2, p. 190.

[14] *The Collected Works of Abraham Lincoln,* edited by Roy P. Basler (Rutgers, 1955), vol. 4, p. 151.

[15] *Speeches and Writings, vol. 2, p. 615.*

[16] Hannibal *Courier-Post,* March 1, 1835.

[17] Francis B. Carpenter, *Six Months at the White House* (Riverside Press, 1877), p. 234.

[18] Lane Cooper, the classicist, noted Lincoln's striking asyndeton in *The Rhetoric of Aristotle* (Appleton-Century, 1932), p. xxxiii.

Despite the suggestive images of birth, testing, and rebirth, the speech   10
is surprisingly bare of ornament. The language is itself made strenuous,
its musculature easily traced, so even the grammar becomes a form of
rhetoric. By repeating the antecedent as often as possible, instead of referring to it indirectly by pronouns like "it" or "they," or by backward
referential words like "former" and "latter," Lincoln interlocks his sentences, making of them a constantly self-referential system. This linking
up by explicit repetition amounts to a kind of hook-and-eye method for
joining the parts of his address. The rhetorical devices are almost invisible,
since they use no figurative language or formal tropes.

> Four score and seven years ago our fathers brought forth on this
> continent, *a new nation, conceived* in Liberty *and dedicated* to the
> proposition that all men are created equal.
>   Now we are engaged in A GREAT CIVIL WAR, testing whether *that
> nation,* or any nation *so conceived and so dedicated,* can long endure.
>   We are met on a great <u>battle-field</u> of THAT WAR.
>   We have come to <u>dedicate</u> a portion of *that field,* as a final resting
> place for those who here gave their lives that *that nation* might live. It
> is altogether fitting and proper that we should do this.
>   But, in a larger sense, we can not <u>dedicate</u>—we can not <u>consecrate</u>—
> we cannot hallow—this ground.
>   The brave men, living and dead, who struggled here, have <u>consecrated</u>
> it, far above our poor power to add or detract. The world will little
> note, nor long remember, what we say here, but it can never forget what
> they did here.
>   It is for us, the living, rather, to be <u>dedicated</u> here to the unfinished
> work which they **who fought here** have thus far so nobly advanced. It
> is, rather, for us to be here <u>dedicated</u> to the great task remaining before
> us—that from **THESE HONORED DEAD** we take increased devotion
> to that cause for which they gave the last full measure of devotion—
>   that we here highly resolve that **THESE DEAD** shall not have died
> in vain—that this nation, under God, shall have a new birth of free-
> dom—and that government of the people, by the people, for the peo-
> ple, shall not perish from the earth.

Each of the paragraphs printed separately here is bound to the pre-   11
ceding and the following by some resumptive element. Only the first and
last paragraph do not (because they cannot) have this two-way connection to their setting. Not all of these "pointer" phrases replace
grammatical antecedents in the technical sense. But Lincoln makes them

perform analogous work. The nation is declared, again, to be "consecrated" and "dedicated" before each of these terms is given a further two (separate) uses for individuals present at the ceremony, who repeat (as it were) the national consecration. By this reliance on a few words in different contexts, the compactness of the themes is emphasized. A similar linking process is performed, almost subliminally, by the repeated pinning of statements to *that* field, *these* dead, who died *here*, for *that* (kind of) nation. The reverential touching, over and over, of the charged moment and place leads Lincoln to use "here" six times in the short text, the adjectival "that" five times, "this" four times.[19] The spare vocabulary is not impoverishing because of the subtly interfused constructions, in which Charles Smiley identifies "six antitheses, six instances of balanced sentence structure, two cases of anaphora, and four alliterations." "Plain speech" was never less artless. Lincoln forged a new lean language to humanize and redeem the first modern war.

Some have claimed, simplistically, that Lincoln achieved a "down-to-earth" style by using short Anglo-Saxon words rather than long Latin ones in the Address. Such people cannot have read the Address with care. Lincoln talks of a nation "conceived in Liberty," not born in freedom; of one "dedicated to [a] proposition," not vowed to a truth; of a "consecrated" nation whose soldiers show their "devotion"—Latinate terms all. Lincoln was even criticized, in the past, for using so "unliterary" a word as "proposition."[20] These criticisms are based on a misunderstanding. Though Lincoln used fertility *imagery* from the cemetery movement, his *message* was telegraphic (itself a Latin term, from the Greek). He liked to talk of the theorems and axioms of democracy, comparing them to Euclid's "propositions."[21] He was a Transcendentalist without the fuzziness. He spoke a modern language because he was dealing with a scientific age, for which abstract words are appropriate. His urgency was more a matter of the speech's internal "wiring" and *workability* than

12

---

[19] Lincoln, conscious of the repeated "here," took out a seventh use in the phrase "they [here] gave the last full measure of devotion" (*Collected Works*, vol. 7, p. 23). The frequency of "that" in the speech was criticized by William E. Barton (*Lincoln at Gettysburg* [Bobbs-Merrill, 1930], p. 147).

[20] Cf. Barton, *Lincoln at Gettysburg*, p. 148; Louis A. Warren, *Lincoln's Gettysburg Declaration* (Lincoln National Life Foundation, 1964), p. 106. Lincoln's fondness for the word "proposition" is apparent at *Speeches and Writings*, vol. 1, p. 277, 683, 732, 741.

[21] *Speeches and Writings*, vol. 2, p. 19.

of anything so crude as "calling a spade a spade." He was not addressing an agrarian future but a mechanical one. His speech is economical,
taut, interconnected, like the machinery he tested and developed for battle. Words were weapons, for him, even though he meant them to be
weapons of peace in the midst of war.

This was the perfect medium for changing the way most Americans   13
thought about the nation's founding acts. Lincoln does not argue law or
history, as Daniel Webster did. He *makes* history. He does not come to
present a theory, but to impose a symbol, one tested in experience and
appealing to national values, with an emotional urgency entirely expressed
in calm abstractions (fire in ice). He came to change the world, to effect
an intellectual revolution. No other words could have done it. The miracle
is that these words did. In his brief time before the crowd at Gettysburg
he wove a spell that has not, yet, been broken—he called up a new nation
out of the blood and trauma.

VOCABULARY

paragraph 1: perspicuity
paragraph 2: disjunctive, concessive, permutation, theorems
paragraph 4: deferential, dogmatic, norms
paragraph 6: cognate
paragraph 7: waffling, hyperbole
paragraph 8: languid, staccato
paragraph 10: tropes
paragraph 11: resumptive
paragraph 12: Transcendentalist

QUESTIONS

1. How do the opening paragraphs of the letter to Horace Greeley "perform the classical role of an exordium, limiting one's task, disarming hostility, finding common ground with one's audience"?

2. In the letter to Greeley, Wills says, Lincoln sounds "deferential rather
than dogmatic, yet he is in fact precluding all norms but his own" (paragraph 4)? How does Lincoln do so?

3. What "suggestive images of birth, testing, and rebirth" do you find in the Gettysburg Address?

4. What instances of antithesis and exact parallelism or balance do you find?

5. How does Wills explain Lincoln's stripped-down style in the address and other writings? What does he point to in Lincoln's character and beliefs?

6. Why was the language Lincoln spoke and wrote "the perfect medium for changing the way most Americans thought about the nation's founding acts" (paragraph 13)?

SUGGESTIONS FOR WRITING

1. Analyze sample paragraphs from another of Lincoln's addresses—for example, that at the Cooper Union in 1860 or the first or second Inaugural Address—to test the points Wills makes.

2. Wills says that "well-focused words were the medium through which Grant and Lincoln achieved their amazing degree of mutual sympathy and military accord." Compare one of Grant's letters to Lincoln with one of Lincoln's to Grant to test this statement.

3. Discuss what the style of one or two paragraphs of one of the following suggests about the character of the author:

a. Thomas Paine, *Common Sense*

b. George Washington, Farewell Address

c. Thomas Jefferson, First Inaugural Address

d. William Jennings Bryan, Address to the 1896 Democratic National Convention

e. Franklin D. Roosevelt, First Inaugural Address

f. Dwight D. Eisenhower, First Inaugural Address

g. John F. Kennedy, Inaugural Address

h. Martin Luther King, Jr., Letter from Birmingham Jail, "I Have a Dream"

VI

ESSAYS ON WRITING

INTRODUCTION

In the first essay that follows, Mark Twain stresses the unconscious powers of mind that come into play in the act of composition. Twain refers to "an automatically-working taste . . . which selects and rejects without asking you for any help, and patiently and steadily improves itself without troubling you to approve or applaud." But that taste has been shaped by what the writer has read; Twain takes note of the "model-chamber" in which writers store those effective sentences they find as they read. Though writers shape their sentences unconsciously, drawing upon these model sentences, the act of writing becomes conscious when they reject sentences that don't make sense and experiment with sentences that are different from the ones they usually write.

John Ciardi agrees with Twain that reading is essential to the writer: "No writer can produce good writing without a sure sense of what has been accomplished in the past within his form." But, Ciardi adds, the writer does not adhere to the past but rather innovates: "it is impossible to venture meaningful innovation unless one knows what he is *innovating from*." But more so than Twain, Ciardi stresses the conscious side of creativity, which he defines as "the imaginatively gifted recombination of known elements into something new." Practiced writers possess a power of mind akin to that described by Twain—in Ciardi's words, "a second attention lurking in the mind at the very moment [writers] have felt the need to be most indivisibly absorbed in what they are doing." The competent writer, like the competent reader, must possess "fluency," which Ciardi defines as "the ability to receive more than one impression at the same time."

Walker Gibson deals with a different kind of decision—that of the style the author chooses, sometimes unconsciously, sometimes deliberately. He states in his book on prose styles, *Tough, Sweet, and Stuffy,* that each choice "is significant in dramatizing a personality or voice, with a particular center of concern and a particular relation to the person he is addressing." The author may have reason to question the style of a piece of writing under review, sensing that the piece does not "sound right," though the content seems satisfactory. We have all had this experience in beginning a letter, then starting again, sensing we are writing in a style—or voice—that conveys a false impression or image of ourselves. We continue experimenting until our sentences establish the desirable relation to the person addressed. The main job of revision, we sometimes discover, is to find the appropriate style or voice.

In his essay on revision, William Zinsser focuses on what happens in the course of writing and afterwards, as we rethink and revise initial drafts. Zinsser gives the same advice that George Orwell does in his classic essay "Politics and the English Language." In his discussion of how to avoid ready-made words and phrases, Orwell suggests how these words and phrases find their way into a piece of writing: "When you think of something abstract you are more inclined to use words from the start, and unless you make a conscious effort to prevent it, the existing dialect will come rushing in and do the job for you, at the expense of blurring or even changing your meaning." Zinsser shows how to deal with this problem of ready-made words and ideas. "The secret of good writing is to strip every sentence to its cleanest components," he states, and he illustrates how to do so.

These four essayists by no means suggest all the ways writers proceed or engage in writing and revision. They agree, however, that the act of writing is not aimless or undirected. Zinsser and Gibson in particular show that writers give attention to what they have written—to its clarity and effectiveness—at some stage in the process and sometimes at all stages.

MARK TWAIN

MARK TWAIN's description of life in the Missouri river town where he grew up and his experience as a cub pilot on a Mississippi steamboat appear earlier in this book. His numerous stories, novels, sketches, and essays seem the work of a writer who lets a tale or comment develop leisurely, in the manner of the relaxed yarn spinner. This impression is deceptive, for Twain was attentive to the craft, as all good storytellers and writers must be. Yet, he tells us in this short statement on writing, he allowed his imagination to shape the work, without constant awareness of means and effects. Rather, he depended on the "model-chamber" he describes and on "an automatically-working taste" that came to him through wide reading. Twain suggests one way that writers develop their craft.

The Art of Composition

Your inquiry has set me thinking, but, so far, my thought fails to materialize. I mean that, upon consideration, I am not sure that I have methods in composition. I do suppose I have—I suppose I must have—but they somehow refuse to take shape in my mind; their details refuse to separate and submit to classification and description; they remain a jumble—visible, like the fragments of glass when you look in at the wrong end of a kaleidoscope, but still a jumble. If I could turn the whole thing around and look in at the other end, why then the figures would flash into form out of the chaos, and I shouldn't have any more trouble. But my head isn't right for that today, apparently. It might have been, maybe, if I had slept last night.

However, let us try guessing. Let us guess that whenever we read a sentence and like it, we unconsciously store it away in our model-chamber; and it goes with the myriad of its fellows to the building, brick by brick, of the eventful edifice which we call our style. And let us guess that whenever we run across other forms—bricks—whose color, or some other defect, offends us, we unconsciously reject these, and so one never finds them in our edifice. If I have subjected myself to any training processes, and no doubt I have, it must have been in this unconscious or half-conscious fashion. I think it unlikely that deliberate and consciously methodical training is usual with the craft. I think it likely that the training most in use is of this unconscious sort, and is guided and governed and made by-and-by unconsciously systematic, by an automatically-working taste—a taste which selects and rejects without asking you for any help, and patiently and steadily improves itself without troubling you to approve or applaud. Yes, and likely enough when the structure is at last

1

2

pretty well up, and attracts attention, *you* feel complimented, whereas you didn't build it, and didn't even consciously superintend. Yes; one notices, for instance, that long, involved sentences confuse him, and that he is obliged to re-read them to get the sense. Unconsciously, then, he rejects that brick. Unconsciously he accustoms himself to writing short sentences as a rule. At times he may indulge himself with a long one, but he will make sure that there are no folds in it, no vaguenesses, no parenthetical interruptions of its view as a whole; when he is done with it, it won't be a sea-serpent, with half of its arches under the water, it will be a torch-light procession.

Well, also he will notice in the course of time, as his reading goes on, that the difference between the *almost right* word and the *right* word is really a large matter—'tis the difference between the lightningbug and the lightning. After that, of course, that exceedingly important brick, the *exact* word—however, this is running into an essay, and I beg pardon. So I seem to have arrived at this: doubtless I have methods, but they begot themselves, in which case I am only their proprietor, not their father.

J O H N   C I A R D I

Poet, editor, and translator JOHN CIARDI (1916–1986) was the author of forty books of poetry and criticism. He was poetry editor for *Saturday Review* from 1956 to 1972, writing a column "Manner of Speaking" for that magazine. These columns and other essays are collected in *Dialogue with an Audience* (1963) and *Manner of Speaking* (1972). His distinguished translation of Dante's *Divine Comedy* was published in its full edition in 1977. Ciardi was director of the Bread Loaf Writers' Conference at Middlebury College from 1955 to 1972. The essay that follows was presented to the conference in its inaugural year.

WHAT EVERY WRITER MUST LEARN

The teaching of writing has become practically a profession by now. There is hardly a college in the land that does not offer at least one course in "creative writing" (whatever that is) by some "teacher of writing" (whoever he is). There are, moreover, at least fifty annual writers' conferences now functioning among us with something like fifty degrees of competence. And there seems to be no way of counting the number of literary counselors, good and bad, who are prepared to promise that they can teach a writer what he needs to know.

I am myself a "teacher of writing," but though it be taken as a confession of fraud I must insist, in the face of all this "teaching" apparatus, that writing cannot in fact be taught. What a writer must have above all else is inventiveness. Dedication, commitment, passion—whatever one chooses to call the writer's human motivation—must be there, to be sure. But to require human motivation is only to assume that the writer is a human being—certainly not a very hard assumption to make. Art, however, is not humanity but the *expression* of humanity, and for enduring expression the one gift above all is inventiveness.   2

But where, in what curriculum ever, has there been, or can there be, a course in inventiveness—which is to say, in creativity? The truly creative—whether in art, in science, or in philosophy—is always, and precisely, that which cannot be taught. And yet, though it seems paradoxical, creativity cannot spring from the untaught. Creativity is the imaginatively gifted recombination of known elements into something new.   3

And so, it may seem, there is no real paradox. The elements of an invention or of a creation can be taught, but the creativity must be self-discovered and self-disciplined. A good teacher—whether in a college classroom, a Parisian café, or a Greek market place—can marvelously assist the learning. But in writing, as in all creativity, it is the gift that must learn itself.   4

The good teacher will be able to itemize a tremendous amount of essential lore. He can tell a would-be novelist that if an incidental character is given a name that character had best reappear in the later action, and that if he is not going to reappear he should be identified simply as "the supply sergeant," "the big blond," "the man in the red waistcoat," or whatever. He can point out that good dialogue avoids "he averred," "he bellowed," "he boomed," "he interpolated," and that it is wise to write simply "he said," indicating any important direction for the tone of voice in a separate sentence. He can demonstrate that in all fiction the action must be perceived by someone, and he can defend in theory and support by endless instances that in effective fiction one does not allow more than one means of perception within a single scene. He can point out to would-be poets that traditional rhyme and traditional metrics are   5 not indispensable, but that once a pattern has been established the writer must respect it. And he can then point out that within the pattern established at the start of the student's poem certain lines are metrically deficient and certain rhymes forced.

He may "teach" (or preach) any number of such particulars. And if he is a good man for the job he will never forget that these particulars are simply rules of thumb, any one of which may be violated by a master, but none of which may be safely ignored by a writer who has not yet learned they exist.   6

Belaboring such particulars is a useful device to the would-be writer, who under a competent teacher may save himself years of floundering trial-and-error. Writers are forever being produced by literary groups of one sort or another, and one of the most important things a writer acquires in the give-and-take of a good literary group is a headful of precisely such particulars. The most important thing a teacher of writing can do is to create a literary group in which he teaches minimums while the most talented of his students learn maximums—very largely from fighting with one another (rarely, if ever, from mutual admiration).   7

But if writing requires a starting talent that a man either has or has not and which he cannot learn, and if the teachable elements are not enough to make a writer of him, what is it he must learn? What are the measures by which his gift comes to know itself?   8

The answers to that question must be given separately, and if they are so given they must be put down one after the other with some sort of natural implication that the order in which they are given is keyed to their importance. Such mechanical necessity (and it is one of the most constant seductions of the classroom) must not be allowed to obscure the far greater likelihood that the answers all exist at the same time in the behavior of a good writer, and that all are equally important. That, too, is part of what must be learned. As is the fact that no one set of generalizations will ever suffice. But one must begin somewhere. I offer the following six points as the most meaningful and the most central I have been able to locate.   9

1. Something to Write About

"You have to give them something to write about," Robert Frost once said in discussing his classroom principles. His own poems are full of stunning examples of the central truth that good writers deal in information, and that even the lofty (if they are lofty) acreages of poetry are sown to fact. Consider the opening lines of "Mending Wall":

Something there is that doesn't love a wall,
That sends the frozen-groundswell under it,
And spills the upper boulders in the sun;
And makes gaps even two can pass abreast.
The work of hunters is another thing:
I have come after them and made repair
Where they have left not one stone on a stone,
But they would have the rabbit out of hiding,
To please the yelping dogs. The gaps I mean,
No one has seen them made or heard them made,
But at spring mending-time we find them there . . .

I intend no elaborate critique of this passage. I want simply to make the point that it contains as much specific information about stone walls as one could hope to find in a Department of Agriculture pamphlet.

Frost states his passion for the *things* of the world both in example and in precept. "The fact is the sweetest dream the labor knows," he writes in "The Mowing." One has only to compare that line with R. P. T. Coffin's "Nothing so crude as fact could enter here" to understand an important part of the difference between a poet and something less than a poet.

Even so mystical a poet as Gerard Manley Hopkins (I misuse the word "mystical" in order to save three paragraphs, but let me at least file an apology) is gorgeously given to the fact of the thing. Consider: "And blue bleak embers, ah my dear, / Fall, gall themselves, and gash gold-vermilion." (I.e., "Coal embers in a grate, their outside surfaces burned out and blue-bleak, sift down, fall through the grate, strike the surface below, and are gashed open to reveal the gold-vermilion fire still glowing at their core.")

The writer of fiction deals his facts in a different way, but it will not do to say that he is more bound to fact than is the poet: he simply is not required to keep his facts under poetic compression; keep hard to them he still must. Consider Melville's passion for the details of whaling; or Defoe's for the details of criminality, of ransoming an English merchant captured by a French ship, or of Robinson Crusoe's carpentry. The passion for fact was powerful enough in these masters to lure them into shattering the pace of their own best fiction, and to do so time and time again. And who is to say that a man reading for more than amusement, a man passionate to touch the writer's mind in his writing, has any real objection to having the pace so shattered? All those self-blooming, lovingly managed, chunky, touchable facts!

For a writer is a man who must know something better than anyone   14
else does, be it so little as his own goldfish or so much as himself. True, he is not required to know any one specific thing. Not at least until he begins to write about it. But once he has chosen to write about X then he is responsible for knowing everything the writing needs to know about X. I know of no writer of any consequence whatever who did not treasure the world enough to gather to himself a strange and wonderful headful and soulful of facts about its going and coming.

2. An Outside Eye

Nothing is more difficult than for the writer to ride his passion while still   15
managing to observe it critically. The memoirs of good writers of every sort are studded with long thoughts on this essential duplicity, this sense of aesthetic detachment, of a second attention lurking in the mind at the very moment they have felt the need to be most indivisibly absorbed in what they are doing.

The writer absolutely must learn to develop that eye outside himself,   16
for the last action every writer must perform for his writing is to become its reader. It is not easy to approach one's own output as if he were coming on it fresh. Yet unless the writer turns that trick any communication that happens will either be by accident or by such genius as transcends the possibility of discussion.

For the writer's relation to his writing is a developing relation. The   17
writing starts as a conceptual buzz. Approaching the writing thus with the buzz loud in the head, one may easily believe that anything he sets down is actually full of that starting buzz. But one must remember that the buzz is there before the writing, and that should some accident interfere with the actual writing the buzz would still be there. A writer in a really heightened state could jot down telephone numbers and actually believe that he has set down a piece of writing that accurately conveys his original impulse.

The reader, however, is in a very different situation. He comes to   18
writing committed to no prior emotion. There is no starting buzz in his head, except by irrelevant accident. It is the writer's job to make that reader buzz. Not, to be sure, to make every reader buzz—the world

is full of the practically unbuzzable—but to make the competent reader buzz. Simply to say, "I buzz," is not enough. To make the reader experience the original buzz with nothing but the writing to create the buzz within him—that is the function of every sort of literature, the communication of experience in experienceable terms. The disciplines of any art form are among other things ways of estimating the amount of buzz the form is transmitting.

3. Fluency

As noted, one does not hope to reach all readers, but only the competent. In one way the qualifications of a good reader are the same as those of a competent writer. Both must achieve fluency. By fluency I mean the ability to receive more than one impression at the same time. To create or to experience art one must be both technically and emotionally fluent. 19

A pun is a simple example of the necessity for technical fluency. The two or more faces of a pun must be received at the same instant or all is lost. The news comes over the radio that the Communist leader of Pisa has been chastised by Moscow for making overtures to the left-center parties for a unified front, and the happy punster says, "Aha, a Lenin tower of a-Pisa-ment!" then settles back in his moment of personal splendor. This golden instant from my autobiography—but what good is even glory if it has to be explained? "I don't get it," says the guest who will never be invited again, and the evening is ruined. 20

The pun, of course, is only the simplest example of the need for technical fluency. Unless the writer and the reader have in common the necessary language of simultaneity in its millions of shadings, the best will die en route. 21

The need for emotional fluency is analogous. Good writing constantly requires the writer to perceive and the reader to receive different sets of feelings at the same instant. Both the writer and the reader must be equal to the emotion of the subject dealt with. Shakespeare can put a world into *Hamlet*, but where is that world when a five-year-old child or an emotionally-five-year-old adult attempts to read or to see the play? Whatever he may see, it is certainly not Shakespeare. A reader who is emotionally immature, or who is too psychically rigid (the same thing really) to enter into the simultaneity of the human experiences commonly portrayed in literature, is simply not capable of any sort of writing with the 22 possible exception of the technical report, the statistical summary, or that semi-literate combination, the Ph.D. thesis.

4. *A Sense of the Past*

No painter can produce a good canvas without a broad knowledge of what has been painted before him, no architect can plan a meaningful building except as he has pondered the architecture of the past, and no writer can produce good writing without a sure sense of what has been accomplished in the past within his form.

There are legions of poets today who are trying belatedly to be Wordsworth, and legions of fictioneers who are trying to be Louisa May Alcott. I imply no attack here on either Wordsworth or Alcott. I simply make the point that it is too late to be either of them again. Both of them, moreover, did a better job of being themselves than any of their imitators can aspire to. As the Kitty-cat bird in Theodore Roethke's poem said: "Whoever you are, be sure it's you."

Nor does one learn the past of his form only to adhere to it. Such an adherence, if overdedicated, would be a death in itself. I mean, rather, that it is impossible to venture meaningful innovation unless one knows what he is *innovating from*. With no exception I am able to think of, the best innovators in our literature have been those who best knew their past tradition.

I am saying simply that a writer must learn to read. He must read widely and thoughtfully, and he must learn to read not as an amateur spectator but as an engaged professional. Just as the football coach sees more of the play than do the coeds, so the writer must learn to see more of what is happening under the surface of the illusion than does the reader who simply yields to the illusion. William Dean Howells, then editor of *The Atlantic,* paid what he intended as a supreme compliment to one of Mark Twain's books when he reported that he had begun the book and for the first time in many years had found himself reading as a reader rather than as an editor. A happy indulgence and a gracious compliment, but once the writer has allowed himself that much it becomes his duty to reread the book with his glasses on—not only to enter into the illusion of the writing, but to identify the devices (*i.e.,* the inventions) by which the illusion was created and made to work upon him. And here, too, he must experience his essential duplicity, for the best reading is exactly that reading in which the passion of the illusion and the awareness of its technical management arrive at the same time.

5. A Sense of the Age

The true writer, that is to say the writer who is something more than a   27
competent technician, has a yet more difficult thing to learn. He must not only know his human and artistic past; he must learn to read the mood of his world under its own names for itself. He must become an instrument, tuned by devices he can never wholly understand, to the reception of a sense of his age, its mood, its climate of ideas, its human position, and its potential of action. And he must not let himself be deceived into thinking that the world answers to the names it gives itself. Hitler's agencies once gave a great deal of attention to what they called "Strength-through-Joy." It was the product of this Strength-through-Joy that Lord Beaverbrook called at the time "the stalwart young Nazis of Germany." The names were "strength," "joy," and "stalwarts." Yet any man today can see that those who answered to these shining names contained within themselves possibilities for action that must answer to much darker names. Any man can see it—now. I think it is very much to the point that all of the best writers sensed it then, and that the better the German writers were, the earlier they left Germany. Good writing must be of its times and must contain within itself—God knows how but the writer must learn for himself—a sense of what Hippolyte Taine called "the moral temperature of the times," what the Germans call "der Zeitgeist," and what English and American writers have come to call "the climate."

6. Art Is Artifice

And along with all else, as an essential part of his duplicity, his commit-   28
ment, his fluency, and his sense of past and present, the writer must learn beyond any flicker of doubt within himself that art is not life itself but a made representation of life. He must learn that it is no defense of a piece of fiction, for example, to argue, "But that's the way it happened." The fact that it happened that way in the world of the *Daily News* does not make it happen to the reader within the world of the writing.

The writer's subject is reality but his medium is illusion. Only by   29
illusory means can the sense of reality be transmitted in an art form. That

complex of pigment-on-canvas is not four maidens dancing, but it is the managed illusion whereby Botticelli transmits his real vision of the four seasons. Those words on paper are not Emma Bovary, but they are the elements of the illusion whereby we experience her as a living creation. The writer, like every artist, deals in what I have come to call the AS-IF. As-IF is the mode of all poetry and of all imaginative writing Is is the mode of what passes for reality and of all information-prose. Is IS more real than AS-IF? One must ask: "More real for what purposes?" I have no argument with, for example, the research chemists. I mean rather to hold them in considerable admiration. But though many of them think of themselves as the IS-iest men in the world, which of them has ever determined a piece of truth except by setting up and pursuing a starting hypothesis (let me leave accident out of consideration)? And what is a starting hypothesis but an AS-IF? "Let us act AS-IF this hypothesis were true," says the researcher, "and then see how it checks out." At the end of ten, or a hundred, or ten thousand starting AS-IF's lurks the nailed-down IS of valence, or quanta, or transmutation of elements. Maybe. And then only until the next revolution in IS outdates the researcher's results.

At the far end of all the AS-IF's a man, and particularly a writer, can summon from himself, there lurks that final IS (maybe) that will be a truth for him. But not all of the truth will be told at one time. Part of the truth, I think the most truth, a writer must learn is that writing is not a decorative act, but a specific, disciplined, and infinitely viable means of knowledge. Poetry and fiction, like all the arts, are ways of perceiving and of understanding the world. Good writing is as positive a search for truth as is any part of science, and it deals with kinds of truth that must forever be beyond science. The writer must learn, necessarily of himself and within himself, that his subject is the nature of reality, that good writing always increases the amount of human knowledge available, and that the one key to that knowledge of reality is AS-IF. His breadth and depth as a human being are measured by the number of AS-IF's he has managed to experience; his stature as a writer, by the number he has managed to bring to life in his work.

For no man in any one lifetime can hope to learn by physical experience (IS) all that he must know and all that he must have experienced in order to be an adequate human being. No writer can hope to engage physically enough worlds of IS to make his imagination and his humanity pertinent. Only by his vicarious assumptions of AS-IF can the writer learn his real human dimension, and only as he dedicates his writing to the creation of a meaningful and experienceable new AS-IF can he hope to write well—to write as no school can teach him to write, but he must learn for himself if he cares enough, and if he has gift enough.

WILLIAM ZINSSER

WILLIAM ZINSSER, whose essay "The Right to Fail" appears earlier in this book, has had a long and varied career as a journalist, critic, columnist, and teacher of writing. His numerous essays are collected in *The Lunacy Boom* (1970) and other books. In this essay from his book *On Writing Well* (6th ed., 1998), Zinsser discusses the clutter that infects so much American writing today, and he emphasizes the importance of revision and editing in the act of writing. In the sample extract included in the essay, Zinsser gives an example of his own revising and editing.

SIMPLICITY

Clutter is the disease of American writing. We are a society strangling in unnecessary words, circular constructions, pompous frills and meaning-less jargon.

Who can understand the clotted language of everyday American com-merce: the memo, the corporation report, the business letter, the notice from the bank explaining its latest "simplified" statement? What mem-ber of an insurance or medical plan can decipher the brochure explain-ing his costs and benefits? What father or mother can put together a child's toy from the instructions on the box? Our national tendency is to inflate and thereby sound important. The airline pilot who announces that he is presently anticipating experiencing considerable precipitation wouldn't think of saying it may rain. The sentence is too simple—there must be something wrong with it.

But the secret of good writing is to strip every sentence to its cleanest components. Every word that serves no function, every long word that could be a short word, every adverb that carries the same meaning that's already in the verb, every passive construction that leaves the reader unsure of who is doing what—these are the thousand and one adulterants that weaken the strength of a sentence. And they usually occur in proportion to education and rank.

During the 1960s the president of my university wrote a letter to mollify the alumni after a spell of campus unrest. "You are probably aware," he began, "that we have been experiencing very considerable potentially explosive expressions of dissatisfaction on issues only partially related." He meant that the students had been hassling them about different things. I was far more upset by the president's English than by the students' potentially explosive expressions of dissatisfaction. I would have preferred the presidential approach taken by Franklin D. Roosevelt when he tried to convert into English his own government's memos, such as this blackout order of 1942:

> Such preparations shall be made as will completely obscure all Federal buildings and non-Federal buildings occupied by the Federal government during an air raid for any period of time from visibility by reason of internal or external illumination.

"Tell them," Roosevelt said, "that in buildings where they have to keep the work going to put something across the windows."

Simplify, simplify. Thoreau said it, as we are so often reminded, and no American writer more consistently practiced what he preached. Open *Walden* to any page and you will find a man saying in a plain and orderly way what is on his mind:

> I went to the woods because I wished to live deliberately, to front only the essential facts of life, and see if I could not learn what it had to teach, and not, when I came to die, discover that I had not lived.

How can the rest of us achieve such enviable freedom from clutter? The answer is to clear our heads of clutter. Clear thinking becomes clear writing; one can't exist without the other. It's impossible for a muddy thinker to write good English. He may get away with it for a paragraph or two, but soon the reader will be lost, and there's no sin so grave, for the reader will not easily be lured back.

Who is this elusive creature, the reader? The reader is someone with an attention span of about 30 seconds—a person assailed by many forces competing for attention. At one time those forces were relatively few: newspapers, magazines, radio, spouse, children, pets. Today they also include a "home entertainment center" (television, VCR, tapes, CDs), e-mail, the Internet, the cellular phone, the fax machine, a fitness program, a pool, a lawn, and that most potent of competitors, sleep. The man or woman snoozing in a chair with a magazine or a book is a person who was being given too much unnecessary trouble by the writer.

It won't do to say that the reader is too dumb or too lazy to keep pace with the train of thought. If the reader is lost, it's usually because the writer hasn't been careful enough. That carelessness can take any number of forms. Perhaps a sentence is so excessively cluttered that the reader, hacking through the verbiage, simply doesn't know what it means. Perhaps a sentence has been so shoddily constructed that the reader could read it in several ways. Perhaps the writer has switched pronouns in mid-sentence, or has switched tenses, so the reader loses track of who is talking or when the action took place. Perhaps Sentence B is not a logical sequel to Sentence A; the writer, in whose head the connection is clear, hasn't bothered to provide the missing link. Perhaps the writer has used a word incorrectly by not taking the trouble to look it up. He or she may think "sanguine" and "sanguinary" mean the same thing, but the difference is a bloody big one. The reader can only infer (speaking of big differences) what the writer is trying to imply.

Faced with such obstacles, readers are at first tenacious. They blame themselves—they obviously missed something, and they go back over the mystifying sentence, or over the whole paragraph, piecing it out like an ancient rune, making guesses and moving on. But they won't do that for long. The writer is making them work too hard, and they will look for one who is better at the craft.

Writers must therefore constantly ask: what am I trying to say? Surprisingly often they don't know. Then they must look at what they have written and ask: have I said it? Is it clear to someone encountering the subject for the first time? If it's not, some fuzz has worked its way into the machinery. The clear writer is someone clearheaded enough to see this stuff for what it is: fuzz.

I don't mean that some people are born clearheaded and are therefore natural writers, whereas others are naturally fuzzy and will never write well. Thinking clearly is a conscious act that writers must force on themselves, as if they were working on any other project that requires logic: making a shopping list or doing an algebra problem. Good writing doesn't come naturally, though most people seem to think it does. Professional writers are constantly bearded by people who say they'd like to

5 --

is too dumb or too lazy to keep pace with the ~~writer's~~ train of thought. My sympathies are ~~entirely~~ with him. ~~He's not so dumb.~~ If the reader is lost, it is generally because the writer ~~of the article~~ has not been careful enough to keep him on the ~~proper~~ path.

This carelessness can take any number of ~~different~~ forms. Perhaps a sentence is so excessively ~~long and~~ cluttered that the reader, hacking his way through ~~all~~ the verbiage, simply doesn't know what it ~~the writer~~ means. Perhaps a sentence has been so shoddily constructed that the reader could read it in any of several ~~two or three different~~ ways. ~~He thinks he knows what the writer is trying to say, but he's not sure.~~ Perhaps the writer has switched pronouns in mid-sentence, or ~~perhaps he~~ has switched tenses, so the reader loses track of who is talking ~~to whom~~ or ~~exactly~~ when the action took place. Perhaps Sentence B is not a logical sequel to Sentence A -- the writer, in whose head the connection is ~~perfectly~~ clear, has not bothered to provide ~~given enough thought to providing~~ the missing link. Perhaps the writer has used an important word incorrectly by not taking the trouble to look it up ~~and make sure.~~ He may think that "sanguine" and "sanguinary" mean the same thing, but ~~I can assure you that~~ the difference is a bloody big one ~~to the reader.~~ The reader ~~He~~ can only ~~try to~~ infer ~~what~~ (speaking of big differences) what the writer is trying to imply.

Faced with these ~~such a variety of~~ obstacles, the reader is at first a remarkably tenacious bird. He ~~tends to~~ blames himself. ~~He~~ obviously missed something, ~~he thinks,~~ and he goes back over the mystifying sentence, or over the whole paragraph,

6 --

piecing it out like an ancient rune, making guesses and moving
on. But he won't do this for long. ~~He will soon run out of patience.~~ The writer is making him work too hard ~~-- harder than he should have to work --~~ and the reader will look for
~~a writer~~ one who is better at his craft.

The writer must therefore constantly ask himself: What am
I trying to say? ~~in this sentence?~~ Surprisingly often, he
doesn't know. ~~And~~ Then he must look at what he has ~~just~~
written and ask: Have I said it? Is it clear to someone
encountering ~~who is coming upon~~ the subject for the first time? If it's
not, ~~clear,~~ it is because some fuzz has worked its way into the
machinery. The clear writer is a person ~~who is~~ clear-headed
enough to see this stuff for what it is: fuzz.

I don't mean ~~to suggest~~ that some people are born
clear-headed and are therefore natural· writers, whereas
others ~~other people~~ are naturally fuzzy and will ~~therefore~~ never write
well. Thinking clearly is ~~an entirely~~ conscious act that the
writer must force ~~keep forcing~~ upon himself, just as if he were
embarking ~~starting out~~ on any other ~~kind of~~ project that requires ~~calls for~~ logic:
adding up a laundry list or doing an algebra problem ~~or playing chess.~~ Good writing doesn't ~~just~~ come naturally, though most
people obviously think it does. ~~it's as easy as walking.~~ The professiona

Two pages of the final manuscript of this chapter from the First Edition of *On Writing
Well*. Although they look like a first draft, they had already been rewritten and retyped
— like almost every other page — four or five times. With each rewrite I try to make
what I have written tighter, stronger and more precise, eliminating every element that's
not doing useful work. Then I go over it once more, reading it aloud, and am always
amazed at how much clutter can still be cut. (In later editions I eliminated the sexist
pronoun "he" denoting "the writer" and "the reader.")

"try a little writing sometime"—meaning when they retire from their real profession, like insurance or real estate, which is hard. Or they say, "I could write a book about that." I doubt it.

Writing is hard work. A clear sentence is no accident. Very few sentences come out right the first time, or even the third time. Remember this in moments of despair. If you find that writing is hard, it's because it is hard.

WALKER GIBSON

In *Tough, Sweet, and Stuffy* (1966), **WALKER GIBSON** describes three kinds of talker—the Tough Talker, a person who is "centrally concerned with himself" whose style is "I-talk"; the Sweet Talker, who makes a special effort to be nice to us and whose style is "you-talk"; and the Stuffy Talker, who "expresses no concern either for himself or his reader." Gibson states that "these are three extreme possibilities: the way we write at any given moment can be seen as an adjustment or compromise among these three styles of identifying ourselves and defining our relation with others." In the following chapter, Gibson describes the Stuffy Talker and analyzes typical stuffy writing.

STUFFY TALK:
THE RHETORIC OF HOLLOW MEN

Leaning together,
Headpiece filled with straw. Alas!

The voice we hear in an ad is not the official voice of the corporation that pays the bill. The voice in the ad is a highly fictitious created person, speaking as an individual in a particular situation. In a bathtub, for instance. No corporation could ever say, officially, "I never, never bathe without Sardo." The official voice of a corporation appears, I suppose, in its periodic reports to its stockholders, or in its communications with government agencies.

I define official prose, accordingly, as language whose voice speaks 2
for an organization rather than for an individual. And nobody says a
good word for it, not even its authors. The composing of officialese suffers
from circumstances, however, that make the job especially difficult, and
possibly some small sympathy is in order. For just as such prose speaks
for a group of people rather than for a single writer, so in its actual composition a number of people are likely to be lending a hand. And in writing, two hands are usually worse than one.[1]

Anyone who has worked on a committee preparing a document to 3
be signed by all fellowwriters knows some of the difficulties. Disagree-
ments of opinion and emphasis can produce a voice that is hardly a voice
at all. Constant qualification makes for weakness. The various writers,
all too aware of their audience as real people, may try to anticipate hopelessly conflicting prejudices and objections. Everybody has a point he
wants included, but what is worse, no one feels any personal responsibility for the tone of the whole. Nobody cares, really. Contrast the situation of the single writer alone at his desk, who can establish a single
speaking voice and an ideal assumed reader to listen to it. Yet a great
deal of modern prose is written, or at any rate rewritten, not at a lonely
desk but around a table where everybody talks at once. The loss of
personality almost inevitable under such circumstances should cause us
anguish whenever, as so often happens, we have to read or write the prose
of organization life. When we speak of official prose as *stuffy*, we are
referring, I think, directly to this loss of personality. (Not that you need
a committee to produce stuffiness.) Stuffiness may imply, by way of the
stuffed shirt, that the speaker has no insides, no humanity. It is scarecrow prose. Other familiar metaphors also seem to recognize an emptiness within; thus we speak of the "inflated" language of officialese, the
speaker in that case being filled with gas, or hot air.

What is the rhetoric of such hollow men, and how can it be improved, 4
if it can?

---

[1] Actually, in various works on the subject, there has been precious little sympathy for the
writers of officialese, who are an easy mark for critical abuse. Among numerous discussions of official style, all fairly bloodthirsty. I recommend: George Orwell's famous essay,
"Politics and the English Language," in *Shooting an Elephant and Other Essays* (1950),
Robert Graves and Alan Hodge, *The Reader over Your Shoulder* (1946), and Robert Wad-
dell, *Grammar and Style* (1951), which contains an entertaining "grammar of Basic Jargon." See also, for an earlier attack, Sir Arthur Quiller-Couch, *On the Art of Writing* (1916).

Take a handy example, the federal government's much-publicized report, "Smoking and Health," issued early in 1964. The text quoted in the newspapers ("Summary and Conclusions") begins this way:

> In previous studies the use of tobacco, especially cigarette smoking, has been causally linked to several diseases. Such use has been associated with increased deaths from lung cancer and other diseases, notably coronary artery disease, chronic bronchitis, and emphysema. These widely reported findings, which have been the cause of much public concern over the past decade, have been accepted in many countries by official health agencies, medical associations, and voluntary health organizations.
>
> The potential hazard is great because these diseases are major causes of death and disability. In 1962, over 500,000 people in the United States died of arteriosclerotic heart disease (principally coronary artery disease), 41,000 died of lung cancer, and 15,000 died of bronchitis and emphysema.
>
> Another cause of concern is that deaths from some of these diseases have been increasing with great rapidity over the past few decades.
>
> Lung cancer deaths, less than 3,000 in 1930, increased to 18,000 in 1950. In the short period since 1955, deaths from lung cancer rose from less than 27,000 to the 1962 total of 41,000. This extraordinary rise has not been recorded for cancer of any other site. While part of the rising trend for lung cancers is attributable to improvements in diagnosis and the changing age-composition and size of the population, the evidence leaves little doubt that a true increase in the lung cancer has taken place.

This is by no means an extreme example of stuffiness, and I quote it to give the official voice its due. And I reaffirm my modest sympathy with the authors, who must have had to compose this document under difficult circumstances. There were ten of them on the committee, professional experts chosen by the Surgeon General, presumably strong-minded men of varying opinions. A separate committee staff was also involved. There must have been considerable debate about phrasing as well as more "substantial" matters, and no doubt uneasy compromises had to be made. A consciousness of audience must have been high in the writers' minds. On one hand the document had to be acceptable to the scientific community, particularly to those scientists who had participated in various earlier projects on which this report was based. On another hand, the document was surely addressed to legislators and officials with the expectation of their taking the "remedial action" called for. On still a third hand, these multidextrous writers must have wished to reach the smoking public directly, and they surely anticipated the reprinting of key passages like this one in the daily press. We may, as I say, sympathize with the practical difficulties of multiple authorship and multiple readership, but it does not follow that we have to like the results. For this is a Stuffy voice.

For a harder look at the created personality, I take a shorter passage   11
from the page in the committee's report where one might suppose both writer and reader to be especially attentive. It is a point where, if anywhere, the committee might be expected to speak directly and plainly, with a minimum of hot air.[2] Here is the much-quoted conclusion under the heading "Lung Cancer":

> Cigarette smoking is causally related to lung cancer in men; the magni-   12
> tude of the effect of cigarette smoking far outweighs all other factors. The data for women, though less extensive, point in the same direction.
>
>   The risk of developing lung cancer increases with duration of smok-   13
> ing and the number of cigarettes smoked per day, and is diminished by discontinuing smoking.
>
>   The risk of developing cancer of the lung for the combined group of   14
> pipe smokers, cigar smokers, and pipe and cigar smokers is greater than for nonsmokers, but much less than for cigarette smokers.
>
>   The data are insufficient to warrant a conclusion for each group   15
> individually.

"Cigarette smoking is causally related to lung cancer in men. . . ."   16
Causally related? Probably there is some good reason why the committee could not say simply "Cigarette smoking causes lung cancer in men." What good reason could there be? Perhaps the latter phrasing suggests that smoking is the *only* cause of lung cancer? Perhaps it suggests that all smoking necessarily causes lung cancer? But our faint understanding of the committee's anxiety for caution and clarity, in the light of its complex audience, should not prevent us from deploring the alternative. For by using the passive verb (*is related to*) and its odd modifier (*causally*), the writers deprive their language not only of strength but of responsibility.

---

[2] In the version published in book form, the following prefatory remark describes the intention in this section of the report: "Realizing that for the convenience of all types of serious readers it would be desirable to simplify language, condense chapters, and bring opinions to the forefront, the Committee offers Part I as such a presentation." *Smoking and Health*, Public Health Service Publication No. 1103, U. S. Government Printing Office, p. 5.

Note that in this sentence the committee's voice isn't doing any relating itself; all it's saying is that something is or has been related to something —by someone else. Very scientific, very "objective." Then we read on (to finish the first sentence): "the magnitude of the effect far outweighs all other factors." The magnitude is doing the outweighing, not the austere members of this committee. The choice of language in the following sentence ("data . . . point in the same direction") is of course similar. An abstraction (data) is pointing, not a human finger. Explained in these terms, we can understand why the voice in this first paragraph sounds so disembodied and the wording sounds so awkward.[3]

A key characteristic of Stuffy rhetoric is just this refusal to assume personal responsibility. It is accomplished by at least two stylistic techniques, both of which we have just witnessed. One is the use of the passive verb. (Military prose, among others, is full of this gambit: *it is ordered that . . . it is desired that. . . .* Who ordered, who desired? With such rhetoric, buck-passing becomes child's play.) The other technique is a preference for abstract nouns as the subjects of active verbs. The doer of the action is not a human somebody, certainly not the speaker himself. It is Magnitude, or Data, buzzing along while the speaker merely notes the unarguable results.

It is as if the speaker, in this first paragraph, had made a determined effort to keep *people* out of the discussion, including himself. Whether this was done to promote a kind of official tone for the sake of legislators, or to sound mathematical and cautious for the sake of scientists, or simply out of stuffy habit, I cannot tell. But the effort partly breaks down in the second paragraph. "The risk of developing lung cancer increases with duration of smoking." This is still clothed in pretty abstract dress, but there has been a significant change, for now we are suddenly seeing the situation almost from an individual smoker's point of view. The statement seems far less rigorously mathematical when the subject of the sentence is a

---

[3] The pussyfooting language seems at odds with the conviction about *cause* that the Committee evidently did feel. The book version of the report contains a statement about this conviction, after some cautious warning about the Committee's use of the word "cause." "No member was so naive as to insist upon monoetiology in pathological processes or in vital phenomena." Nevertheless, "granted these complexities were recognized, it is to be noted clearly that the Committee's considered decision to use the words 'a cause,' or 'a major cause,' or a significant cause,' or 'a causal association' in certain conclusions about smoking and health affirms their conviction." (*Smoking and Health*, p. 21.) What interests me here is that this conviction is affirmed in language that almost removes the affirmers from the scene.

word like *risk,* though of course the riskiness is based on numbers. And the writers' own risk seems abruptly much greater, for now they do seem to be taking responsibility for a more ambitious assertion: "the risk increases." It is hard to understand why they had to be so awkwardly impersonal and cautious in their first paragraph, if they were going to come out so flatly in their second.

In the third paragraph the voice continues, rather woodenly, with "risk," 19 and then moves into a terrible tangle as the writers, trying to deal with three groups of smokers, produce an almost unreadable mess. "Pipe smokers, cigar smokers, and pipe and cigar smokers." This sort of thing is easily perpetrated by a voice that cares as little about its reader as this one does. Then in the final sentence of the passage the voice backs away again into its posture of impersonal no-responsibility. "The data are sufficient to warrant a conclusion. . . ." Data are insufficient only if somebody says so. Once again, the subject of the verb is the data, not the interpreters of the data.

No doubt the data are insufficient to warrant a conclusion, but I find 20 insurmountable the temptation to rewrite the committee's prose into plainer English, and politer.

> Cigarette smoking is the major cause of lung cancer in men, and probably 21 in women too.
>
> The longer one smokes, and the more cigarettes one smokes per day, 22 the greater the chance of developing lung cancer. This risk is reduced when one stops smoking.
>
> People who smoke pipes or cigars, or both, also risk cancer, but to 23 a lesser degree than cigarette smokers. We cannot say exactly what the risk is for each of these groups.

For any number of reasons, possibly even good reasons, this version 24 might be unacceptable to the advisory committee. But at least we can examine some of the ways in which the revision was accomplished, and so focus on some rhetorical characteristics of Stuffiness. In the first place, of course, human responsibility has been introduced, in the opening sentence, by the simple tactic of removing the passive verb and making a more positive statement. (The statement *seems* to be justified by the original.) The original's willingness to speak of "the risk" in its second paragraph is retained in the revision, and the smoker's own involvement in the situation is further encouraged by the introduction of "people" in the revised third paragraph. Finally, the committee's responsibility is made explicit in the revised last sentence, by changing "The data are insufficient to warrant . . ." into "We cannot say exactly what. . . ."

These changes suggest that I have tried to make a scarecrow into a hu- 2.
man being. By what other means can one humanize the quality of a Stuffy
voice? One way is to reduce sharply the sheer number of words, in this
case by something over one-quarter. Stuffy voices talk too much, although
for sheer gratuitous verbosity a Sweet voice does pretty well too. The Stuffy
voice characteristically uses longer words, and the revision shows a clear
rise in proportion of monosyllables, and an even clearer drop in proportion of words of more than two syllables. Stuffy voices modify nouns almost as generously as adwriters, and they are exceedingly fond of the noun
adjunct construction. Whereas the original contained nine adjectives and
nine noun adjuncts (like *cigarette smoking*), the revision contains three of
each. Finally, repetition in the original is very high (the "wooden" effect
alluded to), and this repetition, while still present in the revision, has been
reduced. A list of this information may be of interest:

	ORIGINAL	REVISION
Total number of words	106	76
Average sentence length	21	15
Proportion of monosyllables	57%	69%
Proportion of words over two syllables	18%	5%
Adjectives and noun adjuncts	18	6

Such "rules" as these figures suggest are familiar enough, and many   2
a popular treatise on writing has been based on the simpleminded proposition that simple words and sentences are always better than complex
ones.[4] But that is not the point at all. It depends! In true Stuffy Talk, we
feel a disparity between the simplicity of the situation, as we feel it ought

---

[4] Extraordinary efforts, over the past quarter century and more, have been devoted by psychologists and others to devising formulas for measuring "readability." The best-known of
these formulas are those constructed by Rudolph Flesch (*The Art of Plain Talk,* etc.). Readability or Reading Ease (Flesch's term), refers entirely to the comfort and efficiency of the
reader in "understanding" the words in front of him. Most of the formulas proposed to
measure this quality depend heavily on simple computations of sentence length and word
length. These formulas, as their inventors usually concede, are not concerned with style in
my sense, as the expression of a personality on paper. No doubt such formulas may be
helpful to some writers in improving style—especially the style of Stuffy Talk—but the experts in readability are not worried about what happens to the voice when their formulas
are applied. See George R. Klare, *The Measurement of Readability* (Ames, Iowa, 1963).

to be defined, and the pretentiousness of the lingo. As so often in literary matters, we have to appeal finally to extraliterary considerations—our sense of a "proper" definition of the circumstances. Thus we resent a voice haranguing us from a high horse, not just because his horse is high, but because the situation seems to us to be worthy of a more modest perch. If you are composing a preamble to a new nation's constitution, you have a perfect right to climb up on a high horse. On the other hand, if you're trying to get people to stop smoking. . . .

But this is not to say at all that the problem of cancer and smoking is frivolous: the tone of my revision remains serious, even though I have brought the voice down from on high and into closer contact with the listener. I did not go so far as to invoke the intimacy of the Sweet Talker, or even the Tough Talker. The occasion remains, as it must, official and formal. Nevertheless it is true that in revising I have imposed upon the committee's style some of the Tough Talker's manners. A little Tough Talk goes a long way, sometimes, as an antidote to Stuffy Talk, and I have no doubt that most committee reports would be more palatable if the language could be brought somewhat into line with Tough Talk's rhetoric. But easy does it. Whereas a little Toughness can be wholesome, a little Sweetness can be sickening. How facile it would be to reduce an official voice to mere cuteness, in a flurry of public-relations informality. For instance take this sentence from the original committee report:

> The risk of developing lung cancer increases with duration of smoking and the number of cigarettes smoked per day, and is diminished by discontinuing smoking.

My revision offered this alternative:

> The longer one smokes, and the more cigarettes one smokes per day, the greater the chance of developing lung cancer. This risk is reduced when one stops smoking.

A reviser interested in promoting informality could easily become too interested. He could, for instance, bring the voice still closer to the reader by the simple introduction of the second-person pronoun:

> The longer you smoke, and the more cigarettes you smoke per day, the greater your chance of developing lung cancer. This risk is reduced when you stop smoking.

This begins now to look like the clubbiness of Sweet Talk—a degree of admonitory intimacy that the members of the committee would no doubt,

and rightly, consider beneath their dignity. And from here it is only a step
to the full saccharine flavor of Sweet Talk itself:

> No doubt about it—when you smoke cigarettes you're running a sci-
> entifically-proved risk of lung cancer. That is, if you're a man. And if
> you're a woman, you're probably running a risk that's almost as certain.
>
> Fact is, the longer you've smoked, and the more cigarettes you smoke
> every day, the likelier you are to develop cancer. But scientific data
> demonstrate that you can lower that risk any time you care to—just
> stop smoking.
>
> If you smoke cigars or a pipe (or both), you're still risking cancer.
> But a good deal less than you are if you stick to those cigarettes.
>
> So why not cut out expensive, evil-smelling, disease-laden cigarette
> smoking for good? Like the Surgeon General says you should.

Examples of Stuffy Talk abound. Of our three styles, it is the easiest
to recognize and define; perhaps it is easy to compose too. Consider another example, from another branch of government. Not long ago the
pay envelopes of academicians included a document stating a new ruling
by the Internal Revenue Service. This ruling, a welcome one to its recipients, concerned certain deductible expenses on the part of professors. It
began this way; and it needs no comment:

REVENUE

> Advice has been requested concerning the deductibility for Federal in-
> come tax purposes of research expenses, including traveling expenses,
> incurred by college and university professors in their capacity as edu-
> cators.
>
> The facts presented are that the duties of a professor encompass not
> only the usual lecture and teaching duties but also the communication
> and advancement of knowledge through research and publication.
> Appointments are commonly made to college and university faculties
> with the expectation that the individuals involved will carry on inde-
> pendent research in their fields of competence and will put that research
> to use in advancing the body of learning in that area by teaching, lec-
> turing, and writing. It is customary, therefore, for professors to engage
> in research for the above purposes. Where the research is undertaken
> with a view to scholarly publication, the expenses for such purposes
> cannot usually be considered to have been incurred for the purpose of
> producing a specific income-producing asset. . . .

Based on the facts presented, it is held that research expenses, 35
including traveling expenses properly allottable thereto, incurred by a
professor for the purposes of teaching, lecturing, or writing and publishing in this area of competence, as a means of carrying out the duties
expected of him in his capacity as a professor and without expectation
of profit apart from his salary, represent ordinary and necessary business
expenses incurred in that capacity and are therefore deductible under
section 162(e) of the Code.

I take a final example of Stuffy Talk from another end of academic life. 36
Here is the voice of the academic institution itself, a passage from the catalogue of a liberal arts college setting forth its policy on admissions.

ADMISSIONS

Admission to X College is a selective process, since each year many 37
more qualified candidates apply for admission than can possibly be ac-
commodated. In considering the factors involved in the selections, academic ability, and achievement, community citizenship and leadership,
character, and personality are considered most important. Special emphasis is placed on the candidate's record of achievement throughout
his secondary school years. Specifically, selection of candidates is based
on information obtained from the following sources: (1) the secondary
school record, including rank in class; (2) the College Entrance Examination Board's Scholastic Aptitude and Achievement Tests; (3) a personal interview with a member of the Admissions staff, or with a designated representative; (4) the recommendation of the school.

X College admits undergraduates for the Bachelor of Arts degree 38
only. For practical reasons of adjustment to college life and the proper
arrangements of a program of study, X admits freshman students only
in September, at the beginning of the fall semester. The freshman class
is limited by the capacity of the dormitories. An early application is advised. It is expected that candidates who live within a reasonable distance of the College will visit X sometime before January of their senior year of secondary school.

The Admissions office is open for appointments throughout the year 39
except on Saturday afternoons and Sundays. (During the months of July
and August appointments and interviews are not scheduled on Saturdays.) An appointment with the Admissions Officer may be arranged
by writing or phoning the Admissions Office at least two weeks in advance of the intended visit.

As every parent, teacher, and teenager knows, admission to college   40
these days is a desperate business. But the assumed author here could
hardly care less. Certainly he admits no difficulties on his part, and his
passive verbs do their efficient work of evading responsibility. "Special
emphasis is *placed* . . . , selection of candidates is *based*. . . " Note that
it is quite possible to be Stuffy within a very short sentence: "An early
application is *advised*." In the face of all these passives, the poor appli-
cant has nobody to argue with. The machine grinds on. There is no hint
here about what actually happens in the "admissions process"—who
pores over the documents, how he or they do make decisions, what the
relative importance may be of the four sources of information. Furthermore an interview with an Officer whose very title rates a capital O is
already a formidable undertaking. Surely teenagers have enough troubles,
without having to face the blank face of prose like this.

Glossary

allusion An indirect reference to a presumably well-known literary work or a historical event or figure. The phrase "the Waterloo of his political career" is a reference to Napoleon's disastrous defeat at the Battle of Waterloo in 1815. The allusion implies that the career of the politician under discussion has come to a dramatic end.

analogy A point-by-point comparison between two unlike things or activities (writing an essay and building a house) for the purpose of illustration or argument. Unlike a comparison (or contrast), which compares things of equal importance, analogy exists for the purpose of illustrating or arguing the nature of one of the things, not both.

antithesis The arrangement of contrasting ideas in grammatically similar phrases and clauses (*The world will little note, nor long remember, what we say here, but it can never forget what they did here.*—Lincoln, *Gettysburg Address*). See *parallelism.*

argument Proving the truth or falseness of a statement. Arguments are traditionally classified as *inductive* or *deductive*. See *inductive argument* and *deductive argument.* Argument can be used for different purposes in writing. See *purpose.*

autobiography Writing about a person's own experiences, often those of growing up and making one's way in the world. The autobiographical writings of Mary E. Mebane and Eudora Welty describe their childhood in the South.

balanced sentence A sentence containing parallel phrases and clauses of approximately the same length and wording. (*You can fool all the people some of the time, and some of the people all the time, but you can't fool all the people all the time.*—Lincoln).

cause and effect Analysis of the conditions that must be present for an event to occur (*cause*) and of the results or consequences of the event (*effect*). An essay may deal with causes or with effects only.

classification and division *Classification* arranges individual objects into groups or classes (GM cars, Chrysler cars, Ford cars). *Division* arranges a broad class into subclasses according to various principles (the broad class

GM *cars* can be divided on the basis of their transmission or manufacturing unit).

cliché A once colorful expression made stale through overuse (*putting on the dog, mad as a wet hen*).

coherence The sense, as we read, that the details and ideas of a work connect clearly. A paragraph or essay that does not hold together seems incoherent. Transitions are a means of coherence. See *transition*.

colloquialism An everyday expression in speech and informal writing. Colloquialisms are not substandard or "illiterate" English. They are common in informal English and occur sometimes in formal English.

comparison and contrast The analysis of similarities and differences between two or more persons, objects, or events (A and B) for the purpose of a relative estimate. The word *comparison* sometimes refers to the analysis of similarities and differences in both. *Block comparison* presents each thing being compared as a whole (if the comparison is between A and B, then a, b, c of A, followed by a, b, c of B). *Alternating* or *point-by-point comparison* presents the comparable features one by one (a, a, b, b, c, c).

complex sentence A sentence consisting of one main or independent clause and one or more subordinate or dependent clauses (*The rain began when she stepped outside*).

compound sentence A sentence consisting of coordinated independent clauses (*She stepped outside, and then the rain began*).

compound–complex sentence A sentence consisting of two or more main or independent clauses and at least one subordinate or dependent clause (*She stepped outside as the rain began, but she did not return to the house*).

concrete and abstract words Concrete words refer to particular objects, people, and events (Valley Forge, Franklin Delano Roosevelt, the Rocky Mountains); abstract words refer to general shared qualities (heroism, courage, beauty). Concrete writing makes abstract ideas perceptible to the senses through details and images.

concreteness Making an idea exist through the senses. Writing can be concrete at all three levels—informal, general, and formal. See also *concrete and abstract words*.

connotation Feelings, images, and ideas associated with a word. Connotations change from reader to reader, although some words probably have the same associations for everybody.

context The surrounding words or sentences that suggest the meaning of a word or phrase. Writers may dispense with formal definition if the context clarifies the meaning of a word.

coordinate sentence A sentence that joins clauses of the same weight and importance through the conjunctions *and, but, for, or, nor,* or *yet,* or through conjunctive adverbs and adverbial phrases (*however, therefore, nevertheless, in fact*) following a semicolon.

deductive argument Reasoning from statements assumed to be true or factually well-established. These statements or assumptions are thought to be sufficient to guarantee the truth of the inferences or conclusions. In formal arguments, they are called *premises*. A valid argument reasons correctly from the premises to the conclusion. A sound argument is true in its premises and valid in its reasoning. See *enthymeme, syllogism*.

definition Explaining the current meaning of a word through its etymology or derivation, its denotation, or its connotations. Denotative or "real" definitions single out a word from all other words (or things) like it by giving *genus* and *specific difference*. Connotative definitions give the associations people make to the word. See *connotation*.

description A picture, in words, of people, objects, and events. Description often combines with narration, and it may serve exposition and persuasion.

division See *classification*.

enthymeme A deductive argument that does not state the conclusion or one of the premises directly. The following statement is an enthymeme: *Citizens in a democracy, who refuse to register for the draft, are not acting responsibly*. The implied premise is that the responsible citizen obeys all laws, even repugnant ones. See also *deductive argument*.

essay A carefully organized composition that develops a single idea or impression or several related ideas or impressions. The word sometimes describes a beginning or trial attempt that explores the central idea or impression instead of developing it completely.

example A picture or illustration of an idea, or one of many instances or occurrences that is typical of the rest.

exposition An explanation or unfolding or setting forth of an idea, usually for the purpose of giving information. Exposition is usually an important part of persuasive writing. Example, process analysis, causal analysis, definition, classification and division, and comparison and contrast are forms of exposition.

expressive writing Essays, diaries, journals, letters, and other kinds of writing that present personal feelings and beliefs for their own sake. The expressive writer is not primarily concerned with informing or persuading readers.

figures of speech A word or phrase that departs from its usual meaning. Figures of speech make statements vivid and capture the attention of readers. The most common figures are based on similarity among things. See *metaphor, personification, simile*. Other figures are based on relationship. See *allusion*. *Metonymy* refers to a thing by one of its qualities (*the Hill* as a reference to the U.S. Congress). *Synecdoche* refers to a thing by one of its parts (for example, *wheels* as a reference to racing cars). Other figures are based on contrast between statements and realities. See *irony*. Related to irony is *understatement,* or saying less than is appropriate (*Napoleon's career ended unhappily at Waterloo*). *Hyperbole* means deliberate exaggeration (*crazy about ice cream*). *Paradox* states an apparent contradiction (*All great truths begin as blasphemies*—G. B. Shaw). *Oxymoron,* a kind of paradox, joins opposite qualities into a single image (*lake of fire*).

formal English Spoken and written English, often abstract in content, with sentences tighter than spoken ones, and an abstract and sometimes technical vocabulary. See *general English* and *informal English.*

general English A spoken and written standard that has features of informal and formal English and avoids the extremes of both. See *formal English* and *informal English.*

focus The limitation of subject in an essay. The focus may be broad, as in a panoramic view of the mountains, or it may be narrow, as in a view of a particular peak. A writer may focus broadly on the contribution to scientific thought of scientists from various fields, or focus narrowly on the achievements of astronomers or chemists or medical researchers, or more narrowly on the achievements of Albert Einstein as representative of twentieth-century science.

image A picture in words of an object, a scene, or a person. Although visual images are common in writing, they are not the only kind. Images can also be auditory, tactile, gustatory, and olfactory. Keats's line *With beaded bubbles winking at the brim* appeals to our hearing and taste as well as to our sight. His phrase *coming musk-rose* appeals to our sense of smell. Images help to make feelings concrete.

implied thesis The central idea of the essay, suggested by the details and discussion rather than stated directly. See *thesis.*

inductive argument Inductive arguments reason from particulars of experience to general ideas—from observation, personal experience, and experimental testing to probable conclusions. Inductive arguments make predictions on the basis of past and present experience. An argumentative analogy is a form of inductive argument because it is based on limited observation and experience and therefore can claim probability only. Analysis of causes and effects is inductive when used in argument.

"inductive leap" Making the decision that sufficient inductive evidence (personal experience, observation, experimental testing) exists to draw a conclusion. Sometimes writers of argument make the leap too quickly and bases their conclusions on insufficient evidence.

informal English Written English, usually concrete in content, tighter than the loose sentences of spoken English, but looser in sentence construction than formal English. The word *informal* refers to the occasion of its use. A letter to a friend is usually informal; a letter of application is usually formal. See *formal English* and *general English.*

irony A term generally descriptive of statements and events. An ironic statement says the opposite of what the speaker or writer means, or implies that something more is meant than is stated, or says the unexpected (*He has a great future behind him*). An ironic event is unexpected or is so coincidental that it seems impossible (*The fireboat burned and sank*).

jargon The technical words of a trade or profession (in computer jargon, the terms *input* and *word process*). Unclear, clumsy, or repetitive words or phrasing, sometimes the result of misplaced technical words (*He gave his input into the decision process*).

loose sentence A sentence that introduces the main idea close to the beginning and concludes with a series of modifiers (*The car left the expressway, slowing on the ramp and coming to a stop at the crossroad*). See *periodic sentence*.

metaphor An implied comparison that attributes the qualities of one thing to another (the word *mainstream* to describe the opinions or activities of most people).

mixed metaphor The incongruous use of two metaphors in the same context (*the roar of protest was stopped in its tracks*).

narration The chronological presentation of events. Narration often combines with description, and it may serve exposition or persuasion.

order of ideas The presentation of ideas in a paragraph or an essay according to a plan. The order may be *spatial*, perhaps moving from background to foreground, or from top to bottom, or from side to side; or the order may be *temporal* or chronological (the order of time). The presentation may be in the order of *importance*, or if the details and build intensively, the order of *climax*. The paragraph or essay may move from *problem* to *solution* or from the *specific* to the *general*. Some of these orders occur together, for example, a chronological presentation of details that builds to a climax.

parallelism Grammatically similar words, phrases, and clauses arranged to highlight similar ideas (*There are streets where, on January nights, fires burn on every floor of every house, sending fragrant smoke through the cold black trees. There are meadows and fields, long rows of old oaks, bridges that sparkle from afar, ships about to leave for Asia, lakes, horses and islands in the marsh.* —Mark Helprin). See *antithesis*.

paraphrase A rendering of a passage in different words that retain the sense, the tone, and the order of ideas.

periodic sentence A sentence that builds to the main idea (*Building speed as it curved down the ramp, the car sped into the crowded expressway*). See *loose sentence*.

personification Giving animate or human qualities to something animate or inhuman (*The sun smiled at the earth*).

persuasion The use of argument or satire or some other means to change thinking and feeling about an issue.

point of view   The place or vantage point from which an event is seen and described. The term sometimes refers to the mental attitude of the viewer in narrative. Mark Twain's *Huckleberry Finn* narrates the adventures of a boy in slave-owning Missouri from the point of view of the boy, not from that of an adult.

premise   see *syllogism*.

process   An activity or operation containing steps usually performed in the same order. The process may be mechanical (changing a tire), natural (the circulation of the blood), or historical (the rise and spread of a specific epidemic disease like bubonic plague at various times of history).

purpose   The aim of the essay as distinguished from the means used to develop it. The purposes or aims of writing are many. They include expressing personal feelings and ideas, giving information, persuading readers to change their thinking about an issue, inspiring readers to take action, giving pleasure. These purposes may be achieved through description, narrative, exposition, or argument. These means may be used alone or in combination, and an essay may contain more than one purpose.

reflection   An essay that explores ideas without necessarily bringing the exploration to completion. The reflective essay can take the form of a loosely organized series of musings or tightly organized arguments.

satire   Ridicule of foolish or vicious behavior or ideas for the purpose of correcting them. *Social satire* concerns foolish but not dangerous behavior and ideas, for example, coarse table manners, pretentious talk, harmless gossip. George Bernard Shaw's *Arms and the Man* is a social satire. *Ethical satire* attacks vicious or dangerous behavior or ideas—religious or racial bigotry, greed, political corruption. Mark Twain's *Huckleberry Finn* is an ethical satire.

simile   A direct comparison between two things (*A growing child is like a young tree*). See *figure of speech, metaphor*.

simple sentence   A sentence consisting of a single main or independent clause and no subordinate or dependent clauses (*The rain started at nightfall*).

slang   Colorful and sometimes short-lived expressions peculiar to a group of people, usually informal in usage, and almost always unacceptable in formal usage (*nerd, goof off*).

style   A distinctive manner of speaking and writing. A writing style may be plain in its lack of metaphor and other figures of speech. Another writing style may be highly colorful or ornate.

subordinate clause   A clause that completes a main clause or attaches to it as a modifier (She saw *that the rain had begun; When it rains*, it pours).

syllogism   The formal arrangement of premises and conclusion of a deductive argument. The premises are the general assumptions (*All reptiles are cold-blooded vertebrates, All snakes are reptiles*), from which particular conclusions are drawn (*All snakes* *are cold-blooded vertebrates*). This formal arrangement helps to test the validity or correctness of the reasoning from premises to conclusion. See *deductive argument, enthymeme.*

symbol An object that represents an abstract idea. The features of the symbol (the fifty stars and thirteen horizontal stripes of the American flag) suggest characteristics of the object symbolized (the fifty states of the Union, the original confederation of thirteen states). A sign need not have this representative quality: a green light signals "go" and red light "stop" by conventional agreement.

thesis The central idea that organizes the many smaller ideas and details of the essay.

tone The phrasing or words that express the attitude or feeling of the speaker or writer. The tone of a statement ranges from the angry, exasperated, and sarcastic, to the wondering or approving. An ironic tone suggests that the speaker or writer means more than the words actually state.

topic sentence Usually the main or central idea of the paragraph that organizes details and subordinate ideas. Although it often opens the paragraph, the topic sentence can appear later—in the middle or at the end of the paragraph.

transition A word or phrase (*however, thus, in fact*) that connects clauses and sentences. Parallel structure is an important means of transition.

unity The connection of ideas and details to a central controlling idea of the essay. A unified essay deals with one idea at a time.

INDEX

* See *Glossary* for additional definition of asterisked words

PERMISSIONS AND ACKNOWLEDGMENTS

Diane Ackerman, "Watching a Night Launch of the Space Shuttle," from *A Natural History of the Senses*. Copyright © 1990 by Diane Ackerman. Reprinted by permission of Random House, Inc.

Irving Lewis Allen, "Newspapers," from *The City in Slang: New York Life and Popular Speech*. Copyright 1995 by Oxford University Press, Inc. Reprinted by permission of Oxford University Press, Inc.

Anonymous, "Who Am I?" from *Educating the Mexican American* by Henry Sioux Johnson and William J. Hernandez. Valley Forge: Judson Press, 1970. Reprinted by permission of the publisher.

Brooks Atkinson, "The Warfare in the Forest Is Not Wanton." Copyright © 1968 by The New York Times Co. Reprinted by permission.

Russell Baker, "Little Red Riding Hood Revisited." Copyright © 1980 by The New York Times Co. Reprinted by permission.

William J. Bennett and C. DeLores Tucker, "Wal-Mart's Free Choice." Copyright © 1996 by The New York Times Co. Reprinted by permission.

Carol Bly, "Monkeying," from *Letters from the Country*. Copyright 1999 by University of Minnesota Press. Reprinted by permission. Selection title by editor.

John Brooks, "The Telephone," from *The Telephone: The First Hundred Years* pp. 8–9. Copyright © 1975, 1976 by John Brooks. Reprinted by permission of HarperCollins Publishers, Inc. Selection title by editor.

Stanley C. Brubaker, "In Praise of Censorship." by Stanley C. Brubaker. Reprinted with permission of the author from *The Public Trust*, No. 114 (Winter 1994), pp. 57–64. Copyright © 1994 by National Affairs, Inc.

William F. Buckley, Jr., "Internet: The Lost Fight," From *On the Right* column, William F. Buckley, Jr. Copyright © 1997. Distributed by Universal Press Syndicate. Reprinted by permission. All rights reserved.

Sally Carrighar, "The Blast Furnace," from *Home to the Wilderness*. Copyright © 1944 by Sally Carrighar; renewed 1973 by I.C.E. Ltd. Reprinted by permission of Houghton Mifflin Co. All rights reserved.

Rachel Carson, "The Rocky Shores," from "The Rocky Coast," *The Edge of the Sea*. Copyright © 1955 by Rachel L. Carson, © renewed 1983 by Roger Christie. Reprinted by permission of Houghton Mifflin Co. All rights reserved.

Stephen L. Carter, "Computer Viruses," from *Civility: Manners and Morals and the Etiquette of Democracy*. Copyright © 1998 by Stephen L. Carter. Reprinted by permission of Basic Books, a member of Perseus Books, LLC. Selection title by editor.

John Ciardi, "What Every Writer Must Learn," from *Dialogue with an Audience.* Philadelphia: Lippincott, 1963. Copyright © the Ciardi Family Publishing Trust. Permission granted by the Ciardi Family Publishing Trust.

Kenneth B. Clark, "The Limits of Relevance," from *Pathos of Power* pp. 50–52. Copyright © 1974 by Kenneth B. Clark. Reprinted by permission of Harper-Collins Publishers, Inc.

I. Bernard Cohen, "What Columbus 'Saw' in 1492." Copyright © 1992 by Scientific American, Inc. Reprinted by permission. All rights reserved.

Norman Cousins, "Who Killed Benny Paret?" from *Present Tense.* New York: McGraw-Hill, 1967. Reprinted by permission of the author's estate.

Alan M. Dershowitz, "The Case for Medicalizing Heroin," from *Contrary to Popular Opinion.* Pharos Books, 1992. Reprinted by permission of the author. Alan M. Dershowitz is a professor of law at Harvard Law School.

Hilary de Vries, "I Think I Will Not Forget This." *The Christian Science Monitor,* September 17, 1987. Reprinted by permission of the author.

Joan Didion, "Marrying Absurd," from *Slouching Toward Bethlehem.* Copyright © 1966, 1968, renewed 1996 by Joan Didion. Reprinted by permission of Farrar, Straus, and Giroux LLC.

Annie Dillard, "At Tinker Creek," from *Pilgrim at Tinker Creek.* pp. 21–23. Copyright © 1974. Reprinted by permission of HarperCollins Publishers, Inc. Selection title by editor.

Michael Dorris, "For Indians, No Thanksgiving." *New York Times,* November 25, 1988. Copyright © 1988 by The New York Times Co. Reprinted by permission.

Gretel Ehrlich, "Excerpts," from *The Solace of Open Spaces.* Copyright © 1985 by Gretel Ehrlich. Used by permission of Viking Penguin, a division of Penguin Putnam Inc.

Loren Eiseley, "What Makes a Writer," from *The Invisible Pyramid.* Copyright © 1970 by Loren Eiseley. Reprinted with the permission of Scribner, a Division of Simon & Schuster. Selection title by editor.

Loren Eiseley, "The Cosmic Prison," from *All the Strange Hours.* Copyright © 1975 by Loren Eiseley. Reprinted with the permission of Scribner, a Division of Simon & Schuster. Selection title by editor.

William Finnegan, "Surfing." Copyright © 1992 William Finnegan. Reprinted by permission of International Creative Management, Inc. Originally appeared in *The New Yorker.*

Lawrence M. Friedman, "Crime," from *Crime and Punishment in American History.* Copyright © 1993 by Lawrence M. Friedman. Reprinted by permission of Basic Books, a member of Perseus Books LLC.

Ernesto Galarza, "Boyhood in a Sacramento Barrio," from *Barrio Boy.* Copyright © 1971 by University of Notre Dame Press. Reprinted by permission of the publisher. Selection title by editor.

Herbert Gans, "The Underclass," from "So Much for the Underclass?" *Washington Post,* September 10, 1990. Copyright © by *Washington Post.* Reprinted by permission of the author.

Walker Gibson, "Stuffy Talk," from *Tough, Sweet and Stuffy.* Copyright © 1966 by Indiana University Press. Reprinted by permission of the publisher.

Ellen Goodman, "Wait a Minute," Copyright © 1993, The Boston Globe Newspaper Co./Washington Post Writers Group. Reprinted by permission.

Edward T. Hall, "The English and the Americans," from *The Hidden Dimension.* Copyright 1966, 1982 by Edward T. Hall. Used by permission of Doubleday, a division of Random House, Inc. Selection title by editor.

Philip Hamburger, "The Sooners," from *An American Notebook.* New York: Knopf, 1965. Reprinted by permission of the author. Selection title by editor.

Marvin Harris, "Why Nothing Works," from *America Now: The Anthropology of Changing Culture.* Copyright © 1981 by Marvin Harris. Reprinted with permission of Simon & Schuster. Selection title by editor.

Sydney J. Harris, "Freedom and Security," from *For the Time Being.* Copyright © 1972 by Sydney J. Harris; 1969, 1970, 1971, 1972 by Publishers-Hall Syndicate. Reprinted by permission of Houghton Mifflin Company. All rights reserved.

Sydney J. Harris, "Nipping Clichés in the Bud," from *Clearing the Ground.* Copyright © 1968 by Sydney J. Harris. Reprinted by permission of Houghton Mifflin Company. All rights reserved.

Vicki Hearne, "Max into Maximilian," from *Animal Happiness,* pp. 42–43. Copyright © 1994 by Vicki Hearne. Reprinted by permission of Harper-Collins Publishers Inc.

Herbert Hendin, "Students and Drugs," from *The Age of Sensation: A Psychoanalytic Exploration.* Copyright © 1975 by Herbert Hendin. Reprinted by permission of W. W. Norton & Company, Inc.

Edward Hoagland, "City People and Country People," from "The Ridge-Slope Fox and the Knife Thrower." *Heart's Desire.* (collection of essays by the author). Originally appeared in *Harper's.* Copyright © 1977, 1988 by Edward Hoagland. This usage granted by permission of Lescher & Lescher, Ltd. Selection title by editor.

David Holahan, "Why Did I Ever Play Football?" *Newsweek,* December 2, 1985. Reprinted by permission of the author.

John Holt, "Kinds of Discipline," from *Freedom and Beyond.* New York: Dutton, 1972. Copyright © 1972 by John Holt, 1991 by Holt Associates, Inc. Selection title by editor.

Jane Jacobs, "Hudson Street," from *The Death and Life of Great American Cities.* Copyright © 1961 by Jane Jacobs. Reprinted by permission of Random House, Inc.

Michio Kaku, "The Education of a Physicist," from *Hyperspace: A Scientific Odyssey Through Parallel Universes, Time Warps, and the Tenth Dimension.* Copyright © 1994 by Oxford University Press, Inc. Reprinted by permission.

Garrison Keillor, "Hoppers," from *We Are Still Married: Stories and Letters.* Copyright © 1988 by Garrison Keillor, Used by permission of Viking Penguin, a division of Penguin Putnam Inc.

Martin Luther King, Jr., "Nonviolent Resistance," from *Stride Toward Freedom.* Copyright 1958 by Martin Luther King, Jr., copyright renewed 1966 by Coretta Scott King. Reprinted by arrangement with The Heirs to the Estate of Martin Luther King, Jr. c/o Writer's House, Inc. as agent for the proprietor. Selection title by editor.

Perri Klass, "Learning the Language," from *A Not Entirely Benign Procedure.* Copyright © 1987 by Perri Klass. Used by permission of Putnam Berkley, a division of Penguin Putnam Inc.

Leonard Kriegel, "The Purpose of Lifting," from *Falling into Life.* New York: North Point Press, 1991. Copyright © 1989 by Leonard Kriegel. Reprinted by permission of the author.

George Lakoff and Mark Johnson, "Time is Money," from *Metaphors We Live By.* © 1980 by The University of Chicago Press. All rights reserved. Selection title by editor.

Richard A. Lanham, "Digital Literacy." Copyright © 1995 by Scientific American, Inc. Reprinted with permission. All rights reserved.

Patrick D. Maines, "The New Censorship." *Editor and Publisher,* September 14, 1996. Reprinted by permission of the author.

Joshua Micah Marshall, "Will Free Speech Get Tangled in the Net?" Reprinted with permission from *The American Prospect* (Number 36, January-February 1998). Copyright © 1998 by *The American Prospect.* P.O. Box 772, Boston, MA 02102–0772. All rights reserved.

John McPhee, "The World's Largest Pile of Scrap Tires," excerpt from "Duty of Care," *Irons in the Fire.* Copyright © 1997 by John McPhee. Reprinted by permission of Farrar, Straus and Giroux, LLC. Selection title by editor.

Margaret Mead and Rhoda Metraux, "Discipline—To What End?" from *A Way of Seeing* pp. 211–213. Copyright © 1961 . . . 70 by Margaret Mead and Rhoda Metraux. Reprinted by permission.

Mary E. Mebane, "Mary," from *Mary.* Copyright © 1981 by Mary Elizabeth Mebane. Used by permission of Viking Penguin, a division of Penguin Putnam, Inc.

H.L. Mencken, "Reflections on War," from *Minority Report.* Copyright © 1956 by Alfred A. Knopf, Inc. Reprinted by permission of Alfred A. Knopf, a division of Random House, Inc.

W.S. Merwin, "The Buick," from *Unframed Originals.* New York: Atheneum, 1982. Copyright © 1982 by W.S. Merwin. Reprinted with the permission of The Wylie Agency, Inc. Selection title by editor.

Casey Miller and Kate Swift, "Manly and Womanly," from *Words and Women.* New York: HarperCollins, 1991. Copyright © 1976, 1991 by Casey Miller and Kate Swift. Selection title by editor.

N. Scott Momaday, from *The Man Made of Words:* Essays, Stories, Passages. Copyright © by N. Scott Momaday. Reprinted by permission of St. Martin's Press, LLC.

William Least Heat Moon, "In the Land of Coke-Cola," from *Blue Highways.* Copyright © 1982 by William Least Heat Moon. By permission of Little Brown and Company. Selection title by editor.

Mark H. Moore, "Actually, Prohibition Was a Success." Copyright © 1989 by the New York Times Co. Reprinted by permission.

Richard Moran, "More Police, Less Crime, Right? Wrong." Copyright © 1995 by the New York Times Co. Reprinted by permission.

Allan Nevins, "The Newspaper," from *Allan Nevins on History,* compiled and introduced by Ray Allen Billington. Copyright © 1975 by Columbia University. Reprinted by permission of Scribner, a Division of Simon & Schuster. Selection title by editor.

Newsweek, "Being Cool," from *Newsweek,* Special Issue. Spring 1983, Copyright © 1983 Newsweek, Inc. All rights reserved. Reprinted by permission. Selection title by editor.

George Orwell, "Shooting an Elephant," from *Shooting an Elephant and Other Essays.* Copyright © 1950 by Sonia Brownell Orwell and renewed by 1978 by Sonia Pitt-Rivers. Reprinted by permission of Harcourt, Inc.

George Plimpton, "Fireworks," five pages from *The Best of Plimpton* by George Plimpton. Copyright © 1990 by George Plimpton. by permission of Grove/Atlantic Inc.

Mary Helen Ponce, "Hoyt Street," from *Hoyt Street.* Copyright © 1993 University of New Mexico Press. Reprinted by permission.

Anna Quindlen, "Homeless," from *Living Out Loud.* Copyright © 1987 by Anna Quindlen. Reprinted by permission of Random House, Inc.

Charles B. Rangel, "Legalize Drugs? Not On Your Life." Copyright © 1988 by the New York Times Co. Reprinted by permission.

William Raspberry, "Who Deserves the Death Penalty?" Copyright © 1993,

The Washington Post Writers Group. Reprinted with permission.

John Richards, "How the Spider Spins Its Web," from *The Hidden Country.* Copyright © 1973 by John Richards. Reprinted by permission of S.C. Phillips, Inc. Selection title by editor.

Leanne G. Rivlin, "A New Look at the Homeless," adapted from an invited address for the Society of the Psychological Study of Social Issues, presented at the American Psychological Association meeting, August, 1985. Reprinted by permission of *Social Policy,* Social Policy Corporation, publisher, New York, NY 10016 Copyright © 1986 by Social Policy Corporation.

James Salter, "Flying," from "You Must," *Esquire,* December, 1992. By permissions of the author. Selection title by editor.

Esmeralda Santiago, "The American Invasion of Macún," from *When I Was Puerto Rican.* Copyright © 1983 by Esmeralda Santiago. Reprinted by permission of Perseus Books Publishers, a member of Perseus Books, LLC. Selection title by editor.

Karl L. Schilling and Karen Maitland Schilling, "Final Exams Discourage True Learning," *Chronicle of Higher Education,* February 2, 1994. Reprinted by permission of the authors.

Eric Sevareid, "Velva, North Dakota," in *This is Eric Sevareid,* Published by McGraw-Hill, 1964. Copyright © 1964 by Eric Sevareid. Reprinted by permission of Don Congdon Associates, Inc. Selection title by editor.

Mark Singer, "Osu!" from *The New Yorker,* May 26, 1986. Reprinted with permission of the author.

John Steinbeck, "The Turtle," from *The Grapes of Wrath,* chapter 3. Copyright © 1939, 1967 by John Steinbeck. Reprinted by permission of Viking Penguin, a division of Penguin Putnam Inc. Selection title by editor.

Roger D. Stone, "Why Save Tropical Forests?" Copyright © 1986 by the New York Times Co. Reprinted by permission.

Lytton Strachey, "Queen Victoria at the End of Her Life," from *Queen Victoria.* New York: Harcourt Brace and Company, 1921. Selection title by editor.

Peggy and Pierre Streit, "A Well in India." Copyright © 1959 by the New York Times Co. Reprinted by permission.

Robert Sullivan, "A Memo from Dad," from *The New Yorker.* Copyright © 1996 by Robert Sullivan. Reprinted with permission of The Wylie Agency, Inc.

Ronald Takaki, "The Barrio," from *A Different Mirror.* Copyright © 1993 by Ronald Takaki. By permission of Little Brown and Company. Selection title by editor.

Deborah Tannen, "Asymmetries," from *You Just Don't Understand* pp. 62–71 by Deborah Tannen. Copyright © 1990 by Deborah Tannen. Reprinted by permission of HarperCollins Publishers, Inc.

Edward Tenner, "Revenge Theory," from *Harvard Magazine,* March-April 1991. Reprinted by permission of Edward Tenner.

Lewis Thomas, "On Matters of Doubt," from *Late Night Thoughts on Listening to Mahler's Ninth.* Copyright © 1983 by Lewis Thomas. Reprinted by permission of Viking Penguin, a division of Penguin Putnam Inc.

Lewis Thomas, "Communication," from *The Fragile Species.* Copyright © 1992 by Lewis Thomas. Reprinted by permission of Scribner, a division of Simon & Schuster. Selection title by editor.

Susan Allen Toth, "Mountain Day," from *Ivy Days.* Copyright © 1984 by Susan Allen Toth. By permission of Little, Brown and Company. Selection title by editor.

James Trefil, "The Growth of Cities," from *A Scientist in the City.* Copyright

Text 1994 by James Trefil, III, 1994 by Judith Peatross. Reprinted by permission of Doubleday, a division of Random House, Inc. Selection title by editor.

Calvin Trillin, "Ben & Jerry's." From "Competitors" by Calvin Trillin. Appears in the author's collection entitled *American Stories* (collection by the author). Originally appeared in *The New Yorker*. Copyright © 1985, 1991 by Calvin Trillin. This usage granted by Lescher & Lescher, Ltd. Selection title by editor.

John Updike, "My Grandmother," from *The Carpentered Hen and Other Tame Creatures*. Copyright © 1962 by John Updike. Reprinted by permission of Alfred A. Knopf, a division of Random House, Inc. Selection title by editor.

Jearl Walker, "Outdoor Cooking." from "The Amateur Scientist." *Scientific American*, August 1985. Reprinted with permission of the author. Selection title by editor.

Eudora Welty, "Learning to See," from *One Writer's Beginnings*. Cambridge: Harvard University Press. Copyright © 1983, 1984 by Eudora Welty. Reprinted by permission of the publisher.

Alan Wertheimer, "Statistical Lives." Copyright © 1980 by the New York Times Co. Reprinted by permission.

Bailey White, "Mortality," from *Mama Makes Up Her Mind and Other Dangers of Southern Living*. Copyright © 1993 by Bailey White. Reprinted by permission of Perseus Book Publishers, a member of Perseus Books, LLC.

E.B. White, "In an Elevator," from *The Second Tree from the Corner*. Copyright © 1935, 1936, 1937, 1938, 1939, 1940, 1941, 1942, 1943, 1944, 1945, 1946, 1947, 1948, 1949, 1950, 1951, 1952, 1953, 1954 by E.B. White. Reprinted by permission of HarperCollins Publishers, Inc.

E.B. White, "New York," from *Here Is New York*. Copyright © 1949 by E.B. White. Reprinted by permission of International Creative Management, Inc. Selection title by editor.

George F. Will, "'Extreme Fighting' and the Morals of the Marketplace." Copyright © 1995, The Washington Post Writers Group. Reprinted with permission.

George F. Will, "Sex, Fat and Responsibility." *Newsweek*, July 7, 1997. Copyright © GFW, Inc. Reprinted with permission.

Garry Wills, "The Gettysburg Address," from *Lincoln at Gettysburg: The Words that Remade America*. Copyright © 1992 by Literary Research, Inc. Reprinted with the permission of Simon & Schuster.

Marie Winn, "Excerpt" from *The Plug-in Drug*, revised edition. Copyright © 1977, 1985 by Marie Winn Miller. Reprinted by permission of Viking Penguin, a division of Penguin Putnam, Inc.

Tom Wolfe, "Thursday Morning in a New York Subway Station," excerpt from "A Sunday Kind of Love." *The Kandy-Kolored Tangerine-Flake Streamline Baby*. Copyright © 1964 and copyright renewed © 1993 by Tom Wolfe. Reprinted by permission of Farrar, Straus and Giroux, LLC. Selection title by editor.

William Zinsser, "The Right to Fail," from *The Lunacy Boom*. Copyright © 1969, 1970 by William K. Zinsser. Reprinted by permission of the author.

William Zinsser, "Simplicity," from *On Writing Well*, 6th Edition. Copyright © 1976, 1980, 1985, 1988, 1990, 1994, 1998. Reprinted by permission of the author.